The Olympic Marathon

David E. Martin, PhD
Regents' Professor of Health Sciences
Georgia State University

Roger W.H. Gynn
Marathon Statistician
Association of Track & Field Statisticians

Human Kinetics

Library of Congress Cataloging-in-Publication Data

Martin, David E., 1939-
The Olympic marathon / David E. Martin, Roger W.H. Gynn.
p. cm.
Includes bibliographical references and index.
ISBN 0-88011-969-1
1. Marathon running--History. 2. Olympics--History. I. Gynn, Roger W.H. II. Title.

GV1065 .M39 2000

99-057645

ISBN: 0-88011-969-1

Acquisitions Editors: Steve Pope, PhD, and Martin Barnard; **Developmental Editor:** Spencer J. Cotkin, PhD; **Assistant Editors:** Amanda S. Ewing and Mark Zulauf; **Copyeditor:** Marc Jennings; **Proofreader:** Bob Replinger; **Indexer:** L. Pilar Wyman; **Permission Manager:** Heather Munson; **Graphic Designer:** Robert Reuther; **Graphic Artists:** Judy Henderson and Tara Welsch; **Cover Designer:** Jack W. Davis; **Photographers (cover):** Photo of Emil Zatopek © Archive Photos, Photo of Joan Benoit © Claus Andersen; **Illustrator:** Bob Letson; **Printer:** United Graphics

Human Kinetics books are available at special discounts for bulk purchase. Special editions or book excerpts can also be created to specification. For details, contact the Special Sales Manager at Human Kinetics.

Printed in the United States of America 10 9 8 7 6 5 4 3 2 1

Human Kinetics
Web site: http://www.humankinetics.com/

United States: Human Kinetics, P.O. Box 5076, Champaign, IL 61825-5076
1-800-747-4457
e-mail: humank@hkusa.com

Canada: Human Kinetics, 475 Devonshire Road Unit 100, Windsor, ON N8Y 2L5
1-800-465-7301 (in Canada only)
e-mail: humank@hkcanada.com

Europe: Human Kinetics, P.O. Box IW14, Leeds LS16 6TR, United Kingdom
+44 (0)113-278 1708
e-mail: humank@hkeurope.com

Australia: Human Kinetics, 57A Price Avenue, Lower Mitcham, South Australia 5062
(08) 82771555
e-mail: liahka@senet.com.au

New Zealand: Human Kinetics, P.O. Box 105-231, Auckland Central
09-523-3462
e-mail: humank@hknewz.com

To the Olympic marathon champions—shining examples of excellence in the most challenging distance-running event of the modern Olympic Games:

Spiridon Louis
Michel Théato
Thomas Hicks
(William Sherring—Intercalated Games)
John Hayes
Kennedy McArthur
Johannes Kolehmainen
Albin Stenroos
Boughera El Ouafi
Juan Zabala
Kitei Son
Delfo Cabrera
Emil Zátopek
Alain Mimoun
Abebe Bikila
Mamo Wolde
Frank Shorter
Waldemar Cierpinski
Carlos Lopes
Joan Benoit (Samuelson)
Gelindo Bordin
Rosa Mota
Hwang Young-cho
Valentina Yegorova
Josiah Thugwane
Fatuma Roba

Contents

Olympic Marathon Miscellany Finder

Page #

Course Sketch Finder

Foreword

I have been honored in being asked to write the foreword to *The Olympic Marathon*. But I must preface such a foreword by admitting that I am what some term an "Olympic apologist." With the recent scandals that have beset the Olympic movement, it is popular to belittle everything of Olympic origin. But I believe there is much good in the Olympic movement and that the Olympic Games can still be a force for good in today's world.

The basic premise of the Olympic movement is to bring together the youth of the world in peaceful coexistence. Jim McKay, the well-known sports announcer, has correctly stated that the Olympic Games constitute the "largest peacetime gathering of humanity in the history of the world." It is also true that people cannot get along well unless they can meet and understand one another, and this is the true purpose of the Olympic movement—to allow the youth of all countries to meet and try to understand each other better.

Every four years, the Olympic movement accomplishes this via a great spectacle—the Olympic Games. It is a spectacle that is now seen by billions of people worldwide, thanks to television. And at each Olympic Games, one of the most highly awaited events is the marathon footrace. The marathon is a drama that lasts for over two hours, and the whole world watches expectantly. Twenty-eight times this drama has been enacted, and now, for the first time, we have the complete story of the Olympic marathon available to us.

The story is told superbly by Dave Martin and Roger Gynn, and one could not ask for better authors to tell this story of the Olympic marathon. In the world of sports history, there exists a group that devotes itself specifically to studying the Olympics, and another devoted to the study of track and field. Martin and Gynn have distinguished themselves between both groups. They are the acknowledged experts in the field of marathon history.

At the end of the first century of the Olympic movement, we ask for more in hoping that the movement will reach its goals, and that people will understand those goals better. But we cannot ask for more concerning the Olympic marathon. It has brought us great drama and pathos, sorrow and joy. And we can ask for no more than this book on the Olympic marathon. Dave Martin and Roger Gynn have written the definitive history—one you will surely enjoy as much as I did.

Bill Mallon, MD
Vice President
International Society of Olympic Historians (ISOH)
Durham, North Carolina
May 1999

Preface

If there is an athletic event that is uniquely "Olympic," it is the marathon. It was created for the first modern Olympic Games at Athens in 1896 as a commemoration of the legendary run by Pheidippides (or Philippides), who in 776 B.C. brought news of a Greek victory over the invading Persians. The unique nature of the marathon—a footrace over varying terrain of a length that virtually exhausts the energy reserves of its competitors—adds to the intrigue of the event. The summer Olympic Games are typically staged in warm, humid maritime cities, where performance results depend on an intricate interplay between the physics of heat accumulation and the physiology of fitness. The number of runners who did not finish (DNF) for most Olympic events has been minimal—athletes are fit, injuries are few, and the distance to be covered is fairly short. But for the marathoners, it is different. Over the span of the 24 Olympic men's marathons (and one Intercalated Games marathon) held between 1896 and 1996, only 73.5 percent of the starters actually finished their race, and one of the men even died trying! For the women in their four Olympic marathons, the number of finishers is a somewhat better 84.1 percent.

Olympic marathon history has just passed the century mark, and we believe it is appropriate to recognize the achievements of the 1,497 different athletes (1,276 men and 221 women) who have toed the starting line from Athens in 1896 through Atlanta in 1996. Some of these athletes participated in more than one Olympic marathon, giving a total number of 1,795 performances (1,541 by men and 254 by women). Accordingly, we have prepared this book that we hope will serve as a definitive reference that describes the exploits of these athletes. We hope it will both inform and entertain Olympics enthusiasts, sports historians, marathoners and other runners, and those interested in sports statistics.

This is not the first time that Olympic marathons have been described in book format. In an earlier text (Martin and Gynn 1979) we chronicled the history of the marathon as an event, and a brief summary of each Olympic Games marathon was an integral part of that effort. Continuing our friendship, we have "reunited" after 20 years and focus our attention just on the Olympic marathons. However, during the buildup toward the 1996 Atlanta Centennial Olympic Games, several other books appeared with titles that suggest a discussion of 100 years of Olympic marathon races (Escamilla 1996; Haumann 1996; Phillips and Gynn 1996; Sheridan 1996). All were brief in their presentation, and none covered the Atlanta Olympic marathons, as the books appeared prior to those Games. Another book emerged following the Atlanta Olympic Games (Lovett 1997), but its coverage of the event was again limited.

If this book has a thesis, it is that during the course of more than a century, the marathon and the Olympic movement have endured together. Each marathon and each Olympic Games has been presented with its own unique challenges with which athletes have had to cope. The Olympic movement has survived, and although many Olympic events have come and gone, the marathon has also survived, being contested at every Olympic Games. Although it has varied in distance and now women have their own marathon as well, the historical decisions that produced the current "standard" distance of 42,195 meters, and the creation of a separate race for women, are interesting stories in themselves.

The book's format is simple. Each Olympic Games has its own chapter. The Intercalated Games at Athens in 1906 were not Games of an Olympiad, but were of equivalent importance at the time to Olympic Games and were conducted under the auspices of the International Olympic Committee (IOC). Thus, we give the Intercalated Games marathon equal status with its own chapter.

Each chapter briefly summarizes the geographical setting and contemporary political climate of the Olympic movement, as these often influenced the dynamics of marathon preparation and competition. The reader interested in further details of each Games should consult the many available references (e.g., Killanin and Rodda 1976; Lucas 1992; Guttmann 1994; Wallechinsky 1996; Senn 1999). A course sketch and, where known, detailed street information is supplied for each Olympic marathon route. We then provide a general overview of how athlete selection proceeded for each Olympic marathon race, and we identify some of the significant competitors. Following a narrative of the race itself, we give a brief biographical profile of the top three finishers. Also, we provide a career marathon summary for the winners. Each chapter concludes with a "Looking Ahead" section that summarizes major marathon highlights during the years leading up to the next Olympic marathon. Accompanying photos provide additional perspective. Complete results are in the appendixes.

Changing traditions and Olympic politics during the 100-plus year history of the modern Olympic Games frustrate the application of a uniform usage of terminology and concepts. For example, some texts erroneously refer to the top three finishers of all of the Olympic marathons as "medalists." In 1896, only the first two runners received medals, and in 1900 pottery, rather than medals, was awarded. Also, the winners of Olympic marathons for years other than 1900 cannot all be referred to as gold medalists, because at Athens in 1896, the winner, Spiridon Louis, received silver!

Similarly, some texts incorrectly categorize athlete participation according to the nations they represented at the Olympic Games (Kamper and Mallon 1992; Wallechinsky 1996). In the very early Games, although athletes had a national identity, when assembled at the Games they did not necessarily participate as a national team. Eventually it became customary for athletes to be selected not by their nations of residence but by their National Olympic Committees (NOCs). These NOCs were established only gradually; the first six were the United States (1894), Greece (1895), Germany (1895), Great Britain (1905), Belgium (1906), and Finland (1907). Not all NOCs represent an entire nation, however. Guam, for example, is an unincorporated territory of the United States with its own NOC. Puerto Rico is a self-governing commonwealth of the United States with its own NOC. In addition to this complexity, other modes of athlete representation have occurred. At the Barcelona Olympic Games in 1992, for example, although Yugoslavia had an NOC, only its athletes in nonteam sports were permitted to compete, and they did so under the category of Independent Olympic Participant (IOP).

The IOC has devised a three-letter identification for each of its NOCs and other participating entities. Similarly, the International Amateur Athletic Federation (IAAF), the world governing body for track and field (the sport is known more globally as athletics), has also assigned three-letter abbreviations to its member federations, some of which also do not have full national status. Unfortunately, these two sets of three-letter abbreviations are not consistent with each other. Adding still more confusion in athlete identity is that, over time, nations have changed names, split apart, or merged with other nations. Thus, in the various appendixes and chapter summaries, we use a three-letter descriptor to identify what we refer to as the appropriate geopolitical entity (GPE) that most meaningfully identifies each athlete. Thus, GPE is more all-inclusive than NOC and nation, which have many exceptions. We do, however, use NOC and nation in the text where their use is appropriate. The GPE abbreviations are given in appendix A.

We are indebted to Bob Letson of San Diego for producing most of the course sketches. An engineer by profession, he was one of the pioneers in United States road racecourse certification during the 1970s and 1980s, and he has been active ever since. Held in high esteem by his technical colleagues in road race measurement, his name appears on the official 1984 Los Angeles Olympic marathon course documentation as the co-certifier (with 1952 marathon Olympian Ted Corbitt). Thanks to his collaboration, this is the first time that a complete set of Olympic marathon course sketches has appeared in one place.

Appendixes D and E will be a delight to track and field record-keepers, as they record all of the Olympic marathon performances by men and women in chronological order. We used Lyberg's (1993) documentation of Olympic competitors, as well as the marathon databases of Borre Lilloe and Arild Gjerde, to verify initial completeness, and we have added new information since those compilations, thanks to global assistance from our colleagues in the Association of Track and Field Statisticians (ATFS). Despite its being the most complete and accurate compilation of Olympic marathon results to date, there is no such thing as a perfect list. We enthusiastically invite readers to help us finish the task of identifying the missing birth dates and first names.

Plenty of fascinating facts and stories reside in the halls of Olympic marathon history, and we hope readers will enjoy learning them. A few one-liners may serve to whet some appetites:

- In one marathon there were two athletes named Fast and Champion, neither of whom was fast enough to become Olympic champion.

- Although three United States marathoners have earned gold medals, none had the honor of entering the stadium first.
- One of the marathons had—can you imagine?—a false start.
- For one medalist, the Olympic marathon was the only race at that distance that he ever ran.
- One gold medalist ran the entire course barefoot.
- Considering the current concern about illegal use of performance-enhancing drugs, in one of the early Olympic marathons, the use of such was publicly stated and admitted as providing performance benefit.
- Three gold medalists won the Olympic marathon on their first attempts at covering the distance. Three marathoners who won the Olympic marathon qualified to compete in the following Olympic marathon but had to drop out.

In explaining these and many more such factoids, we hope that this book will serve adequately to chronicle the performance and recognize the courage of this special group of athletes who can call themselves Olympic marathoners.

References

Escamilla, P. 1996. *100 años de maratón Olímpica.* Madrid: Real Federación Española de Atletismo.

Guttmann, A. 1994. *The Olympics: A history of the modern Games.* Champaign, IL: University of Illinois Press.

Haumann, R. 1996. *Century of the marathon 1896-1996.* Cape Town: Human & Rousseau Ltd.

Kamper, E., and B. Mallon. 1992. *The golden book of the Olympic Games.* Milano: Vallardi & Associati Editrice.

Killanin, L., and J. Rodda. 1976. *The Olympic Games.* New York: Collier Books.

Lovett, C. 1997. *Olympic Marathon: A centennial history of the Games' most storied race.* Westport, Conn.: Praeger.

Lucas, J.A. 1992. *Future of the Olympic Games.* Champaign, IL: Human Kinetics.

Lyberg, W.S. 1993. *The athletes of the Games of the Olympiad, 1896-1992.* Vol. 1-4, *The 73,000 participants.*

Martin, D.E., and R.W.H. Gynn. 1979. *The marathon footrace.* Springfield, IL: Charles C Thomas.

Phillips, B., and R. Gynn. 1996. *100 years of the Olympic marathon.* Abertillery, Gwent: National Union of Track Statisticians.

Senn, A.E. 1999. *Power, politics, and the Olympic Games.* Champaign, IL: Human Kinetics.

Sheridan, M. 1996. *Good reasons.* Private publisher.

Wallechinsky, D. 1996. *The complete book of the Summer Olympics.* 1996 edition. New York: Little, Brown & Company.

Acknowledgments

We have been blessed with the friendship of a devoted group of colleagues in sport—some for more than 25 years—who have helped us document the Olympic marathon story. These experts fit essentially into two categories: "track and field stats nuts" and "Olympic track and field history buffs," with some overlapping both areas.

We have been active members of the Association of Track and Field Statisticians (ATFS) for collectively more than 50 years. Our many friends in that global organization have "endured" our unending nit-picking statistical queries about athletes, and about the Games held in their respective countries. Our way of saying "Thanks for your patience and assistance" is by recognizing them here, alphabetically by country: Argentina—Luis Vinker; Australia—Paul Jenes; Belgium—Andre de Hooghe; Brazil—Ulf Lagerström; Denmark—Erik Laursen; Finland—Matti Hannus; France—Alain Bouille; Germany—Klaus Amrhein and Otto Verhöven; Hungary—Gabriel Szabó; Italy—Raul Leoni; Japan—Yoshimasa Noguchi; Poland—Henryk Paskal; South Africa—Riël Hauman; Sweden—Rooney Magnusson; United Kingdom—Ian Buchanan, Richard Hymans, Tony Isaacs, Peter Lovesey, Mike Sheridan, Dave Terry, and Norris McWhirter; United States—Hal Bateman, Ken Nakamura, and Bill Mallon.

Although not members of the ATFS, the following have made a substantial contribution by translating early newspapers and other documents, rechecking athlete name spellings and birth dates, and offering informed "leads" for answering difficult questions: Belgium—Noël Devis and Roland Renson; Canada—David Blaikie and Floyd Williston; Ireland—Noel Henry; Japan—Yoo Honda; Netherlands—Frieda Michiels and Wim van Hemert; Newfoundland—Ed O'Toole; South Africa—Floris van der Merwe; United Kingdom—Andy Milroy; United States—John C. Furla II and John Hoyle; Zambia—Phil Kubombela (Zambian AAF).

Some of these individuals, together with others, deserve very special mention, however, for their beyond-the-ordinary contribution of time, new materials, and translation skills:

- Dave Cundy and Paul Jenes [AUS] (note that abbreviations for these geopolitical entities are given in appendix A) have been of unique assistance with all aspects of the Australian Olympic marathons at Sydney and Melbourne, respectively.
- Josep "Bep" Solé, Josep Antentas, and Pedro Pujol, MD [ESP], the respective marathon course measurer, race director, and medical director at

Barcelona, with whom David was privileged to work before and during those Games.

- Matti Hannus [FIN], a respected friend, has been a gold mine of information about details of Finnish Olympic athletes and the story of the Helsinki marathon, and introduced us to specialists in the Helsinki sport museum.
- Alain Bouille [FRA] has been of great value particularly in researching Paris 1900.
- Horst and Mark Milde and Tom Steffens [GER] have been especially helpful in providing unique course materials for the Berlin and Munich marathons, respectively.
- Bob Phillips [GBR], track and field commentator for BBC radio and for 30 years a good friend of Roger's, current editor of *Track Stats*; he and Roger compiled *100 Years of the Olympic Marathon* prior to the Atlanta Games.
- Takao Tomioka [JPN], of the Asahi Shimbun, a friend of Roger's for more than 25 years, has been particularly generous in providing photographs.
- Professor César Moreno [MEX] has helped us research the route of the Mexico City Olympic marathon course; now an IAAF Council member, he was a technical delegate at those Games.
- Sue Richardson and Karen Myers in the IAAF office at Monte Carlo provided detailed answers to historical questions regarding minutes of early IAAF Council meetings.
- Jan Ludeker in Amsterdam and his cousin Tom Mulder in Belgium have been of inestimable value with research on the Amsterdam and Antwerp marathons. They translated early documents from local government and library collections, read chapter drafts, and, in addition, contacted local Belgian village historians to verify details of the Antwerp course, thus enabling us to produce what may be the first map describing it.
- Borre Lilloe and Arild Gjerde [NOR] kindly allowed Roger access to their extensive marathon statistics data base.
- Sergey Tikhonov [RUS] has substantially improved our knowledge of the Moscow Olympic marathon.
- The late Fulvio Regli [SUI], one of the founders of the ATFS, shared with Roger his unique archives of Swiss and Italian data only weeks before his death.
- Rooney Magnusson [SWE] for many years has been a source of special encouragement both with his unfailing demand for accuracy and his ever-helpful responses to many challenging queries.
- Shirley Ito [USA], librarian at the Amateur Athletic Foundation of Los Angeles, has been a genuine joy to work with as she helped David locate photographs and research details using the foundation's immense collection of original Olympic material.
- Don Kardong and Ted Corbitt [USA] have generously provided us with

thoughtful reminiscences of their experiences as Olympians at Montréal and Helsinki, respectively.

- Ken Nakamura [JPN], residing in California but making frequent trips to his native Japan, has devoted many hours in the Chichibu Memorial Sports Library at the National Stadium in Tokyo, helping us research questions about Japanese athlete participation through Games history. Chief Librarian Junko Sudo has been particularly helpful with discovering elusive details.

Despite this assistance from our colleagues worldwide, as authors we of course accept full responsibility for the accuracy of what we have written. We realize that the likelihood of errors creeping into a manuscript with such a mass of detail is inevitable, and would be delighted if readers who do find any would make us aware of them. As with the marathoners in training for their next Olympic race, ours and theirs is a work in progress. A gold medal perfect performance is rare indeed, but it is what we all seek!

Origin of the Olympic Marathon Footrace

The word "marathon" did not appear in English language dictionaries prior to the mid-1890s. Today it refers either to a footrace run on a predetermined course—typically 42,195 meters (42.195 kilometers) or 26 miles, 385 yards in length—or to some other event or activity of great duration. Thus, there are "marathon sessions of Parliament or Congress" that extend for many hours. And there is the "Comrades Marathon," a South African footrace of roughly 90 kilometers (56 miles) between Durban and Pietermaritzburg. A little thought will bring to mind many more examples of usage. The word originates from a village in Greece, roughly 40 kilometers northeast of Athens, known for an important ancient battle.

The Legend of Pheidippides (Philippides)

Herodotus tells us that King Darius of Persia landed a force of 20,000 men onshore near Marathon, planning to conquer the Greeks and punish them for helping the Ionians (who lived in western Asia Minor) revolt against Darius's rule. The Greeks were under the direction of a very competent general, Miltiades, but being outnumbered nearly two to one, they needed reinforcements. Cornelius Nepos, a Roman historian and biographer in the first century B.C., reported that "the Athenians, distressed by this war so near and so great, in their own land, sought aid nowhere other than from the Lacedaemonians (Spartans) and sent Phidippidus, a runner of that class known as hemerodromoi, to report how urgent was the need of aid." The hemerodromoi were trained distance runners.

A later source (Solinus) gave the distance from Athens to Sparta as 1,240 stades. A stade was the length of a stadium, which in cities such as Athens and Olympia was 185 meters (607 feet). This would suggest a distance of 229 kilometers. On today's highways, the distance from Athens to Sparta is a similar 245 kilometers. Ancient evidence leans toward the name of Philippides for this runner, but there is some manuscript evidence for Pheidippides as well. It is not clear from Herodotus whether it was an entirely different runner who traveled from Marathon to Athens to announce that soldiers from Sparta were needed, or whether this same runner, after arriving and conferring with authorities, continued on from Athens to Sparta.

Herodotus does mention that the runner reached Sparta "on the very next day." If taken strictly, this trip from Athens to Sparta implies "within 24 hours," but if taken loosely it suggests "within two calendar days." Either feat is humanly possible, but both are stupendous efforts, particularly when one realizes that (1) the terrain is hilly and (2) he returned soon afterward (again, it is not clear whether he returned just to Athens, with an additional runner dispatched to Marathon, or whether the same runner covered the entire distance). Interestingly, ever since 1983, an ultradistance competition has been staged between Athens and Sparta to commemorate this legendary run. This so-called Spartathlon is held in September, with worldwide participation, and the current course record for the one-way trip from Athens to Sparta is 20 hours and 25 minutes by a Greek, Yannis Kouros.

The Spartan support forces did not reach Marathon in time to assist General Miltiades in his struggle, due to their preoccupation with a religious festival (Martyn 1997). Fortunately for the Greeks, they were not needed. Miltiades faced the Persians squarely and soundly defeated them. In the battle, the Greeks lost only 192 men, many fewer than the 6,400 Persians who died. A large tomb, allegedly holding the remains of these 192 Greeks, can still be seen at the site of the old battlefield.

According to legend (but not mentioned by Herodotus), after the battle an Athenian soldier gifted at running, again known as Philippides or Pheidippides (potentially the same individual who had run to Sparta), was sent to announce the news of the victory to the king in Athens. Reportedly, after his arrival and gasp of the single Greek word "Nenikhkamen" ("We have won!"), he collapsed and died. Others who relate the legend say that "Rejoice, we have conquered" was more accurate. Because it was in Greek, the translation will never be quite precise. One wonders how this final run from Marathon to Athens was omitted by Herodotus in his reporting of events (Kyle 1998)—it would have been the perfect end to a great story.

The legendary run from Marathon to Athens could have taken one of two routes (Ioannides 1976). The longer choice, about 40 kilometers (25 miles) in length, is flat initially, extends south along the sun-baked seacoast past Mati and Raphena, then turns west and eventually crosses the mountains surrounding Athens. Cresting in Stavros at an elevation of 240 meters (788 feet) above sea level, the final several kilometers then descend into the city. The shorter route, about 34 kilometers (21 miles), proceeds immediately westward into the mountains outside Marathon, climbing to an elevation of 350 meters (1,150 feet) in the first nine kilometers. Passing the Dionysos stream provides a source of fresh water. A long gentle descent toward the southwest through cooler pine-filled forests then allows entry into Athens via the suburbs of Kifisia and Amaroussion. Thus, the total ascent using this latter route is greater, but it occurs during the early portion, when runners are fresh, and the route is 15 percent shorter in total distance.

The Modern Olympic Games

When the ancient Games of Olympia were about to be reborn in Athens during 1896 in the form of a global sports competition, it became appropriate for this legendary run from Marathon to Athens to assume a modern reality as part of the sport competition program. The plan was to have a competitive long-distance footrace over roughly 40 kilometers (~25 miles), called "the marathon race," starting at the Marathon battlefield and ending in the Panathenaikon stadium, which was rebuilt for these Games. Two days later, there would also be a "marathon cycle race" of 87 kilometers (54 miles), starting in Athens, going to Marathon, returning, and finishing in the New Phaleron Cycle Track.

Some very brief historical perspective on a few relevant issues may help readers appreciate the setting in which these modern Olympian Games found themselves. First, during the ancient Greek national sports festivals—at Olympia, Nemea, Delphi, and Isthmia—long-distance running events were not included, so a competitive long-distance race in an Olympic Games context was an entirely new concept. The primary running competition in these early Games was the stade—a sprint along the length of the stadium. There also was a diaulos, or down-and-back. The longest event had been the dolichos, or 24 stades, which would not have exceeded 4,800 meters (about three miles).

Second, although the ancient Greeks kept their stadium games to shorter-distance dashes, long-distance running and walking were indeed increasing in popularity during the latter half of the nineteenth century, particularly in the British Isles and in America, creating a sport known as pedestrianism (Quercetani 1990). Contests to see how far one could walk, or run-walk, in an hour, or a day, or a week, became fashionable (Dodd 1997; Cooper 1998). Professional contests even saw sizable sums of money exchanged in betting.

Amateur distance racing was also important at the public school and university level, again particularly in England and the United States. In England especially, track and field competitions with specific established rules provided a basis for competitive sport to develop. In the United States, using such rules, the National Association of Amateur Athletes of America (NAAAA) initiated an annual men's championship over five miles in 1880. This series has continued to the present day, changing names to match variations in the name of the national governing body under whose direction the event was conducted.

Third, nearly a dozen local-level national sports festivals with the name "Olympic" attached to them occurred in Europe during the 1800s (Rühl 1997), notably in Greece and England. It was the Frenchman Pierre Frédy, the Baron de Coubertin, who successfully brought into reality the idea of having nations come together for friendly sport competition. However, at least two other gentlemen deserve considerable credit for developing an environment that permitted de Coubertin's enthusiasm to flourish (Young 1996).

William Penny Brookes was an English physician, writer, and sports enthusiast who organized in 1850 a local sporting competition in his home village of Much Wenlock. His Much Wenlock Games grew into an annual festival, and an expanded version called the Olympian Games started in London in 1866. Meanwhile, in 1859, Evangelis Zappas, a wealthy Greek of Romanian descent, organized the first Zappian Olympic Games in Athens (Chrysaphes 1930). There were four such Games open to Pan Hellenic participants, that is, Greeks or people of Greek descent from Asia Minor and Italy. On November 15, 1859, at these first Zappian Games, there was a dolichos event (24 stades). At the Second Zappian Games, on October 18, 1870, the longest race was the diaulos (two stades). On June 22, 1875, a diaulos was again contested at the Third Zappian Games. Only the stade was contested at the final Zappian Games on April 31, 1889.

Both Brookes and Zappas were aware of each other's activities, and they shared their experiences and ideas with a view toward improving the quality of their respective festivals. According to Young (1996), in 1880 Brookes may have been the first to suggest the idea of an international Olympic Games held in Greece every four years. His problem was finding someone in Greece to help him implement the concept. In failing to do so, he was unintentionally upstaged by Baron de Coubertin, who later also envisioned a similar festival but who was better connected in Athens.

Born in 1863, de Coubertin developed during the 1880s an academic interest in how school systems could best develop optimum social values among children. He was particularly intrigued by the English and American public school systems, and how their philosophy of integrating physical exercise with academics differed fundamentally from that in France. In England, sport was seen as essential for teaching fair play, ethical conduct, and personal interaction, and as such, should intertwine with academics. The French view was that physical activity stifled intellectual thought.

At this same time, de Coubertin also perceived a degradation in the role of sport itself as a positive social force. Two issues in particular worried him. One was a developing dislike by athletes in one sport for those playing other sports—caused, as he saw it, by too much intensity in focus. Another was the commercial invasion into sport, particularly the specter of the outcome of competitions being influenced by paying athletes to lose. He sought to "purify" and "unify" sport rather than allow it to become a purely commercial enterprise.

To stimulate more discussion of these problems and differences, de Coubertin organized an international conference on physical education for November 25, 1892, in Paris. He proposed a "restoration" of the Olympic Games (Mallon and Widlund 1998), which received only a lukewarm reception. Undaunted, he organized another congress lasting nine days at the Sorbonne, starting on June 16, 1894. This became the inaugural Olympic Congress, wherein he hoped to solidify a conceptual framework for his proposed reorganization of the Olympic Games. As de Coubertin declared (1896), the mission of this Olympic movement was "[to] create competitions at regular periodical intervals at which representatives of all countries and all sports would be invited under the aegis of the same authority, which would impart to them a halo of grandeur and glory, that is the patronage of classical antiquity. To do this was to revive the Olympic Games: the name imposed itself: It was not even possible to find another." While William Penny Brookes had proposed such an idea years before, de Coubertin had a friend in Athens, Demetrius Vikelas, who helped make it happen. Vikelas became the first president of the International Olympic Committee, serving from 1894 through 1896. He was appointed by, and then succeeded by, de Coubertin himself.

Athens was the logical venue choice for the initial modern Olympic Games, with Paris the appropriate follow-up. The ancient Greeks probably never envisioned a worldwide sports competition—and it was a novel concept to contemporary Greeks as well. They warmly welcomed the idea as a logical outgrowth of their several national "Olympian Games" organized earlier in the 19th century.

Creating the First Olympic Marathon Footrace

The idea for the marathon race did not originate in Greece, but rather from Michel Breál, an associate of Baron de Coubertin. Breál was born in 1832 in what then was Bavaria; his parents were Jews of French descent, but they spoke German at home (Lennartz 1998). After the death of his father, when he was five, the family moved to the French Alsace, where Bréal quickly learned French. In fact, he learned several languages as he progressed through his years of academic study, majoring in philology and mythology. His interest in mythology brought him to a consideration of Greek culture, and he became fascinated with the ancient Greek Olympic Games. He eventually became head of France's educational system, and this, combined with his interest in ancient mythology, inevitably led to his attending the Sorbonne Olympic Congress.

Being well versed in both sport and politics, Bréal believed that the Greek enthusiasm for hosting these Olympic Games would be enhanced even further by the inclusion of a sporting event relevant to Greek history. Bréal outlined his ideas on a handwritten, four-page letter to de Coubertin written in French. A rough translation of the key paragraph is, "Since you are going to Athens, see if you can't organize a marathon race from Marathon to the Pnyx. If we knew the time that the Greek warrior took, we would be able to establish the record. For my part I would beg the honor of presenting a Marathon Cup." He was referring to the engraved silver cup shown in figure 0.1.

The Pnyx is a steep hill in Athens that was used as a social congregating place. Perhaps Bréal envisioned the race as starting or finishing there—we don't know. And also, of course, no one knew how long it took Pheidippides (or Philippides) to cover whatever route he used from Marathon to inform the king of victory, so it wasn't possible to identify a record time to be broken. Nonetheless, the event was placed on the program, and the first Olympic marathon was set to be run.

Figure 0.1 **The silver cup of Michel Bréal, presented to the winner of the first modern Olympic Games marathon at Athens. The engraved caption reads, "Olympic Games, marathon event, given by Michel Bréal."** Reprinted, by permission, from K. Lennartz.

Julian Versus Gregorian Calendars Brings Olympic Confusion

The date of the first Athens Olympic marathon is given in the 1896 official Games report as Friday, March 29. This date is also reported in local Greek newspapers of that period. Other authoritative sources (Wallechinsky 1996) use April 10. Both are correct, which points to one of the many confusions surrounding documentation of Olympic details. At the time, Greece was using the Julian calendar, whereas much of the rest of the Western world (including most of the world today) was (and still is) using the Gregorian calendar. Some explanation is useful.

The first modern calendar was put into use in 45 B.C. by Julius Caesar, who decreed that there should be three years of 365 days each, and then one year of 366 days, in perpetual cycle. Known as the Julian calendar, this started the practice of adding one day to the end of February every fourth (leap) year. Although an improvement over previous systems, this scheme is inadequate, because one solar year (one revolution of the Earth around the sun) requires 365 days, 5 hours, 48 minutes, 46 seconds—about 11 minutes shorter than 365¼ days.

In 1582, Pope Gregory XIII proposed a correction to the Julian calendar. The new, improved version became known as the Gregorian calendar. First, to correct for all the days that had accumulated since the start of the Julian calendar, it was decreed that 10 days would be removed from 1582. The day after October 4 thus became October 15. He then also instituted a so-called Leap Year Rule: One day is dropped from each centesimal year (ending in 00) whose number cannot be divided by 400. Thus, a day was dropped in 1700, 1800, and 1900, and they were not leap years. A day was not dropped in 2000, so February of 2000 had 29 days.

After the decree in 1582, primarily Roman Catholic countries initially adopted the new calendar. Protestant countries joined later. The American colonies switched in 1752 when the entire British Empire changed. By that time, however, an 11-days adjustment was required. Many countries were slow to adopt the Gregorian calendar. Japan adopted it in 1873, China in 1912, and Greece not until 1924. By the time of the 1896 Olympic Games, the adjustment was 12 days, which explains why Athenian newspapers were 12 days behind the newspapers from many other parts of the world. Thus, the date of March 29 on the Julian calendar used in Greece during the first Olympic Games corresponds to April 10 on the Gregorian calendar.

Some other dates for these first Olympic Games are also relevant. The Opening Ceremonies were on Sunday, March 24 Julian (April 5 Gregorian). There was a specific reason that de Coubertin wanted the competitions to start on the following day. In 1896, the Christian and Eastern Orthodox Easters coincided,

and thus his "resurrection" of the Olympic Games on Easter Monday for both religions was especially symbolic (MacAloon 1981). This was also the Independence Day of Greece. The marathon occurred on the fifth day of competition and was the last contested event in athletics (track and field). The final day of competition was April 3 Julian (April 15 Gregorian), with the Closing Ceremonies one day later.

References

Chrysaphes, I. 1930. *The modern Olympic Games.* Athens: Gergiadon Publishing Co.

Cooper, P. 1998. *The American marathon.* Syracuse: Syracuse University Press.

Dodd, E. 1997. The great six-day races. *Marathon and Beyond* 1 (1): 73-89.

de Coubertin, P. 1896. The Olympic Games of 1896. In *The Olympic Games, 776 B.C.-1896 A.D.*, ed. C. Beck. Translated 1966. London: H. Grevel & Co.

Herodotus. *The Histories. Book VI.* Translated by G. Rawlinson. Everyman's Library. New York: Random House

Ioannides, I. 1976. The true course run by the marathon messenger. *Olympic Review* 109-110: 599-602.

Kyle, D. 1998. *Dictionary of world biography: The ancient world.* Edited by F.N. Magill. Hackensack, NJ: Salem Press.

Lennartz, K. 1998. Following the footsteps of Bréal. *Journal of Olympic History* 6 (2): 8-10.

MacAloon, J.J. 1981. *This great symbol: Pierre de Coubertin and the origin of the modern Olympic Games.* Chicago: University of Chicago Press.

Mallon, B. and T. Widlund. 1998. *The 1896 Olympic Games.* Jefferson, NC: McFarland & Co., Inc., Publishers.

Martyn, S.G. 1997. Book review. *Olympika* 6: 129-136.

Nepos, C. *Miltiades,* 4.

Quercetani, R.L. 1990. *Athletics: A history of modern track & field athletics (1860-1990).* Milano: Vallardi & Associati.

Rühl, J. 1997. The Olympian Games at Athens in the year 1877. *Journal of Olympic History* 5 (3): 26-34.

Solinus. *Collectanea rerum memorabilium.* Book I.

Wallechinsky, D. 1996. *The complete book of the Summer Olympics.* 1996 edition. New York: Little, Brown & Company.

Young, D.C. 1996. *The modern Olympics: A struggle for revival.* Baltimore: Johns Hopkins University Press.

CHAPTER I

1896—ATHENS

Spiridon Louis Victorious for Greece

Selection of the First Marathon Course

The reconstructed Panathenaikon stadium in Athens (figure 1.1) was the centerpiece for the first modern Olympic Games, so there was little doubt that the marathon competition would finish there. The original stadium on that site was constructed in ca. 330 B.C. It fell into disrepair but was rebuilt 500 years later by Herodis Atticus. That second version also disintegrated with time and was buried until 1870, when excavations first revealed its dimensions to modern Greece. The rebuilt 19th century stadium was modeled after the stadium of Atticus, with 100 meters straightaways and 65 meters turns that produced an inside-lane track circumference of 333.33 meters (zur Megede 1999). An estimate of its spectator capacity can be made from the reported sales of 71,800 tickets for the day of the marathon, when the stadium was full (Horton 1999). Other estimates range from 50,000 upward (Mallon and Widlund 1998). Visitors to the stadium

Figure 1.1 **The Panathenaikon stadium as it appeared in the 1960s. Marathoners approached the open end of the stadium from the right along the roadway and proceeded along the southwest straightaway (the left side in the photo), ending at the sphendone (a semicircular end of a Greek stadium). The athletes' tunnel used for recuperation following the race is seen on the near end of the right (northeast) straightaway.** Reprinted, by permission, from Hellenic Olympic Committee.

today are impressed with its marble construction, but not all of this was in place in 1896, and many spectators sat on wooden seats.

In 1896 an unpaved road connected Athens with the village of Marathon. The Olympic organizing committee chose a starting point in the village of Marathon, near a bridge over a low point in the roadway. Estimates of the total race distance are placed consistently at 40 kilometers, and we presume the measurement was done by local surveyors, or perhaps even civil engineers. The bicycle wheel revolution counters first used for measuring road race courses in the 1970s did not exist then, and neither did automobile odometers.

We also do not know why the longer seacoast route was selected in preference to the shorter mountainous route. Perhaps it was because the distance of 40 kilometers is also familiar to nations accustomed to the Imperial measurement system. Forty kilometers is close to 25 miles. To make the necessary conversions, recall that one inch = 2.54 centimeters. Thus, 1 mile = 5,280 feet = 63,360 inches = 1,609.344 meters. Then, 24 miles = 38.624 kilometers and 25 miles = 40.234 kilometers. Conversely, 40 kilometers = 24.85 miles, which is 234 meters (256 yards) less than 25 miles.

The course sketch illustrated in figure 1.2 helps to clarify the dynamics of the race. Starting at an elevation of about 25 meters (82 feet) above sea level, the route is mainly flat for the first 15 kilometers, as it extends southward along the coastal plain. At Nea Makri, the route (now National Highway Number 83) comes quite close to the sea and then continues southward a few kilometers inland, passing by the villages of Mati and Rafina. Turning westward, the course ascends gradually into the Athenian hills, with gentle ascents and descents initially. From approximately 18 through 30 kilometers (11.2 through 18.6 miles), passing through the villages of Pikermi and Pallini, the route becomes steeper and more challenging. In this segment, the course ascends 200 meters (656 feet), cresting near Stavros at 240 meters (788 feet) above sea level. Afterward, the course descends for about 10 kilometers into Athens, through suburban Agia Paraskevi and Holargos, finishing at an elevation of about 75 meters (246 feet). This is one of four Olympic marathon courses with a net uphill gradient, or more ascent than descent. (The others are those at Mexico City in 1968, Los Angeles in 1984, and Barcelona in 1992.)

From a competitor's viewpoint, the course design did have some redeeming qualities despite its difficulty. The initial level portion permitted athletes to develop a sense of efficient race pace. The grade increase in midcourse was reasonably steady, with only a few sharper inclines. And the long sloping downhill finish permitted a pace increase for the very fit, while easing the discomfort for those not having a good day.

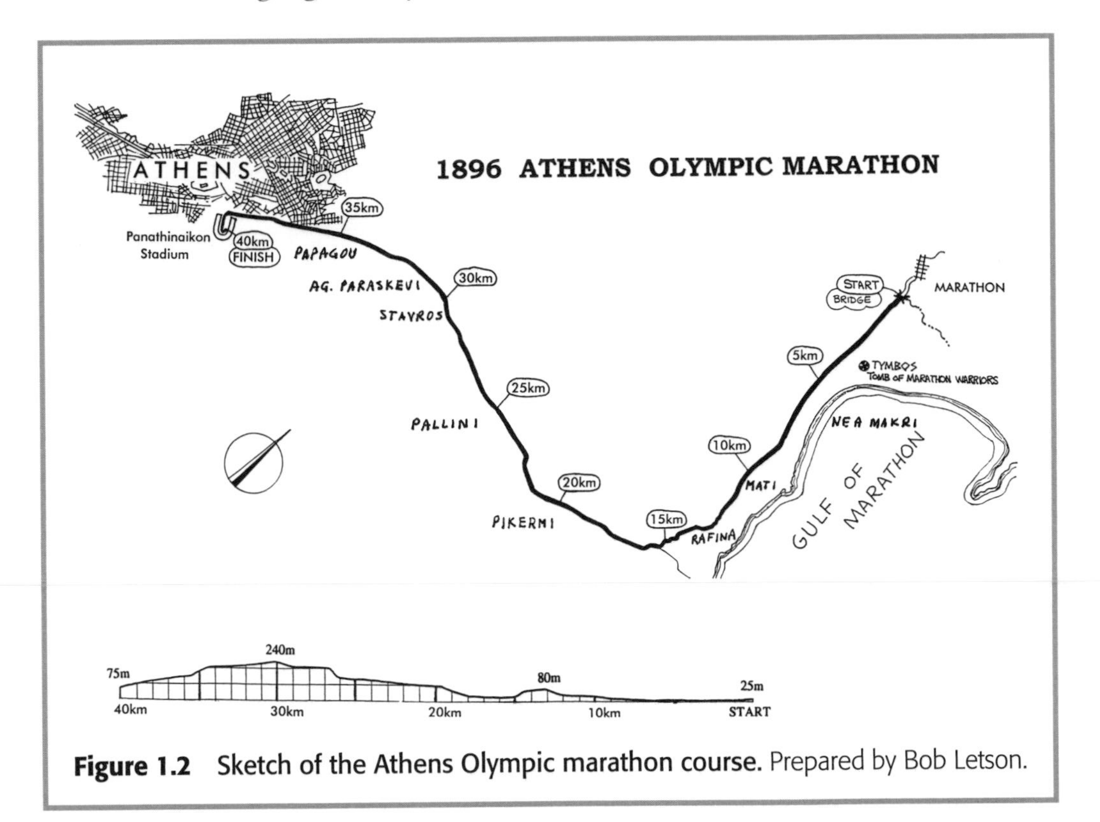

Figure 1.2 Sketch of the Athens Olympic marathon course. Prepared by Bob Letson.

Selecting the Greek Marathon Team

The Greeks were keenly interested in winning this first Olympic marathon race. Ostensibly to help in athlete preparation, and also to determine the best-qualified athletes, two selection races were held on the actual Olympic course within one month of the Olympic Games. It could be argued that such a short time period was insufficient for these athletes to recover for their Olympic race. Thus, the Greeks may have given themselves more liabilities than benefits. Little was known about training for such events in those days.

The first Greek selection race was held on February 27 Julian (March 10 Gregorian; 1896 was a leap year) as part of the Pan Hellenic Sport Celebration. All 12 contestants were members of Greek sports clubs. Only the times of the top 6 athletes are known; it is not known even if the others finished. The fastest finishers were Kharilaos Vasilakos (3:18:00), Spiridon Belokas (3:21:00), Dimitrios Deligiannis (3:33:00), Dimitrios Khristopoulos (3:33:50), Georgios Grigoriou (3:36:00), and Evangelos Gerakakis (3:37:07). All 6 earned a place on Greece's Olympic team.

Two weeks later, on March 12 Julian (March 24 Gregorian), another race was held and was actually called an Olympic trial. This time 38 athletes competed. To be selected for the Greek Olympic team from this event, athletes were told they had to better the time of the Panhellenic Games winner (3:18:00). Again, only the names and times of the first 6 finishers are known: Ioannis Lavrentis (3:11:27), Ioannis Vrettos (3:12:30), Eleitherios Papasimeon (3:13:37), Ilias Kafetzis (3:15:50), Spiridon Louis (3:18:27), and Stamatios Masouris (3:19:15). Louis had declared his entry only a few hours before the race. Louis and Masouris finished outside the time limit, but for at least two reasons were also selected to the Olympic team. First, they were close to the fourth-placed trial finisher. Second, the trial conditions were wretched—rainy, foggy, chilly, and a very muddy course. An additional athlete, Sokratis Lagoudakis, was added to the Greek roster, but it is not known whether his fitness had been tested at these trial races.

The First Olympic Marathon Competition

Many first-person accounts of the Athens Olympic marathon race exist. Bijkerk and Young (1999) collected nearly two dozen such accounts from observers both inside the stadium and outside along the course. It is interesting that these accounts vary considerably one from another, even though the observers were describing the same event. Evidently the emotions from the experience affected each person's sensibilities uniquely and profoundly (see figure 1.3).

The most complete description of the race was by Charalambos Anninos, whose account is in the Official Report (Anninos 1896). Although it is difficult to know if this is the most accurate description of the race, we will use it as a starting point and offer plausible modifications as appropriate. In retrospect, the Official Report of the 1896 Games is relatively detailed; similar reports of subsequent Games give only cursory marathon coverage at best.

Figure 1.3 Artist's sketch of Spiridon Louis approaching the sphendone accompanied by one of the crown princes, who is tipping his hat in salute to the winner. Courtesy of Amateur Athletic Foundation Sports Library.

Athletes were transported to the village of Marathon on Thursday afternoon, March 28 Julian (April 9 Gregorian)—the day before their race. They remained there overnight under the care of a special team from the organizing committee. Anninos does not list the participants, but it appears (Balck 1999) that of the 18 entries, 17 started (1 unidentified German athlete remained behind). Thirteen starters were Greeks, with one each from Australia (Edwin "Teddy" Flack), France (Albin Lermusiaux), Hungary (Gyula Kellner), and the United States (Arthur Blake). Flack won the 800 meters final (2:11) on the same day that he traveled to Marathon! In the 1,500 meters run held two days before that, 3 of the marathoners had taken the top three spots as well: Flack (4:33.2), Blake (4:34.0), and Lermusiaux (4:36.0). Among the foreigners, only Kellner had previously run the marathon distance. He had completed a 40 kilometers time trial at Budapest in three hours.

Anninos (1896) reports that the runners were arranged into two rows, but there were four rows according to both an unknown contemporary writer (Bijkerk and Young 1999) and a present-day Greek journalist-historian (Morites 1997). Karolos Morites lists the sequence of athletes. In row one it was Deligiannis, Flack, Belokas, Lermusiaux, and Khristopoulos. In row two it was Kellner, Vasilakos, Blake, Gerakakis, and Grigoriou. In row three it was Lagoudakis, Lavrentis, Vrettos, Papasimeon, and Kafetzis. And in row four it was Louis and Masouris.

There was a short patriotic speech, in Greek, that translated approximately as: "Men, think of your country; think of your flag on the pole inside the stadium; that flag wants you to do honor for her; Hooray for your country, Hooray for the Olympic Games" (Morites 1997). Lagoudakis, a medical student who spoke French, followed this with a comment to the foreign athletes: "If you win, we will still think of you as brothers."

With the formalities completed, at 1400 (2:00 p.m.) on this cool but sunny afternoon, Colonel G. Papadiamantopoulos fired the starting pistol, and the race began. No more than a few hundred spectators witnessed this historic revival of a legend that dated back 24 centuries, but these local peasant farmers were well aware of the Olympic Games and their significance. Because Greek athletes had not won an event in track and field up to that time (they had won in fencing), the crowd cheered on the potential local heroes with a mix of excitement and anxiety. Fortunately, chilly rains and unseasonably cool weather earlier in the week had settled the roadway dust that otherwise would have added frustration for the runners. Each athlete was permitted one attendant to help along the way.

An interesting account of Australian participation in the Olympic Games (Gordon 1994) contains some colorful commentary on the start of the Athens Olympic marathon. It describes Australia's lone entry, Edwin Flack: "As the runners cantered away backed by an odd caravan of attendants, there he was, a tall and angular figure among so many smaller, swarthier ones, with his chest cased in his old school vest (dark blue with a white miter on the chest) and his head protected by a small tasseled cap, attended by the faithful Delves-Broughton, pedalling a pushbike and looking thoroughly incongruous in a bowler hat." V. W. Delves-Broughton was in fact a staff member from the British embassy who had attended school in Australia when his father was master of the Melbourne mint.

As described by Anninos, foreign runners initially took the lead, Lermusiaux setting the pace through the first half of the race. The village of Pikermi, at about 20 kilometers, was reportedly reached in 52 minutes, with Lermusiaux in the lead, but this is clearly impossible as it suggests a pace of four minutes 11 seconds per mile, or two minutes and 36 seconds per kilometer. Lermusiaux led by 3 kilometers over Flack, followed by Blake (erroneously referred to as Black by Anninos), and then Kellner. The first Greek runners were the Olympic trial winner, Ioannis Lavrentis, and Ilias Kafetzis, but they dropped out at this point. This left their Pan Hellenic Games winner, Kharilaos Vasilakos, and Spiridon Louis running close together, still in contact with the lead foreign athletes. Louis reportedly quaffed a full glass of wine from the roadside inn at Pikermi, queried the spectators about who was in front of him, and confidently predicted that he would be victorious!

The uphill segment soon started taking its toll. As the runners reached the village of Harvati at about 25 kilometers, (also written as Palini, Pallini, and Charbati), athletes were strung out in single file. The anonymous contemporary writer mentioned above (Bijkerk and Young 1999) reported race times for the leaders: Lermusiaux 94 minutes, Flack 95 minutes, Blake 98 minutes, Vasilakos

101 minutes, Louis 101½ minutes, and Kellner 104 minutes, with Deligiannis and the Greek teenager Spiridon Belokas together at 105 minutes.

These intermediate times seem more plausible than the result reported at Pikermi. Lermusiaux's time suggests a pace of six minutes and 3 seconds per mile, or three minutes and 46 seconds per kilometer. The overall winner's race pace was seven minutes and 12 seconds per mile, or four minutes and 28 seconds per kilometer, no doubt slowed in the final stages by the hills and dehydration. Other confusion arises, however, as Anninos reports that Blake dropped out before arriving at Harvati, whereas a time for him is given by the unknown 1896 journalist.

The townspeople in Harvati had built an archway across the street to welcome the runners, and they put a crown of leaves on the head of the leader (Lermusiaux) as he passed, in a symbolic gesture of potential victory. This was clearly premature, for Lermusiaux was paying dearly the price of a fast early start, and the others were catching him. After leaving the village, Lermusiaux had to stop during a noticeable incline to receive an alcohol rubdown from his accompanist, the French cyclist Guisel, according to the official report. However, this handler was probably Alphonse Grisel, who participated in both gymnastics and track and field, as there was no athlete by the name of Guisel at the Games (Mallon and Widlund 1998). This allowed Flack to take the lead. Lermusiaux never did recover, retiring to one of several horse-drawn carriages following behind the athletes to transport officials, timers, and medical people.

Louis eventually caught Vasilakos and they ran together for a while, but as Vasilakos began to slow, Louis continued alone. He then caught Flack at 34 kilometers as they descended into the city. The two stayed in contact through 36 kilometers, Louis typically about 20 paces in front. During this period, Gyula Kellner moved into third place, ahead of Vasilakos. Belokas, appearing unusually fresh, now moved into fifth.

Just outside the village of Ambelokipi (also known as Ampelokipoi) at 37 kilometers, Louis took some orange slices from his girlfriend, who was waiting alongside the route to cheer him on. He then picked up the pace. The steady descent made such a pace change easier, but still it must have been difficult, as the others did not respond. Flack shortly thereafter became another retiree for the recovery carriages. As Louis entered the city limits of Athens, near the Rizarios School, a pistol shot announced his arrival.

Meanwhile, back at the stadium, no one knew whether the race had started on time. Also, no one knew the lead pace, so an arrival time could not be estimated. Fortunately, the pole vault was being contested, which kept people's attention in the interim. A German cyclist, August Goedrich, who would place second in the marathon cycle race two days later, finally arrived with the story that Flack was leading the race. This sent a groan through the biased crowds at the full stadium. Subsequently, the starter arrived on horseback, covered with dust from his long ride, and dashed directly to the royal throne to inform His Majesty King Georgios that in fact Louis was in the lead. This new version also spread quickly throughout the stadium, and the crowd went wild with enthusiasm. Attention was turned toward the open entrance to get the first glimpse of the winner.

According to Anninos (1896), "a man wearing white, sun-burnt, and covered in perspiration, is seen to enter" the stadium. This is another indication that the weather must have been sunny and moderate, in contrast to the chilly, rainy, cloudy weather that had characterized previous days. Indeed it was Spiridon Louis, wearing number 17, entering the stadium and running down its southwest straightaway—the left side as viewed in figure 1.1.

No illustrations of the stadium interior show a definite painted finish line or other indicator, such as a finish tape or cord. However, Richardson (1999) reported that "a string was stretched out at the sphendone," most likely at its apex. (A sphendone is a semicircular area at the end of an ancient Greek stadium. The sphendone of Panathenaikon stadium is in the lower part of the photograph in figure 1.1.) Crown Prince Konstantinos and Prince Georgios ran beside Louis along the stadium straightaway. One of these princes may be depicted in figure 1.3, an artist's rendering of the final moment of the race. In the sketch, Louis is being escorted toward the finish by a man who is tipping his hat in acknowledging the winner. Louis stopped in front of the king, presumably also at the finish line in the sphendone, and bowed, while a band played the Greek anthem. It was surely a momentous occasion.

Louis finished the race in 2:58:50. Seven minutes and 13 seconds later, Kharilaos Vasilakos entered the stadium, finishing in 3:06:03, and it was bedlam all over again. That time difference between the winner and runner-up remains the largest in Olympic marathon history. Just as Vasilakos finished, Spiridon Belokas entered the stadium, and then Gyula Kellner, the latter two athletes finishing only 5 seconds apart. Eventually, another six athletes finished the race, and the last one (Lagoudakis) arrived "an hour behind the winner" (Anonymous 1999), which would be just under four hours. After determining that no other runners were on the course, the pole vault competition was resumed, having been temporarily halted due to the general pandemonium.

Louis was led into the tunnel near the end of the northeast straightaway of the stadium, leading up to the top, which was used as a recovery area. He asked for a cup of coffee, suggesting he cooled quickly on this day with moderate temperatures. As Louis was finishing his second cup of coffee, Queen Olga and others of the royal family came over to congratulate him. Olga embraced him and kissed his forehead, but as she shook his hand she expressed amazement at how callused it was. According to Morites (1997), when she learned that he was a common laborer, she gave him the rings from her fingers, saying the equivalent of, "The honor you have given to Greece is worth far more than these simple rings."

Kellner lodged a protest shortly after finishing, alleging that Belokas completed part of the course in a carriage. The crown prince assigned Prince Georgios to investigate and learn the details, as he chaired the Committee on Judges. Results of the investigation were not printed in the Official Report, but indeed Belokas was disqualified, and Kellner was awarded third place. Table 1.1 summarizes the race.

TABLE 1.1

1896 Athens Olympic Marathon at a Glance

Date: 29 March Julian (10 April Gregorian)
Start time: 1400
Course: Point-to-point
Course distance: 40 km
Weather: Cool, sunny
Starters: 17
Finishers: 10 (including one DQ)
GPEs: 5

TOP RESULTS:

Place	*Athlete*	*GPE*	*Date of birth*	*Time*
1	Spiridon Louis	GRE	12 Jan. 1873	2:58:50
2	Kharilaos Vasilakos	GRE	1871	3:06:03
3	Gyula Kellner	HUN	11 Apr. 1871	3:06:35
4	Ioannis Vrettos	GRE		no time
5	Eleitherios Papasimeon	GRE		no time
6	Dimitrios Deligiannis	GRE		no time
7	Evangelos Gerakakis	GRE		no time
8	Stamatios Masouris	GRE		no time
9	Sokratis Lagoudakis	GRE		~3:58:50

[Spiridon Belokas [GRE] finished third (3:06:30) and was later disqualified (DQ)]
Inaugural geopolitical entities: Greece [GRE], Hungary [HUN], Australia [AUS], France [FRA], United States [USA]
Team score (unofficial): 1. GRE 7 points (1-2-4)

Notes on the Top Three Finishers

As one can imagine, **Spiridon Louis** was a grand hero, instantly famous. Little was known of him before the race, but newspapers the next day had plenty of details. Born on December 31, 1872 Julian (January 12, 1873 Gregorian), he was 23 years old at the time of his victory. He was the fifth and last child of Athanasios and Kalomira Louis, who lived in nearby Amaroussion. Now often shortened as Maroussi, this small town was home to three other Olympic marathoners: Lavrentis, Papasimeon, and Masouris (Lennartz 1999). Amaroussion is also the location of Greece's magnificent marble Olympic stadium complex that will be the centerpiece for the 2004 Olympic Games.

Louis was tall and thin—the ideal build for a distance runner. Figure 1.4 shows Louis in his local ceremonial costume. However, he was not an athlete in terms of training and competition. Louis received only an elementary school education and became a day laborer, rather than moving on to a skilled profession. As a

Figure 1.4 Spiridon Louis dressed in his formal celebratory costume after receiving his winner's medal at the first Olympic Games.

young adult, Louis worked with his father in transporting barrels of fresh water from natural springs near Amaroussion to Athens. For this journey, a distance of 14 kilometers, Spiridon would trot beside their horse-pulled load. This work allowed Louis to develop considerable endurance fitness without being an athlete per se. He had also served as a soldier in an infantry regiment of the Greek army; in fact, the starter of the race was his commanding officer. Following his Olympic victory, Louis was offered all sorts of gifts from Greeks who were full of pride in his achievement. Even King Georgios offered him a gift: whatever he desired! He requested little more than a better cart and another horse so he could continue to transport fresh water into the city of Athens.

Louis never competed again. On April 7, 1897 Julian (April 19, 1897 Gregorian), he married his girlfriend, Eleni, who had cheered him on at 37 kilometers, and their first son, Panagiotis, arrived about a year later. They had two more boys, Georgios and Nikolaos, who all did quite well in life. Unfortunately, Louis did not, eventually falling on financial hard times. He was arrested for forgery in 1925 and jailed, but was found innocent and acquitted in March 1926. Then came the death (from diabetes) of his beloved wife in 1927, after which he suffered miserably, as they had been very close. He was one of the guests of honor at the 1936 Berlin Olympic Games, celebrating 40 years of modern Olympic competition. He died on March 26, 1940, apparently of a heart attack, at the age of 67, and his grave is in the local cemetery in Amaroussion (see figure 1.5).

Kharilaos Vasilakos is one of the most important but least-known marathoners in history. In part, this lack of awareness resulted from Louis's victory being the dominant focus of attention. But also, little was known of the two marathon selection races held in Greece just prior to the Olympic Games.

Because he won the first of these, he therefore has the distinction of being the first known finisher of a race at the distance commonly called the marathon. It is remarkable that he improved his personal best by 11 minutes and 57 seconds at the Olympic race after only 31 days of recovery.

He was born in Pasalamani in 1871. The exact date is not known, so he was either 25 or 26 years old when he ran the Olympic marathon. A champion race-walker as well as runner, he was a serious athlete, in contrast to Louis, who was a laborer. He lived for many years in the Plaka district of Athens, known now to tourists as the very picturesque "old-town" region of the city, at the foot of the Acropolis.

Vasilakos eventually became a customs office director. There, his sportsmanship apparently carried over into his working life, as he had a special reputation for honesty and integrity in a position that often found such virtues difficult to preserve. He died in 1963 at the ripe old age of 92.

The only foreigner to officially finish the marathon, **Gyula Kellner** placed third (after the dismissal of Belokas). Born in Budapest, Kellner had dropped out of the first Hungarian marathon championship, which was held in 1896. He did go on, however, to win the second edition held in 1897. His time in that race was 3:52:00 for 41 kilometers.

Figure 1.5 The grave of Spiridon Louis in the local cemetery at Amaroussion. Courtesy Alexandros Savvidis.

Separating Fact From Fiction

Several errors have crept into the story of the first marathon at these inaugural Olympic Games, and we can correct a few of them here. First, Spiridon Louis did not receive his winner's medal as he crossed the finish line. The prize-giving ceremonies were held for all the athletes five days later, on the concluding day of the Olympic Games (Wednesday, April 3 Julian; April 15 Gregorian).

Second, the awarding of prizes did not occur in the royal palace, but adjacent to the royal seats in the Panathenaikon stadium. There, the king presented the awards for each event. All the winners were introduced first, and then the runners-up. There was no public address system in this large stadium, but thanks to the great booming voice of an artillery captain, Kharilaos Hadjipetros, who served as announcer, spectators could both see and hear who was being honored. After the prizes were awarded, and a short parade, the Games were declared closed, and the world looked forward to Paris.

Third, unlike the present Olympic Games format, the top three athletes were not honored with gold, silver, and bronze medals. Only the top two athletes received medals—silver and bronze—along with a diploma. Each winner also received a branch of wild olive, and each runner-up received a branch of laurel. Louis, of course, was additionally presented with the silver cup of Professor Bréal (figure 0.1, in the Introduction). Also, he received an ancient ceramic vase from the collection of a Mr. John Lambros, with a dolichos runner in full stride painted on the side. Thus, he had a handful to carry off the podium.

Where is the cup today? Thanks to a combination of chance and good sleuthing, it was "rediscovered" in 1989 (Lennartz 1998). It has never left Amaroussion and is tucked away in a closet in the home of Louis's only living daughter-in-law, Eutychia Louis. Although darkened with age from oxidation, it has only slight damage; otherwise, the 25-centimeters-tall trophy is intact.

Did Women Compete in Athens?

A persistent and fascinating modern legend suggests that a woman named Melpomeni (also written as Melpomene) competed in the 1896 Olympic marathon. This is another myth that is contrary to the fact that only men ran the race. Recent Olympic historians (Lennartz 1994; Tarasouleas 1994, 1997) and journalists (Tamini 1993) have concluded, however, that at least one Greek woman—maybe two (but perhaps they were the same)—did run the marathon distance near the time of the 1896 Olympic Games.

First, there is the story of Melpomeni. A French-language newspaper in Athens reported in its March 2 Julian (March 14 Gregorian) issue (Lennartz 1999) that "There was talk of a woman who had enrolled as a participant in the Marathon race. In the test run which she completed on her own on Thursday (late in February), she took 4½ hours to run the distance of 42 kilometers (sic) which separates Marathon from Athens."

Olympic Marathon Miscellany 1.1

In the Beginning There Were Professionals...

Only one athlete represented Italy at the 1896 Olympic Games (Kamper and Mallon 1992). As far as the marathon was concerned, however, the efforts of one Italian athlete, Carlo Airoldi, to achieve Olympic selection were nothing less than heroic (Quercetani 1990). Born in 1869 in Saronno, Airoldi was a top-quality ultradistance runner intent on taking part in the Olympic marathon. On February 28 Julian (March 12 Gregorian), he left Milan on foot and 20 days later arrived in Ragusa (now Dubrovnik), Croatia. He then traveled by boat to Corfu and then to Patrasso in Greece, and walked to Athens, eventually arriving on March 31 Julian (April 12 Gregorian). He had covered 1,338 kilometers on foot! Despite a personal appeal to the Greek authorities, he was refused permission to run because he was a professional. Indeed, he had raced for money—in some local Italian road races, and against horses and cyclists in Buffalo Bill's Wild West Show—and that was his undoing.

Professionalism had thus entered the Olympic picture in the very first modern Olympic Games. In 1908, the United States considered Canadian Tom Longboat, an Onondaga Indian, to be a professional, but the allegation was unsubstantiated and Longboat ran in the London Olympic marathon (see chapter 5). No such luck occurred for Finland's Paavo Nurmi, who was not permitted to compete in the 1932 Los Angeles Games (see chapter 10). Today, the distinction between amateur and professional in Olympic circles has been largely neutralized by the realization that all athletes at the highest levels are in fact professional in both knowledge of their events and in sport participation for their means of livelihood.

Later that year, Franz Kémény, founding IOC member from Hungary, wrote in German (Lennartz 1994) that "indeed a lady, Miss Melpomene, completed the 40 kilometers marathon race in 4½ hours and requested an entry into the Olympic Games competition. This was reportedly denied by the commission" because the Games competition format was for men only. A peculiarity here is why there is no first name for Melpomeni; Greeks used two names, not one.

Second, there is the story of Stamata Revithi. From accounts in contemporary newspapers—three in Athens (*Asti*, *New Aristophanes*, and *Acropoli*) and also in the New York City Greek-language newspaper *Atlantida*—Tarasouleas (1994) summarized what apparently occurred. Revithi was 30 years old, lived in poverty in Piraeus, was the mother of a 17-months-old baby, and as well had a seven-years-old boy who had died in 1895. A few days prior to the Olympic marathon, while walking to Athens to find work, she encountered a male runner along the road who gave her some money. He told her, apparently in jest, that the best way to get rich was to run the marathon and win!

She must have decided then and there to follow his advice, as she had enjoyed long-distance running as a child. She found her way to Marathon the day before the men's Olympic marathon and met the assembled athletes. As with Carlo Airoldi, she too was refused entry into the race by the Olympic Organizing Committee, not because she was a professional but because she was a woman.

The day following the marathon, at 0800 (8 a.m.) on March 30 Julian (April 11 Gregorian), she started out on her own, getting a signed statement from the mayor and magistrate as to the time she departed from Marathon. She arrived in Athens five and one-half hours later, at what now is the location of Evangelismos Hospital (near the Athens Hilton Hotel), at 1330 (1:30 p.m.). She again found witnesses to sign their names and verify the five-and-one-half-hours running time. Revithi intended to present this documentation to the Hellenic Olympic Committee, hoping that they would recognize her talent and achievement. Neither her documents nor reports from the Hellenic Olympic Committee have been discovered to provide corroboration.

Recently, it has been suggested (Tarasouleas 1997) that Melpomeni and Revithi may be the same woman. No contemporary press reports in Greek newspapers mention Melpomeni by name; this was described in foreign reports many years later. A contemporary account referring to Revithi as a well-known marathon runner could explain the earlier run by a woman over the marathon course—that was by Revithi herself, not Melpomeni.

Looking Ahead: Brief Highlights 1896-1899

1896: Following the Athens marathon, inaugural races were staged in France (Paris to Conflans, 40 kilometers, July 19, winner Len Hurst [GBR] in 2:31:29.8), United States (Stamford to New York City, 25 miles, September 20, winner John McDermott [USA] in 3:25:56), Hungary (Aszod, 40 kilometers, October 4, winner Bela Janko [HUN] in 3:29:00), Norway (Kristiania, 40.2 kilometers, October 4, winner Hallstein Bjerke [NOR] in 3:34:36), and Denmark (Copenhagen, 40 kilometers, October 25, winner Christian Andersen [DEN] 3:26:30). The French race was for professionals only.

1897: The first Boston Marathon was held on April 19 between Ashland and Boston over a distance purported to be 24 miles, 1,232 yards (39.7 kilometers) but probably shorter, won by McDermott in 2:55:10.

1898: Germany became the seventh nation to stage a marathon (Leipzig, 40 kilometers, July 3, winner Arthur Techtow [GER] in 3:19:05). Italy was the eighth (Milan, 40 kilometers, October 30, winner Ettore Zilia [ITA] in 2:44:40).

1899: The ninth nation to hold a marathon was Sweden (Södertälje to Stockholm, 40 kilometers, August 13, winner Johan Nyström [SWE] in 2:54:14.2).

References

Anninos, C. 1896. Description of the Games. In *The Olympic Games 776 B.C.-1896 A.D.*, ed. C. Beck. Translated 1966. London: H. Grevel & Co.

Balck, V.G. 1999. De olympiska spelen i Athens 5-14 april 1896. In That memorable first marathon, Bijkerk, A.T., and D.C. Young. *Journal of Olympic History* 7 (1): 15-17.

Bijkerk, A.T., and D.C. Young. 1999. That memorable first marathon. *Journal of Olympic History* 7 (1): 5-27.

Gordon, H. 1994. *Australia and the Olympic Games*. St. Lucia: University of Queensland Press.

Horton, G. 1999. The recent Olympian Games. In That memorable first marathon, Bijkerk, A.T., and D.C. Young. *Journal of Olympic History* 7 (1): 10-11.

Kamper, E., and B. Mallon. 1992. *The golden book of the Olympic Games*. Milano: Vallardi & Associati, Editrice.

Lennartz, K. 1994. Two women ran the marathon in 1896. *Citius, Altius, Fortius: The ISOH Journal* 2 (1): 19-20.

Lennartz, K. 1998. Following the footsteps of Bréal. *Journal of Olympic History* 6 (2): 8-10.

Lennartz, K. 1999. Olympic champion of the 1896 marathon race narrates. In That memorable first marathon, Bijkerk, A.T., and D.C.Young. *Journal of Olympic History* 7 (1): 10-11.

Mallon, M., and T. Widlund. 1998. *The 1896 Olympic Games*. Jefferson, NC: McFarland.

Morites, K. 1997. *Spiridon Louis – a legend in the Olympic Games 1896-1996*. Athens: John Fazdekis.

Quercetani, R.L. 1990. *Athletics: A history of modern track & field athletics (1860-1990)*. Milano: Vallardi & Associati.

Richardson, R. 1999. The new Olympian Games. In That memorable first marathon, Bijkerk, A.T., and D.C. Young. *Journal of Olympic History* 7 (1): 11-12.

Tamini, N. 1993. Women always ran the race. *Olympic Review* 307: 204-208.

Tarasouleas, A. 1994. The female Spiridon Louis. *Citius, Altius, Fortius: The ISOH Journal*, 1 (3): 11-12.

Tarasouleas, A. 1997. Stamata Revithi, "Alias Melpomeni." *Olympic Review* 26 (17): 53-55.

zur Megede, E. 1999. *The first Olympic marathon century 1896/1996*. Köln: Deutsche Gesellschaft für Leichtathletik-Dokumentation.

Chapter 2

1900—Paris

Michel Théato Triumphs in Torrid Paris Race

The Olympic Games as Part of an Exposition

It was logical that the second Olympic Games be awarded to Paris, recognizing the enormous contributions of de Coubertin, Bréal, and others to develop the concept of a worldwide four-year sports celebration. However, organizational problems soon arose between de Coubertin and officials of the French athletics association as to who would ultimately control the competition. In the officials' view, de Coubertin placed too much focus on preserving the Greek historical legacy. They also preferred not to be closely controlled by the IOC.

Paris had also been selected as the site of the 1900 Exposition Universelle Internationale, intended as a grand combination of country fair and commercial trade show. Attempting to avoid continuing controversy with French athletics officials, de Coubertin proposed to merge the Olympic sporting events with the exposition, thereby giving him and the IOC greater control over details. Both hoped that the Olympic Games' identity and value would not be lost in this multifaceted extravaganza, thus preserving the continuity of a four-year Olympic Games cycle.

Unfortunately, the Paris Olympic Games did lose much of their identity, both to spectators and even to those who chronicled sport. In the Official Report of the exposition, they were simply called the "Concours internationaux d' Exercices physiques et de Sports," or "International Competitions of Physical Exercises and Sports," with no mention of the word "Olympic." As shown in figure 2.1, the IOC did publish a list of events within each of its sports, entitled "Programme des Jeux Olympiques de 1900 Paris" in boldface type, for spectators as well as for the historical record. Interestingly, however, the marathon was omitted from the list of events in track and field. The exposition extended from April 15 to November 12, 1900, but those competitions that were eventually considered as "Olympic events" took place from May 14 to October 28 (Mallon 1998).

A new stadium holding 70,000 spectators was constructed for this exposition, but it was not termed an Olympic Stadium and there were no opening and closing ceremonies. This facility was entirely inappropriate for many sports, such as underwater swimming, hot air ballooning, motor car racing, and fishing, but athletes in some sports, such as cricket and croquet, did use it. Many sporting activities were entirely unrelated to the Olympic events contested at Athens.

Advertisements of planned events often did not distinguish whether they were part of the Olympic Games program or part of the exposition. Track and field events were held on July 14, 15, 16, 19, and 22. The most notable track and field Olympian from these Games was Alvin Kraenzlein of the United States, who, in the space of three days (July 14-16), won individual gold medals in the 110 meters hurdles, long jump, 60 meters dash, and 200 meters hurdles. That record in track and field events for a single Olympic Games still stands.

The exposition organizers did not possess the kind of facilities needed to permit quality track and field competition. The IOC unfortunately could not achieve the necessary improvements to the facilities provided because it had no jurisdictional control over them. They belonged to the Racing Club de France. Formed in 1882 and located in the Bois de Boulogne, its property included a 500 meters grass-covered oval in a forested setting. It did not have cinders or dirt for a competition surface, and it was not even flat, so the sprinters ran over undulating ground. The setting was also unsatisfactory for field event competition because the implements for the throwing contests got caught in the branches of the grove of trees. This competition environment was far inferior to the Panathenaikon stadium, but nevertheless, athletes endured.

In de Coubertin's view, another awkward occurrence was the integration of amateurs and professionals. His concept of the Olympic Games was that they were intended solely for amateurs. Always the pragmatist, however, he eventually, though reluctantly, agreed to participation by both groups in some events at the 1900 Games. The discussions ensuing between de Coubertin and the

PROGRAMME

DES

JEUX OLYMPIQUES DE 1900

PARIS

Comité International des Jeux Olympiques

Président. . . . . . . M. le Baron PIERRE DE COUBERTIN. . . . . *Paris.*

MEMBRES. MM. LORD AMPTHILL. . . . . *Londres.*
Le Commandant V. BALCK. . . *Stockholm.*
D. BIKELAS. . . . . *Athènes.*
Le Comte BRUNETTA D'USSEAUX. *Turin.*
Le Comte M. DE BOUSIES. . . . *Bruxelles.*
Le Général DE BOUTOWSKI . . . *Saint-Pétersbourg.*
E CALLOT. . . . . *Paris.*
L. A. CUFF . . . . *Christ Church (N.-Zélande).*

MM. le Docteur W. GEBHARDT. . . . . *Berlin.*
le Docteur JIRI GUTH. . . . . *Prague.*
C. HERBERT . . . . *Londres.*
Fr. KÉMÉNY . . . . *Budapest.*
W. M. SLOANE . . . . *New-York.*
Le Baron F. W. DE TUYLL . . . . *Velsen (Pays-Bas).*
J. B. ZUBIAUR. . . . . *Conception del Uruguay (Rép. Argentine).*

Comité d'Organisation des Jeux Olympiques de 1900

Président : M. le Vicomte de la ROCHEFOUCAULD. **Secrétaire général :** M. Robert FOURNIER-SARLOVÈZE.

MEMBRES : MM. le Comte PHILIPPE D'ALSACE
G. BAUGRAND.
* le Baron JEAN DE BELLET (*Lawn-Tennis*).
le Cte A. DE BERTHIER DE SAUVIGNY (*Tir à l'arc*).
* P. DE BOULONGUE (*Yachting*).
* GEORGES BOURDON (*Sports athlétiques*).
BOUSSOD.
le Duc DE BRISSAC.
* BRUNEAU DE LABORIE (*Boxe*).
* E. CAILLAT (*Aviron*).
Charles CAMBEFORT.
le Baron DE CARAYON LA TOUR.

MM. le Comte CHANDON DE BRIAILLES.
le Marquis de CHASSELOUP-LAUBAT.
* M. DUBONNET (*Aviron*).
R. DUPUYTREM, député.
le Comte D'ESTERNO.
le Baron ANDRÉ DE FLEURY.
ALFRED GALLARD.
le Comte A. DE GUÉBRIANT (*Yachting*).
GORDON BENNETT.
J. J. JUSSERAND.
le Baron LA CAZE.
* le Baron LEJEUNE (*Polo*).

MM. le Duc DE LORGE.
FRÉDÉRIC MALLET
* le Comte F. DE MAILLÉ (*Vélocipédie*).
F. DE NEUFVILLE.
* ARTHUR O'CONNOR (*Courte Paume*).
* le Comte N. POSOCKI (*Escrime*).
* le Comte JACQUES DE POURTALÈS (*Golf*).
* CH. RICHEFEU (*Longue Paume*).
ANDRÉ TOUTAIN.
le Comte TURQUET DE LA BOISSERIE.
* HÉBRARD DE VILLENEUVE (*Escrime*).

N. B. — Les Noms des Commissaires sportifs sont précédés d'une astérisque. Les Commissaires pour la gymnastique, la natation, le foot-ball, etc..., seront ultérieurement nommés.

Programme des Jeux

Sports athlétiques. — *Courses à pied :* 100 m., 400 m., 800 m., 1500 mètres (courses plates), 110 mètres (courses de haies).
Concours : Sauts en longueur et en hauteur (running long et high jumps).
Saut à la perche (Pole vault).
Lancement du poids (Putting the weight) et du disque.
Pentathle (Championnat général d'athlétisme) 4 épreuves : 100 et 400 m., 800 et 1500 mètres. — Saut en hauteur, en longueur ou à la perche. — Lancement du poids ou du disque.
(*Règlements de l'Union des Sociétés françaises des Sports athlétiques*).

Gymnastique. — *Exercices individuels :* Corde lisse en traction des bras. — Rétablissements divers à la barre fixe. — Mouvements aux anneaux. — Barres parallèles profondes — Saut au cheval. — Travail des poids.

Escrimes. — Assauts de fleuret, de sabre et d'épée. — (Amateurs), Professeurs civils et militaires). (*Règlements de la Société d'Encouragement de l'Escrime*).
Assauts de boxe anglaise et de boxe française.
Assauts de canne et de baton.
Lutte : suisse et romaine.

Sports nautiques. — *Yachting :* Courses à la voile en rivière (Yachts au-dessous de 5 tonneaux). — Courses à la voile en mer (Yachts de 20 tonneaux).
(*Règlements du Cercle de la Voile de Paris et de l'Union des Yachts français*).
Aviron : Un rameur : 2000 mètres sans virage (Skiffs).
Deux rameurs de pointe : 2400 mètres sans virage (Outriggers).
Quatre rameurs » » »
Huit rameurs » » »

Natation : Courses de vitesse : 100 mètres.
» fond et vitesse : 500 mètres.
» fond : 1000 mètres.
Concours de plongeon et de sauvetage.
Water-Polo.

Vélocipédie. — Course de vitesse : 2000 m., sur piste, sans entraîneurs.
Course de fond : 100 kilomètres, sur piste, avec entraîneurs.
(*L'entraînement mécanique sera prohibé*).
Courses de tandems : 3000 mètres, sur piste, sans entraîneurs.

Sport hippique — *Polo* (*Règlements des Clubs de Hurlingham et Paris*).

Jeux. — *Foot-Ball* (Rugby et Association).
Cricket.
Golf (*Règlements de Saint-Andrew, modifié selon les nécessités locales*).
Lawn-Tennis (simple et double).
Croquet.
Hockey.
Longue-Paume.
Courte-Paume.

Alpinisme — Un prix olympique sera décerné à l'auteur de l'ascension la plus remarquable accomplie sur un point quelconque du globe depuis la célébration des Jeux olympiques de 1896.

Tir à l'arc. — (Un réglement de concours est à l'étude).

Patinage. — id.

N. B. — Conformément aux décisions fondamentales du Congrès International de 1894, les Concours olympiques sont réservés aux seuls amateurs répondant aux définitions adoptées par l'Union des Sports athlétiques, l'Amateur Athlétic Association d'Angleterre et les autres Sociétés d'Amateurs du monde.

Les concours sont tous des *championnats.*

Les dates et lieux des concours ainsi que les dates de clôture des engagements, bien que déjà fixés, seront publiés ultérieurement, le Comité d'organisation se réservant d'introduire s'il y a lieu quelques modifications dans cette partie du programme.

Les prix consisteront en objets d'art, exclusivement.

Toutes les communications relatives aux Jeux olympiques de 1900, doivent être adressées :

17, Rue de Varennes — Paris.

PARIS — IMP. A. QUELQUEJEU, RUE GERBERT, 10 AFFICHE D'INTÉRIEUR

Figure 2.1 The front page of the program for the Paris Olympic Games of 1900. Notice in the list of events under "Sports athletiques," or track and field, there is no mention of the existence of a marathon. Courtesy Alain Bouille.

organizers were complex and lengthy (Mallon 1998), but the essence is that de Coubertin rationalized that at least the two groups of athletes could see each other compete, which he thought would be beneficial. If professional performances were better than those of the amateurs, this might stimulate the amateurs to work a little harder. Despite all these frustrations, however, the Games did experience a considerable increase in participants. Best estimates report 1,566 men and 22 women representing 30 geopolitical entities (Mallon 1998), compared with 245 from 15 such entities in 1896.

Marathon Running Goes Global After the 1896 Olympic Games

North America

When athletes returned in 1896 from Athens to their respective countries and described the excitement of participating in the marathon race, interest blossomed in having such races locally. Between 1896 and 1899, nine nations organized marathon races—eight in Europe and one in North America. In North America, most of the interest in long-distance running was in the northeastern part of the United States and adjacent eastern Canada. Most of the Canadian Olympic athletes lived in its eastern region, and Canada had also organized an Around the Bay race in 1894 in Hamilton, Ontario. Then more than 19 miles in length, the event is still contested today but uses a slightly shorter 30 kilometers route. Ten of the 14 United States Olympic track and field athletes in 1896 were from either the Boston Athletic Association or Princeton University.

The first marathon race held in North America was a run from Stamford, Connecticut, to Columbia Oval in New York City on September 20, 1896. It was organized as part of the schedule of events at the fall meeting of the New York Knickerbocker Athletic Club. While track and field events were in progress, 30 runners took a train to Stamford and then ran back along a route of 25 miles, arriving in midafternoon. The winner was John McDermott (3:25:55.6), the time rather slow due in part to a muddy course from morning rains.

Several months later, McDermott won the first Boston Marathon, the second such event developed on the continent. Conceived during the fall and winter of 1896/1897, its debut race was April 19, 1897, when 15 runners toed the starting line. The course ran parallel to much of the railroad line from Ashland to Boston in Massachusetts. Estimated to be between 24 and 25 miles in length, this Boston Marathon course profile bore some resemblance to the Athens marathon route in that the final 6 miles were downhill into the city of Boston, preceded by a long steady climb uphill. However, the 5 miles of uphill climb on the Boston course through the city of Newton were not nearly so difficult as the longer and steeper climb on the Athens course (it would, however, become far more famous, with its name of Heartbreak Hill).

At Boston, the elevation rise through the hills of Newton is 56 meters over a distance of 8 kilometers, or 7 meters per kilometer (185 feet over 5 miles, or 37 feet per mile). At Athens, it was a 200 meters rise over a distance of 12 kilometers, or 16.6 meters per kilometer (656 feet over 7.5 miles, or 89 feet per mile). The first 12 miles (19 kilometers) of the Boston course were rolling, with a net descent.

The Boston Marathon became an early focal point for amateur athletes in eastern North America to test their skills. Highway construction, remeasurement, and subtle repositioning of the start and finish have changed the course length several times. The Boston Athletic Association has continued every year to conduct a marathon race over various versions of this course, and the event celebrated its centenary in 1997. The longevity of this race, together with its many epic competitions, gives it a premier global prestige. Canadian Ronald MacDonald, winner of the 1898 race, and American Richard Grant, second in 1899 and eighth in 1900, both competed in the 1900 Paris Olympic marathon.

Europe

In France, long-distance racing had been popular for many years, even before the revival of the Olympic Games. For example, there was a 38 kilometers race from Paris to Versailles on April 11, 1885, won by Louis Saussus in 2:36:30. In 1896, following the Olympic Games, a 40 kilometers marathon race was organized for professionals only, from Paris to Conflans. The idea was to beat the so-called amateur record of Spiridon Louis. There were 191 starters in this French event, and indeed the British star Len Hurst considerably exceeded Louis's time with a fast 2:31:29.8. In 1900 the course changed direction, from Conflans to Paris. Hurst again set a course record, winning in 2:26:47.4. Whether these courses were the same distance from year to year, and whether they were even close to the distance stated, will likely never be known.

Because Hurst was a professional, however, he was not eligible for Olympic competition, as de Coubertin's philosophy of restricting the participants of the Games's track and field events to only amateur athletes was firmly enforced. Second place in the 1900 Paris-to-Conflans race was Georges Touquet-Denis, in 2:38:00. Although he was an amateur, the race included professionals as well. He would later compete in the Paris Olympic marathon representing France.

A Flat Loop Course Tours the City

The Official Report provides no details regarding the marathon course, the weather, the competition, or the results. Thus, what we do know has been pieced together from local newspapers and magazines of the period. Figure 2.2 shows the route as drawn from a 1900 street map of Paris. The course distance is typically reported as 40,260 meters—26 meters longer than 25 miles, making it slightly longer than the approximately 40 kilometers route at Athens. The race began with four laps around the 500 meters grassy oval that encircled the Racing Club de France. Then, exiting these grounds, runners continued for 1,600 meters in the beautiful Bois de Boulogne, a magnificent forested park in Paris. After this portion, which was similar to cross country running, the athletes reached the first control point, at the Porte de Passy. (Using today's streets, the equivalent route would extend from the Racing Club grounds southward along the Chemin de Ceinture du Lac Interieur, and then east along the Route d'Hippodrome, which becomes the Route d'Lacs a Passy to the Place de la Porte de Passy.) This "porte" marked the start of a large loop around the entire city of Paris, along a wide boulevard that essentially followed one of the old city walls.

Paris had been a walled city since the 3rd century A.D. As it grew, its fortifications were extended, once near the start of the 11th century and again near the end of the 14th century. Between 1784 and 1791, the so-called Farmers General Wall was constructed to protect a much larger city holding roughly a half-million people. It had 57 entryways or "portes." Because the boulevard used for the marathon was parallel to the wall, being just inside it, the marathon course was sometimes referred to quite logically as the "Marathon de Fortifs."

At the Porte de Passy, race officials established the first of seven observational control points, to ensure that runners ran correctly. These points are identified in the course details and numbered on the sketch in figure 2.2. Medical facilities and drinking fluids were planned for each point, but we do not know what was actually provided. Runners initially proceeded northward and then continued clockwise around the loop, returning to the Porte de Passy. Then they retraced their steps to the 500 meters oval for a three-lap finish.

Street names along the route changed frequently, especially when major thoroughfares were crossed. Thus, from the Porte de Passy to the Porte Maillot (2.4 kilometers), runners proceeded along Boulevards Suchet and Lannes. Between the Porte Maillot and the Porte de la Villette (8.2 kilometers), runners ran along Boulevards Gouvion de St. Cyr, Berthier, Bessières, and Ney. Then, from the Porte de la Villette to the Porte de Vincennes (6.1 kilometers) there were Boulevards Macdonald, Sérurier, Mortier, and Davout. From the Porte de Vincennes to the Porte de Châtillon (9.2 kilometers) there were Boulevards Soult and Poniatowski. Then the runners crossed the River Seine using the Pont National, and the course continued down Boulevards Masséna, Kellermann, Jourdan, and Brune. From the Porte de Châtillon to the Point du Jour (4.0 kilometers) there were Boulevards Lefèbvre and Victor, a recrossing of the River Seine using the Viaduc d'Auteuil, and then a short journey along the Boulevard Murat. From the Point du Jour, returning to the Porte de Passy (3.5 kilometers), runners traversed Boulevards Murat and Suchet before reentering the Bois de Boulogne.

In modern-day Paris, a multilane thoroughfare called the Boulevard Peripherique has essentially replaced the ancient wall. Within this city ring road, the same small streets enumerated above still exist, with a few name changes, and thus the route can be followed successfully with a current street map.

The Hottest Olympic Marathon in History

The best descriptions of the race come from two eyewitness accounts written in French by Frantz Reichel and Géorges Lefèvre for the *Journal des Sports* on July

Course Details

The 1900 Paris Olympic Marathon

Start—500 meters oval, Racing Club de France (0 kilometers)

4 laps around the grassy oval (2 kilometers)

Through the Bois de Boulogne

To Porte de Passy—control point one (3.6 kilometers)

To Porte Maillot—control point two (6.0 kilometers)

To Porte de la Villette—control point three (14.2 kilometers)

To Porte de Vincennes—control point four (20.3 kilometers)

To Porte de Châtillon—control point five (29.5 kilometers)

To Point du Jour—control point six (33.5 kilometers)

To Porte de Passy—control point seven (37.0 kilometers)

Through the Bois de Boulogne to the track (38.7 kilometers)

Three laps of the grassy oval to the finish (40.2 kilometers)

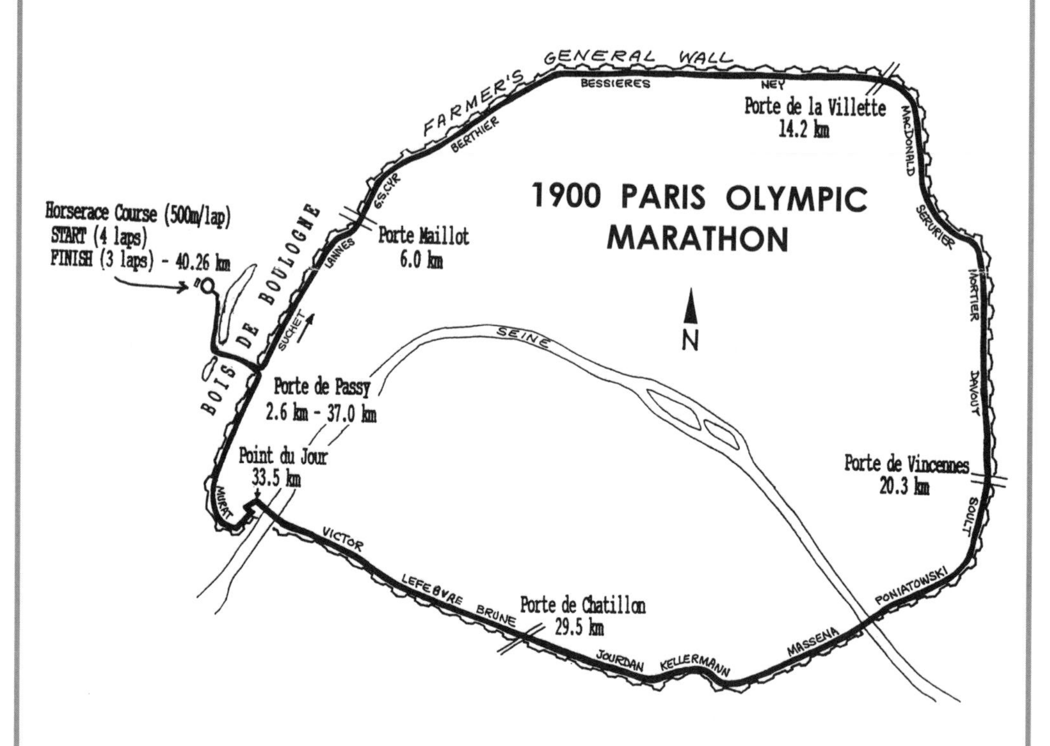

Figure 2.2 Sketch of the Paris Olympic marathon course. Prepared by Bob Letson.

19 and 20, 1900. These have been summarized recently in German (Lennartz 1996). Race-time temperature was reported as between 35°C and 39°C (95°F and 102°F) on this hot day, which was merely a continuation of what had been a very warm summer throughout France that year. Reichel provided biographical sketches for 20 entrants representing seven nations: 1 Canadian, 4 Britons, 4 from the United States, 2 Italians, a Bohemian, 2 Swedes, and 6 athletes representing French clubs. There were no Greeks. Reichel mentions that 17 of the 20 athletes started the race (figure 2.3). One of the nonstarters was Tom Hicks of the United States, who had placed sixth in his marathon debut at Boston in April. Reichel lists the United States's John Cregan as an entrant, but he could not have been there, as he participated instead in an 800 meters handicap event that day (Mallon 1998). Cregan won his heat earlier in the day and ran in the final at 1500 (3:00 p.m.)—30 minutes after the marathon began. Thus, in appendix D, we include 16 athlete participants instead of 17.

The start of this race is shown in figure 2.3, which may be the only surviving photograph of this scene. It is evident that the race began in bright sunshine. The start time was 1436 (2:36 p.m.) and Fernand Meiers fired the starter's pistol—he was the 1892 French 1,500 meters champion. Later research by Raymond Pointu (1979) has suggested that several professional runners also joined in once the race got under way. How many there were, and their fate, isn't known. According to Lefèvre's report, the Swede, Nyström, got one lap around the track and dropped out with illness. One of the Frenchmen, Auguste Marchais, led the pack out of the oval and through the Bois du Boulogne, with Georges Touquet-Denis, Ernst Fast, and Emile Champion close behind. As they went through the Porte de Passy, athletes should have turned left, but the route was not specifically marked, and course marshals were sparse. Fast turned to the right in error and then had to hustle to catch the group, but this kind of jockeying because of unclear markings characterized much of the route.

At the Porte Maillot (near 6 kilometers—where the Concorde La Fayette Hotel stands today), the sequence was Touquet-Denis, Fast, Champion, and Newton, with Marchais 400 meters behind. No intermediate times are available, so the initial pace is unknown. The 3 British entrants retired within 6 kilometers of running, again indicative of the brutal conditions. These were all excellent athletes, having taken the first three places in the 1899 London-to-Brighton ultradistance race. They later reported considerable on-course congestion, including bicyclists, motorcyclists, automobiles, and pedestrians, showing a general lack of awareness by officials regarding the event. With only 16 competitors and the event not being listed on the program, it is likely that, except for officials at the control points, little additional race support was provided. Figure 2.4 gives an impression of this congestion, with cyclists and others accompanying Emile Champion (number 2).

At the Porte d'Ornano, near 12 kilometers, Touquet-Denis stopped by a café for a drink, having run an extra 400 meters by going the wrong way. He ended up finding only beer, drank two, and retired from the race. At the Porte Villette (14 kilometers), site of the Paris abattoir (slaughterhouse), the road was further congested by wandering sheep and cows. As runners passed the Porte de Pantin

Figure 2.3 The start of the Paris Olympic marathon. Note the dense tree cover within the 500 meters oval. Third from the left, dressed in white, is Ernst Fast [SWE] (number 14), and to his left is Auguste Marchais [FRA] (number 13). Immediately to his left, dressed in black, are two British runners, Derek Randall (number 11) and William Saward (number 9). The next, with bib number 8, is Sweden's Johan Nyström, but the two beside him are unidentified. The short runner dressed all in white (number 4) is Arthur Newton [USA]. To his left, taller and darkly dressed, is the eventual winner, Michel Théato (number 3). The runner-up, Emile Champion (number 2) is beside Théato, wearing a white top and dark trousers. Another French runner, Georges Touquet-Daunis (number 1), is to the left of Théato, and an unidentified runner is behind this pair. Courtesy American Historical Review.

at 15 kilometers, Fast was in the lead, with Champion close behind, and Newton in third. It was in this region that the road surface included a kilometer of rough cobblestones, adding to the difficulty.

At the Porte de Vincennes, just short of halfway, Michel Théato and Eugène Besse caught the leaders, passing first Champion and then Fast. Shortly thereafter, Fast was hobbled by a cramp, had to walk for a while, and eventually resumed running. At the Porte de Châtillon, Théato was still ahead of Champion, with Fast still in third and Besse not far behind. This sequence remained unchanged for the duration of the race. Figure 2.5 shows the continuing congestion as Théato pushed onward.

Théato won in 2:59:45 (figure 2.6), averaging a pace of 7:11 per mile (4:28 per kilometer). Champion was 3 minutes and 32 seconds behind. Fast slowed considerably in the later stages, finishing almost 23 minutes behind Champion, but by then only 4 other athletes out of the original 16 were still on the course.

Figure 2.4 **Emile Champion (number 2), along the marathon course. Presumably, the bicyclist is an accompanying official, and it may be hoped the person drinking from the bottle is a trainer who will save some refreshment for Champion!** Photo courtesy Alain Bouille, from *La Vie au Grand Air*, July 29, 1900.

Figure 2.5 **Passing along the Boulevard Murat in the final stages of the race, near 34 kilometers, eventual winner Michel Théato (number 3) is surrounded by both pedestrians and cycling well-wishers.** Photo courtesy Alain Bouille, from *La Vie au Grand Air*, July 29, 1900.

Frenchman Eugène Besse finished just after four hours, followed by the highly regarded American Arthur Newton, known for his winning a 15 miles race on June 17 in 1:28:54.4.

The finish times of Ronald MacDonald and Richard Grant remain an enigma. From Lefèvre's report, Lennartz notes that the last runner finished at 1900 (7:00 p.m.). According to Pointu (1979), Grant was seventh, putting MacDonald in sixth. Pointu reports that the start time was precisely 1436:37 (2:36:37 p.m.). Assuming Grant's finish time as 1900 (7:00 p.m.), we can thus estimate his

Figure 2.6 **Crossing the finish line for the final lap around the oval of the Racing Club de France, winner Michel Théato is congratulated as the winner.** Photo courtesy Alain Bouille, from *La Vie au Grand Air*, July 29, 1900.

marathon performance time as 4:24. Published as part of the report of the exposition, the official results are of no assistance, as only the winners of the track and field events are provided (Anonymous 1900). Even then, only the family name Théato appears, with the rounded finish time of 2:59:00—it was most likely 2:59:45 (see table 2.1).

Olympic Marathon Miscellany 2.1

Nationalities of Olympic Marathon Winners

Michel Théato was listed as a Frenchman for many years, until recent research by Alain Bouille (1990) documented that Théato was born in Luxembourg on March 22, 1878. He thus became the first modern Olympic marathon runner who finished among the top three and represented a country other than that of his birth. Because he lived in Paris and spoke French, apparently few were aware that he was not a native Frenchman, and it remained for Bouille's discovery nearly 90 years after the race to have the facts emerge. Ironically, there have been two other French Olympic marathon winners during this first century of competition, and neither was a native Frenchman: Boughera El Ouafi (1928) and Alain Mimoun (1956) were born in Algeria, a French colony until 1962.

Actually, four other Olympic marathon champions were not born in the countries that they eventually represented when they competed. Thomas Hicks was born in England and was on the United States team in 1904. Kennedy McArthur was born in Ireland but competed for South Africa in 1912. Kitei Son represented Japan in 1936 but was born in Korea, where he was known as Sohn Kee-Chung. And Frank Shorter was born in Munich but competed for the United States in 1972. Shorter's parents were U.S. citizens but had temporary German residence when their son was born, because his father was a military doctor.

TABLE 2.1

1900 Paris Olympic Marathon at a Glance

Date: 19 July
Start time: 1436
Course: Loop
Couse distance: 40.26 km

Weather: Sunny, hot—35°C to 39°C (95°F to 102°F)
Starters: 16
Finishers: 7
GPEs: 8

TOP RESULTS:

Place	*Athlete*	*GPE*	*Date of birth*	*Time*
1	Michel Théato	LUX	22 Mar. 1878	2:59:45
2	Emile Champion	FRA	1879	3:04:17
3	Ernst Fast	SWE	21 Jan. 1881	3:37:14
4	Eugène Besse	FRA		4:00:43
5	Arthur Newton	USA	31 Jan. 1883	4:04:12
6	Ronald MacDonald	CAN	27 Sept. 1874	no time
7	Richard Grant	USA	3 Aug. 1878	~4:24:00

New geopolitical entities represented: Luxembourg [LUX], Sweden [SWE], Canada [CAN], Great Britain [GBR], Bohemia [BOH], Italy [ITA]

Team score (unofficial): No nation had three finishers.

Notes on the Prize Winners

One of the more enduring myths about the 1900 Paris Olympic marathon is that 22-years-old **Michel Johann Théato** was a baker, and thus was accustomed to tolerating great heat in his work (Wallechinsky 1996). By delivering croissants through the streets of Paris, he allegedly knew the city so well that he could perhaps take a few short cuts and extend his lead in the race. Research by recent Olympic historians (Lennartz 1996) has shown that the correct story is somewhat different. First, Théato was a woodworker, not a baker. Second, Parisians went to the bakery themselves in the morning to buy their fresh croissants; they were not delivered. Third, as seen in figure 2.2, the course was a large loop around the whole of Paris, encompassing a much larger region than local shopkeepers would cover in purveying their products. Thus, Théato was not a cheat; he won because he had a very good day in unbearable conditions.

We cannot refer to Théato, Champion, and Fast as Olympic medalists, as they received no medals. Instead, they were awarded porcelain pottery pieces. It was not until 1904 that presenting medals to the top three athletes became standard procedure. Also, at the presentation of prizes following the marathon, no mention was made that these athletes were Olympians. Recall that the Olympic Games were but a small part of the Exposition Universelle, and the marathon had not even been listed on the Olympic program. It wasn't until preparations for the 1912 Olympic Games were well under way that a systematic review of prior Games' results was made to define which competitions would be considered henceforth as "Olympic events," and thus identify "Olympic records" that could serve as goals to surpass at Stockholm. Only when the marathon was included on this list did Théato realize officially—more than a decade later—that he was indeed an Olympic champion.

Prior to the Paris Olympic Games, Théato had little distinction as an athlete. He was first noticed near the end of 1898 when he participated in a one-hour track race (averaging 3:23 per kilometer, or 5:27 per mile). A year later he placed fourth in a 15 kilometers track event. Théato competed in the Olympic Games wearing the colors of the Club Athletique Sportive de Sainte Mandé, but he was also a member of the Racing Club de France. After the Games, he set a French record of 35:13 for 10 kilometers en route to a 53:27 victory for the Prix Gondrand over 10 miles on November 11, 1900. Then, on June 4, 1901, at Lyon, he set an unofficial French record of 8,860 meters on the track for the half-hour run. Later that year, on October 13, he placed third (2:42:43.4) in the second edition of the Tour de France Marathon (40 kilometers), despite falling and injuring his knee. In 1902, Théato turned professional and entered a 41.2 kilometers marathon from Acheres to Paris on July 6. This had replaced the Paris-to-Conflans race as an annual event. He got his first taste of the better preparation of professional runners than that of the amateurs, finishing only ninth (3:18:30). The winner was Albert Charbonnel in 2:52:05.

As to the other two prize-winners, 21-years-old **Emile Champion** was not the champion, and 19-years-old **Ernst Fast** wasn't fast enough to win, either! Little else is known of Champion's athletic endeavors. It was his brother Francois who had won the 1898 Paris-to-Conflans race in 2:30:10. The nearly 30 minutes time difference in results between this and the Paris Olympic race shows the influence of the heat on performance, as the two courses were similar in distance.

Although Swedish, Fast ran only one marathon in Sweden, which he did not finish. He did, however, run in the inaugural Danish marathon championship (40.2 kilometers) on April 24, 1898 in Copenhagen, placing fourth (3:11:31) at the young age of 17 years. In 1902, he again competed in and won the Danish marathon championship in Copenhagen (2:50:30) and set another Swedish national record. Born in Stockholm, he remains the youngest Olympic marathoner to finish among the top three (19 years, 179 days). In fact, this trio of top three finishers remains the youngest ever seen in this first century of the event.

Looking Ahead: Brief Highlights 1900-1903

1900: The route for the Paris Marathon was reversed in direction (Conflans to Paris, July 8) and won again by Hurst in a very fast 2:26:47.4.

1901: Jack Caffery [CAN] won his second consecutive Boston Marathon (April 19) in a record 2:29:23.6. Two more nations started marathons: Austria (Vienna, 40 kilometers, July 14, won by Fritz Luft [AUT] in 3:59:00.4) and Switzerland (Geneva, 40 kilometers, October 27, won by Albert Charbonnel [FRA] in 2:47:25). Charbonnel had won the 1899 Paris Marathon, and won there again in 1902 and 1903. Buffalo became the third venue in the United States, after New York and Boston, to stage a marathon. Samuel Mellor [USA] won it in 3:16.39.4 on July 4 over a 25 miles course.

References

Anonymous. 1900. *Exposition Universelle Internationale de 1900 à Paris.* Concours internationaux d'exercices physiques et de sports. Paris: Imprimerie Nationale.

Bouille, A. 1990. Il était une fois Théato le mystérieux. *La lettre de l'athlétisme* (May): 39.

Lennartz, K. 1996. Der Marathonlauf bei den Olympischenspiele 1900 in Paris. *Deutsche Gesellschaft für Leichtathletik-Dokumentation Bulletin* 5 (17): 37-56.

Mallon, B. 1998. *The 1900 Olympic Games.* Jefferson, NC: McFarland & Co., Inc., Publishers.

Pointu, R. 1979. *42.195 km.: Grandeurs et misères des marathon olympiques.* Paris: Seuil.

Wallechinsky, D. 1996. *The complete book of the Summer Olympics.* 1996 edition. New York: Little, Brown & Company.

Chapter 3

1904—St. Louis

Tom Hicks Conquers Heat Wave in St. Louis

The Olympic Games Travel to North America

The success of American athletes at both the 1896 and 1900 Olympic Games made it appropriate to consider moving the Games to the United States in 1904. The country's economy was strong, and it was a world leader in technology. Its educational system emphasized both athletics and academics, which fit nicely into de Coubertin's own philosophy. Prominent supporters of the Olympic movement in the United States favored Chicago as an appropriate host city and sent representatives to the IOC session held in May 1901 to proclaim its interest in hosting the Olympic Games. On May 22, Chicago was voted as the unanimous choice (Lyberg 1996). An interesting series of events that occurred in St. Louis, however, caused an eventual transfer of the Olympic Games to that city, which very nearly caused their demise.

St. Louis had been planning a mammoth World Exposition to celebrate the centennial of the Louisiana Purchase, the biggest real estate deal in history.

Thomas Jefferson and Napoleon Bonaparte were the principals signing the treaty that transferred one million square miles of land from France to the United States for a cost of $15 million. St. Louis was the capital of the territory annexed by the purchase. The exposition was planned for 1903 and was organized to include a broad range of sporting events as part of its Department of Physical Culture. Financial problems with implementing such a huge event forced a delay until 1904, but with the Chicago Olympic Games scheduled for the same year, the St. Louis organizers believed it would be prudent to combine the two events. Chicago and St. Louis are only 289 miles (465 kilometers) apart, and neither venue would benefit if they each were competing for spectators at their respective extravaganzas. Chicago, however, did not desire to give up its Games.

James E. Sullivan, who was both Olympic Games director and secretary-treasurer of the United States Amateur Athletic Union (AAU), was also chief of the Department of Physical Culture at the Louisiana Purchase Exposition. As a result of Sullivan's joint involvement, the United States national track and field championships, which were organized by the AAU, had been awarded to St. Louis as well. Having an Olympic Games in Chicago, with essentially no American team participation due to a conflicting national championships in St. Louis, would have been inappropriate. The St. Louis organizers thus aggressively sought to have the Olympic Games moved. It appears that they were even prepared to expand the sporting aspect of the Exposition to substantially diminish the stature of the Chicago Olympic Games if additional momentum was required (Barney 1992). In an attempt to resolve the impasse between the two cities, the ultimate decision for the Games' venue was eventually given back to the IOC. Interestingly, despite IOC member preference to keep the Games in Chicago, de Coubertin himself decided otherwise, and the Games were moved to St. Louis (Mallon 1999).

Global travel was difficult in that period, especially to the center of North America. Even de Coubertin stayed home. For this reason, Olympic Games participation in terms of numbers took a step backward. There were only 630 athletes present (only six women), from 12 geopolitical entities. In the marathon, however, the number of such entities represented was similar to previous Olympic Games: five in 1896 (from three continents), seven in 1900 (from two continents), and five in 1904 (from three continents). The Exposition extended from April 30 through December 1, but the so-called Olympic Championships extended only from July 1 through November 23, with the marathon on August 30. As with Paris, the intermingling of an Olympic Games with a world's fair was more of a step backward than forward for the Olympic movement itself.

The Athletes: A Fascinating Cast of Characters

The athlete participants in this marathon comprised an interesting mix of talent. Particularly because there was no limit on the number of athletes representing each nation, the United States contingent was logically the largest: 18

athletes out of 32 starters. They included some experienced and well-known stars. Thomas J. Hicks, of the Cambridgeport YMCA in Massachusetts, had run four of the past five Boston Marathons, placing very well in three: sixth in 1900 and 1901, and second in 1904. Fred Lorz, from the Mohawk Athletic Club in New York, placed fourth at the Boston Marathon in 1903 and fifth in 1904. Olympian Arthur Newton placed fifth at the Paris Olympic race in its infamous heat wave.

In addition to Hicks, Lorz, and Newton, several other outstanding American runners competed in the St. Louis Marathon, making this race for the first time a true United States championship. A Yonkers, New York native, Samuel Mellor Jr., was third at Boston in 1901, and he went on to win the Pan American Exposition Marathon at Buffalo, New York on July 4, 1901, with 3:16:39.4 over 25 miles. In 1902, he was victorious at Boston in a race that featured strong winds and blowing dust. In 1903, Mellor lost at Boston to John Lorden, one of Hicks's Cambridgeport teammates (Lorden had been fifth at Boston in 1901 and third in 1902). Third at that 1903 Boston race was Michael Spring, from New York's Pastime Athletic Club, who won in 1904.

The international entrants were difficult to put into a performance perspective, due in part to little race experience, but also in part because some were not really athletes. There were nine Greeks, all of whom were living in the United States and were in various stages of achieving citizenship. Virtually nothing was known about their capabilities. Albert Corey, from France, had moved to the United States in 1903 and was just starting to build his athletic reputation in the Chicago area. There were three South Africans (see Olympic Marathon Miscellany 3.1) and a Cuban, Felix Carvajal de Soto—whose athletic "credentials" defied anyone to predict how they might perform.

Olympic Marathon Miscellany 3.1

A Mystery Finally Solved

Figure 3.1 shows two so-called Zulu tribesmen, long known only by the names Lentauw (number 35) and Yamasani (number 36), who, along with Robert Harris, represented South Africa. So far as can be determined, neither of these tribesmen had previously run a marathon. They were part of a contingent of veterans of the Anglo-Boer War of 1899-1902 who were participating in an exhibit entitled The Boer War, and thus were actually employees at the fairgrounds. During the Boer War, there had been messenger runners, most likely for General Piet Cronje, and these athletes were two examples. Nothing more was known about them until recently.

Research by Floris van der Merwe, Department of Movement Studies of the University of Stellenbosch, has determined that these athletes were not Zulus but probably Tswanas (van der Merwe 1999). Also, their names were not Lentauw

Figure 3.1 Two Tswana tribesmen who represented their homeland of South Africa at St. Louis. They are Jan Mashiani (number 36) at the left and Len Tau (number 35), barefoot. Courtesy the Missouri Historical Society.

and Yamasani but Len Tau and Jan Mashiani. And so, after 92 years of being referred to by names erroneously entered into the official Olympic program, it is appropriate here to correct the record and reveal these athletes' true identities.

Cuba's lone marathon participant, Felix Carvajal de Soto, was only five feet tall (152 centimeters). Born in San Antonio de los Baños, near Havana, he was about to run his first marathon at the age of 29. In his native Cuba he was a mail carrier instead of a competitive athlete, running long distances across the island carrying letters. Using entrepreneurial expertise fueled by Olympic aspirations, he gave demonstrations of his running abilities in Cuba to earn money for his boat trip to New Orleans en route to the Olympic Games. He then hitchhiked to St. Louis, learning some English along the way, and arrived ready for the race of his life.

A Challenging Course and Another Hot Day

As with most of the early Olympic Games marathon courses, neither the course measurer nor the technique of measurement are known—was it surveyed by an engineer, or measured using an automobile odometer, or was some other technique used? Presumably the measurement was done imperially with a metric conversion because the Imperial system of measurement predominated in the United States. Charles P. Lucas, about whom very little is known in terms of his official role with the Games, witnessed the entirety of the marathon as the personal manager of the eventual winner. He wrote a book about the Games (Lucas 1904) and stated that the course was 24 miles 1,500 yards (24.85 miles), which is equivalent to 39,995.86 meters. The daily program for August 30, 1904, makes a slightly inaccurate reference to the marathon as "40 kilometers (24 miles, 1,500 yards)." This error of 4 meters, though small, has been perpetuated in most articles describing the event. More recently, two St. Louis area locals, June Wuest Becht and Wayne McFarland (Mallon 1999), suggested that the course distance was closer to 42.3 kilometers. But no specific course measurement details have been discovered from original Olympic documents.

The course (see figure 3.2) started and finished in the Francis track and field stadium of Washington University. Named for David Rowland Francis, the president of the Louisiana Purchase Exposition, it was specially constructed for the Olympic Games. Personal communication with the university archivist (Prietto 1998) has provided some details of this most unusual stadium, shown in figure 3.3. It still exists, and it remains the smallest and least imposing of all the modern Olympic stadia. Built of precast reinforced concrete with wooden seating, it accommodated about 9,000 spectators. The track had six lanes and was one-third mile around (586.67 yards, or 536.44 meters). Its shape was unique: one long straightaway and three shorter straightaways. As shown, for these to be connected, two turns were obtuse angles (>90°) and two were acute angles (<90°). Greater intimacy between spectators and competitors was obtained by arranging the seating alongside the short straights, as seen at the left on the left of figure 3.3. The press box was in the center of the short middle section, and apparently this is where the marathon race started and finished.

The runners began the marathon on the short straightaway on the south side of the track (on the left, as viewed in figure 3.3). Running clockwise, the participants completed four laps before exiting the stadium at the east gate (to the right in figure 3.3) on the fifth lap. After negotiating streets on the university campus, the runners entered the city of Clayton and eventually moved out into the rural countryside for one large loop, run clockwise. On return back to the stadium, they ran in the opposite direction—approximately one-quarter mile counterclockwise down the long straightaway and around to the finish beside the press box.

The route shown in figure 3.2 and described in the course details is based on a map published in the *St. Louis Globe-Democrat* (Anonymous 1904a) and augmented by a present-day street map, as well as with supplementary information obtained elsewhere (Mallon 1999). Most of the route can be covered today by visitors to St. Louis.

A few other course discrepancies have yet to be resolved. For example, Lucas (1904) suggested that there were "no less than seven hills, varying from 100 to 300 feet high. . . ." He does not identify their locations or indicate how he knew their height. Mallon (1999) described a downhill from Sappington Drive to North and South Road, and then a very steep uphill on North and South Road (now Brentwood Boulevard) before turning onto Manchester Road. Lucas described two steep hills within the final one and one-half miles on the return trip. Because athletes retraced their steps, presumably these would also have been negotiated on the outbound portion of the race.

Road conditions along the route in several places were poor. Unlike the macadam paving along most of the Boston Marathon route, this course was mostly over rural roads west of St. Louis. According to Lucas (1904), in some stretches the roadway was made of crushed rock rather than the combination of packed dirt, sand, and pebbles found on unpaved rural roads around the world today. While this was unlikely to wash away during the summertime thunderstorms that can strike this area, the uneven surface was difficult for running. Other sections of the roadway were smoother but had stretches covered by a thick layer of powdery soil. This resulted from road traffic that crushed rutty lumps of earth that were created during earlier rainy periods. Horses and cars caused clouds of this choking dust to rise as they passed through it. If published reports are even partly correct, this contest must have been a most extraordinary challenge.

A Race of Attrition and Assistance

The marathon at the 1904 St. Louis Olympics was given thorough coverage, at least in comparison with treatment of the marathon in Paris. Lucas, who is not listed as an Olympic official (Mallon 1999), devoted a 23-page chapter to the event in his book on the Olympic Games (Lucas 1904). Unfortunately, this chapter has numerous inaccuracies and confounding biases that sometimes cause fact and fiction to merge indistinguishably. The question could even be asked as to how this author was permitted to engage in the behavior he describes, as it materially (some might call it unfairly) affected the outcome. Fortunately, a race description in the *St. Louis Star* for August 31, 1904, contains additional coverage, which allows some checking of facts (Anonymous 1904b).

The essence of the race is familiar to most Olympic track and field aficionados. In short, the first athlete entering the stadium was not the winner—and we shall learn that in two subsequent Olympic marathons this same phenomenon

Course Details

The 1904 St. Louis Olympic Marathon

Start—Track, Francis Stadium, Washington University

Run five laps of the track, clockwise

Exit the stadium east gate onto Olympian Way

Right on Olympian Way to Forsyth Boulevard

Right onto Forsyth to South Meramec

Left onto South Meramec to Sappington Drive (now Shaw Park Drive)

Angle from Sappington onto North and South Road (now South Brentwood Boulevard)

Continue on North and South Road to Manchester Road

Right onto Manchester to Ballas Road

Right onto Ballas to Clayton Road

Right onto Clayton to Denny Road (now Lindbergh Boulevard)

Left onto Denny to Olive Street Road (now Olive Boulevard)

Right onto Olive Street to North and South Road

Right onto North and South Road

North and South becomes North Meramec Avenue (now Meramec Avenue)

Continue on North Meramec to Forsyth Boulevard

Left onto Forsyth to Olympian Way

Left onto Olympian Way to east stadium gate

Left through the gate and onto stadium track

Continue one-quarter mile counterclockwise to finish alongside press box

has occurred. This athlete was indeed a bona fide competitor, but he had not run the full distance. He was actually a good runner, known for his free-spirited demeanor, who thought he was being a jokester until he realized too late that his antics were misinterpreted and unappreciated.

The real star of the race should logically be the eventual Olympic gold medalist—Thomas J. Hicks, of Boston Marathon fame. He endured dust, dehydration, heat, and the challenge of running the distance, and he emerged victorious. However, some of the luster of this potential shining star has been removed, for he received unfair assistance from none other than Charles Lucas himself. Lucas administered "performance-enhancing agents" to aid Hicks along the way. This assistance, given by someone accompanying one athlete, was denied to other athletes. If today's rules of good sportsmanship had prevailed back in those days, Hicks would likely have been disqualified.

Some of the participants are shown in figure 3.4 just prior to the start of the race. Lucas reported that 10,000 people assembled in Francis stadium to witness the start. Figure 3.3 however, shows plenty of empty seats in this 9,000-seat stadium. The start was at 1503 (3:03 p.m.), in the heat of the day. The tempera-

Figure 3.2 Sketch of the St. Louis Olympic marathon course. Prepared by Bob Letson.

ture was about 28°C (82°F) in the shade—but the route was bathed in sunshine. Fred Lorz led the field of 32 starters from the gun, but by the first mile, Thomas Hicks (figure 3.5) edged ahead of him. His lead was short-lived. At three of the early checkpoints, some details exist regarding the sequence of leaders. At 3 miles, alongside the Clayton Court House, the sequence was as follows: Mike Spring, Edward Carr, Sam Mellor Jr., Fred Lorz, Arthur Newton, William Garcia, Tom Hicks, David Kneeland, Albert Corey, Len Tau, Henry Brawley, Joe Fowler, and a lone Greek, Christos Zekhouritis. At 6 miles, the sequence was Arthur Newton, Sam Mellor Jr., Edward Carr, Mike Spring, Fred Lorz, and Tom Hicks. Then, at 13 miles, in the village of Des Peres, Sam Mellor Jr. was in the lead, followed by Arthur Newton, Tom Hicks, Albert Corey, William Garcia, Felix Carvajal de Soto, and David Kneeland (Carr had retired).

However, simply listing a sequence of runners does not describe the real flavor of the situation on race day. Several specific details provide an important perspective. First, the only places where fluids were available to athletes along the course were a water tower at 6 miles and a roadside well 12 miles into the race. We do not know how athletes obtained water at these two points. Were

Figure 3.3 The St. Louis Olympic stadium, looking northwest, with the short straightaway on the left, the long straightaway on the far right. Courtesy Washington University Archives, St. Louis, MO.

Figure 3.4 Athletes at the starting line for the 1904 St. Louis Olympic marathon include, from left, Tom Hicks (number 20), Fred Lorz (number 31), Sidney Hatch (number 39), Fred Lorden (between number 39 and number 3), Felix Carvajal (number 3), Christos Zekhouritis (number 6), Albert Corey (number 7), Frank Pierce (number 9), Sam Mellor Jr. (number 10), Edward Carr (number 11), and Arthur Newton (number 12). Courtesy the Missouri Historical Society.

there volunteers to dispense water cups or to provide sponges? Was there simply water flowing freely from a hose connected to a pump? Fluid and electrolyte beverage stations, which are routine today at marathon races, were far less common in these early races, and often were poorly equipped to provide amenities.

Second, as runners proceeded and began to suffer from dehydration, debilitating muscle cramping was the typical cause for them to drop out of the race. Those who had not consumed adequate fluids before the race became dehydrated—and paid the price. This in fact happened to Fred Lorz at 9 miles, and he retired to an automobile moving along with the runners. Also, not long after 13 miles, just onto Ballas Road, Corey and Hicks began to tire noticeably. Mellor had a stitch, and Garcia had fallen to the side of the road. After leaving Denny Road, Hicks overtook Mellor, who retired shortly thereafter. This was at two hours and four minutes into the race, or at about 14.5 miles.

Third, the runners were accompanied by cars, which raised dust and produced uncomfortable and unhealthy conditions for the athletes. Lucas wrote: "Accompanying the runners were a number of automobiles, which raised a great quantity of dust, obscuring the runners many times, and choking the men until they were forced off the road, or causing them to choke and cough until they cleared their throats. Had it not been for the automobiles, the race would have been run under three hours instead of three hours and 28 minutes." Race officials thus could have reduced this problem by either curtailing auto traffic or positioning cars away from the runners (well in front or in back) to permit the dust to settle. Such was not done.

William Garcia, from California, almost became the first fatality of an Olympic marathon due to the choking dust. A dropout, he was later hospitalized with stomach hemorrhaging due to inhaling large quantities of dust that coated his esophagus and entered into his stomach.

Fourth, some of the runners were given preferential treatment. An excerpt from Lucas's (1904) report describes this: "From the 10-mile mark to the finish, the winner, Hicks, was under the personal care of Hugh C. McGrath, of Charlesbank Gymnasium, Boston, Mass., and the author. Hicks was far from being the best man physically in the race, for there were three men who should have defeated him . . . but they lacked proper care on the road. . . . Carvajal was the best physically. . . . On one occasion he stopped at the author's automobile, where a party were eating peaches, and begged for some. Being refused, he playfully snatched two, and ran along the road, eating them as he ran." Thus, Lucas publicly noted that his athlete may not have been as gifted as some of the others, yet he considered it entirely fair for him to have won, thanks to special help being provided. This assistance included water for drinking and sponging, available from a bag kept alongside the engine block.

In addition to water, Hicks was also administered ostensibly performance-enhancing agents. "The Marathon race, from a medical standpoint, demonstrated that drugs are of much benefit to athletes along the road," says Lucas. Knowing what Hicks in fact was given, we wonder how much faster he might have run if Lucas had *not* assisted him. Lucas reported that at 19 miles he "was forced to administer 1/60th grain of sulphate of strychnine, by the mouth, besides the white of an egg. Although French brandy was in the possession of the party, it was deemed best to abstain from further stimulants so long as possible."

Drinking raw egg whites seems difficult to imagine under any conditions, let alone at this point in a marathon. Furthermore, Lucas's understanding of the effects of alcohol was in error. Alcohol is a central nervous system *depressant*, not a stimulant. And in sufficient quantity, it is also a diuretic. What Hicks needed was plenty of water—one liter per hour—not strychnine, egg whites, and brandy! Strychnine has been used for centuries as a rat poison and is a central nervous system stimulant. In small doses, it increases spinal cord reflex excitability, causing a coordinated but exaggerated muscle response. The dose must be carefully monitored because if it is excessive, all coordination is lost and spinal convulsions can occur.

By 19 miles, Hicks, who had been alternately walking and jogging, had the urge to retire due to exhaustion, even though he was already one and one-half miles ahead of Albert Corey and could afford to slow his pace even more. Anyone who has run a marathon and encountered its debilitating, profound fatigue can well identify with Hicks's situation. Shortly after 20 miles, Lucas looked at Hicks and saw that "his color began to become ashen pale, and then another tablet of 1/60th grain of strychnine was administered him, and two more eggs, besides a sip of brandy. His entire body was bathed in warm water, including his head... and he appeared to revive and jogged along once more." Once again, Hicks was receiving preferential treatment unavailable to other athletes in the competition.

While it would be malpractice to condone Lucas's "nutritional" tactics, perceptive readers will notice an interesting implication about the weather. We know clearly that the day was sunny and hot, but also that the humidity must have been low. Evaporation of water is a cooling process, and increases as the humidity decreases. Hicks's reported prompt improvement after extensive sponging with water implies substantial evaporative cooling effects occurring on a dry day with low humidity.

Lucas's description of the final one and one-half miles of the race puts into even clearer perspective the unknowing incompetence of those providing Hicks with alleged assistance. Two sizable hills remained. Lucas writes: "As the brandy carried by the party had been exhausted, Ernie Hjertberg, of New York, kindly replenished Hicks's canteen, and, though the Cambridge man had beef tea with him, he was refused this liquid, as no chance of upsetting his stomach was to be taken. After he had partaken of two more eggs, again bathed, and given some brandy, Hicks walked up the first of the last two hills, and then jogged down on the incline. This was repeated on the last hill, and as he swung into the stadium, Hicks bravely tried to increase his speed, but could not, for, as it was, he scarcely had strength enough left to run the last 440 yards of the distance."

As Hicks entered the stadium, he was cheered enthusiastically by the assembled spectators, who were delighted that, as they saw it, he had finished in second place with a time of 3:28:53. It was at this same moment that Alice

Roosevelt, wife of United States president Theodore Roosevelt, was about to present the gold medal to Fred Lorz, who had finished nearly 16 minutes earlier. Officials accompanying Hicks were incredulous and immediately rushed to inform the appropriate officials that something terribly wrong was happening—obviously Hicks had won the race.

Fred Lorz (wearing bib number 31 in figure 3.4, ironically standing next to Tom Hicks at the starting line) had dropped out at 9 miles. He rode in a car until nearly 19 miles, at which point the car broke down. By this time, he had recovered sufficiently that he decided to leave the beleaguered car and driver, and run into the stadium rather than remain out in the hot sun wondering when help would arrive to fix the car. Passing Hicks shortly after 19 miles, he finished in an estimated time of 3:13:00 and accepted the cheers of those in the stadium as he proceeded around the track. Those applauding assumed he was the Olympic champion.

When confronted, Lorz readily admitted that he had not run the entire course. He had always been the practical jokester, and this was vintage Lorz behavior. Officials did not see it that way, however, and fumed with embarrassment. The

Figure 3.5 **As the marathon began, runners circled the track clockwise. Shown here are Frank Pierce, an American Indian from New York's Pastime Athletic Club (number 9); Henrikos Jenakas, from Greece (number 32); Arthur Newton, who eventually won the bronze medal (number 12); and winner Tom Hicks (number 20).** Courtesy the Missouri Historical Society.

wife of the president had almost presented the winner's medal to the wrong person! In the ensuing emotional aftermath, Lorz was banned from sport for life by the AAU, but this was later rescinded. He resumed racing, performed quite well, and in 1905 won the Boston Marathon (2:38:25).

Following Hicks into the stadium by about 6 minutes was Albert Corey—looking more like the fresh Fred Lorz than the exhausted Tom Hicks, and who had covered the distance without assistance. A little more than 12 minutes later came Arthur Newton, the first athlete to finish two Olympic marathons. Felix Carvajal de Soto also entered appearing quite fresh, but no time was recorded. Reportedly, he had stopped occasionally along the way, once to pick some apples for replenishment of fluids and energy, and at other times to query bystanders about the course. Others had not been so fortunate. John Lorden was vomiting within half a mile after starting, and he never finished the race. Edward Carr retired at Des Peres, near the halfway point, another victim of sickness. It was a race none of the athletes would soon forget. The results are summarized in table 3.1.

TABLE 3.1

1904 St. Louis Olympic Marathon at a Glance

Date: 30 August
Start time: 1503
Course: Square Loop
Course distance: 24.85 miles (39.996 km)

Weather: Very warm—27.8°C (82°F)
Starters: 32
Finishers: 15 (including one DQ)
GPEs: 5

TOP RESULTS:

Place	*Athlete*	*GPE*	*Date of birth*	*Time*
1	Thomas Hicks	USA	7 Jan. 1875	3:28:53
2	Albert Corey	FRA	1878	3:34:52
3	Arthur Newton	USA	31 Jan. 1883	3:47:33
4	Felix Carvajal	CUB	18 Mar. 1875	no time
5	Demetrios Velouis	GRE		no time
6	David Kneeland	USA		no time
7	Henry Brawley	USA	25 Aug. 1880	no time
8	Sidney Hatch	USA	6 Dec. 1885	no time
9	Len Tau	SOA		no time
10	Christos Zekhouritis	GRE		no time

(Frederick Lorz [USA] finished first (~3:13:00) but was later disqualified. Although he ran only part-way, he is included as a finisher.)

New geopolitical entities represented: Cuba [CUB], South Africa [SOA]

Team score (unofficial):

1. USA	10 points	(1-3-6)
2. GRE	29 points	(5-10-14)

Figure 3.6 shows Hicks in an automobile after the race, about to be driven away for medical assistance. His blank stare suggests that indeed he may have endured more than simply a marathon footrace. He had averaged a dismally slow pace of 8:24 per mile (5:13 per kilometer). The Department of Physical Culture at the Exposition carried out what apparently was the first even quasi-scientific study of the effects of endurance running on the human body. As reported in the *St. Louis Star* (Anonymous 1904b), the athletes were weighed before and after the race, and observed throughout. Hicks stood 68 inches tall (173 centimeters) and weighed 133 pounds (60.5 kilograms), and lost 10 pounds (4.5 kilograms) during the event. That is 7.5 percent of his body weight. It is well known that even a 5 percent reduction in body weight lowers the ability to perform aerobic work by 30 percent or more (Wilmore and Costill 1994).

Interestingly, the story of this marathon does not end with the presentation of Hicks's gold medal. A subsequent protest was lodged by Chicago Athletic

Figure 3.6 Gold medalist Tom Hicks with a blank stare showing the grueling effects of his just-completed effort in winning the St. Louis Olympic marathon. Courtesy the Missouri Historical Society.

Association chairman Everett Brown against Hicks's receiving inappropriate and unfair assistance that wasn't available to others. The protest moved up the channels of communication and eventually reached the Olympic Games director himself, James Sullivan. He refused to consider it, and Hicks remained champion (Dyerson 1998).

OLYMPIC MARATHON MISCELLANY 3.2

Olympic "DQs"

Frederick Lorz was the second of several athletes in Olympic marathon competitions who crossed the finish line only to be disqualified. Recall that in 1896, third-placed Spiridon Belokas was disqualified for riding partway in a vehicle. Lorz did that as well in 1904, entering the stadium nearly 16 minutes before the real winner, Tom Hicks. Although various stimulants had been administered to athletes during the early Games, including the 1904 winner Hicks, it was not until 1992 that a marathon athlete was disqualified for drug abuse. That was Madina Biktagirova, representing the Unified Team from the Commonwealth of Independent States (Equipe Unifiée or EUN) (see page 390).

In 1908, Italy's Dorando Pietri was also disqualified. He received unfair assistance from officials, who helped him to his feet on several occasions (after he had collapsed) as he approached the finish line in first place.

In 1972, an imposter at Munich entered the marathon course near the end, ahead of the real gold medalist, Frank Shorter. Finally, in 1996, two women marathoners completed the course in all respects as athletes, but their performances were forever purged from official results because of administrative oversights. They, too, deserve to be remembered, and they will be identified in chapter 24 to help complete the record of this first Olympic marathon century.

Notes on the Medalists

For the first time in the Olympic Games, the top three finishers were presented with medals. As described in chapters 1 and 2, two medals were awarded in 1896 with porcelain pottery presented in 1900. The first two medals at St. Louis were made of silver, and the third was of bronze. Because the first-place medal was gold-plated (gilt), it is often referred to as a gold medal. **Thomas John Hicks** was 29 years old when he won his at St. Louis. Born in Birmingham, England, he was thus the second Olympic champion to represent a nation other than that in which he was born. His performance is the closest that Britain has ever come to winning an Olympic marathon. And he was the third Olympic marathon champion whose Games race was his first marathon victory. There is no record of him competing in shorter-distance events. He did not retire from racing after the St. Louis Olympics, for we know of at least six marathons in which he competed after those Games. His career marathon record is listed in table 3.2.

The runner-up, **Albert Louis Corey**, is usually listed as being from the United States. However, he was born in France near Paris, arrived in the United States in 1903, and did not have time to complete citizenship requirements before his Olympic race. Prior to arrival, he had run at least three marathons in France. He settled in Chicago, where he was a successful runner, particularly after the Games. He finished 4th and 10th in two local Chicago Marathons (25 miles) during 1906, placed 2nd in 1907, and won the race in 1908 with a course personal best (2:57:30). His overall marathon best for the 25 miles distance was a 2:38:47 at the Missouri Athletic Club Marathon in 1908, where he finished 4th. He turned pro at the end of 1908.

Arthur Lewis Newton was born in Upton, Massachusetts, and ran for the New York Athletic Club. He competed in two events at Paris in 1900—the marathon, where he finished fifth, and the 2,500 meters steeplechase held four days earlier, where he placed fourth. Thus, the St. Louis Games were his second Olympics. He was also the AAU champion at five miles in 1900 and in the steeplechase in 1902. At St. Louis, he again doubled in the marathon and 2,500 meters steeplechase, placing third in both events. The steeplechase preceded the marathon by one day.

TABLE 3.2

Career Marathon Record of Thomas Hicks

Date	*Venue*	*Place*	*Time*	*Comments*
19 Apr. 1900	Boston	6th	3:07:19.2	
19 Apr. 1901	Boston	6th	2:52:32.4	
19 Apr. 1902	Boston		DNF?	
19 Apr. 1904	Boston	2nd	2:39:34.2	
30 Aug. 1904	St. Louis	1st	3:28:53	Olympic Games
19 Apr. 1905	Boston		DNF?	
19 Apr. 1906	Boston		DNF?	
30 June 1906	Chicago	1st	3:02:00	
19 Apr. 1907	Boston	13th	2:46:05	
21 Sept. 1907	Chicago	6th	3:28:25	
19 Sept. 1908	Chicago	16th	3:47:00	
16 Jan. 1909	Chicago		DNF	

Looking Ahead: Brief Highlights 1905-1907

1905: The Missouri Athletic Club of St. Louis staged a marathon over its Olympic venue (May 6, 25 miles, won by Joe Forshaw [USA] in 3:16:57.4). This became an annual race for several years. Chicago became the fifth United States city to hold such an event (25 miles, September 23, won by Rhud Metzner [USA] in 3:16:00).

1906: Finland held its first marathon (Oulunkylä, 40.2 kilometers, September 16, won by Kaarlo Nieminen [FIN]—who won his first seven marathons!).

1907: Canadian Indian Tom Longboat won the Boston Marathon (April 19) in a record 2:24:24.

References

Anonymous, 1904a. *The St. Louis Globe-Democrat.* August 30. Anonymous, 1904b. *St. Louis Star.* August 31.

Barney, R.K. 1992. Born from dilemma: America awakens to the modern Olympic Games, 1901-1903. *Olympika* 1: 92-135.

Dyerson, M. 1998. *Making the American team.* Urbana: University of Illinois Press.

Lucas, C.J.P. 1905. *The Olympic Games 1904.* St. Louis: Woodward & Tiernan Printing Co.

Lyberg, W. 1996. *Fabulous 100 years of the IOC: Facts, figures, and much, much more.* Lausanne: International Olympic Committee.

Mallon, B. 1999. *The 1904 Olympic Games.* Jefferson, NC: McFarland & Co., Inc., Publishers.

Prietto, C. 1998. Personal communication.

van der Merwe, F.J.G. 1999. Africa's first encounter with the Olympic Games in...1904. *Journal of Olympic History* 7 (5): 29-34.

Wilmore, J.H., and D.L. Costill. 1994. *Physiology of sport and exercise.* Champaign, IL: Human Kinetics.

Chapter 4

1906—Athens

Billy Sherring Speeds to Victory in the Intercalated Games

The Games Return to Athens

Baron de Coubertin sensed a declining global interest in the IOC's four-year Games spectacle, not because they were a bad idea, but more because their intermingling with two world expositions had confused and disguised their identity. The notion of moving the Olympic Games around the world was indeed perceived as good, but many Greeks preferred a permanent periodic festival of sports commemoration at the site of their origination.

One obvious solution was to have both: develop a four-year global sports festival in Athens sanctioned by the IOC, stage it during the even-numbered year between each officially designated Olympic Games, and ensure that neither event was "contaminated" by another ongoing major exposition. This would provide an Olympic-style competition every two years, giving more visibility and continuity to this global amateur sport movement. The Games in Athens, however, could not officially be called "Olympic Games." As described by the IOC (Anonymous 1984): "the Olympic Games consecrate an 'Olympiad,' meaning a period of four successive years, and are held at the beginning of the Olympiad they are meant to celebrate." The 1906 Athens Games occurred in the middle of the third Olympiad, and thus could not be numbered in sequence with the standard four-year Olympic Games pattern. They thus came to be known as the Intercalated Games, or Interim Games (Greenberg 1996). They were the first Games where all the athletes marched together into the Olympic stadium according to their respective national flags—cheered on by a full Panathenaikon stadium crowd.

Athens was delighted to accept the challenge of hosting a world sports festival as a celebration of the 10th anniversary of the Olympic Games' revival. It developed that these would be the only such Interim Games. Continuing military strife and political instability in this Balkan region made it impossible to stage another such sporting event in 1910. The ensuing death of Archduke Ferdinand eventually initiated the world conflagration that even terminated the Olympic Games temporarily in 1916 (Mallon 1999).

Greece had still not switched to the Gregorian calendar, which adds confusion in dating the various events. Now, 13 days separated the two calendars. These Intercalated Games lasted 11 days, from Monday, April 9 Julian (April 22 Gregorian) through Wednesday, April 19 Julian (May 2 Gregorian). Track and field activities were held on April 13-15 Julian (April 26-28 Gregorian) and on April 17-19 Julian (April 30-May 2 Gregorian). The marathon occurred on Tuesday, April 18 Julian (May 1 Gregorian). As in 1896, the 333 meters track in the Panathenaikon stadium, with its sharp turns and soft cinders, was used for track and field events. Athletes ran clockwise around the track as they did in 1896, although most major meets by this time were switching to have their track events run counterclockwise. Weather conditions were typically favorable for both spectators and competitors throughout the seven days of outdoor competition (Mallon 1999)—except for another very warm marathon day.

Athlete participation at these Games was far superior to the three previous Olympic Games, making this the highest-quality international sporting competition ever seen up to that time. After two previous Olympic Games that were nearly swallowed up by their positioning as part of an international exposition, these Games actually highlighted the fledgling Olympic movement. Baron de Coubertin did not attend these Games, although many IOC members did. The nearly 900 competitors were accommodated in cubicles constructed alongside the Zappeion, a templelike structure adjacent to the stadium (Mathys 1979). Athletes took their meals together in a large hall, and this environment was a forerunner of the future Olympic villages. It was, however, quite primitive, noisy, and crowded, and athletes complained of having to eat an unending diet of tough, tasteless mutton during their stay (Mallon 1999).

Mysteries of the Marathon Course

For the marathon, much at these 1906 Games remained the same as in 1896. There was little that could be changed—the seacoast route from the plain of Marathon to the Panathenaikon stadium was almost hallowed ground. The Greeks fully expected to win again. Continuing elements of mystery, however, surround this 1906 course in relation to that used in 1896.

Were the two courses identical? One standard reference source (Wallechinsky 1996) gives the length of the 1906 route as 41.860 kilometers, compared to the 1896 distance of 40 kilometers. This additional 1,860 meters may have included a deviation that permitted runners to pass the tomb containing the remains of the Greek soldiers lost in the ancient battle on the plain of Marathon. However, no official course maps from either of the organizing committees have been found to permit verification of this, and confusion remains. At variance with Wallechinsky's version, an IOC report (Anonymous 1906) gives the distance as 42 kilometers (26.097 miles). The summary by James E. Sullivan (1906), who was the American commissioner to the Olympic Games, simply reports "about 26 miles," which, if exactly so, would be 41.843 kilometers. Apparently, however, the 1906 course was now paved.

Another interesting question is why the Greek marathoners had not refined their competitive skills better than was demonstrated by their dismal performance at these Games. One could surmise that Spiridon Louis's victory would have created a "running boom" in Greece akin to that in the United States following Frank Shorter's 1972 Munich gold medal victory. This didn't occur in Greece, and it became an embarrassment because when the world's athletes assembled, ready to compete, many had honed their skills in national championship competitions to a level far greater than that seen in 1896. Greece held an Olympic trial competition on March 4 Julian (March 17 Gregorian). The top finishers were Anastasios Koutoulakis (3:04:29.6), Diamantis Kantzias (3:07:14.8), Konstantinos Karvelas (3:07:41.2), Ioannis Alepous (3:10:04.8), T. Dionisyotis (3:11:35), and Khristos Davaris (3:13:05).

A Superb International Field Assembles

Some marathoners worked very hard in their preparations for the Intercalated Games. Canada's William "Billy" Sherring, for example, arrived more than two months before the competition, in order to train on the course and get accustomed to its long steady inclines.

Sweden held its trial race on a windy, snowy day, and only two of eight competitors finished. Gustaf Tornrös won the trial, and of course was selected. Sven Strömberg, second in the trial, could not participate at Athens because of military service. Johan Svanberg led until halfway, but dropped out with a foot injury. He was still selected to compete because of his good performances in 1905, and on the strength of his training form in 1906. Thure Bergvall was also selected to the team without finishing the trial race. Unfortunately, he was not able to compete in the Intercalated Games because his employer refused to give him the time off from work.

Four athletes from the United States competed in the Intercalated Games. This was the first time a so-called American team of athletes was selected (they even wore one standard uniform). The preceding winter months did not permit the staging of a selection race (Mallon 1988), but four athletes were identified as the most talented and fit at that moment. These included Joe Forshaw (first at St. Louis in 1905), Mike Spring (1904 Boston winner, who did not finish in 1905), Robert Fowler (third at Boston in 1905), and William Frank, about whom little is known. According to Mallon (1999), the athletes departed on their 16 days trip to Greece on March 21 Julian (April 3 Gregorian), going by ship from Hoboken to Naples. They arrived on April 3 Julian (April 16 Gregorian). Next, they went by train to Brindisi, then by ship to Patras, and after another train ride, arrived in Athens on April 6 Julian (April 19 Gregorian).

Sherring Steals the Show

The marathon race of the Intercalated Games was the most international of any marathon staged thus far. Twenty-one runners representing 15 geopolitical entities and four continents joined the ranks of 31 Greeks to provide a field of 52 (three times larger than in 1896). Unfortunately, the list of so-called Concurrents in the IOC report (Anonymous 1906) does not reveal whether these are starters, finishers, or entries. The list also provides no nationalities, few first names, and sometimes not even initials of first names. Even now, we can provide little more detail. An additional name appearing in the list but one we do not include in our lists of male participants (see appendix D), is that of A. Tobler, allegedly from Switzerland. The late Fulvio Regli, who devoted essentially a lifetime to researching performances of Swiss and other Olympic athletes, and with whom we had direct correspondence, reported that he was unable to discover any information about such an athlete. Record-keepers from other nations also have not been able to "claim" him.

Three of the starters had competed in a previous Olympic marathon. These included Mike Spring and Robert Fowler, who started but did not finish at St. Louis, along with Greece's Spiridon Belokas, who ran at Athens in 1896 but was disqualified. Sherring was on the entry list for the St. Louis race, but did not participate. Ten European nations sent athletes to Greece. Africa was represented by an Egyptian, Arthur Marson. Australian George Blake was the only participant from Oceania, and later wrote a fascinating account of the race (Blake 1906).

As in 1896, athletes were transported to Marathon the day prior to the race, the idea being to have a nutritious meal, a restful night, and a relaxing morning to prepare for the midafternoon start. As Blake related, the idea was good but the implementation was not very successful. Athletes did not arrive until 2030 (8:30 p.m.), and then they had dinner, which delayed their finally lapsing into a night's sleep. They slept on mattresses laid out on the floor of a farmhouse, but this building was so infested with insects that few slept for more than short periods.

The race began essentially on time, at 1505 (3:05 p.m.), and several stop watches were started to record the official time. The event again was witnessed by only a few hundred local peasant farmers from the area. Once the starting gun was fired and runners were on their way, couriers on horseback transported the official watches to the stadium in Athens. Most weather reports indicate that the day was hot, in contrast to the cooler conditions prevalent during the earlier days of the Games. One source (Blaikie 1984) mentions 33.9°C (93°F), and another (Mallon 1999) gives 27°C (81°F).

The entire course was well patrolled by Greek soldiers to ensure runner safety (Mallon 1999). Every 8 kilometers, there was an emergency aid station set up to care for dropouts and provide fluid refreshment. Mounted officers rode alongside the lead runners, changing horses at the aid stations to ensure fresh mounts. A handler riding on a bicycle accompanied each athlete, identified by a race number pinned on his chest that matched his athlete's number. Only one handler could assist an athlete at any point on the course, but multiple handlers were permitted, each riding partway. The handler could dispense refreshments along the way if his athlete desired such in between the aid stations.

George Blake, William Frank, and Irishman John Daly led the pack initially, continuing together for 8 kilometers. Italy's Dorando Pietri then caught up and joined Frank in the lead. By 10 kilometers, however, the entire field was in single file, Frank in front by about 40 meters. Somewhere between 11 and 13 kilometers, Blake caught Frank, and he moved out in front by 50 meters.

At 24 kilometers, Blake's lead had extended to 1,200 meters, but shortly thereafter a muscle cramp slowed him to a walk. Sherring had been steadily moving up through the field and now caught Blake. As Sherring took the lead, Blake continued to walk and jog, and Frank and the two Swedes passed him—first Svanberg and then Tornrös. Pietri developed stomach cramps at 24 kilometers and retired from the race.

Sherring continued to increase his lead, and by 38.5 kilometers was more than six minutes in front, out of sight to those behind. Svanberg had caught Frank and passed him, but the Greek runner Ioannis Alepous also moved aggressively through the ranks. No one was a match for Sherring, however. Wearing his unmistakable singlet identifying him as a member of Hamilton's Shamrock Athletic Club, he entered the stadium in fine condition, and his 2:51:23.6 victory was more than seven minutes faster than that of Louis 10 years earlier. Sherring averaged a pace of 6:35 per mile (4:06 per kilometer) for the journey.

As described in Sullivan's (1906) report of the race, Sherring "was met at the door by Prince Georgios, who ran with him the entire length of the Stadium, applauding him vigorously. The 80,000 people within the Stadium were Greek sympathizers, but they took their cue from the sportsmanlike conduct of the Prince and cheered Sherring as no victor was ever cheered before in an athletic contest. The King and members of the Royal Family applauded him, and a large bouquet of flowers was sent to him by Queen Olga."

The full stadium gave only a hint, however, of the extent to which the Greek populace turned out to watch the race. The final 8 kilometers of the route along the main thoroughfare leading into the city were lined with spectators on both sides of the street, forming an estimated 150,000-strong cheering line to welcome the runners into the city (Sullivan 1906). This avenue is presently named Mesogeion near the edge of Athens; approaching the stadium, its name changes to Vassilissis Sofias and then to Vassileos Kostandinou.

The two Swedes, Svanberg and Tornrös, were eventually split by the American, William Frank, all finishing within three minutes of each other. Svanberg's time of 2:58:20.8 was 19.2 seconds faster than that of Louis in 1896. The best Greek runner was Ioannis Alepous, in fifth place, only 10 seconds in front of Blake after an aggressive dash down the final track straightaway. The huge Greek contingent otherwise performed quite poorly, with 26 dropouts among 31 starters (84 percent). Table 4.1 provides a summary of the race.

Notes on the Medalists

William John Sherring's convincing victory was well worth his efforts in preparation. A Canadian with Irish ancestry, he was born in Hamilton, Ontario and was a railway brakeman by profession. He was an accomplished distance runner as well. Twice he won the local Hamilton Around the Bay race. His

TABLE 4.1

1906 Athens Intercalated Games Marathon at a Glance

Date: 1 May Gregorian (18 April Julian)
Start time: 1505
Course: Point-to-point
Course distance: 41.86 km

Weather: Very warm
Starters: 52
Finishers: 15
GPEs: 15

TOP RESULTS:

Place	*Athlete*	*GPE*	*Date of birth*	*Time*
1	William Sherring	CAN	19 Sept. 1878	2:51:23.6
2	Johan Svanberg	SWE	01 May 1881	2:58:20.8
3	William Frank	USA	12 Dec. 1879	3:00:46.8
4	Gustaf Tornrös	SWE	18 Mar. 1887	3:01:00.0
5	Ioannis Alepous	GRE		3:09:25.4
6	George Blake	AUS		3:09:35.0
7	Konstantinos Karvelas	GRE		3:15:54.0
8	Andre Roffi	FRA	1882	3:17:49.8
9	Hermann Müller	GER	18 Apr. 1885	3:21:00.0
10	Khristos Davaris	GRE		no time

New geopolitical entities represented: Ireland [IRL], Denmark [DEN], Germany [GER], Belgium [BEL], Austria [AUT], Egypt [EGY]

Team score (unofficial): 1. GRE 22 points (5-7-10)

Figure 4.1 Winner Billy Sherring being applauded by Prince Giorgios as he approaches the finish line in Panathenaikon stadium.

previous marathon best had been a runner-up performance (2:41:31.6) to another Canadian, John "Jack" Peter Caffery, in 1900 at Boston. Sherring was excited about the possibility of representing Canada at the 1906 Games, but as there was no official team with funding, he had to finance the trip himself.

Thanks to two local Hamiltonians—Billy Carroll and Eddie Whyte—Sherring's Olympic dream came true (Blaikie 1984). Carroll had been race director for the Around the Bay race since its inception in 1894. He owned a cigar store but had an undercover horse race betting business on the side. Whyte was a horse trainer who gave Sherring an inside tip to put his money on a horse named Cicely at the local racetrack. Sherring got together Can$ 40 (Canadian) and placed his bet with Carroll at odds of 12 to one. Cicely indeed won the race, and Sherring's Can$ 480 winnings suddenly made his trip to Athens a reality!

Wallechinsky reported in considerable detail Sherring's weight fluctuations as he prepared for the Games. He was 67 inches tall (170 centimeters) and weighed 135 pounds (61.2 kilograms) as he departed Canada for Greece. He was down to 112 pounds (50.9 kilograms) the day of the race, and weighed 98 pounds (44.5 kilograms) after his competition. Presumably different scales were used at each locale, so how much of this variation was due to instrument error is unknown. Also, no mention is made as to why he apparently was the only competitor singled out for such weighing. Sherring lived to the ripe old age of 87 and died in 1964. He will always be a hero in Hamilton.

The fastest European finisher was runner-up **Johan Svanberg**, born in Stockholm, Sweden. A lively competitiveness had developed between him and countryman Gustaf Tornrös, which pushed both to greater excellence. Tornrös had beaten Svanberg easily over 40.2 kilometers in 1905 (3:06:53.8), and then he won the Swedish Olympic trial race in 1906, as mentioned earlier. Tornrös beat Svanberg again in 1907, when he delivered his fastest 40.2 kilometers time of 2:58:03. At Athens, however, in his third marathon, Svanberg beat Tornrös. In 1908, at the London Olympics, Svanberg established Sweden's inaugural 42.195 kilometers marathon record of 3:07:50.8 by finishing eighth. That was his sixth and final marathon as an amateur; he turned professional afterward and raced successfully in the United States. He finished second at New York (2:50:54 on May 8, 1909), winning $2,000, and was victorious three weeks later at Chicago (2:48:11.2 on May 29). He also won a "short course" marathon at Lawrence, Kansas, on August 25, 1910 (2:29:40).

References

Anonymous. 1906. Jeux Olympiques internationaux 1906. Resultats officiels. *Bulletin du Comité de Jeux Olympiques* 4: 82-83.

Anonymous. 1984. *The Olympic movement.* Lausanne: International Olympic Committee.

Blaikie, D. 1984. *Boston—the Canadian story.* Ottawa: Bhakti Press.

Blake, G. 1906. *The Age.* June 14.

Greenberg, S. 1996. *The Guinness book of Olympic facts and feats.* Enfield, Middlesex: Guinness Publishing Ltd.

Mallon, B. 1988. 1988 *U.S. Olympic trials media guide.* Indianapolis: TAC/USA Press Information Department.

Mallon, B. 1999. *The 1906 Olympic Games.* Jefferson, NC: McFarland & Co., Inc., Publishers.

Mathys, F.K. 1979. Those controversial Games of 1906. *Olympic Review* 146: 694-695.

Sullivan, J.E. 1906. The Olympic Games of 1906 at Athens. *Spalding's Athletic Library* 23 (273): 95-101.

CHAPTER 5

1908—LONDON

Pietri Steals the Show as Hayes Captures the Gold

Athletes Prepare for London Instead of Rome

The 1908 Olympic Games had been awarded to Rome, but the powerful eruption of Mount Vesuvius on March 23, 1906, killing at least 2,000 people, brought a severe economic burden to Italy as it turned to reconstructing the destroyed region. At Athens in 1906, Rome reluctantly announced that it could not stage the 1908 Games. Great Britain volunteered on November 19, 1906, to accept the challenge. The British believed they could do a creditable job because amateur sports were already so much a fabric of their society. At the Opening Ceremonies on July 13, 1908, less than two years later, it was clear by the organizational standard and splendor that they were capable hosts.

The mammoth White City Stadium complex, seating 90,000, was completed on time on the grounds of the Franco-British Exhibition at Shepherds Bush in west London. It was dedicated on May 14, allowing both the British Olympic trials and the AAA championships to use the facility as a test run. The London Olympic Games were the first recorded on motion picture film, and much of the action still makes for exciting viewing.

Politics and personalities caused some consternation and confusion during these Games, however, portending what would eventually occur at future Olympic Games. As one example, Finland was a Russian territory, permitted by its controlling government to compete under the Russian flag. The Finns did not like this idea, and thus at the Opening Ceremonies they marched in with no flag at all (Kamper and Mallon 1992). As another example, these were the Games where the United States flag-bearer, shot-putter Ralph Rose, did not dip the flag in recognition when the delegation passed King Edward VII in the royal box—and the tradition continues today. In part, this was due to the American team's irritation at the absence of its flag flying atop the stadium along with those of the other participating nations. The British apologized, saying they couldn't find one—Sweden's was missing also.

A third example involved the incessant bickering between British and American officials. The latter complained that the 400 meters heats were rigged in favor of the former, which was difficult to determine as they were drawn in private. Rancor increased through the week of track and field, culminating the day before the marathon. As eloquently described (Greenberg 1995), John Carpenter of the United States was disqualified for blocking the path of a British runner, Wyndham Halswelle, and the 400 meters final was ordered to be rerun two days hence. The American refused, and on the day after the marathon Halswelle raced alone, becoming the only gold medalist to have won essentially by default (in 50 seconds flat).

Athletes From Around the World Prepare for London

With only two years between the Athens and London Olympic marathons, de Coubertin's idea of keeping the Olympic spirit alive with more frequent Games succeeded. New national marathon championships began, and organizers of events found it desirable from a marketing standpoint to have their races chosen as Olympic team selection races. Athletes set their sights on what even in these early days was simply the grandest world sport spectacle in existence.

Finland

Following the Intercalated Games, Finland was the next to organize and stage a national marathon championship race. This was over a 40.2 kilometers route at Oulunkylä, just north of Helsinki, on September 16, 1906. Kaarlo Nieminen won it in 3:01:06. A year later (June 16, 1907), over a new course at Viipuri, Nieminen won again in a much faster 2:49:15. He enjoyed the marathon so much that he tried yet another two months later—on August 18 at Kuovola—

lowering his personal best again to 2:44:20.2. The next spring, he won the Olympic trial race at Helsinki on May 24, 1908, with a fast 2:47:19.4 over 40.2 kilometers. Having now won seven of the first nine marathons held in Finland, Nieminen was more than ready to challenge the London course as his nation's premier marathon Olympian.

Although the country was sparsely populated, Finland's people loved athletics, as was seen by the rapid development of talent among its athletes. A fascinating rivalry emerged at the previously mentioned Viipuri race with the appearance of the Kolehmainen brothers. The three brothers were fine runners. Two ran the race in Viipuri. Taavetti "Tatu" Heikki Kolehmainen, 22 years old, placed second (3:04:15), with third going to Johannes "Hannes" Petter Kolehmainen, only 17 (3:06:19). Although placing second to Nieminen at the Olympic trial race, Tatu was not selected for the London team, possibly because his finishing 12½ minutes behind suggested to the Finnish officials that he was not sufficiently fit.

A month before the London Games, however, Tatu set a 40.2 kilometers distance record at Viipuri (2:39:04), leaving everyone wondering as to whether he would have been a possible Olympic champion. Further mention of Hannes will occur in chapter 7, where he takes center stage. The third brother, August William "Viljami" Kolehmainen joined the professional ranks of marathoning. Racing on the track, he lowered the world pro record to 2:29:39.2 at Vailsburg, New Jersey, on October 11, 1912.

North America

Canada and the United States had already developed into marathon powerhouses, with the race at Boston showcasing the talent of both nations. At Boston in 1907, on the usual April 19 date, a Canadian teenager named Thomas Longboat—actually an Onondaga Indian—debuted with a course record in driving rain and sleet. A train crossing the route at South Framingham forced all but the top 10 athletes to stop for 75 seconds (Derderian 1994). Longboat was among the lucky front-runners not impeded by the train, and he went on to win. His 2:24:24 on this course, estimated to be 23 miles in length, may have been the first marathon performance faster than a pace of six minutes per mile (5:50.8 if that was indeed the correct distance). Robert Fowler and John Hayes were among those stuck behind the train, but after resuming running, managed to catch everyone but Longboat, placing second and third.

Hayes continued to improve, finishing second (2:26:04) to Tom Morrissey (2:25:43.2) at Boston in 1908, with Fowler third. This was one of two Olympic team trial races in the United States. The other was at St. Louis over 25 miles on May 2, 1908, where Sidney Hatch (2:29:56.4) and Joe Forshaw (2:30:00.4) placed first and second. The United States marathon team bound for London included these two St. Louis athletes, plus four from the Boston Marathon (Morrissey and Hayes, fourth-place racer Mike Ryan, and ninth-place finisher Alton Welton), and Lewis Tewanima.

Canada staged its marathon team trial race on June 6 in Toronto over a course 25 miles long. Only 33 started, vying for eleven team places. By one mile, Harry Lawson had taken a lead that he kept until the finish (2:38:11). Midway into the race, 100 yards behind Lawson was Eddie Carter, with William Wood, William Goldsboro, and an Indian, Fred Simpson, all in single file. Carter fell off the pace, leaving the other three to finish in that order behind Lawson. Tom Longboat didn't participate, but instead ran a special race over three miles (15:21.6) to show fitness—his earlier Boston victory had already earned him a team spot.

Another athlete in the Toronto trial race, who dropped out before halfway but who was also selected to the team, was Jack Caffery. Recall that Caffery had defeated Billy Sherring at Boston in 1900. Retiring from distance running in 1903, he held various jobs—including carpentry, clerking at a hardware store, and selling shoes—while raising his large family of three boys and three girls. Sherring's victory in 1906 stimulated Caffery to emerge from retirement and strive for a place on the 1908 Canadian team. He had just turned 28 two weeks before the trial, and his fitness level was excellent. A foot problem, however, forced him to quit the Toronto trial race, but he, too, was selected to run at London.

Italy

Despite its economic problems, Italy planned to send an Olympic team and staged the country's first national marathon championship over 40 kilometers in Rome on June 3, 1908. This also served as its Olympic trial. Only three athletes finished. Umberto Blasi won (3:01:04) and was named to the Olympic team, along with Augusto Cocca (3:10:00). Dorando Pietri, who was a DNF (did not finish) at Athens in 1906, dropped out again, at 33 kilometers. He was, however, selected to run in London on the basis of a solo 40 kilometers time trial on July 7 at Carpi. His 2:38:00 was the fastest that had been recorded for the distance. Amazingly, he would race in London only 17 days later.

Great Britain

Plans developed for the Olympic marathon route to extend about 26 miles eastward from Windsor Castle to White City Stadium. While the route was being finalized, four marathon team trial races occurred, each over a different distance and venue, the idea being to select the best athletes from these contests. Twelve athletes were eventually chosen for the British team, but we know the details of only seven. The most well-documented of the four races occurred in April, when the Polytechnic Harriers running club staged a 22½ miles race from Windsor to Wembley Park, using part of the Olympic course. Despite cold winds and ankle-deep slush caused by a mixture of rain, hail, and snow, Alex Duncan persevered to win in 2:15:45, ahead of James Beale (2:17:00) and Fred Lord (2:18:04). The top six in that race were selected for Britain's Olympic team, a fitting reward for their demonstrated competitiveness.

The Olympic organizers were so impressed with the Polytechnic Harriers' management of its marathon competition, despite the difficult weather conditions, that the club was invited to assume the honor (and responsibility) of managing the actual Olympic marathon race. This it gladly accepted, and the club attended with great success to every possible detail of course layout, athletes' care, and course management.

Three weeks before the Polytechnic Harriers' race, at Blackheath on April 4, a race occurred over a 24 miles, 670 yards course. For unknown reasons, the winner (E. R. Small, in 2:51:02.2) was not selected for the Olympic team. One month later, at Coventry on May 9, over a 25 miles route, Jack Price won in 2:37:13, filling the seventh spot. These races were the first in Britain over what was termed the "full" marathon distance, or roughly 25 to 26 miles. Then, on May 23, over a course from Windsor/Eton to Wembley, measured as 22 miles, 1,420 yards, the winner (J. B. Powell, in 2:28:23) was also not selected to the Olympic team. Presumably, the remaining five athletes were selected from among these three races, but details remain obscure.

A Course Designed for a Queen and a Princess

Figure 5.1 illustrates the basic plan of the London Marathon course. Starting at Windsor Castle, the route meandered through the villages of Windsor, Eton, Slough, Uxbridge, Ickenham, Ruislip, Pinner, Eastcote, Harrow, Sudbury, and Wembley en route to the White City Stadium finish. The oval cinder running track measured one-third mile (586 yards or 536 meters). It was surrounded by a 660 yards (603 meters) banked concrete cycle track. The stadium track straightaways were oriented northwest-southeast, with two large grandstands along each. The marathon entry tunnel was underneath the grandstand opposite the royal grandstand.

Many explanations have emerged regarding the eventual decision to make the course 26 miles, 385 yards in length. It appears to have happened incidentally as a result of plans for the royal family to participate in the marathon start and finish. Queen Alexandra was to sit in the royal box at the stadium on the side away from the marathon entry tunnel, and the plan was for athletes to finish in front of her. Athletes and spectators both would enjoy this, because it meant running more than half a lap around the track inside a full stadium of cheering spectators.

The queen would also play a role in starting the race. She was to send a signal by telegraph to the starter, Lord Desborough of the British Olympic Association, when the athletes were assembled on the street by Windsor Castle. He would fire the starter's pistol. This plan was eventually modified to allow instead the Princess of Wales to receive the signal from the queen, and she, in turn, would command Lord Desborough to start the race. The princess wanted her children to view these festivities, and so the start point was shifted to the actual castle grounds, on the east terrace under the windows of the nursery, rather than on the street.

Based on these constraints, the course was then measured from the Windsor Castle start point to the stadium. After 26 miles, athletes were just barely inside the stadium. The additional distance to the queen's royal box was 385 yards.

Course Details

The 1908 London Olympic Marathon

Start on the grounds of Windsor Castle on its east terrace, under the windows of the nursery, 700 yards east of Victoria's statue on Castle Hill

Continue to Victoria's statue

Right onto High Street to Thames Street (Windsor)

Right onto Thames Street to High Street (Windsor)

Left onto High Street, cross Windsor Bridge over the Thames River, continue through Eton College to Windsor Road (Eton)

Half right onto Windsor Road (Eton)

Windsor Road (Eton) becomes Slough Road

Slough Road becomes Windsor Road (Slough)

Continue on Windsor Road (Slough) to High Street (Slough)

Right onto High Street to Uxbridge Road (Slough)

Half left onto Uxbridge Road (Slough)

Uxbridge Road becomes Slough Road, eventually crossing the Colne River

Slough Road then becomes St. John's Road

St. John's Road becomes Rockingham Road

Rockingham Road becomes Windsor Street (Uxbridge)

Continue on Windsor Street to High Street (Uxbridge)

Right on High Street to Park Road (Uxbridge)

Left onto Park Road

Park Road becomes Swakeleys Road

Continue on Swakeleys Road to High Road (Ickenham)

Left on High Road (Ickenham)

High Road becomes Ickenham Road

Continue on Ickenham Road to High Street (Ruislip)

Left onto High Street to Eastcote Road (Ruislip)

Right onto Eastcote Road to Field End Road

Right onto Field End Road to Bridle Road (Eastcote)

Half left onto Bridle Road

Bridle Road becomes Eastcote Road

Continue on Eastcote Road to Marsh Road (Pinner)

Right onto Marsh Road to Pinner Road (Pinner)

Half right onto Pinner Road

Pinner Road becomes Lowlands Road (Harrow on the Hill)

Lowlands Road becomes Tyburn Lane (Harrow)

Tyburn Lane becomes Kenton Road (Harrow)

Continue on Kenton to Watford Road (Harrow)

Right onto Watford Road to Harrow Road (Sudbury)

Left on Harrow Road

Harrow Road becomes Harrow High Road (Wembley)

Harrow High Road becomes Harrow Road (Wembley)

Harrow Road becomes Hillside

Hillside becomes Craven Park

Craven Park becomes High Station Road (Harlesden)

High Station Road becomes Old Oak Lane (Harlesden)

Old Oak Lane becomes Old Oak Common Lane

Continue on Old Oak Common Lane to Wormwood Scrubs path

Left on Wormwood Scrubs path to Scrubs Lane

Right on Scrubs Lane to Wood Lane

Scrubs Lane becomes Wood Lane

Continue on Wood Lane to access road for White City Stadium marathon tunnel

Right on access road through stadium tunnel onto the track

Left on stadium track 365 yards to finish beside royal box

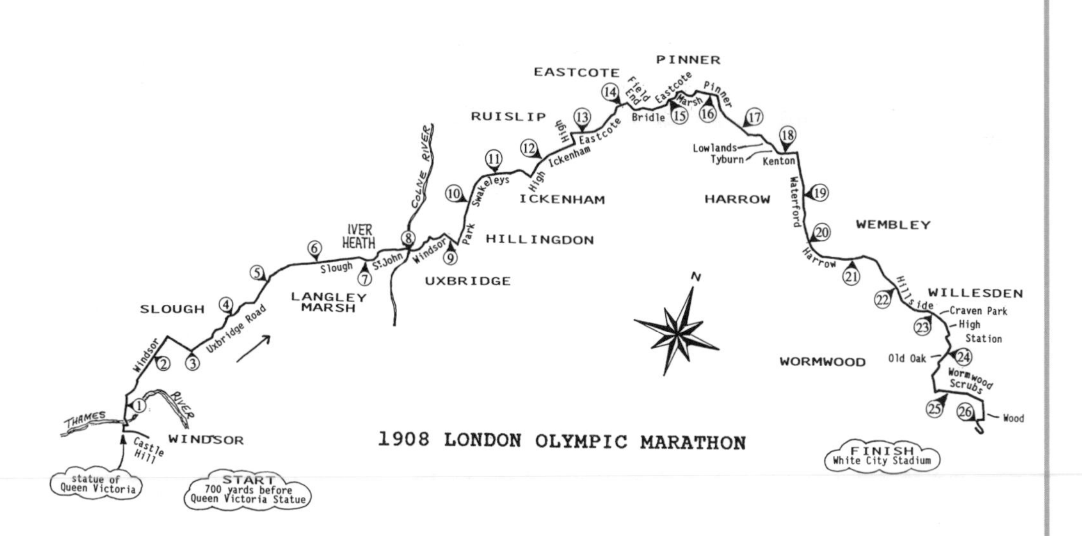

Figure 5.1 Sketch of the London Olympic marathon course. Not all streets are identified, and street descriptors (road, way, lane, street, etc.) have been omitted for simplicity. Prepared by Bob Letson.

There being no standard marathon distance, no attempt was made to tinker with the route and achieve a "rounded" distance, such as 26 miles.

Most roads for this original route remain—except for those adjacent to White City Stadium, which was demolished in 1987/88 to provide for expansion of British Broadcasting Corporation facilities. Other Olympic stadia have been renovated or converted to permit sports other than track and field, but this remains the only one that has disappeared entirely.

The course description from the Olympic Report (Cook 1908) has many grammatical errors and depicts an almost incomprehensible combination of streets and local buildings, as many of the buildings no longer exist. The course details box provides an alternative summary using street names that can be followed with the aid of a current street map. Street widening has of course occurred, more extensively in some areas than others. Consideration is presently being given to organize in 2008 a centennial marathon over this original route.

Two other peculiarities are notable with regard to course measurement. First, the distance markings along the route indicated miles *remaining* rather than miles *traversed*. As an example, at the first mile athletes passed a large "distance tablet" with the number "25" visible, indicating 25 miles remaining. Of course, each of these was in error by 385 yards because, for example, when the runners had completed 26 miles, an additional 385 yards remained between them and the finish line. For two athletes in particular, this added distance made the difference between winning and losing.

Second, on page 69 of the official Olympic Report, below a list of locations of all the mile posts, a summary statement reads simply "26 miles 385 yards = 42,263 meters Full distance." This error (the correct metric equivalent is 42,195 meters) is consistent in early Games documentation, and occurs as well in the "Programme Guide and Route of the Great Marathon Race from Windsor to the Stadium" prepared for spectators. This guide is also confusing due to its many errors regarding athlete identification (McWhirter 1998). As just one example, five Italians were listed but there were really only two. Augusto Cocca did not start. U. (Umberto) Blasi was listed twice with different bib numbers. The other Italian was listed under two different names—Dorando, P. (number 19) and Durendo, P. (number 23)—referring to Dorando Pietri, who raced wearing number 19.

In addition to managing the start and finish details, the Polytechnic Harriers group provided equally meticulous instructions to athletes. The Olympic Report (Cook 1908) provides the flavor of some of this: "Every competitor must wear complete clothing from the shoulder to the knees (i.e., jersey sleeved to the elbows and loose drawers with slips)....The Oxo Company have been appointed Official Caterers and will supply the following free of charge to Competitors: Oxo Athletes' Flask, containing Oxo for immediate use, Oxo hot and cold, Oxo and Soda, Rice Pudding, Raisins, Bananas, Soda and Milk." At four stations en route (Ruislip, Harrow, Sudbury, and Harlesden), Eau de Cologne and sponges were made available at special refreshment booths. Athletes were transported to the start by a special train that departed Paddington Station at 1303 (1:03 p.m.).

Competitors were permitted two attendants riding bicycles along the course, each wearing the same bib number as the athlete to whom they had been assigned. They could observe the start and were then driven quickly to a meeting point 5 miles out on the course to join the race as their athletes passed by.

Pacing and Perseverance Are the Keys to Good Performance

The complex but innovative details of starting the race were carried out flawlessly. The race began at 1433 (2:33 p.m.). Athletes had been assigned to one of four rows, and the field of 55 starters from 16 geopolitical entities was once again the largest and most international field ever seen up to that time. Sixteen entrants, including Augusto Cocca of Italy and Samuel Stevenson of Great Britain, did not start. The field was primarily European, with 31 athletes from 12 nations. North America was represented by only 2 nations, but they brought large teams: Canada had 12 and the United States had 7. The African continent was represented by 2 runners from South Africa. No representation came from Asia or South America. Oceania had 2 athletes from Australia, but in 1908 and 1912 this nation's athletes were combined with New Zealand's into a single geopolitical entity called Australasia.

The weather was sunny, warm, and humid. Temperature details from the meteorological station at Kew Gardens, less than 4 miles from the stadium, indicated 22.2°C (72°F) at 1400 (2:00 p.m.), 25.0°C (77°F) at 1500 (3:00 p.m.), and 25.5°C (78°F) at 1600 (4:00 p.m.), cooling thereafter.

Athletes ran down Castle Hill (figure 5.2) predictably fast, but even after they leveled off onto Thames Street en route toward Eton, the pace still was too fast for the weather. Englishman Thomas Jack led the pack with a 5:01.4 first mile, which, if maintained, would have yielded a finish time of 2:11:44. To put this pace into perspective, it was not until 1953 that Britain's Jim Peters broke even the 2:20:00 time barrier for covering this distance. Jack's second mile was 5:11, and as might be predicted, he did not finish the race. By contrast, those who placed well remained initially near the back of the pack, pacing themselves for a fine finish rather than a fast start.

Amazingly, Jack led through 5 miles (27:01). As he began to tire and drop back, three British runners (Jack Price, Fred Lord, and Alex Duncan), South Africa's Charles Hefferon, and Italy's Dorando Pietri followed in that order. At 10 miles (56:53), Price was leading by 2 seconds over Lord. Hefferon had overtaken Pietri and was 1 second ahead of him (57:12). The two leading Americans, John Hayes and Michael Ryan, were a mile behind, running conservatively. At Ruislip, the approximate halfway point, Price was still in the lead (1:15:13), 41 seconds ahead of Hefferon, who had overtaken Lord for second place. Price now succumbed to his early quick pace, and by 14½ miles Hefferon had taken the lead. At the 15 miles mark, Hefferon (1:28:22) was exactly two minutes in front of Fred Lord, with Pietri only 6 seconds farther back in third

Figure 5.2 Athletes proceeding up Castle Hill to the start point of the London Olympic marathon. Courtesy of Amateur Athletic Foundation Sports Library.

place. Canadian Tom Longboat was in fourth, and thus the lead group presented a truly global battle: four nations and three continents.

While Lord stopped briefly to regroup in the heat and humidity, Longboat and Pietri cruised by. Lord was not a factor thereafter, and Longboat also began to suffer at 17 miles, eventually slowing to a walk and later retiring. Hefferon continued undaunted, passing 20 miles in 2:02:26, three minutes and 52 seconds ahead of Pietri. The Italian, however, quickened his pace (figure 5.3), hoping to catch Hefferon before it was too late. Meanwhile, an American trio of John Hayes, Joe Forshaw, and Alton Welton had started steadily moving up through the ranks. They now found themselves among the top five. Pietri was three minutes and 18 seconds behind at 21 miles, two minutes and 47 seconds back at 22 miles, and only two minutes behind at 24 miles.

With 1 mile remaining, Pietri caught and passed Hefferon. Shortly thereafter, Hayes overtook him as well. Hayes appeared in fine form (figure 5.4), while Hefferon and Pietri verged on exhaustion. As Pietri ran down the sloping ramp under the stadium and then into the thundering vocal roar of the huge packed arena, he became confused, turned right instead of left, then went left and fell onto the soft cinder track just a few meters beyond 26 miles. Had this been the finish line, the gold medal would have been his. Between this point and the finish line, Pietri collapsed five times, each time being urged onward by stadium

Figure 5.3 Dorando Pietri (number 19), accompanied by his handler (on a bicycle at the far left), passing through Harrow at about 18 miles into the race. Courtesy of Amateur Athletic Foundation Sports Library.

personnel crowded around him. Meanwhile, Hayes and then Hefferon entered the stadium track.

Medical personnel were bewildered as to how to proceed. They did not want to provide assistance that would disqualify Pietri, yet they felt obliged to do something lest Pietri experience dire consequences in the presence of the queen and a full stadium. As shown in figure 5.5, at the third of his five falls, officials physically propped him up and encouraged him to continue, clearly in violation of rules for providing assistance to an athlete. He got up, fell once more, and eventually tottered across the finish line, as Hayes approached him. Hayes crossed the finish line 32 seconds later, with Hefferon another 48 seconds behind. Americans and Canadians took the next 5 places, headed by Joe Forshaw in 4th. The two Scandinavians, Svanberg and Nieminen—unaccustomed to warm, humid weather—placed well (9th and 11th).

As Pietri was carried away on a stretcher, United States team officials lodged a protest against his being inappropriately assisted. It was reviewed by the Jury of Appeal and upheld; Pietri was thus disqualified, Hayes won the gold medal, and all the athlete places listed above moved up by one (table 5.1). The assistance given to Pietri was primarily by Jack Andrew, the honorary general secretary of the Polytechnic Harriers and a key organizer of the race. Following instructions of the medical officer for the race, Doctor Bulger, Andrew reported in the August 1908 issue of *The Polytechnic Magazine*: "As regards the finish, most of the reports of same are absolutely erroneous regards my assisting the winner—the doctor's instructions were emphatic, carrying them out caused disqualification; as the animated photos show, I only caught Dorando as he was

Figure 5.4 Johnny Hayes of the United States, accompanied by his handler, running alone in the closing stages of the race. He was eventually declared the winner. Courtesy Amateur Athletic Foundation of Los Angeles.

Figure 5.5 Dorando Pietri being assisted to his feet at the curve in the stadium after falling from near-exhaustion. Dr. Bulger, the medical director, is using the megaphone to request aid for Pietri. In the brimmed hat, kneeling to assist Pietri, is Sir Arthur Conan Doyle, noted writer and creator of detective Sherlock Holmes.

falling at the tape. What I did then I would do again under similar circumstances" (Winter 1969). The continuing friction between British and American officials had many of the latter suggesting that because Hayes was closing in fast, the British were trying to ensure that anybody other than an American would win the race.

Fortunately, Pietri was revived quickly at a nearby hospital and experienced no ill effects from his encounter with what was likely a combination of dehydration and heat stress. At a banquet that evening, Lord Desborough announced that the queen had decided to present Pietri with a special trophy the next day to honor his fighting spirit under adversity (figure 5.6). On it was the simple engraved message: "For P. Dorando, In Remembrance of the Marathon Race. From Windsor to the Stadium, July 24 1908. From Queen Alexandra." The trophy still exists, residing in a safe deposit box at a bank in Carpi, Italy, maintained by Pietri's sport club, the Società Ginnastica La Patria Carpi.

The Pietri issue was not the only protest in the marathon. Prior to the competition, United States officials made at least three protests to the British Olympic

TABLE 5.1

1908 London Olympic Marathon at a Glance

Date: 24 July
Start time: 1430
Course: Point-to-point
Course distance: 26 miles, 385 yards (42,195m)

Weather: Warm and humid, 24.4°C (76°F)
Starters: 55
Finishers: 28 (including one DQ)
GPEs: 16

TOP RESULTS:

Place	*Athlete*	*GPE*	*Date of birth*	*Time*
1	John Hayes	USA	10 Apr. 1886	2:55:18.4
2	Charles Hefferon	SOA	25 Jan. 1878	2:56:06.0
3	Joseph Forshaw	USA	13 May 1881	2:57:10.4
4	Alton Welton	USA	1886	2:59:44.4
5	William Wood	CAN		3:01:44.0
6	Frederick Simpson	CAN	1876	3:04:28.2
7	Harry Lawson	CAN	1888	3:06:47.2
8	Johan Svanberg	SWE	01May 1881	3:07:50.8
9	Lewis Tewanima	USA	1888	3:09:15.0
10	Kaarlo Nieminen	FIN	26 Apr. 1878	3:09:50.8

(Dorando Pietri [ITA] finished first (2:54:46.4) but was later disqualified.)

New geopolitical entities represented: Finland [FIN], Russia [RUS], Netherlands [NED]

Team score (unofficial):

1. USA	8 points	(1-3-4)
2. CAN	18 points	(5-6-7)
3. GBR	40 points	(12-13-15)

Figure 5.6 To honor Dorando Pietri's competitive spirit, the Queen presented him a specially engraved cup.

Council claiming that in their view Canadian Tom Longboat was a professional (Mallon and Buchanan 2000). When asked to provide specific evidence, the United States AAU secretary-treasurer, James E. Sullivan, skirted the issue. As an example, in one letter Sullivan said only that "officials of the (British) AAA can give you information in relation to one Percy Sellen, who has been competing with this Thomas Longboat in America." The Canadian Central Olympic Committee had already studied the matter and found no evidence regarding activities of Longboat as a professional. As recorded in the Olympic Report (Cook 1908), the British Olympic Council decided to deny the protest: "When the governing body which enters a competitor vouches for his amateur status, and that amateur status is contested by a foreign governing body, the mere assertion of the latter body cannot be considered as concluding the case against the competitor."

On the next day, when awards were distributed, the entire United States team was jubilant (figure 5.7), carrying Hayes around as if he was the king of the marathon. On that day, he was! Ironically, however, a young American composer, Irving Berlin, chose to focus on the Pietri incident, writing his first hit song, "Dorando." It popularized marathon running in the United States, although it caused confusion because listeners assumed this was Pietri's family name rather than his first name. Also, many wondered why Hayes wasn't the topic of a tune rather than Pietri; after all, it was Hayes who won the gold medal.

Figure 5.7 Group photo of the jubilant United States team carrying winner Johnny Hayes on a table. Nearest the camera, balancing the front post, is Lewis Tewanima.

Notes on the Medalists

John Joseph Hayes won only one race prior to his London Games performance, and that was at the inaugural 25 miles point-to-point Yonkers Marathon, near New York City, in 1907. He ran the Boston Marathon three times, and his best result was a second place finish in 1908, when it was an Olympic selection race.

Stories abound regarding Hayes's allegedly being employed by Bloomingdale's Department Store as a shipping clerk. Reportedly, he prepared for the Olympic marathon by arduous track training on the roof of its large building in Manhattan. His quality training was really on a track outside the city, and not on the roof.

Following his victory, he then reportedly was promoted to chief of the sporting goods division. It is true that he was paid a salary by Bloomingdale's, but he was not a working employee (Schaap 1963). This was an arrangement made through his Irish-American Athletic Club, and the story about his being a clerk was just that. He drew a salary from a corporation that was sympathetic toward his desire to have the financial security for devoting energy to training. Whether he was a "professional" is thus a matter of interpretation. Following the Games, Hayes did turn professional in the sense of competing for cash, and he improved his London-distance marathon time to 2:41:49 in 1910. His known amateur marathon career record is given in table 5.2.

OLYMPIC MARATHON MISCELLANY 5.1

Johnny Hayes—Irishman or American?

Perusal of even a few books on the history of distance running or the Olympic Games provides confusion as to when and where Hayes was born. One recent article (Phillips 1997) summarized much of the controversy. There is little doubt that the Hayes family was Irish and that the Hayeses lived in or around the village of Nenagh in County Tipperary. Some of Johnny's family emigrated to New York. The question of interest is whether Hayes was actually born in Ireland when it was still part of Great Britain, emigrating later to the United States with his parents, or whether he was born in America after the family had arrived. We know of no birth records for Johnny Hayes in the Nenagh area of Ireland, and no birth certificate for him has been located in either country. However, he died on August 23, 1965, in New York, and the death certificate states clearly that he was born in New York on April 10, 1886, making him 22 years old at the time of his Olympic victory.

TABLE 5.2

Career Marathon Record of Johnny Hayes

Date	*Venue*	*Place*	*Time*	*Comments*
19 Apr. 1906	Boston	5th	2:55:38.8	
19 Apr. 1907	Boston	3rd	2:30:38.6	
28 Nov. 1907	Yonkers	1st	2:44:45	
19 Apr. 1908	Boston	2nd	2:26:04	
24 July 1908	London	1st	2:55:18.4	Olympic Games

Runner-up **Charles Archie Hefferon** was born in Newbury, Berkshire, England, but later moved to South Africa and became one of its citizens. Starting in 1904, he won the first five of South Africa's annual 4 miles championship races. In the Olympic trial race on April 22, 1908, he dropped out at 11 miles, and Kennedy McArthur went on to win. Members of the South African Amateur Athletic Union had so much confidence in Hefferon's abilities that they raised funds to send him to London, ignoring McArthur. After the Olympics, Hefferon won another national title over 4 miles, as well as the 1909 national championship over 10 miles. He also turned professional in the marathon and in 1910 won a marathon track race (183½ laps!) in 3:07:40.

Bronze medalist **Joseph Forshaw** was born in St. Louis, Missouri, and spent his life in the Midwestern United States. He became a three-time Olympian, finishing 12th in 1906, 3rd at the London Olympics, and then 10th at the Stockholm Games in 1912 (2:49:49.4). He qualified for the London Olympics by finishing 2nd at the 1907 St. Louis Marathon (2:30:00.4) behind Sidney Hatch. Forshaw had won the inaugural St. Louis Marathon in 1905 (3:15:57.8), organized by the Missouri Athletic Club, and placed 2nd there also in 1908, 1911, and 1912.

Looking Ahead: Brief Highlights 1908-1911

1908: South Africa, Canada, and Great Britain all staged inaugural marathons over 25 miles prior to the 1908 Olympic Games. Following the Dorando Pietri drama, there dawned an international professional marathon era, particularly popular through 1911. The first such race over the London Olympic marathon distance was held between Windsor and Shepherds Bush in England on October 10. The winner was Henri Siret (2:37:23), who had also won in Milan (2:42:28.4) a fortnight earlier. An inevitable rematch between Pietri and Johnny Hayes occurred at New York's Madison Square Garden on November 25, with an Italian victory (2:44:20.4). In each of three more meetings, Pietri finished ahead of Hayes.

1909: "Marathon fever" swept the athletics world—amateur and professional runners alike—particularly in the United States. This resulted in five successive improvements to the world amateur "record" within eight months over the London Olympic distance. The first three were in the New York City area: Robert Fowler [USA] at Yonkers on January 1 (2:52:45.4), then James Clark [USA] at Brooklyn (2:46:52.8) on February 12, and finally Al Raines [USA] at the Bronx Oval (2:46:04.6) on May 8. On May 26, across the Atlantic, Harry Barrett [GBR] won the inaugural *Sporting Life*/Polytechnic Harriers race between Windsor and Stamford Bridge in Chelsea in an even-faster 2:42:31. Later in the summer, on August 31 at Stockholm, Sweden's Thure Johansson recorded 2:40:34.2 on a 368 meters velodrome track.

References

Cook, T.A. 1908. *The Fourth Olympiad, being the Official Report of the Olympic Games of 1908.* London: British Olympic Association.
Derderian, T. 1994. *Boston Marathon.* Champaign, IL: Human Kinetics.
Greenberg, S. 1995. What special relationship. *The ISOH Journal* 3 (1): 27-29.
Kamper, E., and B. Mallon. 1992. *The golden book of the Olympic Games.* Milano: Vallardi & Associati, Editrice.
Mallon, B., and I. Buchanan. 2000. *The 1908 Olympic Games.* Jefferson, NC: McFarland & Co., Inc., Publishers.
McWhirter, N. 1998. A marathon myth laid to rest. *Track Stats* 36 (1): 57-59.
Phillips, B. 1997. Johnny Hayes: Could he be the eighth Olympic nomad? *Track Stats* 35 (3): 11-13.
Schaap, R. 1963. *An illustrated history of the Olympics.* New York: Alfred A. Knopf.
Winter, A.E.H. 1969. *From the legend to the living.* Rugeley: Benhill Press, Ltd.

CHAPTER 6

1912—STOCKHOLM

A South African Success Spree in Stockholm

Sweden Sets the Stage for a Splendid Olympics

Unlike London, Stockholm had plenty of time to prepare for its Games, and its vigorous support of the Olympic movement suggested that they would be successful. Indeed, using governmental lotteries, the country raised adequate funding to do a first-class job of building facilities and providing excellent accommodations. A record participation by 2,547 athletes (2,490 men and 57 women) from 28 geopolitical entities enhanced the global recognition of these Games. Stockholm's red brick Olympic stadium, the clock tower of which still functions today, was filled for the opening ceremonies. The stadium still stands today and is used routinely for football (soccer). It is also the home of the "DN-Galan," one of the world's great international track and field competitions. The name

DN-Galan refers to its local newspaper sponsor, the *Dagens Nyheter*. The annual Stockholm Marathon also uses the stadium for its finish.

The Stockholm Olympic Games were noted for several innovations that enhanced competition. First, each lane was clearly indicated by a chalk line around the entire track, separating athletes from each other in the shorter-distance races. Previously, each lane was delineated by the use of strings to identify each athlete's running domain; these were subject to breaking. Second, photo-finish timing was first used for better accuracy in identifying winners. This technology could not have arrived at a better moment, as it permitted identification of Abel Kiviat as the victor over Norman Taber in the men's 1,500 meters final—both were timed in 3:56.9. Finally, this was the first time there was a public address system to permit better communication of events to the audience.

Selection of Athletes Provides a Star-Studded Field

Three of the four previous Olympic Games winners had been residents of the host nation. Swedish marathoners were not so experienced, so there was some trepidation that they might not compete favorably against the world's best. Although four had competed at London, two had failed to finish. The other two, however, placed a respectable 8th and 21st. The Canadian and American teams would likely again be very strong. Marathon running continued to increase in popularity in Great Britain, partly fueled by the excitement of the London Games but also because the British did so poorly at these Games that this was embarrassing to Britain, and their desire to do better made runners try harder. The 1908 success of South Africa's Charles Hefferon also raised the level of marathon activity in this far-away land.

United States

The United States used several events to choose its large 1912 Olympic team (figure 6.1). Six of the first 10 finishers at Boston on April 19 were selected. Michael Ryan, who was a DNF at the London Olympic marathon, won the race in a record time of 2:21:18.2—only 19 seconds ahead of Andrew Sockalexis—on roads made slick as ice due to mud from a continuing drizzle. Joseph Erxleben and perennial favorite Joe Forshaw went one-two (2:36:30 and 2:37:32) at the 25 miles Missouri Athletic Club Marathon on May 4, and they were also selected. One entrant, a Hopi Indian named Lewis Tewanima, ran so fast in a 12 miles race (1:09:16) sponsored by the *New York Evening Mail* that he was also added to the team. London Olympic gold medalist Johnny Hayes had turned professional, and so was ineligible to compete, but served as assistant to the American team coach Mike Murphy.

Great Britain, Canada, and South Africa

Canadian James Corkery and South African Christian Gitsham both used an interesting race opportunity in London as their trial race to prove fitness. In

Figure 6.1 The United States marathon team chosen to compete at Stockholm. Front row, from left: Clarence DeMar, Andrew Sockalexis, and Gaston Strobino. Middle row, from left: John Gallagher, Thomas Lilley, Coach Mike Murphy, Lewis Tewanima, and Joseph Erxleben. Back row, from left: Joseph Forshaw, John Reynolds, Richard Piggott, Assistant Coach Johnny Hayes, Harry Smith, and Michael Ryan. Courtesy of Amateur Athletic Foundation Sports Library.

1909, collaboration developed between the Polytechnic Harriers athletic club—who had expertly organized the 1908 Olympic marathon—and a daily newspaper called *The Sporting Life*. The newspaper provided an enormous and valuable silver trophy to the winner of a marathon race that used a large portion of the Olympic route, from Windsor Park to White City Stadium at Shepherds Bush. The idea was to stimulate British distance running by encouraging the best in the world to compete together in Britain, thus capitalizing on the momentum of interest in top-level sport that developed during the London Games. Contested almost annually with few exceptions, the Polytechnic Harriers Marathon has continued to this day.

The 1912 edition of this so-called *Sporting Life*/Polytechnic Harriers Marathon had a superb field with the presence of Corkery and Gitsham. Corkery, from Toronto, placed third at Boston in 1910, but dropped out in 1911. He did not disappoint at the 1912 "Poly," winning impressively (2:36:55.4) on May 18 over Gitsham (2:37:14.6). These runners were on a world record pace: unfortunately, no records resulted because officials inadvertently pointed the runners the wrong direction as they entered the stadium. This resulted in a course that was 360 yards short of the planned 26 miles, 385 yards. Britain's Henry "Harry" Green was third, also with an excellent performance (2:39:22.4). Interestingly, Gitsham commented to those wishing him well that back home in South Africa an even better athlete named McArthur was training hard and would be coming to Stockholm.

Finland

Of all the European countries that were planning to send athletes to the Games, Finland had one of the better chances for success, especially if the weather was cool. Recall the Kolehmainen brothers introduced in chapter 5. At London, the oldest brother, Tatu, had been denied a team spot in favor of Kaarlo Nieminen. For the Stockholm marathon, Nieminen was not selected; he had emigrated to the United States and turned professional. Tatu was indeed selected, and his brother Hannes would be running three other events: 5,000 and 10,000 meters on the track, and cross country. Tatu won the Olympic trial race on May 19, 1912 at Oulunkylä, just north of Helsinki, with a splendid 2:29:07.6 over a muddy 40.2 kilometers course that was part road and part dirt track. He surprised everyone, as his last marathon had been nearly three years before, on September 19, 1909.

A Flat Course Suggests Fast Times

Most marathon courses in Scandinavia were roughly 40.2 kilometers in length. It was not until the Stockholm Games that a worldwide organization to govern track and field was formed—the IAAF—and thus no established "official" Olympic marathon distance existed beforehand. A variety of contested distances existed, most ranging from 40 kilometers to the London Olympic distance of 42.195 kilometers. Swedish organizers thus decided upon a 40.2 kilometers course that started and finished in the main Olympic stadium. However, it would not be until the 1924 Paris Olympic Games that the 42.195 kilometers distance would be selected as the global "standard" distance; see chapter 8.

The Stockholm Olympic stadium had a track that measured 383 meters in length and its long straightaways were oriented in a slightly northwest-to-southeast direction (figure 6.2). Its royal box is along the east straightaway (the same side as the clock tower). The race started and finished on the track, alongside this royal box, so that assembled spectators could see the first and last 350 meters of the competition. Runners proceeded eventually in a northerly direction out of the city, and then through several small villages using the narrow road connecting Stockholm with Uppsala. The road throughout was lined with spectators as well.

The turnaround point occurred just past the main church in the village of Sollentuna and was indicated by a temporary metal marker that was removed after the race. Runners then retraced the route exactly, entering the stadium and simply reversing the direction they used when they left. For this reason, no attendants of any kind, on bicycles or in cars, were permitted. This made perfect sense for preventing accidents in the region near the turnaround as athletes retraced their steps on the narrow road. The course details box provides street details for this truly out-and-back route—the first of its kind for an Olympic Games. With its minor grade changes, if typically cool Scandinavian summertime weather prevailed, the opportunity was good for a fast competition.

Only parts of this marathon course can be followed today. The route near the stadium, as well as the portion in Sollentuna, can be found easily. The E4 highway has become a major route that extends northwest out of Stockholm. Extensive widening and straightening, particularly as the road passes Stockholm's Arlanda International Airport and its associated commercial development, have relegated much of the original route to history except for short stretches that local knowledgeable runners can identify.

Smart Running Essential in a Race of Attrition

While the organization was superb, the race day weather could not have been worse. The race was scheduled for 1345 (1:45 p.m.) on July 14, 1912. It was Sunday and a national holiday, so not only the stadium but much of the route was jammed with spectators either cheering for their favorite 12 Swedish athletes or simply being part of the sport scene. Everyone suffered in the heat. Unconfirmed reports have suggested a temperature of 32°C (89.6°F) in the shade.

When the official roll call was completed and the runners were lined up on the track, the field numbered 68 athletes from 19 geopolitical entities. By far, the majority of the group was European, with 47 athletes from 14 nations. The African, Asian, and Oceanic regions had 3 South Africans, 1 Japanese, and 1 Australian, respectively. The North American contingent included four Canadians and 12 from the United States.

At 1348 (1:48 p.m.) the gun sounded, and as Swede Alexis Ahlgren led the group around the track (figure 6.3) and out onto the streets, the stadium crowd stood and cheered with enthusiasm. Most runners were sensibly dressed in white for reflection of the sunlight, and most had white handkerchiefs or some kind of makeshift white linen headgear to keep balding heads from becoming sunburned.

The road was essentially unpaved outside the city, but the dirt was hard-packed, and all wheeled traffic had been stopped on the road an hour before the competition. It was also swept clean of debris and lightly watered for dust control. As seen in figure 6.4, a sidewalk along some parts of the course provided a smoother running surface than the roadway, and runners took advantage of it.

COURSE DETAILS

The 1912 Stockholm Olympic Marathon

Start on the track, beside the royal box (east side of the stadium)

Run counterclockwise 350 meters and exit the stadium

Right (west) onto Valhallavägen to Drottning Kristinas Väg

Right (north) onto Drottning Kristinas Väg to Björnäsvägen

Left (west) onto Björnäsvägen to Roslagsvägen (now the E18 highway)

Right (north) on Roslagsvägen past Stockholm University to Bergshamravägen

Left (west) on Bergshamravägen past the north shore of the Brunnsviken to Uppsalavägen in the village of Ulriksdal

Right (north) onto Uppsalavägen (now the E4 highway)

Continue northward through the villages of Jarfva, Silfverdal (~10 kilometers), Tureberg (~15 kilometers), Norrviken, and Sollentuna (~20 kilometers) to the turnaround point ~500 meters beyond the main village church in Sollentuna

Turn around at the monument indicator, and remain on the E4 highway (Uppsalavägen) through Sollentuna, Norrviken, Tureberg, Silfverdal, and Jarfva to Bergshamravägen

Left (east) onto Bergshamravägen and pass the north end of the Brunnviken to Roslagsvägen

Right (south) onto Roslagsvägen to Björnäsvägen

Left (east) onto Björnäsvägen to Drottning Kristinas Väg

Right (south) onto Drottning Kristinas Väg to Valhallavägen

Left (east) onto Valhallavägen to Olympic stadium

Left (north) through the tunnel onto the stadium track

Run clockwise 350 meters to finish beside the royal box

By the 5 kilometers point near Stocksund, Ahlgren, Tatu Kolehmainen, and a young Italian, Carlo Speroni—who had turned 17 years old the day before—were in the lead. About 10 meters behind were a Frenchman (Jean Boissière) and the two South Africans (Gitsham and McArthur). Kolehmainen later took the lead and began pushing the pace (figure 6.4), and by the 15 kilometers point at Tureberg he was 13 seconds in front of Gitsham and McArthur. The Official Report (Bergvall 1913) mentions that although fluids (lemonade, water,

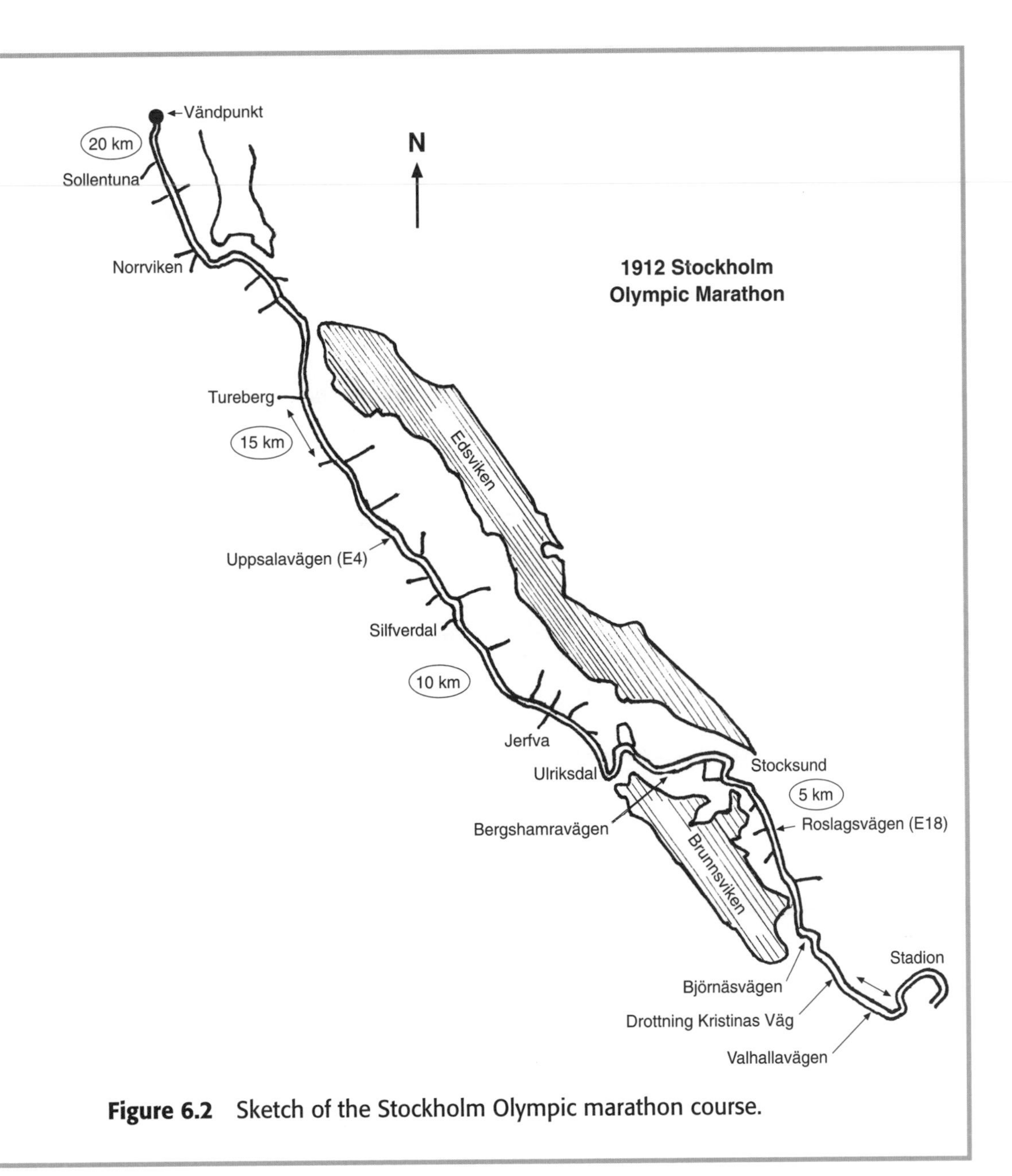

Figure 6.2 Sketch of the Stockholm Olympic marathon course.

and tea) were readily available, only those in the pack took full advantage of them. Those in front passed them by, which was a big mistake. Athletes began dropping out even at Tureberg, 15 kilometers into the race, and continued to do so thereafter.

The Official Report also provides intermediate split times for the top athletes, but an error makes construction of an accurate time sequence for the first half of the race difficult. The start time of 1:48:00 p.m. (1348) is documented in the

Figure 6.3 Sweden's Alexis Ahlgren leads the marathon race as it exits the stadium onto the streets of Stockholm. Courtesy IOC/Olympic Museum Collections.

Official Report, with subsequent real clock times reported for leading athletes in the competition. As an example, the clock time given for the top three running together at Stocksund (5 kilometers) is 2:17:20. Subtracting this time from the race start time (1:48:00) indicates that these leaders covered the first 5 kilometers in 29:20—an extremely slow pace of 9:26 per mile (5:52 per kilometer). However, at 15 kilometers (Tureberg), the clock times for Kolehmainen (2:42:19) and the two South Africans (2:42:32) suggest that they covered their preceding 10 kilometers in 24:59 and 25:12, respectively—faster than the world track record for 10 kilometers even today! Clearly, there was an error in documenting the 5 kilometers time, as the pace over 15 kilometers (5:47.5 per mile, 3:36 per kilometer) is realistic. Britain's Fred Lord was in fourth place, ahead of Ahlgren, who was now being followed closely by a 29-years-old countryman, Sigge Jacobsson, the 1910 Swedish marathon champion.

Although Kolehmainen had earlier enjoyed a 13 seconds lead over Gitsham at Tureberg, Gitsham had caught Kolehmainen just before the turnaround and now was ahead by 15 seconds, with actual race times of 1:12:40 and 1:12:55, respectively. McArthur was in third (1:13:15), in front of Lord (1:14:30). Speroni and Ahlgren had now overtaken Jacobsson, and Jim Corkery moved into eighth place.

Figure 6.4 Finland's Tatu Kolehmainen is pushing the pace out in the countryside between 5 and 10 kilometers, running on the smooth walkway adjacent to the bumpier road surface. Just behind him is Sweden's Alexis Ahlgren (number 6). Courtesy of Amateur Athletic Foundation Sports Library.

Reaching the Tureberg checkpoint on the return, Gitsham and Kolehmainen were now together (1:34:40), with McArthur only a second behind. Speroni was another 15 seconds behind, well ahead of Jacobsson and Lord. Four Americans—Richard Piggott, Lewis Tewanima (10,000 meters silver medalist), 20-years-old Gaston Strobino, and Harry Smith—rounded out the top 10.

Between Tureberg and Stocksund, Kolehmainen retired, putting Gitsham and McArthur in front (2:14:22) at the Stocksund checkpoint. Next came Strobino, half a minute behind the leader, with Jacobsson another 90 seconds behind. Canadian James Duffy had now moved up into fifth, alongside Carlo Speroni (2:21:19). Six Americans then followed behind Duffy and Speroni (Tewanima, Sockalexis, Erxleben, John Gallagher, Thomas Lilley, and Richard Piggott). This suggested their better heat acclimatization as a group, as American summer weather is generally much warmer than that in most of northern Europe.

Thanks to excellent organization by the Swedes, the full stadium throng had been kept informed regarding the progress of the race by radio transmission of information from each checkpoint. The crowd knew that two South Africans were leading, with an essentially unknown American in third. On Drottning Kristinas Väg, approaching Valhallavägen, at the start of a gradual incline, Gitsham stopped for a drink. McArthur continued onward without stopping and developed a lead that ensured his capturing the gold medal.

Spectators dressed in their Sunday finest lined the road as McArthur approached the stadium (figure 6.5), amazed that he had endured so well in the heat. He entered the stadium unchallenged, and it was fortunate that he was still in good condition, as an immense wreath was thrown around his neck, which he had to manage as he went around the track. It was a South African double, as McArthur (2:36:54.8) finished just short of a minute ahead of Gitsham (2:37:52.0) (figure 6.6). Of course, both were nearly exhausted from their ordeal, but officials had expected far worse.

Strobino and Sockalexis passed their older rival Jacobsson in the final few kilometers to take third and fourth places. Duffy also finished strongly, relegating Jacobsson to sixth as the fastest European. Nine of the first 12 across the line were North Americans. In the end, 34 finished and 34 dropped out, indicating the horrific conditions. One of the more notable dropouts was Swede Gustaf Tornrös, fourth in the 1906 Athens marathon. The race summary is given in table 6.1.

Figure 6.5 **Approaching the stadium near the end of the marathon, South Africa's Ken McArthur (number 613) is seen with the Springbok emblem on his jersey.** Courtesy IOC/Olympic Museum Collections.

Figure 6.6 South African Chris Gitsham (number 471) finishes with a silver medal at Stockholm. Courtesy IOC/Olympic Museum Collections.

Olympic Marathon Miscellany 6.1

Stockholm Mourns the Olympics' Only Marathon Death

For one runner who dropped out of the Stockholm marathon, his ordeal only worsened. Somewhere around 30 kilometers, a catastrophe occurred. As stated in the Official Report (Bergvall 1913), the lone Portuguese entrant, Francisco Lazaro "suddenly staggered and fell, and after being attended to by the medical men who were immediately called to the spot, was taken to the Seraphim Hospital (which no longer exists). There the doctors did their utmost for the unfortunate man, no means for his restoration being left untried. All these efforts were in vain, however, and Lazaro died early on Monday morning." Information from Portuguese officials along the course reported that he had been in 27th place at 15 kilometers, and in 18th at 25 kilometers.

(continued)

Hospital records have been unobtainable, and it is not known whether an autopsy was performed. The cause of death, occurring at 0620 (6:20 a.m.) and released 14 hours afterward, was "possibly meningitis, brought on by heat exhaustion." Although a heart problem could always be considered a possibility, one would think this unlikely—he was only 21 years old. His is the only death in the annals of this first century of Olympic marathon history.

The big red stadium in Stockholm still remains, as does the church at Sollentuna. Near the turnaround point is a fluted, Doric column seven meters tall, carved locally from the Gylsboda Quarries in North Scania (figure 6.7). The Official Report (Bergvall 1913) states that the column was of "black granite," but granite *per se* cannot be black, as the quartz and feldspar minerals composing granite are light-colored. Most likely, the material is actually gabbro or larvekite, which is common in the region. It was erected the year following the Games to commemorate the marathon. At the top of the column, on one side, is simply the date "1912," and on the opposite is the word "Vändpunkten" ("Turn point"),

TABLE 6.1

1912 Stockholm Olympic Marathon at a Glance

Date:	14 July	**Weather:**	Hot, about 30°C (86°F)
Start time:	1348	**Starters:**	68
Course:	Out-and-back	**Finishers:**	34
Course distance:	40.2 km	**GPEs:**	19

TOP RESULTS:

Place	***Athlete***	***GPE***	***Date of birth***	***Time***
1	Kennedy McArthur	SOA	10 Feb. 1882	2:36:54.8
2	Christian Gitsham	SOA	15 Oct. 1888	2:37:52.0
3	Gaston Strobino	USA	23 Aug. 1891	2:38:42.4
4	Andrew Sockalexis	USA	11 Jan. 1891	2:42:07.9
5	James Duffy	CAN	01 May 1890	2:42:18.8
6	Sigfrid Jacobsson	SWE	04 June 1883	2:43:24.9
7	John Gallagher	USA	13 Apr. 1890	2:44:19.4
8	Joseph Erxleben	USA	15 Sept. 1889	2:45:47.2
9	Richard Piggott	USA	06 July 1888	2:46:40.7
10	Joseph Forshaw	USA	13 May 1881	2:49:49.4

New geopolitical entities represented: Norway [NOR], Japan [JPN], Portugal [POR], Serbia [SER]

Team score (unofficial):	1. USA	14 points	(3-4-7)
	2. CAN	31 points	(5-11-15)
	3. SWE	52 points	(6-22-24)

Figure 6.7 The church at Sollentuna with the commemorative turnaround marker visible at the far right, at a distance of approximately 500 meters. A close-up of this stone column is shown in the inset. Photos courtesy David Martin.

while on the other two sides viewers see the word "Marathon." Only 3 of the 11 out-and-back marathon courses designed during this first century of the Olympic marathon have such markers; the others are at the turnarounds along the 1952 Helsinki and 1956 Melbourne routes.

Notes on the Medalists

The Stockholm Olympic champion, **Kennedy Kane McArthur**, was born in Dervock, County Antrim, Ireland. This race was his first athletic success after a four-year pattern of bad luck. In 1907 and 1908, he had raced well enough to compete with other marathoners at the London Olympic marathon. But as mentioned in chapter 5, he was skipped over in the selection process in favor of Charles Hefferon—even though he had won the 1908 trials race in torrid heat.

Undaunted, McArthur traveled abroad again in 1910 to seek good competition. It was his hope to compete in both the Intercalated Games marathon in Athens and the *Sporting Life*/Polytechnic Harriers Marathon in London. Both of these were canceled. Ironically, his best success came at home, where he ran his personal best in November 1910 at Cape Town. It was actually the fastest performance recorded over the London-length out-and-back distance up to that time—a pace of 6:17 per mile (3:54 per kilometer). So far as can be determined, McArthur never lost a marathon. His career record is in table 6.2.

Fellow countryman **Christian William Gitsham**, born in Pietermaritzburg, South Africa, was a dropout in the 1910 Cape Town race won by McArthur. Prior to the Olympic Games, however, he managed a fine second place in the 1912 *Sporting Life*/Polytechnic Harriers Marathon. As mentioned earlier, his time would have been a new African continental record, but the runners went short of the full distance used at London. He had won five national track titles (three at 4 miles and two at 10 miles) between 1910 and 1913. At the 1920 Antwerp Olympic marathon, he led for 35 kilometers before dropping out.

The surprise third-place finisher, **Gaston Strobino**, was born in Biela, Italy, and may be the only Olympic marathon medalist to run just one marathon race in his entire career. A naturalized United States citizen living in Paterson, New Jersey, he qualified for the Stockholm Games by placing second in a competition estimated at 12 to 12½ miles in New York City on May 4. His time was 1:09:20, and the winner of that race, Louis Scott (1:08:28.4), competed at Stockholm in the 5,000 meters, 10,000 meters, and cross country events, but not the marathon. Strobino had run the same event in 1911, finishing fourth behind Lewis Tewanima. Otherwise, he remains a mystery, and after the Games he never competed again. According to the *New York Times* (Anonymous 1979), following the Stockholm race "his feet were skinned and bleeding, and he was suffering great pain." Perhaps it is understandable that he was uninterested in racing more marathons. After the games, he moved to Illinois where he continued to work as an apprentice machinist. Eventually, he reached the top of his profession as a tool maker.

TABLE 6.2

Career Marathon Record of Kennedy Kane McArthur

Date	*Venue*	*Place*	*Time*	*Comments*
11 Apr. 1908	Johannesburg	1st	2:20:30	22 miles/35.4 kilometers
22 Apr. 1908	Cape Town	1st	3:18:27.4	25 miles/40.2 kilometers
04 Sept. 1909	Johannesburg	1st	3:03:54.2	
25 Oct. 1909	Durban	1st	2:44:36	25¼ miles/40.6 kilometers
05 Nov. 1910	Cape Town	1st	2:42:58.2	26 miles, 385 yards/42.195 kilometers
14 July 1912	Stockholm	1st	2:36:54.8	Olympic Games; 40.2 kilometers

Looking Ahead: Brief Highlights 1912-1919

1912: The professional era came to a close with two more record performances: Canadian Hans Holmer's 2:32:21.8 at Edinburgh on January 3 and Willie Kolehmainen's 2:29:39.2 at Vailsburg on October 20.

1913: After a track marathon record performance of 2:38:16.2 by Harry Green on May 12 at Stamford Bridge (London), Sweden's Alexis Ahlgren won the *Sporting Life*/Polytechnic Harriers race on May 31 in another world record time of 2:36:06.6. The previous year, on September 22, 1912, Ahlgren had run 2:24:15 over 40 kilometers at Helsingborg. World War I caused an understandable reduction in marathon racing activity during the ensuing years.

References

Anonymous, 1979. *The complete book of track and field.* New York: New York Times.

Bergvall, E. 1913. *The fifth Olympiad: The Official Report of the Olympic Games of Stockholm 1912.* Translated by Edward Adams-Ray. Stockholm: Wahlström & Widstrand.

Chapter 7

1920—Antwerp

World Best for Hannes Kolehmainen

Olympic Sport Endures as a Shattered Europe Rebuilds

Berlin had been awarded the privilege of organizing the 1916 Olympic Games, but World War I halted such sporting activities. This created a problem. As mentioned in chapter 4, according to Olympic organizational structure, the Olympic Games are numbered according to the Olympiad, which they initiate every four years, and thus cannot be postponed. If the Games are not held, that Olympiad still occurs, and the numbering continues sequentially. Thus, the 6th Olympiad had no Games (and later on, neither would the 12th and 13th Olympiads in 1940 and 1944). The 7th Olympiad would begin with the Games of 1920.

As early as 1914, the IOC had considered a number of cities as possible hosts for the 1920 Olympic Games, but the final choice became a decision between

Antwerp and Lyon, with Antwerp being selected in 1918 (Renson 1995). In terms of worldwide linkage via rail and ship, Antwerp meant superior travel ease for far-away delegations. Politics probably played a role in the final decision, as only five years before, Belgium had been the victim of invasion by Germany, and Belgium's selection could be seen as a gesture of recognition for its regained independence. Once selected, Belgium then became responsible for extending invitations to participating nations. Neither Germany nor Hungary received one, although Budapest had also been a candidate city.

Despite financial and time limitations, the Belgians did an adequate job of preparing venues and hosting athletes in a hospitable and sporting manner. Once again, a new stadium was constructed, this one with a six-lanes, 389.80 meters cinder track and a capacity of 30,000. Athletes were housed in various areas of the city, primarily in schools, and transported to their appropriate sport venues in open trucks, cheered on by townspeople as they passed by. Despite the absence of the 1916 Games due to war, athlete participation was comparable to that at Stockholm, with 2,591 men and 78 women representing 29 geopolitical entities.

The Olympic oath was first added to the Opening Ceremonies protocol at these Games. Belgian fencer Victor Boin, who eventually became head of his nation's Olympic Committee, proudly uttered a simple but symbolic statement of the goal for all athletes to abide by fair play (Wendl 1995). The text has been changed frequently since, but delivering the oath remains an important element of the ceremonies.

These were also the first Games to use the five intertwined Olympic rings arranged together on a new Olympic flag. De Coubertin developed the idea in 1913 and displayed it in Paris in 1914 on the 20th anniversary of the reestablishment of the Games, but World War I delayed its formal use at the Olympic Games until 1920. Symbolizing the five continents linked in unity, the colors of blue, yellow, black, green, and red were chosen because at that time at least one of those colors appeared in the flag of every participating geopolitical entity. The rings have subsequently become the world's most well-known insignia.

Selection Races Choose Good Teams

Athletes were selected to compete in the Olympic marathon in various ways. Some were simply picked by their NOC because they were clearly the best in their country. Others were chosen based upon quality performances in one or more trial races held in their homeland, typically a national championship. Sometimes, however, athletes living in one country but native to another ran in a local marathon race and then submitted the results to their NOC for consideration.

The United States used four marathon races to determine its team. A wintertime race 25 miles in length was held on February 22 in Brooklyn and was won by 27-years-old Frank Zuna. His finish time (2:57:53.2) was so slow, however, that he wasn't selected as a team member. Two spring races were held. The first was from Pontiac to Detroit, Michigan on April 3 over 25 miles, and the second was at Boston on April 19 over approximately 24 miles. Charles "Chuck" Mellor won at Detroit in 2:30:04 and was given a team berth. The winner at Boston was Peter Trivoulidas, a Greek employed by the John Wanamaker Department Store in New York. Trivoulidas finished strongly (2:29:31) to defeat two locals, Arthur Roth and Carl Linder. All three top finishers at Boston would compete in Antwerp (Trivoulidas for Greece), although only Linder would finish.

Finally, there was an early summer race on June 5, sponsored by the New York Athletic Club over a course measured as 26.5 miles. Three Finns living in the United States used this race as their Olympic trial—Hannes Kolehmainen (1912 track and cross country Olympian), Juho Tuomikoski (ninth at Boston), and Willie Kyrönen. The course was difficult, and summertime warmth slowed times as well. Kolehmainen's 2:47:49.4 victory—his first marathon in more than three years—let the world know he was ready for Antwerp. Finishing second was American Joseph LeRoy Organ (2:51:06.2), and Tuomikoski was third, one minute behind. Both Organ and Tuomikoski were selected to represent their respective nations. One week later, Finland selected two more team members at its trial race in Hyvinkää over a 40.2 kilometers course. Hannes's 35-years-old brother Tatu won by one minute and 48 seconds over Urho Tallgren in a fast 2:39:03.5.

Five weeks before the Games, on July 17, England staged its annual *Sporting Life*/Polytechnic Harriers Marathon and again had gathered together a quality international field. Valerio Arri, 28, the Italian marathon champion, found himself challenging an inexperienced 26-years-old English farmer named Arthur Robert "Bobby" Mills. One of the newcomers in Britain's efforts to regain the respect in distance running that it had enjoyed a few years earlier, he was a twin, and both brothers served with distinction in World War I. Mills scored a brilliant debut win (2:37:40.4) over Arri (2:44:46). Both were selected for their respective teams bound for Antwerp, and as well, Mills was now the new British marathon record-holder.

A Fast but Long Course Challenges the Olympians

The Antwerp marathon course started and finished in the Olympic stadium, which still stands. Its cinder track also remains, and its infield eventually became the venue for the football (soccer) club Beerschot, which explains the present-day name of Beerschot Stadium. As sketched in figure 7.1, the general plan of the route shows it extending southward out of the city, passing through the villages of Wilrijk, Aartselaar, Reet, and Rumst, and then turning northward back toward Antwerp through Waarloos before reaching the turnaround point in the village of Kontich (Renson 1995). Then, just as at Stockholm, athletes retraced the route back to the stadium.

It was common practice in those days for marathon courses to be away from congested city streets, so this route into the countryside made sense. Precise details of the course have only recently been pieced together (Ludeker 1998) as a result of searches through the archives of the various villages and discussions with local officials. Largely unknown, however, are details of the number of aid stations, the kinds of provisions at such stations, and the "rules of the course"—for example, whether athletes were permitted to have attendants on the route, as at London. It is known that many of the runners carried sponges tucked into their shorts, and some had small bags sewn to their shorts, presumably carrying first aid or refreshments.

The course details box provides street details of the route using present-day names, so that those interested can follow it. After one and one-half laps inside the Olympic stadium, runners exited onto two small streets that provided access to Boomsesteenweg. Although a narrow street back in 1920, this today is a four-lane dual highway extending south out of Antwerp, through and past Aartselaar. Turning east onto Hoevelei in Aartselaar, the remainder of the course is also on small two-lane roads, which, of course, are much better maintained now than in 1920. At that time, the route had cobblestoned streets, essentially one lane, often with a footpath alongside (figure 7.2). From Wilrijk to Rumst, a tramway bordered the road.

The route was fairly flat, except for two moderate grades. One was just north of Rumst, near the old brick-producing factories that still exist today on the west side of the road. The other was just east of Rumst as the route turned toward what today is highway N1, the Antwerpsesteenweg, known at that time as the Chausee Anvers-Bruxelles. Along this segment of the course was a moderate hill called Vosberg. Atop the hill, on the north side of the roadway, was the Eikenhof Castle, which no longer exists. In those days, this region was sparsely inhabited and appeared bleak on the dreary, cloudy afternoon of race day.

The Antwerpsesteenweg extended north-south and changed names a few times before the turnaround point just outside the village of Kontich. This point was beside the Chapel of Our Holy Virgin of the Snow (Onze Lieve Vrouwe ter Sneeuw, in Dutch), the patroness of sufferers from Hansen's disease (sometimes called leprosy). It is also known as the Reepkens Kapel or Reepkens Chapel, referring to the southernmost part of built-up Kontich (known as "De Reep" or "the strip"). The original chapel was built in 1440 and rebuilt in 1756. Pictured in figure 7.3, this chapel is an important landmark for those interested in following the course.

Returning from the chapel, athletes retraced their route back to Antwerp exactly. The course distance is reported consistently by all sources, including the Official Report (Anonymous 1920a) as 42,750 meters (26 miles, 992 yards). This was certainly the longest Olympic marathon route designed up to that time—555 meters (607 yards) longer than the London course. As mentioned in chapter 6, no standardized marathon course distance existed, and details of course layout and measurement were at the discretion of each Olympic organizing committee.

Course Details

The 1920 Antwerp Olympic Marathon

One and one-half laps counterclockwise in the Olympic stadium, exiting through the marathon tunnel onto Marathonstraat

Continue one block on Marathonstraat to De Bosschaertstraat (0.7 kilometer)

Half right on De Bosschaertstraat to Boomsesteenweg (1.3 kilometers)

Continue southbound on Boomsesteenweg (now the A12) through Antwerp and Wilrijk into Aartselaar

Half left onto Hoevelei (6.2 kilometers), which becomes Kapellestraat as it passes through Aartselaar

Departing Aartselaar, Kapellestraat becomes Reetsesteenweg (8.1 kilometers), which becomes Pierstraat, which becomes Eikenstraat as it continues south into Reet

At the Reet city center, Eikenstraat becomes Rumstsestraat (11.4 kilometers) and continues south out of Reet toward Rumst

Rumstsestraat becomes Hollebeekstraat (13.5 kilometers) as it passes the old brick factories (on the right)

Entering Rumst, Hollebeekstraat becomes Molenbergstraat, which continues south to the city center

At the city center, left on Kazernestraat (14.2 kilometers), which becomes Kerkstraat (14.3 kilometers) proceeding east

Kerkstraat becomes Tiburstraat, which becomes Bussestraat to Antwerpsesteenweg intersection (16.0 kilometers)

Left onto Antwerpsesteenweg (Highway N1), which becomes Grotesteenweg (17.1 kilometers), which becomes Mechelsesteenweg (19.0 kilometers)

Continue on Mechelsesteenweg until the turnaround point (21.375 kilometers) at the Reepkens Kapel on the west side of the street at the southern village limits of Kontich

Turn around and retrace the route exactly, through Rumst, Reet, Aartselaar, and Wilrijk, reentering Antwerp and then the stadium

Continue counterclockwise one and one-half laps to the start/finish line

Cool Weather Stimulates Excellent Competition

Race day was Sunday, August 22, when Belgian summer weather is typically pleasant, but sometimes warm and humid. The scheduled starting time of 1610 (4:10 p.m.) was midafternoon prime-time viewing for spectators. How-

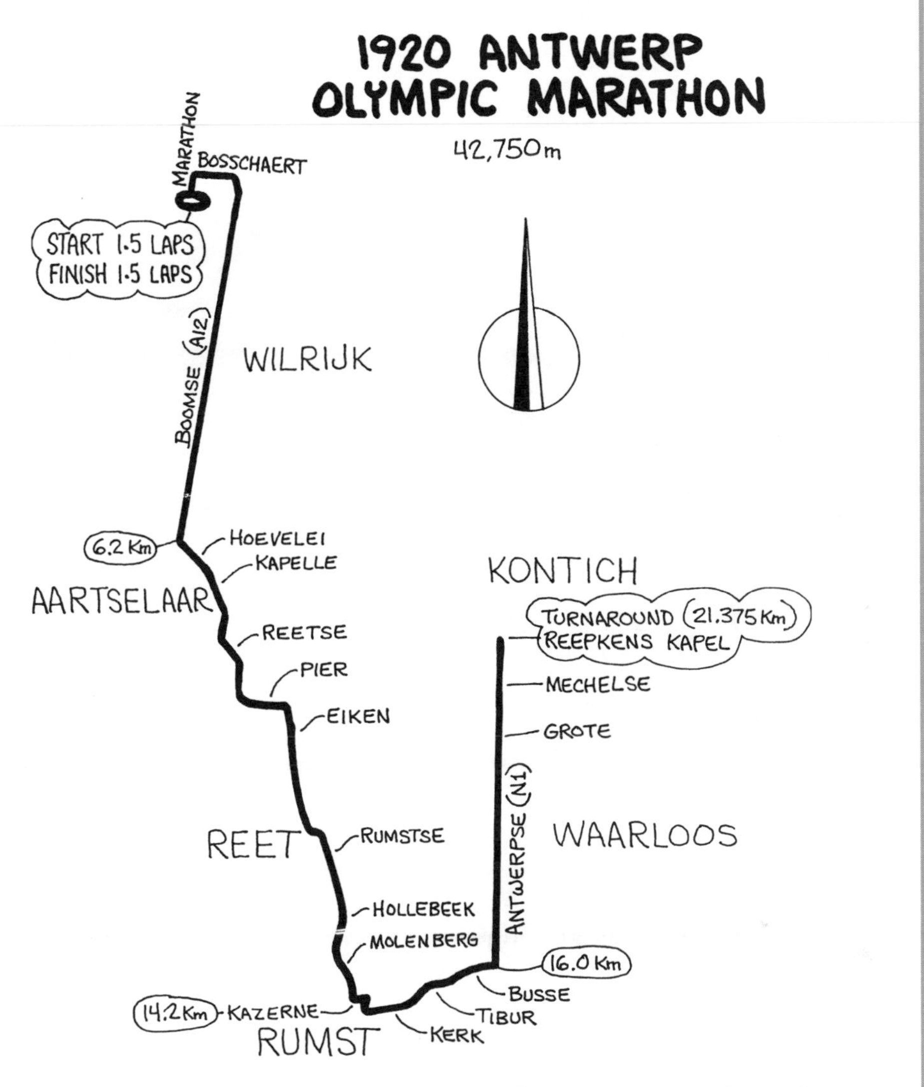

Figure 7.1 **Sketch of the Antwerp Olympic marathon course. Descriptors for street identification (straat, steenweg, etc.) are omitted for clarity.** Prepared by Bob Letson.

ever, instead of the seemingly habitual heat and sun that had plagued four of the five Olympic marathons previously described, this day was cool and damp, often with a drizzling rain, making the road muddy in places. The cooler conditions would allow athletes to finally race the entire distance rather than being concerned with just finishing. After the usual introductions and athlete placements at the starting line, the starter's gun sounded at 1612 (4:12 p.m.) (Mallon 1992).

Figure 7.2 Tatu Kolehmainen is just about to reach the course midpoint and circle around the Olympic flag positioned on Mechselsesteenweg near the Reepkens Chapel. Courtesy Charles Du Houx.

Figure 7.4 shows the large field of 48 athletes from 18 geopolitical entities proceeding counterclockwise around the stadium track. Five continental regions were represented: 30 Europeans from 11 nations (including Greece), 8 from North America (4 Canadians, 4 Americans), a South African, a Chilean, an Australian, 6 Asians (4 from Japan and 2 from India), and a runner from Newfoundland who confuses continental categorization (see Olympic Marathon Miscellany 7.1).

Olympic Marathon Miscellany 7.1

A Forgotten Land Newly Found

Newfoundland was one of the oldest independent colonies of the former British Empire until it joined Canada in 1949. It was never a member of the IOC or the IAAF, but its athletes competed successfully in the 1930 and 1934 Empire Games. The last finisher at Antwerp, Eric Mackenzie Robertson, born in St. John's, Newfoundland, was initially invited by the Canadian marathon squad to be a reserve fifth member, although he was not a Canadian citizen. Only four athletes per nation were permitted to compete. All four Canadian team members, in fact, ran the race. So did Robertson.

The mystery of how he managed to compete in Antwerp has finally been solved. He had seen military action on the Somme during World War I, where he was wounded. After the war, he worked in London and befriended some runners who were members of the Polytechnic Harriers running club. However, a search through the files of the Harriers club can produce no evidence that Robertson competed in either cross country or road races sponsored by the group. In 1920, Robertson traveled to Antwerp on his own and found his Polytechnic running buddies, who had been selected to the British Olympic team.

(continued)

Figure 7.3 The Reepkens Chapel just outside the village of Kontich marks the turnaround point for the Antwerp Olympic marathon. Courtesy Tom Mulder.

They had only three marathon athletes, with four entries permitted. The British team manager offered Robertson the remaining fourth spot.

And so Robertson ran, finishing 35th in 3:55:00, wearing a race number for the NOC of Britain, although he was not a British citizen. He thus complicates the picture for those attempting to list the identity of participants in the Olympic marathon. At Antwerp, athletes represented 17 nations with respect to bib number identification, but they represented 18 geopolitical entities in terms of their citizenship. Robertson was the first Newfoundland-born athlete to finish an Olympic marathon. He was not, however, the first Newfoundland-born Olympic marathoner. That was Robert Fowler, who later became a United States citizen living in Boston; he failed to finish either of his races in 1904 and 1906.

Following the 1920 Olympics, Eric Robertson was presented with a silver medal by the Harriers club, inscribed simply: "The Polytechnic Sports Club. Awarded to Eric Robertson, Olympic competitor 1920."

As runners exited the stadium onto the roadway (figure 7.5), Frenchman Henri Teyssedou was leading (number 371), followed closely by the two British runners dressed in white (Bobby Mills, number 409, and George Piper, number 416). Just behind them, on the outside, is Hannes Kolehmainen (number 263) in

Figure 7.4 Start of the Antwerp Olympic marathon in Beerschot Stadium. Courtesy of Amateur Athletic Foundation Sports Library.

Figure 7.5 The Antwerp Olympic marathoners on Maraathonstraat. The runners have just left the Olympic stadium and are about to turn right onto De Bosschaertstraat. In the lead is Henri Teyssedou [FRA] (number 371). Courtesy of Amateur Athletic Foundation Sports Library.

the dark top and white shorts, and behind him is Estonian Jüri Lossman (number 680), with white shirt and shorts.

Intermediate split times were apparently not taken as part of the austerity measures to minimize expenses in staging the Games, but contemporary newspaper accounts give the essential race details (Anonymous 1920b).

By the first checkpoint at 3 kilometers, in Wilrijk, South African Chris Gitsham and Belgian Auguste Broos were pushing the pace. Only time would tell if Gitsham was racing too quickly. He had arrived weeks early and knew every kilometer of the course from training. Hannes Kolehmainen and Italian Ettore Blasi were not far behind. By 10 kilometers, just before entering Reet, this lead group was still in contention. Gitsham was in front, followed by Blasi, Broos, and Hannes Kolehmainen. Not far behind were Jüri Lossman and Juho Tuomikoski.

At the 15 kilometers checkpoint in Rumst, Hannes Kolehmainen had joined Gitsham in the lead. Broos, Blasi, Tuomikoski, and Lossman were still in contact. Now, however, Tatu Kolehmainen had moved into seventh, Chile's Juan Jorquera into eighth, and the Italian, Valerio Arri, into ninth.

Times taken at the halfway point near the Reepkens Chapel in Kontich show that Gitsham and Hannes Kolehmainen passed in 1:13:10, with Broos and Blasi

48 seconds behind. Lossman had now overtaken Tuomikoski and was in fifth. Gitsham soon faltered, reportedly because one of his shoes tore open, causing a foot problem (Wallechinsky 1996). At 25 kilometers, in Waarloos, Gitsham and Hannes remained together, with Lossman now in third place as Broos and Blasi began to tire and slow their pace.

At 27 kilometers (1:30:00), just past the village of Rumst, Hannes Kolehmainen, perhaps stimulated by the familiar pungent odors from the brick kilns (he started out as a builder), moved out in front of Gitsham, with Lossman not far behind in third. Blasi and Broos were still in fourth and fifth, followed by Tuomikoski and Tatu Kolehmainen. By 30 kilometers, on the north side of Rumst, runners started to spread out from each other, forming a single line. Gitsham was an estimated 300 meters behind Kolehmainen, and Lossman about 500 meters behind Gitsham; Broos was alone in fourth. This sequence remained through 35 kilometers.

At around 37 kilometers, on Kapellestraat, Gitsham faltered, fading to fifth, and eventually retired from the race. Lossman now began a noticeable pace increase in an attempt to catch Hannes Kolehmainen. The two were at least 1,500 meters in front of the rest, so there were essentially two races: one for the bronze medal, and a fight for gold versus silver. Valerio Arri had paced himself appropriately for his fitness level, alternating between eighth and ninth positions. Still feeling strong in these closing kilometers, he quickened his pace and methodically passed a string of six competitors. Eventually he found himself in a kind of runner's "no-man's-land"—the bronze medal was his, he was fresher than those behind, but he was still too far away from the leaders to catch them.

Hannes Kolehmainen raced strongly to the finish (figure 7.6). He had little choice, because Lossman was extremely determined mentally, in great shape physically, and was closing the gap. In fact, it took a world record to prevent Lossman from winning. Hannes crossed the line in an amazing 2:32:35.8—faster than any previous performance, even those on a shorter 42.195 kilometers course! Lossman was less than 13 seconds behind, however, and the drama of these two men racing nearly together around the track was unforgettable. It was the closest Olympic finish up to that time. Valerio Arri was similarly delighted with his third place, which he celebrated by performing three cartwheel somersaults at the finish line. Kolehmainen took a victory lap wearing his laurel wreath and a Finnish flag draped around his shoulders (figure 7.7), which brought many cheers. Just as memorable was the beautiful rainbow appearing as the sun shone through the breaking clouds with the rain finally passing.

As can be seen in the summary of the results (table 7.1) and complete results (appendix D), this race marked a sudden turnaround of world marathon superiority. The first 6 placers were Europeans—they comprised 8 of the top 10. The reign of Americans and Canadians had been toppled. And the 1st and 10th combined placing for the Kolehmainens has not been surpassed by any other brother or sister combination in this first marathon century.

Table 7.2 summarizes the pace in minutes per mile and minutes per kilometer for the first seven Olympic marathons. Antwerp was indeed the fastest Olympic marathon run up to that time, despite its length; but then, the weather was by

Figure 7.6 Hannes Kolehmainen (number 263) racing through the streets of Antwerp accompanied by an official on a bicycle in the closing kilometers of the Antwerp marathon.

far the coolest. As the accuracy of these course measurements is unknown, the numerical values in table 7.2 are only approximate.

Notes on the Medalists

Johannes Petter Kolehmainen was born at Kuopio, Finland, on the edge of Lake Kalki, and ran his first marathon in 1907 when only 17½ years old. In 1909, he ran three marathons within 18 days during September, showing not only incredible injury resistance but also competitive drive. Two of these were track events, showing clearly his love for this kind of competition venue. In fact, he decided to focus on shorter-distance track racing and cross country at the Stockholm Olympics. There, he was a triple-gold medalist, winning the 5,000 and 10,000 meters on the track, and the 12 kilometers cross country, all between July 9 and 15. Including heats in the two track events, his racing effort totaled 42,000 meters—a marathon in itself.

Figure 7.7 Juri Lossman (number 680) and Hannes Kolehmainen receiving congratulations from officials and spectators after their race. Courtesy of Amateur Athletic Foundation Sports Library.

By the end of the Stockholm Games, Hannes Kolehmainen held world records at 2,000, 3,000, and 5,000 meters. He moved to New York, raced quite successfully, and became a naturalized American citizen. However, at Antwerp he competed for Finland. The reason for this is summarized in the American Olympic Report (Anonymous 1920c): "The International Amateur Athletic Federation rules state that an athlete who has once competed for his native land in an Olympic meet cannot thereafter run for an adopted country. Therefore, Kolehmainen had no choice in the matter, as eight years previous he had competed in the Olympic Games at Stockholm for Finland."

Following the Antwerp Games, Hannes returned to Finland, continued racing, and set world records at 25 and 30 kilometers, but he never regained his marathon racing skills. He started the 1924 Paris Olympic race but did not finish, and in 1928 he dropped out of the Finnish Olympic trial for the Amsterdam Games. His marathon career record is listed in table 7.3.

Silver medalist and almost champion, **Jüri Lossman** was born in the Köo district of Estonia and was only two years younger than Hannes Kolehmainen. There the similarity ended. He raced infrequently, but in training he ran as

TABLE 7.1

1920 Antwerp Olympic Marathon at a Glance

Date: 22 August
Start time: 1612
Course: Out-and-back
Course distance: 42.75 km

Weather: Cool, damp
Starters: 48
Finishers: 35
GPEs: 18 (includes Newfoundland)

TOP RESULTS:

Place	*Athlete*	*GPE*	*Date of birth*	*Time*
1	Johannes Kolehmainen	FIN	09 Dec. 1889	2:32:35.8
2	Jüri Lossman	EST	04 Feb. 1891	2:32:48.6
3	Valerio Arri	ITA	22 June 1892	2:36:32.8
4	Auguste Broos	BEL	09 Nov. 1894	2:39:25.8
5	Juho Tuomikoski	FIN	14 Dec. 1888	2:40:10.8
6	Sofus Rose	DEN	10 Apr. 1894	2:41:18.0
7	Joseph Organ	USA	03 Aug. 1892	2:41:30.0
8	Rudolf Hansen	DEN	30 May 1889	2:41:39.4
9	Urho Tallgren	FIN	10 Oct. 1894	2:42:40.0
10	Taavetti Kolehmainen	FIN	21 Apr. 1885	2:44:03.2

New geopolitical entities represented: Estonia [EST], India [IND], Chile [CHI], Newfoundland [NFD]

Team score (unofficial):

1. FIN	15 points	(1-5-9)
2. USA	30 points	(7-11-12)
3. CAN	50 points	(13-15-22)

TABLE 7.2

Race Pace for the First Seven Olympic Marathons

Year	*Venue*	PACE (*min/mile*)	PACE (*min/kilometer*)
1896	Athens	7:11.8	4:28.3
1900	Paris	7:11.1	4:27.9
1904	St. Louis	8:24.3	5:13.4
1908	London	6:41.2	4:09.3
1912	Stockholm	6:16.9	3:54.2
1920	Antwerp	5:44.7	3:34.2
1924	Paris	6:09.3	3:49.5

TABLE 7.3

Career Marathon Record of Hannes Kolehmainen

Date	Venue	Place	Time	Comments
16 June 1907	Viipuri	3rd	3:06:19	40.2 km road
02 Sept. 1907	Helsinki	3rd	2:57:25.4	40.2 km road
21 June 1908	Viipuri	4th	2:52:36	40.2 km road
13 June 1909	Helsinki	2nd	3:05:22	42.195 km track
04 July 1909	Helsinki	4th	3:12:19.3	42.195 km road
31 Aug. 1909	Stockholm	5th	3:09:19	42.195 km track
05 Sept. 1909	Göteborg	3rd	2:42:59	40.2 km track
19 Sept. 1909	Hanko	1st	3:10:31.4	
19 Apr. 1917	Boston	4th	2:31:58.6	23.5 m road
05 June 1920	New York	1st	2:47:49.4	26.5 m road
22 Aug. 1920	Antwerp	1st	2:32:35.8	Olympic Games; 42.75 km
13 July 1924	Paris	DNF		Olympic Games; 42.195 km
17 June 1928	Kauhava	DNF		

many as 120 to 130 kilometers per week, sometimes wearing lead weights on his training shoes. He had won all four of his marathons prior to the Antwerp Olympic Games, and very nearly won there as well.

On more than one occasion, Lossman was known to be critical of both teammates (who did not cheer him on during races) and officials (who seemed amateurish to him). An example of the former occurred at the Antwerp Olympics. His Estonian teammates took a daylong excursion on the day of the marathon, and he criticized them for not coming out to cheer for him along the marathon course. An example of the latter relates to a marathon on September 17, 1922, which he won easily in 2:18:33. A course remeasurement showed it as 38.5 kilometers, not the 40.2 kilometers advertised. Lossman criticized the officials, who, in his view, had little interest in taking the time to attend to such details so that athletes could have a proper competitive environment.

The next year, on July 8, 1923, Lossman lined up in Göteborg with the best Swedes, Finland's Tatu Kolehmainen, and top athletes from several other nations. The occasion was to celebrate Göteborg's tercentenary, and the distance was 40.2 kilometers. Again, Lossman was unbeatable, winning by more than five minutes (2:40:59.7) in 30°C (86°F) weather.

At the Paris Olympic marathon in 1924, he finished 10th and then turned professional, finishing 4th behind Boughera El Ouafi, Joie Ray, and Arthur Newton in a marathon race on the Madison Square Garden indoor track in 1928. Interestingly, his 1920 Olympic Games time of 2:32:48.6 remained the Estonian record until August 12, 1956.

Bronze medalist **Valerio Arri** did not come into public view as an athlete until 1919, when he won both the Turin international race (2:40:47.6 on September 28) and the Italian marathon title (3:13:41 over 48 kilometers on October 5). These were his only marathon victories. Born in Portocomaro, Italy, his marathon career was short-lived, and after Antwerp he never regained similar form.

Looking Ahead: Brief Highlights 1921-1924

1921: Frank Zuna lowered the Boston Marathon record to 2:18:57.6 (April 19), but Clarence DeMar further reduced the record by 47 seconds the following year (2:18:10).

1922: Manuel Plaza [CHI] won the Latin American Championships at Rio de Janeiro on September 16 in 2:57:00.

1923: After three successive wins in the *Sporting Life*/Polytechnic Harriers Marathon, Bobby Mills was beaten by Axel Jensen [DEN]. Jensen's time of 2:40:46.8 was the fastest London Olympic distance time between the 1920 and 1924 Olympic marathons.

References

Anonymous. 1920a. *Viième Olympiade Anvers.*

Anonymous. 1920b. *Gazet van Antwerpen.* August 23.

Anonymous. 1920c. *Report of the American Olympic Committee.* Seventh Olympic Games, Antwerp, Belgium.

Ludeker, J. 1998. Personal communications.

Mallon, B. 1992. *The unofficial report of the 1920 Olympics.* Durham, NC: MOST Publications.

Renson, R. 1995. *The VIIth Olympiad Antwerp 1920 The Games Reborn.*

Wallechinsky, D. 1996. *The complete book of the Summer Olympics.* 1996 edition. New York: Little, Brown & Company.

Wendl, K. 1995. "The Olympic oath—a brief history." *Citius, Altius, Fortius—The ISOH Journal* 3 (1): 4-5.

CHAPTER 8

1924—PARIS

A Surprise Runaway Victory for Stenroos in Paris

An Official Marathon Distance and Another New Stadium Greet the Games

The 1924 Olympic Games were originally scheduled for Amsterdam, but in view of the planned retirement of Baron de Coubertin, the Dutch agreed to a 1928 date so that the final Games of de Coubertin's long career could be held in France. Once again, a new Olympic stadium was constructed, this one large enough for 60,000 spectators. Two covered grandstands, each seating 10,000, were adjacent to the long straightaways of the 500 meters cinder track. In addition, the ends of the stadium were filled in with uncovered stands that each accommodated 20,000. The Olympic complex was constructed in Colombes, 10 kilometers northwest of the center of Paris, as part of an urban rehabilitation plan to improve the use of a weed-covered landfill in this unattractive industrial suburb (Phillips 1996).

An adjacent training stadium and a tennis stadium with practice courts were also part of this complex not far from the river Seine. In addition, an Olympic "day village" was constructed nearby. It consisted of many small wooden huts that athletes could use for rest and final preparations before competition. It was not designed for overnight residence, but the existence of facilities such as a post office, money exchange, and other amenities provided for the first time a kind of village atmosphere where athletes from many countries could mingle. With equestrian, cycling, fencing, pentathlon, and tennis occurring at Colombes in addition to track and field, such a gathering place was not only needed but welcomed by the athletes. Rugby and soccer matches were also played at Colombes, but they were held in May and June, many weeks before the official opening ceremonies on Saturday, July 5. This permitted an initial testing of the facilities to manage large crowds and athletic teams, which, in view of the unprecedented athlete participation (2,956 men and 136 women from 44 geopolitical entities), was both appropriate and useful.

The IOC delegated considerable authority in the preparations for the Paris Olympic Games to the various international sport federations that had developed over the preceding years. The IAAF had been formed with 17 charter members two days following the Stockholm Olympic Games, and its president was Sweden's J. Sigfrid Edström. Edström announced this transferring of authority for conducting Olympic Games sporting events in his opening statement at the Fifth IAAF Congress in Geneva on May 27, 1921 (Anonymous 1921): "Your President has been elected a member of the (International Olympic) Committee, and it is assured that the influence of our Federation on the Olympic Games will be very strong. Also the arrangements of the Athletic competitions will henceforth be in our hands."

It was at this Geneva IAAF congress that the Olympic Games marathon distance was standardized. A list of proposed events was circulated for approval, and the marathon was included on that list (Anonymous 1921). The race's length was given as 42.195 kilometers, or 26 miles, 385 yards—the same as at the 1908 London Olympic Games—but no discussion is provided regarding the rationale for its selection. Senn (1999) suggests that perhaps it was the British influence among members of the IAAF committee who discussed the track and field agenda. Or perhaps it was the extensive publicity regarding the 1908 Olympic marathon race.

Also, no requirements were mandated regarding course layout (e.g., point-to-point, out-and-back, starting and/or finishing inside the stadium, etc.). Debate did occur regarding a motion to reduce athlete entries in the marathon from six to three, in keeping with other events. That motion failed, and the final vote (Anonymous 1921) was to run the Olympic marathon over the London distance using a course deemed appropriate by local organizers, with no more than six runners per team. (In 1932, this marathon entry quota would be reduced to three.)

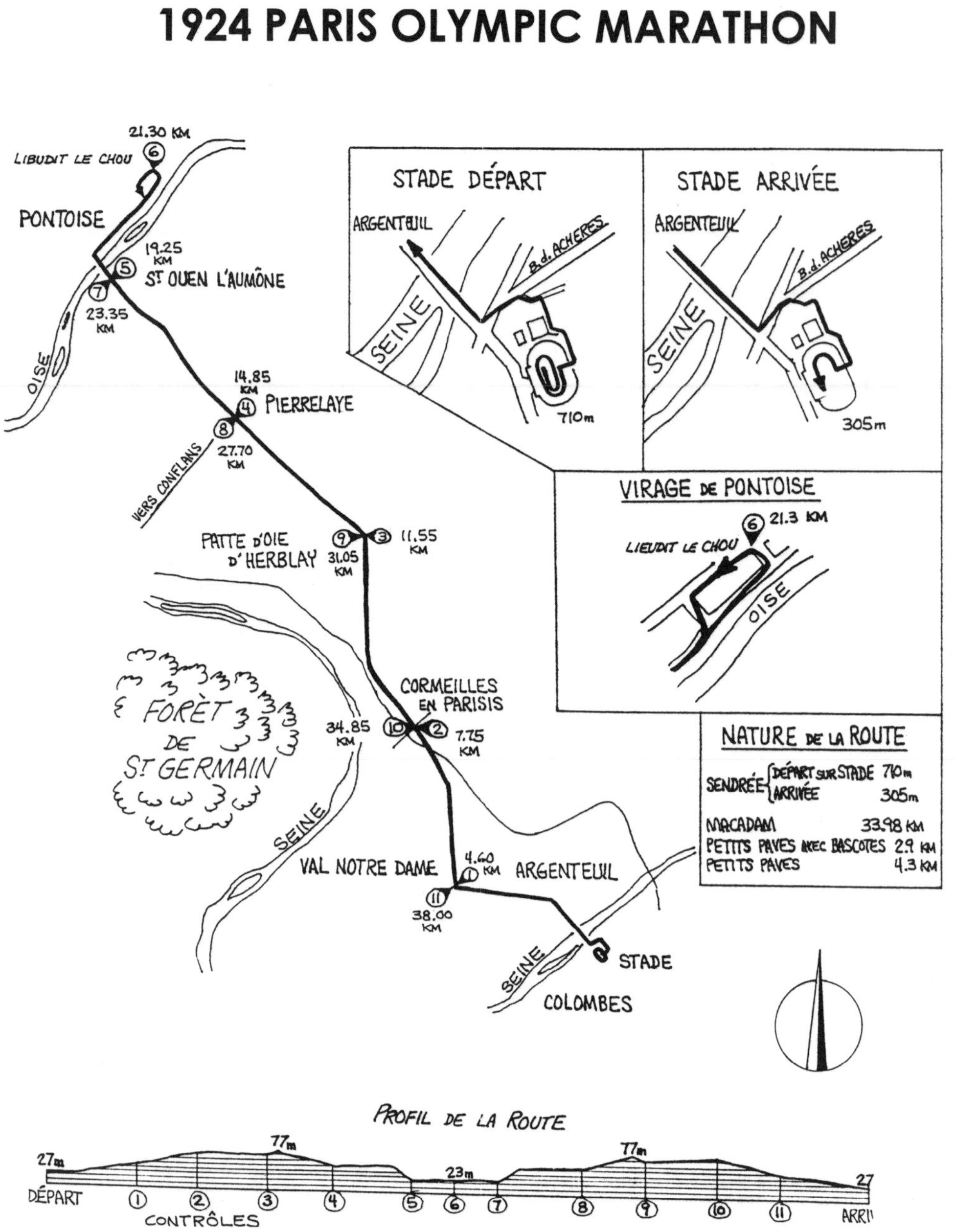

1924 PARIS OLYMPIC MARATHON

Figure 8.1 **Sketch of the Paris Olympic marathon course.** Prepared by Bob Letson.

The Paris Olympic Games marathon began and ended in the Colombes stadium, and it involved a journey into the French countryside northwest of Paris (figure 8.1). The running surface consisted of 1,015 meters on the cinder track, 33,980 meters on macadam (compacted broken stone bound with tar or asphalt), 4,300 meters on unpaved road with small pebbles, and 2,900 meters on cobblestones (Anonymous 1924). Athletes started on the stadium track at its northwest corner and ran 710 meters counterclockwise to the exit tunnel on its northeast side. Upon exiting, athletes made a sharp left turn along the access road in between the practice and Olympic stadia, and then made a half-left turn onto the larger Boulevard d'Acheres. This connected directly to the main road that crossed the river Seine using a bridge known as the Pont d'Argenteuil. After crossing the bridge, athletes ran through the village of Argenteuil and then reached the first of 11 control points on this out-and-back route. On return, the runners crossed back over the Pont d'Argenteuil, retracing their steps into the stadium. Once inside, they ran a final 305 meters counterclockwise, finishing on the southwest corner of the track. The control points are illustrated in figure 8.1 and summarized in table 8.1.

European, Japanese, and American Marathoners Dominate

With the Olympic Games scheduled for the European continent, pre-event hype in local newspapers caused increasing interest among both spectators and

TABLE 8.1

Key Measurement Points: 1924 Paris Marathon Course

Marathon control point	*Distance (km)*	*Altitude (m)*
Stade de Colombes	0	27
Val Notre Dame	4.60	46
Cormeilles en Parisis	7.75	69
Patte d'Oie d'Herblay	11.55	69
Pierrelaye	14.85	48
Saint Ouen l'Aumòne	19.25	27
Pontoise	21.30	27
Saint Ouen l'Aumòne	23.35	27
Pierrelaye	27.70	48
Patte d'Oie d'Herblay	31.05	69
Cormeilles en Parisis	34.85	69
Val Notre Dame	38.00	46
Stade de Colombes	42.20	27

athletes. The Olympic Games were indeed a major sports event, particularly with the attention given to de Coubertin's impending retirement as leader of the Olympic movement.

Finland

Because of Hannes Kolehmainen's Antwerp victory, Finland was the center of discussion whenever the question of a likely marathon gold medalist at Paris was posed. But in addition to the Kolehmainen brothers, this small nation had plenty of other talented distance runners, led by the great "Flying Finn," Paavo Nurmi. Nurmi, who won 12 Olympic medals (still the most by any Olympian) in the 1920s and is arguably the most successful long-distance runner in Olympic history, was not planning on competing in the Paris marathon. The story of how the Finnish team was selected, however, is both complicated and interesting.

The official Olympic trial race was held in Hyvinkää on May 18, 1924, over the 40.2 kilometers distance that was still popular in Scandinavia. Ville "Willie" Kyrönen won this race (2:38:00), Albin Stenroos was a relaxed runner-up (2:39:33), and Väinö Hietakari placed third (2:42:29). These three were given team berths by the selectors. Seventeen men started this trial race, and only eight finished, including 40-years-old Teudor Koskenniemi in fourth (2:43:52), running his first marathon after a long and successful track career. Olympians Aarne Kallberg (DNF at Stockholm) and Urho Tallgren (ninth at Antwerp) were fifth and seventh, respectively, and were not selected to the team. Lauri Halonen had not been racing for several years, but the Olympic year rekindled his desire to train, and his fitness level was good. He led the race, developing a stitch at the halfway mark, which forced him to retire. Gabriel Ruotsalainen was another runner with excellent past credentials who failed to finish.

Halonen and Ruotsalainen were given another chance to race at the Olympic preparation camp during June in Lahti. First, a 25 kilometers race was arranged, and it was Halonen (1:31:25) over Stenroos (1:32:00), with Ruotsalainen another 50 seconds behind. One week later, in miserable weather, a 30 kilometers trial was staged. This time it was Ruotsalainen (1:49:42) over Hietakari (1:50:50), with Halonen another 9 seconds behind. Following these races, the two extra trial winners (Halonen and Ruotsalainen) were added to the team. Hannes Kolehmainen was added as well, despite not having run any of the trials. He had a foot injury that was slow to heal, but he nevertheless had run a solo 27 kilometers in 1:35:00 as a test of fitness.

Interestingly, Koskenniemi was also added to the team in view of his fourth place at the Olympic trial. This gave a total of seven marathoners, but only six could race. Because the rules permitted athletes to switch events after the entry deadline, Ruotsalainen was actually entered as a 110 meters hurdler. Finland thus had the best possible options for fielding a great team on race day. Eventually, Kolehmainen was allowed to race in place of Koskenniemi. This was unfortunate because Kolehmainen had to drop out at about 25 kilometers; his foot simply could not endure the pavement pounding.

Great Britain

The usual heavy participation by international athletes at the British Polytechnic Harriers Marathon dwindled to only one such entrant on May 31, 1924. That was Japan's Yahei Miura. It was Britain's Olympic trial, and the huge field of 80 starters was almost unmanageable on the narrow road used for the race. George Neill was the early pacesetter, but at 11 miles, a 27-years-old Scotsman named Duncan McLeod Wright took the lead. Wright went on to win the race (2:53:17.4). It was his second victory in two starts.

A young airman named Samuel Ferris also was impressive with his superb sense of pace, starting sensibly and then finishing strongly. He was in fifth place at 15 miles, just behind Antwerp veteran Bobby Mills. By 23 miles, Ferris had moved into second. He had been five and one-half minutes behind the leader at 20 miles, came to within 100 seconds by 25 miles, and was only 45 seconds behind Wright at the finish. Wright, Mills, and Ferris were selected for the British team, along with Jack McKenna, who had collapsed at 25 miles but until then had been quite competitive. In addition, Ernie Leatherland (2:48:43.8) and Tony Farrimond finished first and second at Manchester on May 31, completing the British team. If any team could cope with the Finns, Britain could.

Japan

The Japanese Olympic marathon trial was at Tokyo on April 13, 1924. Shizo Kanaguri again demonstrated potential medal-quality fitness with his superb 2:36:10 victory—good enough for another Asian and Japanese national record. It was also the fastest time in the world for 1924. He had competed at both Stockholm (DNF) and Antwerp (16th). His Belgian performance also had been an Asian record, which got lowered subsequently by two other Japanese runners in 1922 and 1923. The Japanese Olympic team would consist of Kanaguri, Yahei Miura, who had competed at the "Poly," and a relative unknown, Kikonosuke Tashiro. One can only imagine the travel stress that these athletes must have experienced in reaching Paris from Japan.

United States

The United States used three races in the spring of 1924 to select its team: Laurel-to-Baltimore on March 8, Pontiac-to-Detroit on March 29, and Hopkinton-to-Boston on April 19. Frank Zuna won at both Baltimore (2:41:39.4) and Detroit (2:42:56), and was selected; six weeks later he ran Boston as a training effort. Clarence DeMar did the opposite, running at Baltimore but performing poorly due to a recurrence of some knee and back problems that had bothered him on and off for years. He recovered soon thereafter and delivered a brilliant 2:29:40.2 in Boston to soundly defeat Charles Mellor of Chicago (2:35:04.6). Mellor had also placed second at Detroit (2:43:32.4). All courses had been lengthened ostensibly to 42.195 kilometers in compliance with the new IAAF standards. But because course measurement technology was in its infancy, with little if any course documentation available to review, it is likely that some variability existed. Although DeMar's time was touted as a new world record, subsequent remeasurement again found the Boston course at least 176 yards (161 meters) short (26 miles, 209 yards). Other unsubstantiated claims have the course distance approximating 25 miles (~40.2 kilometers).

A decision was made to send the first six Americans at Boston, plus Frank Zuna, as the Olympic team, with a final selection race to eliminate one of them occurring in Europe about three weeks before the Games marathon. The Boston group included (in order of their finish) DeMar, Mellor, Frank Wendling of Buffalo, William Churchill of San Francisco, Carl Linder of Boston, and Ralph Williams of Quincy. A bitter controversy developed over the details of the final on-site selection race, described in both the official United States team report (Thompson 1924) and in DeMar's autobiography (DeMar 1937). It is likely that similar problems occurred over the years with other teams, but this one has been well documented and is worthy of summary.

The American team sailed from New York on May 24 on the steamship *Leviathan*, arriving at Cherbourg on May 30. The marathoners were accompanied by team manager and trainer Michael Ryan, a two-time Olympic marathoner who did not finish at either London or Stockholm. Thus, he knew the sadness of having a bad race and worked diligently to care for every possible need of his team. His athletes did very little training on the trip over so that they could recover from their hard racing in the United States and get mentally fresh for the upcoming supreme challenge six weeks away.

Ryan had booked the team into the American Hotel, just two blocks from the magnificently forested Bois de Boulogne, where many of the 1900 Paris Olympic venues were located. But after two weeks the Paris police objected to their training in the forest, for reasons not clear. Ryan found another hotel for the athletes near the St. Germain forest, in the village of Maisions Laffitte, close to the Val de Marne control point on the marathon course. This was a useful arrangement because athletes could train on the course or in the forest, and it was here that the 15 miles time trial was held on June 25, using a grass track. The plan was for manager Ryan to determine the athlete least likely to perform well in the Olympic Games. Paris was having an unusually warm summer, and this was one of those days. The order of finish was DeMar, Wendling, Churchill, Linder, and Zuna. Williams quit after three miles, and Ryan pulled Mellor off the course at 12 miles because he was the thinnest of the group and his excellent heat adaptation response through sweating was risking a loss of too much weight if he ran the full distance. Ryan's recommendation was to eliminate Williams from the start list.

But Ryan was overruled (Thompson 1924) by "the head coach and the chairman of the Selection Committee," who "were of the opinion that Williams had greater possibilities of winning the race than Linder had and that they were in favor of playing the greatest possibilities." DeMar, in his autobiography, addresses the distress that likely affected team performance: "I have always wondered just which of the Olympic officials wanted to gamble on a youngster like Williams (23 years old) winning the big race as a dark horse, knowing that while Linder (34 years old and a veteran of Antwerp) would run a good race, he had no chance of winning. But Linder had won a place as a regular member of the team, and he was still in good condition. Williams had not shown that he was any better than seventh man and a sub. This trick destroyed any hope and morale that any of the men had left." And so Linder did not start the Paris marathon. Williams did, but did not finish.

The Competition: A Runaway Victory for Stenroos

The marathon was scheduled for Sunday, July 13, the ninth day of the Games, the eighth and final day of athletics, and one week before the Closing Ceremonies on July 20. It was the day after the horrendously hot 10,000 meters cross country race that sent several to the hospital, and which caused officials to remove the event from future Olympic competition. Race officials decided to delay the 1500 (3:00 p.m.) marathon start for two hours, reducing somewhat the effects of radiant heating on the participants. Fortunately, a weather front moved through and made the day warm rather than hot, and there was even a small breeze that helped cool the 58 starters from 20 geopolitical entities. It was primarily a European race, with 43 athletes representing 13 nations. From Africa came one lone South African, and from South America came one each from Chile and Ecuador. Three runners from Japan and one from India represented Asia. North America had six from the United States and two from Canada.

The race actually began at 1723 (5:23 p.m.), and as the runners exited the stadium and entered the countryside, each of the 11 control points was able to provide radio communication back to the stadium. Rather than intermediate split times being taken, runner positions were recorded and announced periodically over the stadium loudspeaker system. This gave the assembled spectators an awareness of race developments, especially among the lead runners.

As usual, the early leaders suffered the consequences of their quick pace, and they either did not finish at all or placed well back of the eventual top stars. A Greek, Alexandros Kranis, had the lead at Val Notre Dame (4.6 kilometers), 50 meters ahead of Canadian John Cuthbert. Surprisingly, Hannes Kolehmainen (wearing number 308 at the front of one of the lagging packs in figure 8.2) was already two minutes behind the leaders, in 43rd position. Kranis increased his lead over Cuthbert by the checkpoint at Cormeilles en Parisis at 7.75 kilometers (29:18.8), with the rest of the pack strung out behind. He remained in the lead through the 11.55 kilometers checkpoint at Patte d'Oie d'Herblay. Clarence DeMar of the United States had moved into 2nd place, 32 seconds behind. The leading Finn at this point was not Kolehmainen (now three and one-half minutes behind, and who eventually dropped out—see Olympic Marathon Miscellany 8.1) or Lauri Halonen, but track star Albin Stenroos, in 12th place.

Kranis began to falter, faded to 3rd at 14.85 kilometers (Pierrelaye) behind DeMar, slowed rapidly thereafter, and retired after 23 kilometers. He was replaced in the lead by France's Georges Verger, who had steadily moved through the field of competitors from 18th place. American Charles Mellor was in 4th

Figure 8.2 During the early stages of the race, Hannes Kolehmainen (number 308, on the right side of the photograph) was already well behind the leaders. To his right is Duncan McLeod Wright [GBR](number 456). Behind these runners, from left to right, it is Antal Lovas [HUN] (number 547), Sam Ferris [GBR] (number 439), Ernest Leatherland [GBR] (number 450), and Gabriel Ruotsalainen [FIN] (number 330). Kolehmainen was already two minutes behind the leader by the 4.6 kilometers checkpoint. Courtesy of Amateur Athletic Foundation Sports Library.

place, hoping to maintain contact with DeMar. In the ensuing 4 kilometers downhill to the fifth control point near the bridge over the river Oise at Saint Ouen l'Aumône, Verger maintained his lead. But Stenroos moved into 2nd, 4 seconds behind, and 17 seconds ahead of DeMar. The Italian Ettore Blasi, never too far from contention (in 7th place from 11 kilometers onward), was now in 4th. As with Kranis, however, Blasi also developed problems and retired after 23 kilometers.

Just before the midpoint, near the Auberge Le Chou and still along the river Oise, Stenroos suddenly took the lead from Verger, opening a gap before the Frenchman realized what was occurring. At Pontoise (21.3 kilometers), Stenroos was timed in 1:20:06, 30 seconds ahead of Verger, and 58 seconds ahead of DeMar. In 4th place, Italy's Romeo Bertini had opened a gap over Blasi, France's Jean Manhes, and Lauri Halonen. On the return to the stadium, it became increasingly a one-man race for the gold medal as Stenroos steadily increased his lead. By 27.75 kilometers at Pierrelaye, he was two minutes and 50 seconds in front of DeMar, who, in turn, was just ahead of Bertini. Antwerp silver medalist Jüri Lossman steadily moved up through the pack, from 35th initially to 6th place at this point. Duncan McLeod Wright had also paced himself well, coming from 39th initially to 5th. The story emerged after the race that Wright had run with his ankles wrapped in order to provide support on the nearly 3 kilometers of cobblestoned pavement (Fairlie 1924). His feet started to swell from the effects of the 190 steps-per-minute pounding on the warm pavement. Shortly after 31 kilometers, he stopped to remove the wrappings. His hamstring muscles cramped so badly as he bent down that he could run no more. It was his only recorded DNF in a marathon.

By 31.05 kilometers (Patte d'Oie d'Herblay), three other runners now caught the attention of stadium spectators listening to the announcements of athletes passing the various checkpoints. A Chilean runner, Manuel Plaza, had moved from 19th to 11th and now to 7th through checkpoints seven, eight, and nine. Similarly, Britain's Sam Ferris had moved from 27th to 17th to 13th. Also, an Algerian-born Frenchman, Boughera El Ouafi, had been running steadily in 7th and 9th place for much of the race. By the next checkpoint, at 34.85 kilometers, Ferris had improved from 13th to 9th, with Plaza moving ahead of Ouafi into 6th place. Which of these well-paced athletes would now move into the medal positions?

Figure 8.3 Albin Stenroos (number 334), well out in front during the later stages en route to becoming the Olympic champion.

Stenroos continued to build on his huge lead (figure 8.3), and it became obvious that the gold medal was his. However, the real competition was for the other medals. It developed that the sequence of Bertini, DeMar, and Halonen was set at 31 kilometers, and this order remained to the end of the race. By 38 kilometers (Val de Notre Dame) Plaza had moved up a few places, into fifth, and Ferris had moved into sixth. Lossman slowed in the heat and eventually fell back to ninth. In the final few kilometers, Ferris caught and passed Plaza, finishing fifth. A better view of these changing positions is provided in table 8.2.

Stenroos's entry into the stadium was announced by bugle. He appeared fit and relatively fresh as he completed the final 305 meters of his journey before the cheering crowd in the full stadium. Just short of six minutes later, as Stenroos finished his victory lap and disappeared into the dressing room, Bertini entered, also looking unfazed by the ordeal, and then DeMar arrived nearly another minute behind. Decent performances by two other Americans, Frank Wendling (16th) and Frank Zuna (18th), gave the United States the best overall performance as a nation, followed by France and Great Britain. The results of the race are summarized in table 8.3. Despite the fairly healthy appearance of those who finished, the rolling course and warm weather took a heavy toll. Only 30 out of the 58 athletes finished. For some nations, it was a disaster: no Japanese, Greeks, or Czechs finished the race, and four of the six Finns and three of the six British athletes dropped out.

TABLE 8.2

Order of Top Placers Through Control Points

Control point	*Miles*	*Kilometers*	*Stenroos*	*Bertini*	*DeMar*	*Halonen*	*Ferris*	*Plaza*
Val Notre Dame	2.86	4.60	16	15	17	26	40	45
Cormeilles	4.82	7.75	12	10	13	19	41	42
Patte d'Oie	7.18	11.55	12	11	2	10	40	41
Pierrelaye	9.23	14.85	8	10	2	9	40	38
Saint-Ouen	11.96	19.25	2	5	3	6	33	28
Pontoise	13.24	21.30	1	3	4	6	30	23
Saint-Ouen	14.51	23.35	1	3	2	5	27	19
Pierrelaye	17.22	27.70	1	3	2	4	17	11
Patte d'Oie	18.37	31.05	1	2	3	4	13	7
Cormeilles	21.66	34.85	1	2	3	4	9	6
Val Notre Dame	23.62	38.00	1	2	3	4	6	5
Stade de Colombes	26.22	42.195	1	2	3	4	5	6

TABLE 8.3

1924 Paris Olympic Marathon at a Glance

Date:	13 July	**Weather:**	Warm, breezy
Start time:	1723	**Starters:**	58
Course:	Out-and-back	**Finishers:**	30
Course distance:	42.195 km	**GPEs:**	20

TOP RESULTS:

Place	*Athlete*	*GPE*	*Date of birth*	*Time*
1	Albin Stenroos	FIN	24 Feb. 1889	2:41:22.6
2	Romeo Bertini	ITA	21 Apr. 1893	2:47:19.6
3	Clarence DeMar	USA	07 June 1888	2:48:14.0
4	Lauri Halonen	FIN	24 Mar. 1894	2:49:47.4
5	Samuel Ferris	GBR	29 Aug. 1900	2:52:26.0
6	Manuel Plaza	CHI	19 Mar. 1902	2:52:54.0
7	Boughera El Ouafi	FRA	18 Oct. 1898	2:54:19.6
8	Gustav Kinn	SWE	10 June 1895	2:54:33.4
9	Dionisio Carreras	ESP	09 Oct. 1890	2:57:18.4
10	Jüri Lossman	EST	04 Feb. 1891	2:57:54.6

New geopolitical entities represented: Spain [ESP], Czechoslovakia [TCH], Ecuador [ECU]

Team score (unofficial):			
	1. USA	37 points	(3-16-18)
	2. FRA	43 points	(7-12-24)
	3. GBR	49 points	(5-17-27)

OLYMPIC MARATHON MISCELLANY 8.1

From Riches to Rags—Olympic Gold to DNF

Probably no athletic victory is so treasured anywhere on the planet as an individual Olympic gold medal. Very simply, on the given day, this athlete is the best in the world. But human failings are also part of life, and it thus must be a uniquely profound sense of disappointment when an Olympic gold medalist tries again but fails even to finish the race. It might be unimaginable that someone so good one year could meet such a fate four years later, but the marathon is merciless in its toll on participants who exceed their performance limits.

Hannes Kolehmainen's Antwerp gold and Paris DNF (did not finish) provided the first such pairing of Olympic marathon supremacy and disappointment. It would occur on three more occasions during this first marathon century. The

(continued)

next athlete to experience such a fate was Juan Carlos Zabala of Argentina (gold at Los Angeles in 1932, DNF at Berlin). Perhaps the most famous example has been Ethiopian Abebe Bikila (victories at both Rome and Tokyo, but a Mexico City DNF due to injury). The fourth is Italy's Gelindo Bordin (Seoul gold and Barcelona DNF).

The reverse has also occurred, where an athlete who did not finish in his first Olympic marathon came back to conquer in his next attempt. Mamo Wolde was a DNF at Tokyo but won the gold at Mexico City.

Notes on the Medalists

Born in Vehmaa, Finland, and 35 years old when he won his gold medal, **Albin Stenroos** had a long but inconsistent career. He was either out of the running scene or at the very top of his game—there was little in between. He was a woodworker by profession (Wallechinsky 1996), and he had a powerful frame (68 inches or 173 centimeters, 141 pounds or 64 kilograms) that helped increase his success as a runner. He set national records on the track in both the 5,000 and 10,000 meters events. He ran only two marathons over the now-standard 42.195 kilometers distance in addition to his race at Paris. His athletic excellence was often overshadowed by results of the other great Finnish distance runners. As just one example, perhaps his most competitive non-Olympic marathon experience was on July 4, 1909, when he ran 3:03:54. He had all three Kolehmainen brothers to deal with in that race, and he was the only athlete to separate them. Tatu and Willie Kolehmainen placed first and second, and Stenroos was third, eight minutes ahead of Hannes Kolehmainen.

Following that race, Stenroos stayed away from the marathon for 15 years and emphasized track running. At the Stockholm Olympic Games, he was the bronze medalist for Finland at 10,000 meters (behind Hannes Kolehmainen and Lewis Tewanima). He set a world best for 30 kilometers (1:48:06.2) in 1915 and then lapsed from the running scene, entering only minor races in 1917, and neither training nor racing between 1918 and 1920. He resumed training in 1921, competed occasionally through 1921 and 1922, and then suddenly rose to the top once again with a world best over 20 kilometers in 1923 (1:07:11.2). He continued to train hard through 1923 and 1924, with walking (as much as 120 kilometers per week) being a mainstay of his training. His superb fitness became very clear at the Paris Olympic Games, after which he then went on to set another world best for 30 kilometers (1:46:11.6).

Stenroos lived in the United States during 1925 and 1926, and he was runner-up to Canadian Johnny Miles in the 1926 Boston Marathon, beating DeMar again. Stenroos retired in 1928 after failing to make the marathon team for Amsterdam. Over his long career he captured 15 Finnish long-distance running titles. His only victory in a marathon was the one at the Paris Games. His marathon record is given in table 8.4.

TABLE 8.4

Career Marathon Record of Albin Stenroos

Date	Venue	Place	Time	Comments
02 Sept. 1907	Helsinki	DNF		40.2 km
06 Oct. 1907	Helsinki	DNF		40.2 km
04 July 1909	Helsinki	3rd	3:03:54.7	42.195 km
03 Oct. 1909	Helsinki	2nd	3:14:59	42.195 km track
25 Sept. 1910	Stockholm	DNF		42.195 km
18 May 1924	Hyvinkää	2nd	2:39:33	40.2 km
13 July 1924	Paris	1st	2:41:22.6	Olympic Games; 42.195 km
19 Apr. 1926	Boston	2nd	2:29:40	26 m(?)
02 June 1926	Philadelphia	DNF		42.195 km
17 June 1928	Kauhava	DNF		42.195 km
09 July 1928	Helsinki	2nd	2:37:05.6	41.6 km

The silver medalist, Italian **Romeo Bertini**, 31, was born in Gessate, near Milan. He made his marathon debut in 1913 but did not run another marathon until the 1924 Olympic trial race on a short (37 kilometers) course, where he placed second. Thus, the Paris Olympic race was his third marathon. After returning home, Bertini's excellent fitness provided him with a very successful fall racing season. He won his national marathon championship at Florence on September 14, 1924 over 42.75 kilometers. His time was slow (3:00:36), but conditions were not conducive to fast times, and he finished nearly six minutes ahead of the runner-up. Recovering amazingly well, he then entered the fifth annual Turin Marathon on October 26, winning handily with 2:49:55.4, only 67 seconds away from a course record. He was never again able to recapture this level of fitness, and he did not finish the 1928 Olympic marathon.

Bronze medalist **Clarence DeMar**, born in Madeira, Ohio, was the oldest of the three medalists. At 36 years old, he was by far the most experienced and was in the prime of an already extraordinary career. This was his second Olympic marathon, having placed 12th at Stockholm. He was 3rd in the 1910 Boston Marathon and won it in 1911. Soon after that, he was diagnosed with a heart murmur. Concerned about his heart, DeMar developed other interests and put running on the back burner for five years. In 1917 he resumed training, in part because his heart murmur could not be confirmed and his competitive instincts were still strong.

He won at Boston in 1922, 1923, and 1924, and his selection to the United States team for Paris was to be expected. Following the Paris Olympic Games, DeMar went on to win at Boston three more times (1927, 1928, and 1930). He became a three-time Olympian at Amsterdam, his 27th place coming at the age of 40 (see Olympic Marathon Miscellany 9.1).

Looking Ahead: Brief Highlights 1925-1928

1925: At least five nations started annual national marathon championships: the United States (Chuck Mellor at Boston on April 19), Britain (Sam Ferris at the "Poly" on May 30), Germany (Paul Hempel at Leipzig on September 6), Hungary (Pal Kiraly in Budapest on September 13), and Czechoslovakia (Jozef Maly at Prague on September 27). Albert "Whitey" Michelsen set a 42.195 kilometers marathon best of 2:29:01.8 between Columbus Circle in New York City and Liberty Square in suburban Port Chester on October 12, finishing more than two minutes ahead of DeMar. The two competed at this venue for six years, with Michelsen beating DeMar four times.

1926: Canadian Johnny Miles scored a Boston Marathon course record (2:25:40.4) in his marathon debut (and would win again in 1929).

1927: Whitey Michelsen achieved the year's fastest time (2:31:11) at Port Chester, New York on October 8.

References

Anonymous. 1921. *Handbook: International Amateur Athletic Federation 1912-1921.*
Anonymous. 1924. *Les Jeux de la viii^e Olympiade, Paris 1924.* Librairie de France: Paris.
DeMar, C.H. 1937. *Marathon.* Brattleboro, VT: Stephen Daye.
Fairlie, F.G.L. 1924. *The Official Report of the VIIIth Olympiad, Paris, 1924.* London: British Olympic Association.
Phillips, E. 1996. *The VIII Olympiad.* Vol. 8, *The Olympic Century.* Los Angeles: World Sport Research & Publications, Inc.
Senn, A.E. 1999. *Power, politics, and the Olympic Games.* Champaign, IL: Human Kinetics.
Thompson, R.M. 1924. *Report on VIII Olympiad Paris, France, 1924.* New York: American Olympic Committee.
Wallechinsky, D. 1996. *The complete book of the Summer Olympics.* 1996 edition. New York: Little Brown & Company.

CHAPTER 9

1928—AMSTERDAM

French Algerian El Ouafi Wins at Amsterdam

New Traditions and Events for Women Add Glamour to the Games

The Dutch welcomed the opportunity to host the Olympic Games in Amsterdam and engaged in a mammoth construction project to provide adequate facilities. Most of this western region of the Netherlands is either at or below sea level. To meet the needs of an increasing population, a project was begun in the 1920s to reclaim land from the sea. An enclosing dike was built to separate the Zuider Zee from the North Sea. Inflow of fresh water reduced its salinity, and it was gradually drained. Large land parcels called polders resulted; when drained, these were available for urbanization. Near Amsterdam, a drained freshwater lake (40 acres or 16 hectares) at the southwestern edge of the city became the focal point for Olympic Games construction.

The centerpiece of this Olympic site was a track and field stadium large enough for 40,000 spectators. It included a tall, architecturally pleasant tower bearing a large cauldron on top. Catacombs inside the stadium provided state-of-the-art meeting room facilities for all the various aspects of conducting a major competition. Track and field athletes were of course delighted with a new cinder track and a thick grass infield. For the first time in Olympic history, the running track was 400 meters, a standard dimension that has been used ever since (zur Megede 1999). But marathon runners were also happy with Amsterdam because they knew the course would be flat and the weather, they hoped, would be cool.

Participation by 2,724 men and 290 women from 46 geopolitical entities set a record, exceeding the 3,000 mark for the first time. Teams were housed all over the city in a variety of living accommodations. The American team, for example, lived aboard the *S. S. President Roosevelt,* on which it had sailed from New York. This ensured familiar food, training facilities, and appropriate security, as women were on the team along with men, making their Olympic debut in track and field. Their contested events included the 100 meters, 800 meters, 4 × 100 meters relay, high jump, and discus.

Another Olympic first saw an official team marching sequence put in place for the Opening Ceremonies. Greece and the host nation marched in first and last, respectively. Between them, the other participating teams were arranged in alphabetical order by geopolitical entity, using the host nation's language. This tradition continues today. As a symbolic touch to demarcate the Games period, a so-called Olympic flame was lit in the cauldron high atop the main stadium tower during the Opening Ceremonies. It remained lit until the Games ended, and at night the flame could be seen from a long distance. In 1936, at Berlin, considerably more ceremony would be added to the concept of an Olympic flame at the Games by lighting it in Greece and transporting it via relay to the host city.

In 1925, Pierre de Coubertin resigned from the presidency of the IOC. He had been in poor health, and this was the official explanation provided for his stepping down. But it was well known that he was not at all in favor of women's athletic participation. He also was not enamored by an increasing addition of team sports to the program. He steadfastly maintained that the Games should (a) be reserved for men, and (b) be individual contests of skill. For the first time since 1904, De Coubertin did not attend the Games, and the new IOC president, Count Henri de Baillet-Latour, from neighboring Belgium, presided over the festivities.

It may be that the first scandal of exploitation occurred at these Olympic Games. The organizing committee sold rights to take photographs of the Games to a commercial company, thereby preventing even spectators from snapping photos for their albums at home. Spectators had to check their cameras before entering the sport arenas, with searches outside these venues to ensure that they had not snapped photographs even of the ancillary festivities. This became impossible to implement, and eventually the organizing committee was not paid because the company declared that the terms of its agreement requiring no unauthorized filming had not been observed. Such funding would have been welcome. Using 1928 values for Netherlands guilders (NLG) and U.S. dollars, the new stadium cost U.S.$968,094 (NLG 2,371,830) to build—and revenue from gate receipts only totaled U.S.$585,854 (NLG 1,435,343). Because other Olympic Games had not been profitable, there was no complaint that these failed to turn a profit either, but it was becoming clear that such commercialization strategies would be the only way that a profit could emerge.

The United States outperformed the rest of the participating teams, with 22 gold, 18 silver, and 16 bronze medals in all. Germany was second, with 10 gold, 7 silver, and 14 bronze medals. Still, the United States track-and-field coaches were disappointed because only a single medal was won by American men in a nonhurdle track event from 100 meters through the marathon, that being Ray Barbuti's 47.8 seconds in the 400 meters dash. This was particularly embarrassing as it followed the confident declaration (Schaap 1963) of the recently elected president of its Olympic Committee, Major General Douglas MacArthur: "Without exception, our athletes have come through the long grind of training into superb condition. They are prepared both mentally and physically for the great test. America can rest serene and assured. . . ." Schaap goes on to comment that "most observers agreed that the Americans sagged because of four excesses: they were overcoached, overtrained, overfed, and overconfident."

The first gold medal won by a woman in track and field was awarded to Elizabeth Robinson of the United States for the 100 meters. She was also the youngest female gold medalist in 1928, at 16 years and 343 days. The women's 800 meters event was also a fine competition—the three medalists all ran faster than the existing world record. But a few of the women fell to the track in exhaustion, much as men do, causing such consternation among IAAF officials that they decided to ban the event from future Olympic Games. It wasn't until 1960 that the women's 800 meters was reinstated, with the 1,500 meters event added 12 years later.

A Flat Course Along the Dikes Promises Fast Racing

Marathon organizers decided upon a midafternoon start as optimum for spectator viewing and acceptable for the weather, as this part of Europe typically has a temperate summer climate. The marathon race director, Charles "Kelly" Kellenbach, the 1892 Dutch 100 meters sprint champion, examined the course carefully to ensure that athletes had the best possibilities for a good competition. The route was completely closed to all traffic starting at 1400 (2:00 p.m.), with a start planned for 1500 (3:00 p.m.).

Along the course, signboards with orange flags flying overhead indicated each five kilometers point. At each turn, course marshals waving blue flags guided runners in the proper direction. The army supplied them with field telephones for communication with each other and back to the stadium. These were supplemented as well by families living along the course who had telephones in their homes and made them available. Thus, the stadium spectators had ongoing knowledge of the race as it progressed.

Figure 9.1 illustrates the marathon route. It was essentially an out-and-back course just south of the city, including one initial lap within the stadium and a 200 meters half-lap finish. The roadway had a variety of surfaces, because in some places the route was heavily trafficked and in others it was a semirural country lane. These surfaces included macadam (10,768 meters); gravel (11,211 meters); clinkers, a kind of brick used for paving but not for buildings (13,084 meters); and cobbles (6,541 meters) in addition to the track cinders (591 meters) (van Rossen 1928). Much of the course ran along dikes that either helped contain the Amstel River flow or drained the polders, some of which are named in figure 9.1.

Runners were given a detailed set of rules for the competition, most of which were both familiar and expected. They could wear a watch and they had to wear competitor numbers on their vests, front and back. They had to stay on the roadway and could not accept assistance from anyone. Perhaps the most interesting rule (Sullivan 1928) was number seven: "the competitor is not allowed to run in the Amstel for a bath."

The course details box outlines both the individual street details and the locations of control points. These points were at specific major street intersections, and thus were not necessarily at evenly spaced 5 or 10 kilometers intervals. At a few of these points during the competition, the time for the leader was relayed back to the stadium, and these times will be mentioned later. Complete lists of athlete sequence and performance times at each checkpoint apparently were not compiled as the race progressed. However, to help athletes realize where they were in the competition, the time for the leader was written on a large board at control point G.

Additionally, control points C, E, and G provided refreshment stations—making five stops in all, as runners also passed points E and C in that sequence on the return to the stadium. The variety of refreshments was reminiscent of those provided at London in 1908 (see chapter 5): warm or cold water, white or chocolate milk, coffee and tea along with sugar, peeled bananas and grapes, peeled slices of lemons and oranges, and even sandwiches and peeled hard-boiled eggs (van Rossen 1928). In addition, this is apparently the first Olympic marathon at which athletes could also prepare their own special drinks prior to the competition and bring them to the stadium for subsequent delivery to specific refreshment stations as desired.

This entire marathon route is accessible today by either running or bicycling. In August 1998, the route was used for the Gay Games marathon, with the start near point C. Two portions are presently inaccessible to automobiles: between points C and D (6.3 to 7.7 kilometers) outbound and between points D to C to J (37.8 to 41.3 kilometers) on return, along the Amsteldijk and through a residential area. The Olympic stadium is currently undergoing a renovation, having been saved from demolition through vigorous lobbying by those who wanted the edifice preserved (Bijkerk 1997). It had been enlarged in 1937 to hold 65,000 spectators, but the current renovation, due to be completed in 2000 at a cost of U.S.$13,500,000 (NLG 23 million), will only seat 22,500. It will contain an eight-lanes athletics track surrounding a soccer field. A multi-sport gala is planned for May 13, 2000, to celebrate its restoration. Thus far, of the 22 modern Olympic stadia constructed from 1896 through 1996, only one has been demolished, that being London's (1908) White City Stadium.

Various Selection Strategies Produce Strong Teams

Although marathon racing was a global phenomenon, the hotbeds of activity in the mid-to-late 1920s were in Europe and the northeastern United States. Japan, however, was a pioneer in the Asian region regarding the development of opportunities for distance runners interested in quality competition. Its annual national championship race was well attended by the best runners, and when that also became Japan's 1928 Olympic selection event, runners truly were in top form. That race was held at Osaka on May 20, 1928 and was won by 26-years-old Kanematsu Yamada (2:43:22), followed by Seiichiro Tsuda. Although virtual unknowns to European and American athletes, they were equals in talent. Japan's selection method typified that used by many nations, a so-called first-past-the-post system where the entire team was chosen from the finish sequence of one competition.

Finland

Finland attempted to use a single trial race concept, but it was not as successful as planned. A full Olympic distance course was developed at Kauhava, and on June 17, 1928, 31-years-old Martti Marttelin was the convincing winner (2:38:56) over a classy field of Finland's finest. However, three runners behind him—Verner Laaksonen, Eino Rastas, and Ilmari Kuokka—intentionally crossed the finish line side by side, with the identical time of 2:40:40, so that they all would be selected. Finland decided to send these four athletes, plus fifth-placed Väinö Sipilä, who finished 62 seconds behind them. The 1924 gold medalist Albin Stenroos did not finish, however, so he was given one more chance to qualify, at a race over 41.6 kilometers held in Helsinki on July 9. He lost to Yrjö Korholin-Koski (2:35:11.3) by nearly two minutes. Korholin-Koski was then also added to the Finnish team, and Stenroos stayed home.

United States

The United States continued its habit of an announced series of trial races from which the best were selected by committee. No time standards had to be met because of the vagaries of weather and course difficulty. Instead, athletes thus had to "impress the selectors" with the quality of their performances in relation to those of other athletes. Unless someone won an event outright, he had to either gamble that his place would be among the very best or run another

Course Details

The 1928 Amsterdam Olympic Marathon

Start on stadium cinder track beside exit tunnel

Run one lap counterclockwise (.391 kilometer) and exit stadium

Outside the stadium, turn left onto Stadionplein to Stadionweg

Right onto Stadionweg to Olympia Weg

Half left onto Olympia Weg to Apollolaan

Half right onto Apollolaan

Apollolaan becomes Amstellaan (now called Churchill Laan and then Vrijheidslaan)

Continue on Amstellaan to intersection with Amsteldijk (4.865 kilometers at control point B)

Right onto Amsteldijk to intersection with Nieuwe-Wandelweg (6.276 kilometers) at control point C

Continue on Amsteldijk to control point D (8.318 kilometers) in 't Kalfje

Continue on Amsteldijk to control point E (12.818 kilometers) in the village of Ouderkerk

Continue on Amsteldijk to intersection with Nesser-laan (15.885 kilometers) at control point F alongside the Bovenkerker polder

Continue on Amsteldijk to intersection with Thamerdijk (20.519 kilometers) at control point G near the village of Uithoorn

Right onto Thamerdijk to intersection with Bovenkerkerdijk (21.895 kilometers) at control point H (midpoint)

Right onto Bovenkerkerweg to intersection with Nesser-laan (25.292 kilometers) at control point I alongside the Bovenkerker polder

Right onto Nesser-laan to intersection with Amsteldijk (28.225 kilometers) at control point F

Left onto Amsteldijk to control point E (31.292 kilometers) in the village of Ouderkerk

Continue on Amsteldijk to control point D (35.792 kilometers) in 't Kalfje

Continue on Amsteldijk to intersection with Nieuwe-Wandelweg (37.834 kilometers) at control point C

Left onto Nieuwe Wandelweg (now called Zuidelijke Wandelweg, which becomes De Groene Zoom, then Prinses Irenestraat, and finally Frederik Roeske Straat) to intersection with Amstelveensche Weg (41.339 kilometers) at control point J

Right turn onto Amstelveensche Weg to Stadionplein

Left turn through stadium tunnel onto track (41.995 kilometers)

Right turn and 200 meters around to finish line at the "Eretribune" ("Grandstand of Honor") and the royal box

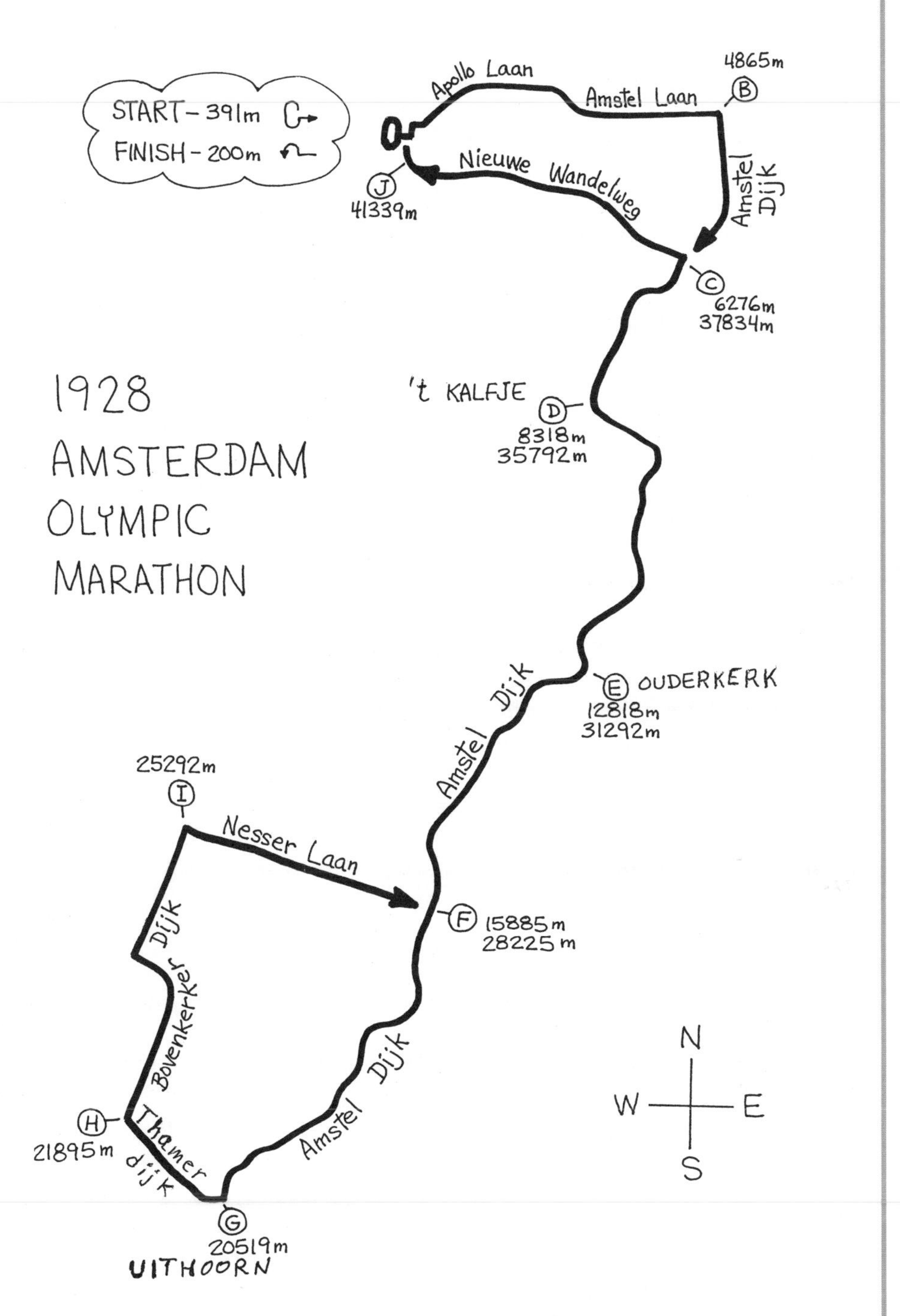

Figure 9.1 **Sketch of the Amsterdam Olympic marathon course.** Prepared by Bob Letson.

marathon. The risk of this strategy, of course, is that an athlete may overrace or sustain injury, and then, if selected, deliver a poor Olympic performance due to insufficient physical and mental recovery time.

The United States used three events for its team selection: the Boston Marathon, a marathon from New York City to Long Beach, and the Baltimore Marathon. Boston came first, on April 19. The winner was almost predictable. Clarence DeMar took his sixth victory (2:37:07.8) by nearly four minutes. The more interesting struggle ensued between the second and third places. It was between two very different athletes. Jimmy Henigan had been racing marathons since 1911—but only finished one. In his passion for competition, he typically started out too fast and faltered near the end. Joie Ray, on the other hand, had never run a marathon at all. He was a middle-distance track star with a 4:12 mile to his credit. Both finished this marathon, however, with Henigan (2:41:01) over Ray (2:41:56.8), and both were placed on the team.

In May, Ray won the New York-to-Long Beach Marathon, beating the far more experienced Whitey Michelsen. As a result, Michelsen decided he had better run at Baltimore in June, and win, to ensure selection. It was his fourth marathon that spring, as he had won the Woonsocket-to-Pawtucket Marathon in Rhode Island earlier in March, and then delivered a poor performance (35th) at Boston. He did not win at Baltimore, however, as William Agee secured a probable team spot by beating Harvey Frick, who had earlier finished 5th at Boston. Michelsen was back in 3rd. The American Olympic Committee eventually decided to bring DeMar, Ray, Agee, Frick, Henigan, and Michelsen. They all certainly had done their best to show they were quality athletes with a driving passion to represent their country in sport. All indeed did finish the Olympic marathon, but as mentioned in the committee's final report (Sullivan 1928), this no longer was considered an acceptable format. It was "too much of a strain on any class of competitors to keep men in condition over a period of four or five months up to the time for final selection."

Great Britain

In Britain, the team selection was also based upon results of three races. On May 19, the Manchester title went to Harry Wood (2:39:29.2) with the third fastest time in British history over the full distance. He won by 11½ minutes! A week later, at the Polytechnic Harriers race, Sam Ferris showed his superb fitness with an unprecedented fourth victory by almost 10 minutes (2:41:02.2) over S. S. Jones and Herbert Bignall. Ferris sustained a slight injury and missed the Amateur Athletic Association championship race on July 6, held over the same course. In only his second marathon, Harry Payne ran a course record 2:34:34 to defeat Ernie Harper (2:37:10), Scotsman Duncan McLeod Wright, and Bignall. Britain decided to send its three winners (Wood, Ferris, and Payne), plus the next three at the AAA race (Wright, Harper, and Bignall)—arguably the strongest team at the Games. Figure 9.2 shows some of these athletes on a training run before the Olympic marathon race.

Figure 9.2 **Members of the British marathon team on a training run in Amsterdam prior to the Olympic Games. From left are Harold Wood, Ernie Harper, Herb Bignall, Sam Ferris, and Duncan McLeod Wright. On the right is the one-armed South African Marthinus Stetyler. Hidden behind Ferris is probably Harry Payne, the sixth British team member.** Courtesy Roy Wood.

A Damp, Breezy Race Day Challenges the Runners

A contemporary journalist nicely described the setting of the race (Williams 1928): "Seemingly half the population of Holland, lining the course of more than 26 miles this damp, chilly afternoon, watched a son of the sun, a native of Algeria wearing the tricolor of France, win the grand prize of the ninth Olympic Games, the marathon. As the runner sped across the typical Dutch landscape, between grim dikes and beside desolate marshes, punctured with tiny flower-decked windmills, under heavy, watery skies through which the sun was unable to cast a single cheering ray, he was greeted with cheers by the Hollanders who braved a wind that forecast autumn."

This story is not quite accurate, as the "desolate marshes" had already been drained and the region, although rural, was indeed populated. The weather on

Sunday, August 5, as documented by the Royal Dutch Meteorological Institute (Ludeker 1998), was mild. The temperature at start time was close to the high for the day—16.1°C (61.0°F)—and the humidity was a high 93 percent. A strong breeze was blowing from the north-northwest at 7.0 meters per second (15.6 miles per hour). Thus, runners encountered a cross tailwind (from the right) from 4.8 kilometers through 20.5 kilometers, a headwind from 20.5 to 25.2 kilometers, a cross tailwind (from the left) from 25.2 to 28.2 kilometers, and a cross headwind to a full headwind for the remainder of the route back to the stadium.

The race began at 1514 (3:14 p.m.), 14 minutes late, on the final day of track and field. Spectators in the stadium were able to watch the relays and several field events, as well as a lacrosse demonstration, while the marathoners were on the course. The starting field of 69 made it the largest Olympic marathon up to that time. European countries dominated (51 athletes from 17 nations), but there were 13 athletes from North America (the United States, Canada, and Mexico), and 3 from Japan composed the Asian contingent. There was 1 South African and 1 South American.

After running slightly less than one lap counterclockwise in the stadium, the marathoners, led by the one-armed South African farmer Marthinus Steytler, exited the stadium through the marathon tunnel. Figure 9.3 shows Britain's Ernie Harper (number 461) in the lead, with the Union Jack logo on his singlet. Flanked on his left are two Belgians—Joseph Marien (number 622) and Jean Linsen (number 619). Newspaper reports (Williams 1928) indicated that the American, Joie Ray, was first out of the stadium portal, in front of Harper, so he was already out of camera view when this photo was taken.

Runners then made a sharp left turn onto the plaza in front of the stadium, called Stadionplein, and in figure 9.4, Ray (number 546) is now visible wearing a sweatshirt for the chill, to the right of Harper. (He is erroneously listed as number 556 in the official list of participants.) The two Belgians are just behind. Stadionplein was originally given the name of Van Tuyllplein in honor of the Dutch Olympic Committee's first president, Frederik W. C. H. Baron Van Tuyll van Serooskerken. For obvious reasons, a simpler street name was preferred, and Stadionplein has been used ever since.

As athletes reached the Amsteldijk at control point B, Kanematsu Yamada led the pack. They now turned southward, and Yamada continued to lead past control point C. With thousands of cheering spectators standing along the roadside, the lead now changed hands frequently. Beyond control point C, runners no longer had a tree-protected residential area to break the wind as they entered the rural environs outside the city.

At control point D, as runners passed through 't Kalfje, it was Finland's Eino Rastas (28:25 for 8.3 kilometers) in front of Germany's Franz Wanderer and two other Finns, Marttelin and Korholin-Koski. A time of 28:25 was announced for Rastas; this represents a pace of 5:30 per mile, or 3:25 per kilometer. The winning pace for this marathon turned out to be 5:50 per mile, or 3:37 per kilometer, so this suggests that athletes may have been favorably influenced by the tailwind from the north-northwest.

Figure 9.3 Runners coming through the tunnel leading out of the stadium to the city streets. Athletes identifiable include Ernie Harper [GBR] (number 461), Leon Broers [BEL] (number 607), Joseph Marien [BEL] (number 622), Jean Linsen [BEL] (number 619), Franz Wanderer [GER] (number 746), Hans Schneider [GER] (number 735), Sam Ferris [GBR] (number 452), Martti Marttelin [FIN] (number 796), Kanematsu Yamada [JPN] (number 264), Marcel Denis [FRA] (number 69), and Axel Elofs [SWE] (number 845). Courtesy IOC/Olympic Museum Collections.

In the village of Ouderkerk, at control point E, Jean Linsen had the lead, and his time is reported as 41:00 at 12.8 kilometers. This gives a net pace of 5:09 per mile, or 3:12 per kilometer, again a quickening of pace, likely due to the continuing tailwind. On the return, the pace was correspondingly slowed as the fatiguing competitors endured what now was a headwind. Just behind Linsen came Wanderer, Tsuda and his fellow countryman Junichi Nagatani, and Joie Ray. Bricker was sixth and Michelsen seventh.

Franz Wanderer passed control point F (15.8 kilometers) in the lead, with a reported time of 1:04:00. Here it was Tsuda just behind Wanderer, followed by Ray, Yamada, three Finns (Väinö Laaksonen, Marttelin, and Rastas), and Nagatani.

Near the village of Uithoorn, control point G (20.5 kilometers) was established to direct runners off the Amsteldijk with a right turn onto the Thamerdijk. Although this was not precisely the race midpoint, this was the most distant point away from the stadium. Tsuda was now out in front, just ahead of Yamada. Following were Marttelin, Bricker, and Ray. At this point, Ferris had fallen back to 18th place.

Figure 9.4 On Stadionplein just outside Olympic stadium, it is Joie Ray [USA] in the lead (number 546), with Ernie Harper [GBR] (number 461) just to his left. Just behind are two Belgians, Joseph Marien (number 622) and Jean Linsen (number 619). Other athletes visible back in the pack include Martti Marttelin [FIN] (number 796), Len Broers [BEL] (number 607), Kanematsu Yamada [JPN] (number 264), Karl Schneider [GER] (number 735), Verner Laaksonen [FIN] (number 791), Romeo Bertini [ITA] (number 222), Sam Ferris [GBR] (number 452), Emilio Ferrer [ESP] (number 230), Gerardus Steurs [BEL] (number 627), and Clarence De Mar [USA] (number 521). Courtesy IOC/Olympic Museum Collections.

No significant change occurred among this lead group through control points H (the midpoint), I, and then F, where the runners again reached the Amsteldijk. This was now familiar terrain, but it must have all looked the same, with the constancy of the rural roads along the dikes and polders. Between control points E (31.2 kilometers) and D (35.7 kilometers), Tsuda started to slow his pace, but Ray strongly moved into second behind Yamada, with Martellin in fourth. Approaching Tsuda fairly quickly now appeared the French Algerian Boughera El Ouafi, who, in turn, was being shadowed by Chile's Manuel Plaza. Four years earlier, at Paris, Plaza had used similar tactics in following El Ouafi, and then passed him near the finish to take sixth place.

Ray led briefly, but by control point C (37.8 kilometers), as the runners turned to the northwest and into the head wind, Yamada overtook him, and a classic duel began to see who would falter first. El Ouafi, however, was also racing strongly and soon found himself in between them, with Marttelin holding onto fourth. Suddenly Yamada slowed his pace, stumbled to the side of the road and fell onto the grass with cramps in one thigh. Each runner had a bicycle escort, and Yamada's, having experience with massage, dashed over to assist. Fortunately for Yamada, a race official from Finland witnessed the scene and intervened to keep the assistant from touching the runner, lest he be disqualified. As this was occurring, El Ouafi, Plaza, and Marttelin passed Yamada. Although he resumed running momentarily, he was suddenly out of contention for a medal. Ray also was slowed by painful muscle cramps.

As trumpets sounded from atop the stadium tower above the marathon entry tunnel, El Ouafi entered the stadium track (figure 9.5), his light blue shirt with its French Gallic cock dampened with sweat. His 2:32:57.0 was, at that time, the third fastest marathon in Olympic history. It would be 28 years until another Frenchman, again Algerian-born, would win an Olympic marathon gold medal for France. Plaza followed El Ouafi 26 seconds later (figure 9.6). Marttelin captured the bronze medal, and Yamada's fourth place effort was the fastest up to that time by an Asian marathoner.

Figure 9.5 Boughera El Ouafi (number 71) emerges from the marathon tunnel onto the stadium track en route to his Olympic victory. Courtesy IOC/Olympic Museum Collections.

Marttelin's bronze medal performance drew attention to the excellent overall performance by Finnish marathoners, as their 7th- and 12th-place finishers combined to make them the best-performing full team in the competition. Britain's Sam Ferris, who placed 8th, mentioned after the race that he ran conservatively so as not to cause problems with leg muscle twinges that had been bothering him since May. With Wood in 11th and Payne in 13th, Britain had the second best finish as a team. The United States placed 3rd as a team, with Ray in 5th, Michelsen in 9th, and DeMar in 27th. The race is summarized in table 9.1. As a testament both to the improved quality of Olympic marathon athletes and to the decent weather, 57 of the 69 starters completed the journey (82.6 percent), the best finish rate thus far. The Official Report lists 68 starters; it failed to list Franz Wanderer, who clearly is pictured in figure 9.3 wearing number 746. Also, Canadian Harold Webster was entered but does not appear in the official result list, and no photographic evidence has shown him competing.

A visit to the postrace recovery room showed the varying effects of the competition on the participants. El Ouafi was relaxed, drinking some water and milk, and asking for a cigarette. Joie Ray was grimacing with the agony of leg muscle cramps, either from dehydration or electrolyte imbalance, and then started

Figure 9.6 Silver medalist Manuel Plaza (number 686) has to settle for second place at Amsterdam. Courtesy IOC/Olympic Museum Collections.

TABLE 9.1

1928 Amsterdam Olympic Marathon at a Glance

Date:	05 August	**Weather:**	Cool, damp, cloudy, 16.1°C (61.0°F)
Start time:	1515	**Starters:**	69
Course:	Out-and-back with one loop	**Finishers:**	57
Course distance:	42.195 km	**GPEs:**	23

TOP RESULTS:

Place	*Athlete*	*GPE*	*Date of birth*	*Time*
1	Boughera El Ouafi	FRA	18 Oct. 1898	2:32:57
2	Manuel Plaza Reyes	CHI	19 Mar. 1902	2:33:23
3	Martti Marttelin	FIN	18 June 1897	2:35:02
4	Kanematsu Yamada	JPN	16 Sept. 1903	2:35:29
5	Joie Ray	USA	13 Apr. 1894	2:36:04
6	Seiichiro Tsuda	JPN	26 July 1906	2:36:20
7	Yrjö Korholin-Koski	FIN	03 May 1900	2:36:40
8	Samuel Ferris	GBR	29 Aug. 1900	2:37:41
9	Albert Michelsen	USA	16 Dec. 1893	2:38:56
10	Clifford Bricker	CAN	23 Apr. 1904	2:39:24

New geopolitical entities represented: Mexico [MEX], Latvia [LAT], Yugoslavia [YUG], Romania [ROM]

Team score (unofficial):			
	1. FIN	22 points	(3-7-12)
	2. GBR	32 points	(8-11-13)
	3. USA	41 points	(5-9-27)

shivering uncontrollably from hypothermia. "The Frenchman got the better of the argument," he remarked (Williams 1928), "so there's nothing to say." Clarence DeMar commented that the wind was indeed a factor in the race. "There weren't any hills—that's what floored me. This isn't my kind of a course."

Notes on the Medalists

Boughera El Ouafi was the first native-African Olympic marathon champion—in only his second try at the distance. An Arab born in Ould-El-Cadan (sometimes transliterated as Ould-Djleb) near Biskra, Algeria, he was a date-grower. He first started running at the age of 23 years and set an Algerian one-hour track record (16.899 kilometers or 10.49 miles). He then moved to France, joined an athletics club in Paris, got caught up in the Olympic spirit with the 1924 Games coming to his adopted hometown, and decided to focus on the marathon. During May and June of 1924 he lost races over 15, 25, and 30 kilometers, each time to France's star, Jean Manhes. At the French national marathon championship in 1924—the Olympic trial race—Manhes failed to finish, and El Ouafi won the event in 2:50:52.8. Both were awarded Olympic team spots. Manhes placed 12th at Paris, and El Ouafi, at the age of 25, placed 7th.

Following the Paris Games, El Ouafi competed very little. He returned to Algeria, where he became a dispatch carrier for the French army in the war against Abd El Krim in 1926. Running long distances in the hot, dry desert thus toughened him for sport competition, and in 1927 his desire to compete in another Olympic Games brought him back to France. Wintertime cross country training helped him build initial endurance, running with the colors of the French club C. O. Billancourt. His first real test of fitness on April 1, 1928, showed him returning to form, with a 2:18:30 victory in a 35 kilometers road race at Bruay-les-Mines. As in 1924, he then raced several more times without winning but suddenly returned to fine form when it was needed. The occasion was the national marathon championship at Melun on July 8, over 38.5 kilometers. He won in 2:20:03 only one month before the Amsterdam Olympic Games. He defeated two rising French stars, Jean Gerault (2:21:20) and Guillaume Tell (2:25:17), and all three were selected to the French team. His teammates finished back in the pack, but El Ouafi once again demonstrated that rare talent of training very intensively for a relatively short period of time, remaining injury-free, and reaching a physical and emotional peak at the right moment. His Amsterdam victory, at the age of 29, climaxed his athletic career.

After Amsterdam, El Ouafi turned professional and came to the United States for racing opportunities. At one classic event on Madison Square Garden's indoor track in New York City, El Ouafi faced an incredible field: Antwerp silver medalist Jüri Lossman, fifth-at-Amsterdam Joie Ray, Britain's Arthur Newton, and the great Willie Kolehmainen. Over the now standard Olympic distance, El Ouafi won by a quarter mile in 2:44:55.4 and captured the huge prize of $4,000. The runner-up was Joie Ray.

Manuel Plaza Reyes brought the first Olympic marathon medal to the South American continent. Plaza developed from an earlier track background at shorter distances, moving up to the marathon as he got older and sought new challenges. At the third South American championship in Buenos Aires in 1924, he won the 3,000, 5,000, and 10,000 meters races on the track, as well as the cross country race. Marathon racing was not popular in South America during this period, but he was given a berth on Chile's Olympic marathon team at Paris in 1924 on the strength of this long-distance track expertise and the fact that he had run one marathon race. That race was at Rio de Janeiro, where he won the Latin American championship (2:57:00) on September 16, 1922. His fine sixth place at Paris showed an excellent ability to adapt to the longer distance.

Winning the same four track events again at the South American championships of 1926 and 1927 prepared him nicely for his silver medal performance at Amsterdam. At 26 years of age, he was in his prime. He continued to race long after these Olympics, and he won the first South American half marathon championship at Montevideo, Uruguay, in 1933, which was held as part of the Eighth South American Athletics Championships.

Martti Marttelin was born in Nummi, Finland, and ran his first marathon (over 40.2 kilometers) in 1926, at the age of 28. His Olympic Games bronze medal at Amsterdam was his first marathon loss in five races. Following these Games, he set a world record for 25 kilometers, which he improved on in 1930. He also won the talent-loaded Turin international marathon (2:41:24.2), beating Sam Ferris. In turn, Ferris took his revenge when the two met again at the 1930 AAA marathon championship. Marttelin did not finish the 1932 Olympic trial, which was his 10th marathon attempt. His career included six victories. During World War II, he was killed in military action (see Olympic Marathon Miscellany 17.2).

Olympic Marathon Miscellany 9.1

Mr. DeMarathon's Olympic Career Closes

Clarence DeMar's 16-years span of Olympic marathon participation is the longest of any such athlete. Four Olympic marathoners competed in four Games during this first century, but these were consecutive, and thus achieved over 12 years. DeMar was a three-timer (along with 18 others). He placed 12th at Stockholm, and there were no Games in 1916. He missed Antwerp, then reattained world-class fitness in the early 1920s and won the silver medal at Paris. His 27th place at Amsterdam came at the age of 40. It was also his 27th marathon, 12 of which were victories. By the end of 1930, the last of his winning years at Boston, he had stood on the victory podium for 17 of 40 marathons.

Similarly, his lifetime racing career is one of the longest on record. He ran his first race in 1909, a cross country race. His earlier career leading up to and just after his Paris bronze medal performance was described in chapter 8. Following Paris, he willingly participated in early medical research investigating the physiological adaptations to high-level endurance exercise. At the Harvard Fatigue Laboratory, the pioneering physiologist David B. Dill and colleagues discovered that one of DeMar's "secrets" to running so well was a high anaerobic threshold (Dill 1965). Thus, he had a resistance to blood lactic acid accumulation at paces that for others would have brought a rapid rise, with subsequent slowing of performance. He won 7 Boston Marathon races (out of 34 starts), a feat still unequalled in the race's 100-plus year history. In 1954, at the age of 65, he still managed to place 78th among 113 starters! There is no known record of him ever dropping out of a race.

Nicknamed "Mr. DeMarathon" by the articulate *Boston Globe* sportswriter Jerry Nason, he died on June 11, 1958, of metastatic rectal carcinoma, at the age of 70. In a eulogy published by the *Boston Globe* (Derderian 1994), it was written that he "lived simply, always had a farm, and earned his living as a

(continued)

printer.... Occasionally a career like his comes as a reminder of what human nature can achieve when great ability is united with strong character and single-minded devotion to essential values."

An autopsy of DeMar (Currens and White 1961) revealed a striking anatomic feature in his heart: "the coronary arteries were estimated to be two or three times normal size." While showing signs of lipid obstruction characteristic of aging hearts, his coronary arteries were so large that his cardiac performance was protected from such aging effects.

Looking Ahead: Brief Highlights 1928-1932

1929: Harry Payne won the British Amateur Athletic Association title in a European record time of 2:30:57.6 over the Windsor-to-Stamford Bridge course on July 5.

1930: DeMar won his sixth Boston Marathon, a feat unequalled up to that time in race history. Scotsman Duncan McLeod Wright won the inaugural British Empire Games (now Commonwealth Games) title at Hamilton, Ontario (August 21) in 2:43:43, comfortably ahead of Sam Ferris (eight-time winner of the *Sporting Life*/Polytechnic Harriers Marathon) and Johnny Miles, Boston Marathon winner from Canada in 1926 and 1929.

1931: In his debut over the marathon distance, a developing Argentine star, Juan Zabala, won the eighth annual Košice Marathon in Czechoslovakia on October 28. He set a course record of 2:33:19, which was so fast that it stood until 1950.

References

Bijkerk, T. 1997. Demolition of Amsterdam Olympic stadium averted at the last moment. *Citius, Altius, Fortius* 4 (3): 19-20.

Currens, J.H., and P.D. White. 1961. Half a century of running: Clinical, physiological and autopsy findings in the case of Clarence DeMar ("Mr. Marathon"). *New England Journal of Medicine* 265: 988-993.

Derderian, T. 1994. *Boston Marathon.* Champaign, IL: Human Kinetics.

Dill, D.B. 1965. Marathoner DeMar: physiological studies. *Journal of the National Cancer Institute* 35: 185-191.

Ludeker, J. 1998. Personal communication.

Schaap, R. 1963. *An illustrated history of the Olympics.* New York: Alfred A. Knopf.

Sullivan, T.J. 1928. Report of manager of marathon team. *Report of the American Olympic Committee, IX Olympiad, Amsterdam, 1928.* New York: American Olympic Committee.

van Rossen, G. 1928. *The ninth Olympiad, being the Official Report of the Olympic Games of 1928 celebrated at Amsterdam.* Translated by Sydney W. Fleming. Amsterdam: J.H. de Bussy Ltd.

Williams, W. 1928. *The New York Times*, August 5.

zur Megede, E. 1999. *The first Olympic marathon century 1896/1996.* Köln: Deutsche Gesellschaft für Leichtathletik-Dokumentation.

CHAPTER 10

1932—Los Angeles

Zabala Takes Gold as Ferris Closes Fast in Los Angeles

Good Weather and Facilities Provide a Favorable Environment

The Los Angeles basin of southern California can experience hot weather during the summer and presently has air pollution as an added potential health concern. But in 1932, a consistent pattern of low humidity, cool Pacific breezes, and mild sunny days provided an unprecedented ideal climate for finely tuned athletes to compete well. Previous Olympic Games had not been so fortunate, with everything from heat waves and muggy weather to cold spells and rain plaguing this outdoor sports spectacle.

One new feature was an Olympic village for athlete residence—a city unto itself constructed in suburban Baldwin Hills, 12 miles (19 kilometers) southwest of downtown Los Angeles. It occupied 321 acres (130 hectares) and had 550 residential bungalows. Forty kitchens provided a wide variety of ethnic cuisines. The 1,281 male athletes stayed here, while the 127 female athletes were housed in Los Angeles hotels.

Another unique feature was the 400 meters track. It was without question the fastest ever constructed. Built of a special crushed peat mixture, it made athletes feel like they were running on a springboard. It packed nicely when rolled flat and did not cake between the spikes on runners' shoes. It could never be used in Europe or other areas where rain is frequent, because it would stick much like cement. Rain did not occur during these Olympic Games, and this surface remained marvelously consistent. Twenty-two men's track and field events were repeated from previous Olympics, and new Olympic records were established in all but three events (hammer throw, broad jump, and high jump).

These were the first Summer Olympic Games to have athletes ascend a victory podium to receive their medals. The tradition started at the Lake Placid Winter Games earlier in the year. At previous Games, athletes simply paraded past a royal box or formally decorated elevated platform, from which appropriate dignitaries handed out the medals. The mystery of just who ordered this change in format, which became an elegant and worthy part of Olympic ceremonial protocol, has recently been explained (Barney 1998). It was none other than the IOC president himself. In a letter dated May 8, 1931 to the secretaries of the two United States organizing committees, Count Henri de Baillet-Latour gave instructions to build a pedestal with three platforms reserved for medal ceremonies. At Los Angeles, each tier was numbered, and the podium resided in the Coliseum. Track and field medalists were recognized there on the day of their competition, following verification of results. Athletes who had competed at other venues assembled the day after their events in the Coliseum in order to receive their medals.

The centerpiece for these Olympic Games was the Los Angeles Coliseum, first opened on May 1, 1923, after 17 months of construction. This was the same year that the IOC, at its meeting in Rome, voted to award the Games to Los Angeles. A subsequent 15-months renovation project completed on May 11, 1931 enlarged the seating capacity to 101,574, by far the largest Olympic stadium up to that time. During the Games, it was used for the ceremonies as well as track and field. On only one day was it full for competition, but the daily average attendance of 60,000 spectators in the stadium was unprecedented.

With such a marvelous competition environment, athletes faced only two challenges: getting fit and getting to Los Angeles. Even for teams from the United States, Mexico, and Canada, a lengthy train ride was required, as the major North American population centers were either in the eastern regions of Canada and the United States, or in Mexico City. For only the second time in modern Olympic history, all the European nations had to join the rest of the world in undertaking arduous journeys to reach the site of the Olympic Games. For example, the Finnish team traveled relatively directly. These athletes took a nine-days boat ride from Helsinki to New York, recovered for two days, and then crossed the American continent in five days by train.

In contrast to the direct route taken by the Finns, the British team, one of the major powers in the marathon, took much longer to reach Los Angeles. The team left Southampton, England, on Wednesday July 13 aboard the steamship *Empress of Britain*, traveling in tourist third class, and sailed to Quebec. After a five-days voyage and a train ride from Quebec to Toronto, they stayed at the Royal York Hotel for three days of training.

On July 21, the British team left Toronto using the Canadian National Railways and journeyed to Chicago. This was a special Olympic train; also aboard were the Canadian and South African teams, as well as part of the Hungarian and Belgian delegations. A 12-hours stopover in Chicago permitted a vigorous training session. Next, the teams transferred to the Santa Fe Railway and traveled to Albuquerque, where they disembarked for exercise and a shower. They reached Los Angeles at midday on Monday, July 25, and spent the afternoon getting transported either to the Olympic village (men) or to the appropriate hotels (women). Athletes of today might cringe at the thought of a 12-days trek, but at least one problem was solved: time-zone acclimatization occurred gradually en route instead of on arrival.

Pre-Game Hype Suggests Four Nations in Contention for Marathon Medals

Four nations on three continents were developing talented marathoners whose credentials appeared above the rest: Japan, Britain, Finland, and the United States. However, isolated individual athletic excellence in other nations provided just enough uncertainty to make it risky to suggest an outcome.

Japan

Japan probably had the largest number of top-level marathon runners, with a steady changing of positions on performance lists as athletes improved. By the fall of 1931, Japan could have fielded several teams of three Olympic-caliber athletes. On October 4, 1931, Seiji Takahashi lowered the Asian and Japanese record to 2:34:30 at Tokyo. But a month later, on November 3, Tamao Shiaku improved upon that (2:34:04.4) at the Tokyo national championship. Then, on April 30, 1932, also in Tokyo, on a course from Jingu Stadium to Rokugo Bridge and return, Tanji Yahagi's 2:31:31 set a world best for out-and-back courses. It ended up as the year's fastest performance by 5 seconds. Takahashi was second, and Amsterdam Olympian Seiichiro Tsuda was third—all three were faster than Shiaku's November mark! The next day, Shiaku ran a probably short-course marathon at Sakaide City, and won. Norio Suzuki did the same at Kashiwazaki a week later under similar circumstances.

Thus, the Japanese Olympic trial race on May 25 was pressure-packed—only three would go to Los Angeles, and so many had comparable talent. The final result caused even more confusion. Seiichiro Tsuda qualified with his third place finish of 2:38:03.2. Finishing first and second, however, were two previously unheralded athletes: 26-years-old Taika Gon (2:36:49.6) and 18-years-old Onbai Kin, 67 seconds behind in a personal best. These athletes were from

Korea, which had been annexed in 1910 by Japan (their Korean names were Kwon Tae-ha and Kim Eun-bai, respectively). The unlucky fourth-placer was the consistent Seiji Takahashi. Initially, this result suggested a possible disadvantage of using a single-race trial rather than a selection system; one could only await the outcome in Los Angeles.

Great Britain

Britain used its two major marathons for selection purposes—the "Poly," held May 28, and its national (AAA) championship on July 1, over the same course. In contrast to 1931, the "Poly" had an international field—South African Tommy Lalande, two-time Košice Marathon winner from Germany Paul Hempel, and his countryman Erich Geisler. How the British ranked in comparison to these international athletes was unknown. Britain's Sam Ferris, however, had won the 1931 edition in his now-famous come-from-behind style that characterized his excellent pace judgment. In 1932, Ferris and Lalande led from 15 miles, and 2 miles later Ferris quickened his pace. He finished confidently and unchallenged (2:36:32.4), with Lalande nearly seven minutes behind.

Satisfied that he had a team berth secured, Ferris opted not to run the AAA championship. The best of Britain all were there, including two Scotsmen from the Maryhill Harriers, Duncan McLeod Wright and Donald McNab Robertson. They ran patiently in the early miles, but just before 20 miles took the lead together. In a truly epic battle, they raced shoulder-to-shoulder for the final 10 kilometers. Robertson beat Wright by a mere 1.4 seconds at the finish in an impressive 2:34:32.6. Work and family commitments prevented Robertson from accepting his invitation to run in Los Angeles. He was a coach painter with the Glasgow Corporation and was not allowed the necessary leave time. This was unfortunate; as a six-time national (AAA) marathon champion, he was one of the most consistent and enduring British runners of the period. He later died in his sleep at the young age of 43. The British team thus was not a full complement of three, with only Ferris and Wright.

Finland

The world eagerly awaited the decision of Finland's Paavo Nurmi to run the marathon. This was the only event remaining for him to be the first to complete a collection of gold medals in Olympic long-distance running. At Antwerp he took gold in the cross country and 10,000 meters events, with a silver medal in the 5,000 meters. At Paris, he captured individual gold medals at 1,500 and 5,000 meters on the track and cross country, and was on his country's gold medal 3,000 meters team. At Amsterdam, he won gold at 10,000 meters, with silver medals at the steeplechase and 5,000 meters. He indeed decided to enter the Finnish Olympic marathon trial, held at Viipuri on June 26, 1932.

A most peculiar, confusing, interesting, and unfortunate set of circumstances ensued. First, Nurmi wore spikes for the race, because he wanted to feel as light as possible. True, the first and final 10 kilometers were run on the Papula sports ground cinders, with the middle 22 kilometers on nearby dirt roads, and he indeed desired good traction—but running 42 kilometers in spikes? Second, he did not drink a drop of fluid all through the race, again suggesting that he really had not thought much about the huge difference between a marathon and the much shorter track races. Third, although he ran a superb effort, was never challenged, and was ahead by several minutes in the final stages, he announced to officials that he would stop at 40.2 kilometers because of an irritated Achilles tendon. This had been the popular Scandinavian version of the marathon distance for years, being only 33 meters short of 25 miles. His time was a very fast 2:22:03.8, equivalent to around 2:29:00 for the full marathon distance. The winner, Armas Toivonen, ran 2:35:50.2. Both were declared on the team, along with Willie Kyrönen, who finished farther behind. Nonfinishers included 1928 medalist Martti Marttelin (33 kilometers) and Canadian-based Dave Komonen (29 kilometers).

However, although Nurmi traveled to Los Angeles with the team, he did not run in the Olympic marathon. On July 28, three days before the Opening Ceremonies, the 35-years-old Finn was suspended from the Olympic Games at the end of an all-day, 11th-hour meeting of the seven-member Executive Council of the IAAF. It was contended that during September and October 1931, Nurmi had run five exhibition races in Germany for which he had received remuneration in excess of his actual expenses. There was little doubt that Nurmi had profited during his incredible career, but so had many others.

By IAAF policy, its council, headed by President J. Sigfrid Edström of Sweden, had the sole power to accept or reject entries, and its decision did not permit appeal. The communiqué issued provided no details concerning the case itself, thereby allowing no possibility for debate. As reported in *The New York Times* (Anonymous 1932b): "The Commission appointed by the International Amateur Athletic Federation pursuant to its rules to manage the track and field events of the 10th Olympiad, having carefully reviewed the evidence before it and the representatives of Finland, has unanimously rejected the entry of Paavo Nurmi, under authority given it in the seventh paragraph of Rule 2 of its general rules for Olympic events." Apparently the evidence against Nurmi was sufficiently incriminating that his case could serve as a warning to athletes of the world against the "evils of professionalism," as after all, the Games were still "reserved for amateurs," at least in the eyes of policymakers.

Nurmi watched the race from the Olympic stadium, and never ran another marathon. He was replaced on the marathon team by Lauri Virtanen, who had not previously run the event. In addition to his inexperience, there was concern that he may not have recovered from his excellent track racing. He had won the bronze medal in the 10,000 meters on July 31, qualified for the 5,000 meters final on August 2, and earned the 5,000 meters bronze medal on August 5. Now, with only one day of rest, he would face the marathon distance on August 7.

Other Nations

The United States once again used a selection committee to choose the traveling team based on performances from three races (Rubien 1932). Two were in the spring—logical choices for those desiring to recover and resume training. The Boston Marathon on April 19 started the series, followed on May 28 with the Cambridge-to-Salisbury Marathon on Maryland's eastern shore. The final race was the fourth edition of the *Los Angeles Times* Marathon, scheduled for June 25, only six weeks before the Games. Foreign-born runners living or training in the United States were also interested in using these events to test their fitness and establish qualifying performances, which helped make these races quite competitive.

A good example was the 1932 Boston Marathon. A 24-years-old German ex-sailor, Paul de Bruyn, living in New York and working as a boiler room stoker at the Hotel Wellington, defeated the American James "Jimmy" Henigan by less than a minute (2:33:36.4 to 2:34:32). In the previous year, Henigan had won at Boston with de Bruyn back in eighth place, so their rivalry was keen. Finland's Willie Kyrönen placed third and thus had an early indication of developing fitness for his nation's upcoming June Olympic trial. In fourth was Olympian Whitey Michelsen, ninth at Amsterdam and rounding into form nicely. Germany eventually selected de Bruyn as its sole marathon entrant. As part of a rather unusual training regimen, he regularly dashed up and down the 26 floors of the hotel in performing building repairs.

At the Maryland trial race, Michelsen again participated, not knowing whether the selectors would consider his fourth place at Boston acceptable. He lost by five minutes and 45 seconds, this time to Hans Oldag (2:38:00), an up-and-coming new star from Buffalo. Knowing that Oldag would certainly be selected, Michelsen felt obliged to attempt the third trial race in Los Angeles, again hoping for a victory. He and de Bruyn journeyed to California together by train, stopping in Chicago to test their fitness with an attempt at the world and United States 15 miles track records. When they arrived, they learned that they now would also be facing Argentina's young star, Juan Zabala.

Having impressed the world the preceding fall with a victory at the annual international marathon in Košice, Czechoslovakia, Zabala was now living in the United States to acclimatize to time zones and further his training. Zabala quickly took the lead in this Chicago race, as was his usual style, and in the closing stages it became evident that indeed the world record would fall. However, Zabala either misjudged his pace or became complacent in listening to encouragement along the way. He missed breaking Fred Appleby's 1902 mark of 1:20:04.4, set in London, by only 33 seconds. But he did set a new American all-comers record, beating Charles Pores' 1:23:24.4 set at New York in 1918. Michelsen was 6:12.4 behind Zabala—both frustrated and disappointed. He knew he simply had to win in Los Angeles to be selected.

The *Los Angeles Times* Marathon started at noon in front of its downtown headquarters building. It was a large loop around the city, and contrary to previous reports (Martin & Gynn 1979; Wallechinsky 1996), did not include any of the Olympic marathon course. The race finished in front of City Hall. It was a hot day, with only three refreshment stops along the entire route. Only 11 runners finished. Again, Zabala took the lead, passing the first mile in 4:45, 5 miles in 24:30, and 10 miles in 51:30! At one point, Zabala was nine minutes ahead of the pack.

Unfortunately, Zabala paid for this excessive enthusiasm. He faltered badly as he encountered some hills on Beverly Boulevard. He also experienced some painful foot problems, and at 19 miles (30.5 kilometers) his coach told him to quit the race. Neither he nor his shoes were accustomed to the pounding on macadam, with unpaved surfaces being the rule in Argentina. Showing fitness and maturity, Michelsen ran within himself and took plenty of fluids at the drink stations. With Zabala now not a factor, it became clear that Michelsen was the best of the field, and he won the race with 2:44:11. He was both overjoyed and apprehensive, because he now needed to recover from his three marathons in three months in order to be competitive for the big day. Zabala needed to get both his feet and his mind recovered, as there is little worse than entering a supreme test of fitness with either an injury or a fear of failure, or both.

A Fast Marathon Course Tours the City

Race organizers devised a roughly square marathon route, starting and finishing within the stadium, as shown in figure 10.1. In the Official Report of the Olympic Games (Anonymous 1932a) is the statement that "Since the Marathon was required, by edict of the International Athletic Federation (sic), to start and finish in the Olympic stadium, it remained only to pick out the most suitable course from the standpoint of traffic control, to prepare for this historic event." This appears to be erroneous, as was indicated in chapter 8. The IAAF Congress minutes of 1921 only stipulated the course distance, with local organizers arranging the route.

On the marathon course at Los Angeles, runners initially proceeded south using established Los Angeles city streets and then ran westward into a relatively rural region now occupied by the cities of Gardena and Hawthorne. Turning back north, they continued through the rural Los Angeles area into Inglewood, passing what is presently an entirely urbanized region, including the Los Angeles International Airport. Reentering the city of Los Angeles, runners then completed their loop, retracing the final 3 miles (4.8 kilometers) to the Olympic stadium.

Even in these earlier days, the per capita density of automobiles in Los Angeles surpassed that of any community in the world. This caused a policing problem beyond the initial comprehension of event organizers, which caused some worry. This concern paid off, however, because both spectator crowds and traffic rerouting requirements were managed without incident.

The road surface was primarily concrete, with some smooth unpaved dirt stretches in the early portions of the second half. The stadium sits at an altitude of 164 feet (50 meters) above sea level, but athletes had to climb 20 feet (6.1 meters) in leaving the stadium to reach the adjacent street level. There were eight descents and eight ascents, all gradual, and relatively minor. The high point of the course was 200 feet (61 meters) above sea level, reached at two points: on Vermont Avenue at 114th Street (9.5 miles or 15.3 kilometers), and at the intersection of West Boulevard and Slauson Avenue (21.8 miles or 35.1 kilometers). The lowest point was at 50 feet (15 meters) above sea level at 11 miles (17.7 kilometers). Thus, only two sections of the course posed even a

Course Details

The 1932 Los Angeles Olympic Marathon

Start—Stadium track finish line

Two and three-quarters circuits around the track, counterclockwise, to the marathon (southwest) tunnel

Exit the stadium onto Menlo Avenue

Left on Menlo Avenue to Santa Barbara Boulevard (now M. L. King Jr. Boulevard)

Right onto Santa Barbara Boulevard to Normandie Avenue

Left onto Normandie Avenue to Florence Avenue

Right onto Florence Avenue to Western Avenue

Left onto Western Avenue to Manchester Avenue

Left onto Manchester Avenue to Vermont Street

Right onto Vermont Street to Ballona Avenue (now El Segundo Boulevard)

Right onto Ballona Avenue to Inglewood-Redondo Road (now Aviation Boulevard)

Right onto Inglewood-Redondo Road to Arbor Vitae Street

Right onto Arbor Vitae Street to Prairie Avenue

Left onto Prairie Avenue to Florence Avenue

Half right onto Florence Avenue to Redondo Boulevard overpass over Atchison, Topeka, and Santa Fe Railway

Half left onto Redondo Boulevard overpass, then right, continuing on Redondo Boulevard to West Boulevard

Left onto West Boulevard to Slauson Avenue

Right onto Slauson Avenue to Normandie Avenue

Left onto Normandie Avenue to Santa Barbara Boulevard

Right onto Santa Barbara Boulevard to Menlo Avenue

Left onto Menlo Avenue to stadium tunnel entrance

Right through tunnel onto stadium track

Three-quarters circuit around the track to finish line

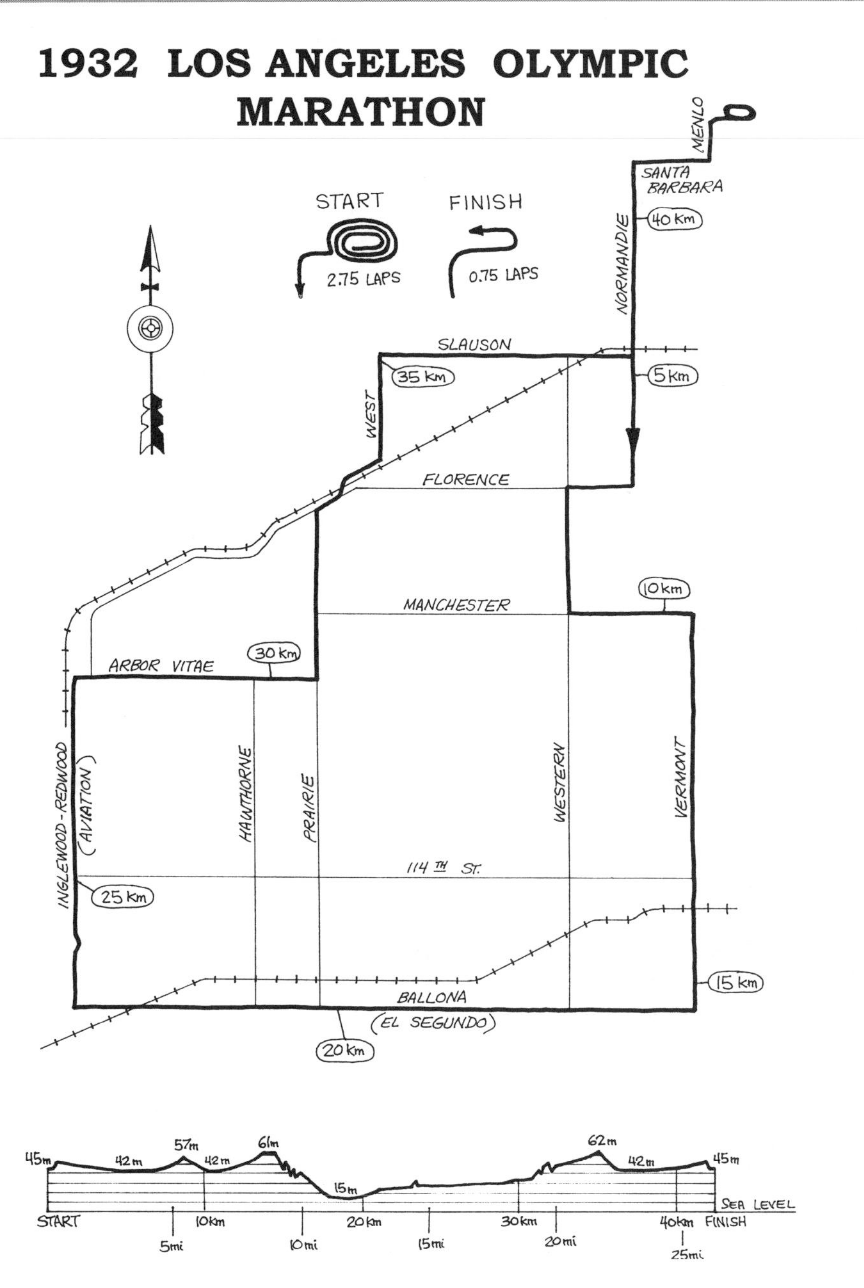

Figure 10.1 Sketch of the Los Angeles Olympic marathon course. Prepared by Bob Letson.

modest challenge in terms of terrain: a descent of 150 feet (46 meters) between 9 miles (14.5 kilometers) and 11 miles (17.7 kilometers), and a rise of 100 feet (30 meters) between 18.5 miles (29.8 kilometers) and 21.8 miles (35.1 kilometers). The course details box provides street details of the route.

Virtually the entire Olympic marathon route is negotiable by car today. Only a four-block section of what is now Aviation Boulevard just before the 17-miles mark has been displaced one block as it intersects with Arbor Vitae Street. The Los Angeles International Airport did not exist during the 1932 Olympic Games, so the region from 14.5 through 17 miles has changed entirely in appearance.

At the seven control stations, the sequence of athletes was recorded, along with a few intermediate times, which permitted an assessment of how the event progressed. From reports published in the *Los Angeles Times* (Dyer 1932), it is also known that tea and milk were available, and presumably water, although additional details are lacking.

With No Race Favorite, a Surprise Winner Is Guaranteed

At 1525 (3:25 p.m.) on Sunday, August 7, the marathoners were brought onto the Coliseum track and given their final opportunity to loosen up and jog before setting forth. They were arranged in two rows across the track, and at 1538 (3:38 p.m.) starter Franz Miller fired the gun. An estimated 80,000 spectators were on hand for this final day of track and field, with plenty of excitement occurring in other events while the marathoners were touring the city. Approaching the start of the marathon, for example, the outstanding woman high jumper Mildred "Babe" Didrikson was in the tie-breaking part of her well-known competition against Jean Shiley, and about to be disqualified because of her controversial "diving" style of approaching the bar. Periodic radio communication from the five control stations provided updates to the spectators regarding progress of the marathon competition while these track events were proceeding.

The starting field of 29 from 15 geopolitical entities and four continents was the smallest since the 17 known starters at both Athens in 1896 and Paris in 1900. Five full teams of 3 athletes were entered. They were from Argentina, Finland, Japan, Canada, and the United States. Eight European nations contributed 14 athletes, and Japan was the sole Asian representative. No representation came from Africa. South America was represented by Brazil and Colombia in addition to Argentina, and Mexico was also a North American participant. The small showing was due in part to the world economic crisis, but also to the difficulty of traveling to Los Angeles. But the world's marathon stars, including Nurmi (who could not compete), were all there.

Argentina's Juan Zabala immediately took the lead and was the first out of the stadium. Immediately behind him were Italy's Michele Fanelli, Mexico's Margarito Pomposo, Germany's Paul De Bruyn, and Canada's Cliff Bricker. The throngs of cheering spectators continued outside the stadium and all along the entire course in a mammoth outpouring of interest in watching this competition unfold. By the second control station (4.5 miles or 7.2 kilometers) runners had warmed up and were into the kind of "cruise mode" that permits them to focus on efficient running for as long as possible. Zabala remained in the lead (~25:30), followed by Pomposo 15 yards back. Next was a group consisting of Bricker; another Argentine (Jose Ribas); Whitey Michelsen; the Japanese trio of Seiichiro Tsuda, Taika Gon, and Onbai Kin; and the Dane Anders Andersen.

At approximately 9 miles, Pomposo took the lead from Zabala, who appeared to be struggling. But this was only temporary. By the third control station (9.5 miles or 15.3 kilometers), Zabala had regained the lead (57:00) and was 30 seconds in front. Pomposo was dropping back, leaving Bricker in second, and now Gon in third (58:00), followed by Ribas, and then Michelsen in fifth.

The fourth control station was just past the halfway point, at 14.5 miles (23.3 kilometers). Runners here were as far away from the stadium as the course would take them, about to turn northward from Ballona Avenue onto Inglewood-Redondo Road. Zabala was still in the lead (1:20:00), but now in second place was Finland's Lauri Virtanen (1:21:00), seemingly unfazed by his 15,000 meters of track competition in the preceding days. In third place was another Finn, Armas Toivonen (1:21:30), followed 30 seconds later by Tsuda. Bricker was in fifth, and Michelsen still held onto sixth. Hans Oldag had moved into seventh. Shortly thereafter, the duo of Toivonen and Tsuda passed by.

Virtanen surged forward at 16 miles (25.7 kilometers), passing Zabala. At control station five (19.5 miles or 31.4 kilometers), shortly after the start of the 100 feet (30 meters) climb over 3.3 miles (5.3 kilometers), Virtanen was still in the lead (1:50:00) and stopped briefly to drink a glass of milk. At this point, it was Toivonen in third, followed by Duncan McLeod Wright in fourth, and then Tsuda, with Sam Ferris in sixth. It had been Wright's prerace strategy to take the lead at around 20 miles (32.2 kilometers) and hold on from there. Indeed, he was out in front, timed in 2:06:00 at control station six (22 miles or 35.4 kilometers). Zabala, Toivonen, and Tsuda were each one minute behind, with Ferris now in fifth. Virtanen's surging caused him problems and he started to slow, eventually retiring at 23 miles (37 kilometers).

Wright could no longer maintain the lead pace and had slowed, putting Zabala back in front, but both were feeling miserable. As runners reached control station seven (24 miles or 38.6 kilometers) and now started retracing their steps to the stadium, the final drama unfolded. The sequence of the top five athletes was Zabala, Wright, Toivonen, Ferris, and Tsuda, with only three minutes separating first from fifth. Ferris was still fresh enough to quicken his pace, steadily gaining on Toivonen. Both passed Wright.

With a late afternoon sun casting long shadows and Pacific breezes cooling the air, 75,000 spectators were still watching and waiting when the sounds of trumpeters from atop the stadium heralded the arriving champion. Clothed in his white singlet and pale blue running trunks edged in white, and still wearing his white handkerchief over his head to prevent sunburn, the dark-skinned

Zabala entered the stadium. Zabala was near utter exhaustion as he completed the final three quarters of a lap. As he crossed the finish line, three other athletes were on the track. Roughly 100 yards (90 meters) behind Zabala was Ferris, then 90 yards (80 meters) farther back was Toivonen, and 150 additional yards (140 meters) back was Wright. The time difference between Zabala and Ferris was 19 seconds, between Ferris and Toivonen 17 seconds, and between Toivonen and Wright 29 seconds. No Olympic marathon finish up to that time had been more intensely contested.

Ferris, finishing second (figure 10.2), had started his final surge too late, running out of distance before he could catch Zabala. Although five nations had a full team complement of three athletes, only Japan and Canada had three who finished. Japan's team performed magnificently, easily winning the informal team title with finishers in fifth (Seiichiro Tsuda—sixth at Amsterdam), sixth (Onbai Kin), and ninth (Taika Gon). British runners placed second and fourth; if Britain had sent one more good runner, it may have surpassed Japan as a team. The first American was Whitey Michelsen in seventh—in his fourth marathon in three and one-half months. The race summary is given in table 10.1.

Figure 10.2 Britain's Sam Ferris takes the silver medal with his fine 2:31:55, 19 seconds behind Zabala. Courtesy IOC/Olympic Museum Collections.

TABLE 10.1

1932 Los Angeles Olympic Marathon at a Glance

Date:	07 August	**Weather:**	22.2°C (72°F) at start; clear skies
Start time:	1538	**Starters:**	29
Course:	Square loop	**Finishers:**	20
Course distance:	42.195 km	**GPEs:**	15

TOP RESULTS:

Place	*Athlete*	*GPE*	*Date of birth*	*Time*
1	Juan Zabala	ARG	21 Sept. 1911	2:31:36
2	Samuel Ferris	GBR	29 Aug. 1900	2:31:55
3	Armas Toivonen	FIN	20 Jan. 1899	2:32:12
4	Duncan McLeod Wright	GBR	22 Sept. 1896	2:32:41
5	Seiichiro Tsuda	JPN	26 July 1906	2:35:42
6	Onbai Kin (Kim Eun-bai)	JPN	21 Aug. 1913	2:37:28
7	Albert Michelsen	USA	16 Dec. 1893	2:39:38
8	Oskar Heks	TCH	10 Apr. 1908	2:41:35
9	Taika Gon (Kwon Tae-ha)	JPN	02 June 1906	2:42:52
10	Anders Andersen	DEN	01 Feb. 1907	2:44:38

New geopolitical entities represented: Argentina [ARG], Brazil [BRA], Colombia [COL]

Team score (unofficial):	1. JPN	20 points	(5-6-9)
	2. CAN	44 points	(12-14-18)

Zabala was totally consumed by his efforts (figure 10.3) and had to be supported by one of his countrymen as another helped him put on his bright red sweats to keep warm in the late afternoon shade and cool breeze. He recovered enough to remain at midfield for another hour, holding and waving his blue Argentine flag in a state of confused euphoria that only a gold medalist could appreciate. As the renowned sportswriter Damon Runyon penned so poignantly on the front page of the *Los Angeles Examiner* the next day (Runyon 1932): "In spirit, in heart, and in endurance, Juan C. Zabala, a slim young son of Argentina, was the modern reincarnation of Pheidippides of old." Indeed, he was slim (120 pounds or 54.5 kilograms) and young—at 20 years, 9 months, he remains the youngest Olympic marathon champion in this first century of competition. Along with 16 world records set in this outstanding track and field competition, his 2:31:36 was the 25th Olympic record.

Notes on the Medalists

Juan Carlos Zabala was born in Buenos Aires and orphaned at an early age. At 13 years, while attending a school for such children, he was befriended by

Figure 10.3 Just following his race, an exhausted gold medalist Juan Zabala is assisted in putting on his sweats. Courtesy IOC/Olympic Museum Collections.

Alexander Stirling, the school's physical training instructor. Stirling realized early on that Zabala was a potential running prodigy, and the two developed an abiding friendship. In 1931, at the age of 20, Zabala won the South American 10,000 meters track championship (31:19.0), and his coach decided to bring Zabala to Europe for world-class competition. Zabala was welcomed, as his presence added even more to the international flavor of Europe's athletic environment.

His flair for the longer distances became evident on October 10, 1931, when he set a world 30 kilometers best track time of 1:42:30.4 at Vienna. Only 18 days later, Zabala decided to capitalize on his fitness and attempt his first marathon at Košice, Czechoslovakia. Now in its eighth year, this event had already developed a reputation for attracting excellent competition. The race continues presently and celebrated its 75th anniversary in 1999. Hungary's Jozsef Galambos had won the previous two editions and was there again to defend. What occurred took the entire running world by surprise. Zabala surged into the lead when the starting gun fired, delivering course-record splits throughout. His finish time of 2:33:19 had only been beaten on an out-and-back course by Kolehmainen, Lossman, and El Ouafi. Galambos was nearly 15 minutes behind, and Zabala's course record stood at Košice for 19 years.

Thus, Zabala was poised for greatness at the Los Angeles Games, provided he could recover from his pre-Olympic practice run, where he stopped at 19 miles (30.5 kilometers) due to shoe problems. He did recover, and his gold medal performance was magnificent. But here his career essentially ended. He attempted two more marathons, one on the track 20 days after the Olympics, which he did not finish. He disappeared from the running scene until 1936, when he regained attention by setting a world best 20 kilometers track performance early in the year. This gave him a spot on the Argentine team bound for Berlin. He subsequently broke off his previously successful relationship with Alexander Stirling, but could not muster the momentum to successfully defend his Olympic title and dropped out at Berlin. Thus, his marathon career was very erratic (table 10.2).

Samuel Ferris was born in Dromore, Northern Ireland, and served in the Royal Air Force from 1918 to 1950. In his early days as an airman he served in India, and here his interest in distance running blossomed as a means of keeping fit. On return to England, he joined the Shettleston Harriers as a club-mate of Duncan McLeod Wright. He ran his first marathon on May 31, 1924—the Polytechnic Harriers race—and placed second. In 1930 he placed second (to Wright) in the British Empire Games. Prior to his Olympic Games career-best

TABLE 10.2

Career Marathon Record of Juan Zabala

Date	*Venue*	*Place*	*Time*	*Comments*
28 Oct. 1931	Košice	1st	2:33:19	
25 June 1932	Los Angeles	DNF		
07 Aug. 1932	Los Angeles	1st	2:31:36	Olympic Games
27 Aug. 1932	Boston	DNF		track
09 Aug. 1936	Berlin	DNF		Olympic Games

performance, his best time had been a British record 2:33:00 in the 1928 Liverpool Marathon. Ferris was one of those highly gifted athletes who knew how to prepare for top-level competition and arrive in perfect form physically and mentally on the day—and he did it at three Olympic Games (see Olympic Marathon Miscellany 10.1).

Ferris recalled much later, when in his 70s, that had the marathon distance in Los Angeles been another kilometer longer, he might have won the gold medal, for he was gaining rapidly on Zabala in the closing stages. On a training run over the marathon course, he had seen a large milk advertisement about a mile from the finish. He intended to use that sign as a marker for starting his final push if needed, but a viewing stand erected just before the race covered it up, and he did not see it. Ferris ran one more marathon after Los Angeles and scored a record eighth win at the "Poly" in 1933. In all, he ran 21 marathons, winning 12—indeed amazing when one realizes that his weekly training volume rarely exceeded 40 miles per week (Webster 1932).

Armas Toivonen, born in Halikko, Finland, also ran a personal best in winning the bronze medal. Twelve years older than Zabala, but only a year older than Ferris, Toivonen was a real late bloomer. Even at 23 years of age, his personal best for 10,000 meters was only 39 minutes. Five years later, he captured the Finnish 25 kilometers track championship title in 1927, and he repeated in 1930. He started in seven marathon races, dropping out of the first two, which were the Olympic trial marathon races in 1928. In 1931, he finally finished one, at Viipuri, and it was an excellent 2:35:55.8. He also won the 1932 Olympic trial race, and at Los Angeles he joined Zabala and Ferris in running faster than countryman Kolehmainen's Antwerp Olympic record. Unlike Zabala, Toivonen had post-Olympic success, winning the European championships in 1934 at Turin over a long course. However, he failed to finish the 1936 Finnish Olympic trial race over 36.5 kilometers.

Olympic Marathon Miscellany 10.1

Olympic Marathon Career Excellence

Most Olympians consider it a rare achievement just to qualify for one team. To compete at two or more Olympics, especially in an event so demanding as the marathon, is indeed unusual. To finish all Olympic marathons entered is even more amazing, and to place among the top ten in each race is historic in significance. Sam Ferris did just that. Only three others have managed similar showings since.

The grand master of the men Olympians is Belgium's Karel Lismont. He finished 2nd at Munich, 3rd at Montréal, 9th at Moscow, and 24th at Los Angeles. Lismont's closest rival is Australia's Rob De Castella (10th at Moscow, 5th at Los Angeles, 8th at Seoul, and 26th at Barcelona). The other two quadruple marathon Olympians are Djibouti's Ahmed Salah Hussein and Nepal's Baikuntha Manandhar.

Among those who have started three Olympic marathons, Sam Ferris is tied with Japan's Kenji Kimihara in overall quality. Ferris finished fifth at Paris, eighth at Amsterdam, and second at Los Angeles. Kimihara placed eighth at Tokyo, second at Mexico City, and fifth at Munich. Of the 27 who have started three Olympic marathons, only 16 finished all three.

Looking Ahead: Brief Highlights 1933-1935

1933: Les Pawson won the Boston Marathon in a record 2:31:01.6 on April 19. He would win twice more.

1934: Harold Webster [CAN] won the second British Empire Games marathon (London, August 7) in 2:40:36, with defending champion Duncan Wright a distant third. Armas Toivonen, Los Angeles bronze medalist, became the first European champion (at Turin, September 9) in 2:52:29 over a long (42.75 kilometers) course. Dave Komonen [CAN] won both the USA/AAU and Canadian titles for the second consecutive year, and he also won at Boston (2:32:53.8).

1935: This exciting pre-Olympic year was highlighted by world records from Japanese stars Fusashige Suzuki (2:27:49 at Tokyo, March 31), Yasuo Ikenaka (2:26:42 at Tokyo, April 3), and Korean-born Kitei Son (Sohn Kee-chung) (2:26:42 at the national championship race in Tokyo on December 3).

References

Anonymous. 1932a. *The Games of the Xth Olympiad, Los Angeles, 1932*. Los Angeles: Xth Olympiad Committee of the Games of Los Angeles.

Anonymous. 1932b. *The New York Times*. July 29.

Barney, R.K. 1998. The great transformation: Olympic victory ceremonies and the victory platform. *Olympika* 7: 89-112.

Dyer, B. 1932. *Los Angeles Times*. August 8.

Martin, D.E., and R.W.H. Gynn, 1979. *The marathon footrace*. Springfield, IL: Charles C Thomas.

Rubien, F.W. 1932. *Report of the American Olympic Committee: Games of the Xth Olympiad, Los Angeles, California*. New York: American Olympic Committee.

Runyon, D. 1932. *Los Angeles Examiner*. August 8.

Wallechinsky, D. 1996. *The complete book of the Summer Olympics*. 1996 edition. New York: Little, Brown & Company.

Webster, F.A.M. 1932. *The Official Report of the Xth Olympiad Los Angeles 1932*. London: British Olympic Association.

CHAPTER II

1936—BERLIN

Korea's Son Triumphs in Japanese Colors

Olympic Preparations Strive for Perfection

The IOC met in Barcelona in April 1931 to determine the site of the Games for the 11th Olympiad in 1936. Berlin and Barcelona were the only bidding cities. Due to small attendance at the meeting, a postal vote was held to ensure greater participation, and on May 13, 1931, it was officially announced that Berlin had won by a vote of 43 to 16. One year later, the Los Angeles Games were a great success, and the Germans developed an enthusiasm for trying to make theirs even more superb. Estimates approaching $30 million indicate the magnitude of investment required to prepare the venues and the German team (Constable 1996).

Knowing no more, one might consider this as exemplifying a delightful German recovery following its defeat in World War I. Unforeseen political events occurred rapidly in the few years prior to the Olympic Games, however. The first meeting of the Berlin Olympic Organizing Committee was held on January

24, 1933, but on January 30 the Reich Chancellorship was awarded to Adolf Hitler. This resulted in the formation of a new government, which eventually embraced fully the Olympic sports pageant as a tool of great propaganda value. Movements to boycott the Olympic Games because of German persecution of Jews came to a head in 1934-35, when Hitler publicly promised that everyone would be welcome.

The unprecedented investment of money and energy provided an unsurpassed physical environment for athlete housing and competition. On the western edge of the city, a huge 325 acres (132 hectares) tract of land (the Reichssportfeld) served as the center of Olympic activities. It included a gymnasium, a polo field, basketball courts, swimming pools (one seating 18,000 spectators!), a theater, and four stadia. The 328 female Olympians also lived on the premises.

The centerpiece of this area was the new Olympic stadium, designed by architect Werner March. Built in only two years using mostly natural stone and up to 2,600 workers per day, it showcased track and field as well as the ceremonies, with a spectator capacity of 76,005 (Anonymous 1985). The old stadium was demolished, except for part of the old marathon tunnel. Instead of cinders or peat, this time the seven-lanes, 400 meters track had an eight-centimeters-thick surface of 80 percent coarse slag and 20 percent clay (Anonymous 1936b)—perfect for the climate. Underneath this was a packed red-earth-and-clay combination that helped make the surface extremely fast. Adjoining the stadium to the west was the immense Maifeld (May Field). This was a grassy area used for everything from polo games to gymnastics exhibitions to dressage riding, and it was also part of the marathon course. The Olympic stadium would have been a complete oval except for a 25 meters (82 feet) wide gap in its upper ring to permit a view of this field with its 75 meters (247 feet) high bell tower at its western end. The tower's bell, weighing 9,635 kilograms (21,197 pounds) first rang on New Year's Day 1936. The marathoners ran under this tower as they exited the sports venue and entered the city streets.

The Olympic Village, constructed on the former Döberitz parade ground, could not quite match the Pacific shoreline beauty of suburban Los Angeles, but the quality of construction was superior. The brick-and-stucco cottages were each named after a German city, and the 139 acres (56 hectares) complex provided ample space for the record 49 geopolitical entities and 3,738 male athletes using it. After the Olympic Games it became a military officers' club. Many traditional delights from a variety of cultures were included as village amenities: saunas for the Finns, steam baths for the Japanese, several separate kitchens each specializing in different ethnic cuisines, and even wine at the dinner table for the French athletes. A fleet of 200 buses transported athletes to and from the various venues.

The marvels of modern technology were implemented as never before, to ensure that these Olympic Games were made visible to the public. The first live radio broadcast from an Olympic Games occurred here. And the Games were televised, although this was restricted to closed circuit broadcasts in special halls throughout Germany.

The general secretary of the Organizing Committee, Carl Diem, was well known in world sport circles, and he was blessed with a natural talent for drama as well as organization. It was his idea to have a flaming torch relay that for the first time would link in a real way ancient Olympia with the host city during the Olympic Games. During the 1928 and 1932 Games, a cauldron at the Olympic stadium had "Olympic flames" burning, but such a personal connection between Olympia and the Games site had not been considered. And so, before the Temple of Hera at ancient Olympia on July 20, a group of Greek women dressed as ancient priestesses initiated a very private and formal ceremony that ever since has started the countdown to each Olympic Games.

The priestesses focused the sun's rays onto some grasses and twigs that were placed into a highly polished steel parabolic mirror created by the German company Zeiss Optik. The resulting fire ignited a torch that was carried out of the sacred area into public view. The high priestess then transferred the flame to a torch held by the first relay runner, Konstantin Koudylis, and the relay began. Running one kilometer, he passed the torch to the next runner. This exchange continued in a nearly unbroken sequence for a distance of 3,075 kilometers. First from Olympia to Athens, and eventually through Delphi, Thessaloniki, Sofia, Belgrade, Budapest, Vienna, Prague, and Dresden, the torch moved with precision, reaching the Olympic stadium at 1720 (5:20 p.m.) on August 1, 1936.

German middle-distance star Fritz Schilgren was selected as the final torchbearer to light the Olympic flame, reportedly because of his unusually smooth running style. This tradition continues today as the culminating emotional focal point of the Olympic Games Opening Ceremony. Whereas the cauldron in Los Angeles used natural gas from local wells, in Berlin a new gas called propane was used for the first time, giving a beautiful color with no noticeable odor or smoke.

As if any more drama was needed, the ultimate was achieved by the presence of Spiridon Louis himself, to celebrate the 40th anniversary of his famous run to victory. During the traditional parade of athletes, with the Greek delegation leading off, it was the 63-years-old Louis who carried his nation's flag. But the stadium masses did not know he was there! After Schilgren kindled the flame in the Olympic cauldron, the presence of Louis was announced. After being escorted to Hitler's viewing box, Louis gave Hitler an olive branch from the Sacred Grove of Zeus at Olympia. It was a striking contrast—Hitler in his military uniform with long-legged leather boots, Louis in his simple native Greek costume. Unfortunately, the 73-years-old Baron de Coubertin, in failing health, could not join IOC president Henri Baillet-Latour to enjoy the moment.

The Top Marathon Nations Prepare Their Teams

Several nations brought complete three-man marathon teams, notably Great Britain, South Africa, Finland, Japan, and the United States. There were, of course, individual athletes from other nations who also figured prominently. One of these was the 1932 Olympic champion from Argentina, Juan Zabala, but he no longer had a close working relationship with his coach, Alexander Stirling, who had cared very well for his needs in earlier years. However, Zabala's experience as well as his talent put him high on the list of athletes likely to race well. He had arranged his training and racing for several months in Germany to ensure optimal time zone adaptation and some competitive opportunities. He had improved the South American track 10,000 meters record and, as well, had delivered a world 20 kilometers track best of 64:00.2.

South Africa and Great Britain

On the weekend before the Boston Marathon, in the South African championship race at Port Elizabeth on April 11, 25-years-old Johannes Coleman and 21-years-old Henry "Jack" Gibson waged a terrific battle. It became one of the fastest marathon races of the entire Olympic year. It was a cool 0800 (8 a.m.) start for the small group of 13 runners, and these 2 were the class of the field. Gibson had won the 1935 South African Marathon championship at Pretoria, and Coleman had run a South African record 2:38:32 at Durban. From the 20 miles mark onward, the two athletes raced nearly together and ended up in a final 300 yards sprint on the finishing track. Coleman won by 20 yards with an African continental best time of 2:31:57.4. Gibson was also under the previous African record with 2:32:09. Both athletes were considered top candidates for a good performance at Berlin.

In Britain, the "Poly" and the AAA championship served jointly as selection races (Anonymous 1937). The "Poly" was contested on June 11 on a wet course, due to an overnight rain. Bert Norris was the defending champion and confidently assumed the lead at 8½ miles. By 10 miles (59:38), however, four athletes had caught up with him, including Ernie Harper and South African Tommy Lalande (who wanted to join Coleman and Gibson at Berlin). At around 19 miles, Norris and Lalande picked up the pace, with Duncan McLeod Wright in third; Harper had fallen behind. Shortly after 20 miles, Norris moved away from Lalande and went on to win in 2:35:20, with Lalande only 58 seconds behind. It was fitting that these two were selected to their respective Olympic teams. Wright overtook Harper and placed third, but neither was selected, so they had to race again.

The AAA championship was just short of one month later, on July 11. Norris was already selected, so he did not compete. Harper was determined to make the team, but it was not until the 20 miles point that he managed to catch Donald McNab Robertson, who wanted a team berth as well. The two runners matched strides for several miles. They came onto the White City Stadium track together, and the enthusiastic crowd cheered them onward. Robertson lengthened his stride and got slightly ahead of Harper, but then Harper found another gear, and it was a sprint to the finish. Robertson barely beat Harper, 2:35:02.4 to 2:35:03.6, and both were placed on the Great Britain team. They now moved up to fourth and fifth on the British all-time list, behind Harry Payne, Sam Ferris, and Duncan Wright.

United States

Two races selected the United States team—the Boston Marathon on April 20 and the AAU championship six weeks later at Washington (Hymans 1996). The Boston race was incredibly competitive. A 22-years-old Narragansett Indian named Ellison Brown—known as "Tarzan" because he enjoyed swinging from tree branches at home—started the race with a quick 55 minutes for the first 11 miles. It was his seventh marathon and his fourth Boston run, so he should have known better. At the start of the net uphill stretch through suburban Newton, John Adelbert Kelley finally caught Brown and overtook him. (John A. Kelley eventually became known as "Johnny the Elder" to distinguish him from the unrelated John Joseph Kelley, who also was to demonstrate his superb marathon racing skills during the 1950s.) Brown was not to be beaten, and the two raced side by side up the hills. It nearly destroyed them both. At one point, Kelley stopped to walk, as did Brown. Brown eventually won the race (2:33:40.8), but William "Billy" McMahon, Mel Porter, and Leo Girard passed Kelley. He thus finished fifth.

Kelley, Porter, and McMahon raced again in Washington on May 30, but the short time period for recovery gave them all worry due to a quality field of other athletes also seeking team positions. McMahon again beat Kelley, 2:38:14.2 to 2:40:07, and both were selected to the team. Mel Porter was third, and some questioned whether he ought to have been selected over Kelley due to his consistent performance among the top three in almost every marathon he ran. In the end, Kelley proved to a capable competitor as he was the only United States marathoner to finish at Berlin (Anonymous 1936a).

Japan

Because of hot, humid weather in Japan during the summer and early fall, Japan's marathon season logically extends from November through March. Cool, dry weather and generally flat courses in coastal cities provide a perfect environment for athletes to race well. Japan's athletes developed a keen interest in the marathon soon after its inception, perhaps because of their nation's ancient tradition of using distance-running messengers to provide communication. By the mid-1930s, Japan was the world's top-ranked country in both athlete numbers and quality of fast performances. As seen in table 11.1, 7 of the all-time top 10 fastest times belonged to Japan, and 6 had been achieved in 1935.

A special trial race was held on April 18 from Jingu Stadium to Rokugo Bridge and back. Four of the athletes listed in table 11.1 competed together. Kitei Son won (2:28:32) over Shinichi Nakamura and Fusashige Suzuki; Tamao Shiaku did not finish. Japan's final Olympic trial was held on May 21, 1936, over the same Tokyo course. Conditions were not ideal due to springtime warming, which kept times slow despite the highly competitive race. Only three athletes could make the team, but another half dozen also would have been worthy Olympians. The early leader in this final trial race was Chosun Ryu, but by the turnaround (1:18:24), Shiaku had replaced him. Kitei Son took the lead for a while on the return trip, but Nan stayed with him, and in fact ran away from

TABLE 11.1

Ten Fastest Marathon Performances as of Jan. 1, 1936

Time	*Athlete*	*GPE*	*Venue*	*Place*	*Date*
2:26:42	Kitei Son	JPN	Tokyo	1st	03 Nov. 1935
2:26:44	Yasuo Ikenaka	JPN	Tokyo	1st	03 Apr. 1935
2:27:49	Fusashige Suzuki	JPN	Tokyo	1st	31 Mar. 1935
2:29:01.8	Albert Michelsen	USA	Port Chester	1st	12 Oct. 1925
2:29:55	Shinichi Nakamura	JPN	Nishinomiya	1st	23 Nov. 1935
2:30:57.6	Harry Payne	GBR	London	1st	05 July 1929
2:31:01.6	Leslie Pawson	USA	Boston	1st	19 Apr. 1933
2:31:10	Kozo Kusunoki	JPN	Tokyo	1st	03 Nov. 1933
2:31:21	Tamao Shiaku	JPN	Tokyo	2nd	03 Nov. 1935
2:31:27	Chosun Ryu	JPN	Seoul	1st	18 Oct. 1935

Son, winning (2:36:03) by nearly two minutes (2:38:02). Suzuki held onto third place (2:39:41), defeating Shiaku by only 69 seconds. Yasuo Ikenaka, who had beaten Ryu late in March, was a dropout, along with Nakamura and other notables. As with the United States in 1924, Japan sent more than the number who could compete (four in this case), leaving the decision to the trainer as to which would be the better three. Suzuki was eventually the athlete who did not run.

Ryu, Son, and Nan were actually from Korea, but running for Japan. As a result of victory in the Russo-Japanese war of 1904-1905, Japan occupied the Korean peninsula, formally annexing it as a colony in 1910. Imposing the Japanese language upon the Korean people meant that Yoo Jang-chun became Chosun Ryu, Sohn Kee-chung became Kitei Son, and Nam Sung-yong became Shoryu Nan.

Using Forest and Auto Speedway, a Unique Olympic Course Emerges

Organizers decided to start and finish the Olympic marathon within the track and field stadium, optimizing the opportunities for spectator viewing. As seen in figure 11.1, the long axis of the oval stadium was oriented east-to-west, and the sprint straightaway extended along the south side. The sprint start line was also the marathon start line. The marathon tunnel began from behind the sprint starting area, on the southwest side, and continued underground for about 200 meters, becoming part of a service road leading out of the stadium.

The road portion of the course was similar to the Stockholm, Antwerp, and Paris marathons in that the outbound portion was exactly retraced on the return.

COURSE DETAILS

The 1936 Berlin Olympic Marathon

Start in stadium at sprint start line

One and three-quarters laps counterclockwise in stadium to marathon exit tunnel

Upon exit through the tunnel, two sharp right turns, and then a left turn to climb onto the grassy surface of the Maifeld

Run along the Maifeld adjacent to the Olympic stadium until abreast of the stadium opening, then left, continuing on the Maifeld toward the Olympic bell tower

Run through the passageway beneath the bell tower and onto Glockenturmstraße

Continue on Glockenturmstraße to Angenburg-Allee

Right on Angenburg-Allee to Havelchaussee

Left on Havelchaussee and continue until kilometer 13, at the entrance to the Avusrennstrecke

Left onto the Avus, continuing its entire length, eventually returning just after 30 kilometers

Right to exit the Avus and reenter Havelchaussee

Continue on Havelchaussee to Angenburg-Allee

Right onto Angenburg-Allee to Glockenturmstraße

Left on Glockenturmstraße to the Olympic bell tower

Run through the passageway beneath the bell tower onto the Maifeld

Continue on the Maifeld toward the stadium, then right, remaining on the grassy field along the stadium to the tunnel access road

Turn right, then left, then left again to reenter the marathon tunnel

Continue through the tunnel onto the stadium track

Turn right onto the track and run 150 meters along its sprint side, ending at the distance event finish line

The first and last 12 kilometers were on the shaded asphalt roadway called the Havelchaussee, which meandered through the well-forested Grunewald alongside Lake Havel (the Havelsee). The middle 17 kilometers were partially shaded, and they utilized a perfectly straight section of hard concrete road known as the Avusrennstrecke (Avus raceway). It was used for automobile racing. Note also that the course curved back on itself such that the turnaround point was actually less than 2 kilometers from the stadium! Returning by the same route to the Maifeld and then through the marathon tunnel, athletes ended their run at the finish line used for track events. The course details box provides the specifics of the route.

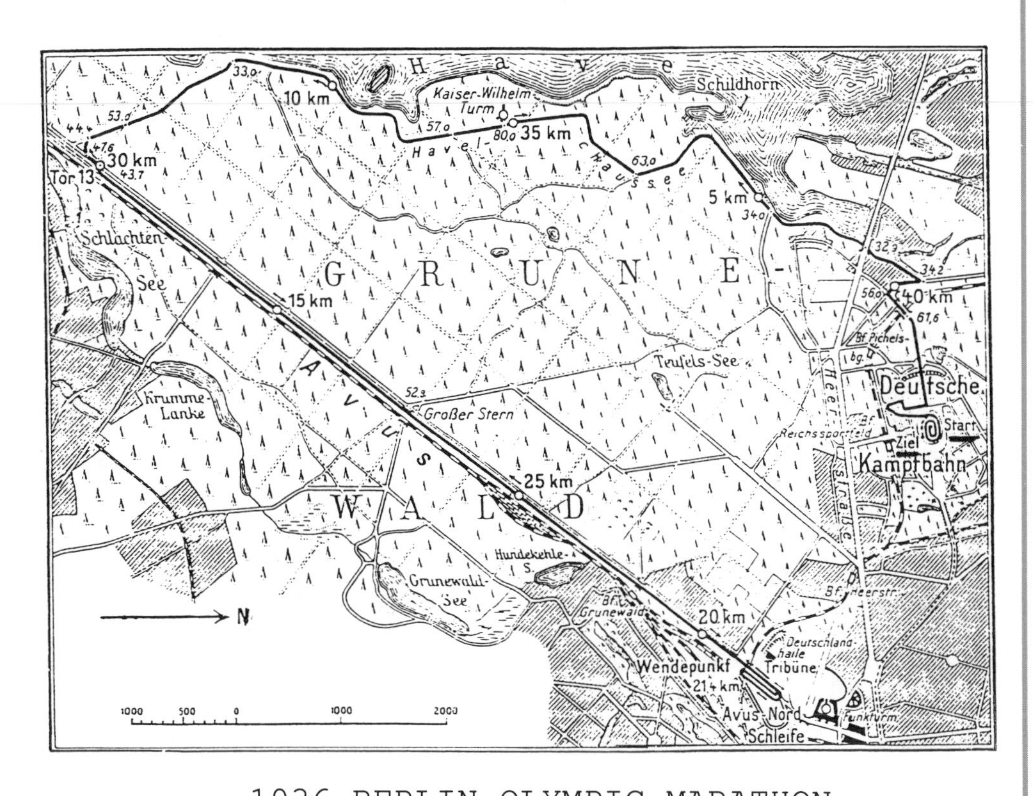

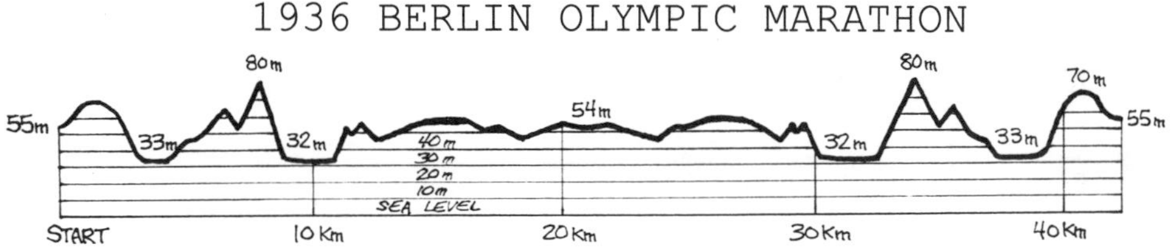

Figure 11.1 Sketch of the Berlin Olympic marathon course. Prepared by Bob Letson.

Berlin is only slightly above sea level and relatively flat. Thus, the course was only slightly rolling, varying between 31.6 meters (104 feet) and 80.0 meters (263 feet) above sea level. The stadium elevation was 55.6 meters (182 feet). There was only one notable hill—on the outbound route from 4.7 kilometers (2.9 miles) to 8.0 kilometers (5.0 miles) and on the return route from 33.2 kilometers (20.6 miles) to 34.2 kilometers (21.3 miles).

In keeping with the meticulous planning that characterized these Olympic Games, 15 checkpoints were established at roughly 3 kilometers intervals. At these points, fluid refreshments and medical services were provided, and intermediate split times were also recorded for participating athletes.

A Global Battle on a Warm Day Produces an Olympic Record

At Antwerp and Amsterdam the weather had been chilly, and occasionally rainy. However, Sunday, August 9 dawned sunny and dry, with race-time temperatures ranging from 22.3°C (72.1°F) at the 1500 (3:00 p.m.) start to 21°C (69.8°F) at the finish. It was the final day of athletics, but not the final day of the Olympic Games; Closing Ceremonies were on August 16. The stadium was jammed, and according to *The New York Times* for August 10, "fairly conservative estimates of the number of spectators who lined the route set the figures at more than 1,000,000."

The starting field of 56 athletes was predominantly European—36 athletes from 18 geopolitical entities. A scattering of entries came from the other four continents—Africa (3 South Africans), North America (3 each from Canada and the United States), Asia (3 Japanese, 1 each from India and China), and South America (3 Peruvians, 2 Argentines, and 1 from Chile). In particular, the Japanese team was strong. And, as mentioned earlier, there was the defending Los Angeles gold medalist, Argentina's Juan Zabala, who had placed sixth in the 10,000 meters event on August 2 one week earlier.

Covering his head with a white kerchief to prevent sunburn as he had done in 1932, Zabala led the field out of the stadium and onto the polo fields. At the 4 kilometers checkpoint, Zabala was 30 seconds ahead of Portugal's Manuel Dias. Lalande was in third, Tarzan Brown in fourth. However, by 6 kilometers Harper and Son had taken over third and fourth places and were in contact with Zabala (figure 11.2). From the 5th through 8th kilometers, Zabala pushed the pace up the only sizable hill on the course, near the Kaiser Wilhelm Tower. This hill had a rise of 46 meters (151 feet) over 3,300 meters (two miles), or 14 meters per kilometer (74 feet per mile). The downhill portion was shorter, and thus steeper. By the crest of the hill, Zabala was 43 seconds ahead of Dias. Now it was Brown's turn to surge forward, moving into third place by 10 kilometers, 40 seconds behind Dias and 85 seconds behind Zabala.

At 15 kilometers, Zabala (49:45) was still 100 seconds ahead of Dias, but Son and Harper were now only 30 seconds behind Dias and steadily coming closer. Brown was in fifth, followed by Sweden's Thore Enochsson. By 18 kilometers, Enochsson had replaced Brown in fifth, with Coleman now in sixth.

Shortly after 20 kilometers, both Dias and Zabala began to slow their pace. At the turnaround point near the northeast end of the Avus racecourse, Zabala (1:11:29) was 50 seconds in front of Son and Harper, both of whom had passed Dias. Just behind Dias was Enochsson, with Coleman and Gibson almost on his shoulder. Tarzan Brown looked strong, having apparently recovered from the effects of his earlier surge.

Zabala also recovered briefly, accelerating slightly to give him a 92 seconds lead at 25 kilometers (1:23:17) over Harper and Son. Brown surged again on this flat portion along the Avus raceway, edging into fourth place ahead of Coleman, Enochsson, Dias, and Gibson, each running alone. Son quickened his

Figure 11.2 **Ernie Harper (#265), left, running beside Kitei Son (#382), right, along the Avusrennstrecke.** Courtesy Asahi Shimbun.

pace at 28 kilometers, breaking clear of Harper by 10 meters in an attempt to catch Zabala. Coleman overtook Brown for fourth, with Gibson in sixth. Two new faces were now approaching: Finland's Väinö Muinonen and Erkki Tamila in seventh and eighth.

Just after 28 kilometers, approaching the north end of the Avus raceway, Zabala tripped and fell, and recovered just slowly enough that Son and Harper both passed him. Back into the Grunewald, having turned right off the raceway, and back onto the shaded Havelchaussee, Son passed 31 kilometers (1:46:20), 16 seconds up on Harper, with the valiant Zabala trying to regain his rhythm. Coleman was in fourth, closely pursued by the entire Finnish team of Tamila, Muinonen, and Mauno Tarkiainen. It was Tarkianinen's first full-distance marathon because the Finnish trial race at Ilmajoki—which he won—was only 36.5 kilometers.

Zabala officially quit the race at 32 kilometers, just before ascending the 46 meters (151 feet) hill along the Havelsee shoreline. Son was now racing strongly, establishing a lead of 25 seconds over Harper by 33 kilometers. At this point, it appeared that Son and Harper might capture the top two medals. The trio of Muinonen, Tamila, and Coleman was three minutes behind, running together; Gibson remained in sixth. But the bronze medal would not go to any of these athletes! The real threat at this point in the race turned out to be Shoryu Nan, who by 35 kilometers had systematically passed them all and moved into third. Son's time at 35 kilometers was 45 seconds faster than Harper and three minutes and 45 seconds faster than Nan. Muinonen was in fourth, just ahead of Tamila, with Coleman following. Britain's Donald McNab Robertson had been maintaining a very steady pace to conserve energy on this warm day, and it paid off as he now moved into seventh at 39 kilometers (Anonymous 1937).

Son passed 40 kilometers in 2:19:40, leading Harper by 87 seconds. Nan was another 90 seconds back. Encountering several turns along the small streets approaching the stadium, the sequence of medalists remained unaltered. In the final kilometer, very near the stadium, a private duel for eighth place ensued between Gibson and Tarkiainen. Gibson won it shortly before entering.

An estimated 100,000 people had jammed the stadium on this final afternoon of athletics not only to see the marathon, but an outstanding program of track and field finals as well. At 1725 (5:25 p.m.) the 4 × 400 meters relay event was contested, with bedlam reigning as spectators cheered a world record time of 39.8 seconds. It was their last chance to see America's Jesse Owens, who led off, passing to Ralph Metcalfe. Foy Draper and Frank Wyhoff added two more quick laps to give the team a victory by 14 meters (15 yards).

Now, amid the stadium uproar, came the sound of bugles. They announced the arrival at the west end of the stadium of Kitei Son, and the crowd cheered wildly once again. Emerging from the marathon tunnel, with but 150 meters to reach the standard track event finish line, Son looked almost like a sprinter as his bowed legs covered the final 100 meters in 13.3 seconds, for a time of 2:29:19.2. Harper was 600 meters behind, and so the two never were on the stadium track together. Harper and Nan were, however, but only briefly, finishing 19 seconds apart. Table 11.2 summarizes the relative positions of the top six finishers during the race, and table 11.3 provides a summary of the race.

Son's remarkable victory made him the first Olympian under two and one-half hours at the Games. This was Japan's first Olympic gold medal, and it was Son's third sub-2:30:00 marathon. Harper's magnificent personal best ranked him number two on Britain's all-time list, behind Harry Payne. Nan also achieved a personal best. At the postrace press conference, it became clear that Son understood some English, for he and Harper had a conversation during the race. As reported in *The New York Times* (Daley 1936), when asked to describe the race, Son replied through an interpreter: "Much credit for my victory must go to Harper of England. From the time we started he kept telling me not to worry about Zabala, but to let him run himself out."

Notes on the Medalists

Kitei Son (Kee Chung-sohn) was born in Sinuiju, a small, poverty-burdened farming and lumbering village along the Yalu River in what is now the Demo-

TABLE 11.2

Order of Top Placers Through Selected Control Points

	Son	*Harper*	*Nan*	*Tamila*	*Muinonen*	*Coleman*
10 km Havelchaussee	5	4	33	18	16	13
12 km Entry to Avus	5	4	28	14	15	10
15 km Avus raceway	3	4	25	14	13	8
18 km Avus raceway	4	3	16	12	11	6
Turnaround	2	3	15	12	11	6
25 km Avus raceway	3	2	13	10	9	5
28 km Avus raceway	2	3	11	8	7	4
31 km Havelchaussee	1	2	10	5	6	4
33 km Havelchaussee	1	2	7	4	3	5
35 km K. W. Tower	1	2	3	5	4	6
37 km Havelchaussee	1	2	3	4	5	6
40 km Angerburg-Allee	1	2	3	4	5	6
Finish	1	2	3	4	5	6

cratic People's Republic of North Korea, near the Chinese border. It was, and still is, one of the most primitive regions of Asia. The modernizing influence of Japanese rule had not reached these hinterlands, and the locals were scarcely aware of the Olympic Games. It was just those rugged hills in that wooded mountainous region that toughened Son into a most formidable competitor. He earned his gold medal at the young age of 22 years.

He achieved early success on the track over distances from 800 meters through 5,000 meters, and when he turned his attention to the marathon, he won his first three races. They were all in Seoul, over a probably short course, and the first two were national championships. In 1935, he ran seven marathons: four in Seoul, three in Tokyo, and his November world best performance put him high on the list of media favorites in Berlin. He remains the only athlete to have won an Olympic marathon as the reigning world record-holder. Hannes Kolehmainen's Antwerp gold *became* the world's fastest performance, and Johnny Hayes set a world best *at* the inaugural 42.195 km distance. After the Berlin Olympics, Son retired, having won 10 of his 13 marathons in a short but superb career, which table 11.4 summarizes.

Ernest "Ernie" Harper was 13 years older than Kitei Son, but when the two appeared together, the boyish youthfulness of Son was such a contrast to Harper's mature appearance that the age difference seemed much larger. This was Harper's second Olympics; he had placed 22nd at Amsterdam. He ran no marathons between 1928 and 1936, preferring to focus on the track. During this period he competed very well: he won the IAAF International Cross Country Championship in 1926, and was four times the British AAA champion over 10 miles. He set a new world 25 kilometers track best in 1929 at Berlin, and he won a silver

TABLE 11.3

1936 Berlin Olympic Marathon at a Glance

Date:	09 August	**Weather:**	24°C (75°F)
Start time:	1500	**Starters:**	56
Course:	Out-and-back	**Finishers:**	42
Course distance:	42.195 km	**GPEs:**	27

TOP RESULTS:

Place	*Athlete*	*GPE*	*Date of birth*	*Time*
1	Kitei Son (Kee Chung-sohn)	JPN	29 Aug. 1914	2:29:19.2
2	Ernest Harper	GBR	02 Aug. 1902	2:31:23.2
3	Shoryu Nan (Nam Sung-yong)	JPN	23 Nov. 1912	2:31:42.0
4	Erkki Tamila	FIN	05 May 1911	2:32:45.0
5	Väinö Muinonen	FIN	30 Dec. 1898	2:33:46.0
6	Johannes Coleman	SOA	05 June 1910	2:36:17.0
7	Donald McNab Robertson	GBR	07 Oct. 1905	2:37:06.2
8	Henry Gibson	SOA	31 Mar. 1914	2:38:04.0
9	Mauno Tarkiainen	FIN	18 Aug. 1904	2:39:33.0
10	Thore Enochsson	SWE	17 Nov. 1908	2:43:12.0

New geopolitical entities: Poland [POL], Peru [PER], Bulgaria [BUL], China [CHN], Switzerland [SUI]

Team score (unofficial):			
	1. FIN	18 points	(4-5-9)
	2. SOA	41 points	(6-8-27)
	3. FRA	68 points	(12-16-31)

medal at the 1930 British Empire Games over six miles. His inexperience at the marathon distance was thus amply compensated through his being a true veteran of many years of high-level long-distance competition. His 4th place at London on June 13, runner-up at the AAA trial race on July 11, and then his silver medal at Berlin on August 9 indicated his superior knowledge of himself—how to balance training, racing, and recovery to remain fit and fresh, and improve at the same time. Few athletes have ever perfected those skills, and it was fitting that everything came together for him at this pinnacle of his career.

Shoryu Nan (Nam Sung-yong) was a relative unknown among the top marathoners at Berlin. He first came to prominence in 1933, placing second at Tokyo on November 3 (2:32:35). He ran another marathon at Tokyo October 13, 1935, placing second again (2:39:05). This race was quite close in time to the Japanese national championship on November 3, also at Tokyo, and his fourth place 2:36:52 there may have reflected an incomplete recovery. It was his unexpected victory over the favored Kitei Son at the Olympic trial race in May of 1936 that announced to the world that, as a nation, Japan could take two or more medals at the Berlin Games. Along with Harper's, Nan's marathon personal best came at these Berlin Games.

TABLE 11.4

Career Marathon Record of Kitei Son (Kee Chung-sohn)

Date	Venue	Place	Time	Comments
10 Oct. 1933	Seoul	1st	2:29:34.4*	
22 Apr. 1934	Seoul	1st	2:24:51.2*	
08 Oct. 1934	Seoul	1st	2:32:19.8*	
23 Mar. 1935	Tokyo	1st	2:26:14*	
03 Apr. 1935	Tokyo	3rd	2:39:34	
27 Apr. 1935	Seoul	1st	2:25:14*	
18 May 1935	Seoul	1st	2:24:28*	
29 Sep. 1935	Seoul	1st	2:42:02	
08 Oct. 1935	Seoul	2nd	2:33:39	
03 Nov. 1935	Tokyo	1st	2:26:42	
18 Apr. 1936	Tokyo	1st	2:28:02	
21 May 1936	Tokyo	2nd	2:38:12	
09 Aug. 1936	Berlin	1st	2:29:19.2	Olympic Games

*probable short course

OLYMPIC MARATHON MISCELLANY 11.1

From Silent Protest to Highest Honor

The Olympic movement has traditionally emphasized individual athlete or team participation with the goal of performance excellence itself, without national identification. Tallies of which geopolitical entity wins the most medals (typically by an NOC) have largely been a media creation, to the dismay of the IOC. Any NOC is of course very proud when members of its delegation earn medals, and national pride runs high when citizens see "one of their own" reach the victory stand. Athletes themselves take pride in wearing their nation's colors and emblem on their competition vest. Sohn Kee-chung was such an athlete—an intensely proud Korean. Few could identify with the depths of his emotions in having to endure competing under Japanese colors, and with a name different from his own.

Notice in figure 11.3a that Son and his countryman Nam Sung-yong (who ran as Shoryu Nan) bowed their heads as the Japanese anthem was played while they were on the podium. As Son later told reporters (Constable 1996), this was not in reverence to the flag or the anthem, but in polite but silent "shame and outrage" that their nation lived under Japanese domination. The next day, in the major Seoul daily newspaper *Dong-a Ilbo*, the victory dais photo had been retouched (figure 11.3b), with the Japanese rising sun removed from Son's sweatshirt. Japanese authorities in Korea were furious and took action against the newspaper by reportedly jailing some of its employees and forcing the newspaper to suspend publication for nine months (Wallechinsky 1996).

The duel between Son and Ernie Harper was such an epic battle that the two athletes were brought back to Berlin following the Olympic Games so that the famed cinematographer Leni Riefenstahl could re-create parts of the race for her cameras. She had already exposed 250 miles (402 kilometers) of film shooting all 136 competition events using an 80-person film crew. These additional inserts helped to make her film *Olympia* a classic sports documentary. Of course, Son had to wear his Japanese team uniform yet again, and it pained him immeasurably. Son retired after the Berlin Games and was appointed manager of Korea's developing marathon athletes. He had to wait until the end of World War II for Korea to regain its independence.

Time has a habit of healing wounds, and for Son, as well as for all Koreans, 1988 brought something very special. One of the most poignant moments in

Figure 11.3a On the victory podium, from left, are bronze medalist Shoryu Nan, gold medalist Kitei Son, and silver medalist Ernie Harper. Courtesy IOC/ Olympic Museum Collections.

(continued)

Figure 11.3b Photo of Kitei Son as presented in the Korean daily newspaper *Dong-a Ilbo* the day following his victory. Notice that the Japanese flag has been removed. Courtesy Korean Amateur Athletic Federation.

marathon history during this first modern Olympic century came at the Opening Ceremonies of the Seoul Olympic Games. Now 73 years old, Sohn Kee-chung ran into the stadium carrying the Olympic flame. Fifty-two years after becoming Olympic champion, at last he was running on an Olympic track wearing his Korean colors! The 88,000 spectators filling Olympic Stadium were completely surprised and rose to their feet to give prolonged applause. Seemingly taking energy from these emotions, Kee, weeping with immeasurable joy, ran so proudly and vigorously that he looked almost as young as in Berlin. Few in attendance will forget it.

Looking Ahead: Brief Highlights 1937-1947

1937: African and European continental records by, respectively, Jack Gibson (South Africa, 2:30:45 at Bloemfontein on March 27) and Manuel Dias (Portugal, 2:30:38 at Lisbon on March 28) topped the year's rankings. Frank "Pat" Dengis [USA], later one of America's most consistent runners, won the Pan American Games title (2:42:43 at Dallas on July 18), with Canadian Walter Young, winner at Boston, a nonfinisher. Baron Pierre de Coubertin died on September 2 of a stroke; buried in Lausanne, his heart was transferred to Olympia and placed in a commemorative stele.

1938: Johannes Coleman (South Africa) won the Third Empire Games marathon title in 2:30:49.8 at Sydney on February 7, beating arch-rival Gibson into third place. In their six marathon clashes, Coleman triumphed over Gibson four times. Väinö Muinonen of Finland won the European Athletics Championships marathon (2:37:28.8 at Paris on September 4).

1939: Ellison "Tarzan" Brown became the first to better 2:30:00 over a full-length Boston course (2:28:51.8 on April 19). Dengis won his third AAU title (2:33:45.2 at Yonkers on November 12) and set a course record that stood until 1955; it was his last race before a plane crash caused his untimely death. Although never winning at Boston, Dengis won 12 of 14 marathons between Dallas in 1937 and Yonkers in 1939.

1940: Gerard Côté [CAN] won the first of four Boston races in a record 2:28:28.6. He also won the United States AAU title—and repeated this double in 1943. Many feel that, had the Games been held in 1940 and 1944, he would have been a prime contender for possibly even a medal. Spiridon Louis died on March 26.

1941-45: Marathon activity was limited outside the United States during the war years. Bernard "Joe" Smith [USA] set a new Boston record of 2:26:51.2 on April 19, 1942, and "Johnny The Elder" Kelley, seven-time runner-up in Boston, won in 1945, adding to his previous win 10 years earlier. International Olympic Committee president (for 17 years) Count Henri de Baillet-Latour died in 1942, on January 6, of a stroke. Named to succeed him was J. Sigfrid Edström, who had been the first president of the IAAF.

1946: A third consecutive European Athletics Championships victory went to a Finnish marathoner, this time Mikko Hietanen (2:24:55) finishing ahead of defending champion Muinonen (now 47 years old!) in Oslo on August 22 over 40.2 kilometers. Stylianos Kyriakidis [GRE], winner at Boston with a European record (2:29:27), was a nonfinisher at Oslo.

1947: Mikko Hietanen traveled to Boston and narrowly missed a new European record with his 2:29:39, but was still four minutes behind Korean Suh Yun-bok, whose 2:25:39 was a world best.

References

Anonymous. 1985. *Olympia-Stadion Berlin.* Berlin: Felgentreff & Goebel.

Anonymous. 1937. *The Official Report of the XIth Olympiad Berlin 1936.* London: British Olympic Association.

Anonymons. 1936a. *Report of the American Olympic Committee, Games of the XIth Olympiad.* New York: American Olympic Committee.

Anonymous. 1936b. *The XIth Olympic Games, Berlin, 1936, Official Report.* Vol. 1. Berlin: Publ. Wilhelm Limpert.

Constable, G. 1996. *The XI, XII, and XIII Olympiads.* Los Angeles: World Sport Research & Publications, Inc.

Daley, A.J. 1936. *The New York Times,* August 10.

Hymans, R. 1996. *A history of the U. S. Olympic trials for track and field.* Indianapolis: USA Track & Field.

Wallechinsky, D. 1996. *The complete book of the Summer Olympics.* 1996 edition. New York: Little, Brown & Company.

CHAPTER 12

1948—LONDON

Cabrera Victorious in Postwar Games Revival at London

The Olympic Games Resume After a 12-Year Hiatus

Wartime activities caused cancellation of the Games of the 12th and 13th Olympiads. The IOC awarded Games of the 12th Olympiad (1940) to Tokyo in 1936 at its meeting in Berlin. Helsinki and Tokyo had been the only cities in contention. In 1938, however, the Japanese government ordered the Tokyo Organizing Committee to cease its Olympic preparations as a result of its expanding Sino-Japanese War activities. The Games were then transferred to Helsinki, but when the Soviets invaded Finland, the Olympic Games were canceled altogether. Continuing global strife made it impossible to stage the 1944 Olympic Games as well.

In August of 1945, with the war just over, new IOC president J. Sigfrid Edström from Sweden met with Avery Brundage, now an IOC vice president, and Executive Board colleague Lord Aberdare to assess the future of the Olympic movement. To their credit, they felt strongly that—especially in view of the recent world conflict—the ideal of nations working together for a common goal of international brotherhood was even more essential than ever before. Thus, the question was never whether there should be Games of the 14th Olympiad; it was simply where.

As the ravages of war were absent there, four sites in the United States were considered: Baltimore, Minneapolis, Los Angeles, and Philadelphia. However, in 1939 London had been awarded the 1944 Olympic Games over Detroit, Lausanne, and Rome. World War II brought a halt to the staging of these Games as well, but London became a logical favorite for 1948 in view of its earlier selection. In 1946, the result of a postal vote among the IOC members indeed gave London the Olympic Games, with Lausanne chosen as the future site for the IOC headquarters. The talented Carl Diem, who had directed an International Olympic Institute in Berlin—now destroyed—was asked to relocate it to Lausanne and to eventually establish a sports university in Cologne. Thus, the Olympic movement once again had an identifiable continuity.

Once again, London faced the challenge of hosting the Olympic Games on short notice. It rose to the occasion with vigor equal to that in 1908. Thanks to the organizational skills and love of sport of British Olympic Committee chair David Cecil, Lord Burghley, the Sixth Marquis of Exeter (the Olympic 400 meters hurdles champion in 1928 and fourth in 1932), the job was completed superbly, albeit in a spartan fashion. Existing facilities were renovated and/or repaired to ensure that they were in good order. The huge Empire Stadium (also called Wembley Stadium) became the focal point for the ceremonies, as well as track and field. Completed in 1923, it became one of the most famous soccer stadiums in the world. Track and field activities had not occurred in it for more than 20 years, so an entirely new track and infield facility needed design and construction. Because of pre-Games events occurring in the stadium until July 10, only 19 days were available for this complex project (Anonymous 1951).

Constructing a new Olympic Village was out of the question due to lack of building supplies, so the male athletes stayed in various army and air force camps, including Uxbridge and Richmond Park. Southlands College opened its dormitories for the women athletes. German and Japanese teams were not invited due to their aggressor nation status, but still a record 59 geopolitical entities sent athletes: 3,714 men and 385 women. King George VI led a long list of dignitaries joining the 85,000 who watched the Opening Ceremonies in the Empire Stadium on Thursday, July 29. The ceremonial Olympic flame arrived on schedule, successfully making its 3,160 kilometers journey via two boat rides and 1,688 relay couriers from Olympia. It traveled through Italy, Switzerland, France, Luxembourg, and Belgium, reentered France, crossed the English Channel, and finally found its way into the stadium in Wembley.

On some days, such as for the Opening Ceremonies and the first day of track and field competition, London weather was wonderful—sunny and warm. But on other days, drenching rains and blustery winds produced wretched conditions. For some of the track races, competitor numbers were scarcely legible due to mud-splash from the cinder track. Partly due to weather, but also due to the profound loss of continuity in training for top-level athletes—some of whom were soldiers—these Olympic Games produced an historical low in record improvements. Among track and field events, there were just seven. The overall track and field star of these Olympic Games had to be Holland's Fanny Blankers Koen, who won gold medals in the 100 meters, 200 meters, 80 meters hurdles, and 400 meters relay—a feat still unmatched among women Olympians.

Quality Athletes Identified Despite Wartime Interference

Finland

Finnish athletes won the unofficial Olympic marathon team title in 1936, and their country did not suffer extensive wartime destruction, so sportswriters predicted that the Finns would perform well at London. Just less than a month before the Olympic Games, on July 11, the Finnish Olympic trial was held at Vuoksenniska to select three athletes. Mikko Hietanen was superior, winning (2:31:02) over Jussi Kurikkala by five minutes and 39 seconds. Both were given team berths. Although 29-years-old Martti Urpalainen was third (2:38:01), he was passed over in favor of Viljo Heino—the reigning world record-holder at six miles, 10,000 meters, and the one-hour run (the first man ever to exceed 12 miles in that period). Heino did the double at these Olympic Games in both the 10,000 meters and the marathon.

Great Britain

British selectors simplified their athlete identification process as well, using a single trial that incorporated the AAA championship as part of the Polytechnic Harriers Marathon on June 19. Since it was staged over its usual route from Windsor to Chiswick, British athletes did not have the opportunity to compete on the newly developed Olympic course. Jack Holden had emerged as the postwar star and proved his continuing excellence with a 2:36:44.6; that time was 77 seconds ahead of runner-up Tom Richards. The real battle was for the third team position. This went to Polytechnic Harrier Stan Jones, who beat John Henning of Northern Ireland by the slim margin of 10 seconds!

Soviet Union

Interestingly, marathoners from the Soviet Union had shown great promise with their recent results. In 1947, Vasiliy Gordienko set a new Russian record (2:37:00), beating Feodosiy Vanin by nearly three minutes. In 1948, Vanin won (in a very fast 2:31:55) by 29 seconds over runner-up Gordienko in a field of 65 runners. These two would have very much enjoyed competing at London. Only coaches and technical officials attended, however. They snapped photos by the hundreds, and they wrote volumes of notes. An integral facet of justifying the value of the communist form of government involved a demonstration of "human excellence" by having their youth perform well athletically on the world stage. The Soviet Union could not afford to fail on its inaugural appearance, and so opted for another Olympic quadrennial of preparation before entering the world sporting arena.

Canada and the United Sates

North America continued to have its dominant marathon activity in the northeastern region, as most of the marathoners resided in eastern Canada and New England. The United States again decided to select its athletes from three races: the 1947 and 1948 editions of the Boston Marathon, and the 1947 AAU championship at Yonkers on October 26. Athletes had to run in all three races, and the best overall performance determined team membership (Hymans 1996). Theodore "Ted" Vogel was the sportswriters' favorite—best American at Boston in 1947, and later the AAU winner. At Boston in 1948, the top Canadians also competed, the most famous of whom was Gérard Côté. Vogel and Côté dueled together for 23 miles before Côté gradually edged in front, winning by only 44 seconds (2:31:02). Vogel was thus the first choice for the American team, and Côté was selected to represent Canada. Johnny Kelley and Finnish-American Aulis Olavi "Ollie" Manninen placed fourth and fifth at Boston. Together with their other two race results, this ensured their selection to the American team. Canada also selected its two remaining team members from the 1948 Boston race—Lloyd Evans of Montréal (sixth) and Walter Fedorick of Hamilton (seventh).

Côté ran two more marathons before the Olympic race, which either attested to an exceptional ability to manage travel, competition, and recovery, or else suggested that his London racing would be slowed from doing too much. He crossed the North American continent and won the warm-weather Los Angeles Coliseum Relays Marathon on May 22 in a manner that was vintage Côté. The outside stadium entry gates in front of the marathon tunnel were still locked when he arrived. Unfazed, he scaled the fence and dashed into the stadium only to find hurdles in place for a race on the track. He simply ran around them, finished (2:42:07), and lit one of his trademark huge cigars in celebration. Three weeks later he was back on the East Coast, and on June 12 he won the Canadian marathon trial at Hamilton (2:46:06).

South Africa

Another nation expected to give a strong showing was South Africa. Sadly, Jack Gibson, having served with the South African Air Force as a gunner, was killed in a plane crash in 1944, leaving 38-years-old Johannes Coleman, sixth at Berlin, as the "grand master" among a young but developing South African marathon contingent (Hauman 1996). Experience and fitness combined to give him his third national championship victory (2:32:30) at Port Elizabeth on March 27, which doubled as the Olympic trial. He was more than six minutes ahead of 22-years-old Syd Luyt. Debuting the previous November, Luyt had won at Durban (2:39:27), but there was concern that such a young athlete, traveling so far to race at London, might be overwhelmed by the ordeal. Luyt and Coleman developed an abiding friendship, however, and its synergism helped them both perform well.

A New Course Almost Touches the Old

Instead of a point-to-point course as developed in 1908, the Olympic organizers opted for a looping out-and-back route with the start and finish inside the Empire Stadium (figure 12.1). This continued the trend for stadium spectators to enjoy both the start and finish, being apprised of race progress via the stadium public address system, with thousands more fans able to view the happenings along the course. Interestingly, the earlier 1908 London Olympic course, proceeding from west to east, came within one-half mile of the Empire Stadium (figure 12.2) at roughly 21.6 miles (34.8 kilometers). The two courses never intersected, however, as the 1948 route went north from the stadium and then returned.

The Empire Stadium completely surrounded the track, with north and south grandstands alongside the track straightaways, which were oriented east-to-west. The marathon tunnel was located midway along the north grandstand, underneath the royal box. The race started and finished within the stadium.

Once outside the stadium, an initial 11 kilometers outbound section of the course extended north to Stanmore through the suburban areas of Wembley Park, Barn Hill, Kingsbury, and Canons Park (figure 12.1). This route was retraced on the return trip. Then, between 11 and 31 kilometers, a 20 kilometers loop proceeded counterclockwise through Elstree and Radlett, returning to Stanmore. The course details box summarizes the various street and track details of the marathon route.

The road surface was macadam throughout, but the course was continually rolling, with many turns. The stadium was 100 feet (30.5 meters) above sea level, and the course increased in elevation through 18 miles (29 kilometers) shortly after entering Shenley Elstree Way. The elevation at this point was 425 feet (130 meters). The remaining 8 miles (12.8 kilometers) were thus a steady 325 feet (99 meters) downhill on the return to the stadium. Athlete comments following the race suggested that the combination of gusty winds plus hills and undulations made the competition an extremely demanding ordeal.

In accordance with IAAF rules, eight so-called feeding stations were established at 5 kilometers intervals (Anonymous 1951). Provisions at these stations included warm or cold tea (sweetened or unsweetened), warm coffee, barley water, lemonade, carbonated water, sugar cubes, oranges, and lemons (Anonymous 1951). Athletes could also prepare special drinks prior to the race for distribution at these stations as desired.

The course outline remains substantially as it was in 1948. Watford Way has been renamed Edgware Way. Along with Barnet Way, these roads are now multilane highways (known in Britain as dual carriageways). Wembley Stadium still stands, and a thorough renovation has recently been announced.

Course Details

The 1948 London Olympic Marathon

Start at the 100 meters start line at the northeast side of the stadium

Run one complete lap counterclockwise, and then another 50 meters to exit the stadium via the tunnel under the royal box

Continue onto Olympic Way into Wembley Park Village to Brook Avenue

Half left onto Brook Avenue to Forty Avenue

Right onto Forty Avenue over railway bridge to the Town Hall

Left at the Town Hall onto The Paddocks

Half left onto Fryent Way, which becomes Honeypot Lane

Honeypot Lane becomes Marsh Lane

Straight on Marsh Lane to London Road

Right onto London Road, which becomes Spur Road

Straight on Spur Road to Watford Way

Half right onto Watford Way to Barnet Way

Left onto Barnet Way to Shenley Elstree Way

Left onto Shenley Elstree Way to Theobald Street

Right on Theobald Street, crossing under Radlett Railway Bridge to Watling Street

Left onto Watling Street into Elstree High Street

Half left onto Elstree High Street to Watford Way

Half left onto Watford Way to Spur Road

Right onto Spur Road

Spur Road becomes London Road

Left onto London Road to Marsh Lane

Left onto Marsh Lane

Marsh Lane becomes Honeypot Lane

Honeypot Lane becomes Fryent Way to The Paddocks

Half right on The Paddocks to the Town Hall

Right at the Town Hall onto Forty Avenue

Across Railway Bridge on Forty Avenue to Brook Avenue

Left onto Brook Avenue to Wembley Park Village

Half right onto Olympic Way to the Empire Stadium

Enter the stadium track through the tunnel under the royal box

Right turn onto the track, continuing 50 meters to the finish line and then making one complete lap around the track counterclockwise, returning to the finish line

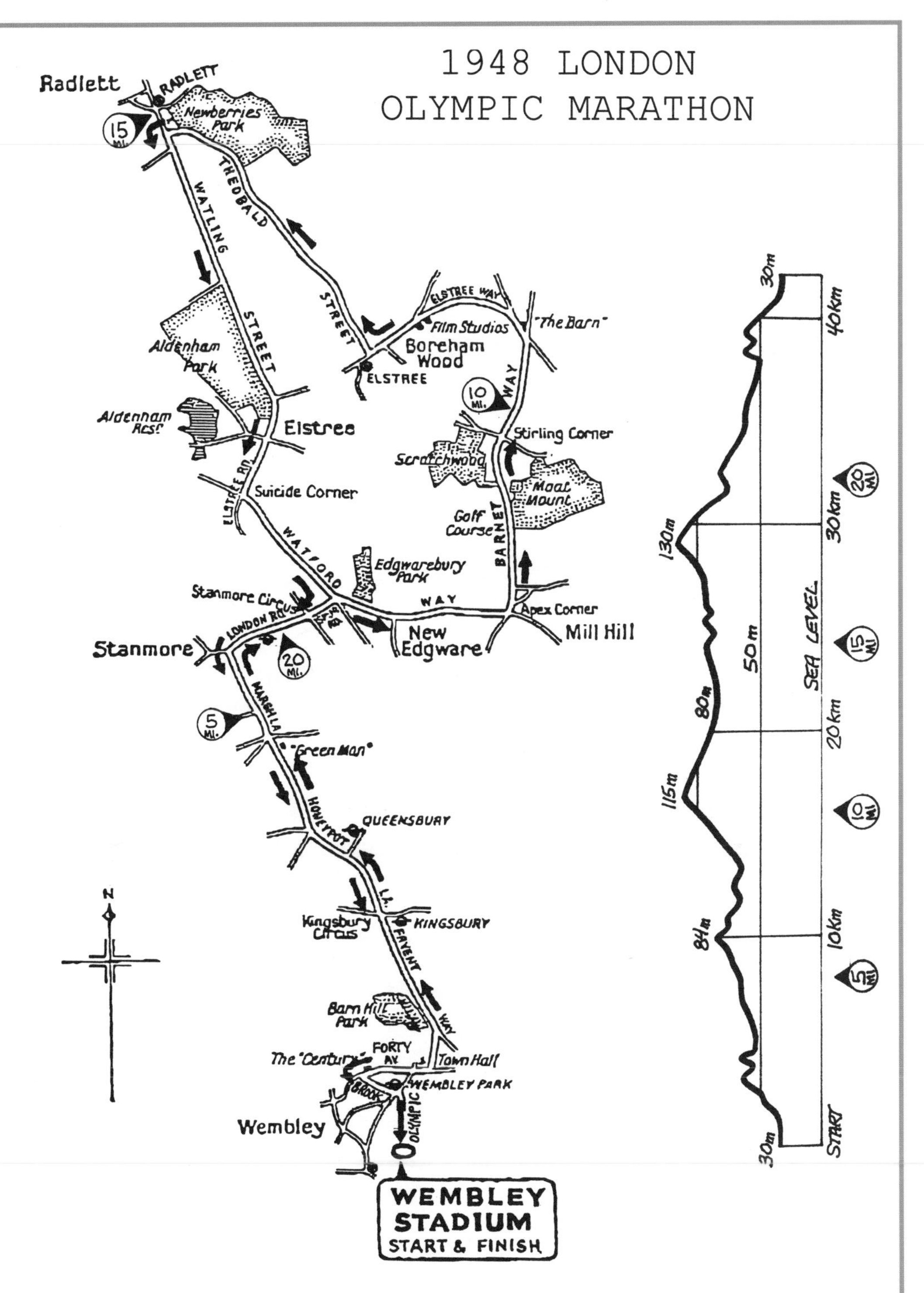

Figure 12.1 Sketch of the London Olympic marathon course. Prepared by Bob Letson.

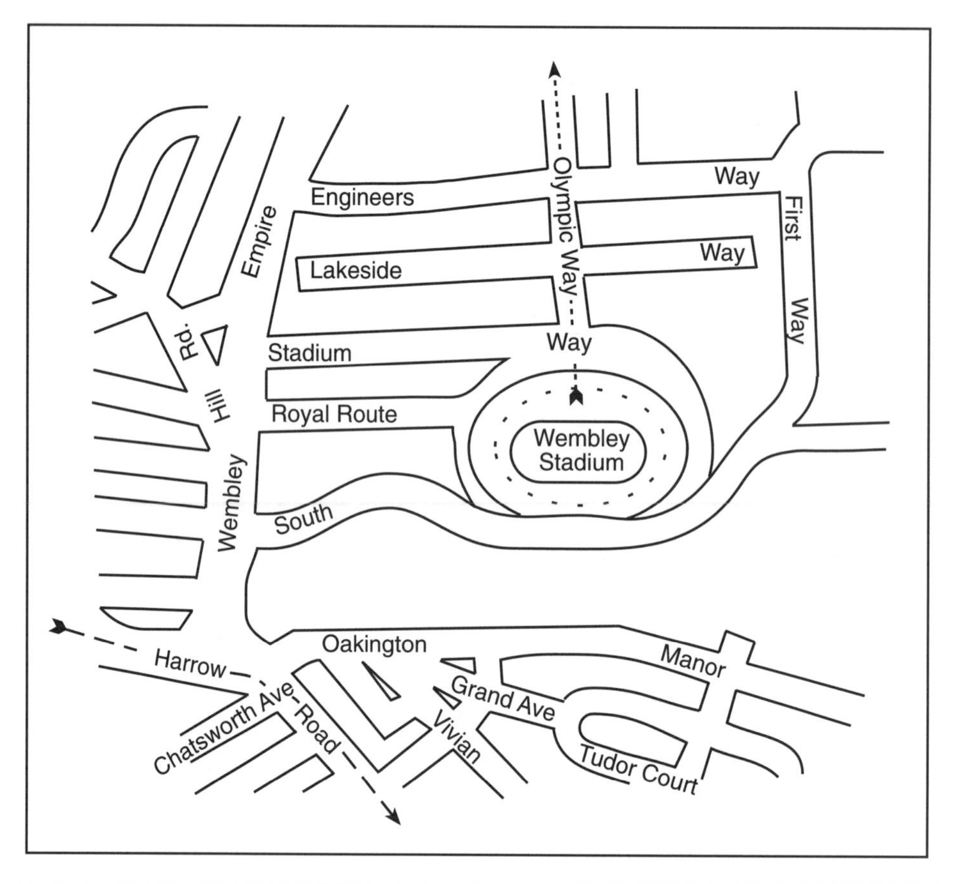

Figure 12.2 Sketch showing the proximity of the 1908 and 1948 Olympic marathon courses. At approximately 21.6 miles into the 1908 course (intersection of Harrow Road with Wembley Hill Road), it is less than a half-mile walk to Empire (Wembley) Stadium.

Cabrera Over Richards and Gailly: Good Pacing Prevails

A warm 22.8°C (73°F), cloudy, humid (60 percent), and windy Saturday, August 7 greeted the athletes as they toed the line and the starting gun fired at 1500 (3:00 p.m.) for their journey through the rolling terrain of northwest London (Meisl 1948). The field of athletes resembled that in Berlin, except slightly smaller: 24 Europeans from 13 nations, and 17 more from four other continents. South America had 3 from Argentina, plus 1 Chilean. Asia had 3 Koreans, and 1 each from China and India. Africa was represented by 2 South Africans, and North America had full teams of 3 each from the United States and Canada. Three athletes who ran in the 1936 Berlin Olympic marathon were entered in this race: South Africa's Johannes Coleman (6th), Greece's Stylianos Kyriakides (11th), and America's John A. Kelley (18th).

Argentina's Eusebio Guiñez took the early lead, but then Belgium's Etienne Gailly surged to the front, passing the 10 kilometers checkpoint (just past the Stanmore metro station) in 34:34, 12 seconds ahead of an unknown from China, Lou Weng-au. Gailly had been a paratrooper during the war, and this was his debut at the marathon distance. Behind Lou by another 19 seconds was the duet of Guiñez and Rene Josset, France's marathon champion. Then came Sweden's Gustav Östling, Finland's Jussi Kurikkala, Choi Yoon-chil of Korea, and Argentina's Delfo Cabrera. Four of the seven top finishers would emerge from this group. Figure 12.3 shows some of the runners farther back in the pack along this portion of the course.

The first major hill came between 8 and 10 miles—a net climb of 165 feet (50 meters). Gailly led, and continued to lead at 20 kilometers or 12.4 miles (1:09:29), with Lou only 24 seconds behind. Guiñez remained just ahead of Josset, with Östling in fifth, and now Cabrera running smoothly in sixth (1:10:51). Just behind Cabrera was Syd Luyt and Choi, and then Jack Holden. Two notable

Figure 12.3 Out on the marathon course, it is Britain's Stan Jones (number 265) and Denmark's Henning Larsen (number 257) just in front of the South African duo of Syd Luyt (number 279) and Johannes Coleman (number 278), with possibly one of the Argentines (Guiñez or Sensini) barely visible farther back. Reprinted, by permission, from the collection of Stan Jones.

dropouts had already occurred—Salvatore Costantino and Pierre Cousin—and Mikko Hietanen had injured his foot and had slowed noticeably.

Crossing the railway bridge in Radlett at 24 kilometers (15 miles), the runners had reached the northernmost point of the course. They turned left and started back toward the stadium. At 25 kilometers, Hietanen was now a DNF, but Gailly was still in the lead (1:27:27), 41 seconds in front of Guiñez. Lou started to slow his pace and was passed by Östling and Cabrera, who now were positioned third and fourth. As the runners started up the next sizable hill—gaining 150 feet over 1 mile (46 meters over 1.6 kilometers)—Choi quickened his pace, and by 30 kilometers had moved from eighth (almost two minutes behind Gailly) to third, only 52 seconds away. Jack Holden retired at 27 kilometers due to blisters.

At 30 kilometers, toward the end of the loop portion of the course, Gailly (1:47:01) was 32 seconds in front of Guiñez. Another 20 seconds back was Choi (1:47:53), with Cabrera a mere second behind him. At their race pace, 1 second of time represents about four and one-half meters of distance. Other athletes with excellent credentials were maintaining their pace. Östling was in 5th, just ahead of Syd Luyt, with Tom Richards in 7th, and Berlin marathon star Johannes Coleman in 11th.

Choi continued to push the pace, and by 35 kilometers, in Canons Park on the out-and-back return portion of the course, Choi was leading Cabrera by 28 seconds. Would it be another Olympic marathon victory by a Korean-born athlete? Just behind Cabrera, by only 3 seconds, was Gailly, his stride visibly stiffening. Guiñez was now in fourth, and Tom Richards had moved into fifth. Luyt had overtaken Östling, and Coleman was now in eighth. Between 36 and 37 kilometers, Choi started to limp visibly for reasons never explained later in the interviews, and he dropped out, apparently from injury. Cabrera was now leading the race, with first Gailly and then Guiñez strung out behind him, several meters separating each. Guiñez now started to slow, his stride losing its fluidity.

Near the 40 kilometers point, the complexion of the race changed substantially. As if recovered from his previous bad patch, Gailly now surged into the lead by catching and passing Cabrera. Tom Richards had quickened his pace, moving from fifth to third, and now established himself as a medal contender for Great Britain. South Africa's Coleman also had accelerated, moving up from eighth to fourth, relegating the tiring Guiñez to fifth.

Unfortunately, Gailly's eccentric pacing had nearly catastrophic results, and his running form degenerated drastically in the final stages outside the stadium; he very nearly could not run at all. A poignant description of what happened next was published in *The Times* of London (Anonymous 1948) on Monday, August 9: ". . . a figure fully as tragic as Dorando's emerged from the tunnel. It was the Belgian, Gailly, so sore of foot and weary of leg and soul that he could hardly make any progress at all. Suddenly, quite close behind him, appeared another figure, that of the strongly built Cabrera, who doubtless was tired too, but looking a fresh and lively sprinter by comparison. The Argentinean passed his man in a few strides (figure 12.4) and set off to complete a lap that must have seemed like 5 miles or more to the poor tottering Belgian. No more than

20 seconds later came the loudly and justly cheered arrival of Richards—a pleasant surprise indeed for most people. Richards had little pace, but he easily passed poor Gailly in the back-stretch and lessened by a little the original 50 yards between himself and Cabrera. Richards finished only 16 seconds behind the winner. Gailly once very nearly pulled up dazed and hopeless with the appalling distance of 60 yards still between him and the tape. Already other gallant runners were appearing, and it was in no grudging spirit that one breathed

Figure 12.4 **Delfo Cabrera (number 233) passing the utterly exhausted Etienne Gailly (number 252) on the cinder track to win Olympic gold. Tom Richards also passed Gailly to capture the silver medal, relegating Gailly to third.** Courtesy Dave Terry.

again when Gailly at long last staggered into third place. He then collapsed and was carried off on a stretcher."

Table 12.1 provides a summary of how the top six athletes proceeded through the race. Never before in an Olympic marathon had three more variant styles of racing topped the victory podium: Cabrera's steady pace throughout (see Olympic Marathon Miscellany 12.2), Richards's conservative come-from-behind quickening, and Gailly's energy-sapping surges all brought success.

Eleven out of the 41 starters failed to finish this challenging event. As the last runner, Britain's Stan Jones, the 30th finisher out of the starting field, entered the stadium (figure 12.5), he received nearly as large an ovation as the winner.

TABLE 12.1

Order of Top Placers Through Control Points

	Cabrera	*Richards*	*Gailly*	*Coleman*	*Guiñez*	*Luyt*
10 km Stanmore	10	14	1	16	4	13
20 km Elstree	6	14	1	12	3	8
25 km Radlett	4	11	1	13	2	5
30 km Elstree	4	7	1	11	2	6
35 km Canon's Park	2	5	3	8	4	6
40 km Wembley Park	2	3	1	4	5	6
Finish	1	2	3	4	5	6

OLYMPIC MARATHON MISCELLANY 12.1

Debuts With Distinction

Such is the peculiarity of the marathon as an event that it is possible to win an Olympic gold medal on one's first effort. Four have done it: Théato in 1900 and Cabrera here in 1948 are two who now are familiar. The only explanation for such an achievement seems to be a combination of (1) genetic talent as demonstrated from previous shorter-distance running excellence, (2) extraordinary fitness on the day, and (3) an unyielding will to win.

Interestingly, Cabrera seemed to set a trend, for improbable as it may seem, a debut marathoner would win the next two Olympic marathons: Emil Zátopek in 1952 and Alain Mimoun in 1956. Similarities in these three athletes help explain their ability to achieve the ultimate victory the first time out. Perhaps just as amazing is that all three members of the 1948 Argentine marathon squad—averaging 35 years of age—were running their first marathon. Their combined finish places gave them the unofficial team title in convincing fashion!

Figure 12.5 The last finisher, Britain's Stan Jones (number 265), responding to the official's instructions to turn right for his final lap to the finish. Reprinted, by permission, from the collection of Stan Jones.

Cabrera brought Argentina its second Olympic marathon gold medal. Only 16 seconds separated gold from silver, with 26 seconds between silver and bronze. Only at Los Angeles in 1932 had there been such a close finish—at both sites, the first four were on the track at the same time. Table 12.2 summarizes the race.

Notes on the Medalists

Delfo Cabrera, born in Cordoba, Argentina, had natural track speed, as seen by his national track championship victory at 1,500 meters in 1940. But he also had excellent endurance, as seen by his later successful switch to a primary focus on the 5,000 and 10,000 meters, taking five bronze medals at the South American championships during 1943-45. Finally, in 1946 he won at 10,000 meters. In 1947, he showed both speed and endurance over a wide range of distances: third place in both 3,000 and 10,000 meters at the South American championships in Rio de Janeiro, and fifth in his national 5,000 meters championship. This extensive experience at faster-than-marathon-pace racing helped

TABLE 12.2

1948 London Olympic Marathon at a Glance

Date: 07 August
Start time: 1500
Course: Out-loop-back
Course distance: 42.195 km
Weather: 22.8°C (73°F); humid, windy
Starters: 41
Finishers: 30
GPEs: 21

TOP RESULTS:

Place	*Athlete*	*GPE*	*Date of birth*	*Time*
1	Delfo Cabrera	ARG	12 Nov. 1919	2:34:51.6
2	Thomas Richards	GBR	15 Mar. 1910	2:35:07.6
3	Etienne Gailly	BEL	26 Nov. 1922	2:35:33.6
4	Johannes Coleman	SOA	05 June 1910	2:36:06.0
5	Eusebio Guiñez	ARG	16 Dec. 1906	2:36:36.0
6	Sydney Luyt	SOA	11 Dec. 1925	2:38:11.0
7	Gustav Östling	SWE	17 Dec. 1914	2:38:40.6
8	John Systad	NOR	20 Mar. 1917	2:38:41.0
9	Armando Sensini	ARG	21 Sept. 1909	2:39:30.0
10	Henning Larsen	DEN	12 Dec. 1910	2:41:22.0

New geopolitical entities: Turkey [TUR], Korea [KOR]

Team score (unofficial):

1. ARG	15 points	(1-5-9)
2. SWE	47 points	(7-12-28)
3. CAN	56 points	(16-17-23)

him greatly at London. For him, marathon pace felt so easy—his mind had only known a race pace of 76 seconds per 400 meters or faster. His London race pace was a much slower 88 seconds per 400 meters. He only needed to practice patience to go the distance successfully, and it appears that he learned very well.

After the London Games, Cabrera won two South American titles over the 20 kilometers (in 1949) and half marathon distances (in 1952). He won the inaugural 1951 Pan American Games marathon by 10 minutes at Buenos Aires (2:35:00.2), and then finished an excellent sixth place at the 1952 Helsinki Olympics. He thus was much more fortunate than two other gold medalists, Kolehmainen and Zabala, who failed to finish in their second Olympic attempts. He retired in 1957 but stayed active with sport, initially as a physical education teacher. Eventually he was elected to the presidency of the Argentine Olympic Association. Cabrera's career marathon record is shown in table 12.3.

Tom Richards, the 38-years-old Welshman born in Monmouth, had won two of the wartime "Polys" (1944 and 1945), as well as the 1947 Rugby Marathon. Also in 1947, he was runner-up in both the "Poly" and the AAA champion-

TABLE 12.3

Career Marathon Record of Delfo Cabrera

Date	Venue	Place	Time	Comments
07 Aug. 1948	London	1st	2:34:51.6	Olympic Games
06 Mar. 1952	Buenos Aires	1st	2:35:00.2	
27 Jul. 1952	Helsinki	6th	2:26:42.4	Olympic Games
19 Apr. 1954	Boston	6th	2:27:50*	
05 Dec. 1954	Kamakura	DNF		

*short course

ships, and was runner-up at the 1948 "Poly" AAA Olympic trial. Jack Holden had won the 1947 and 1948 "Poly" races and had been touted as a potential medalist more than Richards had. The Olympic race was thus enormously satisfying for Richards—a personal best when it counted the most. He continued to perform creditably, recording his career best of 2:29:59 at the 1954 "Poly," where he placed sixth to Jim Peters's world best performance of 2:17:39.4. Between 1950 and 1956, Richards won five Welsh marathon titles.

For **Etienne Gailly**, just as with Cabrera, the 1948 Olympic marathon was a debut at the distance. He had won the 1947 and 1948 Belgian titles, but these were over a distance of 32 kilometers. Subsequently, he finished eighth in the 1950 European championship (2:38:24), and the following month, in Rome, he won a short-course race in 2:36:01.

Looking Ahead: Brief Highlights 1949-1951

1949: Salomon Könönen [FIN] set a European record 2:28:39.4 in winning at Turku on October 2.

1950: Jack Holden [GBR], a 1948 Olympic nonfinisher, won both the Empire Games marathon (2:32:57, at Auckland on February 11) and the European championships (2:32:13.2 at Brussels on August 23), as well as the British title (2:31:03.4).

1951: Two new regional championships started within a week of each other, continuing the global development of marathon racing. As mentioned earlier, Olympic champion Cabrera won the inaugural Pan American Games marathon on March 6, while eight-time Indian marathon champion Chhota Singh upset the favored Japanese in the inaugural Asian Games at New Delhi on March 11 (2:42:58.6).

References

Anonymous. 1948. *The Times (London).* August 9.
Anonymous. 1951. *Official Report of the Organizing Committee for the XIV Olympiad.* London: The Organizing Committee for the XIV Olympiad.
Hauman, R. 1996. *Century of the marathon 1896-1996.* Cape Town: Human & Rousseau.
Hymans, R. 1996. *The United States Olympic Trials for track and field 1908-1992.* Indianapolis: USA Track and Field.
Meisl, W. 1948. *Marathon: British Olympic Association Official Report of the XIV Olympic Games.* London: World Sports.

Chapter 13

1952—Helsinki

Helsinki Hails Triple-Gold Hero Emil Zátopek

Tiny Finland Hosts the Sporting World With Class

When the Olympic Games of 1940 were transferred from Tokyo to Helsinki, the Finns built a magnificent 70,000-capacity stadium in a forested area just north of the downtown area. World War II then halted the Games for two Olympiads. Fittingly, to recognize both its sport-loving citizens and its venerable sporting heritage, and as well to take advantage of an Olympic stadium that had never been used, the IOC in 1947 awarded the 1952 Games to Helsinki. Remote as little Finland was, with fewer than five million people in the far north of Europe, 69 geopolitical entities brought a total of 4,925 athletes (4,407 men and 518 women), and Finnish hospitality was at its best. The venues were magnificent, the organization was professional, and the spectators were knowledgeable.

Postwar recovery in athletic performance showed continuing improvement. At Helsinki, of the 22 standard events of track and field (excluding the walks), 17 Olympic records were broken and 2 were tied.

No sporting event of this magnitude is free of challenges, of course, but increasingly the Olympic Games were experiencing political rather than sporting problems. Politics became an issue here as never before. Postwar division of Europe into an East bloc and a West bloc, separated by what Winston Churchill termed an Iron Curtain, meant that the entire world was divided. It was capitalism versus communism in a kind of "Cold War," pitting the two philosophies against each other. That meant the United States of America versus the Union of Soviet Socialist Republics [URS]. Included within the so-called communist bloc were the "buffer countries" of Bulgaria, Hungary, Poland, Romania, and Czechoslovakia. Who was "better" at sport would be a powerful indicator of which political system was "better" than the other.

Journalists seized upon this idea as well and created a ranking system in Olympic sports competition whereby places one through six were awarded, respectively, a point value of 10, 5, 4, 3, 2, and 1. They then used this to compare the change in performance of individual nations from one Olympic Games to the next. Comparisons *between* nations are meaningless unless population is factored in, but the United States and the Soviet Union were similar in population. Shortly following the Helsinki Games, the new IOC president, Chicago millionaire Avery Brundage, put it bluntly (Schaap 1963): "If this becomes a giant contest between two great nations rich in talent and resources, the spirit of the Olympics will be destroyed."

In other ways, this political wrangling caused frustration, and those who suffered most were the athletes and spectators. As one example, the German Democratic Republic asked the IOC to let its athletes compete as a separate nation. This request was denied—the IOC would recognize only one German nation. As another example, the Soviets created their own Olympic Village in suburban Otaniemi, near the Soviet-owned Porkkala naval base, intended also for athletes from the communist satellite nations. Surrounded by barbed wire, it was well away from the primary Olympic Village for men, nestled in the forested suburb of Kapylä, just 5 kilometers from the stadium complex.

As a third example, Helsinki desired to have the Olympic flame relayed on foot from Greece to Finland. It would have to cross a huge expanse of the communist bloc to reach the Finnish border. The Soviets denied the request. And so the flame took its first ride on an airplane. Kindled in Olympia, run to Athens via relay, and then transferred to a miner's lamp, it was flown from Athens to Copenhagen and brought to Malmö, Sweden, by boat. Here, a 3,612 kilometers journey began, through all of Scandinavia, with 3,042 torchbearers. From the cities and towns in the south to back roads well above the Arctic Circle—where the Olympic flame merged with that from a torch lit by Laplanders using the rays of the sun at midnight—the Olympic spirit traversed the region, arriving on time for the Opening Ceremonies on Saturday, July 19.

A thunderstorm before the ceremonies moderated, and the festivities proceeded through a drippy afternoon. The distance-running legacy of Finland played a delightful role as spectators warmly greeted the legendary Paavo Nurmi, now 55 years old but still smooth of stride despite advancing rheumatism. Entering through the marathon tunnel and carrying the Olympic flame around the track, he lit a huge urn sitting beside the track on the high jump apron. Then, proceeding to the base of the stadium tower rising 72 meters (236 feet) from the southwest corner, he gave the torch to a younger runner who carried it, climbing the stairs, to the top. There, as a fitting climax, 62-years-old Hannes Kolehmainen was waiting, and he lit the cauldron that burned throughout the Olympic Games until August 3. A few IOC dignitaries complained that Nurmi was perhaps a poor choice as a participant, being one of those dreaded professionals, but with Kolehmainen soon taking center stage, it became a minor issue. The Olympic Games could begin, and the marathon race was eight days later.

Key Athletes Get Selected for Competition

The Americas

In April, the now-famous Boston Marathon experienced unusually warm weather (33°C or 88°F). This caused a real problem for local athletes, who had no opportunity for heat acclimatization, having just emerged from the winter season. However, two runners from Guatemala—Doroteo Flores and Luis Velasquez—had just arrived from summertime weather. Typically, the South and Central American nations staged championships over the half marathon distance, so these two athletes came to gain experience in the marathon. Flores, winner of the Central American and Caribbean Games half marathon in 1946, debuted and won (2:31:53); Velasquez took third. Victor Dyrgall of the United States finished between them. Three weeks later, on May 11, at the South American Games in Buenos Aires, over the 21 kilometers distance, a strong trio of Delfo Cabrera (the 1948 London gold medalist), Reinaldo Gorno, and Corsino Fernandez finished in that order and thus formed the Argentine team.

For team selection, the United States used a point system based on results from the 1951 and 1952 AAU races at Yonkers, and also the 1952 Boston Marathon. Dyrgall was the decisive winner at Yonkers in 1952 on May 18 (2:38:28.4) over Tom Jones (2:42:22.2) and Ted Corbitt (2:43:23). Dyrgall's Boston and Yonkers results thus earned him the initial team spot. Tom Jones had two runner-up finishes and a third place, so he was the next-best qualified. Corbitt had run all three races as well and was next in line, becoming the first African-American Olympic marathoner for the United States.

Asia

Asian marathons also were scheduled early in the spring. On March 26 at Pusan, Korea's Choi Yoon-chil proved that he was back into Olympic racing fitness with a 2:26:07, a world best at that time for an out-and-back course. A 1948 London Olympian, he was in the lead at 35 kilometers before dropping out due to injury. This experience, plus a third place finish at Boston in 1950 and a 2:25:16.5 performance over a probably-short course in Asia gave him added confidence that he could perform well on a world sporting stage.

In postwar Japan, a resurgence of distance-running excellence occurred. At Osaka on May 4, Yoshitaka Uchikawa won the Mainichi Marathon. A consistent performer, third at both the 1951 Japanese championship and at Fukuoka, Uchikawa beat a large field of 59 athletes with a convincing 2:29:55.4—the second fastest time in postwar Japan. Katsuo Nishida, Hideo Hamamura, and Keizo Yamada finished within 70 seconds, making team selection difficult, as only three could race. In the end, Hamamura did not travel to Finland.

Europe

European nations typically scheduled their trial races in the early summer, but this would provide marginal recovery time for the July 27 marathon. Britain again used its AAA championship over the Windsor-to-Chiswick course on June 14 to select its Olympic team. Jim Peters, the new star of British marathoning since his debut British record of 2:29:24 at the "Poly" in 1951, was in this race, along with Stan Cox. Both were 1948 Olympians at 10,000 meters in London, and both had switched focus to the marathon. Cox finished second behind Peters in the 1951 "Poly" race. Once again, Peters proved superior (2:20:42.2), with Cox timed at 2:21:42. The finish times were so fast that they prompted a course remeasurement. Actually, the course was a little long, making Peters's performance an astounding world best! In third place was newcomer Geoff Iden (2:26:53.8), giving Britain a potentially formidable team to face the world at Helsinki. However, these runners only had six weeks to recover.

Across the English Channel on that same day, the Belgian championship was held over a course between Waregem and Gent. Although it was common practice in those days to measure road courses in Belgium using an automobile odometer, which typically produced courses short by a kilometer or more, sources close to the event maintained that the course was full distance. Jean Leblond, the 1950 Belgian champion, and Charles DeWachtere, the 1949 winner on a 35 kilometers course, raced each other in a fashion similar to Peters and Cox. In the closing stages, DeWachtere gained a 27 seconds lead, finishing in a time (2:23:07.8) that had been surpassed by Peters and Cox earlier that day. Jean Simonet's 2:28:07 thus gave Belgium an excellent team as well.

Finland's respected long-distance-running heritage and its status as the host of the Olympic Games gave rise to expectations that its marathon athletes would be talented and motivated to perform well. Indeed, Finnish athletes got an initial edge by competing for team positions on the new Olympic course. June 22 was a cool, drizzly day, ideal for racing. Erkki Puolakka won in 2:29:02, well in front of 41-years-old Mikko Hietanen (2:30:24.4) and Eino Pulkkinen.

Frustration developed among the finish line spectators, as they assumed that Veikko Karvonen would be among the top three. He had made a breakthrough to big-time racing in 1950 at the European championship in Brussels, winning a silver medal. He also won the Finnish marathon championship in 1951 with a fast 2:28:46 at Hameenlinna. He eventually arrived, back in sixth, slowed by a leg injury. With less than five weeks before the Olympic marathon, the selectors met with a dilemma. Should they choose Karvonen over Pulkkinen and trust that he would recover, or should they eliminate him in favor of a less-experienced athlete? The selectors took the former option, and Karvonen competed.

Another Out-and-Back Course Provides a Fair Challenge

As at Stockholm, Antwerp, Paris, and Berlin, the organizers decided that the best plan for the marathon competition was to use an out-and-back route (figure 13.1). This minimized traffic congestion and optimized course control. The course was appropriately lengthened for the 50 kilometers walk. The course details box provides street specifics for the portion within Helsinki and more general directions for the portion outside the city (street names in parentheses are the Swedish equivalents, as Finland has two official languages). Most of this route remains and can be followed by car or bicycle, or on foot. A portion of this road leaving Helsinki (National Highway number 137) has been enlarged, providing efficient traffic flow past the airport (now called Helsinki-Vantaa, formerly known as Seutula). The marathon route in this area is on an adjacent smaller road, known locally as "old Tuusulantie." The entire course was on macadam pavement, except for the cinder track. A monument, which still remains, was erected at the turnaround point in Mätäkivi.

As seen on the elevation profile, Helsinki Olympic Stadium sits at 8 meters (26 feet) above sea level. The first 15 kilometers (9.3 miles) of the course were essentially flat, with a transition to rolling terrain causing a net uphill of 30 meters (98 feet) over the next 6 kilometers (3.7 miles). On return, the rolling portion extended from 21 to 27 kilometers, with the remaining portion essentially level. Personal communication from United States Olympian Ted Corbitt (1998) adds some interesting practical perspective: "There was a difference of opinion as to whether it was an easy course. I found it tough every single time that I was out on it except on marathon day. There was always, without exception, a following wind on the way out into the country, and this became a headwind of considerable annoyance on the way back. Sometimes this wind was so strong that it almost stopped you in your tracks."

Several major marathons have been staged in Helsinki since the 1952 Olympics, notably the 1983 World Athletics Championships, the 1994 European Athletics Championships, and the annual Helsinki Marathon. These events have not utilized the Olympic course except for the access road adjacent to the marathon tunnel.

A One-Man Show Brings Triple Gold

A packed stadium witnessed the 1528 (3:28 p.m.) start on Sunday afternoon, July 27, the final day of track and field activities. The last event was the women's

Course Details

The 1952 Helsinki Olympic Marathon

Start at the 100 meters start line at the northwest side of the stadium

Run three and one-half laps counter-clockwise

Exit the stadium through the tunnel near the 1,500 meters start line

Half right onto Hammarskjöldintie (Hammarskjöldsvägen) to Vauhtitie (Fartvägen)

Sharp left (northward) onto Vauhtitie (Fartvägen) (2 kilometers) to Nordenskiöldinkatu (Nordenskiöldsgatan)

Right (eastward) onto Nordenskiöldinkatu (Nordenskiöldsgatan), pass under railway bridge, to Savonkatu (Savolaxgatan)

Left onto Savonkatu (Savolaxgatan) to Kumpulantie (Gumtäksvägen) (3.5 kilometers)

Right onto Kumpulantie (Gumtäksvägen) to Mäkelänkatu (Backasgatan) (4 kilometers)

Left onto Mäkelänkatu (Backasgatan), which continues out of the city

Pass Olympic Village (Olympiakylä) in suburban Käpylä between 5 and 6 kilometers

Mäkelänkatu (Backasgatan) becomes Tuusulantie (Tusbyvägen)

Continue into the countryside (on highway number 137) through Pakinkylä (8 kilometers) and Tuomarinkylä (10 kilometers)

Cross Vantaa River bridge just after 10 kilometers

Pass Helsingin pitäjä (Helsinki Parish Church) at 14 kilometers

Pass through Tikkurila at 15 kilometers

Pass through Ruotsinkylä at 20 kilometers

Reach turnaround point in Mätäkivi

Return by the same route, passing through Tuomarinkylä at 30 kilometers, near the Vantaa River bridge

Pass through Pakinkylä at 35 kilometers

Reenter suburban Helsinki and reenter the stadium via the marathon tunnel

On the track, turn right, continue down the back straightaway, around the back turn, and finish at the standard track event finish line

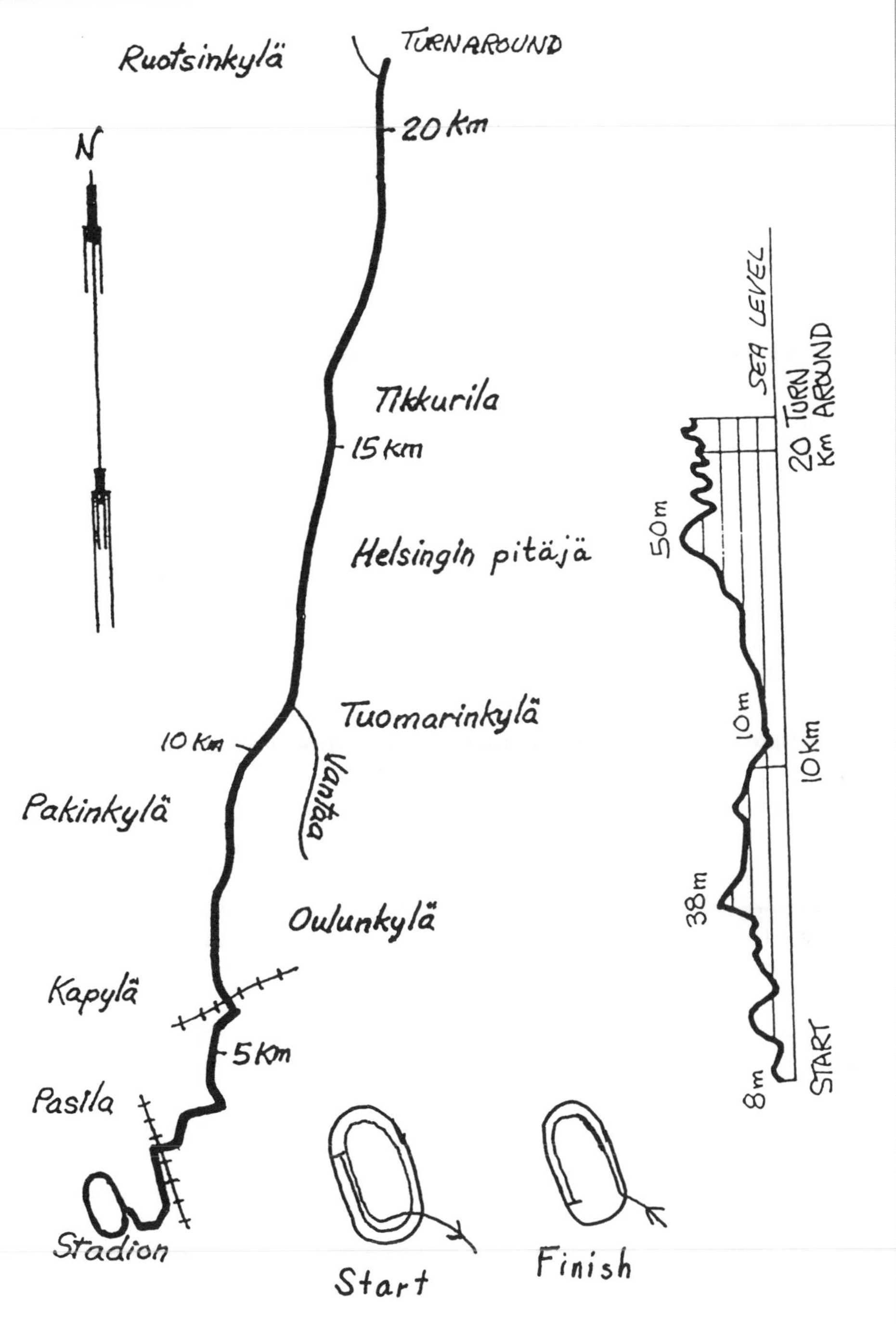

Figure 13.1 **Sketch of the Helsinki Olympic marathon course.** Prepared by Bob Letson.

high jump, starting as the marathon race began and concluding shortly after the marathon runners returned. Announcement of 5 kilometers split times for the first several athletes over the public address system provided an ongoing update of race progress. As Corbitt describes, "marathon day was probably the best day of the Games for track and field events, but as far as I was concerned, too warm for racing the marathon. No traffic or bikes were permitted on the road, and the wind had a cooling effect." The official starting temperature was 18.0°C (64.5°F) (Anonymous 1955).

The assembled field of 66 starters had the usual European domination in numbers: 40 athletes from 20 nations. Five South Americans included a full Argentine team of 3, plus 2 runners from Chile. Nine Asians included athletes from Pakistan and India, plus full teams from Korea and Japan. Four Africans included a full South African team, plus an Egyptian runner. Six North Americans included a full United States team, plus runners from Guatemala and Canada. Two Australian athletes represented Oceania. The 32-years-old defending Olympic champion (Cabrera) headed up a group of 7 who had run at London, including Syd Luyt, Gustav Östling, and Johan Systad, who had finished sixth, seventh, and eighth. Cabrera's teammate Gorno was also a rising star.

But then there was Emil Zátopek, the Czech—speaking five languages, happily greeting fellow athletes in the warm-up area in French, German, English, whatever he needed—in his disarmingly friendly and outgoing style. His competitors wondered whether to take him seriously after what he had accomplished in the previous week.

On July 20 he had won the 10,000 meters run—42.6 seconds faster than his own 1948 London Olympic record. But that was only the start. On July 22 he cruised through the heats of the 5,000 meters run, and on July 24 he won the 5,000 meters final—with another Olympic record! In the audience was Hannes Kolehmainen, watching this wonderful double-gold-medal performance that he, too, had achieved in Stockholm in 1912. Happily, Zátopek then moved into the grandstands to watch his wife, Dana Zátopkova, win the javelin gold medal with a personal best and Olympic record. In this first Olympic century, they remain the only husband and wife to win Olympic gold medals on the same day. Actually, the two had met in London in 1948 and were engaged during those Games (as Dana Ingrova, she placed 7th in the javelin). As an interesting coincidence, they also were born on the same day—September 19, 1922.

Now, three days after his 5,000 meters gold, Zátopek was here warming up for the marathon. His competitors had seen how thoroughly he had thrashed the best distance runners of the world. His racing achievements were well known, but in many ways he was a mystery. When he ran, he seemed from another planet: an excessive counter-rotation of his shoulders, a stiff and high arm action, and strained facial and neck muscles that produced a characteristically agonized countenance as he rolled his head from side to side. Ever quotable, he once remarked: "I am not talented enough to run and smile at the same time." It is true that when he ran, his upper body was a mess. But his strides were quick, short, and smooth—his foot-strikes were light as a feather, making him so efficient he could seemingly run forever.

Details of how he trained were becoming known to his competitors, however, which made many shake their heads in disbelief. Here was an athlete clearly at another level. In one sense, he was like today's Kenyan runners. As a child growing up in the hills and forests of Moravia, he ran everywhere. At the age of 19 years he ran his first race, a factory-sponsored run across town, which he won. Joining a local running club, he liked to run fast, he liked to win, and as he improved, he became inquisitive about what kinds of training would give him more endurance and speed. One thing, he knew, was absolutely essential, and that was hard work. He also knew that training fast made him race fast. Training under difficult conditions made racing in excellent conditions relatively easy. And so, runs of 10 to 20 miles in army boots were not unusual (he was a career army man). A session of 20 × 400 meters at marathon race pace was fun. Over-distance runs at continuously changing paces toughened him for surging in a race.

He eagerly anticipated the marathon, as much for his inquisitiveness as for his inherent love of distance running. He knew about Jim Peters's world record the month before, and so, logically thinking that being the best meant learning from the best, he planned to stay in contact with Peters and use the same tactics. The only thing Zátopek needed were some shoes. After the 5,000 meters race, his shoes were unwearable. According to a reliable source (Ecker 1996), Zátopek bought a pair of local-brand shoes (Karhu), but found them too stiff and tight. The American 10,000 meters Olympian Fred Wilt, whom Zátopek had met at the London Games in 1948, suggested he coat the inside of his shoes with cooking grease, to soften the linings and let them conform to his feet. This apparently solved the problem. Let the race begin!

Jim Peters led the pack out through the stadium tunnel, passing 5 kilometers in 15:43. This pace (75 seconds per 400 meters) was much too fast to be maintained, as it would have produced a 2:11:06 marathon. Zátopek ran together with Cox and Jansson, 19 seconds behind. Another 18 seconds behind was the trio of Yakov Moskachenkov, Reinaldo Gorno, and Doroteo Flores. Moskachenkov was the 1951 Soviet marathon champion and the world record-holder over 30 kilometers. Behind them came a steady stream of athletes, cheered on by huge crowds alongside the roadway (figure 13.2). Although the crowds shown in this photograph were wearing long coats, this is most likely not because it was chilly. Rather, it was only seven years following World War II, and the Finnish people had little choice of clothing due to continuing postwar austerity.

Peters continued to lead at 10 kilometers through the village of Tuomarinkylä (31:55), but still in close contact were Jansson (32:11) and Zátopek (32:12). Cox, Gorno, and Cabrera were now in single file behind. By 15 kilometers, in Tikkurila, Jansson had caught Peters (47:58), but Zátopek was only 2 seconds behind. An appreciable gap had developed behind them, however, with Gorno more than one minute back (49:04), followed by Cox (49:09), and then Cabrera (49:41).

Shortly before 20 kilometers, Jansson and Zátopek caught Peters. It was here that Zátopek reportedly conversed with Peters, asking him what he thought of the pace, as Zátopek was unsure of himself on his debut at the distance.

Figure 13.2 **Early in the race, in Helsinki, huge crowds lined the route to watch the runners pass. Shown here in sequence are Egilberto Martuffi [ITA] (number 251), Yoshitaka Uchikawa [JPN] (number 307), Ted Corbitt [USA] (number 999), Asfo Bussotti [ITA] (number 249), Jozsef Dobronyi [HUN] (number 943), and Victor Olsen [NOR] (number 508).** Courtesy Suomen Urheilumuseo, Helsinki.

Although the exact conversation is most likely lost, some versions get quite entertaining (Wallechinsky 1996). The essence is that when Peters, already verging on exhaustion, gallantly suggested that the pace may be too slow, Zátopek and Jansson edged ahead. By 20 kilometers (1:04:27), they were in front of Peters by 10 seconds. Gorno was now alone in fourth (1:05:50), followed by Cabrera (1:06:34), with Cox 3 seconds farther behind. Shortly thereafter, Cox collapsed and was carried to a waiting ambulance. At the turnaround in Mätäkivi (figure 13.3), Jansson and Zátopek were nearly side by side.

Zátopek continued to race under control, his incredible fitness allowing him to manage the lead pace more comfortably than the others. He passed 25 kilometers in 1:21:30, 5 seconds ahead of Jansson. Peters stubbornly held on, 28 seconds behind Jansson, hoping to recover and at least stay in contention for a medal. Gorno trailed by another 57 seconds, with his teammates in fifth and sixth. At 30 kilometers, with Zátopek still leading, the gap between the top three widened steadily. Zátopek was timed in 1:38:42, Jansson in 1:39:08, and Peters in 1:39:53, with the three Argentines also in single file just behind.

Suddenly, tragedy struck the British champion as a painful left leg muscle cramp forced Peters to a hobble. Ironically, the British 1932 Games marathon silver medalist Sam Ferris had come out to the 20-miles mark, where, as veterans of marathon racing agree, "the real racing begins." Ferris shouted words of encouragement, but after another 200 meters, Peters stopped in his tracks. There is one set of circumstances that might provide an explanation for his muscle cramps. Both Peters and Cox flew to Helsinki on July 24 in a partly converted military bomber, and they endured an icy wind blast on their left from a poorly fitting door during the flight. Cox and Peters both had problems during the race with left-side muscle cramping, and the question remains whether that was related to the bone-chilling cold they had experienced on their flight.

At 35 kilometers (1:56:50), Zátopek had increased his lead over Jansson to 65 seconds. Gorno was only 51 seconds behind Jansson and steadily gaining, in possible medal contention. The experienced Cabrera was also coming closer to Gorno (1:58:46), only 31 seconds separating the two. A new player now entered the scene, as Korea's Choi Yoon-chil improved from 10th at 20 kilometers to 7th at 30 kilometers, and now was in 5th place (2:00:57). Finland's Karvonen also advanced from 9th at 30 kilometers to 6th.

Zátopek passed 40 kilometers in 2:15:10, still not closely challenged. His steadily slowing 10 kilometers split times indicated the price he had paid for trying to match Peters's early fast running: 32:12, 32:15, 34:15, and 36:28. But he was still in control, even chatting with those on bicycles riding alongside on the course.

Figure 13.3 **At the turnaround point in Mätäkivi, Sweden's Gustaf Jansson (number 683) is only a stride ahead of Emil Zátopek (number 903).** Courtesy Suomen Urheilumuseo, Helsinki.

Gorno (2:17:25) had slipped past Jansson into the silver medal slot just after 39 kilometers, taking advantage of the Swede's increasing fatigue. Gorno was two minutes and 15 seconds behind Zátopek and 11 seconds ahead of Jansson. Cabrera held onto fourth, but Choi was gaining on him—would Choi catch him before the race ended? The closing 2 kilometers through the tree-shaded parkland between the Olympic Village and the stadium provided a thrill for the huge crowds lining the route. They saw Choi overtake Cabrera for fourth place. Karvonen, still in sixth, decided to use his track speed to attack Cabrera in the stadium, taking energy from his home crowd to try to finish in fifth. Table 13.1 summarizes how the top six athletes were positioned at major checkpoints through the race, and table 13.2 provides general race results.

When the Czech wearing number 903 entered the stadium, it was sudden bedlam! The knowledgeable spectators well realized that they were about to witness the most stupendous triple in Olympic distance running. Standing and applauding—70,000 cheering as one—"Zá-to-pek!"—in rhythm to his footsteps—they watched as around the stadium he went. Paavo Nurmi and Hannes Kolehmainen were chanting as well, and 63-years-old Albin Stenroos was there, too—he was the head groundsman. Just two months shy of his 30th birthday—winning his third gold medal in seven days' time—with a third Olympic record—Zátopek breasted the tape. Suddenly, and for only a brief instant, his trademark grimace of pain disappeared, and in its place appeared an almost childlike smile (figure 13.4), revealing to the world his inner joy at competing well. His 2:23:03.2 was a world best for an out-and-back course.

Later, Zátopek recalled that he could barely walk the entire next week, so stiff were his legs from the energy depletion and tissue breakdown. "But it was the most pleasant exhaustion I have ever known," he said (Wallechinsky 1996). As written in the Official Report of the British Olympic Association (Meisl 1952): "He had come through hell—and he had reached his Olympic Heaven."

In the moments that followed, the just-victorious Jamaican 4 × 400 meters sprint team members, still celebrating their own greatness, picked up Zátopek and all five took a victory lap. As Gorno, Jansson, and Choi entered, and as Karvonen happily out-sprinted Cabrera to the tape by 0.6 second, knowledgeable journalists in the crowd started to grasp the reality of what they had just witnessed.

TABLE 13.1

Order of Top Placers Through Control Points

	Zátopek	*Gorno*	*Jansson*	*Choi*	*Karvonen*	*Cabrera*
10 km	3	5	2	11	16	6
20 km	1	4	2	10	15	5
30 km	1	4	2	7	9	5
40 km	1	2	3	5	6	4

TABLE 13.2

1952 Helsinki Olympic Marathon at a Glance

Date:	27 July	**Weather:**	18.0°C (64.5°F)
Start time:	1528	**Starters:**	66
Course:	Out-and-back	**Finishers:**	53
Course distance:	42.195 km	**GPEs:**	32

TOP RESULTS:

Place	*Athlete*	*GPE*	*Date of birth*	*Time*
1	Emil Zátopek	CZE	19 Sept. 1922	2:23:03.2
2	Reinaldo Gorno	ARG	18 June 1918	2:25:35.0
3	Gustaf Jansson	SWE	05 Jan. 1922	2:26:07.0
4	Choi Yoon-chil	KOR	19 July 1928	2:26:36.0
5	Veikko Karvonen	FIN	05 Jan. 1926	2:26:41.8
6	Delfo Cabrera	ARG	12 Nov. 1919	2:26:42.4
7	Jozsef Dobronyi	HUN	17 June 1917	2:28:04.8
8	Erkki Puolakka	FIN	17 May 1925	2:29:35.0
9	Geoffrey Iden	GBR	08 Oct. 1914	2:30:42.0
10	Wallace Hayward	SOA	10 July 1908	2:31:50.2

New geopolitical entities represented: Union of Soviet Socialist Republics [URS], Guatemala [GUA], Pakistan [PAK], Federal Republic of Germany [FRG]

Team score (unofficial):			
	1. FIN	30 points	(5-8-17)
	2. SOA	40 points	(10-11-19)
	3. SWE	44 points	(3-12-29)

The facts were simply amazing. Not only did Zátopek surpass Kitei Son's Olympic marathon record set at Berlin, but places two through eight were faster as well! Britain's Geoff Iden—whose time prior to this would have made him the second fastest Olympic marathon performer behind Son—finished in a splendid 2:30:42, but he was back in ninth place. In fact, the top 15 athletes all ran personal bests. For the first time in an Olympic marathon, every finisher was home in less than three hours—53 out of 66 starters—although many were dazed and in pain from their exhausting ordeal.

Zátopek now had five Olympic medals—three from Helsinki, plus his London gold at 10,000 meters and silver at 5,000 meters. Probably the most frustrated distance runner at these Games was Algerian-born Alain Mimoun, competing for France. He had been runner-up to Zátopek in both 10,000 meters races and in the 5,000 meters race, but he didn't run the marathon. There's an adage, however, that if one watches a winner long enough, winning ways will follow. It would happen at Melbourne.

Figure 13.4 Emil Zátopek smiles in delight as he crosses the finish line for an Olympic marathon record performance. Courtesy Popperfoto.

Notes on the Medalists

Emil Zátopek was extraordinary. Born in the small village of Koprivnice in northern Moravia, the son of a poor carpenter, his greatness came in part from his dedication to hard work. Starting as a shoe factory worker, he entered the Czech army and became a career military man, eventually rising to the rank of lieutenant colonel. When he won at Helsinki, he was already the world record holder at 10,000 meters, 10 miles, 20 kilometers, and the one-hour run. Eventually he set 17 world distance records, from 5,000 through 30,000 meters. Between 1949 and 1952, he amassed an unbroken streak of 69 victories over 5,000 and 10,000 meters. He was the first to race faster than 28 minutes for 6 miles and 29 minutes for 10,000 meters. In 1956, he raced the Olympic marathon at Melbourne, equaling Cabrera's achievement of finishing sixth as the defending marathon champion. Most would agree that he and Nurmi are among the greatest long-distance runners of the 20th century. One veteran *The New York Times* sportswriter called him "the Colossus of the Roads" (Danzig 1952). His marathon career was short in quantity of races, but excellent in quality (table 13.3).

Reinaldo Gorno, born in Yapeyu, Argentina, was the runner-up to Delfo Cabrera when Cabrera won the inaugural Pan American Games marathon in 1951. Gorno also finished second to Cabrera in the 1952 South American half marathon championship. Although relegated to second place at Helsinki, behind Zátopek, Gorno finally beat Cabrera, who placed sixth. After the Helsinki Games, Gorno continued to improve, winning the 1953 South American half marathon title and then setting a South American record (2:24:55) in winning the Japanese Asahi Marathon in 1954 at Kamakura. In 1955, two months after a fifth place finish at Boston, he won at Enschede (2:26:33).

Bronze medalist **Gustaf Jansson** was born in Brattfors, in the Swedish province of Värmland, and as a marathoner he was a competitor of consistent quality. Before the Helsinki Games, he was three times the Swedish marathon champion (1951, 1952, and 1953), runner-up at Košice in 1950, and second in the 1951 Nordic championships. After Helsinki, he was again runner-up at Košice in 1954, fifth at the European championships the same year, and sixth at the 1955 Boston Marathon, just behind Gorno. His Helsinki performance, however, his seventh marathon, remained his personal best over the full distance.

TABLE 13.3

Career Marathon Record of Emil Zátopek

Date	Venue	Place	Time	Comments
27 July 1952	Helsinki	1st	2:23:03.2	Olympic Games
01 Dec. 1956	Melbourne	6th	2:29:34.0	Olympic Games

Looking Ahead: Brief Highlights 1952-1955

1953: Marathon performance times continued to be revolutionized by one man: Jim Peters. On the point-to-point "Poly" course from Windsor to Chiswick, Peters became the first runner to better 2:20:00 over a full-length course (2:18:40.2) on June 13. Three months later, he did it again at Enschede, this time for an out-and-back course record.

1954: After yet another world best performance (2:17:39.4 on June 26) on the "Poly" course, Peters suffered in the extreme heat of the British Empire Games at Vancouver on August 7, and he collapsed within sight of the finish. The race was won by an unheralded Scotsman, Joe McGhee (2:39:36). On August 25, the consistent Finnish runner Veikko Karvonen won the European title (2:24:51.6) in Berne after the leader, Ivan Filin [URS], made a wrong turn onto the finishing track.

1955: 1952 Boston winner Doroteo Flores [GUA] won the second Pan American Games marathon at Mexico City on March 19 in an altitude-slowed time of 2:59:09.2.

References

Anonymous. 1955. *The Official Report of the Organizing Committee for the Games of the XV Olympiad, Helsinki 1952.* Helsinki: Werner Soderstrom Usakeyhtio.

Corbitt, T. 1998. Personal communication.

Danzig, A. 1952. *The New York Times,* July 28.

Durantez, C. 1988. *Le flambeau Olympique.* Lausanne: International Olympic Committee.

Ecker, T. 1996. *Olympic facts and fables.* Mountain View, CA: Tafnews Press.

Meisl, W. 1952. *British Olympic Association Official Report of the Helsinki Olympic Games 1952.* London: World Sports.

Schaap, R. 1963. *An illustrated history of the Olympics.* New York: Alfred A. Knopf.

Wallechinsky, D. 1996. *The complete book of the Summer Olympics.* 1996 edition. New York: Little, Brown & Company.

Chapter 14

1956—Melbourne

Mimoun the Best of a Modest Field

Games Preparations Proceed Despite a World in Turmoil

The Olympic Games moved from one sport-loving nation to another in proceeding from Helsinki to Melbourne. Both nations were small in population but rich in resources, and each did an admirable job at staging a successful Games. Melbourne, the capital of Victoria (the smallest mainland state of Australia), staged the first Southern Hemisphere Summer Olympic Games for those "down under," which meant the winter months for those "up top." Until now, the Games had never been held even south of the Tropic of Cancer. The fact that 67 geopolitical entities brought teams to Melbourne, only 2 fewer than at Helsinki, despite journeys of more than 7,000 miles (11,300 kilometers) for many of the nations' top-level athletes, attested to the global importance of the Olympic movement. Total athlete numbers were down, however, due probably to the travel expense.

Many frustrations occurred in the years leading up to the Melbourne Games, however, as internal bickering and power struggles resulted in preparation delays. Eventually, IOC president Avery Brundage made a personal inspection trip and commented that Rome was farther ahead in its preparations for the 1960 Games than Melbourne was for its own. Stung with the specter of world embarrassment, this public note of concern was the needed catalyst for forward progress. The Games were marvelous.

For only the second time in modern Olympic history, a new stadium was not constructed for the Games (in 1948 London's Empire Stadium was refurbished). Instead, the mammoth (103,000 capacity) sports palace called the Melbourne Cricket Ground, or simply the MCG, was deemed adequate (Anonymous 1958). However, the wonderfully manicured green turf within the arena was revered as almost hallowed ground to local sports people who played cricket on it in the summer and Australian-rules football in the winter. Deference to these sporting events prevented construction of the seven-lanes, 400 meters cinder track until only a few weeks prior to the Games.

Another dilemma involved the Australian government's absolute refusal to lift a mandatory six-months quarantine requirement for horses brought in for the equestrian competition. The matter never was resolved, and so, for the only time during this first Olympic century, the Summer Games had venues in two different nations. The equestrian events were contested in Stockholm during its summertime. This was against even the IOC's own rules, which stated that all the events of an Olympic Games must be staged in a single host country. The two venues have caused some confusion in the reported numbers of athlete participants. At Melbourne there were 3,184 (2,813 men, 371 women), while at Stockholm there were 158 (145 men, 13 women).

Transporting the Olympic flame again had its share of intricacies. After the usual ceremonies at Olympia and a relay involving 340 couriers that finally reached the ancient Acropolis, the flame was transferred to a miner's lantern for the transoceanic flight. Stopping en route at Calcutta, Bangkok, Singapore, Jakarta, and then Darwin, the lantern was transferred to a military jet, which sped the flame 909 miles across Australia to Cairns, on its northeast coast (Durantez 1988). Then the relay journey continued on foot for 2,782 miles (4,476 kilometers) through Australia, requiring 3,118 couriers. The total trip was the longest for the flame up to that time. From ignition on November 2 to its arrival at the MCG on November 22, newspaper coverage of its movement predictably united Australia in sporting enthusiasm, and the Opening Ceremonies were awaited eagerly. The stadium erupted in applause when Australia's 19-years-old mile sensation Ron Clarke entered and carried the torch the last quarter-mile. Clarke had failed to make his Olympic team, but his athletic prowess before and after the Games made him a fitting man for the honor. He later competed as an Olympian at Tokyo in the 10,000 meters run and the marathon. Following the pattern set by Zátopek, he was the first to run faster than 27 minutes for six miles, and the first faster than 28 minutes for 10,000 meters.

Construction of the Olympic Village was also managed successfully. Athletes from both East and West blocs lived together and mingled freely, and the 841 nicely landscaped houses alleviated a housing shortage in the Melbourne area following the Games. Even superlong beds were provided for the tall athletes in sports such as basketball.

Opening Ceremonies were scheduled for Thursday, November 22, the American Thanksgiving Day, starting at 1030 (10:30 a.m.). As a special treat to the American athletes, traditional baked turkey dinners had been served to help them feel at home. So vast were the time zone differences, however, that those in New York interested in listening live on radio to the festivities had to tune in on Wednesday evening, November 21 at 1930 (7:30 p.m.). In sport-crazed Australia, 50,000 people camped out around the stadium overnight in hopes of getting standing-room tickets for the already sold-out stadium. Most, of course, remained outside, listening to the pomp and Olympic splendor occurring inside.

Once again, the politics of worldwide turmoil, springing up like wildfires around the globe, impacted noticeably on the Olympic Games as nations used sport to vent their political frustrations. On October 29 Israel invaded the Gaza Strip of Egypt, with the help of Britain and France, in a dispute over the Suez Canal. Egypt, Iraq, and Lebanon withdrew from the Olympic Games in protest, and Israel sent only a token representation.

One week later, on November 4, Soviet tanks entered Budapest to quash a Hungarian nationalist bid for independence. After nearly two weeks of fighting, with Hungarians throwing rocks against an onslaught of tanks, thousands were dead and the rebellion was crushed. Some of the Hungarian team had already left for Melbourne on the Soviet steamer *Gruzia.* The rest were eventually flown to Melbourne, but after the Olympic Games 45 members of the team sought asylum in the West. To protest the Soviets' invasion of Hungary, Switzerland, Spain, and the Netherlands boycotted the Games.

As if that was not enough, there was the Chinese problem. The IOC had invited both communist (mainland) China and nationalist China (Taiwan) to the Olympic Games. Communist China accepted, but then nationalist China declined. Shortly thereafter, nationalist China changed its mind and accepted its invitation, prompting communist China to withdraw. Nationalist China's team did appear, but at the traditional welcoming ceremony in the Olympic Village, officials raised the communist flag by mistake. Before they could correct the oversight, delegation members tore the flag from its pole.

Through it all, IOC president Brundage held strongly to his determination that the Olympic Games must go on despite all these varied political intrusions. And they did, showing that the splendor of the Olympic Games soars above worldly squabbles and local toiling over details. On a positive note, the IOC convinced the two parts of Germany, East and West, to enter a combined team. This recurred in 1960 and 1964. The grandest of many firsts at these Olympic Games came during the Closing Ceremonies. Athletes did not march in according to their geopolitical affiliation but instead entered all together as people unified in their love of sport despite a politically divided world (Anonymous 1958). "A wave of emotion swept over the crowd, the Olympic flame was engulfed in it and died, and (then) a great silence. This, more than any remembered laurel of the Games—was something no one had ever experienced before—not anywhere in the world, not anywhere in time."

Marathoners Selected to Compete "Down Under"

With most of the world's top marathon runners living in the Northern Hemisphere, it was a challenge to prepare optimally. Most major marathons were in the April-to-June time frame, with few races scheduled during the Northern Hemisphere summer months from June to September. Thus, athletes selected early in the year had to design a plan for achieving their supreme competitive peak in early December.

Japan

No top-level Japanese runners traveled to Boston in 1956 because races in their homeland were earmarked as Olympic selection events. Kurao Hiroshima performed well during 1955, and he continued to do so into the 1956 Olympic year. At the Beppu Marathon on February 12, he won a 62 seconds victory (2:26:24) over Katsuo Nishida. On May 6 in Osaka, at the Mainichi Marathon, Yoshiaki Kawashima achieved a personal best 2:27:45, more than five minutes ahead of runner-up Toyohichi Nakata. Hideo Hamamura was third, 23 seconds behind. Hiroshima and Kawashima were selected to the team, and Hamamura was selected over Nakata, in part because Hamamura had also set a national 20 kilometers record in February.

United States

The Boston Marathon on April 19 was a primary selection race, but this year the AAU championship at Yonkers moved from its usual May date to September 30. This provided a nice option for selecting an Olympic team poised to perform well in December. Deciding the best athletes to represent the United States developed as a simple task. Although another fleet Finn, Antti Viskari, caught John J. Kelley in the Newton hills and set a new Boston course record of 2:14:14 over the still-short course, Kelley was only 19 seconds behind. The real duel occurred a few minutes back, with Eino Oksanen (2:17:56) beating schoolteacher Nick Costes by 5 seconds. The next two Americans were Dean Thackwray and Helsinki Olympian Ted Corbitt.

At the fall Yonkers race, it was Kelley, Thackwray, and Costes again, finishing in that order, with Corbitt in sixth, making team selection rather obvious. Kelley was in especially fine form, setting a new record (2:24:52.2) for this difficult course. After being such a powerhouse in these pre-Olympic marathons, hopes were high among Americans that "Johnny the Younger" would win a medal.

Europe

Britain selected its marathon team early, allowing all of its athletes greater individual freedom for balancing recovery and the necessary preparation to perform well in December. The annual "Poly" was the primary selection race, held on June 16. Ron Clark, one of the Herne Hill Harriers (and not to be confused with Australia's track star Ron Clarke!), outlasted Fred Norris from the Bolton Harriers on a cold, raw, wet day. His winning time of 2:20:15.8 was the fastest by a British runner since the days of Jim Peters's top form. Norris also ran well (2:21:48.6), with Arthur Keily third in 2:22:37.2. Finishing with a time equal to Keily was Harry Hicks, who almost caught Keily at the tape.

Determined to achieve team selection, Hicks traveled to Port Sunlight for the British AAA championship on July 28 and performed very well. He won with a good time (2:26:15) ahead of Olympian Stan Cox (2:27:17), and the selectors logically put Hicks on the team, along with Clark and Norris. Hicks had plenty of time to recover, and Keily had little choice but to aim for the next Olympics.

Soviet marathon runners continued to become more visible, both in performance and numbers. Ivan Filin had unfortunately missed the European championship title at Berne in 1954 (he led into the stadium and then went the wrong way), but he took the Soviet marathon championship at Moscow on July 10, 1955 with a record 2:23:09.6. In 1956, the Soviets delayed their trial race to August 12, and Filin won again (2:20:05.2) with another national record. Behind him was Albert Ivanov (2:21:52). These two were selected to run at Melbourne, along with Boris Grishayev, an experienced marathoner who had finished second to Filin at the 1955 championship.

On the same August day as the Soviet trial, the 16th Finnish national championship in Pieksamaki also served as that country's Olympic trial. The day was cool and overcast, with no wind, and the course was a combination of macadam and packed dirt through forested terrain. Finland's elite marathoners raced themselves into history. Whereas only four sub-2:20:00 performances had been delivered during the past three years (by one man—Jim Peters), now Finland delivered four in one day. It was Paavo Kotila who won (2:18:04.8), with the second fastest time in history, an out-and-back world best. His 10 kilometers splits were like a Swiss clock: 33:10, 33:41, 33:05, and 32:32, indicating his good choice of pace as well as a flat course. The next two athletes also were selected to the Olympic team: Eino Oksanen (2:18:51) and Veikko Karvonen (2:18:56.4). In fourth was the unfortunate Eino Pulkkinen (2:19:27), who had to stay home because only three composed a team. A course remeasurement showed an accurate distance. The big question was whether these athletes could keep their fitness until December.

The annual marathon at Košice, traditionally held near the first weekend of October, provided a perfect opportunity for those Europeans who preferred a selection opportunity closer to the December Olympic Games. On a flat course extending out-and-back between Košice and Sena, and with favorable weather, it was a day for speed as 17 runners from all over Europe finished within 2:30. The Swedish star Thomas Nilsson set both a national and a course record with his winning time of 2:22:05.4. In second place was Finland's Olavi Manninen, whose 2:22:09 was similar to his fifth place 2:22:33.8 at Pieksamaki. Karl Hartung (2:23:06), of the German Democratic Republic, narrowly beat Czechoslovakia's Pavel Kantorek by nine seconds for third place. All of these athletes except Manninen were chosen by their respective nations for Melbourne.

Australia

Because Australian athletes rarely got the chance to travel abroad for marathons, neither foreign journalists nor coaches had much of an idea regarding whether Australian marathoners would perform well against the rest of the world. The focus of attention was primarily on Keith Ollerenshaw, of Welsh ancestry, who lived in New South Wales. On September 24, 1955, he had run 2:22:17 for a new national record. Then, in the Australian winter of 1956, on August 4, he bettered his own record (2:22:12), two minutes and 16 seconds ahead of Bruce McKay and John Russell. On September 8, the Australian Olympic trial race was staged in Melbourne. Although Ollerenshaw led through 15 miles, on this day it was Russell's moment to shine, and he won the trial (2:26:37.8) by nearly a minute. These two became the national favorites for the Australian spectators to cheer as the Olympic Games marathon began.

A Painted Line Points the Way

The Melbourne Olympic course was out-and-back, as at Helsinki, and was oriented northwest-southeast. Passing through the suburbs of St. Kilda, Malvern, Caulfield, Carnegie, Murrumbeena, Oakleigh, East Oakleigh, and then Clayton, this population corridor provided a splendid setting. Spectators sat on their lawns under trees to remain in the shade, organized afternoon cheering parties, and enjoyed the excitement of both the outward and return portions of the competition. Parts of the route had been used often before for race-walking and road-racing events of varying distances. It was a smooth bituminous surface (i.e., asphalt), well kept, and thus ideal for racing.

The Melbourne Cricket Ground was a circular stadium, and its track was a temporary installation that could have been configured in any orientation. The arrangement that was chosen was with the long axis of the track in northeast-southwest orientation, which conveniently placed the stadium finish line directly in front of the grandstand reserved for MCG season ticket holders. Athletes thus ran toward the southeast, but because winds in this area are primarily from the south, virtually all the races were run into headwinds. The track had the shortest life span in any Olympic stadium. It could not be installed until after the Australian-rules football grand final in September. Immediately following the Olympic Games, it was dismantled and its cinders were relaid on one of the suburban running tracks.

In the stadium, the marathon start was the same as that used for the 50 kilometers walk and for the 80 meters hurdles. This was 20 meters in front of the start point of the 100 meters races. Athletes then ran two and one-half laps (~980 meters) counterclockwise, departing by the service tunnel adjacent to the 1,500 meters start line. Upon leaving the stadium, as athletes turned left onto Brunton Avenue, they had no need for officials to point them in the correct direction, because they could "follow the green line." See Olympic Marathon Miscellany 14.1.

The stadium track was eight meters (26 feet) above sea level, and the course

Olympic Marathon Miscellany 14.1

A Painted Line Points the Way

For the first time in an Olympic marathon, painted on the street was a green broken line indicating the entire route. In 1904, periodic red flags had been placed along the course. At London in 1908, there were the so-called distance tablets at each mile. But never had a painted line been used.

The man most responsible for the Melbourne green line was Alf Robinson, then president of the Victoria Walkers Club and part of the organizing committee (later a member of the Australian Olympic Committee). Green and gold were the "Aussie colors," but gold (or yellow) was already used in highway markings, so the logical choice was green. Robinson was known for his meticulous attention to detail. He used a police crayon to indicate the route location and then used a specially made paint applicator pulled behind a vehicle to make a broken line, each segment being one foot long and two inches wide, and separated by 10 yards. This was no ordinary paint; it was still visible in certain places 30 years later (Keane 1999).

gradually rose in elevation until its midpoint (figure 14.1). Although there were many small undulations, two significant uphill segments existed. One occurred between 8 and 10.5 kilometers (5 and 6.5 miles)—a rise of 36 meters over 2.5 kilometers (118 feet over 1.6 miles). The other was between 16.5 and 20.5 kilometers (10.3 and 12.7 miles)—a rise of 49 meters over 4 kilometers (161 feet over 2.5 miles). These rises became descents on the return trip, making the outbound portion of the course significantly more difficult. It was also covered during the hottest part of the afternoon. Thus, the best competitive strategy for athletes was to run within themselves on the outbound portion, saving some energy for a quick second half.

The course details box provides details of the marathon route. Present-day road reconstruction has converted the Dandenong Road-Normanby Road-Dandenong Road segment (between 10 and 15 kilometers) into a major thoroughfare called Princes Highway, which continues farther using the same routing as Dandenong Road to the turnaround. East Oakleigh is now known as Huntingdale, and the region at the turnaround point is known locally as Clayton North. The macadam paving is also much better than existed 40-plus years ago. The majority of the Melbourne course is still accessible for those interested in touring it. A turnaround marker was dedicated in November 1999.

Mimoun Finally Beats Zátopek

At 1513 (3:13 p.m.) on December 1, 1956, the 46 starters from 23 geopolitical entities lined up on the track before a crowd of 100,000 to watch the usual

Course Details

The 1956 Melbourne Olympic Marathon

Start at 20 meters in front of 100 meters start line

Run counterclockwise around the track two and one-half laps (~980 meters)

Exit through service tunnel near 1,500 meters start line (southeast side of stadium) onto Brunton Avenue to Punt Road

Right onto Punt Road to Boulton Parade (exit and entrance) for Batman Avenue

Right onto Boulton Parade to Batman Avenue

Continue on Batman Avenue along Yarra River to Swan Street Bridge

Cross Yarra River on Swan Street Bridge

Half right onto Alexandra Avenue to Linlithgow Avenue

Circle left onto Linlithgow Avenue, continuing around through Kings Domain to intersection with Government House Drive

Continue straight through the intersection onto Anzac Avenue to St. Kilda Road

Half left onto St. Kilda Road to St. Kilda Junction (3.8 kilometers)

Half left onto Wellington Street

Wellington Street becomes Dandenong Road after crossing railway bridge (8.6 kilometers)

Continue on Dandenong Road to Normanby Road (12.2 kilometers)

Half right onto Normanby Road to Queens Road (14 kilometers)

Left onto Queens Road to Railway Avenue (14.2 kilometers)

Right onto Railway Avenue to Dandenong Road (14.5 kilometers)

Right onto Dandenong Road to turnaround just past intersection with Surrey Street (21.43 kilometers)

Turn around clockwise, returning on Dandenong Road using the opposite side of the street (the left side) to Railway Avenue (28.5 kilometers)

Half left onto Railway Avenue to Queens Avenue

Left onto Queens Avenue to Normanby Road (28.9 kilometers)

Right onto Normanby Road to Dandenong Road (30.5 kilometers)

Half left onto Dandenong Road

Dandenong Road becomes Wellington Street (34 kilometers)

Continue on Wellington Street to St. Kilda Junction (35 kilometers)

Half right onto St. Kilda Road to Anzac Avenue (38.5 kilometers)

Anzac Avenue to intersection with Government House Drive

Continue through intersection onto Linlithgow Avenue

Circle Right on Linlithgow Avenue around Kings Domain to Alexandra Avenue

Half right onto Alexandra Avenue to Swan Street Bridge

Half left across Yarra River on Swan Street Bridge

Half right onto Batman Drive to Boulton Parade

Half left onto Boulton Parade to Punt Road

Left onto Punt Road to Brunton Avenue

Left onto Brunton Avenue to stadium access tunnel entrance

Right at stadium access tunnel and onto the track

Right along the back straightaway and three-quarters lap around

Finish at track event finish line

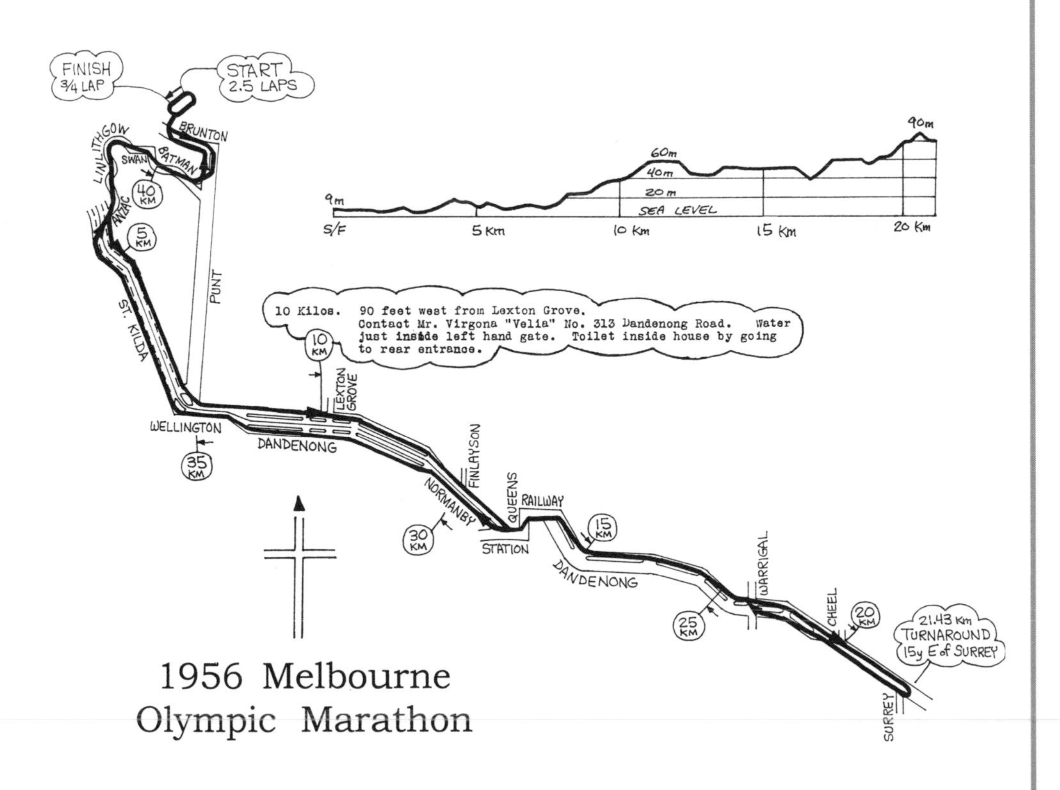

Figure 14.1 Sketch of the Melbourne Olympic marathon course. Note the interesting information provided on the Organizing Committee's map at the 10 kilometers point regarding the availability of water and toilet facilities. Prepared by Bob Letson.

action-packed final day of track and field finals. It was a hot (27°C or 80°F), sunny, summery Saturday afternoon. Despite the long travel distance, Europeans (22 from 11 nations—five full teams) dominated the field. But Asia had five nations, with Japan and Korea fielding full teams. From the Americas, only the United States and Chile sent athletes. From Oceania, although both Australia and New Zealand were represented, only Australia fielded a team. African participation was of considerable interest. In addition to the usually expected South African entries, appearing for the first time were runners from Ethiopia and Kenya.

Not only was the outcome unpredictable—the race was full of the unexpected. A unique event in this first century of Olympic marathoning occurred as the runners toed the line. Colonel Stewart Embling was the starter—an experienced coach as well as an official. In the opinion of several overeager competitors, he waited a little too long before firing his starter's pistol, because a false start occurred. This was the only one in Olympic marathon history and perhaps the only one in any marathon. No specific athletes were charged formally, so they all reassembled, and the second start went without incident. After two track circuits (figure 14.2), runners exited the stadium onto Brunton Avenue and followed the painted green line along the pavement. A diverse duo shared the lead: Finland's experienced Paavo Kotila and Kenya's debuting Arap Sum Kanuti. Just behind followed an equally diverse group: Australian Les Perry; Kurt Hartung, running for the combined German team; the new Italian champion Rino Lavelli; and the unknown Ethiopian Gebru Birkay.

By 10 kilometers, in the midst of the first long uphill from 8 to 10.5 kilometers (5 to 6.5 miles), the lead group was again a mixture of experts and new faces, all hoping that they had selected a pace they could maintain during this very warm afternoon. Kotila was ahead (33:30), but only by 2 seconds, just ahead of Alain Mimoun and two Soviet runners, including Ivan Filin. Another 2 seconds behind was the trio of Bert Norris, Veikko Karvonen, and Kanuti, and then another trio 1 second behind (the Balkan Games marathon winner Franjo Mihalic, Eino Oksanen, and Les Perry). Of this lead group of 10, only half were world-ranked marathoners: Filin, Kotila, Karvonen, Norris, and Oksanen. Emil Zátopek was 17 seconds behind the leader, running his final marathon. Race day was a few months too early for him to reach top form, having not recovered fully from a hernia operation.

At 15 kilometers, Mimoun appeared just in front of Filin, but the scorers gave them the same time (50:37), along with America's John J. Kelley. However, these were but part of a 4 seconds time oval of runners, with Kotila alongside Norris (50:38), and Mihalic, Ivanov, and Johan Nyberg 1 second behind. Zátopek was still in 11th place (50:42), beside Oksanen.

After a short downhill at 16.5 kilometers, the route then commenced to climb 49 meters over the next 3.5 kilometers (161 feet over the next 2.4 miles). This caused the entire field to string out along the sun-swept, seemingly never-ending Dandenong Road toward the turnaround in suburban Clayton. This lead group tried hard to stay in contact with each other, however, and by 20 kilometers (1:08:03) six were together as one—Mimoun, Mihalic, Karvonen, Kelley,

Figure 14.2 After one circuit of the track, in front of a full stadium in Melbourne, the marathon field is already strung out. Courtesy of IOC/Olympic Museum Collection. Photo: Olympic Photo Association.

and two of the Soviet team, Filin and Ivanov. Zátopek was in 10th and Oksanen was in 12th; both were close enough to see the leaders but did not want to risk problems by quickening their pace to catch up.

Almost as if it was planned, near the crest of this long hill Mimoun surged and broke contact. Surprising everyone, he dashed around the turn point and took advantage of the downhill portion in front of him to gain even more distance. By 25 kilometers, having completed the descent, Mimoun was 50 seconds ahead of Mihalic and Karvonen, who were racing together. Behind these two, it was single file. Japan's Kawashima, however, moved from 14th at 20 kilometers to 4th. His 5 kilometers split of 16:38 was only bettered by Mimoun's 16:32 for that net downhill segment. Nyberg and Zátopek had now moved into 5th and 6th, ahead of the two Soviets. Kelley and Kotila were running together in 9th and 10th. Kelley's teammate, Dean Thackwray, had dropped from the race. Many others would also wilt due to the heat.

The dark-skinned Mimoun, wearing a kerchief over his head as protection from the sun—reminiscent of Zabala at Los Angeles—continued to push the pace, passing 30 kilometers in 1:41:47. Kawashima was now sharing 2nd place with Mihalic and Karvonen, although still 72 seconds behind Mimoun. Zátopek had taken the 5th spot away from Nyberg, who had also been passed by Filin. Another Asian, Korea's Lee Chang-hoon, delivered a fast 5 kilometers split on this relatively level portion, bringing him from 18th to 8th. In the heat, this was a risky maneuver; nine athletes had already dropped out.

Between 30 and 35 kilometers (18.6 and 21.8 miles), the course descended another 36 meters (118 feet), and Mimoun seemed well in control at the front. He passed 35 kilometers in 1:59:34, 76 seconds ahead of Mihalic, who had moved ahead of Karvonen by 8 seconds. Kawashima was now in fourth (2:01:36), 20 seconds ahead of Zátopek, with Lee in sixth.

At 40 kilometers Mimoun was timed in 2:17:30, and Mihalic had gained only 2 seconds on him (2:18:44). Karvonen appeared destined for third place, 53 seconds behind, leading Kawashima by 62 seconds. But Lee was still gaining on this group, moving now into fifth place, relegating Zátopek to sixth.

In the final 2 kilometers Mimoun extended his lead to 92 seconds, entering the stadium to a huge roar of approval. The crowd was witnessing an almost unimaginable third debut Olympic marathon victory in as many Games. Wearing number 13 on his bib, this was indeed Mimoun's lucky day. Franjo Mihalic was the next to enter, 75 seconds ahead of bronze medalist Veikko Karvonen. Lee continued to press the pace, overtaking Kawashima for fouth. Zátopek remained in sixth, and as he entered, the cheers of the crowd were so loud it was if he had won. Mimoun shooed away the photographers and officials as they approached him, and he jogged over to give Zátopek congratulations. It was an emotional high point of the Games as the two engaged in an extended embrace as sportsmen. For the first time, Mimoun had beaten him. It was a poignant end to their many-year rivalry, as they never competed against each other again. Later, while he was resting on the infield, bundled in blankets to keep warm as he waited for the medal ceremony, a rare photograph caught Mimoun in a moment of quiet reflection (figure 14.3).

Table 14.1 provides a summary of how the top six athletes performed during the race. Just as amazing as the surprise winner was the overall excellent performance of Scandinavian athletes in these warm conditions. In the unofficial marathon team standings, Finland was first (26 points) and Sweden second (28 points), as indicated in the synopsis of the race (table 14.2).

Notes on the Medalists

Alain Mimoun, born in Telagh, Algeria, joined El Ouafi and Théato as gold medalists wearing the French "tricolor." Continuing the trend, none of these athletes were born in France, Mimoun and El Ouafi coming from the African continent, and Théato from Luxembourg. Mimoun came to Melbourne with the specific assignment of racing the 10,000 meters event, which had only a final on November 23. His performance was utterly dismal—he finished 12th and he was even lapped in the process. Before the race, in the back of his mind he had considered running the marathon, but had mentioned it to no one. To help overcome his track disappointment, he decided indeed to enter the marathon, which was held eight days after the 10,000 meters race. The evening before the

Figure 14.3 Olympic champion Alain Mimoun savoring the delight of victory on the infield following his race in Melbourne. Courtesy Corbis/Bettman-UPI.

TABLE 14.1

Order of Top Placers Through Control Points

	Mimoun	*Mihalic*	*Karvonen*	*Lee*	*Kawashima*	*Zátopek*
10 km	=2-4	=8-10	=5-7	14	36	12
15 km	1	6	9	21	31	11
20 km	=1-6	=1-6	=1-6	19	14	10
25 km	1	=2, 3	=2, 3	18	4	6
30 km	1	=2-4	=2-4	8	=2-4	5
35 km	1	2	3	6	4	5
40 km	1	2	3	5	4	6
Finish	1	2	3	4	5	6

marathon, Mimoun got word that his wife had delivered their child, but an *s* was erroneously affixed to *enfant* on the written message. Mimoun ran the marathon wondering all the while how he would manage the financial demands of supporting twins! Only after the race did he learn that indeed he had only one child, not two.

TABLE 14.2

1956 Melbourne Olympic Marathon at a Glance

Date:	01 December	**Weather:**	27°C (80°F)
Start time:	1515	**Starters:**	46
Course:	Out-and-back	**Finishers:**	33
Course distance:	42.195 km	**GPEs:**	23

TOP RESULTS:

Place	*Athlete*	*GPE*	*Date of birth*	*Time*
1	Alain Mimoun	FRA	01 Jan. 1921	2:25:00
2	Franjo Mihalic	YUG	09 Mar. 1920	2:26:32
3	Veikko Karvonen	FIN	05 Jan. 1926	2:27:47
4	Lee Chang-Hoon	KOR	21 Mar. 1935	2:28:45
5	Yoshiaki Kawashima	JPN	10 May 1934	2:29:19
6	Emil Zátopek	TCH	19 Sept. 1922	2:29:34
7	Ivan Filin	URS	10 Mar. 1926	2:30:37
8	Evert Nyberg	SWE	28 Feb. 1925	2:31:12
9	Thomas Nilsson	SWE	09 Apr. 1926	2:33:33
10	Eino Oksanen	FIN	07 May 1931	2:36:10

New geopolitical entities represented: Burma [BIR], Ethiopia [ETH], Iran [IRN], Kenya [KEN], New Zealand [NZL], German Democratic Republic [GDR]

Team score (unofficial):			
	1. FIN	26 points	(3-10-13)
	2. SWE	28 points	(8-9-11)
	3. JPN	54 points	(5-16-33)

Achieved at the age of 35 years, his victory launched an excellent career at the marathon following his superb record at shorter-distance racing. In addition to the three silver medals he won when competing against Zátopek on the track in two Olympics, he had finished second to Zátopek two other times, during the 1950 European championships in the 5,000 and 10,000 meters races. He won 26 French titles in everything from cross country to 5,000 and 10,000 meters on the track. He also set national records in these two track distances, as well as at 20,000 and 25,000 meters, and one-hour runs also on the track. He was an excellent cross country runner, having won the International Cross Country Championships four times (including 1956).

When he retired at 45 years of age, he had won six national championships. He did not finish the 1958 European championships marathon and was a distant 34th in the Rome Olympics. His marathon personal best was his first national championship win in 1959 (2:33:41) over a short course of about 41.7 kilometers, although he may have averaged a faster pace at a race in 1958 over about 43 kilometers (2:25:29.3). Mimoun's career international championship results are listed in table 14.3.

TABLE 14.3

Career Marathon Record of Alain Mimoun

Date	Venue	Place	Time	Comments
01 Dec. 1956	Melbourne	1st	2:25:00	Olympic Games
24 Aug. 1958	Stockholm	DNF		European championships
10 Sept. 1960	Rome	34th	2:31:20	Olympic Games

Franjo Mihalic, born in Ludina, Yugoslavia, was unheralded back home, for he never won a national marathon championship, and he only once won the Balkan Games title (1956). He became a shining star around the world, however, with impressive international marathon victories over excellent fields of athletes at Athens (1957), Moscow (1957), and Boston (1958). Later in 1958 he placed 3rd at Japan's prestigious Asahi international marathon. At 36 years of age, his Melbourne performance was the pinnacle of his career in terms of quality, although his personal best was a 2:21:23.4 at Moscow on August 4, 1958. He failed to finish the next two European championship marathons, in 1958 and 1962. He did compete in the Rome Olympic marathon, placing 12th.

Veikko Karvonen, born in Sakkola, Finland, was "Mr. Consistency" during his prime racing years, having been ranked number one in the world for the marathon by coauthor Roger Gynn for *Track & Field News* magazine in 1951, 1954, and 1955. Karvonen had sustained a leg injury just before the 1952 Olympics, yet still finished fifth. Between 1949 and 1959 he won 14 of the 34 marathons he started. These included the 1954 European Championship, three Nordic titles (1951, 1953, 1955), and two national championships (1951, 1954). He also won the four top-level marathons of the world at that time at least once: Enschede (1951), Boston (1954), and Athens and Fukuoka (both in 1955). His best time came at 30 years of age during the summer of 1956, almost four months before the Games at Melbourne, when he ran 2:18:56.4 at Pieksamaki, Finland on August 12.

Looking Ahead: Brief Highlights 1957-1959

1957: John J. Kelley became the first American winner at Boston since John A. Kelley in 1945. His time was 2:20:05, a record for the finally full-length course. He went on to win eight consecutive AAU titles at Yonkers between 1956 and 1963.

(continued)

1958: Lee Chang-hoon [KOR] won the Asian Games marathon race at Tokyo on May 27 in 2:32:55.2. Dave Power [AUS] won the Empire and Commonwealth Games at Cardiff on July 24 in 2:22:45.6. Sergey Popov [URS] won the European championship marathon at Stockholm on August 24 in a world record 2:15:17. (He was born in the Asian Russian city of Irkutsk.)

1959: After failing to finish in 1955, John J. Kelley succeeded in taking the Pan American Games title at Chicago on September 2 (2:27:54.2), ahead of countryman Jim Green. Sergey Popov became the first to break 2:20:00 at Košice, Czechoslovakia, on October 11 (2:17:45.2).

References

Anonymous. 1958. *The Official Report of the Organizing Committee for the Games of the XVI Olympiad, Melbourne 1956*. Melbourne: W.M. Houston, Govt. Printer.

Durantez, C. 1988. *Le flambeau Olympique*. Lausanne: International Olympic Committee.

Keane, D. 1999. Personal communication.

CHAPTER 15

1960—ROME

Barefoot Bikila Has a Roman Heyday

Ancient Traditions Link With Modern Celebration

With only five years to prepare, the Rome Olympic Games still developed into one of the most successful sports gatherings in history. The setting could not have been more historic. Dating back to the fifth century B.C., Rome was nearly as old as the ancient Greek Games themselves, and even some of its aged sports venues were used for competition. Wrestling, for example, was contested in the 1,650-years-old Basilica of Maxentius in the Roman Forum. Ironically, however, it had been the Roman emperor Theodosius who issued the edict in A.D. 393 to abolish the ancient Greek Olympic Games (Ecker 1996). How times change!

Just northwest of the Rome city center, where the Tiber River makes a large crescent in its meandering toward the sea, an immense Olympic Games environment was constructed. On the east side of the river several stadia were built, as well as the Olympic Village. Just west of the river was the new 65,000-capacity Olympic stadium, with its magnificent warm-up track alongside. Flanked by 46 marble statues, nestled in a grove of evergreens, connected to the main stadium by a tunnel . . . if this practice venue—called the Stadio del Marmi—did not get athletes inspired to compete, nothing would! Actually, the Stadio del Marmi was built two decades earlier as part of Benito Mussolini's developing dream of bringing the Olympic Games to Rome. The Games arrived a bit late but under more favorable political circumstances.

For the first time, the total number of athletes topped 5,000—4,738 men and 610 women. As usual, some names will always be well remembered. A young boxer of only 18 years won a gold medal. Then called Cassius Clay, he later became Muhammad Ali and would figure in the 1996 Atlanta Games. Among the women, a 20-years-old Tennessee girl from a family of 19 children—a person who could not walk until she was seven years old—won the gold medal at 100 and 200 meters. This was Wilma Rudolph. Tallying the number of nations participating became a challenge because of an 800 meters runner, Wim Essayas, Surinam's only competitor. Unaware of a schedule change, he missed his heat, so never competed. Thus, although 84 geopolitical entities had marchers in the Opening Ceremonies out of a possible 95 who were officially affiliated as NOCs, only 83 were represented in competition.

The Rome Games were unique in many ways. Never before had so many NOCs sent athletes to compete. The unprecedented crowds, estimated at more than one million spectators, enjoyed the festivities due to the popularity of the Games in Italy and in the rest of surrounding Europe. For the first time, television contracts were negotiated for the rights to broadcast the Games. Columbia Broadcasting System (CBS) in the United States paid $394,000 for the telecasting rights. (Compare this to the $456 million that the National Broadcasting Corporation (NBC) paid to broadcast the 1996 Atlanta Games!)

Normally, track and field events are contested early in the Games period, with cycling toward the end. The Italians were superb at cycling, however, and the schedule was reversed to put cycling early. The idea was to heighten public awareness of the Olympic Games and thus increase ticket sales. Not only did the Italian fans arrive in droves to watch, but Italy won both gold medals during the first day of cycling. Sadness followed, however, with the death of 23-years-old Knud Enemark Jensen of Denmark in the 100 kilometers team race. Although the initial cause of death was given as a heatstroke-induced brain hemorrhage, later investigation revealed that he was the Olympic Games' first known death due to a performance-enhancing agent. He had been injected with nicotinyl alcohol for the purpose of enhancing skeletal muscle blood flow (Ryan 1968).

Although the pressure to win was suddenly seen as becoming even death-defying, a partial "thaw" of the Cold War reduced the obsession among journalists and the sporting world to focus solely on comparing medal totals by the United States and the Soviet Union. During the late 1950s, especially with track and field, competitions between these two nations had occurred in each country, and a friendlier rivalry had developed. This improving tone allowed medalists from other nations to gain deserved attention instead of being ignored. Indeed, athletes from smaller nations won more medals than ever before, showing the global growth and success of sport training programs.

At the Closing Ceremonies the intermingling of athletes, which at Melbourne had caused such a positive emotional high for both spectators and athletes, did not occur. In fact, only the flag bearers entered the stadium, with athletes and spectators watching from their seats. The usual traditions of lowering the Olympic flag, extinguishing the flame, and transferring responsibilities to the next host city were all memorable. For the first time, the embroidered "Antwerp flag," presented in 1922 to the IOC as a gift intended to be transferred from venue to venue, was given by the mayor of Rome to the mayor of Tokyo through the hands of the IOC president as part of the ceremonies. Previously, this had been done at private IOC meetings. Then came the fireworks, which provided unexpected excitement as falling embers set fires ablaze in the surrounding forest. Although the Olympic extravaganza was declared an overall success, the Games nevertheless are all about athletes coming together. So moving had been the spectacle of athletes happily intermingling at Melbourne's Closing Ceremonies that it was decided to make this an integral part of succeeding festivities.

Global Preparations by Marathoners Focus on Rome

The Rome Olympic marathon was scheduled for September 10. Because most of the major world marathons occurred during the first eight months of the year, they conveniently served as events from which Olympic team members were identified. There were a few late-year exceptions, however, but for those, the 1959 editions served as selection events.

In this latter category, three 1959 races were noteworthy: Košice (Czechoslovakia), Athens, and Fukuoka. At Košice on October 11, British, Argentine, and Soviet athletes all competed, and the weather was excellent for good racing. Sergey Popov was on world record pace by the halfway point of this out-and-back course. He could not maintain this pace, but his winning time of 2:17:45.2 had only been bettered once on an out-and-back course—by himself, on August 24, 1958, in Stockholm. Britain's Dennis O'Gorman, who had won the June "Poly" from Arthur Keily, was runner-up (2:23:08), with Popov's countryman Ivan Filin third in 2:23:55.4.

The Finns opted to run in Athens on October 26, which brought together an even more diverse international field. Athletes came from Australia and New Zealand, from Korea and South Africa. Kiwi Jeff Julian (his nation's cross country champion) and Finn Eino Oksanen (recent Scandinavian marathon champion) raced together for most of the distance. Oksanen edged ahead to win (2:26:30), with Julian 31 seconds behind. In third was another Finnish hopeful, Jukka Koivumaki, with the well-known Finn Paavo Kotila in fourth and the new Oceania record-holder Bill Baillie (another Kiwi) in fifth.

Closing the 1959 marathon season was the Japanese Asahi international marathon at Fukuoka on November 8, with Finland's Pavel Kantorek as the major invited international athlete. He was runner-up to Japan's Kurao Hiroshima (2:29:34), the first to win this prestigious 13-years-old race twice. Nobuyoshi Sadanaga, the 1960 Mainichi Marathon winner, and Kazumi Watanabe, the 1960 Beppu champion, completed Japan's strong Olympic team.

In the spring of 1960, the April 19 Boston Marathon provided the next great international racing opportunity. Finland's Paavo Kotila came over to race, took the lead near 11 miles, and no one could catch him (2:20:54). "Johnny the Younger" Kelley was expected to give him a fight but was hobbled by a heel blister and dropped out at 20 miles. Gordon McKenzie of the United States was runner-up at 2:22:18. This caused a problem for United States team selection, as Kelley was of Olympic caliber, but stated policy required that athletes desiring a team berth had to finish both the Boston race and the AAU championship at Yonkers on May 22. Kelley went on to win at Yonkers for the fifth time in a course record 2:20:13.6, and McKenzie was runner-up. A Marine, Alex Breckenridge, finished fourth at Boston and third at Yonkers. McKenzie and Breckenridge were named to the United States team, and a recommendation was made that Kelley be the third man on the basis of previous excellence and his recent good performance. This arrangement was approved.

In Britain, although Jim Peters had retired in 1954, hopes were high for a better Olympic showing than at Helsinki and Melbourne. This was because in 1960 four other British athletes broke the 2:20:00 barrier. On April 18, from Doncaster to Sheffield, Arthur Keily covered the distance in 2:19:23, with Peter Wilkinson only 31 seconds behind. Then, at the 47th edition of the "Poly" on June 11, Keily did it again (2:19:06) in a runaway triumph, beating young Brian Kilby on his debut. A few weeks later, on June 30, over a circular course in Liverpool, a close race saw Dennis O'Gorman (2:18:15.6) narrowly defeat Fred Norris (2:19:08). Only Peters, Kotila, and Popov had run faster. O'Gorman, Keily, and Kilby were selected to the British Olympic team.

The Course Provides a Tour Through Roman History

Olympic organizers created a marathon course that was truly an historical classic befitting the ancient traditions of the Games. Dispensing entirely with the modern Olympic Games pattern of either starting or finishing in the Olympic stadium, this course did neither. Instead, the race began and ended at two of the most inspiring of Rome's old monuments within 1 kilometer of each other in the center of the city. In between was a grand tour that showcased both ancient Rome and the modern city.

The start was at the Campidoglio, the most sacred of Rome's seven hills. It is known for its beautiful piazza, designed by Michelangelo, that contains the equestrian statue of Marcus Aurelius. The finish was at the Arch of Constantine, built in A.D. 315, adjacent to the Colosseum. Taking advantage of three major roadways, the course was essentially an equilateral triangle having a north-south leg, a west-east leg, and a southeast-northwest leg, as shown in figure 15.1.

The north-south leg extended for about 20 kilometers outbound to the suburbs. Athletes first ran alongside the old Roman Forum, under the Arch of Constantine, and past the ancient Circus Maximus, where chariot races had been held two thousand years before. Passing alongside the baths of Caracalla, runners then left the old walled city of Rome via its Porta Ardeatina. From here the road widened into a broad avenue, the Via Cristoforo Colombo.

Continuing south, between 9 and 11 kilometers athletes ran through a huge development known to Romans simply as the EUR—Esposizione Universale di Roma. Conceived by Mussolini in the 1940s, it became a splendid multiple-use urban residential area, with fountains, plazas, public housing, and huge public buildings, all tastefully designed and connected. Olympic basketball was played at its mammoth Palazzo dello Sport. Runners traversed the entire length of this subdivision.

Remaining on the Via Cristoforo Colombo, runners then crossed a large highway called the Raccordo Annulare and continued to the course midpoint at the intersection with Via del Risario in the village of Vitinia. The 7 kilometers out-and-back section between the Raccordo and Vitinia permitted course measurers to keep the fixed start and finish points while still achieving the required marathon distance. Returning to the Raccordo Annulare, athletes then proceeded eastward onto the second leg of the triangle.

The west-to-east segment of the course along the Raccordo was 11 kilometers in length. Today this is the Grande Raccordo Anulare (GRA)—a multilane auto throughway encircling the city, which is inappropriate for running.

On the third leg of the triangle, which covered the remaining 11.2 kilometers, the course primarily followed the ancient Roman Appian Way. Quite narrow, lined with large cypress trees and pines, monuments and statues, with ancient cobblestones still existent in many places, the Via Appia Antica is of enormous historical significance. The first 9 kilometers of this route returned runners to the city wall at the Porta San Sebastiano. It then rejoined the outbound route at the baths of Caracalla, only 1 kilometer from the finish under the Arch of Constantine. The course details box summarizes the streets used for the marathon and will be useful for those interested in following this exciting route.

Warm weather was typical for Rome even in mid-September. Thus, the start time was delayed until 1730 (5:30 p.m.). Arrival onto the narrow, tree-shaded Appian Way was projected for 1900 (7:00 p.m.), as dusk was setting in, and runners would finish after sunset. To solve the frustration of television producers seeking adequate illumination—and the need for athletes to clearly see the route—hundreds of torchbearers were put in place along both sides of the road to guide the runners. For spectators, this eerie scene was unforgettable. As they crowded the roadside, they only saw a blur of bodies speeding by and disappearing into the flickering darkness. Captivated by the allure of the Olympic marathon, however, this was unimportant—they were a part of history.

Although Rome sprawled over its legendary seven hills, its marathon course had minimally significant elevation changes. Instead, the heat, the many turns,

Course Details

The 1960 Rome Olympic Marathon

Start at the Piazza de Campidoglio, bottom of the steps, continuing along the Via San Pietro in Carcere to the Via dei Fori Imperiali

Right onto the Via dei Fori Imperiali to the Piazza del Colosseo

Right under the Arco di Costantino onto the Via di San Gregorio

Continue to the Piazza di Porta Capena (2 kilometers)

Half left onto the Via della Terme di Caracalla to the Piazzale Numa Pompilio

Half right onto the Viale della Terme di Caracella to the Via Cristoforo Colombo

Continue on the Via Cristoforo Colombo through the Piazza dei Navigatori

Cross the Viale Guglielmo Marconi (7.3 kilometers)

Continue on the Via Cristoforo Colombo through the Centro Sportivo de Tre Fontaine of EUR, and circle around the Palazzo dello Sport

Continue on the Via Cristoforo Colombo, crossing the Raccordo Anulare (13 kilometers)

Continue on the Via Cristoforo Colombo to the turnaround point at the intersection with the Via del Risario in Vitinia (16.65 kilometers)

Turn around and return on the Via Cristoforo Colombo to the Raccordo Anulare (20.3 kilometers)

Right on the Raccordo Anulare, crossing the Via Appia Mediana (21 kilometers), now the Via Pontina

Cross the Via Laurentina (23.3 kilometers)

Cross the Via Ardeatina (27.9 kilometers)

Left onto the Via Appia Antica at 30.75 kilometers

Cross the Via di Tor Carbone at 34.2 kilometers

Cross the Via Dell'Acqua Santa at 36.4 kilometers (now the Via di Acqua Bullicante)

Pass the Domini Quo Vadis at 39.3 kilometers

Continue on the Via Appia Antica through the Porta San Sebastiano

Via Appia Antica now becomes the Via di Porta San Sebastiano

Continue on the Via di Porta San Sebastiano to the Piazzale Numo Pompilio (40 kilometers)

Straight through the Piazzale Numo Pompilio onto the Via della Terme Di Caracalla to the Piazza di Porta Capena

Right onto the Via di San Gregorio to the finish line underneath the Arco di Costantino

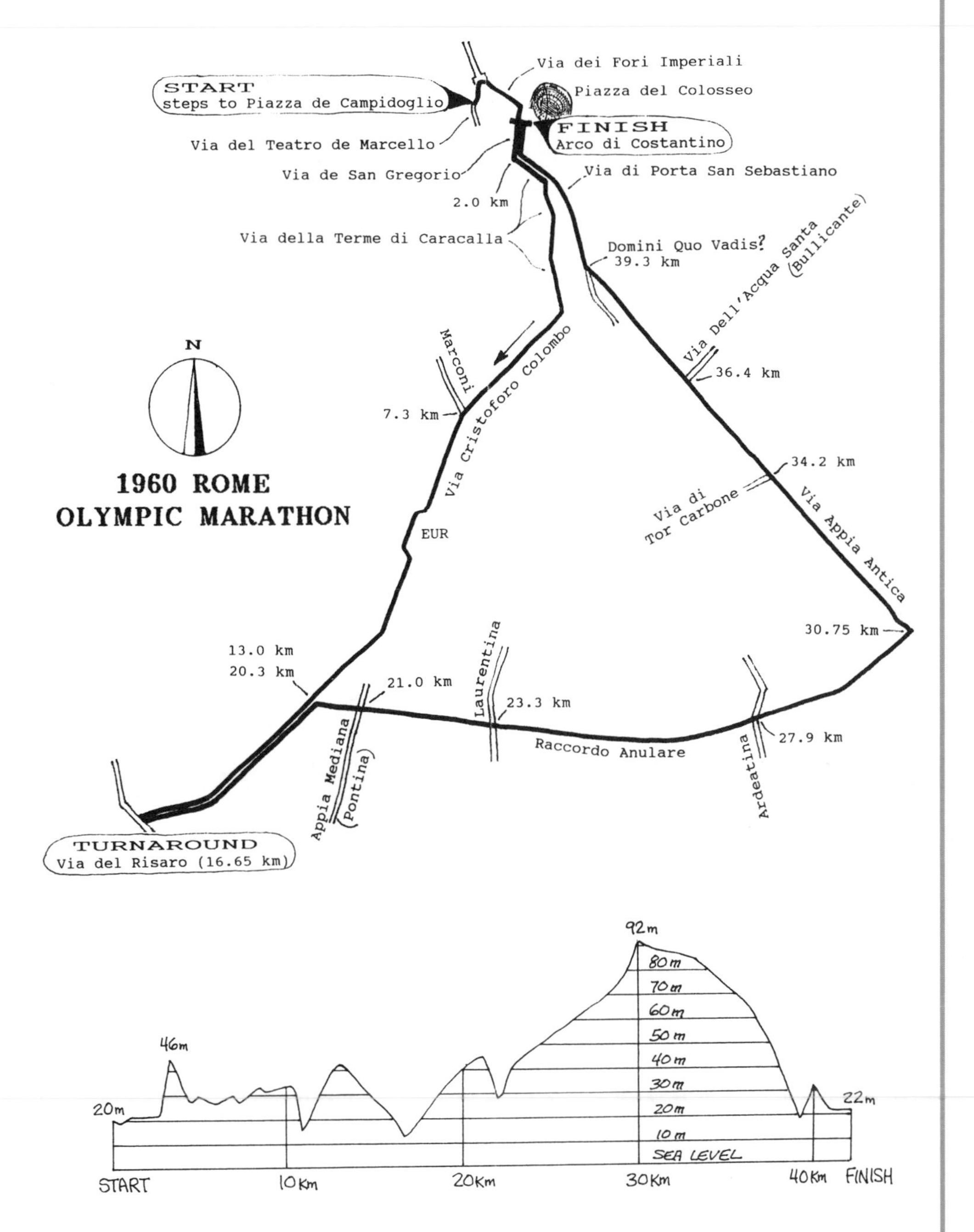

Figure 15.1 Sketch of the Rome Olympic marathon course. Prepared by Bob Letson.

the sometimes very narrow streets (particularly in the final 10 kilometers), and the crowds of spectators were of greatest concern. Runners started at 26 meters above sea level (85.3 feet). For the first 22 kilometers (13.7 miles), in contrast to reports of a steady uphill (Smith 1960), the elevation rolled gently, ranging from 16 meters (52.5 feet) to 40 meters (131 feet). A steady rise then occurred on the Raccordo Anulare for 8 kilometers (5 miles), reaching 90 meters (295 feet) at 30 kilometers (18.6 miles), just before the turnoff at 30.75 kilometers. This represented a rise of 65 meters over 8 kilometers, or 8.1 meters per kilometer (213.3 feet over 5 miles, or 43 feet per mile). The remaining 12 kilometers were a net descent, gradual at first, but then more substantial in the closing kilometer. The Arch of Constantine is 22 meters (72 feet) above sea level, so the course was a net 4 meters (13 feet) downhill.

North Africans Take One-Two in Another Record Run

Never before had the starting list been so global: 35 geopolitical entities from five continents. The usual European majority included 35 athletes from 18 nations. South America (4) had Chile and Argentina represented, while North America (4) had Canada and the United States. From Oceania (5), New Zealand and Australia participated. Five Asian nations contributed a total of 11 runners, and 11 athletes were from the African continent, representing 6 nations. Fourteen full teams of 3 runners were entered. Indeed, the world's stars were present for this race, and others would become so at its completion.

When the race began it was still warm (23.2°C or 72.0°F), and the city buildings radiated heat from daytime warming. During the first few kilometers, the usual confusion of athletes jockeying to identify their optimal race pace was even more complicated because of the need to dash around monuments and across plazas. Four athletes were distinguishable in the lead. Two were already well known: Arthur Keily and Aurele Vandendriessche of Belgium. The latter had won five Belgian marathon titles since 1956 (and would win five more). The other two were unfamiliar to most. One of these was a barefoot Ethiopian, Abebe Bikila, a member of Emperor Haile Selassie's Imperial Palace guards. The other was Morocco's Rhadi ben Abdesselem. Having placed 14th in the 10,000 meters run just two days before, Rhadi was an entirely unknown factor, as this apparently was his first marathon.

A large group, including the above athletes, passed 5 kilometers in 15:35, and by 10 kilometers (31:07), near the basketball stadium in the EUR, it was joined by Brian Kilby and another Moroccan, Allal Saoudi. Vandendriessche dropped back briefly and was not among the top nine, but eventually rejoined them. Three seconds behind this lead group of six came Ireland's lone entrant, its national champion Albert "Bertie" Messitt, winner of the Irish Olympic trial in 2:28:24. He eventually dropped out. This sequence changed continually as athletes jockeyed for position, and figure 15.2 shows them racing together along the Via Cristoforo Colombo.

Figure 15.2 The lead pack heads south along the Via Cristoforo Colombo near the 10 kilometers point. From right are Ireland's Albert Messitt (number 58), Morocco's Allal Saoudi, Britain's Arthur Keily, Belgium's Aurele Vandendriessche (number 36), Morocco's Rhadi ben Abdesselem (number 185), and Ethiopia's Abebe Bikila (number 11). Courtesy AP/Wide World Photos.

Keily and Vandendriessche alternated at the head of the pack, with Rhadi and Bikila only a step behind. Passing 15 kilometers in 48:02, not far from the turnaround point near Vitinia, Saoudi was now 23 seconds behind this group, and losing contact. By 20 kilometers, just before entering the Raccordo Anulare, Bikila and Rhadi had opened a sizable lead, and were timed in 1:02:39. Vandendriessche was nearly half a minute behind (1:03:05), with Keily trailing by another 15 seconds. Behind Keily, however (1:03:41), a pack of four remained together. These included the world's fastest, Sergey Popov; New Zealand's Barry Magee; the recent Dutch champion, Franz Kunen; and Rhadi's countryman, Benaissa Bakir.

At 22 kilometers, runners started their 65 meters (213.3 feet) climb along the Raccordo Anulare. Bikila and Rhadi passed 25 kilometers in 1:20:47.6, to give them a 5 kilometers split of 18:09 between 20 and 25 kilometers. Magee and Popov shared the third and fourth positions, but were out of contact (1:22:11.6) with the leaders. Keily held onto fifth (1:22:34), trailed by Bakir and Franjo Mihalic 2 seconds behind. Vandendriessche was next, but fading fast, and soon retired.

At 30 kilometers (1:34:29), the African duo of Bikila and Rhadi had a two-minute lead over Magee and Popov (1:36:52), partly because they had quickened their pace yet again. Another minute later came Bakir and Mihalic, clocked at 1:37:51. Keily could not endure the fast pace and dropped back. Shortly after 30 kilometers, runners crested the highest hill on the course and turned left off the Raccordo Anulare onto the narrow Via Appia Antica. The leaders passed 35 kilometers in 1:50:27, leaving Magee, in 1:52:29, ahead of Popov (1:53:37). Moving up now into fifth place and challenging Popov was the recent surprise Soviet marathon champion, Konstantin Vorobiev.

At 40 kilometers, athletes left the ancient Appian Way, passed under the old Roman gate of San Sebastian, and soon started retracing their steps toward the finish. Magee's quickening pace brought him to within 86 seconds of Bikila and Rhadi (2:08:33). Vorobiev had caught and overtaken Popov on the steepest part of the descent, between 38 and 39 kilometers. Shortly before the route widened and once again passed the baths of Caracalla, the Moroccan tried to move away from Bikila, but failed. Bikila stayed with him.

Perceptive readers at this point will notice that something is amiss regarding the 5 kilometers split times, which have been calculated from the Official Report of finishers (Anonymous 1963). The seven 5 kilometers splits delivered by the lead runners through 35 kilometers were 15:35, 15:32, 16:55, 14:37, 18:09, 13:41, and 15:58. The 15-to-20 kilometers split is too fast, the 20-to-25 kilometers split is too slow, and the 25-to-30 kilometers split is too fast. While the 20-to-25 kilometers section is indeed uphill, explaining a slowing, the 25-to-30 kilometers section is an even steeper uphill, and that 13:41 5 kilometers split time would have bettered Murray Halberg's 13:43.4 gold medal performance in the 5,000 meters event! We suspect the 20 and 25 kilometers timing stations were placed incorrectly.

At the Piazza di Porta Capena, it was Bikila's turn to surge—figure 15.3 captures the moment when he started to move away. As he related later, Bikila had seen the Obelisco di Azum on this square and was amused, as it been brought back from Ethiopia by the Italians during their invasion in 1936. He was aware of it as a landmark; in the event the race came down to the wire, he hoped he would see it in the darkness, as he knew it was 500 meters from the finish. Lengthening his stride, he surged forward, and Rhadi didn't respond. Extending his arms in victory and as if to embrace the entire Arch of Constantine, he was bathed for only a brief moment in the television illumination. The gold medal was his.

Rhadi crossed the line 25 seconds later, and a little more than one and one-half minutes after that, New Zealand's Magee captured the bronze medal. These other two medalists didn't get quite the attention they deserved, however, as they suddenly appeared out of the darkness to cross the finish line, and the assembled world press was crowding around Bikila for an interview.

For Bikila, his victory (2:15:16.2) over Rhadi was simply marvelous. Bikila's time was a world best by 0.8 second (bettering Popov, who finished fifth). It was obviously another Olympic marathon record—and the first Olympic performance under the 2:20:00 barrier. Four other athletes broke this time barrier

Figure 15.3 Bikila (number 11), on the Piazza di Porta Capena, beginning to move ahead of Rhadi ben Abdesselem (number 185) in the final few hundred meters of the race. Courtesy AP/Wide World Photos.

as well. Never before had so many finished so fast—61 under three hours, compared to 53 at Helsinki. In fact, the first 15 finishers were under Zátopek's Helsinki record of 2:23:03! Excellent fourth and fifth place Soviet finishes contributed to their winning the unofficial team trophy, ahead of Britain, with Morocco a surprising third, as its athletes were largely unknown outside their country. The team from tiny New Zealand was only one point behind, in fourth. Table 15.1 provides a summary of the race.

TABLE 15.1

1960 Rome Olympic Marathon at a Glance

Date:	10 September	**Weather:**	23.2°C (72.0°F)
Start time:	1730	**Starters:**	69
Course:	Triangle	**Finishers:**	62
Course distance:	42.195 km	**GPEs:**	35

TOP RESULTS:

Place	*Athlete*	*GPE*	*Date of birth*	*Time*
1	Abebe Bikila	ETH	07 Aug. 1932	2:15:16.2
2	Rhadi ben Abdesselem	MAR	28 Feb. 1929	2:15:41.6
3	Barrington Magee	NZL	06 Feb. 1934	2:17:18.2
4	Konstantin Vorobiev	URS	30 Oct. 1930	2:19:09.6
5	Sergey Popov	URS	21 Sept. 1930	2:19:18.8
6	Thyge Tögersen	DEN	04 Nov. 1926	2:21:03.4
7	Abebe Wakgira	ETH	21 Oct. 1921	2:21:09.4
8	Benaissa Bakir	MAR	07 Apr. 1931	2:21:21.4
9	Osvaldo Suarez	ARG	17 Mar. 1934	2:21:26.6
10	Franjo Skrinjar	YUG	17 May 1920	2:21:40.2

New geopolitical entities represented: Morocco [MAR], Ceylon [CEY], Tunisia [TUN], Liberia [LBR]

Team score (unofficial):			
	1. URS	20 points	(4-5-11)
	2. GBR	70 points	(16-25-29)
	3. MAR	71 points	(2-8-61)

Four of the top eight finishers were North Africans, although defending Olympic champion Mimoun only placed 34th. Bikila was an instant hero to his people. As they saw it, a million Italian soldiers were required to defeat Ethiopia in 1936, but now a single Ethiopian runner was victorious in Rome on a still-warm Italian evening. One could only wonder whether this demonstration of African excellence in distance running would continue in future years.

Notes on the Medalists

Abebe Bikila was born in Jatta, in Ethiopia's mountainous region of Debre Birhan, on the same day Juan Zabala won the 1932 Los Angeles Olympic marathon (Abebe 1996). Bikila thus accomplished the same feat 28 years later, in an even grander style. His Christian family was disrupted by the 1936 Italian invasion of what was then called Abyssinia, and when they returned to their home village in 1941 he was old enough to work on the farm, herding cattle. On a trip to Addis Ababa as a teenager, he saw the Imperial Palace Body Guard forces in training and was impressed with their elegance. At the age of 19 years he enlisted and was accepted.

Vigorous physical activities were a programmed part of keeping these soldiers fit, and Bikila's natural athleticism showed forth in several sports they routinely played. One day, seeing a group of soldiers with peculiar-looking (but to him, beautiful) uniforms, and learning that they had received them during their stay at the Melbourne Olympic Games, he decided that he, too, would like to have such a uniform. He found distance running easy and soon was competing with the armed forces team at 5,000 and 10,000 meters, representing the Imperial Palace Body Guards. His first marathon was in Addis Ababa in 1959 as part of the Military Forces Day celebrations.

Watching him with interest was a Finn, Onni Niskanen, who had emigrated from Sweden to become Ethiopia's director of athletics under its Ministry of Education. Niskanen began a disciplined program of training for Bikila and others over the standard track distances, as well as the marathon. The program was essentially unfunded, as the government was unhappy with the poor results of its athletes at Melbourne. Niskanen, however, was resourceful and a good coach. His runners got fit, and one month before the Olympic Games in Rome, at the 2,440 meters (8,000 feet) altitude of Addis Ababa, Bikila won the marathon trials with a time (2:21:23) faster than defending Olympic champion Mimoun had achieved at sea level (2:25:00). The emperor was impressed, and a small team was assembled to compete in Rome.

So why did Bikila run barefoot? He had trained both with and without shoes, but when in Rome during the final days prior to competing, the shoes he had brought with him gave out and were simply unusable (Abebe 1996). A trip to a local shoe store produced a pair, but his long, narrow feet did not fit properly, and he was on the verge of blisters. Using the simplest logic, Bikila opted for no shoes rather than shoes he knew would pose a problem. True, Rome streets had plenty of cobbles, but those were less a problem than blisters. Those who work with highly elite athletes realize perfectly well the scenario unfolding here: these athletes are so focused and so resilient in the face of adversity that absolutely nothing interferes with the performance goal at hand. As far as Bikila was concerned, nothing did.

Bikila had an amazing career, winning 12 of the 15 marathons that he entered. Chapter 16 further discusses his marathon record, and table 16.3 lists it.

Rhadi ben Abdesselem was born in Ksar-es Sauk, Morocco. His distance running experience came at shorter lengths. Earlier in this Olympic year, he had won the International Cross Country Championships, and at the Games themselves, as mentioned, he finished 14th in the 10,000 meters run two days before the marathon (there was no qualifying round). The Rome race, which he ran at 25 years of age, was his debut at the distance, and so far as we know he never ran another.

Arthur Barrington "Barry" Magee was two years older than Bikila, and he was part of the success story of tiny New Zealand, along with Peter Snell's gold at 800 meters and Murray Halberg's gold at 5,000 meters. Born in New Plymouth, New Zealand, Magee had run three local marathons prior to the

Olympics, and he subsequently won two New Zealand national titles in 1961 and 1962. But he had a wide range of talents—in 1961 he also was a member of the New Zealand 4 × 1 mile relay team that set a world record at Dublin. He peaked in 1960 with his bronze medal at Rome, and then in December he won the challenging Asahi international marathon at Fukuoka with an event record 2:19:04 on December 4.

Looking Ahead: Brief Highlights 1960-1963

1960: First held in 1947, the Japanese Asahi Marathon eventually developed the reputation of being the "informal world marathon championship" because of invitations extended to all the major marathon winners of the year. This year, in Fukuoka (which would later become its permanent home), Olympic bronze medalist Barry Magee won it in an event record 2:19:04.

1961: Olympic marathon champion Abebe Bikila made it six victories in six races, winning at Athens (2:23:44.6), Osaka (2:29:27), and Košice (2:20:12).

1962: This was a year of important regional championships. Masayuki Nagata [JPN] won the Asian Games marathon at Djakarta (August 29), and five-time British champion Brian Kilby won both the European championship (Belgrade, September 16, 2:23:18.2) and the Commonwealth Games (Perth, November 29, 2:21:17.2) marathons. A distant 12th at Belgrade was Finland's Eino Oksanen, who had earlier won at Boston to add to his 1959 and 1960 victories there.

1963: Toru Terasawa, winner of the 1962 Fukuoka Marathon (December 2, 2:16:18.4), set a new world best of 2:15:15.8 in winning the 12th Beppu race on February 17. Leonard "Buddy" Edelen had ended 1962 with a United States record of 2:18:56.8 behind Terasawa at Fukuoka, and in 1963 he won at Athens (May 19, 2:23:06.8) over the classical course. Later, he won the 50th "Poly" Marathon from Windsor to Chiswick (June 15, 2:14:28—a world best). And he also won at Košice (October 13, 2:15:09.6) over another high-quality field. Fidel Negrete [MEX] took the Pan American Games title at Sao Paulo on May 9 in 2:27:55.6.

References

Abebe, T. 1996. *Triumph and tragedy.* Addis Ababa: Artistic Printers.

Anonymous. 1963. *The Games of the XVII Olympiad, Rome 1960. The Official Report of the Organizing Committee.* Vol. 2, *Competition Summary and Results.* Rome: Carlo Colombo, Publisher.

Ecker, T. 1996. *Olympic facts and fables.* Mountain View, CA: Tafnews Press.

Ryan, A.J. 1968. A medical history of the Olympic Games. *Journal of the American Medical Association* 205: 715-720.

Smith, L. 1960. Two Africans whip field. *Track & Field News* 13 (9): 12.

Chapter 16

1964—Tokyo

Record Repeat for Bikila in Tokyo

Asia Hosts Its First Olympic Games

Tokyo bid for the 1964 Olympic Games in 1959, along with Brussels, Detroit, and Vienna. Tokyo had been awarded the 1940 Games, but Japan's increasing involvement with wartime preparations caused the nation to abandon its Olympic efforts. The Games' venue was switched to Helsinki, but Finland as well succumbed to wartime activities, and thus the Games did not occur during the 12th and 13th Olympiads. London and Helsinki had already been awarded a postwar Games, giving Tokyo a logical advantage due to its prior bidding success. Indeed, in the balloting, Tokyo won on the first round by a sizable margin.

Both the Japanese government and its people desired to convey a better image to the world than that of an imperialist, aggressor nation. Once the Games were awarded, the city undertook such a massive revitalization of its highways and hotels that its appearance in the early 1960s commonly resembled its rebuilding phase following World War II. An Olympic Village for the athletes was built on a former military parade ground that only needed refurbishing of its existing military living quarters. The men's and women's villages were adjacent but separate. Special attention was given to the various cultures, to provide amenities similar to those at home. As just one example, there were 11 kitchens, each specializing in different cuisine and with its own dining room. The result was a magnificent Olympic Games: well organized and full of happiness among both spectators and athletes. But it was indeed expensive, with costs estimated at more than U.S.$500 million (Grombach 1980). In the end, despite the travel distance, participation reached another all-time high, both for number of geopolitical entities (93) and number of athletes (4,457 men, 683 women). One decision emerging from post-Olympic meetings, at which IOC president Avery Brundage was reelected to another term, was to select a site at least six years in advance for future Games, to accommodate the enormous preparations now required.

A new timing system was developed and implemented at the competitions. Fully automatic, it used the highest technology available. Printed results were available quickly using computerized interfacing with the scoring equipment—primitive by today's standards but functional nonetheless. Much to the delight of journalists on deadline, this sophistication worked flawlessly. The Olympic Games were televised worldwide thanks to Telstar, the new communications satellite. The many time zones between Japan and places such as Europe and the United States meant frequent use of tape-delay broadcasts. Inexperience with such matters sometimes caused peculiar viewing times.

Again the Olympic torch was carried initially by plane to the host nation, and then by running relay throughout Japan. However, instead of a well-known athletic figure being honored with the thrill of lighting the Olympic stadium cauldron, it was a 19-years-old Waseda University student who also was a developing 400 meters runner. Symbolizing the combined elements of youth, peace, hope, and understanding for the future, this was Yoshinori Sakai—born 68 kilometers (42 miles) from Hiroshima on the same day the atomic bomb was dropped there (Posey 1996).

The Olympic Games were not devoid of problems, however, which seemed to get ever more complex. There were, of course, the usual political intrusions. Indonesia and North Korea withdrew because several of their athletes were barred from competition for having participated in the Games of the New Emerging Forces (GANEFO) in 1963. The GANEFO, held in Jakarta, had not allowed Israel or Taiwan to participate. To demonstrate disapproval, the international governing bodies for the sports of athletics, shooting, and swimming barred GANEFO competitors from the Tokyo Games. On an entirely different matter, South Africa's participation was suspended in view of its continuing apartheid policy.

A new twist to the festivities was the "shoe company war!" Two German brothers, Adolph and Rudolph Dassler, had produced athletic shoes for many years under the trade name Adidas. They were of high quality and were eagerly sought by athletes. But a rift developed, and Rudolph started a rival brand of his own, known as Puma. At the Tokyo Games, representatives of each company contacted potential medalists to "wear our brand" rather than another. Of course, in this amateur Olympic world, athletes could accept no payments, but payments were made nonetheless, and they were sizable—but never publicized (Ecker 1996).

This activity paled in comparison, however, to what developed as a trend toward use of ergogenic aids by athletes to gain an inappropriate performance advantage. It became clear that the nicotinyl alcohol-related death of the Danish cyclist in 1960 was only the tip of a growing mountain of chemical drug abuse in sport. Apparently, some athletes had used similar stimulants orally as early as 1956. Amphetamines are particularly nasty. By increasing heart rate and blood pressure, they greatly increase cardiac stress. Competing athletes at the top level are already pushing their cardiovascular systems to the limit. But these drugs also affect the nervous system, making raging monsters of those under their influence. With pain masked and emotions at a killer level, it is little wonder that the sad end result could be death while competing. Those interested in the dangers and physiological effects of performance-enhancing drugs will find useful an excellent book by Melvin Williams (1997), a noted authority on the subject.

But now, in addition to amphetamines, the increasing clandestine use of anabolic steroids for building muscle mass also provoked concern, worry, and frustration among the honest members of the sporting world. This, as well, was starting to create two playing fields: one for those using them, one for those who were not. The worlds of sports medicine and sports administration were ill prepared to adequately understand or deal with the issues of drugs in sport. It was hard to imagine such a state of affairs developing. Is this not against the fundamental ethic of fair play? Who was responsible—the athletes, the coaches, the media, or governments? In today's world, as the new millennium begins, such questions seem almost childish, showing just how distorted the sports world has become. Fortunately, neither amphetamines nor steroids were thought to be of much use to long-distance runners. The marathoners, it could be hoped, were drug-free.

Hopeful Olympic Athletes Are Selected to Team Positions

As an example of Japan's organizational foresight, the country staged an international marathon over the Olympic course in the fall of 1963, on October 15, one year ahead of the Games race. (Actually, another race had been held on the course earlier in the year for Japanese athletes to prepare for this one.) Brian Kilby [GBR] was there, and Victor Baikov [URS], along with Pete McArdle [USA], Jeff Julian [NZL], and Aurele Vandendriessche [BEL]. And, of course, high-quality Japanese athletes—Kazumi Watanabe, Kenji Kimihara, and others—competed as well, gaining experience alongside the foreign stars. Kilby caught a bad cold, and so could not run.

It was a Kiwi victory, with Julian well in front (2:18:00.6). Places two through four did not get sorted out until the finish line. Kimihara caught Watanabe just before reaching the stadium, but Vandendriessche was in front of them. On the back straightaway of the track, Kimihara then raced past the Belgian to capture

2nd (by 6.2 seconds) in 2:20:25.2. McArdle had started too fast and faded to 30th; he learned enormously from the experience. Barry Magee, the Rome Olympic Games bronze medalist, decided to run the 10,000 meters at Tokyo, leaving Julian as New Zealand's prime candidate for a future Olympic marathon success story. All were impressed with the potential for fast times on this flat course with few turns.

Japan staged its Olympic trial in the early spring of 1964, on April 12. Again on their nation's Olympic course, Kenji Kimihara (2:17:11.4) proved superior to Toru Terasawa (2:19:43) with a sizable victory. These two athletes had now raced head-to-head on five occasions, producing a popular rivalry. Kimihara had finished ahead of Terasawa three times. But this time, another Japanese newcomer finished in between them—Kokichi Tsuburaya (2:18:20.2), in only his second marathon race. These three composed the Japanese team, but so deep was Japan's list of top performers that just as many of very similar ability remained behind. Later that year, on August 23 at the very warm Sapporo Marathon, Kimihara ran 2:17:12 to defeat Tsuburaya (2:19:50). Then, just four days later, the two raced over 10,000 meters, with Tsuburaya setting a new Japanese record. Some coaches might consider this a dangerous experiment in overracing so close to an Olympics, but the runners recovered, tapered their training, and entered the Games with high spirits.

The United States selected its team on the basis of performances at the AAU championship in Yonkers on May 24 and at the Western Hemisphere Marathon in Culver City, California, which was moved from its usual December date to July 26. It was fortunate that Boston was not a selection race, as its weather was horrendous: sleet, snow, and a raw wind. A large European contingent made the trip to Boston, as usual, but suffered from the weather. Belgium's Vandendriessche won the race (2:19:59) ahead of Finland's Tenho Salakka, who in turn won a close battle with Canada's Ron Wallingford. Canada had 4 runners in the top 10 but did not send a marathon team to Japan for reasons that have never been clear.

The Yonkers Marathon experienced a heat wave: high humidity, 33°C (91°F) at the start, and a scorching sun. Leonard "Buddy" Edelen, the schoolteacher from South Dakota now based in the cool weather of London, came over to try out for the United States team. He had established himself as a high-quality runner in Europe, winning the famous "Poly" on June 15, 1963, with a world record 2:14:28, but few knew him in the United States. He won in the heat, without complaining, in an amazing 2:24:25.6, stopping "Johnny the Younger" Kelley's streak of victories at eight. Kelley placed third, behind an Austrian, Adolph Gruber, who was selected to represent his nation in Tokyo.

The Culver City race was a hot one as well. Pete McArdle won in 2:27:01, but an exciting battle for second and third developed in the final mile as William "Billy" Mills outraced Wayne van Dellen to the tape. Edelen, McArdle, and Mills thus were given berths on the United States team. Mills, an Oglala Lakota born on the Pine Ridge Indian Reservation in South Dakota and orphaned at 13 years of age, was now in the Marine Corps at Camp Pendleton, California. A cross country all-American at the University of Kansas, he used his shorter-distance speed to qualify as well for the 10,000 meters team.

Britain also used a series of races to select its Tokyo marathoners. The annual Polytechnic Harriers Marathon occurred on June 13 over its traditional Windsor-to-Chiswick route. With a large field of athletes (120) and optimum racing conditions, the event was a thriller. Ron Hill led in the early stages, but Basil Heatley and Jim Alder looked to be in good form as well. Heatley appeared fresh even at the finish and broke the tape with a world best time of 2:13:55. Ron Hill (2:14:12) also was faster than the previous world standard. In third was Czechoslovakia's Václav Chudomel, whose 2:15:26 was a national record and also among the top 10 all-time world performances. It was the second world best performance in as many years at the "Poly," Buddy Edelen having won it the previous year.

Two weeks later, the Welsh championship at Port Talbot saw Juan Taylor, from the Coventry Godiva Harriers, score a most convincing victory (2:15:37), with the runner-up position going to Bill Adcocks, one of Taylor's teammates, in his first competitive marathon (2:19:29). Because Heatley and Hill had each been assured a team berth, the AAA title race at Coventry on August 22 determined the third athlete. Taylor and Adcocks were there, of course, hoping to have recovered, but it was another warm day, and neither one even finished. The victory (and Olympic team berth) thus went to Brian Kilby (2:23:01), who finished with blood-soaked feet from broken blisters.

Because the Tokyo Games were in mid-October, the Košice (Czechoslovakia) Marathon race organizers advanced the date of their October race to August 8, thereby permitting Czech athletes to use it as their Olympic qualifier. It was yet another warm day. The two great Czech stars, Pavel Kantorek and Václav Chudomel, were at the front as expected, but an excellent performance by Britain's Dennis Plater split the two. Kantorek won in 2:25:55.4.

What about the African runners from Morocco and Kenya and Ethiopia who had appeared in Rome? Little was known, even regarding Bikila. Because of ongoing military activities in his region of Africa, it is likely that his military obligations kept him at home. During 1962 and 1963 he had raced outside Ethiopia only once. He ran the 1963 Boston Marathon and placed fifth, becoming the seventh Olympic gold medalist to fail to win there. However, in this Olympic year, the sporting world certainly hoped that he would be permitted time to train and opportunities to compete. On May 31, at the high altitude of Addis Ababa, he won a tune-up marathon in 2:23:14.4, testing his fitness. After two months of hard training, at the August 3 trial race also held in Addis Ababa, he was ready to take on his countrymen. He had created a "running revolution" of his own among military men there, who sought to match his talent. He did have some tough competition from Mamo Wolde. The two raced together through the streets of Addis Ababa, Bikila eventually winning in 2:16:18.8, but Wolde was only 0.4 second behind. And this was at an altitude of 2,440 meters (8,000 feet)! In third place was Demissie Wolde (2:19:30). A most impressive team was bound for Tokyo.

A Flat, Fast Course Provides an Ideal Venue

Much of Tokyo lies on a delta formed by rivers that carry mountain silt toward the sea; thus the city resides on a flat plain. The course began and finished at National Stadium, built for the Olympic Games just east of the city center, about 2 kilometers (1.2 miles) from the Imperial Palace, in Shibuya Ward (Shibuya-ku). As illustrated in figure 16.1, athletes exited the stadium via its north gate (known as "N" gate to the security personnel at that time) and were immediately on city streets. They turned onto the street in front of the Sendagaya train station (Sendagaya Ekimae dori) and continued to Meiji Street (Meiji dori). A short run of about 3 kilometers (1.9 miles) brought runners to a major thoroughfare, Koshu Kaido Avenue. They continued westward on Koshu Kaido Avenue for more than 17 kilometers (10.6 miles), through Setagaya-ku and Suginami-ku in the city of Tokyo, and then they entered suburban Chofu. The turnaround point was at 20.54 kilometers (12.8 miles)—555 meters (0.34 miles) before the halfway mark, indicating that the inbound portion would be slightly

COURSE DETAILS

The 1964 Tokyo Olympic Marathon

Start at midpoint of the 100 meters straightaway of stadium track

Run one and three-quarters laps counterclockwise around the track

Exit through Sendagaya gate to Sendagaya Ekimae dori

Left onto Sendagaya Ekimae dori, pass Sendagaya train station, and continue to Meiji dori

Right onto Meiji dori toward Shinjuku train station to Koshu Kaido Avenue

Left onto Koshu Kaido Avenue, passing Shinjuku train station

Continue on Koshu Kaido Avenue westward out of the city to turnaround point in front of Chofu Concrete Corporation

Turn around cone, and retrace same route on Koshu Kaido Avenue to Meiji dori

Right onto Meiji dori to Sendagaya Ekimae dori

Left onto Sendagaya Ekimae dori, past Sendagaya train station, past Sendagaya tunnel entrance to stadium, to Meiji Park Enshu Doro (Circle Road)

Follow Meiji Park Enshu Doro clockwise around Meiji Shrine to access road for Yoyogi gate onto stadium track

Right turn into stadium through Yoyogi gate

Almost one complete lap of the track, counterclockwise

Finish at standard track finish line

longer than the outbound. A large commemorative cone placed in the center of the street marked the turnaround.

Runners then retraced their steps for the next 17 kilometers (10.6 miles) along Koshu Kaido Avenue. Making the same few turns onto Meiji dori and Sendagaya Ekimae dori as previously mentioned, athletes now took a different route into the stadium. As shown in the right inset of the map in figure 16.1, runners followed the oval park road around the adjacent Meiji shrine (Meiji Park Enshu Doro). This additional distance before the stadium reentry explains the longer inbound route as measured from the turnaround point. Stadium entry on return was via its so-called Yoyogi Gate on the south side (known to security officers at the time as the "B" gate). The course details box summarizes the route for those who find themselves in Tokyo and are interested in following it precisely.

The Tokyo Olympic stadium is essentially at sea level. For the first 15 kilometers (9.3 miles), the course was gently uphill, climbing only 22 meters (72 feet). Between 15 kilometers (9.3 miles) and 16.5 kilometers (10.3 miles), an 18 meters (59 feet) descent provided a noticeable change of grade. Then came an 11

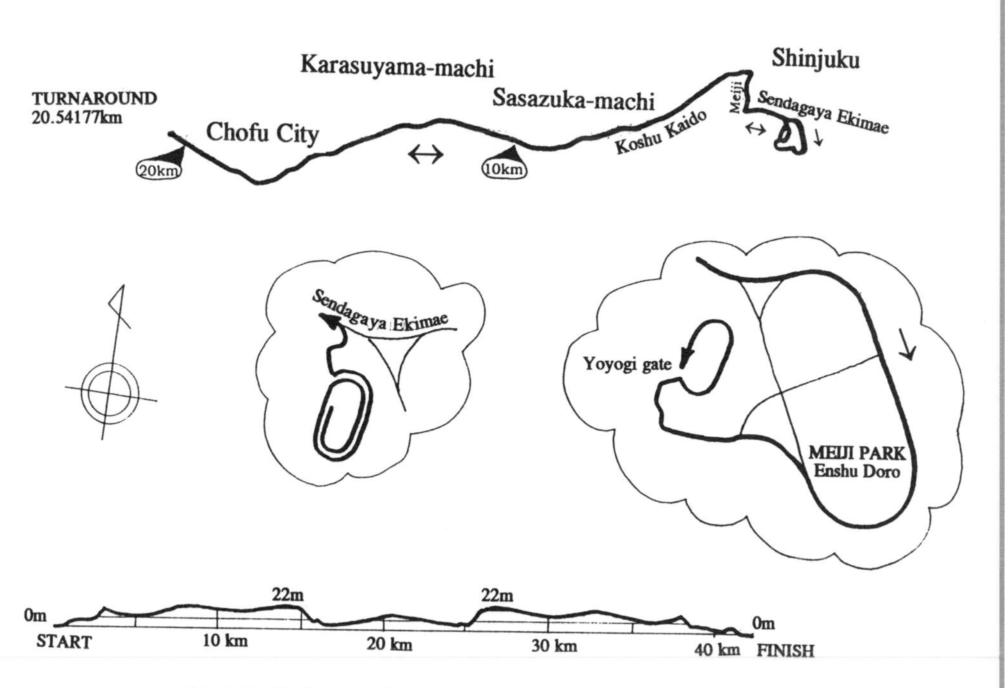

Figure 16.1 **Sketch of the Tokyo Olympic marathon course. Insets illustrate the path taken by runners upon exit from (left) and reentry into (right) the stadium as the marathon progressed.** Prepared by Bob Letson.

meters (36 feet) rise from 16.5 kilometers (10.3 miles) to the turnaround at 20.5 kilometers (12.7 miles).

On the return trip, athletes first descended 11 meters (36 feet) from 20.5 kilometers (12.7 miles) to 24.5 kilometers (15.2 miles), and then they climbed 18 meters (59 feet) again from 24.5 kilometers (15.2 miles) to 26 kilometers (16.2 miles). Then the course descended gradually to the finish. As a result of extensive Olympic Games street renovations, the road surface was smooth macadam throughout, excellent for racing.

Bikila Dons Shoes and Does It Again

The Tokyo Olympic marathon race occurred on Wednesday, October 21, the seventh and final day of the track and field competition. The Games had begun on October 10 and Closing Ceremonies were scheduled for October 24. The weather was typical for early fall (28°C or 68°F), but knowledgeable coaches suggested that the day was too warm for really fast times. Both sunny and rainy days had occurred during the Games, but this one was cloudy and humid. The starting field was large (68) and global, despite the huge travel distance for some. Europeans represented 13 geopolitical entities (GPEs, which were all NOCs) with an appropriately small number of 25 runners. South America had only 2 runners; they were from Chile and Argentina. North America also had few: 6 athletes from 3 NOCs, with only the United States fielding a full team. Africa again had a sizable contingent, with 15 athletes from 7 NOCs—and full teams from Ethiopia, Kenya, and Northern Rhodesia (now Zambia). Asia was, of course, well represented, with 14 athletes and 8 NOCs, Japan and Korea fielding full teams. From Oceania, Australia and New Zealand also sent full teams (Anonymous 1964).

News reporters covering the Olympic Village that morning were amazed to see several of the runners eating beefsteak for breakfast. Others seemed to prefer oatmeal, toast, and coffee. Athletes could prepare their own drinks to be placed along the route or use what was provided. Bikila's coach indicated that, while he had used watermelon juice at Rome, this time he was planning to choose between strawberry juice and orange juice. Much attention was focused on Bikila, who was favored because of his Rome gold medal performance and because of his superb victory at altitude against Mamo Wolde in August. But on September 16, he had undergone an appendectomy, then rested for 11 full days before resuming training. Even his showing up on race day was amazing to some.

The race got under way at 1300 (1:00 p.m.) with runners making just under two circuits of the stadium track. Out on the city streets, at the front of the pack was Australian Ron Clarke (figure 16.2). Those aware of the details of his earlier performance at these Games can imagine why he would be so aggressive. He had earlier been touted as a likely track medalist. Indeed, he did earn the bronze medal at 10,000 meters on October 14, behind the sprint-finish duel between Billy Mills (28:24.4) and the Tunisian Mohamed Gammoudi (28:24.8).

Figure 16.2 The pack of runners at five kilometers. Leading the race is Ron Clarke [AUS] (number 2), with Muhammad Yousaf [PAK] (number 55) to his right, and Hedhili Ben Boubaker [PAK] (number 65) and Mathias Kanda [SRH] (number 57) to his left. Identifiable runners behind this lead group include Ray Puckett [NZL] (number 53), Naftali Temu [KEN] (number 37), Christantus Nyakwayo [KEN] (number 35), Kokichi Tsuburaya [JPN] (number 77), Kenji Kimihara [JPN] (number 75), Armando Aldegalega [POR] (number 56), and Osvaldo Suarez [ARG] (number 1). Courtesy Hideaki Miyagi.

Two days later, Clarke won his heat of the 5,000 meters but finished a dismal ninth in the final after two full days of recovery. Now, terribly frustrated over his poor track performance, and with another two days of recovery, he was anxious to prove himself worthy once again. But the marathon is all about patience, not aggressiveness. Mills was running in the marathon as well (Gammoudi was not), and Clarke was determined to beat him.

Clarke passed 5 kilometers in 15:06, with Ireland's Jim Hogan 2 seconds behind. Two Tunisians then followed—Haddeb Hannachi and Hedhili Ben Boubaker—with Ron Hill close behind. Bikila was 11 seconds behind Clarke, just ahead of Italy's Antonio Ambu. Two Kenyans were there as well: the national record-holder, Christantus Nyakwayo, and an unknown, Naftali Temu.

Clarke's inappropriately fast lead running strung out the field rather quickly as everyone searched for the pace that was best for his own fitness level. At 10 kilometers, Jim Hogan caught Clarke (30:14), with Bikila given the same time but only a step away. Hannachi and Temu maintained contact, 25 seconds behind. Ron Hill had fallen back, just behind a group including Demissie Wolde, Ambu, Nyakwayo, and the new Australian champion Robert "Bob" Vagg.

At 15 kilometers Clarke, Hogan, and Bikila still controlled the race (45:35). The chasing group included Temu, Ambu, Vagg, and a new face, Hungary's József Sütö. This second group was now more than a minute behind (46:41) the leaders. Ethiopia's Demissie Wolde slowed somewhat slightly, and Mamo Wolde would soon retire, leaving the mustachioed Bikila to race without the effectiveness of their teamwork. He did that very well, his long, lean frame (175 centimeters and 55.5 kilograms—69 inches and 122 pounds) picking up the pace slightly and moving away from Hogan and Clarke. Bikila passed 20 kilometers in 1:00:58, 5 seconds ahead of Hogan. Clarke (1:01:39) could not manage this pace, and he slowed appropriately. Demissie Wolde regained his form, getting ahead of Ambu and Sütö. Japan's Kokichi Tsuburaya was alongside Demissie Wolde as they passed 20 kilometers (1:02:46).

Bikila reached the turnaround point in 1:04:28 and appeared in complete control (figure 16.3). Only Hogan was close. By 25 kilometers, Bikila was 15 seconds ahead (1:16:40), but now Clarke, still in third (1:18:02), was being pressed by Tsuburaya, Sütö, and Wolde. Kimihara had slipped into seventh place, together with Billy Mills and the British pair, Brian Kilby and Basil Heatley—nearly three minutes behind the leaders.

Clarke finally began to fall back, as first Tsuburaya and then Sütö challenged him. By 30 kilometers, Clarke was in fifth. Bikila (1:32:50) was now 40 seconds in front of Hogan, who was 29 seconds ahead of Tsuburaya. To clarify this separation, their race pace was about 5.3 meters per second. Sütö was only a few meters behind, but Clarke's continuing tenacity still gave him a narrow advantage over Demissie Wolde. Kilby and Heatley had now overtaken Kimihara and Mills.

The top positions were still unchanged at 35 kilometers. It was Bikila (1:49:01), Hogan (1:51:27), Tsuburaya (1:51:44), and Sütö (1:51:45). Heatley, the reigning world record-holder, had now moved ahead of Kilby into fifth (1:52:13), by 4 seconds. Clarke was in seventh, ahead of Wolde, Vandendriessche, and Buddy

Figure 16.3 Abebe Bikila successfully negotiates the turnaround point, followed closely by Britain's Jim Hogan (number 32). Courtesy Asahi Shimbun.

Edelen, the recent ex-world-record-holder, who also was making a strong late-race surge. Soon after 35 kilometers Hogan retired, simply exhausted from the pace. This meant that by 40 kilometers, Bikila (2:05:10) was three minutes clear of Tsuburaya (2:08:02). Heatley and Kilby picked up the pace, running only 1 second apart, and overtook Sütö. Edelen delivered an even faster 5 kilometers split to move into sixth, just ahead of Vandendriessche. For a summary of the top six finishers through their race, see table 16.1.

Inside the full stadium, it was Bikila on the cinders entirely alone, winning by more than four minutes in 2:12:11.2. Nearly 75,000 cheered him on (figure 16.4). If Athens is where the marathon began, Japan is where it is revered the most. Bikila's demonstration of racing excellence was magnificent. He cavorted around the finish area, doing postrace calisthenics to loosen up, his freshness making this race appear almost easy.

As results flashed onto the scoreboard, spectators could see that Bikila had just broken—no, smashed!—both the Olympic and world records, matching Kolehmainen's feat of 1920. It was the widest Olympic marathon victory margin since the race of Stenroos at Paris in 1924. From being bedridden on September 16 to having a gold medal placed around his neck on the victory podium 35 days later, Bikila extended the imagination of what the human body can achieve.

But the huge Japanese audience was also aware that one of their own—Kokichi Tsuburaya—was in perfect position to take the silver medal. He entered

TABLE 16.1

Order of Top Placers Through Control Points

	Bikila	*Heatley*	*Tsuburaya*	*Kilby*	*Sütö*	*Edelen*
10 km	=1-3	22	=13, 14	=24-29	=11, 12	=16, 17
15 km	=1-3	=18, 19	=10, 11	=20-22	=4-8	=16, 17
20 km	1	12	=5, 6	=17, 18	=6, 7	=14-16
25 km	1	=9, 10	=4-6	=9, 10	=4-6	=12-14
30 km	1	8	3	7	4	=11, 12
35 km	1	5	3	6	4	10
40 km	1	3	2	4	5	6
Finish	1	2	3	4	5	6

Figure 16.4 Abebe Bikila crosses the finish line, the first Olympic marathoner to achieve two successive victories. Courtesy Asahi Shimbun.

the stadium to an ovation the equal of Bikila's, seemingly in fine form. But Basil Heatley then appeared not far behind, still possessed of a devastating kick. Waiting until the final bend, he dashed past Tsuburaya, who simply could not respond. Heatley took the silver, Tsuburaya the bronze—Japan's first marathon medal in 28 years! Ironically, this medal sequence gave Britain the unofficial team victory by one point over Japan. On the podium, it was the first time that all three Olympic medalists were from different continents: Africa, Europe, and Asia (figure 16.5). As with Helsinki, all finishers (58) returned in less than three hours. Table 16.2 gives a synopsis of the race.

The 10,000 meters gold medalist Billy Mills finished a creditable 14th (2:22:56) after falling off pace due to dehydration in the latter 5 miles. As he tells the story (Gambaccini 1999), "I mixed 40 grams of powdered protein with Tang and

Figure 16.5 **On the victory podium, from left, are silver medalist Basil Heatley [GBR], gold medalist Abebe Bikila [ETH], and bronze medalist Kokichi Tsuburaya [JPN].** Courtesy Asahi Shimbun.

TABLE 16.2

1964 Tokyo Olympic Marathon at a Glance

Date: 21 October
Start time: 1300
Course: Out-and-back
Course distance: 42.195 km

Weather: 20°C (68°F)
Starters: 68
Finishers: 58
GPEs: 35

TOP RESULTS:

Place	*Athlete*	*GPE*	*Date of birth*	*Time*
1	Abebe Bikila	ETH	07 Aug. 1932	2:12:11.2
2	Basil Heatley	GBR	25 Dec. 1933	2:16:19.2
3	Kokichi Tsuburaya	JPN	13 May 1940	2:16:22.8
4	Brian Kilby	GBR	26 Feb. 1938	2:17:02.4
5	József Sütö	HUN	09 Sept. 1937	2:17:55.8
6	Leonard Edelen	USA	22 Sept. 1937	2:18:12.4
7	Aurele Vandendriessche	BEL	04 July 1932	2:18:42.6
8	Kenji Kimihara	JPN	20 Mar. 1941	2:19:49.0
9	Ronald Clarke	AUS	21 Feb. 1937	2:20:26.8
10	Demissie Wolde	ETH	08 Mar. 1937	2:21:25.2

New geopolitical entities represented: Luxembourg [LUX], Northern Rhodesia [NRH], Southern Rhodesia [SRH], Tanzania [TAN], Puerto Rico [PUR], Nepal [NEP], Vietnam [VIE], Thailand [THA]

Team score (unofficial):

1. GBR	25 points	(2-4-19)
2. JPN	26 points	(3-8-15)
3. USA	43 points	(6-14-23)

ground up salt tablets and turned that in as my drink for the marathon. At the first two water spots I didn't take any. At 21 miles, I think I moved into 4th place and really thought I was going to win a medal in the marathon. I was on 2:14 pace. At the next stop, they gave me my drink; it was the foulest taste I ever had, and I threw it away. I was dehydrated and at 24.5 miles, I hit the wall."

Notes on the Medalists

Abebe Bikila was the first Olympic marathon gold medalist to repeat—and with both being world best performances, it appears likely that his feat will never be matched. His early achievements and his gold medal run at Rome were outlined in chapter 15. He experienced only one defeat in the 13 marathon races that he completed, namely, on that chilly day in the Boston Marathon of 1963. Aurele Vandendriessche [BEL], "Johnny the Younger" Kelly [USA], Brian Kilby [GBR], and Eino Oksanen [FIN] are the only ones to have beaten him.

Bikila fully expected success at the 1968 Mexico City Olympics. After all, the altitude was entirely familiar to him. He increased his level of training, both in terms of long runs and in pace. He injured a hamstring, however, at a marathon in Zarauz, Spain, in July 1967 and would never recover from it, despite treatment from experts in Germany and elsewhere. Still full of competitive vigor at the age of 36 years, he hoped for the best but didn't finish the Mexico City Olympic marathon. It was his last race at the distance (see Olympic Marathon Miscellany 17.2). Table 16.3 covers Bikila's career marathon record.

Benjamin Basil Heatley, born in Kenilworth, England, started marathon racing early in his career, winning the Midlands regional title in 1956 (2:36:55.2) and 1957 (2:32:01). Between 1957 and 1963, he took a break from marathon racing and focused on shorter distances. He set a world best (47:47) over 10 miles in 1961, for example, and also won the International Cross Country Championship. He returned to marathon racing in 1963, finishing second in the British AAA championship. Then, in the Olympic year, he set a world marathon best in winning the "Poly" in 2:13:55, showing that he was fit to challenge the world at Tokyo.

Kokichi Tsuburaya's bronze medal in the marathon came one week following his sixth place finish in the 10,000 meters run. Thus, he peaked for high-quality competition at the right moment. He ran his first marathon in the Olympic year, finishing fifth at Nagoya (2:23:31) on March 20. Less than a month later (April 12) he improved nicely (2:18:20.2), placing second to Kenji Kimihara and

TABLE 16.3

Career Marathon Record of Abebe Bikila

Date	*Venue*	*Place*	*Time*	*Comments*
? June 1959	Addis Ababa	1st	2:39:50	
? Aug. 1960	Addis Ababa	1st	2:23:00	
10 Sept. 1960	Rome	1st	2:12:16.2	Olympic Games
07 May 1961	Athens	1st	2:23:44.6	
25 June 1961	Osaka	1st	2:29:27	
12 Oct. 1961	Košice	1st	2:20:12	
19 May 1963	Boston	5th	2:24:43	
31 May 1964	Addis Ababa	1st	2:23:14.4	
03 Aug. 1964	Addis Ababa	1st	2:16:18.8	
21 Oct. 1964	Tokyo	1st	2:12:11.2	Olympic Games
09 May 1965	Otsu	1st	2:22:58.8	
24 July 1966	Zarauz	1st	2:20:28.8	
30 Oct. 1966	Seoul	1st	2:17:04	
30 July 1967	Zarauz	DNF		
20 Oct. 1968	Mexico City	DNF		Olympic Games

ahead of the favored Toru Terasawa in the Mainichi Marathon at Tokyo. Injuries terminated his running career prematurely, which caused him enormous disappointment (see Olympic Marathon Miscellany 17.2).

Looking Ahead: Brief Highlights 1965-1967

1965: After winning at Boston (2:16:33), Morio Shigematsu [JPN] set yet another world best (2:12:00) at the Polytechnic Harriers Marathon on June 12. It was an upset over Toru Terasawa (2:13:41) and Buddy Edelen (2:14:34), and it was the third world best on that course in as many years. No other course has seen so many such record performances—nine in all since 1909.

1966: Scotsman Jim Alder overcame the challenge of a start at 0530 (5:30 a.m.) to take the Commonwealth Games marathon title (2:22:07.8) at steamy Kingston, Jamaica, on August 11. Irishman Jim Hogan beat the 1963 and 1964 Boston Marathon winner, Aurele Vandendriessche, for the European Athletics Championship title (2:20:04.6) at Budapest on September 4. At the year's end, Kenji Kimihara beat countryman Morio Shigematsu and captured the Asian Games gold medal (2:33:22.8) at hot, humid Bangkok on December 15.

1967: Canada hosted the Pan American Games for the first time, at Winnipeg. And one of its own, Andy Boychuk, national champion in 1966 and 1967, won the marathon on August 4 (2:23:02.4). This earned him an invitation to the Fukuoka informal world marathon championship on December 3. All the major marathon champions were traditionally invited to compete together in the early days of this Japanese classic. This meant that standing beside Boychuk at the start were the 1966 winner Mike Ryan; Ryan's Kiwi colleague Dave McKenzie, who had won the Boston Marathon in 2:15:45; and the Australian champion, Derek Clayton. The result was an out-and-back world best by Clayton (2:09:36.4), ahead of Seiichiro Sasaki (2:11:17) and McKenzie (2:12:25.8). Clayton thus became the first to break the 2:10:00 barrier.

References

Anonymous. 1964. *The Games of the XVIII Olympiad, Tokyo 1964: The Official Report of the Organizing Committee.* Vol. 2, *Competition summary and results.* Tokyo: Japanese Olympic Committee.

Ecker, T. 1996. *Olympic facts and fables.* Mountain View, CA: Tafnews Press.

Gambaccini, P. 1999. A brief chat with Billy Mills. *Runner's World Online* (June 11): 5-6.

Grombach, J.V. 1980. *The Official 1980 Olympic Guide.* New York: Times Books.

Posey, C.A. 1996. *The XVIII Olympiad.* Vol. 16. Los Angeles: World Sport Research & Publications, Inc.

Williams, M.H. 1997. *The ergogenics edge: Pushing the limits of sports performance.* Champaign, IL: Human Kinetics.

Chapter 17

1968—Mexico City

Wolde Makes It a Threepeat for Ethiopia

World Turmoil Fails to Prevent Record Attendance

Awarding the 1968 Olympic Games to Mexico City brought both delight and criticism. It would be the first time that Latin America would be host to this global sporting spectacle. Central and South America formed a huge landmass, populated by a combination of European Latinos and myriad indigenous cultures, both diverse and united. The Olympic Games needed to come here eventually.

But Mexico City is at altitude—2,240 meters (7,350 feet). While the reduction in air resistance was a delight to sprinters and jumpers, who set world records that lasted for decades (e.g., Bob Beamon's incredible long jump of 29 feet, two and one-half inches (8.90 meters), which lasted as a world record for 23 years), it was devastating to distance runners. The decreased available oxygen slowed times as never before over distances of 800 meters and longer. Also, Mexico was a developing country with enormous poverty. Why bring the Olympic Games to a venue so stressed economically—and so physiologically stressful to so many of the world's athletes?

Vietnam and the United States were engaged in warlike activities, which directly affected not only their youth in sport but the economic fabric of their countries as well. Antiwar and antidraft protests in the United States became particularly divisive. Related to this was an increasing unrest among blacks and whites regarding human rights. In April, Dr. Martin Luther King Jr. was assassinated.

The IOC had a similarly wide-ranging variety of challenges. Early in February of 1968, it voted to invite South Africa to the Games provided its teams were multiracial and selected by fair treatment to all. This invitation was unacceptable to the rest of Africa, whose 33 nations—linked together as the Supreme Council of Sports in Africa—considered boycotting the Games if South Africa participated. Seven Eastern bloc nations supported them.

This pending nonparticipation added to a potential Olympic boycott by a group of black athletes from the United States, first proposed late in 1967 to provide more public attention to racial injustice. Uniting under the name of the Olympic Committee for Human Rights, they received wide support from all sports. Eventually, the IOC reversed its decision, "un-inviting" South Africa, and the looming African-Eastern bloc boycott did not occur. Also, the United States Olympic Committee formed a multiracial Consultant's Committee of Olympians to help improve its team's interpersonal relationships

While the world was immersed in these problems, various factions of the Mexican populace had their own views regarding the upcoming Olympic Games. University students vocally protested their perception of the government's excessive spending on Games preparations in the face of entrenched poverty throughout the land. Indeed, cost estimates were as high as $150 million to cover new and/or improved infrastructure and facilities (Cady 1968). Fortunately, a new Olympic stadium was not needed, as the 80,000-capacity venue built on the campus of the national university in 1955 for the Pan American Games needed only renovations. In the end, an estimated $50 million was recovered through revenues from Olympic Games attendees.

As the Games approached, however, student protesters took to the streets in huge numbers. Amid rumors that these activities could disrupt the Olympic Games as well, IOC president Avery Brundage, still fiery at 81 years of age, sternly warned Mexico's president Gustavo Diaz Ordaz that such could not be tolerated. In an unfortunate show of destructive force at a student protest rally on the Plaza de las Tres Culturas on October 2, student protesters numbering as many as 300,000 (Reineri 1998) found themselves surrounded by the national army. The military opened fire with tear gas, rifles, machine guns, and more. Reports of how many students were actually killed have been downplayed. Casualty estimates range from 260 to more than 400 dead, and more than 1,000 injured (Daniels 1996). Protesters were frightened into total submission, and all resistance stopped. The Olympic Games proceeded without further incident, and eventually a fiestalike atmosphere helped restore the Olympic spirit.

Mexico City streets appeared like an armed camp the day of the Opening Ceremonies, Saturday, October 12. But within the venues it was as if this unstable world was a planet away. Never had so many geopolitical entities participated in the Games: 112 in all. It was also a record for athlete participants—4,750 men and 781 women—the third consecutive Olympic Games total exceeding 5,000. Never before did so many geopolitical entities win gold medals—30—indicating the broadening global excellence of athletic competition.

It was the first time that Olympic track and field athletes competed on an artificial rubberized surface. Produced by the Minnesota Mining and Manufacturing Company (3M), it was called Tartan. The green infield grass combined with the white lane markers on the red track surface to match nicely the colors of the Mexican flag. The track surface was a godsend because the many rainy days would have created a muddy mess without it.

Equally welcomed by athletes but less so by officials was the next level of sophistication of the Tokyo "shoe wars." Mexican Olympic organizers contracted with Adidas as the exclusive shoe distributor within the Olympic Villages, leaving Puma out on the street. Under-the-table payments to athletes for wearing particular brands ran rampant, but little was done to identify or control who got what.

An athletes' testing program to identify those using performance-enhancing drugs was begun for the first time. Urine samples were collected from the top six competitors in each event, plus others randomly chosen. Intended primarily to catch cheaters using steroids and amphetamines, the only positive so-called doping test result came from Sweden's pentathlete Hans-Gunnar Liljenvall, whose blood alcohol level was too high.

In addition, a developing worry about male competitors masquerading as females caused the creation of a so-called femininity control program of the IOC Medical Commission. Chromosomal analysis was carried out on cells obtained by lightly scraping the inside of the mouth of each of the athletes registered as women. No men were found! The idea was to eliminate an embarrassing anatomical exam, but subsequent research has shown that chromosomal testing is also a flawed approach. It has recently been discarded in favor of a physical examination of questionable cases. The matter of "sex-testing" continues to be vigorously debated by the most respected Olympic medical scholars (de la Chapelle 1986).

The flame's journey was again complex (Durantez 1988). It was kindled in the usual manner by Greek women acting as ancient priestesses at the Altar of Hera in Olympia. Runners relayed the flame through Greece to Athens, where it was put aboard a boat to Genoa, birthplace of Christopher Columbus. The flame then followed his route to the New World, proceeding by boat to Barcelona, thence by runner relay through Spain to Puerto de Palos, where Columbus's ships set sail 476 years before. The Spanish ship *Princesa* arrived at the Caribbean port of San Salvador on September 29. Changing ships to the *Durango*, those bringing the flame continued to Veracruz, following this time the route of

Spanish explorer Hernando Cortez. Runners now relayed the torch the length of Mexico from south to north and then returned south to Mexico City, stopping briefly for a pagan ceremony atop the ancient Pyramid of the Moon at San Juan Teotihuacan.

At Estadio Olímpico on October 12, a holiday celebrated as Columbus Day in many countries in the Americas, 100,000 were stuffed into the 80,000-capacity venue for the Opening Ceremonies. They paid as much as $20 for a ticket (contrast this to $600 for an intermediate-price ticket in the 1996 Atlanta Games!). With identity known to only a few, onto the track carrying the blazing torch for its final leg came a most strikingly beautiful female athlete. She was tall (175 centimeters or 69 inches), trim (58 kilograms or 128 pounds), with short black hair, golden-olive skin, a beautiful smile, and a stride so graceful that she appeared to float! It was 20-years-old Norma Enriqueta Basilio from Mexicali, on the United States border. An Olympian (at the 80 meters hurdles, 400 meters, and 4 × 400 meters relay) and a sophomore at the University of Baja California in northern Mexico, her athleticism was obvious as she effortlessly climbed the 90 carpeted stairs in this rarefied air—the first woman to light the cauldron. Competition began on the following day, and the marathon was one week later.

The Challenge of Altitude Affects Athlete Selection

As mentioned, the major pending Olympic challenge for the marathon runners of 1968 was coping successfully with the altitude of Mexico City. The Ethiopians appeared invincible, residing and training at the same altitude, or higher. Abebe Bikila thus led a contingent with both a physiological and a mental performance advantage, although rumors abounded that he was injured.

Just as with Tokyo, these were an October Olympics. Thus, the late 1967 marathons and those occurring through the middle of 1968 were important for athlete selection. Olympic organizers staged an international marathon over their course in October 1967, one year in advance. This gave athletes both an experience in altitude competition and an altitude training opportunity in Mexico. First across the finish line was Belgium's Gaston Roelants (2:19:37.4), two minutes ahead of Japan's Kenji Kimihara. Japan's Akio Usami and Seiichiro Sasaki followed behind Kimihara, with Hungary's József Sütö in fifth. For organizers, this was a useful experience, as they determined their course was 1,200 meters short when comparing the various five kilometers split times. For athletes, it was useful as well. All were drained by the experience, but they had a year to develop a winning strategy. One who attended and almost did win was Kenji Kimihara.

Japan

With marathon talent so deep in Japan, the first several months of 1968 were stressful for its athletes as they attempted to impress selectors. Seiichiro Sasaki certainly deserved a team berth due to his outstanding second place (2:11:17) at the 1967 edition of the Fukuoka International Open Marathon Championship, where Derek Clayton set his world marathon best performance of 2:09:36.4 over an out-and-back course. Sasaki had proven that an altitude training program, which he had carried out in Mexico, was useful for him.

To ensure selection, Sasaki went on to win at Beppu on February 4 (2:13:23.8). Yoshiaki Unetani was nearly two minutes behind, but then came a pack of three only 16 seconds apart: Kenji Kimihara, Tadaaki Ueoka, and Akio Usami. Sasaki did not run in the Olympic trial race at Otsu on April 14, so these and other top-class athletes all had to sort themselves out without him. Up to 30 kilometers, it was a three-man race between Kimihara, Unetani, and Usami, the latter winning by 35 seconds over Unetani in 2:13:49. Eventually, the team selectors opted for Sasaki, Usami, and Kimihara. Unetani was passed over in favor of Kimihara probably because Kimihara also delivered a convincing victory at the "Poly" in England on a hot, sunny June 15, winning (2:15:15) by over four minutes.

The Americas

The United States planned to select its marathon team using a mid-year trial race held at an altitude similar to that of Mexico City. Alamosa, Colorado was the perfect site (2,299 meters or 7,544 feet) for the August 18 race. Among the competitors was the 1968 Boston Marathon winner, Ambrose Burfoot (2:22:17), who had defeated a fine field of Mexicans using the Boston race to test their form (two of them, Alfredo Peñaloza and Pablo Garrido, were selected to their country's Olympic team). The Colorado course was situated on a flat, high-mountain plateau, so competitors at Alamosa were not bothered by hilly terrain that typifies most altitude environments. Still, half of the 129 starters failed to finish. The winner was George Young (2:30:48.6), with Kenny Moore the runner-up in 2:31:47, and Ron Daws (2:33:09) placing third.

This was not the first Olympic marathon qualification race held at altitude, however. That distinction goes to the little-known 2:19:49.8 performance of Irishman Patrick McMahon on February 17 at Artesia, New Mexico (1,152 meters or 3,779 feet). It was an Irish national record.

The Canadian team was selected from a race held June 2 on Belle Isle in Detroit, Michigan. Although in the northern United States, the day was warm (21°C or 70°F). Peter Buniak won (2:23:57.4) in a fairly close race over 1967 Pan American Games champion Andy Boychuk (2:24:22), with Ron Wallingford a distant third. Canada had sent no marathoners to Tokyo in 1964, so this was a welcome North American addition. Buniak later changed his name to Jerome Drayton and became one of the world's premier marathoners. He did not start the Munich marathon but did compete (as Drayton) at Montréal in 1976.

Europe

The Europeans started with their team selections in late springtime. An eight-lap course at Karl-Marx-Stadt in the German Democratic Republic drew a top-class field on May 19. It was a cool, rainy morning with conditions conducive for fast times. Britain's Bill Adcocks set a European and national best time of 2:12:16.8 over Romania's Niculae Mustata (2:13:26.2), another national record. The GDR's Jürgen Busch finished third in 2:13:45.2, another national best. Britain's Jim Alder also scored a personal best (2:14:14.8). In this most amazing race, 14 runners ran their fastest times; national records were set by Hungary (Attila Tormassi), Finland (Pentti Rummakko), and Switzerland (Edgar Friedli) in addition to those mentioned above; and several European Olympic team berths were determined.

The performances of Alder and Adcocks gave ample evidence that a strong British team would be identified. The leading runners bypassed the "Poly" because their trial was the AAA championship on July 27 at Cwmbran in Wales. Not only was the day hot and sunny, but the course had three laps containing some short, steep hills. In the final miles of the race, Tim Johnston and Bill Adcocks found themselves dueling together. Johnston managed a 15 seconds victory margin only near the end (2:15:26). Jim Alder had been with them early in the race, but slowed, then recovered nicely to take third (2:16:37), with Ron Hill 34 seconds farther back. The top three composed the Olympic marathon team, with Ron Hill being awarded a berth on the British 10,000 meters team. Interestingly, Johnston had lived in Mexico for a nine-months period, hoping to perfect the strategy of altitude acclimatization. For him, this effort paid off.

The Course Tours the City but Finishes Uphill

The Mexico City marathon course was point-to-point, starting in the heart of the city on its main city square—the Plaza de la Constitución, known simply as the Zócalo. Passing many downtown landmarks during the first 30 kilometers, one of the route's delights was a run through tree-shaded Chapultepec Park. However, a liability was the large number of sharp turns, shown in the course map (figure 17.1). In the first 33 kilometers of this circuitous course, there were 29 turns of 90°, 5 acute-angle turns, and 2 turnaround points!

The Olympic stadium was near the southern edge of the city, and the final 10 kilometers were essentially a straight route down the broad Avenida Insurgentes Sur to reach it. Unfortunately, after 36 kilometers the elevation increased, making this a net uphill course. This and the original Athens route were the only net uphill Olympic marathon courses up to that time. Here, however, there was the added challenge of altitude. The Zócalo was at 2,228 meters (7,311 feet), and the stadium was at 2,290 meters (7,515 feet). Between 36 and 41.5 kilometers, just outside the stadium, the course climbed from 2,240 meters (7,351 feet) to 2,293 meters (7,525 feet). That is a rate of climb of 9.6 meters per kilometer (51 feet per mile)—not difficult unless one is at altitude and has just raced 36 kilometers! About the only happy note is that runners descended 3 meters (9.8 feet) in accessing the stadium track surface.

The course details box gives the street specifics of the marathon route. It is accessible by car and on foot, except for the area immediately around Avenida Dr. Mora. This was destroyed by the 1985 earthquake, and the reconstruction created a slightly different street pattern.

A Warm Day at Altitude Provides a Supreme Challenge

Sunday, October 20 was the final day of track and field, with only seven events scheduled. The men's high jump began at 1430 (2:30 p.m.), and the marathon began at 1500 (3:00 p.m.), along with the women's shot put final. Then came the men's 1,500 meters final (showcasing the great Kipchoge Keino), and three relays (men's 4 × 100 meters and 4 × 400 meters, and women's 4 × 100 meters). The plan was for the stadium events to finish shortly before the marathoners arrived. Buses transported the marathoners to their starting area on the Zócalo in downtown Mexico City. Race conditions at the start were warm and sunny (22.8°C or 73°F), with a light breeze from the southeast. In this rarefied air, however, once the sun approached the horizon, air cooling from the low humidity (30 percent) was greater than typically found at sea level.

The field of 75 athletes represented 41 geopolitical entities (all NOCs) and six continents, with 10 full teams of 3. Europe had 32 athletes from 17 NOCs. Africa and Asia each contributed 12 athletes, from 7 and 6 NOCs, respectively. Oceania was represented by New Zealand and Australia, each with 2 athletes, one of whom was the world record-holder Derek Clayton. The Americas were poorly represented despite the proximity of the Games. North and Central America fielded only 11 athletes from 5 NOCs, while South America had just 4, each from a different NOC. Still, it was the most global marathon in history.

The start line was in front of the large cathedral on the north side of the Zócalo. There was no doubt that the start would be on time, because it was coordinated with the church bell. It rang three times to sound the hour, and on the third gong of the huge bell, the runners were off. Spectators had a great view of the race, as athletes ran southward from the Zócalo only to turn around and return to it, and then zigzagged toward the broad Paseo de la Reforma. Alongside the historic Alameda, just a few blocks off the Zócalo, Bikila appeared in the lead group, led by Jürgen Busch. They passed in a slow 16:44 caused by the stress of altitude. Moore was also an early leader, along with Gastón Roelants (winner of the pre-Olympic race), Tim Johnston (in only his third marathon), and the two Mexicans, Alfredo Peñaloza and Pablo Garrido, the latter having given the athlete's oath at the Opening Ceremonies.

At 10 kilometers (33:54.8), Moore led along the famed Paseo de la Reforma, with 19 more runners at the front, all under 34 minutes. This included Roelants, Garrido, Johnston, and Australia's John Farrington—Derek Clayton's chief competitor at home. At the end of this group came New Zealand's Mike Ryan, Bill Adcocks, Peñaloza, and Yugoslavia's Nedo Farcic. At 15 kilometers (50:26),

COURSE DETAILS

The 1968 Mexico City Olympic Marathon

Start at the Zócalo (Plaza de la Constitución), in front of the cathedral

Continue east on Plaza to Avenida Pino Suárez

Right onto Avenida Pino Suárez to Avenida Chimalpopoca

Sharp right onto Avenida Chimalpopoca to Avenida 20 de Noviembre

Half right onto Avenida 20 de Noviembre back to Zócalo

Within the Zócalo, left, then right, and left onto Avenida 5 de Mayo to Angela Peralta

Left onto Angela Peralta to Avenida Juárez

Right onto Avenida Juárez to Dr. Mora

Right onto Dr. Mora to Avenida Hidalgo

Right onto Avenida Hidalgo to Valerio Trujano

Left onto Valerio Trujano to Paseo de la Reforma

Half right onto Paseo de la Reforma to Cuitlahuac Monument

Reverse direction at Cuitlahuac monument and return on Paseo de la Reforma to Avenida Ródano

Right onto Avenida Ródano to Avenida Melchor Ocampo

Half right onto Calzada Melchor Ocampo to Avenida Gutemberg

Sharp left onto Avenida Gutemberg to Avenida Ejército Nacional

Right onto Avenida Ejército Nacional to Moliere

Left onto Moliere to Homero

Left onto Homero to Galileo

Right onto Galileo to Horacio

Right onto Horacio (staying on north side of boulevard) to Edgar A. Poe

Reverse direction at Edgar A. Poe and return on south side of boulevard to Galileo

Right onto Galileo to Presidente Masaryk

Right onto Presidente Masaryk to Emilio Castelar

Sharp left onto Emilio Castelar to Edgar A. Poe

Half right on Edgar A. Poe to Luis G. Urbina

Left onto Luis G. Urbina to Aristóteles

Left onto Aristóteles to Avenida Newton

Half right onto Avenida Newton to Homero

Half right onto Avenida Homero to Calzada Mariano Escobedo

Half right onto Calzada Mariano Escobedo to Paseo de la Reforma

Sharp right onto Paseo de la Reforma and enter into Bosque de Chapultepec

Right onto Calzada Mahatma Ghandi through the park, crossing Paseo de la Reforma

Calzada Mahatma Ghandi becomes Calzada Chivatito through the park

Calzado Chivatito becomes Calle Molino del Rey continuing through the park and angling left back to Monumento a Los Niños Héroes

Right at Monumento a Los Niños Héroes to roundabout at intersection of

Avenida Chapultepec and Calzada Tacubaya

Right around the roundabout to Avenida Veracruz

Right onto Avenida Veracruz to Parque España

Left around Parque España to Avenida Sonora

Right onto Avenida Sonora to Amsterdam

Left onto Amsterdam and circle almost completely around Parque General San Martin to Ozuluama

Half left onto Ozuluama to Nuevo León

Sharp right onto Nuevo León back to Parque España

Sharp left onto Tamaulipas to Juanacatlán (now renamed "Alfonso Reyes")

Left onto Juanacatlán to Nuevo León

Half right onto Nuevo León to Avenida Insurgentes Sur

Half right onto Avenida Insurgentes Sur to Olympic stadium access road

Right onto Olympic stadium access road to access ramp and tunnel

Through the tunnel and onto the track at southeast corner (near start point for the 1,500 meters race)

Continue counterclockwise 295 meters around the stadium to finish at standard track event finish line

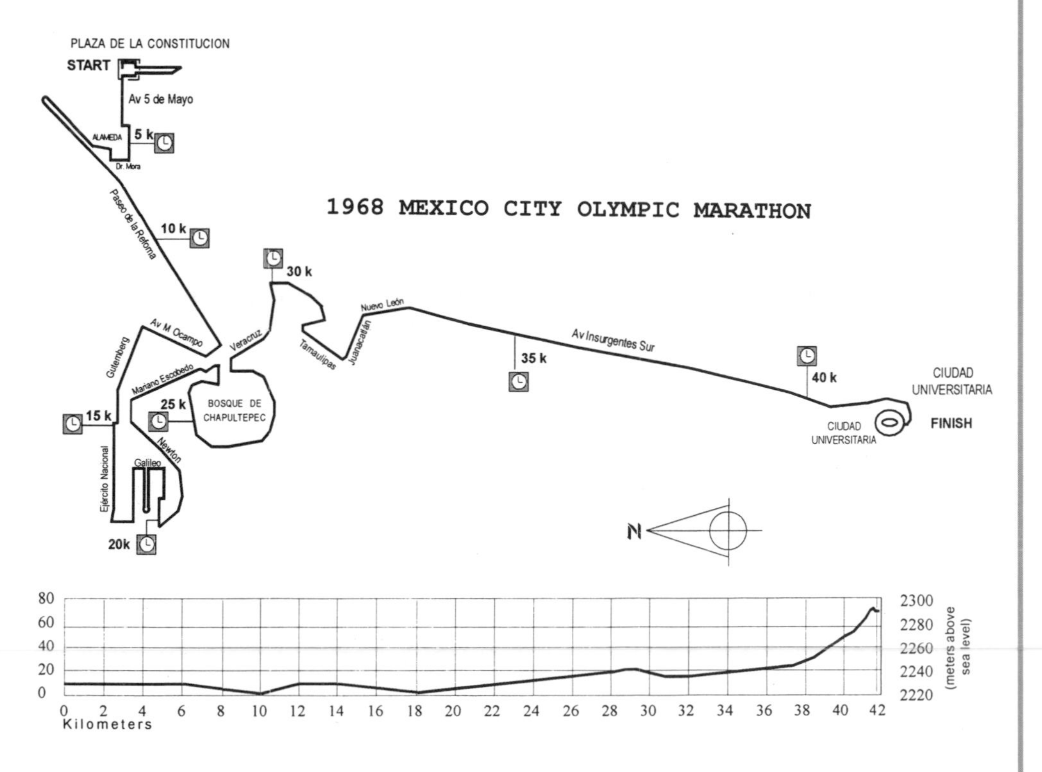

Figure 17.1 Sketch of the Mexico City Olympic marathon course. Prepared by Bob Letson.

Johnston and Farcic had a 1 second lead over Roelants and Seiichiro Sasaki. Moore and Ryan followed in 50:28, and another second behind came a pack of four: Kenya's Naftali Temu, Busch, Turkey's Ismail Akcay, and Ethiopia's Mamo Wolde. Temu had won the gold at 10,000 meters one week earlier. Bikila was well behind (51:23), and he would retire at 17 kilometers.

At 20 kilometers (1:06:02), in the midst of many sharp turns as runners ran back and forth along several parallel streets, Roelants and Johnston led the field, with Temu one step behind. A 17 seconds gap separated these three from the next two, namely Akcay and Ethiopia's Merawi Gebru, who were running together. Ryan was close behind (1:06:21), and then came Sasaki and Wolde another 5 seconds back. Gebru had been impressive during the summer with his victory over Akcay and Wolde at the Zarauz Marathon in Spain. Just behind this trio came Kimihara and Clayton—all content to run as conservatively as possible yet still maintaining contact with the leaders.

By 25 kilometers, within the huge Chapultepec Park, Wolde had moved into silver medal contention, 8 seconds behind Temu, who was leading with 1:22:29. Jim Alder and Tim Johnston were 27 seconds behind Wolde, and 3 seconds ahead of Gebru and Kimihara (1:23:37). Adcocks had slowed considerably and was back in 15th place. It was essentially single file for the next dozen competitors, each selecting his own best pace to prevent lactic acid accumulation in the working muscles (see discussion on page 269 and in chapter 25). Ryan was 6 seconds behind Gebru and Kimihara, followed by Akcay, then Roelants, and finally Garrido and Clayton together. Moore had dropped back to 14th (1:24:40). Fifteen seconds behind him was Adcocks, in 15th. Initially in the top 10, Adcocks realized the pace was too fast for him, slowed to 24th place by 10 kilometers, recovered nicely, and now steadily started moving up through the ranks.

Wolde took the lead just before 30 kilometers (1:39:20), as the runners were about to enter the final confusing twists and turns around the Parc General San Martin. Leaving the park (figure 17.2), Wolde was 6 seconds up on Temu. Kimihara moved into 3rd (1:40:25), but Japan and Britain had each lost a runner due to dropouts by Sasaki and Alder. Ryan moved ahead of Gebru, who was running alongside Johnston, with Akcay just behind. Temu began to feel the fatigue from his earlier 10,000 meters racing, and he slowed almost to a walk. By 35 kilometers, along the wide Avenida Insurgentes Sur, he had dropped to 12th. This sudden departure of the Kenyan from the top ranks put Wolde (1:55:54), Kimihara (1:57:45), and Ryan (1:57:49.6) in the medal positions at 35 kilometers. Between 25 and 30 kilometers, Adcocks had moved up from 15th to 8th, and at 35 kilometers remained there (Anonymous 1968).

At 40 kilometers (2:12:59), midway along the final ascent to the stadium, the medal positions remained unchanged. Wolde was in front by two minutes and 32 seconds, with Kimihara 6 seconds ahead of Ryan. Akcay was 85 seconds behind Ryan, in fourth. Their race pace was at about five meters per second. Adcocks had moved up from eighth to fifth, overtaking Roelants, Gebru, and Johnston, and putting himself only 21 seconds behind Akcay. Table 17.1 summarizes the various positions of the top six athletes during the race.

Figure 17.2 Wearing number 24, Ethiopia's Mamo Wolde follows the marathon line indicating the route, which was completely lined with cheering and applauding spectators. He did not take advantage of the refreshments provided at the right. The lead press vehicle can be seen well in front. Courtesy Corbis/Bettmann-UPI.

TABLE 17.1

Order of Top Placers Through Control Points

	Wolde	*Kimihara*	*Ryan*	*Akcay*	*Adcocks*	*Gebru*
10 km	=11-15	=46, 47	=6-10	=22, 23	=6-10	=11-15
15 km	=7-10	15	=5, 6	=7-10	24	=11, 12
20 km	=8, 9	=8, 9	6	=4, 5	17	=4, 5
25 km	2	=5, 6	7	8	15	=5, 6
30 km	1	2	3	=4-6	8	=4-6
35 km	1	2	3	5	8	7
40 km	1	2	3	4	5	6
Finish	1	2	3	4	5	6

Mamo Wolde reached the Olympic stadium at very close to 1720 (5:20 p.m.). It was still jammed with spectators. Entering near the 1,500 meters start point, wearing bib number 24, he had three quarters of a lap around to reach the finish. Quite logically, he expected applause and cheers of approval as the entering marathon gold medalist. Instead, there were only hushed conversations. He could hear his footsteps as he padded around the track on his lap to the finish. His entrance had scarcely been noticed. Instead, 80,000 pairs of eyes were focused on the high jump pit.

Two competitors remained, both Americans. Each had jumped twice and missed at 2.24 meters (7 feet, four and one-quarter inches), and had one attempt remaining at this height. Typically, during a high-jump competition, athletes take their start positions and rock back and forth to synchronize their minds with their forward momentum. The audience hushes to a whisper, permitting them full concentration. Today was special, because Dick Fosbury had a unique jumping style, twisting at his takeoff point so that he went over the bar not only headfirst but floating on his back in midair (the "Fosbury flop"). Most of the world had only heard about this, and the full stadium was captivated at seeing him in action. Fosbury did clear the bar, and the crowd erupted in cheers that simultaneously merged into a crescendo of congratulations to Wolde, who was making his way toward the finish line. Ed Carruthers failed to clear, so Fosbury was Olympic champion with a record height.

Wolde's 2:20:26.4 was slower than Bikila's times in both Tokyo and Rome (by more than eight and four minutes, respectively). Otherwise, it was the fastest marathon gold medal in Olympic Games history at that time. Given the altitude, it was a fantastic performance. After about three minutes, Kimihara and Ryan entered, and they finished 14 seconds apart (figure 17.3). Behind them, the sight of 54 more finishers entering singly—having just survived a hypoxic hell—was not pretty to watch. Tim Johnston and Akio Usami were within 1.8 seconds apart in placing 8th and 9th, but neither could muster a finishing kick. The United States took the unofficial team title, thanks to fine efforts by Kenny Moore (14th), George Young (16th), and Ron Daws (22nd). Only Moore had been a visible leader early in the marathon. Race details are provided in table 17.2.

At the postrace press conference, the Ethiopian story emerged more fully. Negussie Roba, head coach of the squad, made public for the first time that Bikila had been hobbled by a bone fracture in his left fibula, which not only curtailed his training but gave him intolerable pain during the race. Wolde knew this and, during the race, focused on "being Bikila," not beating Bikila.

The final finisher of the day was Tanzania's John Stephen Akhwari (3:20:46), later identified for special recognition as one who symbolizes Olympic ideals (Greenspan 1995). As he hobbled out of the approaching dusk onto the illuminated track, his right leg bloodied and bandaged at both the knee and thigh, the estimated 10,000 remaining spectators began to clap for him in appreciation. By the time he finished, the crowd had again gone wild; one would have thought he won. He did, in his own way. At his press conference, he was asked why he had not quit once he realized he was in such a sorry state. His reply remains a

Figure 17.3 On the victory podium early in the evening, Japan's Kenji Kimihara shakes the hand of the dignitary who presented him with his silver medal. To his left are the other two smiling medalists, Ethiopia's Mamo Wolde and New Zealand's Michael Ryan. Courtesy Corbis/Bettmann-UPI.

classic: "My country did not send me to start the race. They sent me to finish the race." He would finish an excellent fifth place (2:15:05) in the 1970 Commonwealth Games marathon two years later.

It is true that those who reside and train at altitude do acclimatize significantly to hypoxia. Their kidneys respond by increasing production of a hormone called erythropoietin (EPO). In turn, this directly stimulates their bone marrow to increase red blood cell production. Hemoglobin fills roughly one-third of each red blood cell, and hemoglobin transports 98.5 percent of the blood's oxygen. An accompanying increase in plasma volume keeps the blood thin, so that the work of the heart in pumping blood through the vessels is not increased excessively. But an increase in the work of breathing is still required to bring the rarefied environmental air into contact with the blood. This explains why even altitude-acclimatized people cannot race as fast at altitude as at sea level. In addition to altitude residence acclimatization, athletes also know that they must be very cognizant of pace in long races such as an altitude marathon. They must delay racing faster than their so-called anaerobic threshold pace until the final portion of their race. Otherwise, the debilitating effects of lactic acidosis will slow their pace enormously. Scrutiny of the intermediate split times for all competitors at Mexico City shows clearly that those starting conservatively finished well, whereas those who were more aggressive initially finished very poorly or not at all.

TABLE 17.2

1968 Mexico City Olympic Marathon at a Glance

Date:	20 October	**Weather:**	22.8°C (73°F)
Start time:	1500	**Starters:**	75
Course:	Point-to-point	**Finishers:**	57
Course distance:	42.195 km	**GPEs:**	41

TOP RESULTS:

Place	*Athlete*	*GPE*	*Date of birth*	*Time*
1	Mamo Wolde	ETH	12 June 1932	2:20:26.4
2	Kenji Kimihara	JPN	20 Mar. 1941	2:23:31.0
3	Michael Ryan	NZL	26 Dec. 1941	2:23:45.0
4	Ismail Ackay	TUR	09 July 1942	2:25:18.8
5	William Adcocks	GBR	11 Nov. 1941	2:25:33.0
6	Merawi Gebru	ETH	12 Dec. 1932	2:27:16.8
7	Derek Clayton	AUS	17 Nov. 1942	2:27:23.8
8	Timothy Johnston	GBR	11 Mar. 1941	2:28:04.4
9	Akio Usami	JPN	31 May 1943	2:28:06.2
10	Andrew Boychuk	CAN	17 May 1941	2:28:40.2

New geopolitical entities represented: Sierra Leone [SLE], Philippines [PHI], Guyana [GUY], Nigeria [NGR], Uganda [UGA], Kuwait [KUW], Uruguay [URU], Costa Rica [CRC]

Team score (unofficial):			
	1. USA	52 points	(14-16-22)
	2. FRG	73 points	(17-23-33)
	3. KOR	113 points	(29-38-46)

OLYMPIC MARATHON MISCELLANY 17.1

The Effects of Altitude on Marathon Performance

Only 2 of the top 10 marathon finishers at Mexico City were altitude natives. Mamo Wolde and Merawi Gebru lived in Ethiopia; its capital, Addis Ababa, is on a plateau with an elevation of 2,440 meters (8,000 feet). Despite being acclimatized to altitude, they, as well as the others, discovered that their performances at the similar altitude in Mexico City were considerably slower than their sea-level personal bests prior to the Olympic Games, as shown in table 17.3 (Phillips and Gynn 1996). The variance ranges from 4 to 17 minutes. The primary influencing factor contributing to this slowing is tissue hypoxia (lowered oxygen availability) due to the decreased environmental oxygen. The air is 23 percent less dense at Mexico City than at sea level, so it contains 23 percent less oxygen. Marathon racing is essentially an aerobic event, which means runners work to maintain the fastest pace possible without accumulating lactic acid from anaerobic metabolism.

TABLE 17.3

Comparing Mexico City Performances to Personal Bests

Athlete	*Mexico City*	*Personal best*	*Difference*
Wolde	2:20:26.4	2:16:19.2	+ 4:07.2
Kimihara	2:23:31.0	2:13:33.4	+ 9:57.6
Ryan	2:23:45.0	2:14:04.6	+ 9:40.4
Akcay	2:25:18.8	2:21:09.0	+ 4:09.8
Adcocks	2:25:33.0	2:12:16.8	+13:16.2
Gebru	2:27:16.8	2:18:58.8	+ 8:18.0
Clayton	2:27:23.8	2:09:36.4	+17:47.4
Johnston	2:28:04.4	2:15:26.0	+12:38.4
Usami	2:28:06.2	2:13:49.0	+14:17.2
Boychuk	2:28:40.2	2:17:50.0	+10:50.2

Notes on the Medalists

Degaga (Mamo) Wolde was born in Dirre Jille, Ethiopia, about 60 kilometers south of Addis Ababa, and was 36 years old at the Mexico Games. Both of his parents died when he was very young, and he was raised by a godfather (Van Dyk 1999). His education stopped at the fifth grade level. His hero was Abebe Bikila, and he, too, gained his sporting opportunities as a member of the army. Mexico City was his third Olympics, the first two having been somewhat disastrous. At Melbourne in 1956, he finished last in his heats of the 800 meters, the 1,500 meters, and the 4 × 400 meters relay! As he tells the story, the Ethiopian team flew to Melbourne in DC-3 airplanes, and it took eight days of travel.

At the Tokyo Games he placed 4th in the 10,000 meters final, but then failed to finish in the marathon. He failed to finish two previous marathons as well. At the first African Games, held at Brazzaville (Congo) in July of 1965, there was no track event longer than 5,000 meters, and no marathon. Wolde finished a distant 3rd to Kip Keino and Naftali Temu in that 5,000 meters race. In 1966 he placed 17th in the Košice (Czechoslovakia) Marathon, and in 1967 he won the Zarauz (Spain) Marathon. Wolde was in superb fitness for Mexico City, and his results showed it. He first won the silver medal in the 10,000 meters on October

13. Then, on October 15, he qualified for the final in the heat of the 5,000 meters, scheduled for October 17. He decided not to run in that final, and thus was reasonably fresh for the marathon on October 20. Indeed, it was a good decision.

Wolde's erratic marathon experience includes 17 races over a span of 11 years. He either was beaten soundly or did not finish in 5 of his first 6 marathons, yet 9 of his 17 performances were among the top three places. And two of his finest efforts were when they counted most—in Olympic competition. He competed at Munich in 1972 and won the bronze medal there. Table 17.4 summarizes Wolde's career.

Kenji Kimihara was born in Kokura, Japan (presently combined with four other cities and known as Kita-Kyushu). He won 9 of 18 marathons prior to his Mexico City race. These included two Mainichi Marathons (1963 and 1964), Boston (1966), Beppu (1967), and the "Poly" four months before the Olympic Games. This was his second Olympic appearance, having placed 8th at Tokyo. After the Mexico Games he achieved his personal best, a 2:13:25.8 at the Marathon-to-Athens race in 1969, when he finished second to Bill Adcocks. He won again at Beppu in 1970 and 1971, and he was the Asian Games champion in 1966 and 1970. Kimihara was a successful Olympic competitor in 1972 as well, placing 5th. In fact, only one person has performed so well in Olympic mara-

TABLE 17.4

Career Marathon Record of Mamo Wolde

Date	*Venue*	*Place*	*Time*	*Comments*
02 Dec. 1962	Fukuoka	46th	2:41:27	
19 Apr. 1963	Boston	12th	2:35:09	
03 Aug. 1964	Addis Ababa	2nd	2:16:19.2	
21 Oct. 1964	Tokyo	DNF		Olympic Games
09 May 1965	Osaka	DNF		
02 Oct. 1966	Košice	17th	2:31:22	
30 July 1967	Zarauz	1st	2:21:30	
28 July 1968	Zarauz	3rd	2:19:58.6	
20 Oct. 1968	Mexico City	1st	2:20:26.4	Olympic Games
06 Apr. 1969	Athens	4th	2:15:17.2	
28 Sept. 1969	Seoul	2nd	2:22:07.2	
07 Dec. 1969	Fukuoka	DNF		
10 Apr. 1970	Addis Ababa	1st	2:21:50.4	
04 Sept. 1971	Enschede	7th	2:31:01	
27 May 1972	Addis Ababa	2nd	2:15:34	
10 Sept. 1972	Munich	3rd	2:15:08.4	Olympic Games
14 Jan. 1973	Lagos	1st	2:27:32	African Games

thon competition, namely, Britain's Sam Ferris in the 1924-1932 period (see Olympic Marathon Miscellany 10.1). Kimihara's Olympic marathons were the 7th (1964), 19th (1968), and 29th (1972) in his long and active career.

Michael Robert Ryan was born in Bannockburn, Scotland, and immigrated to New Zealand in 1963. At the 1966 Commonwealth Games in Kingston—his 3rd marathon—he won the bronze medal (2:27:59) in the Jamaican August heat. Near the end of that year he won the prestigious Asahi Marathon at Fukuoka (2:14:04.6) on November 27. It was an epic duel, and he won by only 0.6 second over Hidekuni Hiroshima. His Olympic marathon, at age 26, was the 10th of his career.

Olympic Marathon Miscellany 17.2

Tragic Demises of Olympic Medalists

As we read about the incredible achievements of Olympic marathon medalists, their seeming invincibility hides for a moment their susceptibility to the same kinds of tragedies that happen to the rest of us. Although their accomplishments are special, they are, after all, only human. Thus, when disaster strikes, as it has for several of the medalists, it is especially sad.

Perhaps the best-known experience is the car accident that rendered Abebe Bikila a quadriparetic (referring to a profound *weakness* of all four extremities, as compared to a quadriplegic, referring to a *paralysis* of all four limbs). It occurred on March 22, 1969, five months after his race in Mexico City. According to his daughter (Abebe 1996), while driving alone during darkness to his home 130 kilometers south of Addis Ababa, he swerved his Volkswagen Beetle to the side of the road to avoid collision with a speeding Land Rover coming toward him in the middle of the roadway. He overturned in a ditch and suffered a fracture dislocation of his sixth and seventh vertebrae, at the base of his cervical spine. A passing bus later found him, and he was brought back to Addis Ababa. Flown to Britain's renowned Stoke Mandeville Hospital for spinal cord injury rehabilitation, he never recovered the use of his lower limbs. Being a C-7 quadriparetic, he also had only minimal use of his arms. He still lived an active life and devoted his energies to helping athletes in wheelchair sports. He was a guest of honor at the Munich Olympics, and he died a year later, on October 22, 1973, of a brain hemorrhage at the age of 51 years (Wallechinsky 1996).

The 1948 London Olympic gold medalist—Argentina's Delfo Cabrera—was killed in a car accident on August 2, 1981. Leaving a surviving widow, a son, and two daughters, he was also 51 years of age.

A third gold medalist—Boughera El Ouafi, Amsterdam's marathon hero—died on October 28, 1959, at the age of 61. According to the obituary published in the French sport newspaper *L'Equipe* (Anonymous 1959), he and a partner were at El Ouafi's home, where they both were found shot to death.

(continued)

Bronze medalist (at Amsterdam) Martti Martellin of Finland was also shot, but this occurred during wartime. He was fatally wounded on the eastern front at Taipaleenjoki on March 1, 1940, defending Finland against the Russian invasion. He died later that evening at the age of 43. It was just 10 days before the end of the so-called Winter War.

Another bronze medalist, Kokichi Tsuburaya from the Tokyo Games, committed suicide on January 9, 1968. After Basil Heatley passed him on the final turn of the Tokyo stadium track, he felt so humiliated that he became determined to perform more honorably at Mexico City. In 1967, he injured his right Achilles tendon, which required surgery. During rehabilitation, it became clear that he would never again return to high-level training. Shortly thereafter, he took his own life (Quercetani 1990). As reported by Wallechinsky, he slashed his right carotid artery with a razor blade, leaving a note in which he wrote simply, "Cannot run any more."

Finally, the situation of Mamo Wolde, who won gold at Mexico and bronze at Munich, is especially distressing. Although still alive, he is one of about 3,200 who have been imprisoned in Ethiopia since 1993. These prisoners have never been formally charged (Moore 1995). The present government, which deposed the previous communist regime (known for its civil rights abuses), rounded up thousands to question for possible involvement. Limited economic resources are delaying the investigation of those being held. He remains in the Addis Ababa Central Prison in an isolated section called Alem Bekagne, which translates as "No more the world." (Van Dyk 1999). On weekends, he can talk across a fence to his 27-years-old wife, Aberash, his 6-years-old son, Tabor, and his 8-years-old daughter, Addiss.

Looking Ahead: Brief Highlights 1968-1971

1968: Bill Adcocks added to the laurels of his Olympic fifth place—and his earlier springtime win at the Karl-Marx-Stadt Marathon—by winning at Fukuoka on December 8. His 2:10:47.8 was the second fastest on that course, after Clayton's previous-year world best.

1969: Adcocks started out the year with a superb win at the classical Marathon-to-Athens race on April 6. His course record (2:11:07.2) still stands as this first Olympic marathon century closes. Not even the 1997 IAAF World Championships marathon, which 28 years later brought together the world's best, could improve upon it. Clayton further lowered the world best time to 2:08:33.6 at Antwerp on May 30, but controversy has continued ever since regarding the actual length of the course. Britain's Ron Hill then beat Clayton at Manchester, and he went on to win the European Athletics championship title at Athens on September 21 (2:16:47.8). Here he beat Adcocks as well, who ran despite an injury and had to settle for fifth. Hill then lost at Fukuoka on December 7 to Canadian newcomer Jerome Drayton (2:11:12.8).

1970: Ron Hill was impressive again, starting the year with a Boston Marathon course record 2:10:30 on a chilly, rainy April day. He recovered well, and then he faced an even more difficult contest at the Commonwealth Games in Edinburgh on July 23. Both Jerome Drayton and Derek Clayton were there, together with defending champion Jim Alder. Hill was again victorious (2:09:28) over Alder, as the other two dropped out. At year's end, Kenji Kimihara won his second Asian Games title (2:21:03) at Bangkok on December 15.

1971: Belgium's Karel Lismont upset Hill to win the European Athletics Championship marathon (2:13:09) at Helsinki on August 12. Frank Shorter won the Pan American Games marathon (2:22:40) at Cali, Colombia, on August 5, and then he started a winning streak of four consecutive Fukuoka Marathon races, this one on December 5 (2:12:50.4).

References

Abebe, T. 1996. *Triumph and tragedy.* Addis Ababa: Artistic Printers.

Anonymous. 1959. El Ouafi aura, samedi des obsèques décentes. *L'Equipe,* October 29.

Anonymous. 1968. *The Games of the XIX Olympiad.* Mexico City: Organizing Committee of the XIXth Olympiad.

Cady, S. 1968. *The New York Times,* October 28.

Daniels, G.G. 1996. *The XIX Olympiad.* Los Angeles: World Sport Research & Publications, Inc.

de la Chapelle, A. 1986. Why sex chromatin should be abandoned as a screening method for gender identification of female athletes. *New Studies in Athletics* 2: 49-53.

Durantez, C. 1988. *Le flambeau Olympique.* Lausanne: International Olympic Committee.

Greenspan, B. 1995. *100 greatest moments in Olympic history.* Los Angeles: General Publishing Group, Inc.

Moore, K. 1995. The end of the world. *Sports Illustrated* 83 (24): 78-95.

Phillips, B., and R. Gynn. 1996. *100 years of the Olympic Marathon.* Abertillery, Gwent: National Union of Track Statisticians.

Quercetani, R.L. 1990. *A modern history of track and field athletics.* Milano: Vallardi & Associati.

Reineri, G. 1998. The spirit of 1968. *IAAF Magazine* 13 (3): 40-44.

Van Dyk, J. 1999. Once a gold medallist, now a prisoner. *The New York Times on the Web,* March 24.

Wallechinsky, D. 1996. *The complete book of the Summer Olympics.* 1996 edition. New York: Little, Brown & Company.

CHAPTER 18

1972—MUNICH

Shorter Succeeds for United States in Munich

Terrorist Activities on Site Mar a Splendid Olympic Games Setting

Munich was selected to host the 1972 Olympic Games in 1966 at Rome, in accordance with the then-customary policy of choosing Olympic sites six years in advance, to provide adequate time for preparations. (This policy changed later to seven years, starting with the 1999 Nagano Winter Olympic Games.) Germany had already staged the Games 36 years before, but Munich desired to put forth an entirely different image this time around. Its citizens were renowned for their *gemütlichkeit*—their friendly spirit and love of life—and they hoped these might in the end be known as "the friendly Games."

Willi Daume, a highly successful businessman respected for his outgoing and friendly manner, headed the Organizing Committee and ensured that plans were implemented successfully. He carefully ensured that venue construction was on time and on budget, and the city was indeed transformed. Admittedly, the price tag for this construction and renovation was high—as much as $640 million—three times the outlay for the Mexico festivities. But the city benefited from the new housing, the new subway line, and a wealth of top-class sports facilities.

A huge 740 acres (300 hectares) tract of land 3.8 kilometers northwest of the city center, in suburban Oberwiesenfeld, was converted into the central focus for Olympic activities. This derelict area was much in need of reclamation. Formerly, it had been an airport and a military drill field for soldiers of the Third Reich, and then a landfill for World War II rubble (Daniels 1996). Following the Games, the village became a chic address for those wanting to live in its housing. The fountains, plazas, and parks added beauty to the already aesthetically pleasing architecture. And the athletic venues provided outstanding sporting opportunities.

The centerpiece was the new 80,000-capacity Olympic stadium. The world had never seen anything like it—a suspended tent-like roof of translucent, acrylic plastic panels covering 800,000 square feet (243,902 square meters) that resembled a dragonfly's wing overhead. The roof united not only the stadium but also the adjacent sport hall and swimming stadium. It remains intact today, and the area is a favorite tourist attraction for visitors. Attendance by athletes had never been greater—a record-setting 122 geopolitical entities sent delegations, and the athlete population exceeded 7,000 for the first time, with 6,065 men and 1,058 women.

A new system of automatic timing for the Games was created as part of a joint arrangement with Junghans and Longines. The starter's pistol was constructed in such a way that gas pressure from the exploding blank cartridge activated an electrical contact, which then started the timing system (Anonymous 1973). This was used for all timed events, including the marathon.

It appeared that the Olympic movement would finally be a genuine celebration of sport, relatively free from the world's troubles. To be sure, however, the period prior to the Games was not exactly trouble-free. Groups desirous of using the Games to publicize their dislike of apartheid did so again. The Rhodesian NOC had been invited to participate in the Games. It was a mixed-race nation with a white-rule government. The Rhodesian NOC, however, had stated its intent to send a racially mixed team of athletes, and the Supreme Council for Sport in Africa had earlier agreed that this was acceptable. After Rhodesia had arrived in Munich, however, 21 African nations threatened to withdraw if it participated. The IOC Executive Board voted 36 to 31 in favor of withdrawing Rhodesia's invitation. International Olympic Committee president Avery Brundage, now 85 years old, was outraged at the decision, but could do nothing.

On the day of the Opening Ceremonies, the arrival of the Olympic flame from Greece was especially symbolic, for it was at Berlin in 1936 that this pre-Games journey had been first completed. The flame again traveled overland from Olympia, along a 3,437 miles journey (5,530 kilometers). It was quite different from the Berlin route of 1936. Turkey and Romania were added, Czechoslovakia was omitted, and Bulgaria, Yugoslavia, Hungary, and Austria were retained. Lit on July 28, the flame arrived on August 25, one day before the ceremonies. Another German middle-distance runner with a visually pleasing running style, Günther Zahn, was selected to run the final lap, which he did with the torch held high, before lighting the cauldron.

Once the Olympic Games began, an unfortunate series of problems developed regarding officiating and general administration, involving both NOC and Games personnel. Each snafu seemed by itself somewhat minor until one realized that athlete medal positions often hung in the balance. As just one example, American swimmer Rick Demont tested positive for the stimulant ephedrine after winning the gold in his event, and he was disqualified. It was part of his asthma medication, which he had used for two years. He had informed officials before the Olympic Games exactly what medications he was using, just to be safe. Neither before the Games nor on-site had anyone informed him that he was using a banned substance. As another example, two top American sprinters missed their quarterfinal round of the 100 meters dash because they arrived too late. Their team coach, Stan Wright, had been using a long-outdated event schedule. Other nations knew about the change. Why didn't he?

These frustrations, however, paled in comparison to the disruption that occurred in the predawn hours of Wednesday, September 5, the ninth day of competition. Eight members of a Palestinian terrorist organization called Black September entered the village, made their way to the Israeli floor in the building along Connollystraße, and killed two delegation members on the spot. Taking another nine as hostages, they announced their terms: the Israeli government must release 200 Palestinians held as alleged terrorists in Israel, and the terrorists at the Olympic Games site must be provided with the means to leave Germany. Otherwise, the Israeli athletes and coaches would be killed.

Suddenly the Olympic Games were no longer a festival and sports event, but again a tool for focusing world attention on a sociopolitical problem. Competition was disrupted and eventually suspended, and village life tried to preserve a small modicum of normality. A deal was struck later in the day to transport the terrorists and hostages out to the military airport at Fürstenfeldbruck by helicopter, where an airliner would be provided to fly the terrorists to Egypt. German security at the same time began to develop a counterplan to shoot the terrorists and retrieve the Israelis. The security force leaders put their best sharpshooters at what they believed would be optimal positions for accuracy. The plan almost worked, but it did not—the outcome was horrendous. As the marksmen were rapidly picking off one terrorist after another, remaining terrorists shot four Israelis. One terrorist lobbed a grenade into the helicopter, which contained five more Israelis who were still strapped in. It blew up, and a total of 11 in the Israeli delegation lost their lives.

On the morning of September 6, a memorial service in the Olympic stadium was jammed with those desiring to come together and create some closure to this terrible tragedy. Many urged IOC president Brundage to cancel the rest of the Games. In his wisest judgment, he announced (Daniels 1996) that "We cannot allow a handful of terrorists to destroy this nucleus of international cooperation and goodwill we have in the Olympic movement. The Games must go on, and we must continue our efforts to keep them clean, pure, and honest." Six nations opted to send their delegations home, and Israel withdrew as well. The Games did go on, and Brundage bid farewell to the Games when he closed them five days later. It was a rainy, gray afternoon that some suggested as representing tears from a higher power showing sympathy for what had occurred. Replacing Avery Brundage as IOC president was 58-years-old Michael Morris, third Baron Killanin, of Ireland. It was hoped he would be able to keep the Olympic movement for youth alive for future generations.

The World's Athletes Prepare for a European Olympic Run

Japan

Japan's usual scheduling of its marathon racing season during the first four months of each year made this the first nation to fully select its traveling team. So deep was Japan's talent that two major races were scheduled on February 6. Both had the usual cloudy wintertime Pacific chill in the air, which, for runners, provides excellent racing weather. But this time an accompanying rain provided a challenge to runners to stay warm. At Beppu, Yoshiro Mifune (2:19:10.4) proved superior over Shigeki Seri (2:19:16). And at Kyoto, Susumu Sato managed a faster 2:17:37 to defeat a previously unknown Finn, Matti Vuorenmää, whose 2:18:00 was a personal best.

The actual Japanese Olympic trial race was on March 19 at Otsu, which again had nasty weather. None of the up-and-coming younger athletes upstaged the old guard, however, and the three team spots went to highly experienced stars: Akio Usami (2:20:24), Kenji Kimihara (2:21:06), and Yoshiaki Unetani (2:22:48).

The Americas

In the United States, an increasing interest in running among its masses caused longer-distance road races to spring up seemingly everywhere. In 1972, at least 124 marathons were held, 6 with more than 200 finishers. The only European contests that consistently attracted as large a number of runners as the American races were those at Manchester and Košice. A specific Olympic trial race was planned for Eugene, Oregon, on July 9, and so the top athletes logically stayed away from the springtime marathons in order to be optimally prepared in July.

The Boston Marathon on April 17 was thus largely a Pan-American athlete selection event, with some Europeans also racing. Finland's Olavi Suomalainen debuted there, and proved skillful at managing both pace and the surges applied by his Latin American competitors. He won (2:15:30) over Colombia's Victor Mora (2:15:57), who, in turn, had dashed past Mexico's Jacinto Sabinal on the final downhill after cresting the feared Heartbreak Hill. In fourth and fifth came Sabinal's teammates, Alfredo Peñaloza and Pablo Garrido.

Eugene had long been a running mecca. With weather conducive to training, miles of forested trails, excellent collegiate competition at its University of Oregon campus, which used its renowned Hayward Field Stadium, Eugene was a haven for several of the nation's finest marathoners—and the birthplace of Nike shoes. Oregon's most talented distance runner, Steve Prefontaine, from Coos Bay, had qualified for the Munich team in the 5,000 meters, and the Olympic track trials had only recently finished on the Hayward Field track. Kenny Moore, fourth at Mexico City, was also a star distance runner at the university; he was coached by the Tokyo Olympic Games' 5,000 meters bronze medalist, Bill Dellinger.

Another running mecca, Gainesville, Florida, with its Florida Track Club, had a group of top stars who would certainly challenge Moore. Frank Shorter, Jack Bacheler, and Jeff Galloway all had improved impressively over the previous year, training hard as a group in the favorable Florida weather at Gainesville. It was hard to imagine a tie at the trial, but that's what happened between Moore and Shorter (2:15:57.8). There was little reason for either to attempt a sprint finish. Another tie occurred for third and fourth, at 2:20:29.2, between Galloway and Bacheler. Galloway had already qualified for the 10,000 meters team, so Bacheler became the third athlete on the marathon squad.

Europe

European marathon activities began as the Continent's springtime season blossomed, shortly after the Boston Marathon. During a 24-hours period on April 28 and 29, two national records were lowered in two of the more powerful marathon nations. Igor Shcherbak improved his personal best by eight minutes at Uzhgorod on April 28 with a Soviet record of 2:13:16.2, in front of Leonid Moiseyev (2:13:59) and Vasiliy Sterlyagov (2:15:14). Then, on April 29 on the Karl-Marx-Stadt course, a GDR record of 2:13:19.4 was set by the republic's newest rising star, Eckhard Lesse. His win over such established athletes as Yuriy Volkov, Jürgen Busch, and Seppo Nikkari exempted him from the national championship race at Cottbus on July 2. Although at Cottbus, Busch won convincingly by four minutes (2:16:40.2), only Lesse was selected to race at Munich.

Volkov joined Shcherbak for the Soviet championship race at Novgorod on July 9, and he ran quite well—2:15:21—but the quality of Soviet marathon running relegated him to fifth! The top three made the team: Anatoliy Baranov (2:14:19.6); 1971 national champion, Yuriy Velikorodnikh (2:14:27); and Shcherbak (2:14:43).

The British team trial was conducted at Manchester on June 4 and became the AAA marathon championship. Overseas entrants came to take advantage of an excellent competitive opportunity. The field numbered 279, the largest assembled for a marathon in Europe up to that time. Two West Germans were there: the national champion Lutz Philipp and Paul Angenvoorth. Carlos Perez arrived from Spain, and Ferdi le Grange from South Africa. Le Grange had already been selected to his team as a result of a victory (2:19:02.2) by 16 minutes over a very difficult course on March 6 at Durbanville, near Cape Town. He wanted to get acclimatized to European conditions, and this race fit in as a tune-up, with adequate time to recover.

Supportive spectator cheering along the way and a cool morning start enhanced the competitive environment. It developed that British athletes proved generally superior. Ron Hill and Lutz Philipp found themselves in a two-way battle for first as the race developed. Philipp asserted himself with a last-moment dash to the tape to win by 1 second (2:12:50). Hill was unconcerned about his "loss"; he would save his sprint for Munich. Don Macgregor started conservatively, had a fine second half, and placed third (2:15:06), 11 seconds ahead of Colin Kirkham.

Another City Tour Awaits Runners on Munich's Course

Although Munich, at an elevation (Showers 1989) of 1,706 feet (520 meters), was the second-highest city to stage an Olympic Games, this was insufficient to pose a physiological problem for oxygen delivery to working muscles. Figure 18.1 shows that the route through the city was shaped like the mascot for the 1972 Olympics—the small German dog called a dachshund and affectionately named Waldi. The course was arranged so that the head of the dog faced west. Athletes ran counterclockwise, starting at the back of the dog's neck, and then continued around its ears. The dog's mouth was represented by the path through the Nymphenburg Park. His front feet composed the run through the Hirschgarten. The belly of the dog included the main downtown street of Munich. Its rear feet, rear end, and tail were all in the English Garden, a delightful parkland extending along the Isar River. Athletes then continued along the back of the dog and eventually reached the Olympic stadium. A blue dashed line painted on the roadway indicated the route to both spectators and athletes.

Despite being in proximity to the mountainous region of the Bavarian Alps, this route was essentially flat. The highest point was at 524.4 meters (1,721 feet), with the lowest point at 497 meters (1,631 feet). Organizers received high marks for designing a course that was both flat and shaded. Apart from the 1,706 meters (1.1 miles) within the stadium, fully 18,095 meters (11.2 miles) were run in forested parkland—43 percent of the route! An additional 11,157 meters (6.9 miles) included residential streets with plenty of shade trees. Only 7,466 meters (4.6 miles) were run on broad downtown streets. The course details box provides specifics of this winding tour of the city. The course remains accessible for running or touring by car. Parts of it have been used for city marathons since the Olympic Games. The Munich city marathon between 1983 and 1996 used the final 17 kilometers of the route, so those who ran that event may find the course familiar.

COURSE DETAILS

The 1972 Munich Olympic Marathon

Start at 100 meters start line

Three laps around the track counterclockwise, exiting through the stadium tunnel behind the 100 meters start line

Exit stadium tunnel and turn right onto Spiridon-Louis-Ring

Continue on Spiridon-Louis-Ring to Hanns-Braun-Brücke

Left on Hanns-Braun-Brücke over large traffic artery

Continue straight ahead onto Kusocinskidamm

Cross Landshuter Allee using a bridge, pass between large buildings of the Olympische Einkaufszentrum, turn left along the west façade of the buildings, and continue to Pelkovenstraße

Right onto Pelkovenstraße to Hanauer Straße

Left on Hanauer Straße to Georg-Brauchle-Ring

Right onto Georg-Brauchle-Ring to Allacherstraße (~5.2 kilometers)

Right onto Allacherstraße

Allacherstraße becomes von-Kahr-Straße

Continue on von-Kahr-Straße to Megerlestraße

Left on Megerlestraße to Menzinger Straße

Half left onto Menzinger Straße to Menzinger-Amalienberg Traffic Ring (~10 kilometers)

Enter onto access path into Nymphenburger Park

Continue south on access path past Großer See (keeping on the left), and then north and northeast as it reaches the Nymphenburger Schloß

Right on the access path through Nymphenburger Schloß to Maria-Ward-Straße

Left on Maria-Ward-Straße to Menzinger Straße

Continue straight through intersection to Wintrichring

Continue on Wintrichring to Nederlinger Straße

Right onto Nederlinger Straße to Baldurstraße

Half left onto Baldurstraße to Dantestraße (~15 kilometers)

Right onto Dantestraße

Dantestraße becomes Waisenhausstraße

Continue on Waisenhausstraße to Südliche Auffahrtsallee

Right on Südliche Auffahrtsallee to reflecting pool in front of Nymphenburger Schloß

Left onto Hirschgartenallee to De-la-Paz-Straße

Half left on De-la-Paz-Straße to entry path into Hirschgarten

Left into Hirschgarten, continuing east (~20 kilometers), then north, to Steuben Platz

Continue straight through Steuben Platz onto Washingtonstraße

Continue on Washingtonstraße only a few meters to Wendl-Dietrich-Straße

Right onto Wendl-Dietrich-Straße to Rotkreutzplatz

Right onto Donnerbergerstraße to Arnulfstraße

Left onto Arnulfstraße to Marsstraße

Left onto Marsstraße to Pappenheimstraße

Half left onto Pappenheimstraße to Nymphenburger Straße

Right onto Nymphenburger Straße to Stiglmaierplatz (25 kilometers)

Nymphenburger Straße becomes Brienner Straße

Continue on Brienner Straße to Odeonsplatz

Left onto Ludwigstraße to Geschwister-Scholl-Platz

Right onto Veterinärstraße to Köninginstraße

Right onto Königinstraße to southernmost entry path into Englisher Garten

Left into Englisher Garten and continue northbound the length of the park, keeping Kleinhesseloher See (~30 kilometers) on the left

(continued)

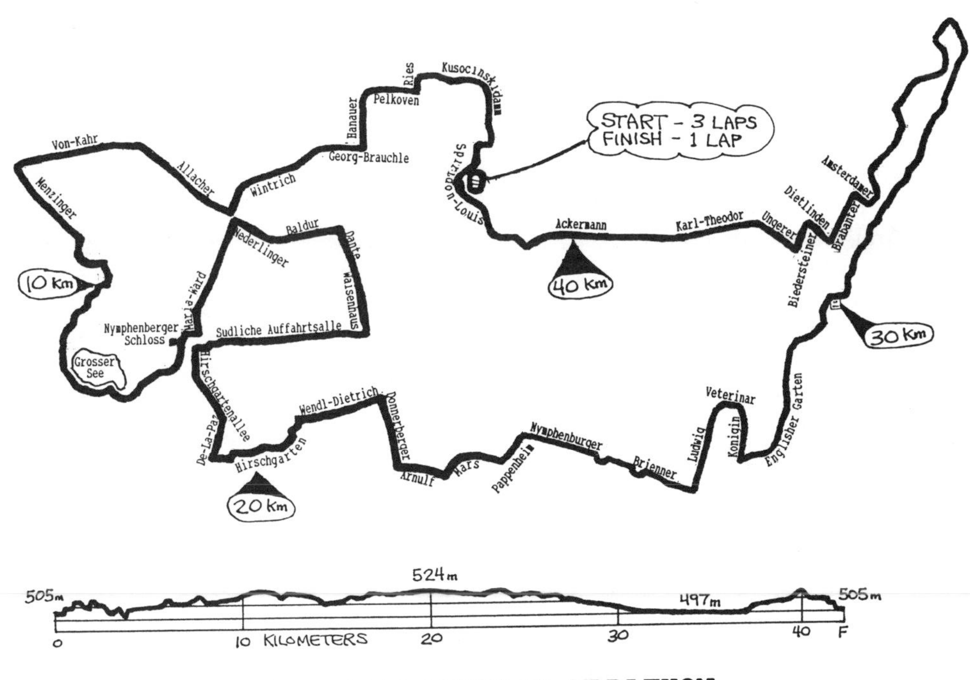

Figure 18.1 Sketch of the Munich Olympic marathon course. Prepared by Bob Letson.

1972 Course Details *(continued)*

At the northernmost end of the park, continue around and southward (~35 kilometers) to the park exit on Ernst-Penzoldt-Weg

Left onto Ernst-Penzoldt-Weg to Osterwaldstraße

Left onto Osterwaldstraße to Amsterdamer Straße

Left on Amsterdamer Straße to Brabanter Straße

Left onto Brabanter Straße

Brabanter Straße becomes Biedersteiner Straße

Continue on Biedersteiner Straße to Dietlindenstraße

Right onto Dietlindenstraße to Ungererstraße

Left on Ungererstraße to Feilitzschplatz

Sharp right across Feilitzschplatz to Karl-Theodor-Straße

Karl-Theodor-Straße becomes Ackermannstraße (~40 kilometers)

Continue on Ackermannstraße to Spiridon-Louis-Ring

Right onto Spiridon-Louis-Ring to entry into Olympic stadium

Continue through stadium tunnel onto stadium track

Continue in midtrack to finish line

Run one complete lap in lane one to finish at track event finish line

Shorter Shows the Way Through the English Garden

The race was scheduled for Sunday afternoon, September 10, when automobile pollution was minimal, but traffic had also been stopped for several hours on the marathon route to help even more. It was the final day of track and field activities, and at 1500 (3:00 p.m.) the 74 athletes from 39 geopolitical entities set forth on their Munich tour. As they ran their three laps around the track and exited, the men's high jump final had just gotten under way, and the relays would add excitement on the track until the marathoners returned, a little before 1715 (5:15 p.m.).

As usual, European nations (16, with 32 athletes) formed the dominant group. Nine athletes came from Asia (5 geopolitical entities, all also NOCs) and 10 from Africa (8 NOCs). Mamo Wolde was prepared to defend his title. From Oceania came the world record-holder, Derek Clayton, as Australia's only representative, while New Zealand fielded a full team (there were 15 teams of 3 in all). South America had 3 NOCs each with a full team of 3 athletes, while North America and Central America had 10 athletes from 5 NOCs (only the United States and Mexico sent full teams). No athletes were overwhelming favorites, so the race again became a fascinating contest to see who would emerge victorious on the day.

The race-day temperature was on the warm side for optimal racing (21.0°C or 70.0°F, with noticeable humidity). A pack of 29 passed the first 5 kilometers in

15:51, and then a gradual sorting of possible top candidates began. At 10 kilometers (31:15), racing along the paths in the huge Nymphenburger Park, Ron Hill shared the lead with Derek Clayton. Hill had gained notice due to his meticulous prerace attention to his clothing and shoes, ensuring they were of minimal weight and optimal for existing race conditions. Fishnet running vests, colorful reflective running shorts that glistened on sunny days, and specially constructed, feather-light running shoes were his trademark. A textile chemist by profession, he worked in the area of color application to apparel fabrics.

Behind Hill and Clayton were three other well-known duos: New Zealand's Jack Foster and Finland's Seppo Nikkari, Gastón Roelants [BEL] and Akio Usami [JPN], and the Ethiopians Mamo and Demissie Wolde. Frank Shorter of the United States, wearing bib number 1014, was amid a 2 seconds oval of five more athletes running 5 seconds behind the Ethiopians: Belgium's Karel Lismont, a third Ethiopian, Lengisse Bedane, and Shorter's two teammates, Moore and Bacheler. Shorter had already placed fifth in the 10,000 meters event a week earlier, on September 3, but because this was the first time that heats were contested since 1920, he had run an additional 10,000 meters on August 31.

As Shorter later recounted (Parker 1972), even this early into the marathon he had developed blisters, as the soles of his shoes were probably too thin. Shorter covered the first two 5 kilometers intervals in 15:51 and 15:33, reaching 10 kilometers in 31:24. Between 10 and 15 kilometers the pace quickened, and Shorter's 5 kilometers split was 14:57. He now found himself at the front of the pack by 5 seconds (46:21). He hadn't planned on being there, but his pace seemed effortless to him. A pack of seven runners was behind him: Lismont, Mamo Wolde, Foster, Nikkari, Usami, Roelants, and Finland's Reino Paukkinen. Surprisingly, Clayton and Hill had lost contact with the leaders, with the two other Americans, Moore and Bacheler, forming the next group behind the pack of seven.

Rather than slow down, Shorter simply continued his pace as he left the Nymphenburg Palace area and headed toward the Hirschgarten parkland. His fourth 5 kilometers split was 15:09. Thus, by 20 kilometers (1:01:30) in the Hirschgarten, he had increased his lead to 29 seconds over Lismont, who was but a second in front of Mamo Wolde, Nikkari, and Usami. Bacheler hung onto this group, with his teammate Moore still in seventh, 9 seconds behind. At 25 kilometers (1:17:05), Shorter's stride seemed easy as he sped down the main street of Munich at Stiglmaierplatz (figure 18.2), where Nymphenburgerstraße becomes Brienner Straße. His lead was now 57 seconds.

Reporters watching Shorter at the 26 kilometers refreshment station (figure 18.3) wondered what he was drinking that made him appear in such fine form. It was a dark fluid in a plastic bottle with the international sign for radiation hazard marked on it. The "magic potion" inside was none other than Coca-Cola that had been allowed to stand overnight and go flat. It provided a tasty source of much-needed fluid and energy replacement.

In second through fourth places at 25 kilometers were Clayton, Moore, and Mamo Wolde, 53 seconds behind Shorter. Bacheler and Lismont were 6 seconds farther back. At approximately 28 kilometers, runners entered the famous

Figure 18.2 Frank Shorter passes 25 kilometers, running smoothly across **Stiglmaierplatz.** Courtesy Dokumentations-und Informationszentrum München GmbH.

Figure 18.3 Shorter grabs a plastic container of de-fizzed Coca-Cola to help replenish fluid and electrolyte losses. Courtesy AP/Wide World Photos.

English Garden for an 8 kilometers run through forested parkland on a wide pedestrian pathway. Because the path was winding, Shorter focused on running the tangents to ensure the shortest route, which was the measured route, and was delighted to be running alone—a group of athletes still together would easily jostle each other. Shorter passed 30 kilometers in 1:32:49 and 35 kilometers in 1:48:40, and it was clear to everyone that he was a potential runaway victor. He appeared fresh, no one was gaining, and, if anything, the separation between the top two was increasing. Thus, at 30 kilometers, Mamo Wolde and Moore were exactly one minute behind Shorter. At 35 kilometers, Shorter was 98 seconds ahead of Mamo Wolde, who, in turn, was 14 seconds ahead of Lismont.

At 40 kilometers (2:05:31) Shorter led by two minutes and 5 seconds and appeared to have victory within his grasp. Now the race for the two remaining medals became a primary focus of attention. Lismont was 5 seconds ahead of Mamo Wolde, with Moore another 39 seconds behind in fourth. Clayton was out of contention. Bacheler slowed significantly, and Kimihara, Hill, Britain's Donald Macgregor, and Jack Foster passed him. From 40 kilometers to the finish, the top six places remained the same. Table 18.1 provides a summary.

Meanwhile, in the stadium, the usual pandemonium had been occurring during the relays—always an exciting finale to the track and field program. At 1645 (3:45 p.m.), it was time for the men's 4 × 400 meters relay, the final track event. In the high jump, athletes were taking their final attempts to decide the competition. As usual, the stadium alternately became quiet and uproarious as spectators shared the concentration of preparation and the outpouring of emotions with each attempt. No German athletes were up front in the marathon, and only intermittent information about Shorter's definitive lead had been announced over the public address system regarding race progress. Just after 1700 (5:00 p.m.) the stadium events concluded, and the audience could focus on the

TABLE 18.1

Order of Top Placers Through Control Points

	Shorter	*Lismont*	*Wolde*	*Moore*	*Kimihara*	*Hill*
5 km	=1-29	=1-29	=1-29	=1-29	=37, 38	=1-29
10 km	=10, 11	9	=7, 8	12	=17-19	=1, 2
15 km	1	=2-8	=2-8	=9, 10	14	13
20 km	1	2	=3-5	7	14	13
25 km	1	=5, 6	=2-4	=2-4	13	12
30 km	1	4	=2, 3	=2, 3	=9, 10	13
35 km	1	3	2	4	5	6
40 km	1	2	3	4	5	6
Finish	1	2	3	4	5	6

arriving marathoners. The appearance of a small athletic figure dashing from the marathon tunnel out onto the track brought the expected roar of cheers and applause befitting the next marathon gold medalist.

But it was not Frank Shorter! It was an imposter. Norbert Südhaus, a 22-years-old West German student, wearing bib number 72, wanted, as he said later, to add a touch of humor to an Olympic Games that was getting entirely too uptight. Waiting in a car outside the stadium, he chose an opportune moment, slipped through the crowd, dashed onto the course, and was quickly mistaken as a bona fide athlete. After all, he was wearing a uniform, had a competitor number, and he ran fast. Anyone aware of the usual gaunt countenance of a fit marathoner, however, would immediately have been suspicious of someone with a stocky build more like a soccer player. Police were unaware of such subtleties, however, and regardless, they had been instructed not to touch or interfere with competing athletes, lest disqualification occur because of unauthorized assistance. Thus unobstructed, Südhaus dashed through the stadium entrance and onto the track.

The tunnel entry allowed athletes onto the track near the start of the sprints. They then used the middle lane to approach and cross the finish line, do one final lap around the track in lane one, and then end their race at the finish line. Südhaus was on the backstretch of his remaining full lap as Shorter entered. Fully expecting a sudden roar of applause and approving cheers as the Munich marathon gold medalist, Shorter instead heard jeering and whistling as the crowd now realized that number 72 was a cruel fake, and voiced disapproval. Shorter remained focused on racing, continuing around the track to finish. Südhaus disappeared back through the entry tunnel without going on to the finish line, having made his point. As Shorter finished (figure 18.4) and then took a victory lap, the crowd finally gave him the cheers he so rightly deserved. Lismont and then Wolde entered the stadium, and as Shorter jogged back to the finish, he learned what had happened. The United States was seemingly in a marathon jinx. None of its three Olympic gold medalists—Hicks in 1904, Hayes in 1908, and now Shorter in 1972—had entered the stadium first!

Shorter certainly deserved congratulations for his grand achievement. It was a personal best and was only 8 seconds slower than Bikila's Tokyo Olympic record. Since the 1912 Games in Stockholm, the United States had achieved only two gold medals in distance running events of 1,500 meters or longer. Those were the 5,000 meters (Bob Schul) and 10,000 meters (Billy Mills) at Tokyo. Finally, it had a third gold medal. Lismont and Wolde had just run the third and fourth fastest Olympic marathons in history.

Shorter is shown in figure 18.5 embracing his teammate Kenny Moore as they exulted in their first and fourth places, but they were even happier after learning that Jack Bacheler had finished ninth, giving the United States the unofficial team title by a substantial margin over Ethiopia. Shortly afterward, a steady rain developed, and the stadium emptied. By the time Haiti's Maurice Charlotin entered as the final finisher (3:29:21), he was virtually alone except for the officials. Table 18.2 summarizes the race.

Figure 18.4 **Crossing the finish line with a personal best, Shorter wins the gold at Munich.** Courtesy AP/Wide World Photos.

Notes on the Medalists

Frank Shorter was born in Munich not far from the marathon course, as his American parents were stationed there on military duty following World War II; his father was an Army surgeon. He grew up in Middletown, New York, and started running at the age of 15. Attending Yale University, he was coached by the renowned Bob Giegengack. In his collegiate days, he was a decent but not outstanding athlete at shorter distances. At the end of his junior year, in 1968, Giegengack told him that he saw the marathon as Shorter's eventual best event.

Figure 18.5 Frank Shorter (left) and Kenny Moore embrace after finishing first and fourth at Munich. Courtesy Dokumentations-und Informationszentrum München GmbH.

Shorter had a wonderfully fluid stride, loved the longer distances, and ran very well in the heat. That was the year of the United States Olympic marathon trials at the high altitude of Alamosa, where he tried but dropped out.

After graduating from Yale, he moved south to Gainesville, Florida, and he eventually entered law school at the University of Florida. But he decided first to focus on getting the most out of himself as a distance runner. He made a breakthrough at the marathon in 1971. He traveled to the West Coast to run in the Kennedy Games on the track in California. He then entered the AAU marathon championship at Eugene and was runner-up to Kenny Moore. This gave him a Pan American Games marathon berth later that year, where he won. In turn, he was invited to compete at Fukuoka for the International Open Marathon Championship, and he won there as well. This set him up for the excitement of 1972. He did much of his training in Gainesville with the now-legendary Florida Track Club. His Munich gold made him the man to beat for the next few years. When he entered the Montréal Games, he had only lost one marathon in that four-years period. Waldemar Cierpinski spoiled his chances for a second gold medal in 1976, but still, owning Olympic gold and silver marathon medals was unique. Only Bikila had performed better!

TABLE 18.2

1972 Munich Olympic Marathon at a Glance

Date:	10 September	**Weather:**	21°C (70°F)
Start time:	1500	**Starters:**	74
Course:	Out-and-back loop	**Finishers:**	62
Course distance:	42.195 km	**GPEs:**	39

TOP RESULTS:

Place	*Athlete*	*GPE*	*Date of birth*	*Time*
1	Frank Shorter	USA	31 Oct. 1947	2:12:19.8
2	Karel Lismont	BEL	08 Mar. 1949	2:14:31.8
3	Mamo Wolde	ETH	12 June 1932	2:15:08.4
4	Kenneth Moore	USA	01 Dec. 1943	2:15:39.8
5	Kenji Kimihara	JPN	20 Mar. 1941	2:16:27.0
6	Ronald Hill	GBR	25 Sept. 1938	2:16:30.6
7	Donald Macgregor	GBR	23 July 1939	2:16:34.4
8	John Foster	NZL	23 May 1932	2:16:56.2
9	Jack Bacheler	USA	30 Dec. 1943	2:17:38.2
10	Bedane Lengisse	ETH	08 May 1945	2:18:36.8

New geopolitical entities represented: Bolivia [BOL], Haiti [HAI], Malawi [MAW], Nicaragua [NCA], North Korea [PRK], Somalia [SOM], Sudan [SUD], Swaziland [SWZ]

Team score (unofficial):			
	1. USA	14 points	(1-4-9)
	2. ETH	31 points	(3-10-18)
	3. GBR	33 points	(6-7-20)

Shorter continued to run marathons long after his highly competitive days, continuing as of this writing. This is highly unusual for Olympic marathon medalists, as most quit running as soon as they found themselves no longer viable at the highest level. Thus, we present in table 18.3 only his complete competitive career and have not listed those races he ran subsequently, most commonly at Honolulu where he has often returned to enjoy the excitement of that international event.

Karel Lismont, born in Borgloon, Belgium, has an overall marathon championship participation and performance record that is unequaled in quality, yet his name is obscure except to the experts. He competed in four Olympic Games, four European championships, and one IAAF/World Championships—winning five medals! His Munich silver medal was his first defeat in four starts, and by Los Angeles, he had won 8 of 21 races. Debuting with a Belgian championship victory in 1970, his career extended through the 1984 Olympic Games. In addition to the major championships, he competed globally and was a consistent top-class performer in big-city marathons, winning at Brussels, Amsterdam, Otsu,

TABLE 18.3

Career Marathon Record of Frank Shorter

Date	Venue	Place	Time	Comments
18 Aug. 1968	Alamosa	DNF		Olympic trial
06 June 1971	Eugene	2nd	2:17:44.6	AAU championships
05 Aug. 1971	Cali	1st	2:22:40	Pan American Games
05 Dec. 1971	Fukuoka	1st	2:12:50.4	
09 July 1972	Eugene	=1st	2:15:57.8	Olympic trial
10 Sept. 1972	Munich	1st	2:12:19.8	Olympic Games
03 Dec. 1972	Fukuoka	1st	2:10:30	
18 Mar. 1973	Otsu	1st	2:12:03	
20 May 1973	Korso	DNF		
02 Dec. 1973	Fukuoka	1st	2:11:45	
08 Dec. 1974	Fukuoka	1st	2:11:31.2	
15 Dec. 1974	Honolulu	4th	2:33:32	
04 Oct. 1975	Crowley	1st	2:16:29	AAU championships
22 May 1976	Eugene	1st	2:11:51	Olympic trial
31 July 1976	Montréal	2nd	2:10:45.8	Olympic Games
24 Oct. 1976	New York	2nd	2:13:12	
17 Apr. 1978	Boston	23rd	2:18:15	
22 Oct. 1978	New York	12th	2:19:32	
21 Oct. 1979	New York	7th	2:16:15	
09 Dec. 1979	Honolulu	2nd	2:17:52	
24 May 1980	Niagara Falls	85th	2:23:23	Olympic trial
27 Sept. 1981	Chicago	3rd	2:17:28	

Berlin, Munich, and Hamburg. For the record, here are Lismont's major achievements:

- European championships: 1st in 1971 (2:13:09), DNF in 1974, 3rd in 1978 (2:12:07.7), 3rd in 1982 (2:16:04)
- Olympic Games: 2nd at Munich (2:14:31.8), 3rd at Montréal (2:11:12.6), 9th at Moscow (2:13:27), 24th at Los Angeles (2:17:09)
- World championships: 9th in 1983 (2:11:24)

Mamo Wolde hoped to emulate his countryman Bikila's feat of winning two successive gold medals. Unfortunately, this was not to be for this now-40-years-old star, the Games' oldest track and field medalist. He was beaten by the youthful vigor of faster men. Shorter was 24 years old and Lismont was 23.

Looking Ahead: Brief Highlights 1973-1975

1972-73: Frank Shorter won the 1972 marathon at Fukuoka (December 3) with what stood as the year's fastest time (2:10:30). He continued successfully into 1973, returning to Japan to win the Mainichi Marathon at Otsu, Japan, on March 18—and his 2:12:03 was a course record. He returned to Fukuoka and won again on December 2 (2:11:45).

1974: This was Ian Thompson's year of excellence in the marathon. He had debuted in 1973 by winning the AAA title in 2:12:40. This gave him a British team berth for the Commonwealth Games at Christchurch, New Zealand, on January 31. He won the race in a splendid 2:09:12. This permitted plenty of time for both mental and physical recovery and preparation for his next feat: namely, a European Athletics Championships marathon victory (2:13:18.8) at Rome on September 8.

1975: Bill Rodgers of the United States finally broke the 2:10:00 barrier at Boston with a splendid 2:09:55 on April 21. This earned him a coveted invitation to run at Fukuoka on December 7. His 2:11:26.4 was of high quality, but only good enough for third place behind Canada's Jerome Drayton (2:10:08.4) and Australia's Dave Chettle (2:10:20). Cuba's Rigoberto Mendoza had surprised the world with his Pan American Games victory (2:25:02.9) at the high altitude of Mexico City on October 20.

References

Anonymous. 1973. *Die Spiele. The Official Report of the Organizing Committee for the Games of the XXth Olympiad Munich 1972.* München: Pro Sport.

Daniels, G.G. 1996. *The XX Olympiad.* Los Angeles: World Sport Research & Publications, Inc.

Parker, J. 1972. *The Frank Shorter Story.* Mountain View, CA: Runner's World Magazine.

Showers, V. 1989. *World Facts and Figures.* 3rd Ed. New York: John Wiley & Sons.

CHAPTER 19

1976—MONTRÉAL

Cierpinski Surprises Shorter in Montréal

Politics Interferes as Games Preparations Proceed

If "tragedy" was the operative word identifying the Munich Games, then "turmoil"—both financial and political—ended up as the descriptor for Montréal. At Amsterdam on May 12, 1970, when the Olympic Games were awarded to Montréal over Moscow and Los Angeles, this was hardly the planned scenario. There was so much good about Montréal. Already a beautiful city on an island at the confluence of the St. Lawrence and Prairie Rivers more than 1,000 kilometers (620 miles) inland from the Atlantic Ocean, the plan was to enhance it with dramatic sports architecture. It was a bilingual city whose residents spoke the Olympic movement's own languages. The world economy was booming, Québec's even more. Prime time TV viewing would feature live coverage into the populous United States markets, a delight to the American Broadcasting Corporation (ABC), which had paid $25 million for the broadcast rights.

A combination of evils lurking too closely together unfortunately caused financial ruin and very nearly brought the movement to its knees. The grand plan of venue construction was so grandiose, meaning expensive, that from a business standpoint everything had to proceed as projected. Little did. Unseasonably bitter cold winters put construction schedules far behind. Labor strikes and overtime work (necessary to meet deadlines) both caused costs to skyrocket. Middle Eastern oil boycotts caused a downturn in the world economy. The price of steel increased six-fold between the start of construction and the final stages of steelwork erection. The unfortunate plight of the architectural masterpiece intended as the Olympic stadium captures the essence of Montréal's struggle. As described in retrospect (Siddons 1995), "The Organizing Committee said it would cost U.S.$ 132.5 million. By the time the Olympics began, the cost was U.S.$ 795.4 million—more than U.S.$ 100 million more than Munich had spent on its entire Olympic preparations—and the stadium wasn't even finished. Not 80 cranes or 2000 workers could complete the 60,000 seat structure and its cabled roof." The completed stadium eventually seated 72,406, but Canadian taxpayers were saddled with paying off their Olympic debts from the cost overruns for many years following the Games.

While the financial challenges were close to home, the political nightmares became global in scope. The first full-scale boycott of the Olympic Games occurred when 24 African and Caribbean nations left the Olympic Village 48 hours before the Opening Ceremonies. The issue concerned a New Zealand rugby team that had been touring and competing in South Africa. A torrent of protest by the vocal Jean-Claude Ganga of Congo, leader of the Supreme Council of Sports in Africa, demanded that New Zealand have its invitation to the Olympic Games retracted for participating in sporting activities in the land of apartheid.

Lord Killanin and his most trusted IOC colleagues debated many hours as to an appropriate response. In some respects, the goings-on were irrelevant to the Olympic movement. First, rugby was not an Olympic sport. Second, other nations had conducted previous sporting tours to South Africa involving non-Olympic sports, for which no protests had been forthcoming. Third, an irony was that the rugby team was in fact multiracial, composed of Maoris and Samoans, and called the "All-Blacks." Hoping the problem would go away, the IOC ignored it, and the stalemate reached a climax when the NOC athlete delegations from the potentially boycotting nations arrived at the Montréal athletes' village. Three days before the Olympic Games began, tears were shed throughout the Olympic Village as governmental orders from the various involved nations ordered their athletes to return home. In a sense, one of the Olympic rings—the black one in the middle—had been removed. For the marathon, it was devastating. Seven African NOCs had sent athletes in 1972.

As assessed by the Organizing Committee following the Games (Anonymous 1978), "the controversies which surround the Games are inevitable. Although it is ironic that a movement based upon the noble ideals of brotherhood, equality, and the unification of mankind should also be such an ongoing object of dispute, it is possibly the price that must be paid for their popularity. . . . Because, with the eyes of the entire world focused upon them, the Games become a readily available stage upon which to parade the tensions and friction of a tormented society. Their very importance makes them a prime showcase for social injustice and discontent."

Canadian politics interfered with the Olympic Games as well, but this involved Asia. The island of Taiwan (sometimes known as nationalist China, with its capital in Taipei) was an IOC member, with its NOC known as the Republic of China (ROC). It planned to send a team in response to its invitation. Mainland China (communist China, with its capital in Beijing) did not have an NOC affiliation with the IOC until 1979. Its athletes first saw Olympic competition at the Lake Placid Winter Games in 1980. In 1972, United States president Richard Nixon visited Beijing, which signaled an improvement in diplomatic relations between mainland China and major Western nations. Canada was instrumental in resuming such ties. Economic reasons were behind this, as Canada had plenty of wheat and the Beijing government had both the funds and a desire to buy it.

Mainland China was opposed to Taiwan's use of ROC (Republic of China) as the designation of its (Taiwan's) Olympic representation and exerted pressure on Canada to prevent Taiwan from competing. Complicating matters, the United States backed Taiwan's right to use the ROC designation. Had the United States withdrawn from the Olympic Games to support Taiwan, the Games themselves could have been in jeopardy, as there would have been little reason for ABC to televise them. Canada buckled to mainland China's political pressure, denying Taiwan from participating as the ROC, and Taiwan's team withdrew.

On the brighter side, a fascinating first for these Olympic Games had two young athletes, not one, share the honors of igniting the cauldron with the Olympic flame. Stéphâne Prefontaine, 15, and Sandra Henderson, 16, represented the two languages of Canada. As they lapped the stadium en route to the cauldron, he held the torch as she supported his arm.

When what remained of the world's athletes finally entered the stadium, their achievements were splendid, as expected. Only 92 geopolitical entities participated, however, compared with 121 at Munich. The number of male athletes was decreased by more than 1,000 from Munich: 4,781 compared with 6,065. But the number of female athletes (1,247 compared with 1,058) continued to grow. This was due primarily to an increase in the number of women's sports: basketball was new, along with rowing and handball. Interestingly, the first member of the British royal family competed in an Olympic Games, in the equestrian event: Her Royal Highness Princess Anne. Although chromosomal sex testing was implemented at Montréal, she was not required to take the test!

Thirty-two world records were established in these Olympic Games, with a large number occurring in track and field: Irena Szewinska [POL] in the 400 meters, Anders Garderud [SWE] in the steeplechase, Edwin Moses [USA] in the 400 meters hurdles, Tatyana Kazankina [URS] and Alberto Juantorena [CUB] in the 800 meters, and Bruce Jenner [USA] in the decathlon, to name a few. Romania's 14-years-old Nadia Comaneci won three gold medals and had seven perfect scores in gymnastics, when never before had even one perfect score been seen!

Then there was Lasse Viren's "double-double"—after winning both the 5,000 and 10,000 meters races at Munich, he did it again in Montréal. For Canada, it was not a good day, as it was the first Olympic Games where the host nation did not win a single gold medal.

The Eastern bloc sports machine stole the show in terms of the gold-silver-bronze medal count. In order of total number of medals won, the final tally was the Soviet Union (49-41-35), the German Democratic Republic (40-25-25), and the United States (34-35-25). Perhaps the Eastern bloc athletes felt at home in this security-rigid environment, as estimates of 10,000 to 16,000 police and soldiers created almost a state of siege to prevent a repeat of the Munich episode at the village. But at a cost of $100 million, what price for peace? In a twist of irony, at the Closing Ceremonies a male streaker eluded this security overkill, darting onto the stadium floor among 500 young ladies dressed in their finest as the festivities began. It was perhaps the Olympic Games' only touch of much-needed humor!

Athletes Prepare Around the World

Asia

The international Asahi Marathon at Fukuoka on December 7, 1975, started the cool-weather pre-Olympic marathon racing season for Japan. Winners of the major world marathons were traditionally invited to this race to duel in almost laboratory conditions: a flat, cool, out-and-back course, excellent organization, and enthusiastic spectator support. The roster was like a Who's Who of those who had raced well in 1975: German Democratic Republic athletes Hans-Joaquim Truppel and Eckhard Lesse, America's Bill Rodgers, Australia's Dave Chettle, Italy's Giuseppe Cindolo, Poland's Jerzy Gross and Edward Legowski, Canada's Jerome Drayton, and others. Its global nature made it almost Olympic in quality. The depth of top performances was unprecedented: a record 29 athletes broke the 2:20:00 barrier, and 10 were under 2:14:00. Drayton set a Canadian record with his victory (2:10:08.4) over Chettle's 2:10:20. Rodgers finished third (2:11:26.4), and Cindolo was fourth at 2:11:45. Gross set a Polish record (2:13:05).

Japan's primary Olympic contenders had their Olympic trial in April, and thus did not participate at Fukuoka. Their philosophical approach to training involves huge volumes of running to achieve optimum fitness, which can only be achieved over many months of focus, uninterrupted by racing. Their trial was the Mainichi Marathon at Otsu held on April 18, the day before the Boston Marathon. Akio Usami again dominated the field. Although it was a warm day, his 2:15:22 was decisive. Usami, together with the next two finishers, Noriyasu Mizukami (2:17:15) and Shigeru So (2:18:05), composed the Japanese team.

Europe

The first of several trial races in Europe occurred at Limerick on April 11, where the Irish team was selected. Daniel McDaid ran a fine 2:13:06 to win over Jim McNamara (2:14:54) and the 1974 Boston Marathon winner Neil Cusack (2:17:07).

On the following weekend came the annual international marathon at Karl-Marx-Stadt, with athletes from Sweden, West Germany, and Poland. This was not the German Democratic Republic Olympic selection race, but German Democratic Republic athletes ran nonetheless to gain experience. While West German Gunter Mielke placed second (2:14:12.8), three of the top four places went to German Democratic Republic athletes. Heading the list was Waldemar Cierpinski at 2:13:57.2, a personal best. A former steeplechaser, he did not seem to be getting faster and thus decided to change events. Only six weeks later he raced again, at the German Democratic Republic trial in Wittenberg. Cierpinski scored another personal best (2:12:21.2). Runner-up Hans-Joaquim Truppel (2:13:44) and Bernd Arnhold (2:14:53.6) also delivered fine performances, but they were left at home. As was rapidly becoming apparent to those who understood the rather secretive but highly developed German Democratic Republic sports system, athletes placed on international traveling teams were expected to place among the top six. Cierpinski was selected for the Montréal team and thus had an enormous responsibility.

Two weeks prior to the race at Wittenberg, the Soviets selected their team. Rather than organize their own trial event, they capitalized on an already well-respected international marathon at Debno in Poland. The well-oiled Soviet sports machine provided a one-two-three finish with Leonid Moiseyev (2:12:19.8), Aleksandr Gozki (2:12:40), and Yuriy Velikorodnikh (2:12:58.2) delivering world-class performances. Poland's Kazimierz Orzel finished fourth (2:13:18.6), a personal best, which gave him confidence for competing well in Montréal.

Britain staged its trial race on May 8 in Rotherham, and an unprecedented field of 370 athletes started. The figure-eight course was traversed twice, and the day was warm. Ian Thompson was the favorite, undefeated in his previous five races. When Thompson surged at 5 miles, intending to separate himself from the rest, Barry Watson went with him. Also known for his self-confidence and aggressive racing tactics, Watson stayed with him, and at 19 miles, as Thompson started to slow with muscle cramps in his legs, Watson took the lead, winning by nine seconds (2:15:08) over Jeff Norman. Keith Angus was close behind as well (2:15:55), forming a surprise team of newcomers. Ron Hill, in fourth, and Thompson, relegated to seventh, stayed home.

United States

In the United States, Eugene was again the selection venue, with a race held on May 22, two weeks after the British trial. To enter, athletes needed to have run faster than 2:23:00 on an approved course during the previous year. Thus, during most of 1975 and early 1976, athletes searched for fast courses and cool weather coming together when their fitness was optimal. Most skipped the 1976 Boston Marathon as it was too close to the trial date. It developed that this was not the year for anyone to use the Boston race to qualify, as the region was engulfed in a springtime heat wave. At the Hopkinton starting line, it was 38°C (100°F) with a broiling sun when the gun fired at noon. Only after cresting Heartbreak Hill at 20 miles (32 kilometers) did runners experience onshore sea breezes that cooled the air to 16°C (60°F).

One particular American marathoner still needed a qualifying time to gain entry to the Olympic trial, and that was Georgetown University student Jack Fultz. Could he do it in the heat? International runners had been given fast time standards to exceed for a team spot in view of this marathon's reputation as a fast course. Hence most started out too quickly. Fultz paced himself properly and eventually found no one remaining in front but himself! He won the race in 2:20:19 and qualified for the Olympic trial.

Fultz thus joined 68 others in Eugene to decide who would represent the United States in Montréal. Obviously, Frank Shorter was the favorite. But another notable was Bill Rodgers from Massachusetts, who had won the 1975 Boston Marathon in a course record 2:09:55. This was the beginning of a golden era in American marathon annals, for Shorter's Munich victory had greatly stimulated long-distance running among top-quality college runners who decided to continue their elite athleticism after graduation. Shorter and Rodgers were in a class by themselves on this May morning, however; only 7 seconds separated the two as Shorter crossed first in 2:11:51. Stanford graduate Don Kardong started conservatively, finishing with a personal best (2:13:54), relegating Anthony Sandoval, also a Stanford athlete, to fourth by 64 seconds.

Another City Tour Promises a Fast Course

Although Montréal has plenty of hills, these are focused mainly around its Mont-Royal, a magnificent forested city park just northwest of the city center. Course designers chose a route that some described rather loosely as a square six miles on a side, just skirting the hills during the latter stages. Figure 19.1 illustrates this course and verifies that it was a roughly square circuit run counterclockwise, starting and finishing at the stadium. The course was not a magnificent tour of city monuments as with the Rome marathon, but resembled instead the Munich course, which encircled the city. It passed through five communities: St. Léonard, Montréal North, Mont-Royal, Outremont, and Montréal. The main street of Montréal, Rue Sherbrooke, was the focal point for spectators watching the finishing stages, but residents lined the entire course to cheer the athletes. Some used the underground Metro to station-hop around the city, popping up here and there to catch a glimpse of the lead pack before dashing back down and traveling to the next appropriate station.

Perhaps more interesting than the route itself was its measurement. For the first time, a bicycle revolution counter was used to measure the length of an Olympic marathon course. The technology for such measurement had been under refinement since the 1960s. John Jewell in Britain and Ted Corbitt in the United States had both suggested that counting the number of revolutions of a bicycle wheel (and fractions thereof) could be both quicker and more accurate than the tedious methods used by professional surveyors. One simply needed to precede the actual course measurement with a check of the wheel circumference using a precisely determined calibration course measured using a steel surveyor's tape.

Course Details

The 1976 Montréal Olympic Marathon

Start at 100 meters sprint start line

Run 2.9 laps counterclockwise to marathon tunnel exit in back of 100 meters start point

Exit marathon tunnel, traverse the access ramps, and reach Rue Sherbrooke

Proceed northeast to Rue Dickson

Left onto Rue Dickson

Rue Dickson merges with Boulevard Lacordaire for only a few meters to intersect with Boulevard Rosemont

Left onto Boulevard Rosemont to Boulevard Viau

Right onto Boulevard Viau to Rue Jean-Talon

Left onto Rue Jean-Talon to Boulevard Provencher

Right onto Boulevard Provencher, following its twists and turns to Rue Jean-Rivard

Left onto Rue Jean-Rivard to Boulevard Pie IX

Right onto Boulevard Pie IX to exit for Boulevard Gouin

Exit half right onto Rue Saint-Julien

Continue on Rue Saint-Julien to Boulevard Gouin

Left onto Boulevard Gouin along Prairie River to Rue Saint-Charles

Right onto Rue Saint-Charles to Avenue Parc Stanley

Left onto Avenue Parc Stanley to Rue Saint-Denis

Left onto Rue Saint-Denis to Boulevard Gouin

Right onto Boulevard Gouin to Boulevard de l'Acadie

Left onto Boulevard de l'Acadie to Avenue Sloane

Right onto Avenue Sloane to Chemin Rockland

Left on Chemin Rockland

Chemin Rockland becomes Avenue Davaar as it crosses over Canadian National Railway tracks

Continue on Avenue Davaar to Chemin de la Côte-Sainte-Catherine

Half left onto Chemin de la Côte-Sainte-Catherine to Avenue du Parc

Half right onto Avenue du Parc to multiple street intersection

Continue straight through the intersection onto Rue Hutchinson

Continue on Rue Hutchinson to Rue Milton

Right onto Rue Milton to University

Left onto University to Sherbrooke

Left onto Sherbrooke to stadium exit road

Continue around and under Sherbrooke to stadium access ramps

Follow access ramps to stadium entrance tunnel

Continue through the tunnel, onto the track, and to the finish line using coned middle lane

Run one complete lap, finishing at normal track finish line

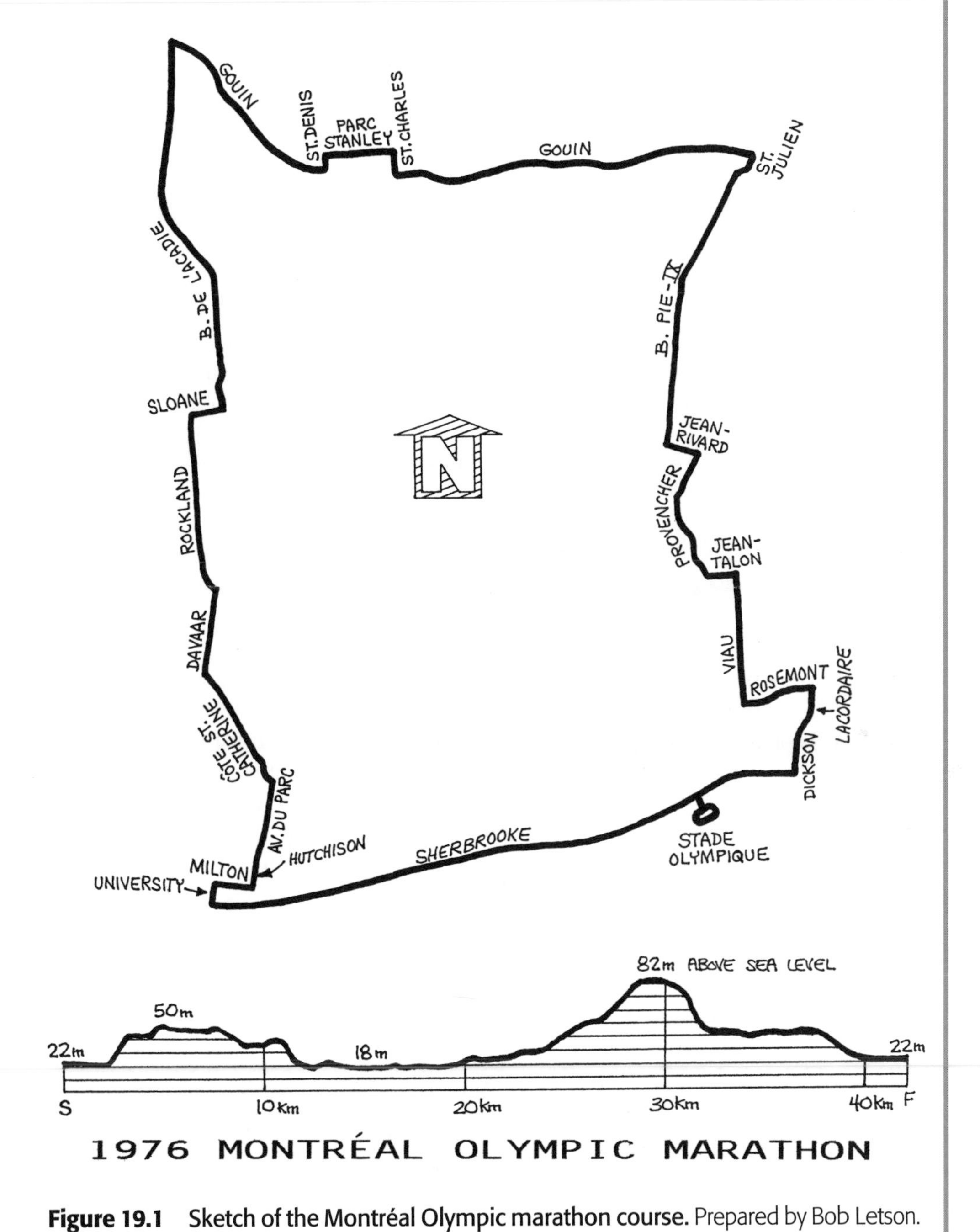

Figure 19.1 **Sketch of the Montréal Olympic marathon course.** Prepared by Bob Letson.

In the 1970-71 period, Alan Jones invented an inexpensive counter that could be mounted easily onto the front wheel of a bicycle. It recorded 20 counts per revolution (Jones 1984). Riding the course along the shortest possible route could be accomplished quickly, with a precision of roughly 0.1 percent (42 meters for the marathon distance). The counter eventually became known as the Clain Jones counter, to recognize Alan's son Clain, who took over much of the assembly detail in producing the counters.

Under the watchful eye of Norm Patenaude, the local Canadian course measurement expert, the Jones counter was used to measure the Montréal course. When compared with the more standard surveying methods, the experience was favorable. The measurers got quick results, with better accuracy measuring around corners and on undulating pavement. Course measurements were done at night using a police escort, not only to reduce traffic interruption but also to take advantage of greater temperature stability over a several-hour period. When the final ramp into the stadium was paved on June 29, the official course measurement using wheel revolution counters was performed, with appropriate adjustments made at key points to ensure the full distance while maintaining the fixed start and finish points within the stadium. A blue line was painted on the pavement to indicate the route. The course details box provides details of the streets utilized; they are still negotiable as of this writing.

Rain Dampens Shorter's Bid for a Repeat Gold

Athletes were permitted to deliver their various drink concoctions to a mixing room in the athletes' village no later than noon on the day of the race, which was July 31. These drinks were stored in insulated coolers until 1400 (2:00 p.m.) and then transported to their various indicated refreshment stations. They were kept chilled until roughly 10 minutes before athletes arrived (Anonymous 1978). The entire route was closed three hours prior to the start, thereby minimizing air pollution in the immediate vicinity. Police were stationed at intervals of 20 meters for crowd security.

As with Munich, this marathon had a stadium start, and it featured a pleasant tour of the city. But there the similarities ended. Although the field had 67 athletes, it would have been deeper had the African nations contributed. Sadly, this entire continent was absent, which denied many marathoners the chance to compete. Nearly half of the athletes (30) were from 16 European countries. Faraway Oceania had the fewest athletes; 7 came from Australia, New Zealand, and Papua New Guinea. From South America came only 4, from 3 nations. The United States and Canada fielded full teams, and 6 other North and Central American nations sent runners. Six Asian nations were represented (11 athletes), with complete teams from North Korea and Japan. In all, 36 geopolitical entities competed, with 11 full teams of 3 athletes.

Two unexpected features added an element of intrigue that defied meaningful prediction of who might win this marathon. One was the presence of the

Finnish policeman from Myrskylä—Lasse Viren, Montréal's version of Zátopek. He had already raced 30,000 meters on the track. On July 23 and 26 he had run the 10,000 meters heat and final, winning the gold. On July 28 and 30 he had run the 5,000 meters heat and final, winning another gold. Now, the next day, here he was again, appearing almost embarrassed to be amongst the group. It was his debut at the marathon! But unlike the openly jovial warmth of Zátopek, Viren was mysterious and quiet, in a real sense a victim of his own excellence.

Newspapers reported (Anderson 1976) that he and others had resorted to "blood doping"—removing a unit of their blood weeks before and then reinfusing it close to race time, thereby increasing its oxygen-carrying capacity and providing a performance edge. Unlike with steroid or amphetamine use, urinalysis could not document such hematological manipulation. It is cruel to insinuate that Viren's greatness was due to something other than talent, training, and competing well. But it was equally cruel for him to compete if he indeed had another card in his deck. Such was the frustration that characterized the ever-increasing specter of performance-enhancing madness in sport. Until proven otherwise, we take the view that his excellent results were just that—a great athlete peaking at the proper moment.

Another oddity was the weather. It was 25°C (77°F) at the 1530 (3:30 p.m.) start time, which by itself suggests conditions perhaps too warm for fast racing. But it was drizzling at the start, and this turned into rain, providing a beneficial cooling effect that increased the likelihood for fast times. However, rain could be devastating to those whose shoes did not fit perfectly, as the slippery pavement would predispose them to blistered feet. Never had an Olympic marathon been run entirely in the rain.

Hundreds of thousands lined the course despite the dampness. In the stadium, a giant video scoreboard provided spectators with an occasional glimpse of the television signal from the lead vehicle. There was no sound, but the quality was sufficient to identify those pictured. This prompted cheers from varying places in the stadium as spectators applauded upon seeing athletes from their respective countries.

The athletes made nearly three laps on the stadium track (figure 19.2) before departing, and then they had to negotiate an intricate set of access ramps from the marathon tunnel up a hill to reach the main roadway, Rue Sherbrooke. Despite the threat of imminent rain, even these ramp access roads were crowded with spectators, content for only two glimpses—out and back—of these great athletes on their historic journey (figure 19.3).

The pack passed 5 kilometers in a quick 15:19. Bill Rodgers headed a most interesting lead pack of nine: Shorter and Lismont of Munich fame, local favorite Drayton, the mysterious Viren, the ex-steeplechaser Cierpinski, India's Shivnath Singh, New Zealand's venerable cyclist Jack Foster (44 years old), Mexico's Rodolfo Gomez, and an unheralded Swede, Goran Bengtsson, running only his second marathon.

Rodgers continued to push the pace with a group of three, which included Bengtsson and Portugal's Anacleto Pinto, through 10 kilometers (30:48). Following the United States trials, Rodgers had sustained a foot injury that had hampered his training, but at the moment he seemed fine. Only 1 second

Figure 19.2 Marathon runners circle the track prior to departing the full stadium for their race through the city streets. From left, identifiable athletes include Jerome Drayton [CAN] (number 37), Akio Usami [JPN] (number 56), Massimo Magnani [ITA] (number 14), Santiago Manguan [ESP] (number 48), Goran Bengtsson [SWE] (number 55), Antonio Baños [ESP] (number 15), Jerzy Gross [POL] (number 45), Giuseppe Cindolo [ITA] (number 13), Aleksandr Gozki [URS] (number 38), and Barry Watson [GBR] (number 16). Frank Shorter is between the two faces that, in turn, are between Bengtsson and Baños. ©IOC/Olympic Museum Collections. Photo: COJ076.

behind, however, was a huge pack of 11—those listed above, plus a few more. One notable athlete not visible was Italy's Giuseppe Cindolo, who had the fastest time for 1976 (2:11:50.6 on April 25 at San Reggio d'Emilia). Unknown to most, he was injured, and he dropped out before 15 kilometers.

At 15 kilometers (46:00), Shorter led a pack of 12, but all were given the same intermediate split time. From 15 to 20 kilometers, he inserted a few surges to test both his own abilities to change pace and, perhaps, to cause a few in front to fall back. This had been his plan at Munich, where it worked well and put him into the lead. He suspected that it might not be so easy this time because there was more talent, and he planned to insert a few more surges after 25 kilometers if necessary. By 20 kilometers (1:01:24), the front pack had reduced itself to eight: Cierpinski, dressed in white, was shadowing Shorter's every move, together with Viren (figure 19.4), and then Lismont, Drayton, Singh, Bengtsson, and Rodgers.

At 25 kilometers (1:16:35), Shorter still controlled the lead group, his intermittent surging reducing to five the number racing alongside him. Cierpinski, Viren,

Figure 19.3 Just outside the mammoth Olympic stadium, runners negotiate access ramps leading to Rue Sherbrooke. Note the presence of spectators filling every available space. The route was tightly protected by connected metal railings and by police, who were positioned every 20 meters. ©IOC/Olympic Museum Collections. Photo: COJ076.

Rodgers, and Singh were running as one, with Drayton 1 second away. Bengtsson and Lismont had now fallen back, by 43 and 62 seconds, respectively. Shorter inserted a quick surge that put him 30 meters in front. Cierpinski was the only runner to respond this time, catching him, so that both went through 30 kilometers in 1:32:08. Drayton and Singh were now 15 seconds behind, Viren 13 seconds farther back, followed by Lismont yet another 8 seconds behind. To help clarify relative positions, athlete race pace was at about 5.4 meters per second.

Just after 30 kilometers, with the continuing rain forming puddles on the street, Cierpinski surprised Shorter with a sudden, sustained burst of speed. Shorter tried to cover the lost distance, but by 35 kilometers Cierpinski (1:47:24) had gained 13 seconds on him. Fifty seconds behind Shorter were Lismont, Viren, and Drayton running together, with America's Don Kardong now visible in sixth, 11 seconds farther back. Rodgers had fallen behind drastically, not due to his foot injury, as he related later, but because the pace had simply been too fast for his fitness level (Prokop 1977).

At 40 kilometers (2:03:42), Cierpinski had a 32 seconds lead over Shorter, and the top two medal spots seemed established. Kardong had moved up into third, thanks to excellent pace judgment, and he was 2 seconds in front of Lismont. Viren, still running smoothly, was in fifth, 58 seconds behind Lismont, and

Figure 19.4 In the early stages, Frank Shorter (number 39) pushes the pace despite a driving rain, with Waldemar Cierpinski (number 51) off his left shoulder. Just in back of Shorter are Lasse Viren on the outside and Bill Rodgers on the inside. Courtesy Corbis/Bettmann-UPI.

Drayton was 13 seconds farther back. Only one change occurred in this sequence of athletes in the remaining kilometer, as seen in the summary of top athlete places in table 19.1. Kardong (1996) described what happened as follows: "Lismont caught me, and I pushed as hard as I could, matching him stride for stride. On our right, the Olympic stadium, heartless megalith, loomed into view. It was a duel to the death, and we both angled for the lethal kick. Turning off the main road and clover-leafing onto a sharp downhill back into the stadium, Lismont surged. I reached deep and found . . . cement. My quads, beaten over 25 miles, were lifeless. Merciless, the Belgian outpaced me on the downward slope and burst into the stadium in third place."

As Cierpinski approached the stadium, he could hear the last bars of his country's national anthem saluting the gold medal victory of the German Demo-

TABLE 19.1

Order of Top Placers Through Control Points

	Cierpinski	*Shorter*	*Lismont*	*Kardong*	*Viren*	*Drayton*
5 km	=1-9	=1-9	=1-9	=10-28	=1-9	=1-9
10 km	=15-20	=4-14	=4-14	22	=4-14	=4-14
15 km	=1-12	=1-12	=1-12	21	=1-12	=1-12
20 km	=1-8	=1-8	=1-8	=14-17	=1-8	=1-8
25 km	=2-5	1	8	9	=2-5	6
30 km	=1, 2	=1, 2	6	7	5	=3, 4
35 km	1	2	=3-5	6	=3-5	=3-5
40 km	1	2	4	3	5	6
Finish	1	2	3	4	5	6

cratic Republic women's 4 × 400 meters relay team. These medalists were walking off the stadium track just as he entered, 40 meters away, and they cheered him on along with spectators in the filled stadium. This time, unlike in Munich and Mexico City, respectively, no imposter intruded, and the men's high jump was over. The track had been coned so that he ran a quarter lap to the track finish line and then made one additional lap in lane one to complete the distance. The lap counter at the finish line thus read "1" as Cierpinski passed, indicating the lap remaining. As he ran down the backstretch, Shorter appeared, and the lap counter remained at "1" to indicate the lap he, too, needed to run. As Cierpinski now approached the finish line again, however, the lap indicator still read "1." Speaking no English or French, to be safe he continued racing past the officials for what he believed was yet another required lap. Meanwhile, Shorter crossed the line knowing his race was completed, and as he quipped later, Cierpinski was probably the only Olympic champion to be greeted by the silver medalist waiting for him at the finish line (Ecker 1996).

The top four performances were all under Bikila's 1964 Tokyo world and Olympic record. Kardong was out of the medals by 3.2 seconds. Only seven athletes failed to finish, and the last finisher was in by two hours and 46 minutes—13 minutes quicker than in Helsinki. Only three athletes in history had run the marathon faster than Cierpinski: Clayton in 1969, Thompson in 1974, and Hill in 1970—with Rodgers equaling the mark with his 2:09:55 at Boston in 1975. Rodgers's slowdown helped the Soviets take the unofficial team title over the United States. Table 19.2 summarizes the race.

The two respected marathon superpowers, Britain and Japan, performed poorly. Britain's top athlete (George "Jeff" Norman) placed 26th, and Japan's best (Shigeru So) was 20th. The Canadians were ecstatic with Drayton's 6th place—the best for them in 64 years. The following day, Drayton's nasal voice confirmed what he had suspected: a viral cold had been developing. Viren's

TABLE 19.2

1976 Montréal Olympic Marathon at a Glance

Date:	31 July	**Weather:**	25°C (77°F), rain
Start time:	1530	**Starters:**	67
Course:	Square	**Finishers:**	60
Course distance:	42.195 km	**GPEs:**	36

TOP RESULTS:

Place	*Athlete*	*GPE*	*Date of birth*	*Time*
1	Waldemar Cierpinski	GDR	03 Aug. 1950	2:09:55.0
2	Frank Shorter	USA	31 Oct. 1947	2:10:45.8
3	Karel Lismont	BEL	08 Mar. 1949	2:11:12.6
4	Donald Kardong	USA	22 Dec. 1948	2:11:15.8
5	Lasse Viren	FIN	22 July 1949	2:13:10.8
6	Jerome Drayton	CAN	10 Jan. 1945	2:13:30.0
7	Leonid Moiseyev	URS	21Oct. 1952	2:13:33.4
8	Franco Fava	ITA	03 Sept. 1952	2:14:24.6
9	Aleksandr Gozki	URS	25 Oct. 1947	2:15:34.0
10	Hendrik Schoofs	BEL	06 Oct. 1950	2:15:52.4

New geopolitical entities represented: Bermuda [BER], Honduras [HON], Paraguay [PAR], Papua New Guinea [PNG]

Team score (unofficial):			
	1. URS	40 points	(7-9-24)
	2. USA	46 points	(2-4-40)
	3. FIN	48 points	(5-16-27)

remarkable two gold medals and a 5th place for 72.195 kilometers of racing in three events came close to matching Zátopek's three gold medals for 62.195 kilometers at Helsinki.

Notes on the Medalists

Waldemar Cierpinski was born in Neugattersleben in the German Democratic Republic. He developed his initial fitness and competitive skills through his country's highly sophisticated sports program. In his earlier track days as a steeplechaser, his personal best was 8:32.4 in 1974. He made his marathon debut that same year, finishing third at Košice. The next year he returned to Košice, placing only seventh but with a time nearly three minutes faster than previously. Despite not winning either race, it was decided that his specialty for the 1976 Olympic Games would be the marathon.

In the spring of 1976, he ran two races within the German Democratic Republic (both victories and personal bests), which raised his confidence. His performance at Wittenberg (2:12:21.2) was world-class and came almost two months before the Montréal Games. He recovered well, and the rest is history. He improved yet again—by close to two and one-half minutes—in capturing the gold medal. His marathon career eventually spanned nine years, including a feat that only Bikila had accomplished, namely, back-to-back marathon gold medals. His entire career record is summarized in chapter 20.

Frank Shorter and **Karel Lismont** were featured in chapter 18, where they first appeared on the Olympic medal scene.

Looking Ahead: Brief Highlights 1976-1979

1976: After five years of seeing loops through New York's Central Park as a race featuring local talent, race director Fred Lebow changed that image by making the New York City Marathon an international race of the highest standard. Traversing all five boroughs of the city and providing unsurpassed views of the skyline in a route that included two of the city's largest bridges, the October 24 New York City Marathon was a huge success. Fittingly, the race, only 12 weeks after the Olympics, featured Frank Shorter and Bill Rodgers in a showdown to challenge the world. Rodgers's foot problem had healed, and perhaps his hunger for victory was stronger, as he won (2:10:09.6) over Shorter (2:13:12). The event remains a late-year world classic, consistently attracting 25,000 or more runners.

1977: Having won the 1976 Fukuoka Marathon (2:12:35), Jerome Drayton won at Boston in 1977 (2:14:46) after Rodgers dropped out. Rodgers bounced back, however, with a win at Amsterdam on May 12, and then he won both the New York City Marathon (2:11:28.2) on October 23 and the Fukuoka Marathon (2:10:55.3) on December 4. Following in the 1973 footsteps of Frank Shorter, his Fukuoka performance became the year's fastest time.

1978: Rodgers continued his streak of victories at Boston (2:10:13) on April 17, and he successfully defended his New York crown (2:12:11.6) on October 22. In between were two major regional championships. Leonid Moiseyev took the European Athletics Championships title at Prague on September 3 by a scant 1.5 seconds (2:11:57.5) after dashing around colleague Nikolay Penzin on the final back turn of the track. Tanzanian Gidamis Shahanga upset Jerome Drayton to win the Commonwealth Games marathon (2:15:39.8) at Edmonton on August 11. At Fukuoka, the rising Japanese star Toshihiko Seko beat all the invited international athletes (2:10:21) on December 3. Rodgers could only finish sixth, and Drayton, who had dropped out at Boston earlier in the year, did the same here.

(continued)

1979: Rodgers recovered and won again at Boston on April 16 with a course record 2:09:27. This victory for him was especially delightful, as Seko was in second place. Rodgers went on to win his fourth consecutive New York Marathon (2:11:42) on October 21. Seko continued to race well, capturing his second of four Fukuoka Marathon titles (2:10:35) on December 2.

1980: Bill Rodgers won his fourth Boston Marathon on April 21 (2:12:11), and less than one week later, Dutchman Gerard Nijboer, in only his third marathon, won the Amsterdam Marathon with a European record 2:09:01.

References

Anderson, D. 1976. The blood scandal. *The New York Times*, August 1.
Anonymous. 1978. *Montréal 1976 Official Report*. Vol. 1, *Organization*. Ottawa: COJO76.
Ecker, T. 1996. *Olympic facts and fables*. Mountain View, CA: Tafnews Press.
Jones, A. 1984. The history of the Clain Jones counter. *RRCA Footnotes* (summer): 4-5.
Kardong, D. 1996. Unfinished business. *Runner's World* 31 (8): 84-87.
Prokop, D. 1977. The long races of Montréal. In *1976 Olympic Games*. Mountain View, CA: Runner's World.
Siddons, L. 1995. *The Olympics at 100: A celebration in pictures*. New York: Macmillan.

CHAPTER 20

1980—MOSCOW

Cierpinski Matches Bikila's Double Gold

Boycott Spoils Soviet Sport Spectacle

When Montréal was selected over Los Angeles and Moscow for the 1976 Games, it would have been logical for the latter two candidates to resubmit their bids for the 1980 Games and compete with additional bidding cities. No other cities bid, however, and Moscow was especially interested. It was a respected world capital, the heart and soul of the communist world, and its social system yearned for world recognition. Many Soviets held respected International Olympic Committee (IOC) positions, and the Soviet Union had fielded quality Olympic teams since 1952. The story has circulated that Soviet premier Leonid Brezhnev and United States president Richard Nixon privately discussed each other's mutual support for hosting the Games (Ecker 1996). However, IOC president Lord Killanin insisted that no such collusion existed among the two nations. Nonetheless, the intermixing of sport and politics during the history of the modern Olympics suggests that almost anything is possible.

Moscow was selected as the 1980 Olympic Games host at the 75th IOC session held in Vienna on October 23, 1974. This gave Moscow its turn to become a construction nightmare for six years. Indeed, the Soviets wanted to showcase their society, their city, and their culture in a grand style. Estimates have suggested that the government spent $9 billion when costs of both athletic venues and city infrastructure were tallied. The facilities were plain, functional, huge, and completed on time.

The showpiece of Olympic venues was the Luzhniki district of Moscow, built along the Moscow River, with its 100,000-capacity V. I. Lenin Central Stadium. Similar to the Mississippi River in New Orleans, although much shorter, the Moscow River snakes through the city. Flowing from northwest to southeast, 80 kilometers (50 miles) of its 473 kilometers (294 miles) length are within the Moscow metro area. One of its more perfectly crescent-shaped bends had been a low-lying marshy area filled with the huts, barns, and small gardens of locals who raised vegetables. During 1954 and 1955 this area was filled in as part of a flood prevention project. Over the next few years, Lenin stadium, two smaller stadia, a swimming center, sports grounds, and gymnasiums were completed on this site for the finals of the First Summer Spartakiade. These facilities in the Luzhniki district were now renovated and upgraded to meet Olympic standards, with modern accoutrements added to the interior of the various stadia to accommodate electronic scoreboards and broadcasting capabilities. The remaining Olympic venues were scattered elsewhere throughout the city (Anonymous 1981).

Although the Cold War still raged between the two superpowers, the United States planned to send a team to compete in Moscow. America therefore proceeded ahead, business as usual, in preparing its teams. As one of the Olympic movement's greatest supporters, where the Games went, so went the United States—until Soviet tanks rolled into Afghanistan the day after Christmas Day in 1979. The Soviets said they were asked to enter and assist with quelling civil disorder threatening Afghanistan's internal stability. The United Nations saw it differently and strongly condemned the Soviet invasion, whose 80,000 troops and armored assistance sought to impose order on a populace clearly not desirous of such, and supported a sympathetic puppet regime. We know now that the bloodshed would continue for years as the Afghanis fought valiantly to prevent a takeover. The immediate issue in January 1980 was a developing global view that the Soviet Union should withdraw its forces immediately from the country.

As had been increasingly popular, the Olympics could provide a lever. What better way to coerce one nation into supporting another's political views than hitting where it hurt the most—preventing its athletes from competing in the Olympic Games? While flattering in that such manipulation demonstrated just how powerful a social force this friendly sport competition was, tampering with the Olympic Games again seemed an inappropriate way to treat the world's athletes.

United States president Jimmy Carter was also the United States Olympic Committee (USOC) honorary president. Early in 1980, he suggested in a letter to the USOC that unless the Soviets cease their aggressive activities immediately, the Olympic Games should (a) be moved from Moscow, (b) be delayed until such aggressiveness ceased, or (c) be canceled entirely. His letter caused no small stirring of emotions. With NBC paying the $71 million rights fee to broadcast the Games, and with the United States providing one of the largest delegations to compete, if the United States and NBC did not participate, the Games would be greatly diminished. Also, if other respected nations supported America's request, the Olympic Games could diminish even more, becoming essentially a communist-bloc all-comers meet.

Some suggested that it was ironic that the United States was fully preparing to welcome the Soviet team to Lake Placid for the Winter Games starting within a few weeks of President Carter's announcement. The United States did not see it that way. Its view was that the Soviet NOC, not the Soviet government, identified and sent the Soviet team. The Soviet NOC's athletes were thus welcome to compete. However, as president, Carter believed it was not in his nation's best interests for world peace to permit his country's athletes to participate in friendly sport competition held in a nation actively engaged in aggressive military activity. The USOC House of Delegates met on April 12 to vote whether to send a team. Should the NOC deliberately defy its honorary president's (and its government's) stated desires? In addition to Carter's clearly expressed request, both houses of Congress had also recommended a boycott until the Soviets moved out of Afghanistan. The USOC decision, made at the Antlers Hotel at Colorado Springs, was 1,604 to 797 in support of the boycott.

Lord Killanin was incensed, but he could do little except state his views: "Politicians had tried to make use of sport and sportsmen for ends they were unable to achieve by political, diplomatic, or economic means." It was reminiscent of an observation the venerable American sportswriter Grantland Rice made years earlier in a poem (Smith 1976): "Wars are made by old men, but oh, how young they are where all the crosses stand."

Carter now sought support from sporting nations around the world, hoping to cause such unanimity against Moscow Games participation that the Soviets would cease their activities in Afghanistan. In the end, 63 geopolitical entities boycotted, including such powerhouses as Japan, Canada, West Germany, and 18 African nations. But 80 such entities did participate, bringing 4,092 men and 1,125 women athletes, giving a total similar to that in 1960, 1964, and 1968. The competition results were excellent: 36 world records were set, compared to 34 in Montréal. If anything, this showed how much better the Olympic Games would have been in Moscow had the whole world assembled. The denial of opportunity to athletes who had prepared for four years was once again a sad moment for them specifically and for the sporting world in general.

These Olympic Games, as with previous recent Games, had increasing problems with officiating. This was due not as much to incompetence as it was to a greater number of events where judging was involved. The fervent nationalism among officials made impartiality difficult, despite their years of training to be otherwise. But athletes performed superlatively, emphasizing to the world that such Olympic Games very much needed to continue.

At last, Ethiopia's Miruts Yifter had his day in the sun, following in the footsteps of Kolehmainen, Zátopek, and Viren. He won both the 5,000 and 10,000 meters events. He had hoped to do the same in Munich, but he became lost in the bowels of the stadium before the 5,000 meters final and missed the race! Then he was denied the chance to compete in the Montréal boycott of African nations. Britain decided not to support the United States and entered a fine team in the Moscow Games. The world will always remember the fascinating duels between Sebastian Coe and Steve Ovett over 800 and 1,500 meters. Ovett surprised Coe, the world record-holder, and won the 800 meters race. Then, Coe upstaged Ovett for the 1,500 meters gold.

At the Closing Ceremonies on Saturday evening, August 2, the tension of two weeks of living in the rigidity of Soviet society caused many to ponder the future of the Olympic movement. The athleticism of participants had been superb, and Lord Killanin traditionally invited the athletes of the world to reassemble four years hence, this time in Los Angeles. Typically, the flags of the two involved nations fly together, in concert with the IOC flag, for this glorious occasion. The United States, however, dutifully substituted for its nation's flag that of the city of Los Angeles, making its boycott of the Moscow Games symbolically as well as physically complete. One could only hope for a better world in 1984.

Athletes Selected Globally: Some to Compete, Others to Stay Home

Japan

The Moscow Olympic marathon was a midsummer event, making the late-1979 and early-1980 marathons appropriate for identifying athlete talent. The cool-weather Japanese marathon season opened with its international classic at Fukuoka on December 2, and it was a thriller. Victorious was Toshihiko Seko (2:10:35), who was followed closely by the twin Soh brothers, Shigeru (2:10:37) and Takeshi (2:10:40). This could have been a terrific Olympic marathon squad, except for two problems. First, this was not the Olympic trial. That was held on March 23 as part of the 64th Japanese championships at Otsu. Second, as news of the Olympic boycott developed, it became clear that Japan would support the United States. These above-mentioned Japanese top athletes thus did not race at Otsu. Hiroshi Yuge fought a stiff headwind alone after 33 kilometers and took that title in a slow 2:14:33. With the marathon being of such great importance in Japan's track and field program, its athletes suffered emotionally from being denied the opportunity to compete in Moscow.

Europe and the World

Key European races for identifying marathon team members began in earnest during March. The entire period from March through mid-May was generally cool and damp, delightful to marathoners. This good racing weather, combined with strong international fields, produced plenty of fast times.

In France, Essonne's sixth international marathon had more than 1,600 participants from 29 nations. For the German Federal Republic and the Netherlands, this was their team selection race. In addition, however, excellent participation from North Korea, China, and Ethiopia provided a wonderful opportunity to see athletes not often visible except at major global events such as the Olympics. Ironically, the top French athletes were absent, as their trial was at Lievin in May. The Ethiopians and North Koreans proved extremely competitive. Ethiopia's Dereje Nedi, Mergessa Tula, and Bedane Lengisse forced the pace until 27 kilometers, when North Korea's Goe Chun-Son caught them. West Germany's Werner Dörrenbacher carefully paced himself and finished strongly. Goe unleashed a strong surge at 35 kilometers and won the race in 2:10:52—the fastest time ever achieved by its marathoners outside North Korea. Only Seko and the Soh twins had ever run faster among Asian competitors. Dörrenbacher (2:12:22) was runner-up, setting a national record, as did the Dutchman Cor Vriend (2:13:20). In fourth was yet another national record, by China's Xu Liang (2:13:32). Mainland China had joined the IOC in 1979, but Xu's performance was irrelevant for Olympic Games selection purposes as the country did not send a team to Moscow. Bedane and Nedi faded to seventh and twelfth places.

Five weeks later at Amsterdam, Vriend's Dutch record was smashed. April 26 was a favorable day for running: sunny, dry, slightly windy, and a 12°C (54°F) temperature. Belgium's José Reveyn, the Netherlands's Gerard Nijboer, and Hungary's Ferenc Szekeres were in the lead by 20 kilometers and pushed each other to the limit. Nijboer's 2:09:01 was not only a Dutch record, but a European record as well! Szekeres set a Hungarian record (2:12:35), and Reveyn (2:12:40) scored a big personal best. Holland and Belgium decided not to support the Olympic boycott, and Hungary was a member of the communist East bloc. Thus, these athletes all knew they had earned a ticket to the Moscow Games.

The Karl-Marx-Stadt Marathon on May 3 used its unusual-but-familiar eight-and-three-quarters-laps parkland course to select the German Democratic Republic team. Several Scandinavian teams used it as well, as its scheduling in late spring was more accommodating to the wintertime training constraints of these athletes from far northern Europe. Even Cuba's Radames Gonzalez, the reigning Pan American Games champion and an Eastern-bloc athlete, was there. This was an opportunity for him to gain experience in cool-weather racing as preparation for Moscow. Little did he know that the eventual Olympic marathon race-day weather would be more like Havana than typical of Moscow.

As might be expected, Waldemar Cierpinski was in the race and ran splendidly. Running patiently within the pack, he quickened his pace in the later stages, and by 40 kilometers he led by 18 seconds over Norway's Øyvind Dahl. The German Democratic Republic's Hans-Joaquim Truppel and Jürgen Eberding, and Finland's Jouni Kortelainen were another 10 seconds behind. This sequence remained, and Cierpinski's 2:11:17 was a course record. Dahl's 2:11:40 was a national record, and Truppel's 2:11:56 put him on the German Democratic

Republic team. Gonzalez scored a Cuban record (2:16:15). An amazing 25 runners were under the 2:20:00 barrier.

Three weeks later, on May 24, the Soviets gave their athletes the opportunity to use the Olympic course, out-and-back from their huge stadium. Serving as the Soviet national championship, the competitive field was nearly 150 strong. The only big name missing was Leonid Moiseyev, but he had apparently been preselected because he was the reigning European and national champion. By 35 kilometers, six athletes were still in contention to win as they reached the Frunzenskaya naberezhnaya (Frunze levee) along the river, en route back to the stadium. Satymkul Dzhumanazarov surged at 37 kilometers, but Vladimir Kotov caught him at 40 kilometers and dashed into the stadium for a national record 2:10:58. Dzhumanazarov was only 18 seconds behind, also under the old record. Along with Moiseyev, these two completed the team. An unprecedented 52 athletes broke the highly esteemed 2:20:00 barrier, and 126 were under 2:30:00.

United States

The United States also scheduled its Olympic trial for May 24, the same day as the Soviet trial. The race began in a small park on the grounds of the Albert-Knox Art Museum in Buffalo, New York. Runners were precleared to pass through Canadian customs, and after a few miles they crossed the Niagara River into Canada. As with the Soviets, they too ran along a river, but not back and forth. Instead, they went downstream to Niagara Falls. It was an idyllic setting—a sunny day alongside the river, through birch-forested parkland just leafing out with springtime growth. The starting field numbered 178 out of 224 who had met the qualifying standard of 2:21:54. In terms of depth of top marathoners, the United States ranked ahead of Japan and equal to the Soviet Union. The diminutive Anthony Sandoval (1.73 meters and 51 kilograms; 68 inches and 112 pounds) unleashed a 4:44 mile between miles 22 and 23 to catch Benji Durden and take the lead. Sandoval's 2:10:18.6 victory was a personal best, as were the times for second (Durden, 2:10:40.3), and third (Kyle Heffner, 2:10:54.1). Amazingly, Ron Tabb was fourth in 2:12:39—his fourth major race in four months. A record 56 runners were under 2:20:00. For the three Olympians, it was indeed unfortunate that they could not compete at the Games.

A Flat Course Suggests a Record Run

The Moscow Olympic marathon course was out-and-back along the Moscow River, with its start and finish inside Lenin Central Stadium. Figure 20.1 illustrates the route. Athletes ran along one side of the river (downstream) toward the central business district, then crossed to the other side via two bridges that went over an island in the river. Reversing direction, they then ran along the other side of the river to a turnaround point near the giant Kiev railway station. Again reversing direction, athletes retraced their steps back into the central business district, across the island, and then back to the stadium. The paved running surface was on the top of levees, called embankments, which had been built to control river overflow.

These embankments were typically tree-lined, and the smooth asphalt and lack of hills except for the occasional grade changes with bridge crossings made this a fast course. The graceful curves of the river reduced the number of sharp turns in the course to the four bridge crossings and the turnaround point. The route certainly was not boring, as it traversed downtown Moscow, passing plenty of well-known structures. The course is still entirely accessible to runners, and thus makes an interesting scenic run.

At an altitude of 167 meters (548 feet), Moscow became the third highest Olympic venue, after Mexico City and Munich. This altitude by itself had no effect on performance, the main limiting factors being the warmth and humidity. Moscow had experienced unseasonably warm weather throughout the Olympic Games, however, and although marathon day dawned cooler than most, it was still too warm for optimal racing conditions.

Soviets Dominate as Cierpinski Gets His Double

The competitive field of marathon athletes (figure 20.2) numbered 74—similar to the previous recent few Olympic Games. Forty geopolitical entities were represented, but as with Montréal, the boycott caused a substantial underrepresentation from certain continents. From North and South America combined, for example, only 4 athletes competed: 1 each from Mexico and Cuba, and 2 from Colombia. From Oceania came only a full team from Australia. However, 11 African nations sent a total of 20 athletes, and 19 European nations sent 37. The European contingent was by far the strongest, headed by Cierpinski. Lasse Viren was back as well, but he had competed in the 10,000 meters qualifying round held in horrific heat on July 24, and then he placed fifth in the final on July 27. With only four days rest, a logical question was whether he had recovered. Asia had no representation from Japan. Six other nations sent a total of 10 athletes, including a full team from North Korea. The absence of marathon-strong nations such as Japan and the United States was particularly sad for their athletes; they each could have fielded two world-class teams.

The scheduled late-afternoon start of 1715 (5:15 p.m.) was a blessing, given the still-warm conditions (26°C or 78°F). An athlete who had few credentials to do so forged ahead from the start. Denmark's Jörn Lauenborg had a 22 seconds lead at 5 kilometers (15:48), but retired before the race was half finished. At 10 kilometers (31:16), the youngest member of the Soviet squad, 22-years-old Vladimir Kotov from the Byelorussian Soviet Federated Socialist Republic (now called Belarus), had a 6 seconds lead over his Asian teammate, Setymkul Dzhumanazarov. In turn, Dzhumanazarov had the new teenaged French sensation on his shoulder—18-years-old Jean-Michel Charbonnel, who had set a French record of 2:12:18 at Lievin on May 1. Then came five runners timed in 31:26

Course Details

The 1980 Moscow Olympic Marathon

Key: "most" = bridge; "naberezhnaya" (nab) = river embankment; "ulitsa" = street; "shosse" = avenue

Start at track event finish line on southeast corner of stadium

Run one and one-quarter laps counterclockwise around the track

Exit the stadium at the midpoint of the turn around the southeast side of the stadium

Turn right and continue for one-quarter turn around the outside of the stadium, then left onto the access road leading to Luzhnetskaya nab

Left onto Luzhnetskaya nab, passing under Metro Most and then Andreyevskiy Most

Luzhnetskaya nab then becomes Frunzenskaya nab

Continue on Frunzenskaya nab, passing under Krymskiy Most

Frunzenskaya nab then becomes Kropotkinskaya nab

Continue on Kropotkinskaya nab under Kameny Most

Kropotskinskaya nab now becomes Kremlevskaya nab

Continue on Kremlevskaya nab to Moskvoretskiy Bolshoy Most

Follow roadway loop rising to the top of the bridge, and cross Moscow River using Moskvoretskiy Bolshoy Most

Follow roadway loop descending back to embankment level

Reverse direction, continuing on Morisa Loreza nab underneath Kameny Most

Follow ramp access to the top of the bridge and cross the island on Ulitsa Serafimovchicha, continuing across the Vodootvodny Kanal to the mainland

Right onto Yakimanskaya nab

Yakimanskaya nab becomes Krymskaya nab, continuing under Krimskiy Most

Krymskaya nab becomes Pushkinskaya nab, going under Andreyevskiy Most

Pushkinskaya nab becomes Andreyevskaya nab

Continue on Andreyevskaya nab under Metro Most

Andreyevskaya nab becomes Vorobyevskaya nab

Continue on Vorobyevskaya nab to Vorobyevskoye shosse

Right onto Vorobyevskoye shosse across Setunskiy Most and then onto Berezhkovskaya nab

Continue on Berezhkovskaya nab to the course turnaround point at the access road for Borodinsky Most

Circle left around the plaza of the Kiev train station and return to Berezhkovskaya nab

Repeat the entire route exactly as described above but in reverse, entering Lenin stadium at the apex of the southeast turn

Continue onto the track in lane one, making three-quarters of a lap to finish at the standard track finish line at the southeast corner

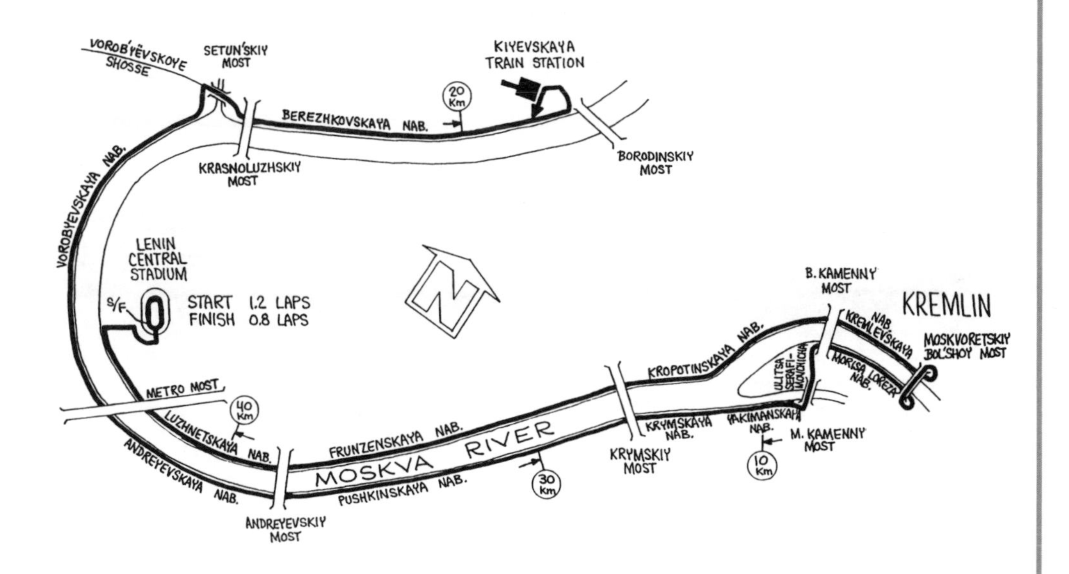

Figure 20.1 Sketch of the Moscow Olympic marathon course. Prepared by Bob Letson.

Figure 20.2 The Moscow men's marathon gets under way in Lenin stadium. Courtesy Sergey Tikhonov.

leading the remainder of the pack. Among these five were Lasse Viren and Mexico's Rodolfo Gomez.

By 15 kilometers, reached in a somewhat leisurely 46:45, the top runners had merged into one oval. At the front were Gerard Nijboer, Gomez, Michael Koussis, Kebede Balcha, and Kotov, with Kotov pushing the pace. Behind by 1 second was a group of six, and then eight more another second behind. The flat course, the top-class field of athletes, and the modest pace accounted for so many staying together.

At 20 kilometers, the first 22 athletes were all given the same time of 1:03:42, but this pace, combined with the weather, began to become intolerable for some. Within 5 kilometers, three well-experienced athletes abandoned the race:

Britain's Ian Thompson, Finland's Jouni Kortelainen, and Ethiopia's Kebede Balcha. A spirited surge by Rodolfo Gomez at 25 kilometers put him into the lead by 6 seconds (1:17:55). Nijboer attempted to follow (1:18:01), and the three Soviets teamed up to cover the move (1:18:04). Five more runners were another 3 seconds behind. After the race it became known that Gomez had seen Viren veer off the course for a "bathroom stop" in some bushes (Hannus and Shearman 1980). Gomez feared Viren more than anyone, and an adrenaline rush sent Gomez dashing ahead hoping to gain some distance. Viren dropped from the race before 30 kilometers.

Gomez's move was similar to what Shorter and Cierpinski had done in 1972 and 1976. Between 25 and 30 kilometers, his lead lengthened to 23 seconds, and a pack of nine was now chasing him: Nijboer, the three Soviets, Ethiopia's Dereje Nedi, Italy's Massimo Magnani, Karel Lismont, and two German Democratic Republic athletes: Hans-Joachim Truppel and Cierpinski. Gomez gallantly continued to lead, but by 35 kilometers (1:49:47) only 3 seconds separated him from the trio of Cierpinski, Nijboer, and Nedi. The Soviet team was 2 seconds farther behind, 1 second in front of Lismont.

As so often occurs in the marathon, the 35-to-40 kilometers section sees a rapid separation between those who had been racing too quickly and those for whom the pace had been manageable. At 37 kilometers, not far from the Kremlin, Nijboer passed Gomez. Then Cierpinski passed them both in succession. Soon the Soviets passed Gomez, and so did Nedi, such that by 40 kilometers Gomez found himself back in seventh place. The intense effort of this lead pack eventually caused it to break up into a file of individual runners as each athlete sought his own manageable pace. Cierpinski (2:04:35) had a 19 seconds lead over the pair of Nijboer and Dzhumanazarov. Moiseyev was in fourth (2:05:09), 23 seconds in front of Kotov. Nedi was 16 seconds behind Kotov, with Gomez 7 seconds farther back and 80 seconds behind Cierpinski. Race pace was at about 5.3 meters per second. In the final kilometer, Moiseyev overtook Kotov to

TABLE 20.1

Order of Top Placers Through Control Points

	Cierpinski	*Nijboer*	*Dzhumanazarov*	*Kotov*	*Moiseyev*	*Gomez*
10 km	=9-39	=9-39	2	1	=9-39	=4-8
15 km	=20-30	=1-5	=6-11	=1-5	=6-11	=1-5
20 km	=1-22	=1-22	=1-22	=1-22	=1-22	=1-22
25 km	20	2	=3-5	=3-5	=3-5	1
30 km	=2-10	=2-10	=2-10	=2-10	=2-10	1
35 km	=2-4	=2-4	=5-7	=5-7	=5-7	1
40 km	1	=2, 3	=2, 3	5	4	7
Finish	1	2	3	4	5	6

take fourth, and Gomez overtook Nedi to take sixth. Table 20.1 summarizes the positions of the top runners throughout the race.

History was made as Cierpinski burst onto the track—Bikila's double-gold-medal streak had been matched! Cierpinski's last 200 meters were in 33.4 seconds (Wojatski 1980). Two days afterward, he celebrated his 30th birthday. The Soviets finished third, fourth, and fifth for the second-best team score in Olympic marathon history, after the first, third, and fourth place finishes of the United States in 1908. It was the best placing for a national team since the three-athlete team limit was invoked in 1932. Nijboer proved that his May European record performance was not a fluke, as the 24-years-old Dutch psychiatric aide beat the entire Soviet juggernaut to take the silver medal. Only six sub-2:13:00 performances had been achieved in all of the Olympic marathons before this race. The Moscow race added seven more despite the heat and humidity. At one point, the second through seventh place finishers were on the track at the same time. All finishers reached the stadium before three hours, but an unfortunate 28 percent had dropped out. Table 20.2 summarizes data for the race.

TABLE 20.2

1980 Moscow Olympic Marathon at a Glance

Date:	01 August	**Weather:**	26°C (78°F)
Start time:	1716	**Starters:**	74
Course:	Out-and-back	**Finishers:**	53
Course distance:	42.195 km	**GPEs:**	40

TOP RESULTS:

Place	*Athlete*	*GPE*	*Date of birth*	*Time*
1	Waldemar Cierpinski	GDR	03 Aug. 1950	2:11:03.0
2	Gerhardus Nijboer	NED	18 Aug. 1955	2:11:20.0
3	Setymkul Dzhumanazarov	URS	17 Sept. 1951	2:11:35.0
4	Vladimir Kotov	URS	21 Feb. 1958	2:12:05.0
5	Leonid Moiseyev	URS	02 Oct. 1952	2:12:14.0
6	Rodolfo Gomez	MEX	30 Oct. 1950	2:12:39.0
7	Dereje Nedi	ETH	10 Oct. 1955	2:12:44.0
8	Massimo Magnani	ITA	04 Oct. 1951	2:13:12.0
9	Karel Lismont	BEL	08 Mar. 1949	2:13:27.0
10	Francois Robert de Castella	AUS	27 Feb. 1957	2:14:31.0

New geopolitical entities represented: Algeria [ALG], Congo [CGO], Lebanon [LBN], Lesotho [LES], Libya [LBY], Madagascar [MAD], Seychelles [SEY]

Team score (unofficial):			
	1. URS	12 points	(3-4-5)
	2. GDR	33 points	(1-11-21)
	3. BEL	40 points	(9-13-18)

While the performances were superb, it was not really a world championship, due to the large absence of notable stars. That would have to wait until December, at Fukuoka, where the winners of major world marathons typically accepted Japan's invitation to compete. In 1972, Shorter beat the world at the Munich Games and won at Fukuoka as well. Would Cierpinski equal that feat? No, he would only place sixth (see Looking Ahead, below).

Notes on the Medalists

Waldemar Cierpinski's first five marathon results were all personal bests, culminating in his Montréal gold medal race, but he never ran faster. He did, however, race well when it counted. He never placed lower than sixth in seven major championships. These included two Olympic Games, one IAAF World Athletics Championships, two European Athletics Championships, and two European Cups. Thus, he pleased his German Democratic Republic sports system when it needed him the most.

One course on which he achieved consistently poor results was at Fukuoka. Only once out of six attempts did he race well there. Coming during the early winter, it didn't mesh well with his normal cycle of training-racing-recovery. The major area championships were in midyear, and what would be his preparation period for the Fukuoka Marathon occurred during his recovery period. His priority was always the major championships. Table 20.3 summarizes Cierpinski's marathon career over nine years.

Gerhardus "Gerard" Nijboer, born at Uffelte in the Netherlands, was a successful marathoner at the highest level, peaking during the second year of a competitive career that spanned a dozen years. His Moscow Olympic race was his fourth marathon. This tendency for marathoners to peak early in their careers seems more prevalent than peaking later (Gynn 1985). His European record of 2:09:01 at Amsterdam just before these Olympic Games was mentioned earlier. He then went on to win the European Athletics Championships marathon in 1982, finished 6th in 1986, but dropped out in 1990. He was a three-time Olympian, dropping out at Los Angeles and finishing 13th at Seoul. In the first world championships in 1983, he finished 29th.

Satymkul Dzhumanazarov, an Asian, was born in Kok-Tyub in the Kirghiz Soviet Federated Socialist Republic (now Kyrgyzstan). He first achieved national recognition for distance running in 1974, but progressed slowly, finishing only 12th in the 1978 European Athletics Championships marathon at Prague. In the Olympic year of 1980, he peaked at the right moment. He was runner-up to Vladimir Kotov in the 1980 Soviet championship with what turned out to be his personal best (2:11:16)—two minutes faster than he had run previously. This gave him a positive mental attitude for the Moscow Olympics. There, he was only 19 seconds off his personal best, and his bronze medal resulted. He was invited to participate at the 1981 Tokyo international marathon and placed 5th with another excellent time, 2:12:31. In his entire career, however, he never won a marathon.

TABLE 20.3

Career Marathon Record of Waldemar Cierpinski

Date	*Venue*	*Place*	*Time*	*Comments*
06 Oct. 1974	Košice	3rd	2:20:28.4	
05 Oct. 1975	Košice	7th	2:17:30.4	
17 Apr. 1976	Karl-Marx-Stadt	1st	2:13:57.2	
30 May 1976	Wittenberg	1st	2:12:21.2	
31 July 1976	Montréal	1st	2:09:55	Olympic Games
05 Dec. 1976	Fukuoka	3rd	2:14:56	
02 Oct. 1977	Košice	3rd	2:16:00.4	
08 May 1978	Prague	1st	2:14:51	
24 June 1978	Boxberg	1st	2:14:57.4	
03 Sept. 1978	Prague	4th	2:12:20	European championships
03 Dec. 1978	Fukuoka	32nd	2:22:49	
01 Sept. 1979	Karl-Marx-Stadt	1st	2:15:50	
02 Dec. 1979	Fukuoka	DNF		
03 May 1980	Karl-Marx-Stadt	1st	2:11:17	
01 Aug. 1980	Moscow	1st	2:11:03	Olympic Games
05 Oct. 1980	Košice	DNF		
07 Dec. 1980	Fukuoka	6th	2:10:24	
13 Sept. 1981	Agen	2nd	2:15:44	European Cup
06 Dec. 1981	Fukuoka	DNF		
31 Jan. 1982	Manila	1st	2:14:27	
30 June 1982	Dresden	1st	2:13:59	
12 Sept. 1982	Athens	6th	2:17:50	European Cup
13 Feb. 1983	Tokyo	7th	2:12:40	
19 June 1983	Laredo	1st	2:12:26	European Cup
14 Aug. 1983	Helsinki	3rd	2:10:37	World championships
04 Dec. 1983	Fukuoka	15th	2:15:13	

Looking Ahead: Brief Highlights 1980-1983

1980: Bill Rodgers's New York City Marathon win streak was brought to an end by Cuban-born United States citizen Alberto Salazar, debuting with a fine 2:09:41 on October 26. Seko triumphed on December 7 at Fukuoka in 2:09:45, relegating Cierpinski to sixth.

1981: Seko was a convincing winner at Boston on April 20 (2:09:26), but the marathons at New York (October 25) and Fukuoka (December 6) provided the real excitement. In "The Big Apple," Alberto Salazar won in 2:08:12.7, apparently a world best time. However, a carefully conducted remeasurement of the shortest possible route that Salazar could have run found that the roadway was 148 meters (486 yards) short of the full distance. Video replays of portions of the race do show Salazar and other athletes clearly running in areas of the roadway that were beyond the shortest possible route. However, record-keeping officials have adamantly held the view that regardless of how far Salazar ran, if the shortest possible route was less than the full distance, the course was deemed short and performances were ineligible for record-keeping purposes. Meanwhile, at the Fukuoka race in Japan, de Castella was slightly slower (2:08:18), and eventually his performance replaced Salazar's on the progression list of world best marathon times.

1982: Salazar became the first sub-2:09:00 runner at Boston with 2:08:51 on April 19 in a thrilling two second win over Dick Beardsley, and he won again at New York on October 24 (2:09:29). The European Athletics Championships (Marathon-to-Athens on September 12) and Commonwealth Games (Brisbane on October 8) titles were won by proven runners Nijboer (2:15:16) and de Castella (2:09:18), respectively.

1983: After Toshihiko Seko won the now-renowned Tokyo Marathon on February 13 (2:08:38), de Castella won a back-and-forth duel with Carlos Lopes at Rotterdam on April 9 by two seconds (2:08:37). De Castella was a worthy winner at the inaugural World Athletics Championships at Helsinki on August 14 (2:10:03), while Seko won his fourth Fukuoka race on December 4 in 2:08:52. An unprecedented number of athletes—five—broke 2:09:00 this year, achieving a total of six such performances.

References

Anonymous. 1981. *Games of the XXII Olympiad Moscow 1980.* Moscow: Fizkultura i Sport.

Gynn, R. 1985. Modern marathon trends. In *International Athletics Annual 1985.* London: Sports World Publications, Ltd.

Hannus, M., and M. Shearman. 1980. *The 1980 Olympics: Track and field.* Croydon: The Sports Market, Ltd.

Smith, R. 1976. Fields of friendly strife. *The New York Times,* August 1.

Wojatski, K. 1980. Marathon. *Track and Field News* 33 (9): 17-18.

CHAPTER 21

1984—LOS ANGELES

Age and Beauty Conquer at Los Angeles

Commercialism Provides a Successful Olympic Environment

Escalating costs of hosting an Olympic Games, with decreasing assurance of recovering the financial outlay over a reasonable time span, caused concern among potential bidding cities to carry on the tradition of the Games beyond Moscow. Canadian taxpayers were not expected to pay off their roughly Can$1 billion deficit until the 1990s. Moscow's Olympic Games took an estimated U.S.$9 billion from its economy to complete the urban redevelopment and Games necessities. It is thus not surprising that in 1977, when the bidding process began for the 1984 Games, few cities participated. There was one weak bid, from Teheran, eventually withdrawn, and one other—from Los Angeles.

The Games were awarded to Los Angeles at the 80th IOC session on May 18, 1978, in Athens. It was only a provisional approval, however, pending a signed contract providing financial backing for the Olympic Games by the City of Los Angeles. Rule four of the Olympic Charter states that the city government and the host country's NOC work together to stage the Games. That means managing the finances as well as Olympic Games implementation. The city refused to comply, and an alternative proposal was offered, suggesting a private organizing committee whose performance would be guaranteed by the United States Olympic Committee (Perelman 1985). The IOC initially was not in favor of such a plan—"commercializing the Games" seemed repugnant. But the IOC had no choice: agree, or seek a new bid city. And there were no other bid cities! After months of delicate negotiations, on October 20, 1978, in the White House, an official signing between the IOC (Lord Killanin) and Los Angeles (Mayor Tom Bradley) made formal the agreement to proceed ahead with, in a real sense, a "private-sector-funded Games."

By early March 1979, a Los Angeles Olympic Organizing Committee (LAOOC) was firmly in place, with its newly elected president, Peter V. Ueberroth, under orders to make the concept work in a manner that ensured both fiscal soundness and the dignity of the Games (Ueberroth 1985). No Summer Olympic Games had made a profit up to that time, so that became a noble goal as well. Three potential sources of funds existed in the private sector: television revenues from the host broadcaster, ticket sales, and corporate sponsorships.

Ueberroth was already an eminently successful businessman, and he relished his new challenge, proving a worthy steward of his city's Olympic Games. He first asked potential bidders for television rights to deposit $750,000 each if they even wanted to be considered! While deciding which network would get the job (ABC did, for an unprecedented $225 million), Ueberroth used the interest to manage early expenses. He next brought on board corporate sponsors: big in name, flush with advertising budgets, and few in number, so as to capture absolute top dollar for permitting their membership in a most exclusive club.

Once a money stream began flowing into the LAOOC, frugality was the watchword, along with quality. Ueberroth's group used existing facilities wherever possible, renovating them so they were first class. The 1932 Los Angeles Memorial Coliseum again served as the main Olympic stadium, and it was refurbished throughout. Instead of building a new Olympic Village, the organizers commandeered three college campuses for the summer: the University of Southern California (USC), the University of California at Los Angeles (UCLA), and the University of California at Santa Barbara (UCSB). Some corporate sponsors themselves paid for the construction of new venues, with their names proudly in place.

Of course, there were challenges, but Ueberroth and his associates managed to defuse, solve, negotiate, and/or compromise wherever appropriate to keep the plan for the Games moving forward. Not always was everyone happy, but Ueberroth was not running a popularity contest. The torch relay, for example, went afoul of the IOC concept of relaying the flame, with all its purity, across the United States to the Olympic Games site. The LAOOC envisioned this event as a potential money-maker. Those desiring to carry the torch should pay for the privilege. Convincing the IOC to "buy the idea" (pun perhaps intended) was not easy and is a fascinating story by itself (Ecker 1996). But it was solved, and the relay netted some $11 million to benefit youth sports programs.

As 1984 began, there was the looming political question of whether Moscow would lead a boycott in retaliation for the United States-led boycott of the 1980 Moscow Olympic Games. On May 8, the Soviet Union formally announced that it would not participate. The primary worry stated in the announcement was that the Soviets did not believe their athletes would be secure in the United States. Other concerns included predictions of a hot, smoggy site, and unpleasant visa problems for some of their personnel. Whatever the reasons, the bottom line was that 14 Soviet-bloc nations formed a Moscow-led boycott.

When 1960 Olympic decathlon gold medalist Rafer Johnson used his torch to light a fuse at the base of the five rings at the peristyle end of the Coliseum, flames burst out around them, and in turn shot up through the chimney that had hadn't seen an "Olympic flame" since 1932. It was an historic moment for the Olympic Games and for Los Angeles. Despite the boycott, two Soviet-bloc nations did participate: Romania and the former Yugoslavia. A record total of 140 geopolitical entities (all of whom were also NOCs) participated (compared to 122 at Munich), and the total number of competitors (5,230 men and 1,567 women) was exceeded only by the Munich Games. These were the Olympic Games when Carl Lewis showed the world his brilliance (and arrogance), winning in four events: 100 meters, 200 meters, long jump, and the 4 × 100 meters relay. Edwin Moses had won the 400 meters hurdles in 1976, was undefeated since 1977, and won again in Los Angeles. Britain's Sebastian Coe was one of the very few athletes who duplicated his Moscow feats: silver in the 800 meters and gold in the 1,500 meters. Others were not so fortunate: Waldemar Cierpinski, for example, the Moscow marathon champion, was deprived of the opportunity to try for a third gold medal.

More than in any previous Olympic Games, women's athletic participation gained global exposure and importance. Mainland Chinese athletes made an impressive first showing in diving and volleyball. New women's sports were added, including synchronized swimming and rhythmic gymnastics. New events were added to other sports already on the calendar. This occurred particularly in track and field, with the women's 400 meters hurdles, the 3,000 meters run, and the marathon.

The tendency of television to focus on the controversial and the sensational put the women's 3,000 meters race in the global spotlight as one of the most remembered Olympic events of the century. On August 10, five days after the women's marathon and two days before the men's, Britain's 18-years-old Zola Budd (formerly of South Africa) tangled legs with America's Mary Decker (Willman 1984). It was just past the halfway point. Budd, running barefoot, had just passed Decker to take the lead. As Decker moved to regain the lead, Budd swerved slightly, and Decker, getting cut off, shortened her stride, stumbled, and spiked Budd's left heel. They tangled, Decker fell to the ground, out of the race, and Budd fell back to seventh. Television coverage focused on replaying "the fall" so much that few knew the medalists. Gold went to Romania's Maricica Puica, with Britain's Wendy Sly and Canada's Lynn Williams taking silver and bronze, respectively.

Drug use continued to be a problem worldwide, with 14 athletes testing positive for banned performance-enhancing substances. Four were in track and field, and one case sent shudders through the distance-running community. After Italy's Alberto Cova narrowly out-sprinted Finland's Martti Vainio to win the 10,000 meters run, Vainio's urine sample tested positive for Primabolin. He protested with the utmost of candor, even on television, emphasizing his innocence. He did admit to blood doping, but there was no way to test for it. The startling conclusion was that he indeed had been using steroids months before, during his training buildup, to help him recover from hard efforts. Reinfusion of the blood, which contained some of the steroids he had been using, caused the positive steroid test. Britain's Mike McLeod was awarded the silver medal.

The concept of commercialism permitted global television to give the gold medalists an unprecedented podium for cashing in on their marketability. It was an intriguing irony that the entrepreneurship making these Games so successful was the antithesis of the idea of amateurism ("sport is for pleasure, not for profit") so entrenched in the Olympic Games' survival in their early years. Wisely, the IOC saw how corporate profits directed into its treasury could provide its own movement with more influence in developing global sporting opportunities for youth.

As the Olympic Games ended, the bottom line was a profit so huge it staggered the imagination: $222,700,000 was announced! This created its own turmoil, as organizations everywhere wanted a piece of the profit. In the end, many worthy projects were funded. The host city portion of the surplus was used to create the Amateur Athletic Foundation of Los Angeles. Interest from its principal is used to maintain a renowned Olympic research library and to provide outreach programs for community athletics and coaching education. The host NOC's portion created a United States Olympic Foundation intended to keep that NOC financially sound for the foreseeable future. A half-century had passed since these Games had come to town, and while the Olympic movement may have been developing nicely then, it now seemed poised to wield an increasingly greater global influence

Course Measurement Becomes a Social Occasion

The only similarity between the 1932 and 1984 Los Angeles marathon courses is that both ended at the Los Angeles Memorial Coliseum track finish line. The road portions were entirely different. In 1932, runners started at the Coliseum and did a loop south of it before returning. In 1984, runners started on the track of Santa Monica City College, west of the Coliseum, and followed a circuitous point-to-point route through the suburbs of Santa Monica, Venice, and Culver City before entering Los Angeles. Air pollution in this part of the by-now heavily populated Los Angeles basin was typically moderate, and a good possibility existed for refreshing onshore ocean breezes due to the typically cool Pacific coastal water.

However, as can be seen from the course profile in figure 21.1, the course was quite hilly at the beginning, making it difficult for runners to maintain an accurate sense of pace. The course also ended at an elevation slightly higher than the start. Recall that a net uphill route also existed with the 1896, 1906, and 1968 Olympic marathon courses. The Santa Monica City College track is at an elevation of 45 meters (148 feet). After two and one-half laps around the track, the course entered city streets and climbed steadily to an elevation of 107 meters (338 feet) approaching 8 kilometers into the race. That is a rise of 9.1 meters per kilometer for 6.8 kilometers (48 feet per mile for 4.2 miles). Following this quite noticeable ascent, a descent occurred to near sea level by the 16 kilometers point. This descent represents 12.7 meters per kilometer for 8 kilometers (67 feet per mile for 5 miles). After another section of about 8 kilometers at essentially sea level, the course began a gradual, undulating rise inland, reaching the stadium at its elevation of 50 meters (164 feet), a net rise of 5 meters (16 feet) (Anonymous 1984).

Accurate road course measurement was a topic of great concern to the distance-running community in the United States. The growing availability of bicycle-mounted Jones revolution counters had increased the ease with which courses could be measured. The national governing body for track and field in the United States began to formulate methodology for both course measurement and course certification to ensure that the intended distance was achieved. The Los Angeles Olympic marathon created an opportunity for many measurement experts to test and compare their skills—and at the same time serve the noble goal of providing the most accurately measured Olympic course up to that time.

A 13-cyclist international "mass ride" occurred on April 24, 1983, at which time six intermediate baseline points were established along the route for rechecking accuracy. Such a technique had never been attempted before (Baumel 1990). A seven-months period of subsequent detailed data analysis was indeed overkill in terms of necessary work, but the lessons learned among road race measurement technicians were valuable. About six months before the mass ride, the decision was made to incorporate a one one-thousandths (0.01 percent) short course prevention factor (SCPF)—for the marathon, a maximum of 42 meters—to minimize the chance that a subsequent remeasurement would reveal a short course. Inclusion of this SCPF is now a standard element of course measurement procedure. The course as finally certified, indicated as a solid blue line on the roadway, thus included an "overage factor" of 28 meters. Figure 21.1 illustrates the route, and the course details box summarizes street details.

While it is possible to drive the course today, it is not possible to run the entire route. This is because the Marina Freeway is a high-speed motorway, with pedestrian access prohibited. This section is from approximately 23.9 through 28.1 kilometers (14.9 to 17.5 miles), making this Olympic marathon course the only one that includes the entirety of a high-speed expressway. No routine vehicle traffic was permitted on the route during the race period.

Women's Marathoning Comes of Age

The year 1984 was an exciting one for women marathoners: They were finally competing in the Olympic Games! Olympic Marathon Miscellany 21.1 briefly summarizes how this came about, but the bottom line was that the women runners of 1984 could finally look forward to the same kind of stresses as the men in securing selection on their respective Olympic teams. It was a stress they relished.

Japan

Women-only marathons had been popular in Japan since 1979, when the first Tokyo women's marathon was held in the autumn. The 1983 winner, Nanae Sasaki (2:37:09), was selected as Japan's first and only competitor in the inaugural Olympic race. In 1982, Osaka staged the first edition of what was to become an annual international classic for women marathoners. There, in 1984, German Democratic Republic runner Katrin Dörre outpaced the home record-holder Akemi Masuda with a German Democratic Republic national record of 2:32:05. Third-place-finisher Karolina Szabo was rewarded with a Hungarian national record of 2:35:23. The Soviet-bloc boycott, however, kept Dörre and Szabo from participating at Los Angeles.

United States

Many athletes took advantage of a pre-Olympic Games race in Los Angeles on February 19, 1984. However, United States runners were preparing for their Olympic team selection race later in the spring, so they stayed away from both Los Angeles and Boston. New Zealand's Anne Audain, running in only her second marathon, set the early pace, but Canadian star Jacqueline Gareau, the 1980 Boston Marathon winner, overtook her. Gareau won by a close 2 seconds (2:31:57). Audain's colleague Mary O'Connor was third. On April 16, the Boston race saw New Zealand's Lorraine Moller, 1980 Avon champion at London, go under the 2:30:00 barrier by 32 seconds for a comfortable win over Sweden's Midde Hamrin. Another Kiwi star, Allison Roe, did not finish. Her double victory at New York and Boston in 1981, in only her second year of marathon racing, showed incredible talent. Achilles tendon problems caused her to miss most of 1982, and she never regained top form.

The United States women's marathon trial was held in the aptly named city of Olympia, the state capital of Washington, nestled in an idyllic forested setting. Joan Benoit achieved global press as the favorite who was about to be hobbled by surgery. She held the world's fastest time (2:22:43 at Boston in 1983), but she needed arthroscopic knee surgery to release a synovial plica (a fold of tissue projecting into the knee joint cavity), and it could not wait. The surgical procedure was performed 17 days before the trial race. An uneventful recovery with proper rehabilitation allowed her not only to compete but also to win (2:31:04) over Julie Brown (2:31:41), with third going to the lesser-known Julie Isphording

Course Details

The 1984 Los Angeles Olympic Marathon

Start at 100 meters start point on Santa Monica City College track

Run two and one-half laps counterclockwise, exiting via northeast gate

Continue onto 17th Street northwest to Olympic Boulevard

Right onto right side of Olympic Boulevard to 26th Street

Left onto 26th Street to Wilshire Boulevard

Right onto Wilshire Boulevard to Bundy Drive

Left onto Bundy Drive to San Vicente Boulevard

Left onto right side of San Vicente Boulevard to Ocean Avenue

Left onto the right side of Ocean Avenue

Ocean Avenue becomes Barnard Way to Pacific Avenue

Right onto Pacific Avenue to Washington Street

Left onto Washington Street to Via Dolce

Right onto Via Dolce to Marquesas Way

Left on Marquesas Way to Via Marina

Right (south) on right side of Via Marina to turnaround at Tahiti

North on right side of Via Marina to Admiralty Way

Right onto the left side of Admiralty Way to Mindanao Way

Left onto Mindanao Way to Highway 90 eastbound

Right onto Highway 90, which becomes Marina Freeway

Continue on Marina Freeway eastbound

Marina Freeway ends at Slauson Avenue

Left onto Slauson Avenue to Hannum Avenue

Half right onto Hannum Avenue to Playa

Half right onto the right side of Playa to Overland Avenue

Half left onto the right side of Overland Avenue to Jefferson Boulevard

Half right onto the right side of Jefferson Boulevard to Rodeo Road

Half right onto the right side of Rodeo Road

Rodeo Road becomes Exposition Boulevard

Continue on Exposition Boulevard to Menlo Avenue

(2:32:26). They formed the United States team. A record 31 competitors were under 2:40:00, and 109 were under 2:50:00. That depth has yet to be matched in any other women's marathon.

Europe

The now classic London Marathon on May 13 saw the women start 10 minutes before the men. Despite this small lead time, Norway's Ingrid Kristiansen kept

Right on Menlo Avenue to stadium tunnel entrance

Sharp left and descent into stadium tunnel onto track

Continue on track counterclockwise one and one-quarter laps to finish line—lane four for one-quarter lap, then lane one for the final lap

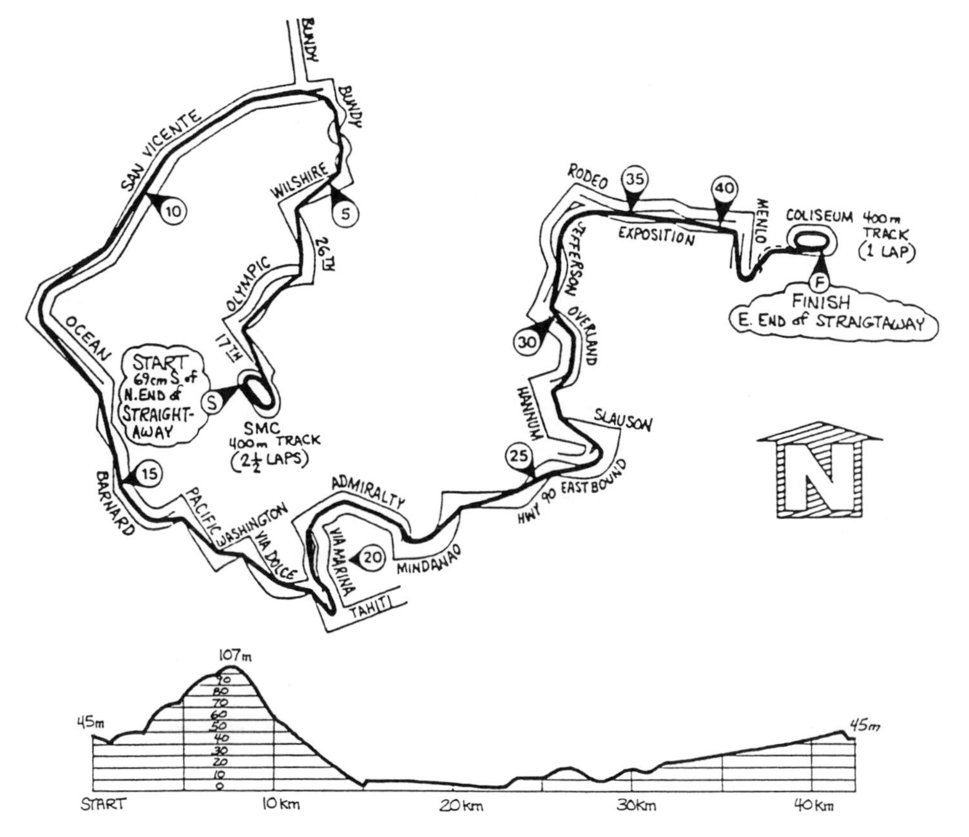

1984 Los Angeles Olympic Marathon

Figure 21.1 Sketch of the Los Angeles Olympic marathon course. Descriptors for street identification (avenue, way, street, etc.) are omitted for clarity. Prepared by Bob Letson.

such a quick pace that she was not caught by the men until 30 kilometers. She had become a mother the previous summer, and had recovered sufficiently to win at Houston on January 15 (2:27:51). She now set a European record of 2:24:26 in defeating Britain's Priscilla Welch (2:30:06), Sarah Rowell (2:31:28), and Veronique Marot (2:33:52). Welch and Rowell were selected as two members of a fine British team that would be led by the enormously talented Joyce Smith. Having won several major races—the Avon race in 1979 at Waldniel, the

The Politics of Inclusion—A Women's Olympic Marathon

How did the women's marathon get approved for the Los Angeles Olympic Games? It was a many-step process. Rule 52 of the IOC Charter (Sports Programme, Admission of Sports, Disciplines, and Events), outlining the requirements, is reprinted below.

> 52.3.2. To be included in the programme of the Olympic Games, events must have a recognized international standing both numerically and geographically, and have been included at least twice in world or continental championships.
>
> 52.3.3. Only events practiced by men in at least fifty countries and on three continents, and by women in at least thirty-five countries and on three continents, may be included in the programme of the Olympic Games.
>
> 52.3.4. Events are admitted four years before specific Olympic Games in respect of which no change shall thereafter be permitted.

Extending into the decade of the 1970s, most national track and field federations forbade women to enter long-distance running competitions. The United States and West Germany pioneered the change in thinking to permit both women's national championships and women-only races. A key person who championed the cause of women's distance running was Dr. Ernst van Aaken, from the German town of Waldniel. A coach and physician, he both encouraged women to run longer distances and lobbied governing bodies to provide women with racing opportunities. He was especially active during the late 1960s and early 1970s, and his influence helped add the women's 1,500 meters run to the Munich Games Olympic program.

On October 28, 1973, van Aaken organized the first West German women's championship in Waldniel. Christa Kofferschläger won (2:59:25.6), and her performance became the first European record. On February 10, 1974, the United States staged its first women's championship at San Mateo. There were 57 starters, and Judy Ikenberry won with 2:55:18.

The world's best women marathoners all reassembled at Waldniel on September 22, 1974, for their first women-only international event. Germany's Liane Winter won (2:50:31.4), and she used this experience to win at Boston in 1975 with the world's fastest time (2:42:24). Christa Vahlensieck (formerly Kofferschläger) won the second such international women-only race, held again at Waldniel, on October 2, 1976, in 2:45:24.4.

Media attention brought by these races, as well as worldwide scientific research into the physiology of human endurance in athletic performance, further increased discussion regarding the question of how fast runners of either sex could run. The scientific community declared that, essentially, women were little different from the men in their competitiveness, trainability, and performance competence. At an international scientific symposium summarizing current research on marathon running, the 500-plus participants agreed to a resolution (Kuscsik 1977) stating, "it is the considered judgment of the participants of this conference that a women's marathon event as well as other long distance races for women be included in the Olympic program forthwith." Although a few scientists have even gone so far as predicting that women will run faster than men (Whipp and Ward 1992), that is unlikely for a variety of physiological reasons.

It was not long before the numbers of both women marathoners and ever-faster performances increased substantially. Whereas not even the three-hours barrier had been broken as 1970 began, by the end of 1979, Norway's Grete Waitz had the world's fastest performance, 2:27:32.6, set at the New York City Marathon that October 21.

At the start of the 1980s, evidence of both a desire and need for top-level women's marathon racing opportunities was clear. And the major sports governing bodies responded. The European Athletic Association planned a woman's marathon in the 1981 edition of its European Marathon Cup and at the 1982 edition of its quadrennial athletics championships at Athens. And the IAAF also planned to include such a race at its inaugural IAAF World Athletics Championships at Helsinki in 1983.

Corporate support for a woman's Olympic marathon had already been providing significant opportunities for women to improve their skills. The Avon International Running Circuit, directed by well-known marathoner Kathrine Switzer, created women-only marathons in Atlanta (1978), Waldniel (1979), London (1980), Ottawa (1981), San Francisco (1982), and Los Angeles (1983) as its contribution to the Olympic cause. For the record, the winners of these events, respectively, were Martha Cooksey [USA], 2:46:15; Joyce Smith [GBR], 2:36:27; Lorraine Moller [NZL], 2:35:11; Nancy Conz [USA], 2:36:45.9; Lorraine Moller [NZL], 2:36:13; and Julie Brown [USA], 2:26:26. This series greatly increased the number and quality of athlete and national participation, both of which were required for adding the event to the Olympic Games program.

Assistance with review of the minutes of past IAAF Council meetings (Myers 1998) gives us a general outline of the deliberation process. John Holt, IAAF general secretary, met with the IOC at Lausanne on April 15, 1980, and he apparently for the first time provided extensive documentation to support the IAAF's request for addition of the 400 meters hurdles, 3,000 meters run, and marathon for women in the 1984 Olympic Games. The IAAF Council then met with the IOC Program Commission at Rome on June 7 and 8, and the item was debated further. As indicated in the minutes of that meeting, the commission was reluctant to accept the women's marathon because it had never previously accepted an event that was not already established worldwide. Mention of the forthcoming international women's championship marathons was thus crucial in providing evidence of rapidly developing global interest. In his report to the

(continued)

IAAF Congress in Moscow on July 21 and 22, 1980, IAAF president Dr. Primo Nebiolo stated that "a decision hung in the balance for one year, subject to the IAAF providing sufficient evidence of the inclusion of this event at the national and championship levels."

No further formal discussion of the marathon occurred at IAAF or IOC committee levels until the IAAF Council meetings of August 30 and 31, and September 3, 1981. There, Item 14 on the agenda was discussion of the Los Angeles Games. Mr. H. D. Thoreau, of the LAOOC, presented three maps for study. One was the marathon course. No written comments are provided in the minutes regarding whether two marathons were planned.

The good news finally occurred at the Executive Board meeting of the IOC, held in Los Angeles on February 23 and 24, 1982 (Anonymous 1982). As recorded in the list of major decisions taken, approval was simply stated: "Women's marathon to be included on the Olympic programme for the Games of the XXIIIrd Olympiad in Los Angeles, but not at the same time as the men's event." With that decision final, the world's women marathon runners could rest assured that they, too, would have an Olympic stage on which to perform.

Tokyo Marathons of 1979 and 1980, and the London Marathons in 1981 and 1982—Smith's personal best of 2:29:43 came at the 1982 London race at 44 years of age! Kristiansen, of course, was selected to the Norwegian team to accompany an equally talented athlete, Grete Waitz, already selected on the basis of her fifth New York City Marathon victory (2:27:00) during the fall of 1983. Sixth at London was Bente Moe, who completed the Norwegian team.

The reigning European champion, Portugal's Rosa Mota, had won the 1983 Chicago Marathon in 2:31:12, her fourth successive time improvement in as many marathons. She, too, was selected. Thus, even for an inaugural event, and even without the Soviet-bloc countries, this first women's marathon promised to be a top-class world championship.

Benoit Leads a Field Deserving Its Place in the Sun

This historic first women's Olympic marathon was on the third day of athletics, on Sunday morning, August 5 at 0800 (8:00 a.m.). The stadium at Santa Monica City College was full for the occasion, and although it was a comfortable 20°C (68°F), there was a characteristic humid Pacific chill that makes this part of the world meteorologically unusual. So close to the ocean, the cold Pacific water causes great fog banks that move inland for a few miles overnight, only to retreat as the morning sun causes their evaporation over land. As soon as this occurs, the hot summer sun can cause as much as a 14°C (25°F) rise in temperature within minutes due to the sudden rise in radiant heat load. The first 25 kilometers of this course were close enough to the shoreline that the overcast coolness prevailed. Then, as runners moved inland, sunshine and a substantial warming occurred in the final stages.

The 49 women starters, representing 28 GPEs (which also were NOCs), formed an impressive first-time field. All the big names were there—11 of the fastest 14 in the young history of women's marathons (Welch 1984) and a global assortment of others who were also worthy competitors. Europeans formed the majority—24 from a dozen NOCs, with full teams from Norway, Portugal, Britain, Italy, and Belgium. The United States, Canada, and Mexico all sent full teams, with 2 additional athletes from other NOCs in Central America. Four athletes each came from Oceania, Asia, and South America. Africa's only representatives were 1 athlete each from Kenya and Nigeria.

Figure 21.2 shows the women on the Santa Monica track as they proceeded two and one-half laps around before exiting onto 17th Street. Leading the group was the Norwegian duo of Waitz and Kristiansen, with Mota on the inside. As soon as the runners departed the stadium, they began into the foothills of suburban Santa Monica. From 45 meters (148 feet) on the track to 107 meters (338 feet) reached just after 6 kilometers, there was never a respite. Predictably, the first 5 kilometers (18:15) were slow, at 5:52 per mile pace (3:39 per kilome-

Figure 21.2 **Starting the women's Olympic marathon on the Santa Monica City College track. In front at the inside edge of lane one is Rosa Mota [POR], and to her right are Ingrid Kristiansen [NOR] (number 286) and Grete Waitz [NOR] (number 289). Other identifiable runners include Sylvia Ruegger [CAN] (number 060), and to her left, Lisa Martin [AUS] (number 016); Nanae Sasaki [JPN] (number 257) and Carla Beurskens [NED] (number 199); Mary Wagaki [KEN] (number 263) and Naydi Nazario [PUR] (number 309). Eventual winner Joan Benoit is immediately next to the left shoulder of Beurskens, on the inside lane.** Courtesy AAF/LPI 1984.

ter). Benoit had moved up to the lead, but only by 5 seconds, ahead of Japan's Akemi Masuda, and the rest of the pack followed.

The next 7 kilometers (4.4 miles) were downhill to the ocean shore via the palm-lined San Vicente Boulevard, and then along Ocean Boulevard. It was a gentle down-slope, and the pace quickened substantially. Benoit still led at 10 kilometers (35:24), having averaged 5:31 per mile (3:26 per kilometer) for her second 5 kilometers interval. The lead group had strung out according to the ease with which each was accustomed to striding downhill. Kristiansen was 4 seconds behind, followed by Sweden's Midde Hamrin (35:32), Waitz in 35:35, Julie Brown and Canada's Sylvie Ruegger together in 35:36, and Lorraine Moller in seventh (35:38). Mota rounded out this lead group (35:39). Behind them, the rest of the field was bunched.

Between 10 and 15 kilometers, Benoit quickened her pace again, averaging 5:16 per mile (3:16 per kilometer) along the ocean for that 5 kilometers interval. Strangely, she found herself alone (51:46), 51 seconds ahead of a pack of five: Waitz, Moller, Ruegger, Brown, and Anne Audain. In turn, they were 1 second ahead of a group of 14 containing all the other major players. Continuing along the shoreline (figure 21.3), Benoit extended her lead to 72 seconds at 20 kilometers (1:08:32), despite having slowed her pace to 5:24 per mile (3:21 per kilometer). Mota had quickened her pace, moving in front of the lead group

Figure 21.3 **Joan Benoit racing alone behind the specially constructed CBS electric camera vehicle, along the shoreline on Barnard Way just as it turns left. One block later, the route turns right onto Pacific Avenue at ~16 kilometers into the race.** Courtesy AAF/LPI 1984.

(1:09:44) in a fruitless attempt to catch Benoit. Kristiansen and Italy's Laura Fogli were in third and fourth (1:09:56), 1 second ahead of Waitz and Ruegger. Another second behind (1:09:58) came Moller and Brown, followed by Britain's Priscilla Welch (1:09:59).

Turning inland and entering onto the Marina Freeway at the 25 kilometers marker, Benoit had increased her lead (1:25:24) to 110 seconds, her 5 kilometers split indicating a pace of 5:26 per mile (3:23 per kilometer). Brown now fell off the pace and was no longer a factor up front. Mota was Benoit's nearest rival (1:27:14), 1 second up on Waitz, Fogli, and Ruegger, who in turn were 1 second ahead of Kristiansen and Finland's Tuija Toivonen.

At 30 kilometers (1:42:23), Benoit's lead remained unchanged at 110 seconds. Waitz, Kristiansen, and Mota were now together (1:14:13), 29 seconds ahead of Welch and Moller. A slight slowing of Benoit's pace during the next 5 kilometers (5:34 per mile; 3:28 per kilometer) and a slight quickening of the pack behind reduced Benoit's lead to 91 seconds at 35 kilometers (1:59:41). The sun now shone brilliantly as they proceeded down Rodeo Road and Exposition Boulevard eastward to the stadium. The roadway was not shaded, so the radiant heating was considerable. Those up front were now all in single file: Kristiansen 20 seconds behind Waitz, Mota 9 seconds behind Kristiansen, Welch one minute behind Mota, and Moller only 2 seconds behind Welch. The separation of these athletes can be best appreciated by knowing that they were racing at a pace of about 4.8 meters per second.

At 40 kilometers, the top two medals were all but decided. It was Benoit (2:17:14), 87 seconds ahead of Waitz. The real struggle was for the bronze medal position. Mota was 38 seconds behind Waitz, but had passed Kristiansen and was ahead of her by only 7 seconds. Moller had now passed Welch, and these two were separated by only 6 seconds. Table 21.1 summarizes the changing order of the top athletes during the race.

Meanwhile, on the morning program at the track, four events had been scheduled in addition to the women's marathon: qualification for the women's javelin

TABLE 21.1

Order of Top Placers Through Control Points

	Benoit	*Waitz*	*Mota*	*Kristiansen*	*Moller*	*Welch*
10 km	1	5	8	3	7	9
15 km	1	=2-6	=7-20	=7-20	=2-6	=7-20
20 km	1	=5, 6	2	=3, 4	=7, 8	9
25 km	1	=3-5	2	=6, 7	9	12
30 km	1	=2-4	=2-4	=2-4	=5, 6	=5, 6
35 km	1	2	4	3	6	5
40 km	1	2	3	4	5	6
Finish	1	2	3	4	5	6

and men's hammer, and initial rounds for two hurdles events—women's 400 meters and men's 110 meters. Such preliminary rounds are not always well attended, but this was no ordinary day. The stadium was bustling with 77,000 awaiting the arrival of the first woman marathoner. The race had been shown on the large video screen inside, so attendees knew what was happening. Benoit made her final dash along Menlo Avenue, and then took the sharp U-turn to the left and downhill into the tunnel leading to the stadium floor. As she emerged, the spectator roar of adulation was so intense that conversation was impossible. Entering onto lane four, she followed the red cones and reached the finish line in lane one. She then had one complete lap around to finish the race. She finished 94 seconds ahead of Waitz, with Mota in third by another 39 seconds. Benoit took a victory lap, flashing a big grin and toting an American flag (figure 21.4).

Figure 21.4 Finishing her victory lap around the stadium, Joan Benoit celebrates. Courtesy AAF/LPI 1984.

The quality of this inaugural event was most impressive. The first set of women's Olympic marathon medalists (figure 21.5), Benoit, Waitz, and Mota were clearly the class of the field, running the third, sixth, and seventh fastest times in the history of this still-young event. Benoit's time was better than 13 of the 20 previous Olympic men's marathons! Welch, who finished 6th, set a world veteran's best at the age of 39. In 11th place, 46-years-old Joyce Smith ran a world best for her age group. The 44 finishers were all back in the stadium so quickly that Brazil's Eleonora Mendonca, in last place with 2:52:19, ran more than six minutes faster than Spiridon Louis back in 1896 over a course more than 2 kilometers shorter. Table 21.2 provides a summary of the women's first Olympic marathon.

At her press conference later, Benoit reasoned that her down time from surgery was probably the secret to her racing so well. As reported (Welch 1984): "I believe I was in the best shape of my life right before the knee injury. I think I would have had the race of my life at the Olympic trials and I think I would have had nothing left for this race. So I feel the injury and the timing were

Figure 21.5 At the historic first Olympic women's marathon medal ceremony, it is Grete Waitz (left, silver), Joan Benoit (middle, gold), and Rosa Mota (right, bronze). Courtesy AAF/LPI 1984.

TABLE 21.2

1984 Los Angeles Olympic Women's Marathon at a Glance

Date:	05 August	**Weather:**	20°C (68°F)
Start time:	0800	**Starters:**	49
Course:	Point-to-point	**Finishers:**	44
Course distance:	42.195 km	**GPEs:**	28

TOP RESULTS:

Place	*Athlete*	*GPE*	*Date of birth*	*Time*
1	Joan Benoit	USA	16 May 1957	2:24:52
2	Grete Waitz	NOR	01 Oct. 1953	2:26:18
3	Rosa Mota	POR	29 June 1958	2:26:57
4	Ingrid Kristiansen	NOR	21 Mar. 1956	2:27:34
5	Lorraine Moller	NZL	01 June 1955	2:28:34
6	Priscilla Welch	GBR	22 Nov. 1944	2:28:54
7	Lisa Martin	AUS	12 May 1960	2:29:03
8	Sylvie Ruegger	CAN	23 Feb. 1961	2:29:09
9	Laura Fogli	ITA	05 Oct. 1959	2:29:28
10	Tuija Toivonen	FIN	22 Sept. 1958	2:32:07

Inaugural geopolitical entities: United States [USA], Norway [NOR], Portugal [POR], New Zealand [NZL], Great Britain [GBR], Australia [AUS], Canada [CAN], Italy [ITA], Finland [FIN], Denmark [DEN], Federal Republic of Germany [FRG], Sweden [SWE], Japan [JPN], Belgium [BEL], the Netherlands [NED], Mexico [MEX], Ireland [IRL], Israel [ISR], Hong Kong [HKG], Chile [CHI], Puerto Rico [PUR], Peru [PER], Switzerland [SUI], Bolivia [BOL], Kenya [KEN], Brazil [BRA], Nigeria [NGR], Honduras [HON]

Team score (unofficial):			
	1. GBR	31 points	(6-11-14)
	2. NOR	32 points	(2-4-26)
	3. ITA	41 points	(9-12-20)

perfect." After first trying to get some experience on the Olympic course in July but finding herself too visible, as later reported (Moore 1984), "she had gone to Eugene, Oregon—Maine away from Maine—and cooled out. Wednesday she'd picked 14 quarts of raspberries. Thursday she'd canned them all. Sunday she found herself running."

Notes on the Women Medalists

Joan Benoit's victory, especially the way she won, was what the women's sporting world needed for enthusiasm and forward progress. She was competitive and set an example for all to follow. Born in Cape Elizabeth, Maine, she attended North Carolina State University briefly, graduated from Bowdoin College, and was relatively undistinguished in collegiate athletics. Her first marathon was in 1979, at Hamilton, Bermuda, as an informal "long run" the day following the annual 10 kilometers road race, which she had run and won. She placed second with 2:50:54. It seemed easy, so she entered the Boston Marathon two and one-half months later, and she won again (2:35:15). Between 1979 and the first United States women's Olympic trial race, she ran 10 marathons, won 5, and set the world's fastest time (2:22:43) at Boston on April 18, 1983.

Following the Olympic Games, she married Scott Samuelson (September 29), and the two subsequently had two children. She continued to train and perform well after having children, as shown by her 4th place 2:26:54 at Boston in 1991. But she missed the 1988 and 1992 United States women's trials due to injuries. Showing her tenacity, she qualified for the 1996 Olympic trials, placing 13th (2:36:54). She continues to be a magnificent role model for women athletes, and in 1998 she switched from athlete to race director, organizing the first elite-level 10 kilometers road race in her home state of Maine. Benoit-Samuelson prides herself on never dropping out of a marathon. Table 21.3 summarizes her career.

Grete Waitz (nee Andersen) epitomized the need for a women's Olympic marathon. Born in Oslo, she developed an interest in competitive distance running, but events for women were limited to 800 and 1,500 meters. She did not progress further than the heats of the 800 meters in the 1971 European Athletics Championships, and she had the same experience in the 1,500 meters at the Munich Olympics in 1972. Marrying her coach, Jack Waitz, in 1975 helped give her stability and a source of coaching guidance. She set world records at 3,000 meters in 1975 and 1976. At the Montréal Olympics she competed again at 1,500 meters, this time reaching the semifinals. She later also excelled at cross country running, winning five IAAF world titles between 1978 and 1983.

Without really focusing on specific marathon training, she accepted an invitation to try the 1978 New York City Marathon, and her 2:32:29.8 was a world best. She returned in 1979 and set another world best of 2:27:32.6. She came back to New York in 1980, and, amazingly, lowered her world standard yet again, to 2:25:41. One year prior to Los Angeles, she won the inaugural world championships marathon in Helsinki (2:28:09). Her silver medal effort at Los Angeles was her second-fastest performance.

Out of 15 completed marathons (another 4 were dropouts), only 2 were slower than 2:30:00, and 13 were victories. Waitz set her personal marathon best (2:24:54) in the 1986 London race, one of her two victories there. The other (2:25:29) was three years earlier.

Rosa Mota's complete marathon career record is detailed in chapter 22. Born in Foz do Douro, Portugal, she was the first woman to win a major marathon title when she debuted at the 1982 European Athletics Championships in Athens (2:36:04). As with Waitz, she demonstrated good track speed early in her long career, with personal bests, for example, of 4:19.53 at 1,500 meters in 1983 and 8:53.84 at 3,000 meters in 1984. But longer distances were her real joy, and

TABLE 21.3

Career Marathon Record of Joan Benoit-Samuelson

Date	Venue	Place	Time	Comments
28 Jan. 1979	Hamilton	2nd	2:50:54	
16 Apr. 1979	Boston	1st	2:35:15	
09 Sept. 1979	Eugene	1st	2:35:41	
03 Feb. 1980	Auckland	1st	2:31:23	
03 Aug. 1980	London	4th	2:38:42	
20 Apr. 1981	Boston	3rd	2:30:16	
23 Aug. 1981	Ottawa	2nd	2:37:24	
11 Oct. 1981	Columbus	2nd	2:39:07	
12 Sept. 1982	Eugene	1st	2:26:11	
18 Apr. 1983	Boston	1st	2:22:43	
12 May 1984	Olympia	1st	2:31:04	Olympic trial
05 Aug. 1984	Los Angeles	1st	2:24:52	Olympic Games
20 Oct. 1985	Chicago	1st	2:21:21	
06 Nov. 1988	New York	3rd	2:32:40	
17 Apr. 1989	Boston	9th	2:37:52	
15 Apr. 1991	Boston	4th	2:26:54	
03 Nov. 1991	New York	6th	2:33:40	
11 Oct. 1992	Columbus	1st	2:32:20	
19 Apr. 1993	Boston	6th	2:35:43	
30 Oct. 1994	Chicago	6th	2:37:09	
08 Jan. 1995	Lake Buena Vista	11th	2:48:31	
10 Feb. 1996	Columbia	13th	2:36:54	Olympic trial
19 Oct. 1997	Chicago	17th	2:46:34	
01 Nov. 1998	New York	12th	2:41:06	

the marathon became her specialty. Her Los Angeles performance, at 26 years of age, was her fifth marathon, with each race at a faster time. Following Los Angeles, she embarked on a "golden odyssey," winning all the big ones: the European Athletics Championships at Stuttgart in 1986, the World Athletics Championships at Rome in 1987, and finally the Seoul Olympic Games in 1988.

City Races and Trials Help Select the Men

Increasingly diverse selection methods were evolving to identify Olympic marathon teams. In part, this was due to the availability of big-city commercial marathons already being staged, omitting the necessity of creating a specific event to select a team. Also, the increasing recovery time required for racing at such a high level made it appropriate to preselect athletes on the basis of proven prior success, thereby giving them time to focus on their Olympic race. Many of the smaller nations, of course, who had perhaps only one or two decent-quality marathoners, simply assigned them to their teams and hoped that the experience gained would help them for the future. And so, particularly for the marathon, the Olympic Games race served essentially two purposes: to let the world's toughest competitors "sort it out on the day" for the medals, and to permit those at a lower level of excellence to savor the experience of world sport participation.

Japan

Japan's star performers in 1980—Toshihiko Seko and the Soh twins (Shigeru and Takeshi)—were victims of the Moscow Games boycott, but they stayed fit, and if anything, got hungrier for Olympic competition. The prestigious Fukuoka Marathon on December 4, 1983, served as the primary Japanese Olympic trial. Seko triumphed (2:08:52), equaling Frank Shorter's string of four victories in the 1970s. Tanzanian Juma Ikangaa set the pace from the start, a common tendency for the African marathoners, and pushed it all the way, even leading as he and Seko entered the stadium. Seko outkicked him by three seconds, but Ikangaa still set a new African record. Shigeru finished third (2:09:11), only six seconds ahead of his brother, with America's Alberto Salazar scoring a fine fifth place in 2:09:21 at this extraordinary race. The Japanese were so thoroughly impressed with Ikangaa's front-running tactics that they invited him back to run the third international Yomiuri race in Tokyo on February 12. Ignoring snow flurries, he ran fast enough to stay warm, beating the German Democratic Republic's Jörg Peter by eight seconds with 2:10:49. Ikangaa was only five seconds slower than his fifth place time at that same venue in 1983. The Japanese would be tough to beat in Los Angeles, and Ikangaa would be right there with them.

United States

Fewer countries were relying on the "sudden death" trial race where the first three finishers qualified. Japan and the United States were among those who still used this method.

The Americans decided to repeat their trial system of 1980 and scheduled a late spring race (May 26) on the gently downhill Buffalo-to-Niagara Falls course. The course was mostly on Canadian soil, in the beautiful park adjacent to the Niagara River. On this occasion, runners had the combined challenges of a headwind and high humidity, so times were slowed. Peter Pfitzinger (2:11:43) edged out Alberto Salazar by a single second, with John Tuttle behind by only another six seconds. Boston Marathon winner Greg Meyer had been favored, along with Bill Rodgers, but the two unfortunately finished seventh and eighth. The United States was similar to Japan in that it had so many top marathon runners that the country could have fielded two quality Olympic teams.

Great Britain

Breaking from recent tradition, Great Britain used a team of selectors to choose its team based upon performance in three existing commercial marathons. Hugh Jones's fifth place 2:11:54 in the Los Angeles pre-Olympic race on February 19 satisfied the selectors, as did Geoff Smith's Boston victory on April 16 (2:10:34) over a moderately deep field. The final spot was decided at the fourth London Marathon, an outgrowth of the invitational Avon-sponsored all-woman marathon held two days after the Moscow Olympics in 1980. This edition was a mega-event, coursing through the heart of the city, and it attracted a world record 16,992 starters! Charlie Spedding, who had debuted at Houston in January with a victory, ran well here also (2:09:57), beating Kevin Forster by one minute and 44 seconds.

Other Countries

The Los Angeles pre-Olympic marathon served as the trial race for Mexico, the Netherlands, and Kenya. Athletes from other countries came as well, hoping to impress their selectors back home and see the Olympic venue at the same time. Tanzania's Gidamis Shahanga, 1978 Commonwealth Games champion, won the race in 2:10:19, and thus joined Ikangaa (who finished sixth) as a Tanzanian teammate. Joseph Nzau placed second (2:10:40), followed by Gerard Nijboer (2:10:53), Jesus Herrera (2:11:00), and world champion Rob de Castella (2:11:09), giving them the lead spots on the Kenyan, Dutch, Mexican, and Australian teams, respectively. Nijboer was the 1980 Games silver medalist and 1982 European champion, and thus became one of the favorites. At Tokyo earlier in the year, Alain Lazare, from New Caledonia in French Polynesia, ran a French national record of 2:11:59 and was selected.

Interestingly, at the Paris Marathon on May 12, Lazare's mark was equaled by local hero Jacques Boxberger, so their trip to Los Angeles was as much to race against each other as to race the world. At that Paris race, however, Boxberger did not win. Two French-speaking Djiboutians added intrigue to Olympic medal possibilities, one winning (Ahmed Salah Hussein, in 2:11:58), the other placing third (Djama Robleh, 2:12:11). Amazingly, Robleh had set a national record of 2:11:25 at Lyon only a month before.

Inexperienced European Marathoners Upstage the Veterans

The men's and women's Olympic marathons used the same course, but there the similarities ended. The women ran in the cooler morning hours, when it was overcast until the sun evaporated the morning fog. The men started at 1700 (5:00 p.m.). In the shade, the temperature was pleasant (23.2°C or 72.0°F), but the course was bathed in sunshine for its entirety, which warmed the runners significantly due to the radiant energy transfer. True, the dry desert air allowed plenty of evaporative cooling, but that increased the risk for dehydration. This was a special problem for runners such as Alberto Salazar, who discovered through laboratory physiological testing that he fell into the minority who sweat excessively in a warm environment. He could lose as much as two to three liters of fluid per hour (Armstrong et al. 1986). That may be fine for evaporative capabilities, but one cannot absorb more than about one liter per hour while racing.

With 107 athletes representing 59 GPEs (all of which again were NOCs), it was history's most global marathon, unlike the women's race, which was predominantly a European affair. Seventeen full teams of 3 composed nearly half the field, the remaining 56 athletes representing 42 NOCs. Eighteen European NOCs sent a total of 35 athletes, with some of the fastest runners on the planet. Africa had 27 athletes from 14 NOCs, notable for their initial front running that produced either victories or dropouts. North America had 17 athletes from 9 entities, including Salazar, with the world's fastest time. Oceania had only 4 representatives from 3 NOCs, but that included the Australian world champion Rob de Castella, who had not lost a marathon in four years. From Asia came 18 athletes from 10 NOCs, including, as usual, a formidable Japanese team. Six athletes represented 5 South American NOCs.

On the Santa Monica track (figure 21.6), African athletes immediately took the initial lead, as expected. The 5 kilometers point was passed in 15:35 by more than half the pack together, and it was not until 10 kilometers (31:09) that even a small separation of a potential lead group emerged. Many of these were the fast-moving Africans: of the dozen African runners up front at this stage, six eventually dropped out. Somalia's Ahmed Ismail led at this point, five seconds in front of Turkey's Mehmet Yurdadon. The eventual stars of the race passed 10 kilometers between 31:19 and 31:20—Charles Spedding, Carlos Lopes, John Treacy, Rob de Castella, and the Japanese team of the Soh brothers and Toshihiko Seko.

At 15 kilometers, the Africans continued to push the pace. Ikangaa, Shahanga, Salah, and Ismail were together (46:00), but only by one second, just ahead of Kenyans Joseph Nzau and Kimurgor Ngeny. Two seconds behind these two were Lopes, de Castella, and Djama. Salazar had already fallen off the lead pace and did not influence the medal positions. Just before 20 kilometers, Takeshi Soh decided to test both himself and the field. He quickened the pace, and his 1:01:20 gave him a six seconds gap. The trio of Lopes, Nzau, and Shahanga kept in contact with him, however, as did a group of five one second behind them: Nijboer, Spedding, Treacy, Ruben Aguiar, and Ralf Salzmann. Another second behind were de Castella, Seko, Djama, and Shigeru Soh. To help in realizing the spatial differences, the athletes were covering 5.4 meters per second.

The pace was seemingly acceptable for this large lead group, as they all maintained their positions within a few seconds of each other. But this pace was nonetheless faster than all but a very few had ever run before: 1:01:26 is 4:56 per mile or 3:04 per kilometer. This was sub-2:09:00 marathon pace! At 25 kilometers (1:17:12), Treacy, Spedding, Ikangaa, and Nzau were together, but they had no perceptible lead, because one second behind came Lopes, Takeshi Soh, de Castella, Djama, and Salah. Similarly, at 30 kilometers (1:33:02), the lead

Figure 21.6 Start of the men's Olympic marathon race at the Santa Monica City College track. In the lead is Juma Ikangaa [TAN] (number 824), followed closely by Takeshi Soh [JPN] (number 566), Carlos Lopes [POR] (number 723) in the middle of the pack on the inside lane, Kjell-Erik Stahl [SWE] (number 814), and Domingo Tibaduiza [COL] (number 191). Following these athletes, others that can be identified include Henrik Jorgensen [DEN] (number 201), Cor Lambregts [NED] (number 445), Vincent Ruguga [UGA] (number 878), Rod Dixon [NZL] (number 688), Gabashane Rakabaele [LES] (number 612), Toshihiko Seko [JPN] (number 563), Shigeru Soh [JPN] (number 565), Ahmet Altun [TUR] (number 860), and Rodolfo Gomez [MEX] (number 638). Courtesy AAF/LPI 1984.

group was Lopes, Spedding, Ikangaa, and Nzau, but only one second behind came Salah, Treacy, Takeshi Soh, de Castella, and Jerry Kiernan. Seko, Shigeru Soh, and Djama were there as well, another second behind. Never had so many good runners been so close together this late in a marathon.

The runners now entered Rodeo Road, which merged with Exposition Boulevard on its straight trek back to the stadium. The relentless fast pacing started taking its toll, and at 35 kilometers (1:48:23), only Spedding, Treacy, and Lopes were together, with Nzau beginning to fade and the rest already falling back. By 37 kilometers it was still Spedding, Treacy, and Lopes. Then Lopes suddenly accelerated. His inherent strength from fast track racing simply let him increase his stride length without quickening his cadence—and no one went with him. By 37.5 kilometers he was well out in front, with Treacy and Spedding not responding. Lopes's 5 kilometers split from 30 to 35 kilometers had been 15:21, but his 35-to-40 kilometers split was 14:33! Spedding and Treacy now could only duel between themselves for silver and bronze. On Menlo Avenue, Treacy gained 7 meters on Spedding just before they U-turned onto the steep descent into the stadium tunnel. Table 21.4 summarizes the various changes in position of top athletes during the race.

Lopes entered the stadium track as both an athlete and an entertainer. The prelude to the Closing Ceremonies started at 1845 (6:45 p.m.) inside the stadium, and it was now 1907 (7:07 p.m.). Seven past Olympic marathon medalists were being introduced to the full stadium crowd to help welcome the runners (Perelman 1985). It was a most impressive group: Son (1936), Gorno (1952), Mimoun (1956), Magee (1960), Heatley (1964), Kimihara (1968), and Shorter (1972 and 1976). The marathon was thus choreographed into the program of the Closing Ceremonies for the first time. How nice to close the Games with the event that was indeed the creation of these modern Games. And what a magnificent way to showcase the sport of track and field, an idea credited to the IAAF's new president, Nebiolo, who was becoming increasingly respected for his keen sense of effective sports promotion. This also could not have been a grander spectacle for the newly crowned Olympic medalists, who now could savor the evening's closing festivities as champions. However, it is likely that most of the marathoners, who were now suffering the searing pain of muscle cramps from energy, fluid, and electrolyte loss, would have preferred that the Closing Ceremonies had been held some hours later, so that they, too, could have enjoyed them.

The Closing Ceremonies choreographers could not have been happier. The three medalists were on the track together. Spedding and Treacy were in single file 200 meters behind Lopes, in that order, but Treacy caught and passed Spedding. Lopes's achievement in victory was no less momentous than that of Benoit. At 37, he was the oldest gold medalist of the 1984 Games (and is still the oldest Olympic marathon gold medalist). His 2:09:21 was an Olympic record, but not a personal best. De Castella had beaten him at Rotterdam in 1983, but

TABLE 21.4

Order of Top Placers Through Control Points

	Lopes	*Treacy*	*Spedding*	*Soh*	*De Castella*	*Ikangaa*
10 km	=20-27	=20-27	=12-19	=12-19	=12-19	=9-11
15 km	=7-9	16	=11-13	=14, 15	=7-9	=1-4
20 km	=2-4	=5-9	=5-9	1	=10-13	15
25 km	=5-9	=1-4	=1-4	=5-9	=5-9	=1-4
30 km	=1-4	=5-9	=1-4	=5-9	=5-9	=1-4
35 km	=1-4	=1-4	=1-4	=5-7	8	=5-7
40 km	1	3	2	4	5	6
Finish	1	2	3	4	5	6

now Lopes was king. From silver in Montréal (in the 10,000 meters) to boycotting Moscow to gold in Los Angeles—Lopes had seen it all. It was a race of superlatives (Phillips and Gynn 1996): there were "the greatest number of starters (107), the most finishers (78) from the widest spectrum of countries (59), and the most under 2:20:00 (34, compared with 25 in both 1976 and 1980) in any Olympic marathon to date." Table 21.5 gives a synopsis of the race.

Statistics experts will note some time and place discrepancies from those normally reported in the men's results summarized in appendix D, especially positions 50 through 55. Two sets of results were distributed following the event, one timed at 2057 (8:57 p.m.), the other at 2318 (11:18 p.m.). Not all the errors that crept into the first version were corrected in the second. More important, in later correspondence with the company handling the results, Ernst & Whinney, some additional corrections were discovered (Sparks 1999) that did not get included in the Official Report. We have included these.

TABLE 21.5

1984 Los Angeles Olympic Men's Marathon at a Glance

Date:	12 August	**Weather:**	23.2°C (72.0°F), sunny
Start time:	1700	**Starters:**	107
Course:	Point-to-point	**Finishers:**	78
Course distance:	42.195 km	**GPEs:**	59

TOP RESULTS:

Place	*Athlete*	*GPE*	*Date of birth*	*Time*
1	Carlos Lopes	POR	18 Feb. 1947	2:09:21
2	John Treacy	IRL	04 June 1957	2:09:56
3	Charles Spedding	GBR	19 May 1952	2:09:58
4	Takeshi Soh	JPN	09 Jan. 1953	2:10:55
5	Francois Robert de Castella	AUS	27 Feb. 1957	2:11:09
6	Juma Ikangaa	TAN	19 July 1960	2:11:10
7	Joseph Nzau	KEN	14 Apr. 1952	2:11:28
8	Djama Robleh	DJI	31 Dec. 1958	2:11:39
9	Jeremiah Kiernan	IRL	31 May 1953	2:12:20
10	Rodney Dixon	NZL	13 July 1950	2:12:57

New geopolitical entities represented: Djibouti [DJI], Jamaica [JAM], Botswana [BOT], Chinese Taipei [TPE], Israel [ISR], Cyprus [CYP], Jordan [JOR], Central African Republic [CAF], British Virgin Islands [ISV], Qatar [QAT], Oman [OMA], Zaire [ZAI]

Team score (unofficial):			
	1. JPN	35 points	(4-14-17)
	2. TAN	49 points	(6-21-22)
	3. DJI	60 points	(8-20-32)

Notes on the Men Medalists

For **Carlos Lopes**, this was his third Olympics. Born in Viseu, Portugal, his early background as an athlete focused on cross country and track. He had essentially only one coach his entire career, Mario Moniz Perreira. At the Munich Olympics, Lopes competed in the 5,000 and 10,000 meters, but did not advance to the finals of these events. In 1976, he won the International Cross Country Championships as a lead-up to the Montréal Games, and he took the silver medal at 10,000 meters behind Viren. He then disappeared from the running scene due to injuries. When he returned in 1982, his inherent track speed showed forth again, as he set a European record at 10,000 meters and placed fourth at the European Athletics championships.

It was then that Lopes tried the marathon, and his record was one of erratic excellence. He did not finish at New York in 1982, and he followed that with a splendid 2:08:39 at Rotterdam in 1983. In the spring of the Olympic year, he entered Rotterdam again soon after winning the IAAF World Cross Country Championships, but dropped out. Mentally, this seemed not to affect him in Los Angeles, as he had again honed his track speed during the early summer months. On July 2, in Stockholm, he had run the second fastest 10,000 meters in history (27:17.48), behind Fernando Mamede's world record. After six weeks of recovery, he was ready to put speed and endurance to work. In Los Angeles, when he made his move near 40 kilometers, the world stayed behind. He joined Alain Mimoun as the only two to have won both the World Cross Country Championships and Olympic marathon gold in the same year.

Lopes managed two more excellent marathon performances after Los Angeles. One was the Chicago showdown in October, where Steve Jones upstaged him. But he returned to his favorite marathon at Rotterdam in 1985 and set a world best that remained the standard for another three years. As shown in table 21.6, it was his last completed marathon.

TABLE 21.6

Career Marathon Record of Carlos Lopes

Date	Venue	Place	Time	Comments
24 Oct. 1982	New York	DNF		
09 Apr. 1983	Rotterdam	2nd	2:08:39	
18 Apr. 1984	Rotterdam	DNF		
12 Aug. 1984	Los Angeles	1st	2:09:21	Olympic Games
21 Oct. 1984	Chicago	2nd	2:09:06	
20 May 1985	Rotterdam	1st	2:07:12	
09 Feb. 1990	Tokyo	DNF		

John Treacy was born in Villierstown, County Waterford, Ireland, and also came from a track background. This was his second Olympics; at Moscow he placed seventh at 5,000 meters and did not reach the finals at 10,000 meters. He attended Providence College in the United States, and he benefited from that country's university-based track and field program. Focusing on cross country during the fall, indoor competition during the winter, and outdoor track racing in the spring, he got fit for returning to Europe during the summer for the top-level meetings.

Treacy's excellent debut performance (and Irish national record) in the Los Angeles Olympics at the age of 27 was a turning point in his career. He continued to train for and compete at shorter distances, but he found marathon racing both enjoyable and financially satisfying. He qualified for two more Olympic marathon teams but was unsuccessful, dropping out at Seoul, and placing 51st at Barcelona. Meanwhile, he placed well at big-city races: 3rd on two occasions at Boston (1988, with a personal best of 2:09:15; and 1989), 3rd at New York (1988), and 2nd at Tokyo (1990). He returned to Los Angeles in 1992 and won its city marathon (2:12:29), setting himself up to place well at Barcelona, but it was not to be.

Charles "Charlie" Spedding was born in Bishop Auckland, County Durham, England. His marathon career started early in the Olympic year when he won the January Houston Marathon (2:11:54). This gave him confidence to try the London race, which was becoming an event approaching Olympic quality. His victory there (2:09:57) earned him a spot on the Olympic team at the age of 32. In Los Angeles, he ran only one second slower in more difficult conditions. He returned to London the year following the Olympics and scored a personal best 2:08:33. He continued to average one excellent marathon performance a year until 1988, when his 10th place 2:12:28 at London again gave him an Olympic team berth. He performed quite well at Seoul, finishing 6th with 2:12:19.

Looking Ahead: Brief Highlights 1985-1988

1984: After the Olympic Games, the race of the year was the Chicago Marathon on October 21, in which several of the Olympic medalists went head-to-head with those hoping to race faster. In the men's race, the unheralded Welshman Steve Jones (he had failed to finish in his only other marathon, at Chicago in 1983) set a magnificent world best 2:08:05 by soundly defeating both the Los Angeles gold medalist (Lopes, 2:09:06) and the Helsinki world champion (de Castella, 2:09:09). In the women's race, Mota (2:26:01) proved superior once again over Kristiansen and Lisa Martin, but this time Martin (2:27:40) was too quick for Kristiansen (2:30:21). Waitz opted for New York and scored her sixth victory there (2:29:30).

1985: Djibouti displayed its marathon-racing prowess in the inaugural IAAF Marathon World Cup at Hiroshima on April 14 as the first three finishers all bettered 2:09:00 (Salah 2:08:09, Nakayama 2:08:15, Robleh 2:08:26), and Djibouti took the team prize (with places one, three, and seven). In Rotterdam one week later, Lopes shattered the world best mark (2:07:12). Steve Jones returned to Chicago, hoping to improve. He did (2:07:13), but missed tying the new world standard by just one second! In between the two Chicago races, Jones had also won at London (April 21) with a superb 2:08:16.

Among the women, the Soviet-bloc boycott kept Katrin Dörre out of the 1984 Games, so her gold medal at the Hiroshima World Cup (April 13, 2:33:30) was especially meaningful. On the following weekend, at London on April 21, Ingrid Kristiansen set a new standard of 2:21:06 for women running on point-to-point courses in mixed races. Waitz scored victory number seven at New York (October 27) with 2:28:34.

1986: Rob de Castella set a new Boston Marathon best performance (2:07:51—the second-fastest time of the year) before going on to win the Commonwealth Games gold medal in Edinburgh (August 1) in 2:10:15. Gelindo Bordin (2:10:54) edged Orlando Pizzolato by three seconds for a one-two Italian sweep of the European Athletics Championships at Stuttgart (August 30). Japan's Takeyuki Nakayama took the Asian Games title in Seoul on October 5, running 2:08:21 essentially alone (only eight were in the race). Two weeks later, at Beijing, two of his countrymen ran the first and third fastest times of the year: Taisuke Kodama (2:07:35) and Kunimitsu Ito (2:07:57).

Grete Waitz won both at London (2:24:54—the year's fastest time) on April 20 and at New York (2:28:06—her eighth victory on that course) on November 2. At Boston (April 21), Ingrid Kristiansen won with the year's second-fastest time, only one second behind Waitz. She also won at Chicago on October 26 (2:27:08). Lisa Martin set her sights on the Commonwealth Games gold, and her 2:26:07, third fastest of the year, was victorious over her chief Oceania competitor, Lorraine Moller (2:28:17). Martin lost to Waitz later on in New York. Rosa Mota focused on winning her second European Athletics Championships and did so at Stuttgart (August 26) in 2:28:38. She then tried the Tokyo Marathon (November 16) on a faster course, and her 2:27:15 was the fifth-fastest performance of the year.

1987: Djiboutian Ahmed Salah won his second IAAF Marathon World Cup title (Seoul, 2:10:55, April 12), beating Kodama, but in turn was upset by Kenya's Douglas Wakiihuri (2:11:48) at Rome (September 6) in the second IAAF World Athletics Championships. The fastest time of the year occurred at the Fukuoka event (December 6) when Takeyuki Nakayama recorded 2:08:18 to impress the selectors using this as the first Japanese race to help choose the Seoul Olympic team.

European women took most of the year's top honors. At the increasingly lucrative big-city marathons, Ingrid Kristiansen was victorious at London (May

(continued)

10) with the year's fastest time (2:22:48). Rosa Mota tried the Boston Marathon (April 20), and her victory (2:25:21) gave her a strong mental edge for the IAAF World Athletics Championships in hot-weather Rome. Although enjoying the benefits of altitude training in Colorado, Mota also competed well in the heat, and she overwhelmed a top field at Rome (August 29) with 2:25:17, giving her two of the year's three fastest times. Katrin Dörre continued to impress, finishing with 2:25:24 at Tokyo (November 15), good for the year's fourth-fastest time.

References

Anonymous. 1982. Meeting of the Executive Board in Los Angeles. *Olympic Review* 161: 139-141.

Anonymous. 1984. *The Official Report of the Games of the XXIIIrd Olympiad, Los Angeles 1984.* Vol. 2, *Competition Summary and Results.*

Armstrong, L.E., R.W. Hubbard, B.H. Jones, and J.T. Daniels. 1986. Preparing Alberto Salazar for the heat of the 1984 Olympic marathon. *Physician and Sportsmedicine* 14 (3): 73-81.

Baumel, B. 1990. Measuring the 1992 Olympic Marathon. *Measurement News* 41: 18-21.

Ecker, T. 1996. *Olympic facts and fables.* Mountain View, CA: Tafnews Press.

Kuscsik, N. 1977. The history of women's participation in the marathon. *Annals of the New York Academy of Sciences* 301: 862-876.

Moore, K. 1984. They got off on the right track. *Sports Illustrated* 61 (8): 60-81.

Myers, K. 1998. Personal communication from IAAF.

Perelman, R.D. 1985. *Olympic retrospective: The Games of Los Angeles.* Los Angeles: The LAOOC.

Phillips, B., and R. Gynn. 1996. *100 years of the Olympic marathon.* Gwent: National Union of Track Statisticians.

Sparks, R. 1999. Personal communication.

Ueberroth, P. 1985. *Made in America.* New York: William Morrow & Co., Inc.

Welch, J. 1984. *Track and Field News* 37 (9): 67.

Whipp, B.J., and S.A. Ward. 1992. Will women soon outrun men? *Nature* 355: 25.

Willman, H. 1984. Puica outruns the disaster. *Track and Field News* 37(8): 62.

Chapter 22

1988—Seoul

Bordin and Mota Score for Europe at Seoul

Korea Shows Its Culture and Capabilities

Seoul was the surprise winner over Nagoya to host the 1988 Olympic Games by a vote of 52 to 27 taken at the 84th IOC Congress in Baden Baden on September 30, 1981 (Anonymous 1981). Nagoya had been favored because of Japan's previously successful Tokyo Games. Korea was a mystery in the minds of many. Although South Korea was a developing economic power among Pacific rim countries, it was better known as (1) a military dictatorship struggling to move toward democracy, (2) a land that had been devastated by war 25 years before, and (3) the site of the planet's most fortified borders—a single culture divided by political differences at the 38th parallel.

Two concerns surfaced immediately despite a praiseworthy bid promising "harmony and progress." One was Seoul's lack of experience in hosting a mega-event such as the Olympic Games, and its accompanying lack of venues, housing, and infrastructure. The promise was only that Seoul was a city of 10 million people who very much wanted the Games to succeed. The other concern was Seoul's ongoing frustration with Pyongyang in the Democratic People's Republic of (North) Korea. Would these Olympic Games simply be a sequel to the Moscow and Los Angeles boycotts? Only recently has the story been made public of at least some of the several years of negotiations between the Olympic movement and the highest levels of various governments (Pound 1994). The story attests to IOC president Juan Antonio Samaranch's negotiating skills as much as to the importance of an IOC president being one who can work with governments at the highest levels.

Samaranch was determined for a boycott not to happen. In a fashion similar to that of 1980, he ordered the IOC itself, rather than the host committee as normal, to send invitations to the NOCs, asking each to send a delegation to the Olympic Games. In the end, only three hard-liners from the communist world refused to come: Democratic People's Republic of Korea, Cuba, and Ethiopia. Albania, a terribly impoverished nation, stayed home; and three others, the Seychelles, Madagascar, and Nicaragua, did not participate for various reasons. For the marathon, this was indeed a loss, because North Korea and Ethiopia in particular had excellent athletes. Ethiopia had won three gold medals and one silver medal in the past eight Olympic Games, a better record than any other nation.

Out of the 167 member geopolitical entities, the 160 participating GPEs (which were all NOCs) exceeded the 140 that participated in Los Angeles—and they brought a record-setting 8,465 athletes (6,279 men and 2,186 women). (Actually, only 159 brought athletes; Brunei had just an official.) It was the first time in 12 years that the "big three" athletic superpowers had come together, and when the gold, silver, and bronze medals were tallied, they led the order of achievement. First came the Soviet Union (55 + 31 + 46 = 132), followed by the German Democratic Republic (37 + 35 + 30 = 102), and then the United States (36 + 31 + 27 = 94). Certainly as noteworthy, however, was the miracle of Korea's athletes. They finished fourth (12 + 10 + 11 = 33). For Samaranch, this bringing of the Olympic spirit into a region relatively undeveloped in terms of sport and fueling its athletic talent to reach for the sky in achievement was truly satisfying.

Commercialization of the Olympic movement increased substantially following the Los Angeles Games. Particularly important was a move to go beyond reliance on United States television network dollars as a primary revenue source for the IOC (although these brought in an unprecedented $408 million). Enter Horst Dassler of Adidas fame. Horst was the son of Adolph, the cobbler from Herzogenaurach whose business acumen and superb product got his wares into the Mexico City village as the contracted athletic equipment supplier. Dassler's global thinking advanced beyond simply the sale of shoes, and in 1983 he established International Sport Leisure (ISL) as a company to market sports events. Dassler convinced the IOC to let ISL serve as its marketing agent on the premise that ISL would return to the NOCs more money than they could acquire by their own negotiations. Wealthy NOCs were more difficult to convince than poorer ones, but eventually everyone saw the logic.

In 1985, Dassler and Samaranch jointly announced a program to provide funding for Seoul and Calgary, the host of the Winter Games. Called simply The Olympic Program (TOP), it was once again a very small group of very large, wealthy corporations benefiting enormously—at a high price—by the visibility associated with their exclusive ties to the five rings. Nine corporations contributed more than $100 million to help these Olympic Games succeed. Although Dassler died in 1987, his legacy lived on with the formation of TOP II for the 1992 Games.

Korea's financial momentum in hosting a successful Olympic Games thus matched the quality of its athlete excellence. Whereas Los Angeles spent $500 million, Korea's total outlay was $3.1 billion: $1.4 billion in direct costs provided by government and civic partners, and $1.7 billion in direct costs provided by the private sector.

Billed as the Games of "Harmony and Progress," they were indeed that. While it sometimes appeared that there were more police than spectators, it was a friendly security, and there were no incidents. The weather was sunny and the temperature cool-to-warm—magnificent for most outdoor events. The streets were lined with flowers and banners as never before, and the people, despite a huge language barrier, communicated with smiles. The Opening Ceremonies combined traditional culture with global themes of sport, art, and music, setting a new standard. The drums, dragons, and colors were unforgettable, but one event in the ceremonies was spellbinding by its simplicity and symbolism. A small boy skipped out onto the then-vacant infield, completely alone, gleefully rolling his plastic hoop. The stadium crowd was hushed in silence, watching and wondering, and was soon informed that this was Yun Tae-ung, born on the day the Olympic Games were awarded to Seoul—representing youth, hope, growth, and sport! And flying in the breeze was the Seoul Olympic flag, replacing the worn version in use since Antwerp. Made of the finest pure Korean silk and hand-dyed, it was unveiled at the 90th IOC session at Berlin in 1985 (Anonymous 1985). The Antwerp flag now rests in the IOC Museum.

In the following days, the athletes put on an unforgettable show. One star of these Olympic Games was Florence Griffith Joyner, or "Flo-Jo." Known as much for her beauty and innovative sprint apparel as for her awesome athleticism, she won gold medals in the 100 and 200 meters—and set two world records in winning the 200 meters. And she was as quick as lightning in the relay events as well.

The men's side had a quite different phenomenon in Canada's Ben Johnson, who destroyed Carl Lewis in the 100 meters final with a world record 9.79 seconds. Could it be real? No, it wasn't! Later that afternoon, Johnson's urine tested positive for stanazolol—a rapidly metabolizable steroid that stayed around a little too long. His gold medal was returned and given to Lewis. Johnson had been booked into a Seoul hotel as John Benson to stay out of the spotlight. Now he could not get out of it. Banished from the Olympic Games and flown back to Canada, his transgressions triggered a governmental investigation, headed by Charles Dubin, into the clandestine world of ergogenics. The report filled a book (Dubin 1990). At Seoul, Johnson was 1 of 10 athletes who tested positive for banned substances, compared to 12 in Los Angeles, 11 at Montréal, 7 at Munich, and 1 at Mexico City (Wallechinsky 1996).

When the Olympic Games closed, in many ways Seoul was a new city. It had a new airport and two new mammoth sports complexes, with nearly a dozen new sports venues that today are used by the masses. An expressway 30 kilometers (18.6 miles) in length was built to connect one of these complexes with the airport. An Olympic Family Town—56 skyscrapers housing Olympic guests—later became comfortable housing for Seoul's burgeoning population. The Olympic Village—86 skyscrapers housing 13,000 athletes and officials—helped alleviate a shortage in another part of the city. The Han River (Han Gang) was cleaned up. The world enjoyed coming to Korea, leaving a positive legacy of untold value. The Olympic movement had again been put into good hands.

Marathon Course Design a Model of Perfection

The Seoul Olympic marathon course was (and probably still is) the most accurately measured in the world. Measurement was managed by the Korean Society of Geodesy, Photogrammetry, and Cartography (Anonymous 1986). The primary project officers were professors from Korea's six universities. All were specialists in their individual assignments, and their education could not have been better. The Seoul Olympic Organizing Committee (SLOOC) decided which streets would be used for the course and used vehicular odometers to determine an approximate distance. Final adjustments could then be made within the stadium by moving the start point and varying the number of track loops. Following IAAF rules, the road route to be measured (i.e., the shortest possible line-of-sight path, allowing 30 centimeters from curbs or edges at turns), was then professionally surveyed and painted with a temporary white line. Other marathons have had lines painted on the roadway to point the way, but Seoul's line was painted *exactly* on the precisely measured route. To enhance accuracy, 12 baselines were embedded along the marathon course, created by an electronic distance meter. Three measurements were made per baseline, accurate to 1/100,000. This is the largest number of embedded baselines in any marathon course in the world today.

After the surveying and painting were completed, 15 expert cyclists from a bicycle-racing club were commissioned to ride the course using Jones counters mounted on their bikes. The cyclists completed these measurements at night, to minimize temperature fluctuations, between May 16 and May 18, 1986. Police escorts reduced traffic congestion; these streets are in a very busy area of Seoul. The cyclists were instructed to ride precisely on top of the painted white line. Once the length of this road distance was established, final adjustments were made to the start line in the stadium to permit athletes to finish at the standard track-event finish line.

As indicated in figure 22.1, the stadium was at 15 meters above sea level (49 feet). Within the first 5 kilometers, a 24 meters climb (62 feet) brought runners to the highest point on the course (39 meters, or 128 feet). Then, within the next 4.2 kilometers, they descended 29 meters (95 feet) to reach the low point (10 meters, or 33 feet). The remainder was continually rolling, with 16 moderate ups and downs in all.

In its 224-page report to the SLOOC, the Korean Society of Geodesy, Photogrammetry, and Cartography reported that the course was "oversized" by only 13 meters (42,208 meters, with 99.95 percent confidence against shortness. By comparison, the Los Angeles marathon Olympic course was certified as 25 meters over the required distance. Before the two Olympic races, the painted white line was carefully repainted in continuous blue. A uniformed police force of 11,000 lined up along the entire course to provide both crowd control and assurance that runners would only run on the marked route. The course details outline the street plan for the Seoul Olympic marathon. Due to heavy traffic, most of the streets would be inappropriate for general running today. However, with a local street map, the entire course can still be driven.

The Women Look Forward to Their Second Olympic Race

Japan

Although 1984 brought much excitement to women's marathoning with its Olympic debut, 1988 brought an even greater excitement as many new stars joined the already established talent pool. The November-to-March Japanese marathon circuit started the selection activity with major headlines. Australia's Lisa Martin came to Osaka ready to race on January 31, and her 2:23:51 was a world best for an out-and-back women-only competition. Her performance was the seventh-fastest run up to that time, and a Commonwealth record as well. No one ran faster in all of 1988. She overshadowed three fine performances by Japanese women, all of whom were selected for their team: Misako Miyahara (2:29:37, for a national record), Kumi Araki (2:31:40), and Eriko Asai (2:32:13). In March, China's Zhao Youfeng won the Nagoya race with an Asian record of 2:27:56, as Carla Beurskens [NED] and Birgit Stephan [GDR] also finished in less than two and one-half hours.

United States

The United States used its "sudden death" selection system at Pittsburgh on May 1, which meant that the Boston Marathon again was essentially devoid of top-level American women. At Boston, Rosa Mota continued her winning ways with a dominating victory (2:24:30) nearly five minutes in front of Finland's Tuija Jousimaa, whose 2:29:26 was still fast enough for a national record and an Olympic team berth. Third-placed Odette Lapierre (2:30:48) made the Canadian team.

At Pittsburgh, Margaret Groos (2:29:50) outlasted Nancy Ditz (2:30:14) and Cathy O'Brien (2:30:18) in a close battle for the top honors. Peaking when it

COURSE DETAILS

The 1988 Seoul Olympic Marathon

Start at apex of top turn of the track (south end of the stadium)

Run 2.9 laps counterclockwise, and exit the marathon tunnel (south end)

Continue on stadium access road past baseball stadium (on the right) to T'eheranno

Right onto T'eheranno to Onjuro

Left onto Onjuro to Yoksamno

Right onto Yoksamno to Kangnamdero

Right onto Kangnamdero to Pongunsaro

Left onto Pongunsaro to Sap'yongno (10 kilometers)

Half right onto Sap'yongno to Hyonch'ungno

Half right onto Hyonch'ungno to Kangnam3no (15 kilometers)

Kangnam3no becomes Kangnam4ro along south side of Han Gang (Han River)

Continue on Kangnam4ro to Taebangno

Right onto Taebangno across canal onto island to Uisadangno

Half left onto Uisadangno to Youido Plaza

Right onto Youido Plaza (20 kilometers)

Cross Youido Plaza and then cross Han Gang via Map'odaegyo (Map'o bridge) to Taegonno

Right onto Taegonno along north side of Han Gang

Taegonno becomes Kangbyon3no (25 kilometers)

Continue on Kangbyon3no to Panp'odaegyo (Panp'o bridge)

Right onto Panp'odaegyo and recross Han Gang

Continue on Panp'oro (30 kilometers) to Sinbanp'oro

Left onto Sinbanp'oro to U-Myonno

Left onto U-Myonno to Chamwonno

Right onto Chamwonno along south side of Han Gang

Chamwonno becomes Apgujongno

Continue on Apgujongno to Onjuro

Left onto Onjuro to Kangnam2ro (35 kilometers)

Right onto Kangnam2ro along south side of Han Gang, crossing Yangaechon (stream) and passing Seoul Sports Complex to Chamsilgil

Right onto Chamsilgil to Olympicno (40 kilometers)

counted the most, all three set personal bests on a difficult course with excellent weather. The unfortunate fourth place went to Lisa Weidenbach, who knew what the feeling was like. She had finished fourth in the 1984 marathon trials as well, and also in the Olympic swimming trials four years before that!

Europe

At London on April 17, Ingrid Kristiansen tasted success for the fourth time, although her victory (2:25:41) was her slowest to date at that venue. She domi-

Right onto Olympicno, recrossing Yangaechon (stream)

Olympicno becomes T'eheranno

Continue onto T'eheranno to Olympic stadium access road

Right onto stadium access road and through entry tunnel to stadium

Run counterclockwise 340 meters to finish at the standard finish line for distance races

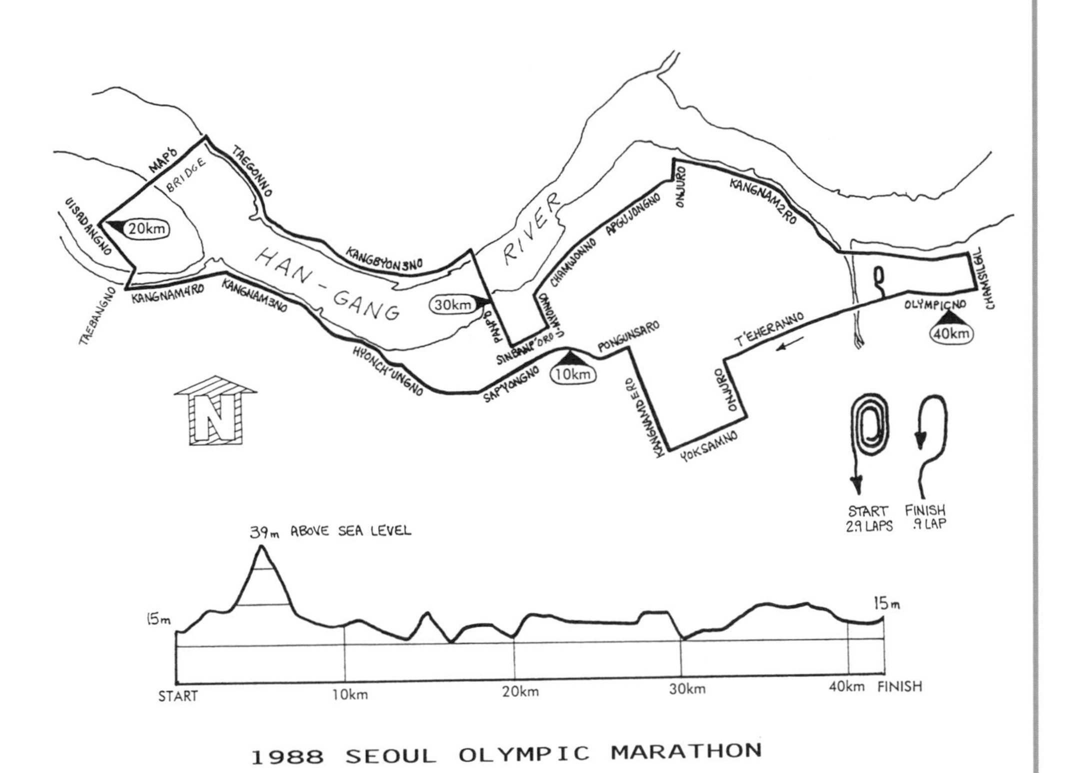

Figure 22.1 Sketch of the Seoul Olympic marathon course. Prepared by Bob Letson.

nated over the rest of her rivals, with Britain's Ann Ford (2:30:38) being the runner-up and given the top spot on her Olympic team. Susan Tooby finished fourth and also was selected to run for Britain along with Angela Pain. Kristiansen joined Grete Waitz on the Norwegian team. Waitz demonstrated her fitness by winning in 2:28:24 on Stockholm's challenging course. After inactivity for much of 1987 with injury, Waitz was delighted with her performance and hoped that she could remain healthy through the long summer, as the Seoul women's marathon was not until September 23.

Two weeks after London, the European Marathon Cup race was staged at Huy in Belgium. Although the ever-consistent Katrin Dörre won it (2:28:28), the event was a runaway success for the Soviets, who took the next four places. The top three composed the Soviet team. The fastest was Raisa Smekhnova (2:28:40), the 1983 IAAF World Athletics Championships bronze medalist. Then followed Zoya Ivanova (2:29:37), the 1987 IAAF Marathon World Cup winner. The final team berth went to Tatyana Polovinskaya, who recovered quickly enough to win the Soviet championship race at Tallinn (2:28:02) two months later, on June 26.

Mota Adds Olympic Gold to Her Growing Collection

Weather conditions at the 0930 (9:30 a.m.) race start time included high (92 percent) humidity, a warm temperature (19.5°C or 67°F), and a sunny sky. In such high humidity, one perspires but does not cool. Fortunately the rising sun dried the air faster than it warmed it, and conditions improved over time. The starting field numbered 69, representing 39 GPEs (all of which were NOCs). As in Los Angeles, Europeans dominated in numbers: 34 from 18 NOCs. North and Central America had 8 NOCs represented, totaling 12 athletes. South America had only 1 athlete, from Brazil. Africa had 5 athletes from 4 NOCs, and Asia had 11 athletes from 5 NOCs. Oceania contributed 5 athletes from 3 NOCs. In all, nine full teams of 3 runners made the team aspect of this race quite competitive (Anonymous 1989).

Most of the world's top women marathoners were ready to race, with two notable exceptions. Joan Benoit-Samuelson took time off to have a baby, and Ingrid Kristiansen had opted to run in the 10,000 meters event. Otherwise, each of the five major players had won her only previous marathon in 1988, and all were poised to win here: Lisa Martin, Katrin Dörre, Zhao Youfeng, Rosa Mota, and Grete Waitz (figure 22.2). It was anyone's guess regarding the outcome.

The rolling nature of the course, the high humidity, and the lack of shade conspired to make this a difficult race. The first (uphill) 5 kilometers (17:10) saw four in front with a 10 seconds gap: Mota, Martin, Dörre, and Smekhnova. This lead was brief, for on the downhill everyone caught up, and by 10 kilometers (34:13) it was a huge lead pack of 21, with the top stars still in contention.

At 15 kilometers (51:30), a group of 14 had opened a separation of about half a minute, with a few isolated runners in between. There were still no surprises in terms of favorites either dropping back or taking the lead. At 20 kilometers (1:08:46), the lead pack was reduced to 13, with Lorraine Moller missing due to problems with dehydration. At 25 kilometers (1:25:55), the pack was down to 12, with Grete Waitz now falling behind. She later said that arthroscopic knee surgery a month earlier had taken the edge off her fitness (Nelson 1988).

Between 20 and 25 kilometers the lead pace was 5:31 per mile (3:26 per kilometer). Between 25 and 30 kilometers the pace did not change, but its

Figure 22.2 **Just outside Olympic stadium as the race gets under way, several of the eventual major players are grouped together. From left, these include Grete Waitz [NOR] (number 438), Rosa Mota [POR] (number 460), Zhao Youfeng [CHN] (number 111), Katrin Dörre [GDR] (number 260), Carla Beurskens [NED] (number 316), Zhong Huandi [CHN] (number 112), Tatyana Polovinskaya [URS] (number 544), Maria Curatolo [ITA] (number 352), Raisa Smekhnova [URS] (number 549), Li Juan [CHN] (number 94), and Gabriela Wolf [FRG] (number 203).** Courtesy Moon-june Lee, The Chosun Ilbo, Ltd.

intensity was too much for all but four: Mota, Martin, Dörre, and Polovinskaya were timed in 1:43:13 at 30 kilometers. They were fully 34 seconds ahead of Zhao, with Zoya Ivanova another 2 seconds behind, and then Laura Fogli 5 seconds farther back. Their race pace averaged 4.8 meters per second, which gives an idea of the separation of runners. Between 30 and 35 kilometers, with more ascent than descent, the pace slowed to 5:46 per mile (3:25 per kilometer), managed by Mota and Dörre (2:01:09), but Martin and Polovinskaya were only a second behind. Zhao had now closed slightly (2:01:37), with Fogli another 23 seconds in back of her. As the temperatures rose, Mota's abilities to run well in the heat gave her an advantage. As she crested the hill at 39 kilometers, knowing it was downhill into the stadium, she kept her cadence but added a little more power to her stride. As runners passed 40 kilometers in 2:18:10, the medal winners were essentially decided, the only question being who would win what. Martin was now behind by just 14 seconds, with Dörre another 1 second back.

Mota entered the stadium track from the marathon tunnel just beyond the track finish line and then had to run nearly a complete lap around to end her race at that finish line (figure 22.3). Her 2:25:40 was not an Olympic record, but it was the first gold medal of the track and field competition. Along with her Los Angeles bronze, she now owned every summer Games medal ever awarded to a Portuguese woman! All three medalists were on the track at one time, Lisa Martin finishing only 15 seconds back, and Katrin Dörre 28 seconds behind her. Amazingly, only 5 of the 69 starters did not finish, and many runners achieved personal bests despite being well out of the medal positions. So great was the depth that the top United States finisher, Nancy Ditz, placing 17th, still recorded her second-fastest time. Athletes with a well-honed sense of pace had some remarkable success. Britain's Angie Pain, for example, moved up from 27th at 25 kilometers to 17th at 35 kilometers, and she was Britain's top finisher with 10th place. Tables 22.1 and 22.2 summarize the changes in order of the top athletes during the competition, along with other details of the race.

Figure 22.3 Rosa Mota approaches the finish line with a smile of Olympic victory.
Courtesy Moon-june Lee, The Chosun Ilbo, Ltd.

TABLE 22.1

Order of Top Placers Through Control Points

	Mota	*Martin*	*Dörre*	*Polovinskaya*	*Zhao*	*Fogli*
5 km	=1-4	=1-4	=1-4	=5-13	=5-13	=14, 15
10 km	=1-21	=1-21	=1-21	=1-21	=1-21	=1-21
15 km	=1-14	=1-14	=1-14	=1-14	=1-14	=1-14
20 km	=1-13	=1-13	=1-13	=1-13	=1-13	=1-13
25 km	=1-12	=1-12	=1-12	=1-12	=1-12	=1-12
30 km	=1-4	=1-4	=1-4	=1-4	5	7
35 km	=1, 2	=3, 4	=1, 2	=3, 4	5	6
40 km	1	2	3	4	5	6
Finish	1	2	3	4	5	6

Notes on the Women Medalists

Rosa Mota's gold capped her already scintillating eight-year career as a marathoner: three European championship gold medals (she would still win another at Split, Croatia, in 1990) and two Olympic medals. Her success at the world championships was not as consistent: fourth in 1983, first in 1987, and a dropout in 1991. But her achievement of 14 victories out of 21 marathons between 1982 and 1992—including most of the biggest of the big-city races—has been approached by only a small handful of the greatest women in the event's history. She was the first Portuguese woman to win an Olympic medal, and in this regard she has served as a positive role model in her country for thousands of women athletes who now can see clearly what hard work and talent can accomplish together. Table 22.3 summarizes her marathon career.

Lisa Martin (nee O'Dea) was born in Gawler, South Australia. As with Waitz and Mota, she, too, came from a shorter-distance track background, attending the University of Oregon and specializing in the 400 meters hurdles. Marrying Ken Martin, United States steeplechase Olympian and, later, top-class marathoner, she soon moved up to the longer distances. Her 2:29:03 at Los Angeles was her third improvement in as many marathons, and she bettered that with 2:27:40 at Chicago later that year (October 21). Although she found big-city marathons to her liking, she was always a threat at the major regional championships. She was selected for the 1986 Commonwealth team, which she won in July at Edinburgh (2:26:07), beating Lorraine Moller. Returning to New York in the fall of 1986, she was again runner-up to Grete Waitz (2:29:12). She followed that with another runner-up performance at Osaka in January 1987, but then failed to finish at the IAAF Rome World Athletics Championships later that year. Returning to Osaka in January 1988, she scored not only a victory (2:23:51) but

TABLE 22.2

1988 Seoul Olympic Women's Marathon at a Glance

Date: 23 September
Start time: 0930
Course: Out-and-back loop
Course distance: 42.195 km

Weather: 19.5°C (67.0°F), 92% humidity
Starters: 69
Finishers: 64
GPEs: 39

TOP RESULTS:

Place	*Athlete*	*GPE*	*Date of birth*	*Time*
1	Rosa Mota	POR	29 June 1958	2:25:40
2	Lisa Martin	AUS	12 May 1960	2:25:53
3	Katrin Dörre	GDR	06 Oct. 1961	2:26:21
4	Tatyana Polovinskaya	URS	14 May 1965	2:27:05
5	Zhao Youfeng	CHN	05 May 1965	2:27:06
6	Laura Fogli	ITA	05 Oct. 1959	2:27:49
7	Daniele Kaber	LUX	20 Apr. 1960	2:29:23
8	Maria Curatolo	ITA	12 Oct. 1963	2:30:14
9	Zoya Ivanova	URS	14 Mar. 1952	2:30:25
10	Angela Pain	GBR	08 Feb. 1962	2:30:51

New geopolitical entities represented: German Democratic Republic [GDR], Soviet Union [URS], People's Republic of China [CHN], Luxembourg [LUX], Hungary [HUN], France [FRA], South Korea [KOR], Poland [POL], Rwanda [RWA], Czechoslovakia [TCH], Mauritius [MRI], Cayman Islands [CAY], Guatemala [GUA], Zimbabwe [ZIM], Aruba [ARU], El Salvador [ESA], Guam [GUM], Nepal [NEP], Grenada [GRN], Burma [BIR]

Team score (unofficial):

1. URS	29 points	(4-9-16)
2. ITA	37 points	(6-8-23)
3. FRA	51 points	(14-18-19)

also her women-only course best performance. This selected her to Australia's team for the Seoul Olympics.

Following Seoul, she continued to race at the top level. Separating from Ken Martin, she then married Kenyan distance star Yobes Ondieki in February 1990, a month after her excellent Commonwealth Games marathon win (2:25:28) in the tropical heat of Auckland. Taking time out to have a daughter, Emma, born in October 1990, the family lived primarily in Flagstaff, Arizona, where altitude training and the climate were favorable for world-class athletics. Finishing third at New York in 1991 (2:29:01), she dropped out of the Barcelona Olympics. Recovering nicely, however, she used her fitness to win at New York later that fall (2:24:40). She used the 1996 Osaka Marathon to qualify (2:30:27) for selection to the Atlanta Olympic team. Here, also, she did not finish, this time due to an Achilles tendon injury. Following that, she separated from Yobes Ondieki and retired from top-level marathon racing.

TABLE 22.3

Career Marathon Record of Rosa Mota

Date	*Venue*	*Place*	*Time*	*Comments*
12 Sept. 1982	Athens	1st	2:36:04	European championships
09 Apr. 1983	Rotterdam	1st	2:32:27	
07 Aug. 1983	Helsinki	4th	2:31:50	World championships
16 Oct. 1983	Chicago	1st	2:31:12	
05 Aug. 1984	Los Angeles	3rd	2:26:57	Olympic Games
21 Oct. 1984	Chicago	1st	2:26:01	
20 Oct. 1985	Chicago	3rd	2:23:29	
26 Aug. 1986	Stuttgart	1st	2:28:38	European championships
16 Nov. 1986	Tokyo	1st	2:27:15	
20 Apr. 1987	Boston	1st	2:25:21	
29 Aug. 1987	Rome	1st	2:25:17	World championships
18 Apr. 1988	Boston	1st	2:24:30	
23 Sept. 1988	Seoul	1st	2:25:40	Olympic Games
29 Jan. 1989	Osaka	DNF		
05 Mar. 1989	Los Angeles	2nd	2:35:27	
28 Jan. 1990	Osaka	1st	2:27:47	
16 Apr. 1990	Boston	1st	2:25:24	
27 Aug. 1990	Split	1st	2:31:27	European championships
15 Apr. 1991	London	1st	2:26:14	World Cup
25 Aug. 1991	Tokyo	DNF		World championships
12 Apr. 1992	London	DNF		

Katrin Dörre was born in Leipzig, in the German Democratic Republic, and thus, like Cierpinski, was a product of its sophisticated athlete development system. Starting in 1982, Dörre has amassed a record of unsurpassed excellence in the women's marathon. In the Olympic Games, she was third at Seoul, and she then went on to place fifth at Barcelona in 1992, and fourth at Atlanta in 1996. In the IAAF Marathon World Cup, she was the inaugural winner in 1985, third at Seoul in 1987, and fourth at London in 1989. In the IAAF World Athletics Championships, she placed third at Tokyo in 1991 and sixth at Stuttgart in 1993. As of late-1999, out of 43 marathons started, she has finished 41 and won 24. Her two dropouts were at the European Athletics Championships in 1986 and 1994. She has had 21 sub-2:30:00 performances—8 more than Waitz, and 9 more than Kristiansen and Mota.

Although her Seoul Olympic race was her 17th marathon, two weeks before her 27th birthday, her personal best was yet to come. That was a splendid 2:24:35 victory (her 24th) at Hamburg on April 25, 1999, nearly 11 years later, at 35 years of age! She thus stands to be a strong contender for a medal at Sydney.

She is married to her long-time coach and mentor, Wolfgang Heinig, and they have a daughter, Katharina, born in August 1989.

Big-City Races and Trial Events Help Select the Men

Selection of athletes for many nations occurred increasingly at big-city races worldwide. Either athletes ran individually, hoping for quality performances that would satisfy a selection committee, or a national governing body would select a particular race as its trial and fly its top athletes to that venue. These selection races were primarily in Japan, North America, or Europe.

Japan

The 1987 Fukuoka Marathon was a primary event for Japan in the selection of athletes to its Olympic team. The depth among its top-level performers meant that its athletes needed to race fast and confidently if they were to achieve a team berth. Takeyuki Nakayama did just that, racing solo—well out in front—and at world record pace for more than half of the race. Unfortunately, a chilling rain began, and it slowed him to "only" 2:08:18. This was his second victory, and he finished well ahead of Hisatoshi Shintaku (2:10:34). Toshihiko Seko was injured but won later in the spring at Otsu (2:12:41), which also was the national championship. The selected team of Nakayama, Shintaku, and Seko would be formidable.

At the Tokyo Marathon in February, an African duo took top honors, Ethiopia's Abebe Mekonnen (2:08:33) edging out Tanzania's Juma Ikangaa by only nine seconds. The German Democratic Republic's Jörg Peter set a national record of 2:08:47 in third place, proving to his selectors that he was ready. Rob de Castella placed fourth, and Douglas Wakiihuri was seventh, but they were essentially racing to practice their skills, as they had been preselected to represent Australia and Kenya, respectively.

North America

The Mexican team was chosen on the basis of best athlete performances at Los Angeles on March 6. Those selected included the winner, Martin Mondragon (2:10:19); the runner-up, Jesus Herrera (2:10:40); and fourth-placed Carlos Retiz (2:11:30). The Boston Marathon served as the combined Kenyan and Tanzanian trials, and thus promised to be a thriller to watch. The 1987 New York winner, Ibrahim Hussein, dueled Juma Ikangaa to within 200 meters of the finish, spurting ahead as they passed a donut shop to win by one second (2:08:43). The 1984 Olympic silver medalist, John Treacy, set another Irish record (2:09:15), finishing ahead of Gelindo Bordin (2:09:27), who lowered the Italian record. Both were selected to race at Seoul.

One week later, at Jersey City, with the Manhattan skyline as a dramatic backdrop, the American men's marathon trial race had no clear-cut favorite. A relatively unknown runner, Mark Conover, from Orinda, California, improved upon his personal best by five minutes to win (2:12:56). Three seconds behind was his Reebok Racing Club teammate, Ed Eyestone, who also improved on his previous best by three minutes. It would be their first Olympic marathon, but Los Angeles veteran Pete Pfitzinger joined them with his third-place 2:13:09 over this hilly course on this blustery day.

Europe

Denmark's Henrik Jorgensen was victorious at the London Marathon (2:10:20) on April 17, but runner-up Kevin Forster [GBR] (2:10:52) was perhaps just as happy because he, too, earned a place on his team. Four years earlier, he also had placed 2nd at London, but did not get selected. Fourth went to Hugh Jones (2:11:08), and a distant 10th was Charlie Spedding. These three were selected, but Spedding's situation was unusual, as there were others with faster times. Dave Long, for example, finished 5th in 2:11:33 and eventually made the team, as Jones opted out. Frustration among athletes renewed the debate of whether they should select themselves on their performance at a one-off race, or whether committees should pick and choose. The debate continues in many countries.

The Rotterdam Marathon was held on the same day as London's, and several of Ethiopia's finest were poised to do battle with the Djiboutians. Sadly, Ethiopia's government had announced shortly before the race that it would boycott Seoul to support the Democratic People's Republic of Korea. The winner, Belayneh Dinsamo, was in the best shape of his life, and he lowered the world marathon best time to 2:06:50. This would stand for 10 years, until the Berlin Marathon in 1998. Third-placed Wodajo Bulti ran a debut marathon best performance of 2:08:44. Abebe Mekonnen ran the race in 2:09:33. On paper, the Ethiopians could be a team hard to beat at Seoul. Interestingly, the Rotterdam runner-up was Djiboutian Ahmed Salah Hussein, also faster than Lopes's previous world best, by five seconds. He lowered his national record to 2:07:07.

With such global quality, one could only imagine that the Seoul race would be hard-fought all the way to the finish. As with the women, there was no real favorite.

Bordin Paces Himself Perfectly

Once again, at the 1430 (2:30 p.m.) start the weather was ideal for *watching* a great marathon, but not ideal for *racing* one: 74 percent humidity, a sunny sky, and a warm temperature (24.5°C; 76.0°F). An Olympic men's field had never been larger—118 athletes from 66 NOCs. For the first time, the African continent dominated the entry list: 36 athletes from 20 NOCs. Europe had 28 athletes from 17 NOCs. North America had 8 NOCs and 19 athletes, but South American representation remained small, with 5 athletes from 4 NOCs. Asia had 19 athletes from 10 NOCs, and Oceania increased its presence significantly, contributing 11 athletes from 7 NOCs. Other than the absence of Ethiopia's world record-holder Belayneh Dinsamo, the best in the world were ready to race—Nakayama and Seko, de Castella and Moneghetti, Salah, Wakiihuri, Spedding, Ikangaa, and Bordin were all on the list. There were 17 full teams of 3 athletes (Anonymous 1989).

With such a huge field of talent prepared to race more than 40 kilometers, the usual scenario is for a huge pack to remain together for the early part of the event (figure 22.4). Indeed, a pack of 19 led through 5 kilometers (15:29), with African runners typically at the front of this group. Juma Ikangaa was most frequently seen up there. At 10 kilometers (30:32), the scene was similar: a pack of 19, with Ikangaa setting the pace. At 15 kilometers (45:57), 33 runners were bunched into a lead oval. The only notable absentee from this group was Gelindo Bordin, who had drifted back into the next group of 11, 15 seconds behind. At their race pace of 5.4 meters per second, the two groups were about 80 meters apart. By 20 kilometers (1:01:21), near the entrance to the first long Han River bridge, this lead pack had split into two groups, 14 in front, and 10 more 1 second behind, with a few drop-offs. Bordin advanced to the second group, along with Ikangaa. John Treacy, silver medalist at Los Angeles, had retired from the race.

Figure 22.4 **The men's marathon race gets under way; athletes are still on the track. At the front is the Tanzanian duo of John Burra (number 967) and Juma Ikangaa (number 968). To their right are Carlos Retiz [MEX] (number 768), Joseph Kipsang [KEN] (number 657), Domingo Aguilar [CHI] (number 191), and Bigboy Matlapeng [BOT] (number 108).** Courtesy Moon-june Lee, The Chosun Ilbo, Ltd.

At 25 kilometers (1:16:57), 13 athletes were out in front, with Ikangaa back in the lead, again dictating the pace. Between 25 and 30 kilometers the intensity of the pace, combined with the warming weather, began to take its toll on athlete performance. At 30 kilometers (1:32:49), only seven remained up front together: Bordin, Wakiihuri, Salah, Nakayama, Spedding, Ikangaa, and Seko (figure 22.5). De Castella was 2 seconds behind and looking fatigued. Moneghetti and Ravil Kashapov were 3 seconds behind him, and also were losing contact. Between 30 and 35 kilometers, it was Seko's turn to struggle under the stress of maintaining pace, and he slowed considerably. That left six in the hunt for medals at 35 kilometers (1:48:25): Bordin, Wakiihuri, Salah, Nakayama, Spedding, and Ikangaa. Moneghetti was all alone in seventh (1:48:47), 6 seconds ahead of de Castella.

Between 35 and 40 kilometers, the steady uphill, combined with dehydration, a warm day, and developing fatigue, began to relegate this talented field to

Figure 22.5 **At 30 kilometers, seven athletes remain in contention: From the head of the pack backward, the runners with visible competitor numbers are Gelindo Bordin [ITA] (number 579), Charlie Spedding [GBR] (number 455), Ahmed Salah [DJI] (number 236), and Rob de Castella [AUS] (number 38). Juma Ikangaa [TAN] is trailing Bordin, and Douglas Wakiihuri [KEN] is trailing Spedding. Toshihiko Seko [JPN] is directly behind Salah, and Takeyuki Nakayama [JPN] is to Seko's left.** Courtesy Moon-june Lee, The Chosun Ilbo, Ltd.

a single line, each athlete tottering on the brink of breakdown. By 40 kilometers (2:03:39), Salah had the lead, with Wakiihuri 4 seconds back, then Bordin another 2 seconds behind. Nakayama followed Bordin by 17 seconds, with Moneghetti 47 seconds farther back.

Bordin was known for his sense of pace, backing off from a pace too quick and even willing to race alone. He proved superior here, moving from the second group back into the lead bunch. In the downhill portion between 40 and 41 kilometers, Bordin caught Salah and passed him. So did Wakiihuri, leaving Salah in third—unless Nakayama's leg speed could also catch him. Into the stadium came Bordin, and he greeted the full stadium crowd with a grin. Briefly, the top four were all on the track together. Crossing the finish line in 2:10:32, the 29-years-old Bordin knelt and kissed the track (Saylors 1988). He was not the first Italian Olympic marathoner to cross the finish line first in an Olympic marathon—Dorando Pietri did that in 1908—but he was the first to bring home a gold medal! His 15 seconds margin of victory was the smallest since Kolehmainen narrowly beat Lossman 68 years earlier. Table 22.4 summarizes the positions of top athletes during the race.

Wakiihuri's 2:10:47 was a personal best. Salah, 31 years old, was just ahead of Nakayama, only 6 seconds separating bronze from fourth. Places five through nine went to great athletes who bravely kept pace despite the conditions: Moneghetti, Spedding, Ikangaa, de Castella, and Seko. It was truly a world-renowned top nine. The Australians finished third as a team, unofficially, with Japan taking top honors and Italy as the runner-up. Table 22.5 summarizes race results.

At the back of the pack were some interesting performances as well. Finishing 20th was Haiti's Dieudonné Lamothe, his 2:16:15 representing a significant improvement from his last-place finish at Los Angeles (2:52:18). The final finisher at Seoul was Belize's Polin Belisle (3:14:02), who actually lived in Los Angeles. Belisle's exploits will be discussed in chapter 23.

TABLE 22.4

Order of Top Placers Through Control Points

	Bordin	*Wakiihuri*	*Salah*	*Nakayama*	*Moneghetti*	*Spedding*
10 km	=1-19	=1-19	=29, 30	=29, 30	=1-19	=1-19
15 km	=34-45	=1-33	=1-33	=1-33	=1-33	=1-33
20 km	=15-24	=1-14	=1-14	=1-14	=1-14	=15-24
25 km	=1-13	=1-13	=1-13	=1-13	=1-13	=1-13
30 km	=1-7	=1-7	=1-7	=1-7	=9, 10	=1-7
35 km	=1-6	=1-6	=1-6	=1-6	7	=1-6
40 km	3	2	1	4	5	=6, 7
Finish	1	2	3	4	5	6

TABLE 22.5

1988 Seoul Olympic Men's Marathon at a Glance

Date: 02 October
Start time: 1435
Course: Out-and-back loop
Course distance: 42.195 km

Weather: 24.5°C (76.0°F)
Starters: 118
Finishers: 98
GPEs: 66

TOP RESULTS:

Place	*Athlete*	*GPE*	*Date of birth*	*Time*
1	Gelindo Bordin	ITA	02 Apr. 1959	2:10:32
2	Douglas Wakiihuri	KEN	26 Sept. 1963	2:10:47
3	Ahmed Salah Hussein	DJI	31 Dec. 1956	2:10:59
4	Takeyuki Nakayama	JPN	20 Dec. 1959	2:11:05
5	Stephen Moneghetti	AUS	26 Sept. 1962	2:11:49
6	Charles Spedding	GBR	19 May 1952	2:12:19
7	Juma Ikangaa	TAN	19 July 1960	2:13:06
8	Francois Robert de Castella	AUS	27 Feb. 1957	2:13:07
9	Toshihiko Seko	JPN	15 July 1956	2:13:41
10	Ravil Kashapov	URS	15 Nov. 1956	2:13:49

New geopolitical entities represented: American Samoa [ASA], Niger [NIG], Angola [ANG], Fiji [FIJ], Belize [BIZ], Guam [GUM], Guinea [GUI], Maldives [MDV], Solomon Islands [SOL], Rwanda [RWA]

Team score (unofficial):			
	1. JPN	30 points	(4-9-17)
	2. ITA	36 points	(1-16-19)
	3. AUS	54 points	(5-8-41)

Notes on the Men Medalists

Gelindo Bordin was born in Longare, Italy, near Venice, and was relatively unimpressive in his early running career. His personal best for 10,000 meters on the track was only 29:00.65, set in 1983. He debuted at the marathon in Milan, close to home, in 1984, and his 2:13:20 victory suggested that his talent resided in the longer distances. He represented Italy in the inaugural IAAF Marathon World Cup at Hiroshima in 1985, scoring another personal best. Racing well in his next two attempts, he honed his skills of proper pacing.

At the European Athletics Championships at Stuttgart in 1986, he surprised the continent with another personal best and a victory over Europe's top talent; it was his sixth marathon. He then earned a bronze medal at the 1987 IAAF World Athletics Championships in Rome, and raised his stature yet another notch with his fourth place at Boston in 1988—another personal best by 86 seconds. His gold medal victory at Seoul was his second-fastest performance up to that time. He used his supreme pace judgment again in the heat of Split, Croatia, in 1990 for the four-lap European Athletics Championships course; he and Mota each won gold medals there. He was past his prime in 1992, however, and dropped out of the Olympic marathon in Barcelona, retiring shortly thereafter. Bordin's marathon career is summarized in table 22.6.

Douglas Wakiihuri is from the Kikuyu tribe and was born in Mombasa, on the Kenyan coast. He became interested in the Japanese training approach to marathon preparation, and in 1983 he traveled to Japan, living for several years under the tutelage of Kiyoshi Nakamura, coach of Toshihiko Seko. He competed with the S&B Foods team, known particularly for its curry. His first marathon performance was 2:16:26 in March 1986 at Otsu, but he rapidly improved to 2:13:34 at Oita one year later. This gave him a Kenyan team spot for the 1987 IAAF World Athletics Championships, which he won in 2:11:48. In turn, that preselected him for the Kenyan Olympic team. Continuing to train in Japan, he used the February 1988 Tokyo Marathon to stay competitive, running 2:11:57 for seventh. His silver medal provided him worldwide racing opportunities, and for a while he did very well, winning at London in 1989 with a personal best of 2:09:03. In 1990 he took the Commonwealth Games marathon title at Auckland

TABLE 22.6

Career Marathon Record of Gelindo Bordin

Date	Venue	Place	Time	Comments
07 Oct. 1984	Milan	1st	2:13:20	
14 Apr. 1985	Hiroshima	12th	2:11:29	World Cup
28 Apr. 1985	Boscochi	1st	2:34:19	
15 Sept. 1985	Rome	7th	2:15:13	European Cup
01 May 1986	Rome	2nd	2:19:42	
30 Aug. 1986	Stuttgart	1st	2:10:53.4	European championships
01 May 1987	Rome	1st	2:16:03	
06 Sept. 1987	Rome	3rd	2:12:40	World championships
11 Oct. 1987	Venice	DNF		
18 Apr. 1988	Boston	4th	2:09:27	
02 Oct. 1988	Seoul	1st	2:10:32	Olympic Games
05 Nov. 1989	New York	3rd	2:09:40	
16 Apr. 1990	Boston	1st	2:08:19	
01 Sept. 1990	Split	1st	2:14:02	European championships
07 Oct. 1990	Venice	1st	2:13:42	
21 Apr. 1991	London	DNF		World Cup
01 Sept. 1991	Tokyo	8th	2:17:03	World championships
09 Aug. 1992	Barcelona	DNF		Olympic Games

with an excellent 2:10:27, his second-best time, in sultry summer conditions. Although he represented Kenya at the Barcelona Olympic Games, his 36th place (2:19:38) signaled a downturn in his career, but he did come back to win the 1995 IAAF World Marathon Cup.

Ahmed Salah, born in Ali Sabieh, Djibouti, was the eldest of nine children. He became Djibouti's first Olympic medalist in any sport. A paratrooper in the Djiboutian army, his military service gave him the opportunity to train. This region of Africa was formerly French Somalia, and thus he spoke French. He did not finish in the inaugural 1983 IAAF World Athletics Championships marathon in Helsinki, but he placed 20th in the Los Angeles Olympics, his sixth marathon. After a training period in France during the winter of 1984-1985, he won the inaugural IAAF Marathon World Cup at Hiroshima (2:08:09), and Djibouti won the team title. He then won the African championship in 1985 as well (2:23:01). Repeating as Marathon World Cup champion in 1987 (2:13:20) in Seoul as a test run over the Olympic course, he later finished second at the Rome world championship in late summer (2:12:30). He was preselected to race at Seoul on the basis of his fine record, which included a sizzling 2:07:07 behind Dinsamo at Rotterdam in the spring of 1988.

Following the Seoul Games, his career continued at the top level. He was again runner-up at the 1991 IAAF World Athletics Championships at Tokyo (2:15:26), and then he entered his third Olympic marathon in Barcelona, finishing 30th (2:19:04). He continues presently as a veteran's (master's) marathon competitor at the highest level in the big-city marathons. At the age of 40 he was runner-up in the 1997 Monte Carlo Marathon (2:12:44), and at 41 he won the 1998 Enschede Marathon with an impressive 2:13:25.

Looking Ahead: Brief Highlights 1989-1992

1988: While most Olympic participants took a well-deserved break after the Games, top-level competition occurred nevertheless, largely among those not selected for Seoul. America's Lisa Weidenbach, fourth at her selection trial, won at Chicago (2:29:17) on October 30. Grete Waitz, who dropped out at Seoul, made amends, winning yet again at New York (2:28:07) on November 6. And Rosa Mota's colleague Aurora Cunha scored an easy victory (2:31:26) by nearly a minute over the German Democratic Republic's Uta Pippig at Tokyo on November 20.

Among the men, Ethiopia's Abebe Mekonnen won at Beijing (2:07:35), Mexico's Alejandro Cruz was victorious at Chicago (2:08:57), and ex-world-record-holder Steve Jones won at New York (2:08:20).

1989: A quiet post-Olympic year was highlighted among the men by Douglas Wakiihuri's win at London (2:09:03) on April 23 and Juma Ikangaa's New York

(continued)

success (2:08:01) on November 5. Mekonnen scored another victory, this time at Boston (2:09:06) on April 17.

On the women's side, Lorraine Moller recovered from her Seoul disappointment, showing fine form with a 2:30:21 victory at Osaka on January 15. Zhao Youfeng waited a few more months before returning to top-level competition, but she won at Nagoya (2:28:20) on March 5. Ingrid Kristiansen achieved the year's fastest time with her 2:24:33 victory at Boston on April 17. She almost matched that (2:25:30) with a New York win on November 5. Meanwhile, Veronique Marot won at London (2:25:56) on April 23.

1990: Douglas Wakiihuri (2:10:27) beat Steve Moneghetti for the Commonwealth Games crown at Auckland on January 30, while Gelindo Bordin (2:14:02) successfully defended his European Athletics Championships title at Split on September 1, ahead of compatriot Gianni Poli, known for his 1986 New York marathon victory. Bordin had also become history's first male Olympic marathon victor to win at Boston (2:08:19), while Moneghetti won at Berlin in the year's fastest time (2:08:16).

Top performances by women started in Asia, with Rosa Mota winning (2:27:47) on January 28 at Osaka, and then, three days later, Lisa Martin capturing the Commonwealth Games title at Auckland with an impressive solo 2:25:28 on a humid summer morning. Poland's Wanda Panfil impressed the world with her 2:31:04 at Nagoya on March 4 over top Japanese women, and then with her victory (2:26:31) at London on April 22. She followed this with a New York City Marathon win (2:30:35) on November 4, relegating Grete Waitz to fourth—Waitz's first loss there in 10 tries! Meanwhile, Rosa Mota won at Boston (2:25:24) over Uta Pippig on April 16, and she recovered in time to take her third consecutive European Athletics Championships title at Split on August 27 with a hot-weather 2:31:27. Pippig went on to win at Berlin (2:28:37) on September 30.

1991: The IAAF Marathon World Cup, held in concert with the London Marathon on April 21, saw ideal racing conditions, and Yakov Tolstikov (2:09:17) was victorious. The IAAF World Athletics Championships held at Tokyo on September 1, however, was slowed by high heat and humidity, with Hiromi Taniguchi taking the gold medal (2:14:57). Other major men's race winners included Koichi Morishita at Beppu (2:08:53), Ibrahim Hussein at Boston (2:11:06), Rob de Castella at Rotterdam (2:09:42), and Salvador Garcia at New York (2:09:28).

Among the women, Wanda Panfil continued her winning ways with the year's fastest time (2:24:18) at Boston on April 15, and then a gold medal at the Tokyo IAAF World Athletics Championships (2:29:53) on August 25. Runner-up at Tokyo was Japan's rising newcomer Sachiko Yamashita, followed by the ever-consistent Katrin Dörre-Heinig, who had earlier won at Osaka (2:27:43) on January 27. The Boston race had been star-studded, with runners-up including Kim Jones of the United States (2:26:40), Pippig (2:26:52), and Benoit-Samuelson (2:26:54). Rosa Mota opted for the IAAF Marathon World Cup in London on

April 21, her 2:26:14 victory serving as the year's second-fastest time. Behind her were America's 38-years-old track star Francie Larrieu-Smith, now turned marathoner (2:27:35), and a consistent Soviet performer, Valentina Yegorova (2:28:18). Britain's track and cross country star Liz McColgan debuted at New York with an impressive victory (2:27:32) on November 3.

References

Anonymous. 1981. The decisions of the 84th session of the IOC. *Olympic Review* 169: 629-630.

Anonymous. 1985. The Seoul flag becomes the new Olympic standard. *Olympic Review* 215: 551-552.

Anonymous. 1986. *Marathon/race walks courses: Study and measurement.* Seoul Olympic Organizing Committee: Korean Society of Geodesy, Photogrammetry, and Cartography.

Anonymous. 1989. *Official Report, Games of the XXIVth Olympiad, Seoul.* Vol. 2, *Competition summary and results.*

Dubin, C.L. 1990. *Commission of inquiry into the use of drugs and banned practices intended to increase athletic performance.* Ottawa: Canadian Government Publishing Centre.

Nelson, B. 1988. Mota picks up tempo late. *Track & Field News* 41 (11): 61.

Pound, R.W. 1994. *Five rings over Korea: The secret negotiations behind the 1988 Olympic Games in Seoul.* New York: Little, Brown & Company.

Saylors, K. 1988. Battling Bordin wins war. *Track & Field News* 41 (11): 24.

Siddons, L. 1995. *The Olympics at 100: A celebration in pictures.* New York: Macmillan.

Wallechinsky, D. 1996. *The complete book of the Summer Olympics.* 1996 edition. New York: Little, Brown & Company.

CHAPTER 23

1992—BARCELONA

Double Surprise Winners Master Montjuïc

Barcelona Impresses the World With Beauty and Quality

After 68 years of waiting, 1992 was Barcelona's year to host the Olympic Games. It first applied in 1924 and failed. It then hosted the 1929 World's Fair that utilized a magnificent Olympic stadium constructed on its forested Montjuïc (Jewish Mountain) near the center of town. Bidding for the Games of 1936, the city lost again. Later, in concert with Madrid, a joint application was made for the 1972 Games, and that bid, too, was unsuccessful. Undaunted, for the 1992 Games Barcelona was one of six competing cities when the 91st IOC Congress convened at Lausanne to vote on October 27, 1986 (Anonymous 1986). Table 23.1 shows the results of the balloting. After three votes, it was a majority for Barcelona, and IOC president Samaranch was delighted. It was his hometown!

TABLE 23.1

Results of the 1992 Olympic Games Vote

City	Round one	Round two	Round three
Barcelona	29	37	47
Paris	19	20	23
Belgrade	13	11	5
Brisbane	11	9	10
Birmingham	8	8	
Amsterdam	5		

The Barcelona Games presented such a successful spectacle of sport and atmosphere that many believe it was the pinnacle of the first Olympic century. First, there was the passion of its residents to enjoy the Games—and to help those attending from far away to enjoy them, too. Second was the weather; for most outdoor events, the heat and humidity were not excessive, although the marathoners, to be sure, did suffer.

Third were the facilities and the general atmosphere of the city. The centerpiece for these Games was Estadi Olympic, used for the ceremonies and for track and field, built along the slope of Montjuïc—totally reconstructed into an arena seating 65,000 that retained its Old World character. Swimming, diving, and gymnastics arenas were constructed within walking distance along the mountainside. Spectacular views of the city from the diving venue made the cover of sport magazines everywhere. A fleet of outdoor escalators transported people up and down the mountainside. Once people descended after the events, Barcelona's beautiful illuminated fountains, with accompanying classical music provided by hidden speakers, became ideal spots for residents and visitors to enjoy the evening together

Fourth, through some innovative political maneuvering, a complete global gathering of athletes was managed. The Soviet Union no longer existed, having been dismantled after the collapse of communist rule. The republics of Latvia, Lithuania, and Estonia were now independent nations, competing as such. The sovereign republics of Russia, Belarus, Ukraine, Armenia, Azerbaijan, Kazakhstan, Kyrgyzstan, Moldova, Tajikistan, Turkmenistan, and Uzbekistan joined to form the Commonwealth of Independent States (CIS). These, along with Georgia, were granted provisional NOC status as of March 9, 1992, and the entire group was permitted to compete at Barcelona as a single geopolitical entity called the Unified Team or Equipe Unifiée (EUN). When athletes from those republics won medals, their respective national anthems were played.

East and West Germany unified into one nation. So did North and South Yemen. Because of ongoing hostilities by Yugoslavia against Croatia and Bosnia and Herzegovina, its athletes were not permitted to compete in team sports. However, in a conciliatory move to bring the world together, individual athletes were allowed to compete under a unique GPE known simply as IOP, or Independent Olympic Participant. South Africa had eliminated apartheid from its constitution and was allowed to compete for the first time since 1960—but could not march with its flag. Albania also finally appeared, following an unprecedented four consecutive boycotts.

Thus, at least for 17 days of sport, the world hung tenuously together, long enough for these Olympic Games to be successful. Another record number of competing athletes—6,659 men and 2,708 women—thrilled the world with their performances. In terms of gold, silver, and bronze medals, it was the Unified Team (45 + 38 + 29 = 112) over the United States (37 + 34 + 37 = 108) and the combined German team (33 + 21 + 28 = 82) who dominated. Interestingly, the combined German team did not perform as well as the former German Democratic Republic team alone in 1988. Just as the Korean athletes starred at Seoul, Spanish athletes performed miracles at Barcelona, winning 13 gold medals compared with only 1 at Seoul and only 4 in all previous Olympic Games combined. And the medals won were in highly competitive events, too. Only three world records were set in track and field, however: the two men's relays and the 400 meters hurdles victory by America's Kevin Young (46.78 seconds). More GPEs than ever before won medals: 64, compared with 52 in Seoul.

As usual, athletic achievements brought many unforgettable moments. As one example, the overwhelming favorite in the men's 1,500 meters run was Morocco's Noureddine Morceli. Few will forget the look on his face as Spain's Fermin Cacho surged forth from the slow initial pace of this race and inhaled the energy of a partisan crowd to capture the gold. And then there were the woman distance runners. The audience sat spellbound as South Africa's Elana Meyer and Ethiopia's Derartu Tulu challenged each other lap for lap in the 10,000 meters run. Showing an African unity and African dominance of distance running as never before, they hugged each other on their joint victory lap. Only 5 seconds had separated their finish. Just as thrilling for the United States was its own Lynn Jennings capturing the 10,000 meters bronze, the first woman from her country to medal in an event longer than 800 meters. Another sensation was Algeria's 24-years-old Hassiba Boulmerka winning the women's 1,500 meters run, equaling the surprise feat of Cacho. If that was not enough for surprises and thrills, the overwhelming favorite in the women's 100 meters hurdles, Gail Devers—who already had won gold in the 100 meters dash—tripped on the last hurdle and crashed to the track. Who won? Greece's first female track gold medalist since the Games began—Paraskevi Patoulidou!

As expected, the price tag for this sports gala was astronomical; $8 billion is a good estimate (Brennan 1993). Similar to the situation in Seoul, much of the funding went to upgrade the city's infrastructure to manage the influx of visitors. Thanks to government contributions and the IOC's healthy fund-raising program, the venture was successful. Barcelona has since benefited enormously from both the publicity and the practical use of its improvements following the Olympic Games. Visitors see evidence of the Olympic legacy seemingly everywhere. There is a new airport, and there are new expressways. The sports complex at Montjuïc is fully used. A large derelict section of factories and run-down buildings along the seacoast, preventing anyone from even realizing that a beach existed, was demolished. In its place rose the Olympic Village, now a fully occupied apartment complex fronting four kilometers of beach that adjoins a revitalized seaside entertainment district. Barcelona was indeed good to the Olympic Games, but the Games did wonders for the city!

A Seacoast Course Ends With a Mountain Finale

A city marathon had existed in Barcelona before the Olympic Games, but several factors required organizers to develop a different course. First, the route wound through busy city streets, which would have caused a massive gridlock. Second, it was crucial to have as pollution-free a route as possible. Third, the mayor of Mataró, just northeast of Barcelona, expressed a desire to showcase his city as the starting point. Thus, the logical solution was a point-to-point route along the seacoast using primarily the national road through the villages of Cabrera, Vilassar, Premia, El Masnou, Montgat, and Badalona. In some places this route is only a few meters from the sea. From Badalona, the route entered Barcelona, passing a number of architectural masterpieces that exhibited the city for world television viewers. Included among these were Gaudi's unfinished church called the Sagrada Familia, the fountain-filled city square known as the Plaça Catalunya, the most famous street in Barcelona called La Rambla, the old city with its narrow passages, and finally, the renovated port district with its ornate statue of Christopher Columbus.

As shown in figure 23.1, the seacoast portion of the course was entirely flat except for a small 15 meters (49 feet) rise through a cut in a cliff that jutted into the sea just past El Masnou. Within the city of Barcelona, another minor rise of 30 meters (98 feet) occurred between 25 and 30 kilometers. This elevation then became a descent in the following 4 kilometers as runners sped through the city center.

The major question for course layout experts was how best to conquer the final 147 meters (482 feet) of elevation required to ascend Montjuïc. The best plan for minimizing athlete stress was to devise a route that minimized the grade by lengthening the run up the mountain. A spiraling route was laid out by creating a few new connecting paths to join existing roads along the forested slopes. Starting at the Christopher Columbus monument, then to Plaça Espanya, and finally moving through switchbacks up the steeper regions, the final route required 6,700 meters of running. Athletes climbed steadily from 35 to 39 kilometers, and then they had a 1 kilometer respite on a level section passing by the cascading fountains alongside the National Palace. A final 1,800 meters ascent then brought them to the stadium entry.

Course measurers began at the finish line within the stadium and then continued backward down the mountain, through the city, and along the seacoast. In this manner, the start line automatically identified itself 42.195 kilometers

Course Details

The 1992 Barcelona Olympic Marathon

Start in Mataró, on Avinguda Maresme (the National Road N II) beside a park, midway between two side streets (Carrer Sant Francesc de Paula and Carrer Sant Joan)

Proceed southwest out of the city toward Barcelona

Continue on National Road through Cabrera (3 kilometers)

Continue on National Road through Vilassar (6 kilometers)

Continue on National Road through Premia (8 kilometers)

Continue on National Road through El Masnou (11 kilometers)

Continue on National Road through Montgat (15 kilometers)

Continue on National Road to city limits of Badalona (15.5 kilometers)

National Road becomes Carretera de Mataró

Carretera de Mataró becomes Carretera Pomar de Baix at 18.3 kilometers

Carretera Pomar de Baix becomes Carretera Sant Bru at 18.7 kilometers

Carretera Sant Bru becomes Carretera Francesc Layret at 19.3 kilometers

Carretera Francesc Layret becomes Carretera de la Creu

Carretera de la Creu crosses Plaça Pep Ventura

Continue through Plaça Pep Ventura onto Avinguda Marques de Mont-roig

Continue on Avinguda Marques de Mont-roig to Avinguda Maresme

Right onto Avinguda Maresme to Avinguda Alfons XIII

Half left onto Avinguda Alfons XIII

Avinguda Alfons XIII becomes Avinguda Pl I Margall, which crosses the Riu Besò at the city limits of Barcelona

Avinguda Pl I Margall becomes Carrer de Mataró

Carrer de Mataró becomes Carrer de Guipuscoa at 24 kilometers

Carrer de Guipuscoa becomes Carrer D'Arago at 26 kilometers

Continue on Carrer D'Arago to Carrer de Cartagena (27.5 kilometers)

Right onto Carrer de Cartagena to Carrer de Mallorca

Left onto Carrer de Mallorca to Avinguda Diagonal (29 kilometers)

Half right onto Avinguda Diagonal to Passeig de Gracia

Sharp left onto Passeig de Gracia to southeast corner of Plaça Catalunya (31 kilometers)

Left along southeast side of Plaça Catalunya to Ramblas

Half left onto Ramblas to Carrer Ferran (32 kilometers)

Continue through Plaça Sant Jaume onto Carrer Princesa

Continue on Carrer Princesa to Comerç (34 kilometers)

Left onto Comerç to Passeig de Picasso

Sharp right onto Passeig de Picasso to Passeig de Pujades

Left onto Passeig de Pujades to Passeig dels Til·lers

Right onto Passeig dels Til·lers (alongside Parc de la Ciutadella) to Avinguda Marques de L'Argentera

Right onto Avinguda Marques de L'Argentera, which becomes Passeig D'Isabel II

Passeig D'Isabel II becomes Passeig de Colom to Plaça del Portal de la Pau (35 kilometers)

Continue through Plaça del Portal de la Pau to Avinguda del Paral·lel

Half right onto Avinguda del Paral·lel to Plaça D'Espanya

Sharp left at Plaça D'Espanya onto Avinguda de la Reina Maria Cristina (37.6 kilometers) to Avinguda Rius I Taulet

Left onto Avinguda Rius I Taulet to Avinguda de la Tecnica

Right onto Avinguda de la Tecnica to Passeig de Santa Madrona

Left onto Passeig de Sant Madrona to Itinerari del Parc Forestier

Right onto Itinerari del Parc Forestier

(continued)

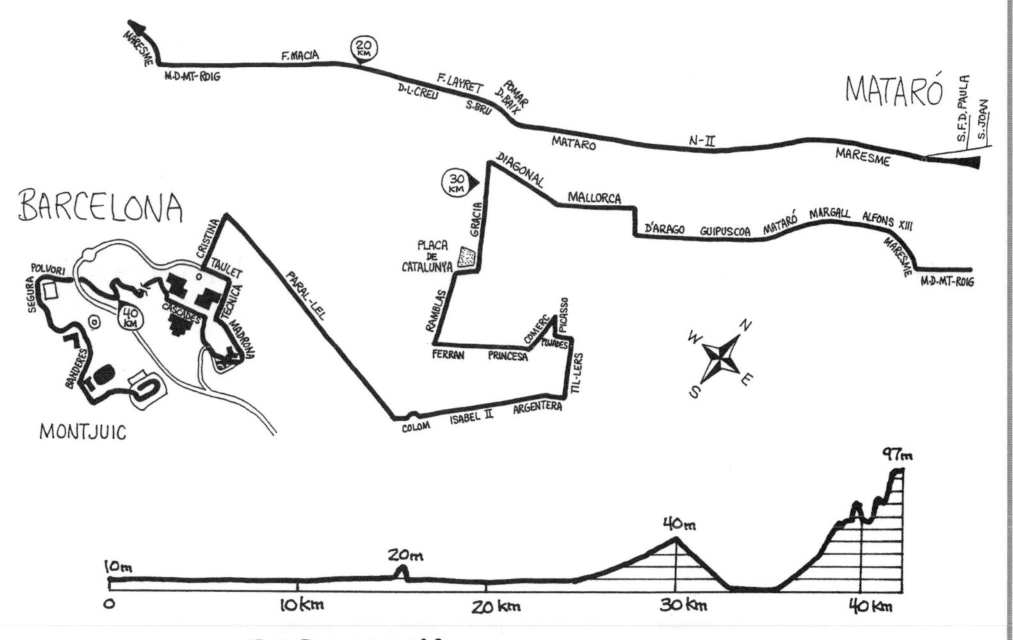

Figure 23.1 Sketch of the Barcelona Olympic marathon course. Note the various street descriptors (avinguda, carrer, passeig, etc.) have been omitted for simplicity. Prepared by Bob Letson.

1992 Course Details *(continued)*

Itinerari del Parc Forestier becomes Passeig de les Cascades

Passeig de les Cascades becomes Lateral Poble Espanyol to Recorregut de la Fuxarda

Left onto Recorregut de la Fuxarda to and through the tunnel

Recorregut de la Fuxarda now becomes Cami del Polvori (Serrahima Stadium on the right)

Continue onto Cami del Polvori to Carrer del Segura

Left onto Carrer del Segura (football stadium on left) to Carretera del Foment i de les Banderes (41 kilometers, baseball stadium on right)

Continue on Carretera del Foment i de les Banderes to Lateral Palau Sant Jordi (alongside gymnastics arena)

Left onto Lateral Palau Sant Jordi to stadium access tunnel

Through stadium tunnel onto the track, continuing one lap counterclockwise to track event finish line

away in downtown Mataró. The course details box summarizes this complex route. The box uses names in the Catalan language because those are on the street signs in Barcelona. The course is entirely accessible today for running, although much of the route along the slopes of Montjuïc is closed to automobile traffic. The way was again marked by a continuous painted blue line.

With a total ascent of 147 meters (482 feet) and 53 meters (174 feet) of descent, the Barcelona marathon course became the third most difficult in the history of the Olympic Games in terms of terrain. Recall that at Athens the difference in elevation between Marathon (25 meters or 82 feet) and the crest over the Athenian hills at Stavros (240 meters or 788 feet) was 215 meters (706 feet). And the Mexico City marathon course was at high altitude, although its ascent toward the finish, 65 meters (214 feet), was modest in comparison to Barcelona.

The expected heat and humidity in Barcelona, together with the mountainous finish, caused considerable concern among athletes regarding optimal preparation and race plan. Long uphill runs, as well as training in the warmer part of the day or at warmer locales for athletes who lived in cool regions were the logical coaching suggestions, but these additional stresses increased the risk of overtraining. Concern by the Olympic Games organizers about providing the best possible medical care for athletes competing under such arduous circumstances was a major focus of the medical director for out-of-stadium road events, Dr. Pedro Pujol-Amat. A marathon runner himself, as well as a research scientist, he brought together an international group of scientists to conduct the first comprehensive documentation of the influence of climatic heat stress on endurance sport performance at a major world competition (Verdaguer-Codina et al. 1995).

Global Racing Selects the Best Women Marathoners

Japan

Top-level racing in this Olympic year started early with the typically superb Osaka International Ladies Marathon on January 26. It was one of Japan's selection races, but runners from around the world were invited as well. Japan's Yumi Kokamo debuted with a national record of 2:26:26. Another debutant, Akemi Matsuno, was runner-up (2:27:02), but she was not selected to the team. The final two spots were awarded to Sachiko Yamashita and Yuko Arimori, whose 2nd and 4th places at the warm and humid 1991 Tokyo IAAF World Athletics Championships gave them the kind of experience needed for Barcelona. Also at Osaka, Katrin Dörre-Heinig had to settle for 3rd despite her fast time of 2:27:34. Two other superstars fared less well. Lorraine Moller, three-time Avon marathon champion in the 1980s, faded to 25th, and Ingrid Kristiansen dropped out at 35 kilometers.

United States

The 1992 United States Olympic trial was an invitation-only event for athletes who satisfied a complex set of qualification criteria (previous marathon Olympian; or run at least 2:45:00 between June 23, 1990, and December 31, 1991; or run at least 32:45 for 10,000 meters on track or roads; or run at least 1:14:00 for the half marathon on roads during the same period). It was staged at Houston on January 26, and victory went to one of America's most experienced athletes, Janis Klecker. The race was a thriller to watch as she dueled with Cathy O'Brien and Francie Larrieu-Smith through a persistent rain. Klecker (2:30:12) was only 12 seconds in front of O'Brien, with Smith another 13 seconds behind. Klecker fell at one point during the race, and O'Brien helped her up in a much-photographed display of outstanding sportsmanship (Negron 1992). For Klecker it was a personal best—and her 35th sub-2:40:00 performance, a record still unmatched by an American woman. In fourth place again, for her 3rd consecutive Olympic marathon trial, was Lisa Weidenbach!

On March 1, the Commonwealth of Independent States used the City of Los Angeles Marathon as the selection event, and its athletes took three of the top four places. Belorussian Madina Biktagirova's 2:26:23 was superior to Russia's Ramilya Burangulova (2:28:12), with Valentina Yegorova (also a Russian) in fourth (2:29:41). Splitting the two Russians was Germany's Kerstin Pressler (2:29:40), but she wasn't selected for her team.

The potential problem with a single selection race became ever more evident at Boston on April 20. There, Russia's Olga Markova scored a national record 2:23:43 that would stand as the year's fastest time. Although her performance was of Olympic team quality, the team had been selected at Los Angeles. In second place was Japan's Yoshiko Yamamoto (2:26:46), also with a national record, and her team selection as well had been completed, so she, too, stayed home. Fourth at Boston was Germany's Uta Pippig (2:27:12), who also did not make her Olympic team. Three athletes from Boston, however, did earn team berths. One was Portugal's Manuela Machado (2:27:42), and the other two were Polish athletes—Malgorzata Birbach (2:28:11) and Wanda Panfil (2:29:29). In 1991, Panfil had won both in Boston and at the warm-and-humid IAAF World Athletics Championships in Tokyo, and thus was well-experienced in hot-weather racing.

Europe

Because many top European runners had taken advantage of the prestigious Japanese and United States races to impress their national team selectors, the European races were somewhat diminished in talent. Portugal's Aurora Cunha had little opposition at Rotterdam on April 5. Winning with a course record of 2:29:14, she was nearly six minutes ahead of Yugoslavia's Suzana Ciric. One week later, at London, it was an exciting duel down to the final mile between Katrin Dörre-Heinig and Poland's Renata Kokowska. Dörre-Heinig won by 20 seconds in 2:29:39.

Yegorova Captures Barcelona Gold With a Duel to the Finish

The third women's Olympic marathon featured 47 runners representing 31 GPEs, nearly half of which were from Europe (21 runners from 12 GPEs). Italy, Great Britain, and the Unified Team fielded full squads, the latter including 2 from Russia and 1 from Belarus. North and Central America had 9 athletes from 6 GPEs (all NOCs); only the United States fielded a full team. From Asia, Japan fielded a complete team, and 3 additional athletes each came from a different NOC. From South America, Brazil had 2 athletes and Peru 1. Oceania also had no full teams; 3 NOCs sent a total of 4 athletes. Africa had 1 athlete each from 4 NOCs. Two women had the distinction of running in their third Olympic marathon: Lisa Martin (now Ondieki), and Lorraine Moller.

Racing conditions for this event were warm and humid at the 1830 (6:30 p.m.) start on Saturday, August 1, the second day of track and field. The sun-drenched seacoast pavement was still adding radiant heat to the somewhat sultry air (27.2°C or 81.0°F), and the low sun angle prompted several runners to don sunglasses as they proceeded southwest. Only a gentle sea breeze wafted inland, so any cooling breeze came from the runners' forward speed. Trepidation abounded regarding the final climb up Montjuïc, so athletes logically started out rather slowly. Ondieki passed 5 kilometers in 17:58, a pace of 5:47 per mile (3:36 per kilometer), which, if maintained, would yield a 2:31:00 finish time. Two seconds behind her was the threesome of Dörre-Heinig, Panfil, and Cunha. Another second behind were Arimori, South Africa's Colleen de Reuck, and Biktagirova of the Unified Team.

At 10 kilometers, Ondieki shared the lead with Dörre-Heinig and Machado (36:27) through the village of Premia de Mar. At this stage, the pace had slowed to 5:51 per mile (3:38 per kilometer), suggesting 2:33:00 if maintained. Behind them by 1 second came Panfil, Biktagirova, and Francie Larrieu-Smith, a United States 1972 1,500 meters Olympian now competing in her fifth Games. Another second behind them were Arimori, de Reuck, and France's Maria Rebelo. Continuing along the flat seacoast, Panfil and Ondieki shared the lead at 15 kilometers (55:28), with the foursome of Dörre-Heinig, de Reuck, Moller, and Italy's Bettina Sabatini 1 second away. Another nine athletes formed the next group 3 seconds behind; it included Cunha, Smith, and Yegorova.

Athletes climbed through the small cut in the rocks just past El Masnou, then returned to the seacoast and reached Badalona (20 kilometers) at 1:14:09. Ondieki still pushed the pace, leading a string of athletes spaced about 1 second apart: Machado, then Biktagirova, and de Reuck. Following these were three athlete pairs: Dörre-Heinig beside Sachiko Yamashita, Yegorova alongside North Korea's Mun Gyung-ae, and then Smith beside Cunha (1:14:15). Another second behind came a trio of Moller, Panfil, and Kokamo. Suddenly, Ondieki fell off the pace. As she related later, she was frustrated with being so fit that she could not maintain such a slow pace but so hot she could not run any faster without overheating. She may also have been overtrained, having endured loads of up to 140 miles (225 kilometers) and having run a personal best (by one minute) at 10,000 meters just one month before the marathon (Burfoot 1992).

Just past 21 kilometers, Biktagirova took the lead, but soon Machado caught her, and then at 23 kilometers, Yegorova moved forward for her turn at the front. By 25 kilometers, as runners were about to leave the seacoast and enter Barcelona streets, Yegorova (1:31:38) was 3 seconds ahead of Biktagirova. Another 3 seconds behind was Machado, followed by de Reuck at 1:31:49. One second behind her came the duo of Panfil and Dörre-Heinig, followed by Yamashita and Arimori another second back, and then Moller. These positions shifted constantly during the race. Figure 23.2 shows Moller, de Reuck, and Arimori in single file at the nearby refreshment station. Between 25 and 30 kilometers, Yegorova pushed the pace up the long grade into the city. She passed 30 kilometers in 1:48:49, already 54 seconds ahead of Biktagirova! Arimori was in third by 1 second, with Moller another 9 seconds behind. Yamashita was 4 seconds farther back, followed by Dörre-Heinig by an equal distance.

Between 30 and 35 kilometers, on the downhill section through the heart of Barcelona, spectators six deep were cheering from both sides of the street. Yegorova was clocked at 35 kilometers in 2:06:36, and Arimori moved into second, 12 seconds behind. Moller was now into the third position (2:07:06), 18 seconds behind Arimori. Then came a steady parade: first Biktagirova (2:07:39), then Dörre-Heinig (2:08:07), and Yamashita 1 second behind her. Farther back were de Reuck (2:08:33) and Machado (2:08:49).

Runners were now at the imposing statue of Columbus on the waterfront, ready to start the 7 kilometers climb to the stadium. Yegorova was in the lead (figure 23.3) as they started up the broad avenue called Paral·lel, but she was trailed closely by Arimori (figure 23.4), who caught her midway along the street.

Figure 23.2 **Passing a refreshment station between 25 and 30 kilometers into the women's race, three top athletes are in single file: Lorraine Moller [NZL] (number 1330), Colleen De Reuck [RSA] (number 1473), and Yuko Arimori [JPN] (number 1075).** Courtesy Montse Garreta.

These two great athletes dueled stride-for-stride, rounding the fountain at the Plaça Espanya, and then up the ever-steeper winding paths in the growing dusk made darker by the groves of evergreens. At 40 kilometers, Yegorova (2:24:54) and Arimori were but a second apart. Meanwhile, Moller (2:07:06) was still secure in third, with Biktagirova, Yamashita, Dörre-Heinig, and Mun behind in single file. The steep incline prevented athletes from quickening their pace and relentlessly beckoned those fatigued to fall back.

The race for silver and gold was not decided until the end, and the packed stadium was ready. After an already full evening of events, the women's 10,000 meters heats would begin after the marathoners arrived. Coming around the gymnastics arena with the stadium in sight, Yegorova took advantage of the brief leveling of the hilly path just before the tunnel entrance into the stadium. She found another gear, and Arimori did not respond. They raced around the track to a cheering throng, and only 8 seconds separated the two at the finish. In the short history of the women's Olympic marathon, this was the closest margin of victory of the three races. Moller was 70 seconds behind Arimori and captured the bronze medal. Table 23.2 summarizes the order of the top finishers during the race.

Figure 23.3 On Avinguda Paral·lel, Valentina Yegorova [EUN] (number 1501) starts the ascent up Montjuïc. Courtesy Montse Garreta.

Figure 23.4 Following closely behind Yegorova at approximately 37 kilometers on Paral·lel is Yuko Arimori [JPN] (number 1075). Courtesy Montse Garreta.

TABLE 23.2

Order of Top Placers Through Control Points

	Yegorova	*Arimori*	*Moller*	*Yamashita*	*Dörre*	*Mun*
5 km	30	=6-8	=19-21	=9-13	=2-5	=19-21
10 km	19	=7, 8	=10, 11	16	=1-3	=10, 11
15 km	=10-12	=16, 17	=3-6	=18, 19	=3-6	=13-15
20 km	=7, 8	14	=11-13	=5, 6	=5, 6	=7, 8
25 km	1	=7, 8	9	=7, 8	=5, 6	11
30 km	1	3	4	5	6	9
35 km	1	2	3	6	5	9
40 km	1	2	3	5	6	7
Finish	1	2	3	4	5	6

Europe, Asia, and Oceania were on the victory podium for the medal ceremony as the Russian anthem played for Yegorova, representing the international concoction that was the Unified Team. The global nature of this event, and the delight of finding a way for all these athletes to compete together, was wonderful to experience. Yegorova recalled the 1990 European Athletics Championships at Split, where she had caught Portugal's Rosa Mota in the final stages, only to have Mota speed away to victory (Hymans 1992). Mota was not here, a late dropout due to sickness, but now Yegorova had her chance to do the same thing and savor victory herself. Arimori and her Japanese teammates captured the unofficial team honors, just ahead of the United States. Biktagirova finished fourth but later tested positive in doping control for the stimulant norephedrine and was disqualified. Table 23.3 summarizes race results.

Notes on the Women Medalists

Valentina Yegorova (nee Vasilyeva) was born in Cheboksary, a city east of Moscow on the Volga River, capital of the Chuvash region of the Russian republic. As with the 1988 medalists, she was an accomplished track runner, integrating her speed with longer-distance training to become a top-level marathoner. She had personal bests of 9:11.2 over 3,000 meters in 1985 and 32:56.13 over 10,000 meters in 1989 (seventh in her national championships). Her marathon debut (2:37:05) in 1988 at Tallinn gave her confidence, and she improved to 2:30:59 later that year. In January 1990, she broke 2:30:00 at Osaka and then took second to Mota at the European Athletics Championships in August. She ran 4 marathons each in 1990, 1991, and 1992, and won the big one at Barcelona. It was only her second victory in 14 marathons.

Following Barcelona, as with most Olympic marathon champions, Yegorova had to pick and choose her marathons carefully, as the outlandish financial

TABLE 23.3

1992 Barcelona Olympic Women's Marathon at a Glance

Date:	01 August	**Weather:**	27.2°C (81.0°F)
Start time:	1830	**Starters:**	47
Course:	Point-to-point	**Finishers:**	38 (including one DQ)
Course distance:	42.195 km	**GPEs:**	31

TOP RESULTS:

Place	*Athlete*	*GPE*	*Date of birth*	*Time*
1	Valentina Yegorova	EUN	16 Feb. 1964	2:32:41
2	Yuko Arimori	JPN	17 Dec. 1966	2:32:49
3	Lorraine Moller	NZL	01 June 1955	2:33:59
4	Sachiko Yamashita	JPN	20 Aug. 1964	2:36:26
5	Katrin Dörre-Heinig	GER	06 Oct. 1961	2:36:48
6	Mun Gyong-Ae	PRK	08 Apr. 1969	2:37:03
7	Maria Manuela Machado	POR	09 Aug. 1963	2:38:22
8	Ramilya Burangulova	EUN	11 July 1961	2:38:46
9	Colleen de Reuck	RSA	13 Apr. 1964	2:39:03
10	Cathy O'Brien	USA	19 July 1967	2:39:42

(Madina Biktagirova [EUN] finished fourth (2:35:39) but was disqualified under doping regulations)

New geopolitical entities represented: Unified Team [EUN], Germany [GER], Democratic People's Republic of Korea [PRK], Republic of South Africa [RSA], Poland [POL], Ethiopia [ETH], Romania [ROM], Costa Rica [CRC], British Virgin Islands [ISV], Zaire [ZAI], Vietnam [VIE]

Team score (unofficial):			
	1. JPN	35 points	(2-4-29)
	2. USA	43 points	(10-12-21)
	3. GBR	56 points	(13-16-27)

proposals from eager race directors hoping to showcase a gold medalist make "just one more marathon" all too tempting. Her favorite big-city race was at Tokyo in November. She ran it six times in seven years starting in 1990, winning twice, and placing second twice. Her success at the Atlanta Games is described in chapter 24. She continues to race actively and will likely be a contender at the Sydney Games. Table 23.4 gives Yegorova's current marathon career.

Yuko Arimori is a graduate of the Nippon College of Physical Education. Born in Okayama City, Japan, her interest in longer-distance road racing and marathon running arose from the combination of her interest in athletics and the popularity of these events in her country. Her marathon debut was at the prestigious Osaka all-woman marathon in 1990, where she placed sixth (2:32:51). She improved the following year to a personal best 2:28:01, good for second place. This resulted in her selection to represent Japan at the 1991 IAAF World

TABLE 23.4

Career Marathon Record of Valentina Yegorova

Date	Venue	Place	Time	Comments
26 June 1988	Tallinn	6th	2:37:05	
10 Sept. 1988	Ufa	1st	2:30:59	
15 Apr. 1989	Milan	15th	2:40:14	World Cup
28 Jan. 1990	Osaka	3rd	2:29:47	
22 Apr. 1990	London	21st	2:35:25	
27 Aug. 1990	Split	2nd	2:31:32	
09 Dec. 1990	Tokyo	4th	2:36:01	
21 Apr. 1991	London	3rd	2:28:18	World Cup
22 June 1991	Leipzig	2nd	2:48:49	
25 Aug. 1991	Tokyo	DNF		World championships
09 Dec. 1991	Tokyo	2nd	2:31:52	
01 Mar. 1992	Los Angeles	4th	2:29:41	
28 Mar. 1992	Paris	12th	2:43:49	
01 Aug. 1992	Barcelona	1st	2:32:41	Olympic Games
15 Nov. 1992	Tokyo	4th	2:31:27	
15 Apr. 1993	Boston	DNF		
21 Nov. 1993	Tokyo	1st	2:26:40	
18 Apr. 1994	Boston	2nd	2:23:33	
20 Nov. 1994	Tokyo	1st	2:30:09	
17 Apr. 1995	Boston	DNF		
19 Nov. 1995	Tokyo	2nd	2:28:48	
10 Mar. 1996	Nagoya	3rd	2:27:53	
28 July 1996	Atlanta	2nd	2:28:05	Olympic Games
26 Jan. 1997	Osaka	DNF		
08 Mar. 1998	Nagoya	6th	2:28:51	
18 Apr. 1999	Nagano	1st	2:28:41	
21 Nov. 1999	Tokyo	3rd	2:28:06	

Athletics Championships in Tokyo, where she placed fourth (2:31:08) on a warm, humid day. She then logically became a favorite for selection to the Barcelona team, and her silver medal resulted. It was her fourth marathon.

After a brief hiatus (see additional biographical information in chapter 24), she returned to top form, winning at the hot summertime Sapporo Marathon in 1995 with 2:29:17. That performance also impressed the selectors, and she was chosen to face another warm, humid competition at Atlanta in 1996, where she earned a bronze medal.

Lorraine Moller was born in Putaruru, New Zealand, and attended the University of Otago, where she received a diploma in physical education. As with many elite-level early marathoners, Moller also started out at shorter distances. Placing fifth at 800 meters in the 1974 Commonwealth Games, she was a bronze medalist at 1,500 meters at the 1983 Commonwealth Games. Finishing fifth at the IAAF World Cross Country Championships in 1985, she began road racing and discovered that her real skills in running were with the longer distances. Her first marathon was a victory, at Duluth, Minnesota (2:37:37) on June 23, 1979. She returned and won there again in June of 1980 (2:38:36). Less than two months later, she won the Avon International Women's Marathon in London (2:35:11) held on August 3, 1980, two days after Cierpinski's gold medal race at Moscow.

Moller continued to race and win; in fact, her first 8 marathons were victories (in all, she won 15 of 28). In 1981, she married 1968 United States marathon Olympian Ron Daws, a native of Minnesota whom she had befriended at Duluth. She supported the Avon International Running Circuit by winning at its 1982 (San Francisco) and 1984 (Paris) editions. She won other big-city marathons as well, notably Boston in 1984 (2:29:28), and the women-only Osaka Ladies Marathon in 1986, 1987, and 1989. Her two fastest performances came in the big meets: 5th at the Los Angeles Olympics in her 14th marathon (2:28:34) and 2nd to Lisa Ondieki at the 1986 Commonwealth Games (2:28:17) 6 marathons later. After placing poorly at Seoul (33rd), her comeback to win the bronze medal at Barcelona was only four days after the death of her husband. One of only two marathoners to qualify for the first four women's Olympic marathons (along with Lisa Ondieki), she placed 46th (2:42:21), giving her the best overall women's performance record in the Games (5-34-3-46 versus 7-2-DNF-DNF for Ondieki).

International Marathons Identify Most of the Top Men

Asia

At the annual top-class marathon race staged between the Japanese cities of Beppu and Oita in Japan on February 2, two invited athletes, each running his third marathon, lowered their national records below 2:09:00. Mexico's Dionicio Ceron (2:08:36) and Korea's Hwang Young-cho (2:08:47) were indeed impressive. Japanese athletes used the similarly-fast Tokyo city marathon as their primary trial. Hiromi Taniguchi had been preselected from his World Athletics Championships victory the previous year. The eventual winner, Koichi Morishita (2:10:19), had run only one marathon before this, also a win (2:08:53) at Beppu in 1991. The runner-up was Takeyuki Nakayama, six seconds behind, and he was also selected.

Korea was also becoming a significant marathon power. On paper, the Korean squad looked as good as the Japanese team: joining Hwang in Barcelona were the top two finishers of the trial at Chunchon on March 22, Kim Jae-ryong (2:09:30) and Kim Wan-ki (2:09:31).

United States

Columbus, Ohio, was the venue for the United States men's Olympic trial on April 11. This continued a recent trend of holding a special invitational race open only to those who met at least one qualifying criterion. Those eligible included (a) being a past marathon Olympian, (b) having run 2:20:00 or faster between November 11, 1990, and March 31, 1992, or (c) being a national road champion from 10 kilometers through the marathon during the same period. Keith Brantly and Bill Reifsnyder set an early quick pace that gave them a 22 seconds lead by 17 miles (Bloom 1992). The warm, humid weather took its toll, however, and the more patient and experienced athletes took the two top spots. Winner Steve Spence (2:12:43) was the 1991 Tokyo IAAF World Athletics Championship bronze medalist, and runner-up Ed Eyestone (2:12:51) was a Seoul Olympian. Third man on the team was medical student Bob Kempainen (2:12:54), only 40 seconds off his personal best and still regaining fitness following injury.

Just over a week later, the usual cosmopolitan lineup at Boston was understandably lacking in American top-level entries, but the event was a showcase for Kenyans, as it was their primary Olympic selection race. Ibrahim Hussein confirmed his place on the Kenyan team (alongside Douglas Wakiihuri and sixth-placed Boniface Merande) with a dominating 2:08:14. It was his third Boston race, but he had run faster there only once. Portugal's Joaquim Pinheiro was a distant second but still ran a fast 2:10:39, ahead of Mexico's Andres Espinosa. Amazingly, the latter was not selected for his Mexican team.

Europe

The reigning Olympic champion Gelindo Bordin experienced a dismal year in 1991, dropping out of the IAAF Marathon World Cup and placing only eighth at the IAAF Tokyo World Athletics Championships. But he was selected nonetheless, as he was improving in fitness. Chosen along with him was Salvatore Bettiol, a consistent performer who placed second at the Italian championship at Carpi on October 27 of the previous year. The winner at Carpi was Brazil's Diamantino dos Santos (2:11:28), who was duly selected to his team. Two others also were given team berths from the Italian championship race: third-placed Saïd Ermili for Morocco and fourth-place runner Paul Davies-Hale for Great Britain.

This pointed to the increasing practice of using results of big-city commercial races to select athletes instead of creating specific national trials. It was thus becoming ever more difficult to keep up with the widely variant national policies, let alone appreciate whether they made sense. The Mexican policy for Barcelona team selection, for example, was simply to select the three fastest athletes during 1992 prior to the cutoff date for entry submission. This put enormous pressure on athletes to (1) find fast races, (2) hope the weather was good, and (3) try again if they were not quite sure that their times were fast enough. The Rotterdam classic was earlier than usual (April 5), and two top Mexicans were there. They finished one and two—Salvador Garcia in 2:09:16 and Isidro Rico in 2:09:28—but then they had to wait for the results of London and Boston to determine whether they were on their team. Fortunately for Garcia and Rico, the three Mexicans at Boston and London ran too slowly. At London on April 12, the pressure to perform was enormous, and only eight seconds separated the first four. Portugal's Antonio Pinto (2:10:02) secured his team spot, ahead of Poland's Jan Huruk (2:10:07), with Tanzania's Thomas Naali another second behind. They all went to Barcelona.

Hwang Adopts the Women's Strategy to Master the Mountain

On Sunday morning, August 9, the final day of the Olympic Games, a predawn thunderstorm left the city with the coolest and clearest air of the Games. But the powerful Mediterranean sun warmed the air rapidly, and the men faced conditions for their 1830 (6:30 p.m.) start (26.6°C or 80.0°F) that were similar to the women's race one week before. The field of 112 runners represented a record 72 GPEs. Africa had the most diverse representation (32 athletes from 22 GPEs), followed by Europe (36 from 18 GPEs), Asia (16 from 12 GPEs), and North America (14 athletes from 10 GPEs). Two regions sparsely represented were South America (8 athletes from 6 GPEs, which were also NOCs) and Oceania (6 athletes from 4 GPEs, which were also NOCs). Fifteen GPEs fielded full teams of 3 runners, 6 coming from Europe. The range of talent was wide; at one end were those among the fastest in the world—the top 5 from Seoul and the top 4 from the Tokyo IAAF World Athletics Championship. At the other end were athletes with very little experience, simply representing their countries or regions in the hope of doing their best. GPEs with no athletes meeting the 2:16:00 time standard could declare one athlete regardless of previous performance.

Complete intermediate split times for the men's race are not available, which prevents our describing the race in depth by 5 kilometers increments. However, a hesitancy of the entire field to race too quickly in the early stages meant that a lead group of 30 ran together until nearly halfway. The 5 kilometers lead split of 16:03 was the slowest of the six Olympic marathons held since Mexico City, and the pace slowed even more as the race progressed. The leading 10 kilometers split of 31:59 was similar to the 31:55 by Jim Peters at Helsinki 40 years earlier, so it was understandable that the lead pack had 50 runners. Typically, it was Hwang and Morishita at the head of the pack, alongside Tanzania's Thomas Naali and South Africa's Zithulele Sinqe. But Taniguchi, Moneghetti, Bordin, Ikangaa, Salah, Mekonnen, and Wakiihuri were alongside as well. All of these except Taniguchi were Olympians. It was an outstanding assembly of stars.

The lead group passed 15 kilometers in 48:18, and although Jan Huruk and Antonio Pinto made a move to take the lead at 18 kilometers, they were reeled in quickly. Moving inland, the group passed the 20 kilometers point near the basketball arena in 1:04:00. Still, the pace was not fast, but the influence of heat and humidity reduced this top field to 30. As runners jostled against each other in this tightly packed group, small gaps opened and a constant shifting of position occurred among these front-runners. They reached the halfway point in a slow 1:07:22, with Naali leading the race.

At the 22.5 kilometers feeding station, tragedy struck. Hiromi Taniguchi tangled legs with someone as he picked up his drink. Falling hard, he lost a shoe in the process. Gelindo Bordin was just behind him and had to leap into the air to avoid trampling him. Bordin strained a groin muscle, and he was out of the race. Taniguchi ran back to retrieve and put on his shoe, and he tried valiantly to catch the group. Unaware of what had occurred, Italy's Salvatore Bettiol made the first decisive attack of the race. It was just before 24 kilometers, and as the lead pack crossed the river into Barcelona, Bettiol was in front. This attack did not last long, however, for at 25 kilometers (1:19:22), Diego Garcia, Kim Wan-ki, Morishita, and Hwang caught him.

Racing through the streets of Barcelona, athletes again found the course lined several deep with cheering spectators. These people could have watched the race live on television in the air-conditioned comfort of their homes, but it was this genuine outpouring of support for the Olympic Games that characterized the people of Barcelona during the entire period. Between 25 and 30 kilometers, the Asian threesome of Kim, Morishita, and Hwang took the lead (figure 23.5), but Germany's Stephan Freigang (figure 23.6) and Takeyuki Nakayama stayed in contact. At 30 kilometers (1:34:42), this sequence remained.

Bedlam reigned through the narrow streets of the old city as this marathon procession passed. First came the string of motorcycles and cars, including the motorcycle-with-sidecar for NBC-TV, and then the runners whooshed by the pressing crowds of cheering fans. Alongside Ciutadella Park, between 33 and 34 kilometers, Kim slowed dramatically (eventually finishing 28th), and as the group departed the narrow streets of the inner city onto the wide waterfront boulevard (the Passeig de Colom), Freigang and Nakayama passed him. At 35 kilometers, near the statue of Columbus, it was Morishita and Hwang at 1:50:02, followed by Freigang 11 seconds behind. Then came Nakayama and Bettiol, 2 and 4 seconds behind, respectively.

As with the women, another memorable struggle began up the mountain. Along Avinguda Paral·lel, Hwang and Morishita raced side by side, making the sharp left turn at the Plaça Espanya and along the avenue of fountains, now illuminated in the growing dusk. Up the winding paths they went, across the level stretch from 39 to 40 kilometers midway up the mountain. The decisive move was made shortly after 40 kilometers, at 2:06:33. Just before entering a tunnel carved through a cliff, the roadway leveled very briefly, and Hwang surged. Emerging from the tunnel, he had already developed a 20 meters gap. It was a shrewd move since the remaining route was uphill to the stadium. Meanwhile, Nakayama and Freigang fought a similar duel, each taking turns surging in an attempt to break the other.

Interestingly, although this was the evening of the Closing Ceremonies, the stadium was only slowly filling, as it had been closed to spectators until only half an hour before the end of the marathon. Nevertheless, the 22-years-old Hwang entered to a cheering throng. Morishita never quite caught up, and the two finished 22 seconds apart. Amazingly, the second half of the route was covered by the lead runners 81 seconds faster than the first half despite the

Figure 23.5 Taking the lead between 25 and 30 kilometers, it was Koichi Morishita [JPN] (number 1087), Hwang Young-Cho [KOR] (number 147), and Kim Wan-Ki [KOR] (number 1152). Courtesy Montse Garreta.

Figure 23.6 Running strongly, Stephan Freigang [GER] (number 800) is being "pursued" by a mobile television crew. Courtesy Montse Garreta.

mountain ascent, showing how conservatively the pack ran early in the race. Freigang and Nakayama entered the stadium together, and Freigang's remaining quickness gave him the bronze medal by a scant 2 seconds. Nakayama had been fourth as well in Seoul, by 6 seconds! No one else has ever been so close to an Olympic marathon medal on two occasions.

At the press conference, Hwang emotionally related that he had absolutely no choice but to be supreme. His mother was back home in a temple praying during the race, and his idol, Sohn Kee-chung, was watching him; he simply could not disappoint either one. At the medal ceremony, it was an interesting juxtaposition of nations from the 1936 Games. Then, the scene was Germany, as a Korean who wore Japanese colors won the race. This evening, it was a German medalist as runner-up to a Korean who defeated a Japanese superstar.

With Taniguchi recovering well enough to place 8th, Japan had a 25 points margin over the Koreans in the unofficial team placing. For the United States,

Steve Spence, Ed Eyestone, and Bob Kempainen finished nearly together—12-13-17 in that order—and placed 3rd as a team, three points behind the Koreans. Despite the oppressive heat and the hills, 37 athletes finished under 2:20:00, compared with 30 at Seoul. Table 23.5 presents race results.

A dilemma of scheduling caused what some perceived as a measure of unfairness to the final five finishing athletes. The start of the formal program of the Closing Ceremonies made it inappropriate for any athletes to enter the stadium after 2115 (9:15 p.m.)—a 2:45:00 finish time. Anticipating this, race organizers had measured an alternative finish line on the final assembly track just outside the Estadi Olympic. Five athletes were directed to this alternate finish line: Benjamin Keleketu [BOT] (2:45:57), Moussa El Hariri [SYR] (2:47:06), Vang Hung Luu [VIE] (2:56:42), Hussain Haleem [MDV] (3:04:16), and Pyambuu Tuul [MGL] (4:00:44).

Tuul's finish time was the third slowest in Olympic history up to that time, but there was a good reason for his slower pace. He had been blinded in a

TABLE 23.5

1992 Barcelona Olympic Men's Marathon at a Glance

Date:	09 August	**Weather:**	26.6°C (80.0°F)
Start time:	1830	**Starters:**	112
Course:	Point-to-point	**Finishers:**	87
Course distance:	42.195 km	**GPEs:**	73

TOP RESULTS:

Place	*Athlete*	*GPE*	*Date of birth*	*Time*
1	Hwang Young-cho	KOR	22 Mar. 1970	2:13:23
2	Koichi Morishita	JPN	05 Sept. 1967	2:13:45
3	Stephan Freigang	GER	27 Sept. 1967	2:14:00
4	Takeyuki Nakayama	JPN	20 Dec. 1959	2:14:02
5	Salvatore Bettiol	ITA	28 Nov. 1961	2:14:15
6	Salah Qoqaiche	MAR	10 July 1967	2:14:25
7	Jan Huruk	POL	27 Jan. 1960	2:14:32
8	Hiromi Taniguchi	JPN	05 Apr. 1960	2:14:42
9	Diego Garcia	ESP	12 Oct. 1961	2:14:56
10	Kim Jae-ryong	KOR	25 Apr. 1966	2:15:01

New geopolitical entities represented: Slovenia [SLO], Cameroon [CMR], Aruba [ARU], Liechtenstein [LIE], Namibia [NAM], Bahrain [BHR], Syria [SYR], Mongolia [MGL], Mauritania [MTN], Unified Team [EUN], San Marino [SMN]

Team score (unofficial):			
	1. JPN	14 points	(2-4-8)
	2. KOR	39 points	(1-10-28)
	3. USA	42 points	(12-13-17)

construction accident in 1980. He was befriended by the Achilles Track Club, a New York City-based group with chapters worldwide that helps physically challenged people achieve self-esteem through distance running. Tuul reportedly finished the New York City race with a guide in a little more than five hours. Helped by a cornea transplant in New York, he still later regained some sight in his right eye. The Mongolian NOC gave him a team berth. He returned to New York in 1994 and placed 17,229th among the men with 4:43:03.

Olympic Marathon Miscellany 23.1

Polin Belisle—A Double Olympic Deception?

Great value is placed upon the Olympic movement as a positive social force, in part because of the known struggle athletes must endure to achieve selection. It is particularly galling, then, to learn that athletes might seek a team berth illegitimately. This may have been done in the marathon, not once but twice, by the same person.

Polin Belisle was born in Honduras, raised in Belize by his Belizean mother, and eventually naturalized in the United States. He lives presently in California with dual United States and Belize citizenship. In 1988, at the Long Beach Marathon, he placed 20th with 2:36:18. Submitting this time, published in the local newspaper, to the Belizean authorities, he was clearly their star marathoner. He competed at Seoul in 1988, finishing in last place (3:14:02).

In 1992, he crossed the finish line of the Los Angeles Marathon with a time of 2:18:38, placing 11th. Subsequently, he was disqualified for not being visible on periodic checkpoint videos, not only there but also at the 1991 Long Beach Marathon, where the official results show him as placing 5th with 2:17:39. Whether he in fact completed the entire 1988 Long Beach Marathon is an unanswered question.

After the 1992 Los Angeles Marathon, Belisle requested and received permission from Honduran Olympic officials to compete in Barcelona. After all, the newspaper clippings showed that he placed very well in an international marathon; he was thus clearly the best marathoner in Honduras! At Barcelona, he was officially entered as Apolinario Belisle Gomez (number 907), whereas at Seoul he was simply Polin Belisle (number 99).

In the Barcelona Olympic Village, Belizean officials noticed Belisle and informed Honduran team staff that Belisle had participated for Belize in 1988. Ordinarily, an athlete cannot compete for different NOCs in successive Olympic Games without mutual NOC consent. Belisle was removed from the Honduran team but kept his identity card. Also, he did not turn back his competitor bib number, and his name was not administratively removed from the final

(continued)

marathon start list. Resourcefully, he reached Mataró on race day and started the race. Here, instead of being the last to finish, he was the first to drop out.

His case provides profound frustration to Olympic record-keepers. Should he be listed as a competitor? Clearly, he did compete—he appears in the official printed results as a DNF and is in the front ranks early in the video of the event. Should Honduras be listed as a participating nation for the 1992 Olympic marathon? There was no other marathon competitor from Honduras.

Notes on the Men Medalists

Hwang Young-cho was born in Samchok, South Korea, and attended Kyungju University. Showing early promise as a young track runner, at only 20 years of age he ran 13:59.70 for 5,000 meters in 1990 and 29:32.01 for 10,000 meters in 1991. Trying the marathon at the young age of five days before his 21st birthday, he won the Seoul international marathon and earned himself a place on the Korean team traveling to the 1991 World University Games at Sheffield, England. He won there as well, and suddenly he saw his future in distance running as being more successful on the road than on the track. In February 1992, he joined the usual top-level marathon field at Beppu, and although most athletes there were considerably more experienced, only Mexico's Ceron ran faster. Hwang's 2:08:47 was a personal best, and it earned him a ticket to Barcelona, where he also did not disappoint! He was Korea's second Olympic marathon gold medalist, although the first to win wearing Korean national colors.

Following Barcelona, he raced sparingly, placing fourth at Boston (2:08:09) in 1994 and later winning the Asian Games title at Hiroshima. Injury prevented Hwang from achieving a place on the Korean Olympic team bound for Atlanta, and he subsequently retired. Table 23.6 summarizes Hwang's marathon career.

Koichi Morishita was born in Yazu Town in the Tottori Prefecture of Japan and was 24 years old at the 1992 Olympic Games. After winning the Asian Games 10,000 meters track title, he attempted his first marathon in 1991, winning with a superb 2:08:53 at Beppu. A year later, he won again, this time at Tokyo (2:10:19). Suddenly he was one of Japan's marathon elite and was selected to the Barcelona team. He raced well at Barcelona, and his silver medal performance represented his only loss in three tries at the distance.

Stephan Timo Freigang was born in Löbau, Saxony, in the former German Democratic Republic and was a long-time member of the Sport Club Cottbus. He, too, was 24 years old at these Olympic Games, making this trio of medalists the second youngest in this first Olympic marathon century (the 1900 Paris winners averaged 21). A sports student, his running career focused on the 10,000 meters and the marathon. First reaching the top ranking lists in 1986 at the 10,000 meters, he tried the marathon in 1987 and won (2:14:34) at Budapest. He

TABLE 23.6

Career Marathon Record of Hwang Young-cho

Date	Venue	Place	Time	Comments
17 Mar. 1991	Seoul	1st	2:12:35	
21 July 1991	Sheffield	1st	2:12:40	World University Games
02 Feb. 1992	Beppu	2nd	2:08:47	
09 Aug. 1992	Barcelona	1st	2:13:23	Olympic Games
18 Apr. 1994	Boston	4th	2:08:09	
09 Oct. 1994	Hiroshima	1st	2:11:13	
28 Oct. 1995	Chunchon	2nd	2:11:32	
24 Mar. 1996	Kyongju	29th	2:25:45	Injured

did not meet the German Democratic Republic's rigid performance standards for the 1988 Olympic Games, and thus hoped he could improve for Barcelona. Not only did his skill improve, but world politics changed as well.

His first top-level international marathon was at Fukuoka in 1988, where he placed eighth (2:12:28). He was a DNF at the 1989 IAAF World Marathon Cup, and subsequently he was injured in a motorbike accident. Returning to form in 1990, he placed fourth at Berlin in September (2:09:45) with what still stands as his personal best. His personal best at 10,000 meters on the track quickened to 28:05 in both 1990 and 1991, which made him stronger for marathon racing. The Barcelona Olympic race was his seventh marathon. He continued to race following the Games and in 1996 ran a respectable 2:11:39 at Rotterdam, placing fifth. This was sufficient to select him for the German team at Atlanta, but he did not finish that marathon.

Looking Ahead: Brief Highlights 1992-1995

1992: Following the Olympic Games, three South African runners made winning headlines. David Tsebe recorded the fastest time for 1992 on September 28 at Berlin (2:08:07) over Portugal's Manuel Mathias (2:08:38). Then Willie Mtolo won the New York Marathon title on November 1 in 2:09:09. The year closed at Fukuoka with Lawrence Peu (2:10:29) finishing second to Ethiopia's Tena Negere (2:09:04) on December 6. These South Africans would have made a formidable team at Barcelona, but their delegation included no marathoners.

Lisa Ondieki avenged her Barcelona disappointment by outclassing Boston winner Olga Markova (2:24:40 versus 2:26:38) at New York on November 1. Two weeks later, Liz McColgan remained undefeated with her second win, this

(continued)

time at Tokyo (2:27:38). Olympic fifth-placer Katrin Dörre-Heinig finished well behind in second (2:30:05).

1993: At the big-city marathon classics, the weekend of April 17-19 was the most memorable. On Sunday, April 18, Britain's Eamonn Martin won in front of a home crowd at London (2:10:50), and Mexico's Dionicio Ceron took the Rotterdam victory with 2:11:06. On the following Monday, Patriot's Day in Boston, Kenya's Cosmas N'Deti won in 2:09:33. In the fall, however, Mexico scored another victory with Andres Espinosa's fine 2:10:04 at New York. Ceron then achieved the year's fastest time at Fukuoka (2:08:51) over South Africa's Gert Thys (2:09:31).

China sent shock waves throughout the women's marathon world on April 4 at Tianjin, as the first 8 runners all bettered 2:26:40! Suddenly there were 4 Chinese on the all-time top-10 list: Wang Junxia (2:24:07), Qu Yunxia (2:24:32), Zhang Linli (2:24:42), and Zhang Lirong (2:24:52). Other top stars achieved fine performances worldwide, but none matched the Chinese. The nearest any other runners in the world came to that level of racing during the year was Olga Markova's second successive Boston victory on April 19 (2:25:27). Poland's Renata Kokowska won at Berlin on September 26 (2:26:20), Uta Pippig won at New York on November 14 (2:26:24), and Valentina Yegorova won at Tokyo on November 21 (2:26:40).

1994: At the Helsinki European Athletics Championships, Spain's Martin Fiz (2:10:31) led a Spanish clean sweep of the medals on August 14, with his teammates Diego Garcia (2:10:46) and Alberto Juzdado (2:11:18) following close behind. Richard Nerurkar continued his impressive performances with a fourth-place finish. Spain easily won the European Marathon Cup trophy that was coupled with the event.

At Boston, the temperature was perfect for racing and a noticeable tailwind assisted in producing fast times. Cosmas N'Deti ran a course record 2:07:15, four seconds ahead of Andres Espinosa, putting them fifth and sixth on the all-time world list. The Barcelona gold medalist Hwang Young-cho finished fourth (2:08:09), one second behind Kenya's Jackson Kipngok. An amazing 7 runners bettered 2:09:00, and 11 were faster than 2:10:00.

But it was not just the breezy Boston course that brought fast times that spring. At London on April 17, Dionicio Ceron's 2:08:53 led a pack with Abebe Mekonnen, German Silva, Salvatore Bettiol, and Grzegorz Gajdus all under 2:10:00. In the autumn, Portugal's Antonio Pinto won at Berlin on September 25 (2:08:31) and Hwang won the Asian Games gold medal at Hiroshima on October 9 (2:11:13). Silva returned to New York on November 6 to win its classic (2:11:21), despite going off course along the south side of Central Park and needing redirection back onto the route.

For the women, the year began with a thriller at Osaka on January 30. Tomoe Abe was delighted with her one second victory (2:26:09) over Junko Asari

(2:26:10), but in between the two was Nobuko Fujimura, given the same time as Asari! Such close finishes were becoming ever more common among both men and women, attesting to the need to develop both speed and endurance in training. At Osaka, eight runners bettered 2:30:00.

The cool, breezy Boston course helped the women achieve fast times as well. Uta Pippig's 2:21:45 was the third fastest time in history, ahead of Valentina Yegorova (2:23:33), Elana Meyer (2:25:15), and the Czech Republic's Alena Peterkova (2:25:19)—all personal bests and all national records. A record four women broke 2:26:00.

Manuela Machado followed in the footsteps of Rosa Mota with her winning ways, taking the European Athletics Championships gold medal on August 7 at Helsinki (2:29:54). Portuguese women now owned all four European Athletics Championships gold medals in this event. In a rare occurrence, Katrin Dörre-Heinig, who had earlier won at London (2:32:34), dropped out at 30 kilometers due to a brief illness. She showed her inherent fitness on September 25, however, with a personal best and national record 2:25:15 at Berlin.

The year closed with two other fine women's performances. Kenya's Tegla Loroupe won at New York on November 6 (2:37:37), her debut at the distance. And Yegorova returned to Tokyo to win again on November 20 in a slightly slower 2:30:09.

1995: The Sixth IAAF World Athletics Championships occurred at Göteborg on August 12, a focal point of the year. European champion Martin Fiz won comfortably with 2:11:41 over Dionicio Ceron (2:12:13) and 1994 Chicago champion Luis dos Santos from Brazil (2:12:49). Earlier in the year, Athens was host for the sixth World Marathon Cup on April 9, which Douglas Wakiihuri won comfortably in 2:12:01 by more than a minute. In the spring, Ceron captured his second London race on April 2 in 2:08:30. The competition was extremely intense—the next two across the line were Steve Moneghetti (2:08:33) and Antonio Pinto (2:08:48). The Boston Marathon saw Cosmas N'Deti capture his third successive victory (2:09:22), and one week later European champion Fiz won at Rotterdam (2:08:57) quite easily.

In the fall, the high-level racing continued as Kenya's Sammy Lelei (2:07:02) and Vincent Rousseau (2:07:20) ran the fastest times for the year at Berlin on September 24. German Silva defended his New York title on November 12 (2:11:00), while Dos Santos won a thrilling duel with Spain's Antonio Serrano by two seconds in 2:09:30 at Fukuoka on December 3. Amazingly, finishing in third, Japan's Masaki Oya was only another second behind!

Among the women, Machado excelled again at the major competitions with a victory at the IAAF World Athletics Championships in Göteborg (2:25:39) over Romania's Anuta Catuna (fifth at the 1994 Helsinki European Athletics Championships) and Italy's Ornella Ferrara (fourth at Helsinki). This capped Machado's finest year, as she had already finished second at both London and Boston!

(continued)

Performance times for the women at Göteborg do not appear on official lists, however, because, due to an organizational error, athletes ran only three of the four 400 meters laps on the track at the start before exiting the stadium.

The final major race of the year, at Tokyo on November 19, saw 1993 world champion Junko Asari (2:28:46) victorious by just two seconds over Barcelona gold medalist Valentina Yegorova.

References

Anonymous. 1986. *The results of the votes.* Olympic Review 229-230.

Bloom, M. 1992. The patient few. *Runner's World* 27 (7): 36-43.

Brennan, C. 1993. Barcelona, the city that never sleeps. In *Barcelona Albertville 1992.* Colorado Springs: U.S. Olympic Committee.

Burfoot, A. 1992. Long slow distance. *Runner's World* 27 (8): 84-85.

Hymans, R. 1992. Yegorova no mistake. *Track and Field News* 45 (10): 62.

Negron, C. 1992. Ups and downs. *Runner's World* 27 (4): 88-93.

Verdaguer-Codina, J., D.E. Martin, P. Pujol-Amat, A. Ruiz, and J.A. Prat. 1995. Climatic heat stress studies at the Barcelona Olympic Games. *Sports Medicine, Training, and Rehabilitation* 6: 167-192.

CHAPTER 24

1996—ATLANTA

Africans Capture the Gold in Atlanta

Atlanta Gets Perfect Attendance at the Centennial Games

If world opinion could have been polled regarding the venue for the 1996 Centennial Olympic Games, celebrating their revival, Athens seemed a logical choice. The Greeks certainly hoped this would occur, having already dedicated in 1982 a glistening marble Olympic stadium intended for track and field activities as well as the ceremonies. It was in suburban Amaroussion, home of Spiridon Louis himself.

However, a diplomat and a dreamer in a far-distant land had entirely different plans, and their small band of devout followers convinced those who *did* vote that *their* city was the better place. The diplomat was the Reverend Andrew Young. Ex-mayor of Atlanta and former United States ambassador to the United Nations, his international ties to Africa were particularly strong. The dreamer was William "Billy" Porter Payne. An ex-collegiate football star from the University of Georgia, his love for sport, his expertise in real estate law, and his unbridled enthusiasm for implementing the improbable gave him the bold idea that Atlanta ought to be host to the Olympic Games.

The details of how these two and their very small inner circle of local friends successfully secured these Olympic Games will likely be discussed for years to come. In the beginning, they scarcely knew any of the voting IOC committee members, let alone understood the complex political machinations of international sports federations. But they had superb business acumen, and they were wonderfully friendly people. The Atlanta Organizing Committee (AOC) focused intently on developing a personal relationship with every IOC member in addition to an effective bid proposal. Along with the usual wining, dining, and gift-giving—which was modest considering their bare-bones budget—they delivered a simple message: we are your friends, we want to join with you to help the world have a wonderful sporting legacy for the next millennium, and if you will entrust us with the Olympic Games they will be successful.

When the IOC members assembled on the evening of September 18, 1990, in the ballroom of the New Takanawa Prince hotel in Tokyo, five separate ballots were required before a majority was reached (table 24.1). Athens began in the lead, but at 2049 (8:49 p.m.) Tokyo time, IOC president Samaranch announced the winner: it was Atlanta. Simultaneously, at 0749 (7:49 a.m.) that same morning Atlanta time, a huge crowd erupted in cheers in its historic old downtown shopping district, viewing the announcement on a big screen. Thus launched a 2,129-days building and planning frenzy that created the largest sports spectacular in history.

The entire Olympic Games had to be financed privately, as no federal or local government bailout money was available if the Games went into debt. A multibillion-dollar corporation called the Atlanta Committee for the Olympic Games (ACOG) replaced the AOC and needed assembly within six years, peaking in size and function during the Games, only to go out of business by the summer of 1999. The primary centerpiece of the Olympic Games was its $235 million oval Olympic stadium, with a seating capacity of 85,600. After the Games it became home to television mogul Ted Turner's Atlanta Braves baseball team. The resulting reconfiguration removed 36,000 seats on its north side and restored Atlanta to its unfortunate status of still lacking a world-class track and field stadium.

TABLE 24.1

Results of the 1996 Centennial Olympic Games Vote

City	*Round one*	*Round two*	*Round three*	*Round four*	*Round five*
Atlanta	19	20	26	34	51
Athens	23	23	26	30	35
Toronto	14	17	18	22	
Melbourne	12	21	16		
Manchester	11	5			
Belgrade	7				

Eleven other major sports venues were also constructed, but in addition, Billy Payne wanted to create a grand gathering area, where no one needed a ticket to be a part and where everyone could congregate to enjoy the Olympic moment. Again dreaming the improbable, and then implementing it, he replaced 21 acres (52 hectares) of dilapidated downtown buildings and nearly vacant lots with a Centennial Olympic Park.

The park's focal point was a sound-and-light Fountain of Rings. Both high tech and beautiful, it remains today as a cooling-off haven for kids on hot summer days. Unfortunately, with the best of dreams comes the risk of a nightmare. The Games endured one of horrific dimensions at 0125 (1:25 a.m.) on the morning of Day 9 (Saturday, July 27) when a crude pipe bomb filled with nails and screws exploded amidst those celebrating in the park, killing 1 and injuring 110. The alleged perpetrator remains at large: Eric Robert Rudolph, charged as well for bombings at abortion clinics in Atlanta (1997) and Birmingham, Alabama (1998).

Meanwhile, 100 days before the Olympic Games began, Billy Payne himself delivered the Olympic flame to United States soil, landing ceremoniously in Los Angeles on a nonstop flight from Athens using an official sponsor, Delta Air Lines. After a 15,000 miles torch relay journey across the contiguous states, the answer to the usual question of who would light the Olympic cauldron remained top secret even as the Opening Ceremonies began. On the track, Atlanta native (and boxing gold medalist) Evander Holyfield shared the torch with Greece's 1992 100 meters gold medalist Paraskevi Patoulidou in a symbolic union of Athens and Atlanta. Swimmer Janet Evans then took the torch and elegantly climbed the stadium stairs to the foot of the bridge connecting the stadium with its adjacent freestanding cauldron. Suddenly spotlighted beside her, having watched the goings-on with delight while no one noticed, Muhammad Ali now took the torch from Evans. The crowd gasped in utter surprise as this boxing gold medalist from the Rome Games—who in 1970 fought Jerry Quarry in Atlanta when no other city would have him—lit the cauldron. The roar of approval climaxed an emotionally powerful beginning for these Centennial Games.

These were billed by some as the "Technology Games" because only the most sophisticated system of communication could keep information flowing among the venues. American corporations were on center stage to showcase their expertise, but there was no opportunity for a dry run. BellSouth's wires carried voice and video from venues to the world perfectly. Swatch Timing documented results flawlessly from the competition arenas. ChampionChip provided computer chips for affixing to the shoes of the marathon runners. These served as transponders and emitted a signal identifiable by a special receiver. Rubber mats containing these receivers were placed at each five kilometers checkpoint along the course. As runners crossed, instant real-time documentation of each race was provided to both journalists and television commentators.

So much technology functioned so well. But during the first few days, IBM's computer results system inconsistently routed results to world news agencies. Over time, the problem was rectified, but during those first few days the absence of anticipated information meant that preassigned print copy space in newspapers was difficult to fill. In frustration, the temptation was simply to fill it with critical commentary.

IOC president Samaranch also complained about rampant commercialism during the Olympic Games, referring to the vendors who turned Atlanta streets into a flea-market atmosphere. It seemed a bit narrow-minded, his criticism of this capitalist spirit. If it were not for a well-funded coterie of megasponsors each anteing up $40 million or more as major sponsors, the Games as a spectacle would have been severely diminished. Perhaps it was simply that he was unwilling to share. In contrast, spectators loved the atmosphere, and the resulting frenzy of pin-trading and souvenir-hunting was an integral part of the world coming together for 17 magic days of friendly competition. At the conclusion of the Olympic Games, Samaranch delivered a stinging rebuke to the organizers, declaring the Games "most exceptional" and not "the best ever" as he had done for all previous Games under his purview (Lyberg 1997). Always with a pleasant word for everyone, ACOG's Andrew Young countered (Saporta 1996): "One thing I've learned is that if everybody is kicking you in the behind, it is only because you are way out in front."

Despite the bombing, the computer glitches, and Samaranch's lament, athlete performances were absolutely spectacular—on the fields, in the pools, and in the arenas. And is that not the real essence of the success of an Olympic Games? The Georgia Institute of Technology campus became a global village for a record number of 10,630 accredited athletes: 7,006 men and 3,624 women (Lyberg 1997). The IOC now had 197 member NOCs, and they *all* participated in the Games—a first. There were no manufactured geopolitical entities like the Independent Olympic Participant and the Unified Team at Barcelona—all GPEs were NOCs. And South Africa marched with its own flag! More NOCs won medals (79) than ever before, and more took home at least one gold (53). In track and field alone, 45 NOCs brought home medals. The top three medal-winning NOCs in track and field were the United States (23), Russia (10), and Germany (7). Never had so many tickets been purchased to attend an Olympic Games: nearly nine million—more than Los Angeles (1984) and Barcelona combined! Never before had so many watched a track and field competition—the eight-days total was 1,164,570 in a stadium having 77,500 spectator seats, compared with 1,129,485 in Los Angeles, whose spectator capacity was 92,607.

Michael Johnson so epitomized Olympic excellence that he caused everyone to rethink the concept of speed with his double victories over 200 and 400 meters. Not only did he become the first man to win gold medals in both, but his world record time of 19.32 seconds in the 200 meters arguably made him the world's fastest human. Though it was specious, his fans noted that he averaged 9.66 seconds *per 100 meters* for 200 meters on that warm August 1 evening, whereas Canadian Donovan Bailey managed "only" 9.84 seconds for just 100 meters in his world record dash five nights earlier. Both became immensely marketable professional athletes, which certainly was fitting, since the IOC had officially deleted the word "amateur" from its charter the year Atlanta won the Olympic Games. But so many others competed solely for pure joy. The oldest competitor was 63, the youngest 12, their names less important than their participation.

Hills and Humidity Create a Challenging Marathon Course

The high altitude of Mexico City caused Olympic marathon runners unquestionably the greatest physiological challenge during this first century. But Atlanta's marathon course ranks a close second in difficulty. It was not the altitude, although indeed, Atlanta's elevation at 300 meters (984 feet) makes it the third highest Olympic city, after Mexico City and Munich. Rather, it was the combination of summertime heat and humidity, plus the numerous hills of Atlanta's terrain, due to its location at the southern end of the Appalachian Mountains. The city was marathon-friendly—its annual marathon dated back to 1963, making it the oldest in the southern United States. It began as ten loops around a golf course, and over the years it underwent three major design changes to eliminate some hills and reduce traffic tie-ups while still showcasing the city. The route being used when the Olympic Games were awarded was unacceptable for Olympic requirements, due to its inclusion of some narrow, tree-lined streets and at least two railroad crossings with the possibility of route closure for passing trains. Also, there was the desire to begin and end the race in the not-yet-existent Olympic stadium.

The Atlanta Track Club had managed the city marathon for most of its history, providing the hordes of volunteers required for such an event to proceed. The club's members enthusiastically accepted the challenge of becoming Olympic volunteers and further refined their skills for the once-in-a-lifetime experience of mothering over the Olympic marathon. After the Games were awarded in 1990, the club did some productive brainstorming, devised a new route, identified a plan for the necessary street closures in the many governmental jurisdictions, and the 1992 edition of the Atlanta Marathon debuted as a kind of Olympic marathon experiment. Starting and finishing beside the baseball stadium just north of the Olympic stadium construction site, it went basically north on Piedmont Avenue and then Peachtree Road, turned around, and then followed Peachtree Road all the way back into the city center (figure 24.1).

The concept was brilliant from many viewpoints. The two streets were multilane, permitting easy access for security, medical, and media vehicles supporting the event. Overhead tree cover was minimal, ensuring uninterrupted broadcast signal transmission. There were very few turns. Spectators desiring to dash from place to place along the course as the race proceeded could use the underground railway system, which largely paralleled it. The route traversed populated neighborhoods, meaning that thousands of spectators had instant free access to the grandest athletic event of them all—twice, to see both the men's and women's races. Only two substantial changes became appropriate. One was the eventual movement of the start and finish lines into the Olympic

Course Details

The 1996 Atlanta Olympic Marathon

Start at 1,500 meters line (southeast side) within the stadium

Run three complete laps counterclockwise, plus an additional nearly 200 meters to exit the marathon tunnel (northwest side)

Cross Ralph D. Abernathy Drive onto Clarke Street

Continue on Clarke Street as it parallels Interstate 75/85 and turns right to intersect Capitol Avenue (now Hank Aaron Way)

Left onto Capitol Avenue

Capitol Avenue passes State Capitol Building (on left) and becomes Piedmont Avenue

Continue on Piedmont Avenue to Auburn Avenue

Right onto Auburn Avenue past Martin Luther King Jr. burial site to Howell Street

Left onto Howell Street to Irwin Street

Left onto Irwin Street to Jackson Street

Right onto Jackson Street to Highland Avenue

Left onto Highland Avenue to Piedmont Avenue

Right onto Piedmont Avenue to Peachtree Road

Right onto Peachtree Road to turnaround point even with Brookhaven Christian Church Driveway

Continue on Peachtree Road to Lanier Drive

Right onto Lanier Drive to Woodrow Way, staying on the right side of the road

Turn around on Lanier, returning to Peachtree Road, again staying on the right side of the road in the direction of running

Continue on Peachtree Road to Edgewood Avenue

Left onto Edgewood Avenue to Gilmer Street

Half right onto Gilmer Street to Courtland Street

Right onto Courtland Street

Courtland Street passes State Capitol (on left) and becomes Washington Street

Continue on Washington Street to Memorial Drive

Left onto Memorial Drive to Capitol Avenue

Right onto Capitol Avenue to Clarke Street

Right onto Clarke Street to intersection with Ralph D. Abernathy Drive adjacent to Olympic stadium

Cross the street and enter access tunnel on northwest side of stadium

Continue through stadium access tunnel to track surface and proceed counterclockwise down the sprint straightaway, using the indicator cones to reach lane one at the finish line

Continue one additional lap (500 meters total on the track) to the standard track event finish line

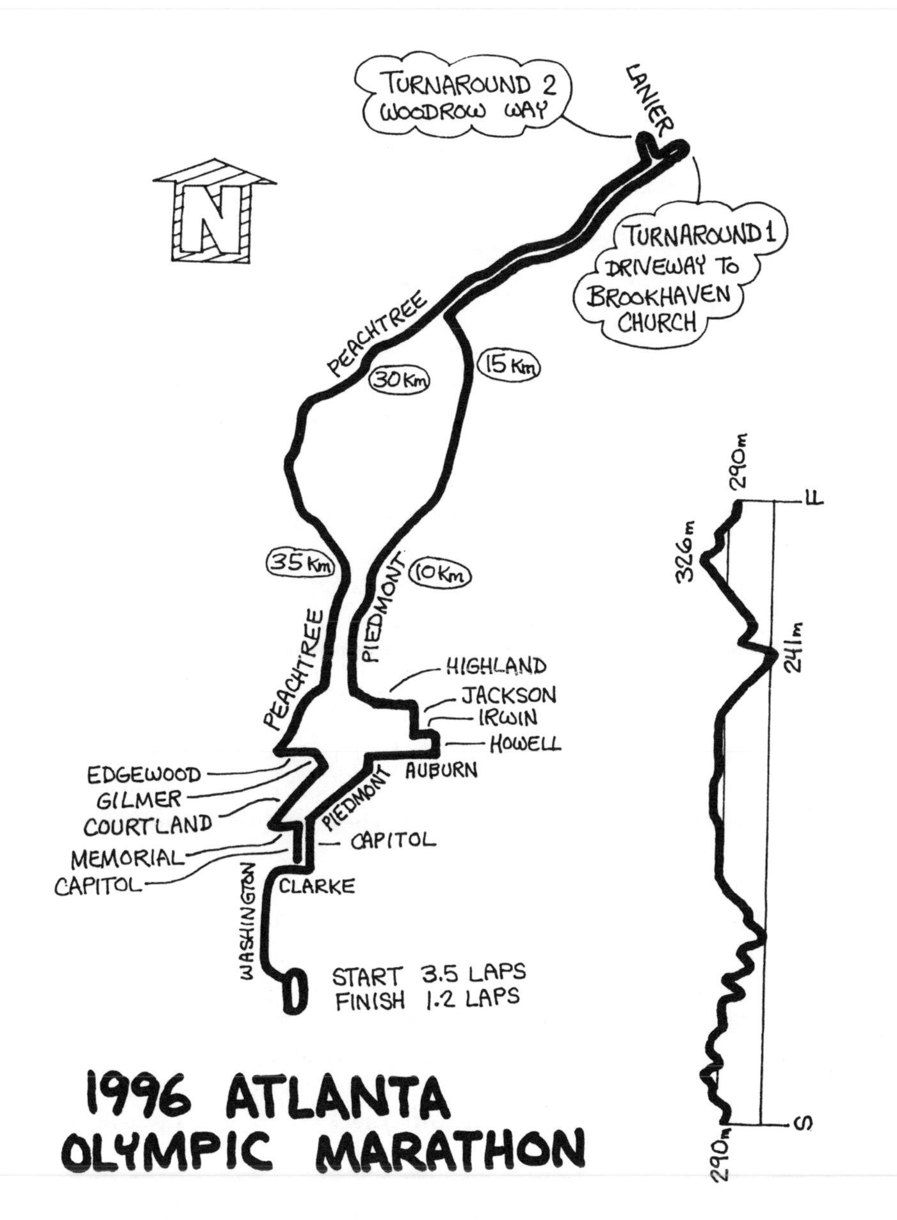

Figure 24.1 Sketch of the Atlanta Olympic marathon course. Note that the various street descriptors (avenue, road, street, etc.) have been omitted for simplicity. Prepared by Bob Letson.

stadium. The other was designing what became known locally as the "MLK extension"—a section of roadway between kilometers four and eight that permitted athletes to run past Martin Luther King Jr.'s gravesite, the Ebenezer Baptist Church where King's father preached, and his birth home.

Figure 24.1 shows Peachtree Creek flowing in an east-to-west direction, essentially bisecting the course. This caused two sets of descents and ascents approximating 61 meters (200 feet) as runners crossed the creek. Whereas the stadium start and finish were at 290 meters (952 feet), the creek bridges were at 244 meters (800 feet). In between, the course reached a maximum elevation of 323 meters (1,060 feet). A preliminary detailed analysis to determine total ascent and descent using topographical maps (Riegel 1995) was supplemented by a second study (Jones 1996). The latter concluded that the total course elevation drop (and gain) was 368 meters (1,208 feet), with 31 percent uphill, 33 percent downhill, and 36 percent flat. These elevation figures can be compared with those of the previously most rolling Olympic marathon course, namely at Athens. There the total ascent was an estimated 270 meters (886 feet) and the total descent was 220 meters (722 feet). Clearly, Atlanta presented an enormous challenge for those in the marathon.

As at Los Angeles in 1984, an "international group ride" by experienced measurement specialists was deemed the best method for making a final check on course accuracy. Twenty-eight experts representing six countries and three continents assembled over the Memorial Day holiday weekend, when traffic was minimal. On Sunday, May 26 they wound their way through Atlanta's city streets. The starting point was the 1,500 meters track start line, with three laps run inside the stadium before departing from the marathon tunnel located behind the 100 meters start line. The finish line, after a little more than one complete final stadium lap, was at the standard track event finish line. Given these constraints, course adjustments were made using the northernmost portion of Peachtree Road to ensure proper distance. The eventual certified course, with built-in short course prevention factor, was 42,247.6 meters in length, which was 52.6 meters too long. As shown in figure 24.1, route designers created a unique double-turnaround arrangement to achieve the required shortening and also ensure that athletes could maintain pace without unduly sharp turns. Prior to the marathon competitions, the entire route was painted with a solid blue line. It is still visible in places as of this writing. The exact street specifics are provided in the course details box. The entire course is negotiable by runners or bicyclists interested in retracing it, except for the entry into the stadium. The marathon tunnel was demolished and bricked in during the stadium's reconfiguration for baseball.

The Best Women Marathoners Prepare

As at Barcelona, depending upon an individual sport governing body's whim, athletes were either preselected by their NOCs on the basis of prior results or required to "show fitness" at a race of their choice, or they were selected on the basis of one or more so-called trial races. Depending upon depth of competition in a particular NOC, one or another system is preferable. Olympic "A" and "B" performance standards also existed. Nations with athletes faster than 2:35:00 could enter three who had bettered that standard between January 1, 1995, and July 16, 1996. Nations with no athletes at the 2:35:00 level could enter a single athlete, provided she had run a 2:50:00 standard within the same time period. Some NOCs had no athletes meeting world performance entry standards in any track and field event, so they were allowed one track and field athlete from each sex in an event of choice.

Japan

Katrin Dörre-Heinig scored her third victory at Osaka on January 28 (2:26:04) with a 23 seconds margin over Japanese debutante Hiromi Suzuki. Suzuki was placed onto Japan's 10,000 meters track team, so the Osaka race became more important for international runners than for the locals. Spain's Monica Pont ran a personal best of 2:27:53 and ensured her team berth, joining two other Spaniards who had finished first and second at San Sebastian the previous October: Ana Isabel Alonso (2:26:51) and Rocio Rios (2:28:20). Lisa Ondieki was not in prime fitness for Osaka, being bothered by a bruised heel, but she nevertheless ran the required Australian time standard with her ninth-place finish (2:30:27). She could now take the time to get healthy and fit.

Izumi Maki won at Nagoya on March 10 with 2:37:32 after a convincing 68:18 half marathon at Tokyo in January. She became the third member of another strong Japanese marathon team. The other two were preselected and included the Barcelona Games runner-up Yuko Arimori and 1995 IAAF World Athletics Champion Junko Asari, who had won at Tokyo in November. The Barcelona gold medalist, Valentina Yegorova, placed third at Nagoya (2:27:53), with Ramilya Burangulova only 5 seconds behind in fourth. This would be their second Olympic Games, the first as bona fide representatives of the Russian federation.

United States

The United States continued with its system of letting the athletes sort themselves out on a given day at a single invitational Olympic trial marathon. This edition was open only to citizens having run 2:50:00 or faster between June 18, 1994, and mid-January 1996. Columbia, South Carolina bid successfully as the host site, and 129 athletes finished the February 10 race. Weather was optimal for racing (7°C or 45°F, sunny, and calm), but the loop course was a real challenge—approaching Atlanta's in its rolling terrain. During the 17th mile, the relatively unknown Jenny Spangler quickened the tempo to 5:20 per mile pace (3:19 per kilometer), and the lead pack suddenly became single file, with only two in close contention behind her. She was the surprise winner with a nearly four-minute improvement in her personal best 2:29:54—a course record as well. Linda Somers also scored a personal best with her runner-up 2:30:06, and Anne Marie Lauck (2:31:18) rounded out the team. Los Angeles champion Joan Samuelson placed 13th with 2:36:54. Just out of the team honors, in 4th, was

Barcelona 10,000 meters Olympian Gwynn Coogan, having recently moved up to the marathon distance.

Here was a situation where a team-selection committee might have picked two-three-four as experienced proven athletes and provided a better chance of success instead of arbitrarily taking the top three placers. Of course, hindsight is always a better judge. Spangler's previous best had come 13 years before, as a collegian. She had been more out of the sport than in during the interim, struggling with injuries and other challenges. But America has a passion for supporting those prevailing over adversity. Spangler became a Cinderella story and a media darling, much to the delight of those surrounding her who capitalized on her sudden rise in commercial value. She also lapsed as quickly back into obscurity, dropping out of the Olympic marathon just after 10 kilometers as a result of an unresolved Achilles tendon injury that had been chronic since the trial race (Spangler 1996). She should have opted out prior to the Games in deference to Coogan, who was both healthy and hungry.

Boston was another important race on American soil that served to select Olympians. This was a most historic event—its 100th running—with a record 35,868 finishers coping with headwinds and cool temperatures on April 15. Kenya's Tegla Loroupe appeared as a likely winner while forging a lead through the Newton Hills, but fatigue caused a dramatic slowdown as she learned the hard way how essential it is to manage pace optimally in the early stages. Germany's Uta Pippig battled gastrointestinal problems but still caught Loroupe at 24 miles and collected her third consecutive Boston victory (2:27:12). Loroupe's 2:28:37 was still top-class, and she captured sixth place in Atlanta at the 10,000 meters event. Back in eighth place, Lorraine Moller's 2:32:02 allowed her to join Lisa Ondieki as the only two women to start all four women's Olympic marathons.

Europe

Several top African marathoners used European races as their Olympic qualifiers. Many had based their training in Europe to take advantage of racing opportunities. Traveling north from Africa gave minimal time zone travel stress. One example was Ethiopia's Fatuma Roba. In January she set a national record (2:30:50) at Marrakech. She then ran an even faster 2:29:05 at Rome on a blustery March 24, well ahead of Italy's Ornella Ferrara (2:31:30). These results gave both athletes Olympic team spots.

At London on April 21, Kenya's Joyce Chepchumba ran a fine 2:30:09 for second, with her colleague Angelina Kanana in fourth. Both were placed on the Kenyan team. Britain's Liz McColgan won with an outstanding 2:27:54 to lead the British marathon squad. She was very happy because she was within half a minute of her 1991 personal best and it was her first victory since 1992 at Tokyo. In third was the 1995 winner from Poland, Malgorzata Sobanska (2:30:17), and she joined the Polish marathon team in Atlanta. One week later, at Rotterdam on April 28, a few other potential Olympic stars verified their readiness. Belgium's Lieve Slegers achieved a national record 2:28:06 with her victory over Mexico's Maria del Carmen Diaz (2:29:48).

Roba Makes Olympic Marathon Racing Look Easy

The women's Olympic marathon started at 0705 (7:05 a.m.) on Sunday morning, July 28. It was the third day of athletics, one day after the Centennial Olympic Park bombing. Hardly a soul was in the stadium because it had been a late-night thriller the evening before. That was when Canada's Donovan Bailey won the men's 100 meters, and when Gail Devers of the United States became the first woman in 28 years to repeat as the 100 meters champion. It was the largest Olympic women's marathon field in the event's short history. Sixteen full teams of 3 athletes toed the stadium start line. Official results tell us that there were 86 starters from 51 NOCs, but if the truth were told, 88 athletes started the race, representing 53 NOCs (see Olympic Marathon Miscellany 24.1). Europe had the greatest representation, as usual, with 44 athletes, 25 NOCs, and nine teams (Belarus, Britain, Germany, Italy, Poland, Portugal, Romania, Russia, and Spain). Asia was also well represented, with 15 athletes, 10 NOCs, and full teams from Japan and Korea. North and Central America were represented by only 8 athletes from Canada, Mexico, and the United States, the latter two fielding teams. South America also had 8 athletes representing 6 NOCs, with only Brazil having a full team. From Africa, Kenya fielded a full team, but Ethiopia, Namibia, and South Africa had 1 lone entrant each. From Oceania, only Australia fielded a full team, and single entrants came from Guam and New Zealand.

The Atlanta course meandered through many ethnic neighborhoods, bringing a continual change in the languages heard and flags waved as people cheered and looked for those from their native lands. Because the race was televised live, spectators found it convenient to watch the drama develop on their TV screens, and then dash out to the street as the athletes raced by their homes. The expected summertime Atlanta heat wave thankfully did not materialize, and weather conditions were better than expected for racing. At the start, it was 21.3°C (70.3°F), foggy and drizzly, with 93 percent humidity (Martin 1999). The fog remained, but as the sun rose, it warmed the air only to 25.1°C (77.2°F) when the winner finished. However, the humidity had dropped to 77 percent. This greater decrease in humidity than increase in temperature actually made racing conditions more favorable as the race progressed; it became easier to lose metabolic heat from sweat evaporation.

It was the fear of an exactly opposite scenario that apparently was in the minds of Germany's Uta Pippig and her shrewd coach Dieter Hogan as she took the lead from the start. Passing 5 kilometers in 17:30, just past the grave of Martin Luther King Jr., she was fully 13 seconds ahead of a huge pack led by Dörre-Heinig and Portugal's Maria Manuela Machado (17:43). This was faster than 2:28:00 pace, which race cognoscenti had not imagined as achievable by women on this course. One notable contender among the group timed in 17:44 was South Africa's Elana Meyer, who would slow drastically after 10 kilometers due to an injured Achilles tendon and retire after 20 kilometers. Australia's Lisa

Ondieki was back in 52nd place, also slowed by injury, and similarly ended her race shortly past 20 kilometers.

At 10 kilometers, Pippig's lead (34:09) had increased to 28 seconds in front of a pack of five: Yegorova, Dörre-Heinig, Romania's Lidia Simon, Machado, and Roba. These five, however, were merely the front of a larger pack, with such notables as Arimori, Asari, Lauck, and Maki 1 second back.

Pippig kept her lead through 15 kilometers, now 20 seconds in front (51:18) of the same lead group of five, with the same pack just behind. Dieter Hogan remarked after the race that they expected the strong summer sun to evaporate the early morning ground fog, making the second half a miserably hot ordeal. Thus they thought it wise to race as quickly as feasible early on, hoping as well to create a substantial gap. The quality of this field, however, was so incredible that, knowing Pippig's credentials, those behind her did not permit such a lead to develop.

At 17 kilometers, the long ascent up Piedmont Road ended, and runners turned right onto the essentially level Peachtree Road, which took them to the turnaround point. Fatuma Roba simply maintained her same running effort on this level portion, and as a result quickened her pace. Easily catching Pippig, she took the lead, and by 20 kilometers (1:08:45) she was 13 seconds ahead of her. But Pippig was not even in second place, for she was also overtaken by Yegorova, Arimori, and Machado (all timed in 1:08:51), and Simon as well, another second behind. Passing the midpoint in 1:12:31, Roba was now 9 seconds up on Yegorova and the others, and her gap slowly widened as the race progressed.

At 25 kilometers (1:25:50), Roba was 28 seconds in front of Yegorova, Arimori, Simon, and Machado. Dörre-Heinig was alone in sixth at this point, 25 seconds behind the foursome and 9 seconds in front of Pippig. In eighth place was Lauck, 50 seconds behind Pippig. The 30 kilometers point on Peachtree Street was midway down a long descent well known to those who have raced the famous 10 kilometers Peachtree Road Race, as this is in its midsection. Roba's lead (1:42:57) had now increased to 61 seconds, with Arimori 1 second ahead of Yegorova, Simon, and Machado. Dörre-Heinig was still in sixth, now 26 seconds behind the threesome. Pippig had fallen back to 1:45:10, 45 seconds behind Dörre-Heinig, with Lauck still holding on to eighth, 42 seconds behind Pippig. To help with spatial orientation of these runners, they were racing at about 4.8 meters per second.

By 35 kilometers, just past the Colony Square micropolis of shops, offices, and apartments, Roba's lead (2:00:46) had extended to 73 seconds, but now athletes were all in single file. It was Yegorova at 2:01:59, 4 seconds ahead of Arimori, and then a gap until Simon passed (2:02:28). Dörre-Heinig was now in fifth, 14 seconds behind Simon, but only 7 seconds ahead of Machado. Pippig had now fallen back to 2:04:37, still in ninth place.

Past the downtown skyscrapers they raced, with Roba seeming to take more energy than the others from the increased crowd support. Ethiopian flags popped up from the crowd, which she occasionally acknowledged. At 40 kilometers, just past the gold-domed State Capitol (figure 24.2), her 2:18:40 was now 105 seconds ahead of Yegorova (2:20:25). The five athletes behind Roba were close enough to each other that a struggle ensued for possession of the remaining two medals. After Yegorova came Arimori (2:20:43), followed by Dörre-Heinig (2:21:02), Simon (2:22:39), and Machado (2:22:48). But Spain's Rocio Rios made a late-race surge and passed both Machado and Simon to capture fifth place. Dörre-Heinig closed her gap with Arimori from 19 seconds at 40 kilometers to 6 seconds by the finish, but it wasn't enough; Yegorova took silver and Arimori

Figure 24.2 **With the gold dome of the State Capitol and the city skyline behind, Fatuma Roba follows the blue line and passes 40.5 kilometers, assured of victory. The specially designed natural-gas vehicles permit media to focus full attention on her final footsteps.** Courtesy *Atlanta Journal-Constitution*/Louie Favorite.

TABLE 24.2

Order of Top Placers Through Control Points

	Roba	***Yegorova***	***Arimori***	***Dörre-Heinig***	***Rios***	***Simon***
5 km	=18-24	=12-17	=4-11	=2, 3	=25-28	=4-11
10 km	=2-6	=2-6	=7-13	=2-6	=22-24	=2-6
15 km	=2-6	=2-6	=2-6	=2-6	=18-21	7
20 km	1	=2-4	=2-4	7	=19-22	5
25 km	1	=2-5	=2-5	6	10	=2-5
30 km	1	3	2	6	9	4
35 km	1	2	3	5	7	4
40 km	1	2	3	4	7	5
Finish	1	2	3	4	5	6

the bronze. Table 24.2 summarizes the order of top athletes as they passed through the various checkpoints.

Roba's 2:26:05 was a national record, bettering her earlier mark set at Rome. She was exactly two minutes ahead of Yegorova and had completed her victory lap in front of a nearly half-full stadium before Yegorova finished (figure 24.3). It was the widest margin of victory for any of the first four women's marathons. Sixty-five athletes finished the race, and thus, 24 percent dropped out, 3 percent more than at Barcelona. Arimori's teammates also ran well, placing 12th (Maki) and 17th (Asari) to give them the unofficial team score (32 points) over Spain and Portugal. Table 24.3 summarizes the race.

Unfortunately, not all of the women had the privilege of finishing in the Olympic stadium. The first round of the men's 100 meters hurdles was scheduled to start at 1045 (10:45 a.m.), 3:40:00 after the start of the women's marathon. As at Barcelona, an alternative finish line outside the stadium had been created. Here, it was the women who had to endure the "punishment" for being too slow to fit within the daily Olympic program. Just before 41 kilometers, instead of turning right off Capitol Avenue onto Clarke Street, runners were directed one additional block on Capitol Avenue, where they turned left onto Fulton Street, reaching 41 kilometers at the intersection of Fulton and Frazier Streets. Turning right on Frazier, they then continued to Georgia Avenue, turned left on Georgia to Amie Street, then turned right on Amie. After passing 42 kilometers, they then turned left and passed through the security gate into the Cheney Stadium athlete check-in facility. Turning right onto the track, they finished midway along its west straightaway. Six athletes were officially scored here: Guylsara Dadabayeva [TJK], Bimala Rana Magar [NEP], Erhemsaihan Davaajargal [MGL], Sirivanh Ketavong [LAO], Marie Benito [GUM], and Virginie Gloum [CAF]. The fate of the latter is described further in Olympic Marathon Miscellany 24.1.

Figure 24.3 Appearing fresh after racing and winning the Atlanta Olympic marathon, a smiling Fatuma Roba waves to the stadium crowd. Courtesy *Atlanta Journal-Constitution*/John Spink.

TABLE 24.3

1996 Atlanta Olympic Women's Marathon at a Glance

Date: 28 July
Start time: 0705
Course: Out-and-back loop
Course distance: 42.195 km
Weather: 21.3°C (70.3°F)
Starters: 86
Finishers: 65 (plus two unofficial)
GPEs: 51 (plus two unofficial)

TOP RESULTS:

Place	*Athlete*	*GPE*	*Date of birth*	*Time*
1	Fatuma Roba	ETH	18 Dec. 1973	2:26:05
2	Valentina Yegorova	RUS	16 Feb. 1964	2:28:05
3	Yuko Arimori	JPN	17 Dec. 1966	2:28:39
4	Katrin Dörre-Heinig	GER	06 Oct. 1961	2:28:45
5	Rocio Rios	ESP	13 Mar. 1969	2:30:50
6	Lidia Simon	ROM	04 Sep. 1973	2:31:04
7	Maria Manuela Machado	POR	09 Aug. 1963	2:31:11
8	Sonja Krolik	GER	24 Feb. 1973	2:31:16
9	Ren Xiujuan	CHN	14 Sep. 1974	2:31:21
10	Anne Marie Lauck	USA	07 Mar 1969	2:31:30

New geopolitical entities represented: Spain [ESP], Argentina [ARG], Kyrgyzstan [KGZ], Colombia [COL], Turkey [TUR], Singapore [SIN], Lithuania [LIT], Greece [GRE], Slovenia [SLO], Yugoslavia [YUG], Namibia [NAM], Tajikistan [TJK], Mongolia [MGL], Lao People's Democratic Republic [LAO], Ukraine [UKR], Ecudaor [ECU], Estonia [EST], Malta [MLT], plus unofficially Moldova [MOL] and Central African Republic [CAF]

Team score (unofficial):			
	1. JPN	32 points	(3-12-17)
	2. ESP	68 points	(5-14-49)
	3. POR	81 points	(7-27-47)

OLYMPIC MARATHON MISCELLANY 24.1

The Mystery of the Missing Female Marathoners

The official result lists 86 women marathoners having participated (Anonymous 1997). In fact, two more started and finished, and except for this writing, most traces of their Olympic identity have been removed. They deserve recognition. The two athletes in question are Valentina Yenaki from Moldova and Virginie Gloum from the Central African Republic. Yenaki's personal best was 2:33:35, but Gloum was not nearly so experienced, having (what remains as) her nation's fastest marathon performance of 3:28:41. Both athletes were bona fide members of their NOC delegations and were housed in the athletes' village. Yenaki was issued bib number 3558 to wear in the race, and Gloum number 3119. Neither was "administratively eligible" to compete due to "infractions," but on race day they nevertheless were "cleared to compete." Comprehending the obvious confusion illustrates how, with a competition as large as the Olympics, the many interacting bureaucracies are not always synchronized.

Both Yenaki and Gloum appeared on the initial printed "Entry List by Name," which provided both the athlete's name and her qualifying mark. Gloum's entry had a fictitious 2:34:08 beside it, far faster than she had ever run. If correct, she would have been eligible to compete by meeting the sub-2:35:00 A-level IAAF standard. However, no athletes from her country had made the standard in any event. Thus, her NOC could only enter one woman athlete, and two days before, Denise Oubangui had finished last (55.74 seconds) in the final heat of the first round of the 400 meters, making Gloum ineligible. Apparently, neither Gloum nor her delegation was confronted with this situation, because on race day, Gloum traveled from the village to the stadium with the other athletes and presented herself (with bib number affixed) for check-in at the Olympic stadium in the predawn hours. She was not on the start list, however, and the humanely appropriate decision was made by the competition management staff to allow her to run. She ran, and because she was the last finisher, she was one of the six diverted to Cheney stadium. Her estimated time of 3:32-plus was within five minutes of her personal best.

In contrast, Yenaki's qualification result was bona fide, but her team management staff did not declare her as an entered athlete the day preceding the competition. Hence, her name, as well, did not appear on the start list prepared the evening prior to the competition. As with Gloum, Yenaki prepared to compete, presented herself at the stadium, was cleared, and ran the race. Her initially reported time was 2:41:30.

During the competition, when the technical delegate's office in the stadium was informed that the two athletes had been permitted to start despite not being on the start list, their names and times were ordered to be excluded from the results. This explains the following cryptic annotation at the bottom of each page of the official marathon results distributed after the competition: "Bib No. 3119 and 3558 were removed. They were not official competitors." Even this mention is deleted in the official Olympic report (Anonymous 1997), however.

This state of affairs leaves perplexing questions for Olympic record-keepers. How many athletes and geopolitical entities really did compete in the marathon? It does appear that Gloum and Yenaki were punished for the shortcomings of associated officials rather than for their own transgressions. Gloum should not have been placed on her Olympic team before travel to Atlanta, and Yenaki's team management should have taken better care of her. For the Olympic historical record, however, and to recognize their achievements in finishing, it is appropriate to tell the story here.

Notes on the Women Medalists

At 22 years of age, **Fatuma Roba** was the youngest of the four women Olympic marathon gold medalists: Benoit was 27, Mota was 30, and Yegorova was 28. Roba was the least known. Four years earlier, in Barcelona, it was Ethiopia's Derartu Tulu who became black Africa's first female Olympic champion (and she placed fourth in Atlanta). Roba was the second such gold medalist, and the two athletes had much in common. Coming from simple backgrounds, they lived in the small town of Bokeji, known for barley and milk production in the agricultural highlands of Ethiopia. Her father was a farmer.

Debuting at the annual Abebe Bikila commemorative marathon in Addis Ababa on July 4, 1993, as a 19-years-old teenager, she won in 2:44:20. Realizing that this was at 2,440 meters altitude (8,000 feet), one was left with a hint of her enormous potential at endurance running. This performance gained her entry into the Paris Marathon on April 24, 1994, where she placed 11th with another personal best (2:35:25). In turn, this qualified her for the 1995 Göteborg IAAF World Athletics Championships, where she placed 18th.

In 1996, it could have been argued that Roba was overracing. She started with another personal best, and a victory, at Marrakech in January. Only two months later, she raced again at Rome, breaking the 2:30:00 barrier and securing a place on the Ethiopian team bound for Atlanta. Instead of overracing, it appears simply that the world was watching an exceptionally gifted endurance runner gain some experience before challenging the deepest women's Olympic marathon field. In Atlanta, she made a 5:24 per mile pace (3:28 per kilometer) over a very hilly course on a warm, humid morning look easy, and for her, it was.

Following Atlanta, she was invited to compete in the lucrative big-city marathons, and those with the biggest budgets secured her talents, most notably Boston in the spring and Tokyo in the fall. The time zones and time of year have suited her better for Boston than for Tokyo. Her victories at Boston in 1997 and 1998 were nearly as spectacular as in Atlanta, with the 1998 Boston effort being another personal best. Tokyo remains her nemesis, however, with one fourth- and two eighth-place finishes. At the 1999 IAAF World Athletics Championships in Seville, she placed a fine fourth (2:28:04), and only three months later ran even faster (2:27:05) at Tokyo, placing second. Thus, she shows definite promise for a good race in Sydney. Table 24.4 lists Roba's career marathon record.

As mentioned in chapter 23, **Valentina Yegorova** raced actively through the interim between the Barcelona and Atlanta Games. Early in March 1996, she delivered her third-fastest time in 19 completed races at Nagoya, finishing third (2:27:53), five seconds ahead of colleague Ramilya Burangulova. Two Japanese were in front of them, but Yegorova was confident after this race that she would also be a tough competitor in Atlanta. Indeed, only Fatuma Roba kept her from another gold medal, and she ran the fourth-fastest performance of her career.

Following the Atlanta Games, she moved to the Gainesville area of Florida in the United States with her husband and coach Yuriy and their 10-years-old son,

TABLE 24.4

Career Marathon Record of Fatuma Roba

Date	Venue	Place	Time	Comments
04 July 1993	Addis Ababa	1st	2:44:20	
24 Apr. 1994	Paris	11th	2:35:25	
05 Aug. 1995	Göteborg	18th	2:39:27	World championships*
14 Jan. 1996	Marrakech	1st	2:30:50	
24 Mar. 1996	Rome	1st	2:29:05	
28 July 1996	Atlanta	1st	2:26:05	Olympic Games
17 Nov. 1996	Tokyo	8th	2:35:54	
21 Apr. 1997	Boston	1st	2:26:23	
09 Aug. 1997	Athens	DNF		World championships
30 Nov. 1997	Tokyo	4th	2:30:39	
20 Apr. 1998	Boston	1st	2:23:21	
15 Nov. 1998	Tokyo	8th	2:36:22	
19 Apr. 1999	Boston	1st	2:23:25	
29 Aug. 1999	Seville	4th	2:28:04	World championships
21 Nov. 1999	Tokyo	2nd	2:27:05	

*400 meters short

Ruslan. This area was also the adopted home of Olga Markova and her coach, and the group of top-level Russian and Ukrainian women marathoners residing there has grown steadily since. In January 1997, Yegorova traveled to Osaka for its prestigious International Ladies Marathon, where she once again faced one of the sport's greatest heroines—Katrin Dörre-Heinig. Yegorova developed problems in the later stages, eventually retiring, and Dörre-Heinig went on to win. Undaunted, Yegorova has continued to train and compete, winning the Nagano international marathon in April 1999 (2:28:41) with her sixth-fastest performance in 22 completed marathons.

Whereas Yegorova competed successfully between Barcelona and Atlanta, bronze medalist **Yuko Arimori** lost momentum from injury and returned to top form only months before the Atlanta Games. Arimori and Yegorova form an interesting contrast. Following Arimori's silver medal performance in Barcelona, she faced enormous local pressure to remain in the limelight. She was a superstar in Japan, and everyone from magazine writers to TV talk-show hosts wanted her time. After racing in the corporate women's ekiden circuit in November 1992, she finally took a break. Returning to racing in April, she continued to participate in smaller road races, some as training sessions, but she did not return to high-level competition.

In the fall of 1993, she injured her right heel, and in trying to train through it, altered her running style and injured her left heel as well. Her problems did not resolve, she lost a full year of training, and she finally underwent surgery in

November 1994. Several months of rehabilitation gave a successful end result. While recovering and resuming training, however, she fell during a training run in May, injuring her right leg, and she lost another full month of training. Frustrated by so many setbacks, when she recovered again she was understandably hungry to resume competition, and she set a goal to enter the warm summertime marathon in Sapporo. Under the guidance of her coach, Yoshio Koide (current coach of Naoko Takahashi and Hiromi Suzuki), and on a day cooler than normal in Sapporo, Arimori set a new course record with an excellent 2:29:17.

This also indicated to Olympic selectors that she might be an excellent choice for Atlanta's expected heat and humidity. She did not want to disappoint them, and her sole goal was to bring home a gold medal. Roba thwarted her ambitions. Nevertheless, her bronze medal performance in Atlanta, combined with her silver at Barcelona, makes her the third best Olympic women's marathoner after Yegorova's first and second, and Mota's first and third. She married American Gabriel Wilson on January 14, 1998, and resumed top-level competition, scoring 2:26:39 for third place at Boston in 1999.

The Best Male Marathoners Prepare

Asia

Japan's well-known marathon racing circuit scheduled from December through March provided an ideal environment for athletes around the world to deliver impressive performances. At Fukuoka on December 3, 1995, Brazil's Luiz Antonio Santos won with a national record (2:09:30). Amazingly, however, runner-up Antonio Serrano's 2:09:32 was not sufficient to place him on the Spanish team, so strong was that nation's talent. His countryman, Diego Garcia, finishing fourth (2:09:51), was given a team berth, however, probably because of his experience; he was sixth at the 1995 IAAF World Athletics Championships in warm weather.

Using similar logic, the Japanese chose Fukuoka third-placer Masaki Oya (2:09:33) for the team, along with Kenjiro Jitsui, who scored 2:08:50 at Tokyo in February. Both performances were personal bests. Also selected for Japan was the venerable Hiromi Taniguchi, who had placed only seventh at Fukuoka, but who in 1991 had won the hot, humid Tokyo IAAF World Athletics Championships. South Africa's Gert Thys won the February 4 marathon between Beppu and Oita with a course record (2:08:30), ahead of Brazil's Valdenor dos Santos (2:10:27). Later in the month, another South African, Josiah Thugwane, won his national championship in Cape Town. Together with Lawrence Peu, selected later from his performance at Paris, these South Africans were eager to prove themselves in Olympic competition; a men's team had not raced at Barcelona in 1992.

At Kyongju, Korea, on March 24, the 1994 European and 1995 IAAF world champion, Martin Fiz, clinched a Spanish team place by edging Lee Bong-ju by one second in 2:08:25. Defending champion Manuel Matias, from Portugal, was relegated to third (2:09:08) but still was given an Atlanta team berth. Finishing strongly in fourth and fifth were two other Koreans, Kim Wan-ki (2:09:19) and Kim Yi-yong (2:09:36), providing as strong a team, at least on paper, as those from the Iberian nations. Alberto Juzdado, who finished third at Tokyo (2:08:46), joined Garcia and Fiz to constitute the Spanish team. This team had swept the three medals at the 1984 Helsinki European Athletics Championships.

While these fast performances were being achieved on flat courses in excellent racing conditions, it was anyone's guess how these athletes would fare in the hills, heat, and humidity of Atlanta.

United States

Below-freezing weather at the invitational Olympic trial race in Charlotte, North Carolina, on February 17 did not deter Bob Kempainen from setting a 2:12:45 course record ahead of colleagues Mark Coogan (2:13:05) and Keith Brantly (2:13:22). Entrants had to have run faster than 2:22:00 between January 1, 1994, and December 1, 1995. This course was as unforgiving as the one they would face in Atlanta, with bitter cold and hills that never stopped. Kempainen was cold-acclimated from living in Minnesota, as was Coogan, who lived in Boulder, Colorado; it was heat-trained Floridian Brantly who found frustration in trying to qualify in a cold-weather race for the chance to show his tolerance to the heat expected six months later. Kempainen's $100,000 first-prize purse was the largest in marathon history, and it helped to pay his medical school bills.

African runners swept the top places at the 100th Boston Marathon on April 15, with Kenyans taking seven of the top eight spots. Only Ethiopia's Abebe Mekonnen split their total domination with a fine sixth place. Not surprisingly, the reason for this dominance was the use of this venue as the Kenyan Olympic trial. From this race, two were selected to combine with the already-chosen Japan-resident Erick Wainaina. He had won the 1995 IAAF World Marathon Cup and was second (2:10:37) at Otsu in Japan earlier in the year. Winning at Boston was Moses Tanui (2:09:15), but he desired to compete in Atlanta at 10,000 meters rather than at the marathon distance. Thus, Kenyan selectors opted for second-place Ezekiel Bitok (2:09:26) and fourth-place Lameck Aguta (2:10:03), leaving third-place Cosmas N'Deti—three-time Boston winner—off the team for reasons unexplained.

Europe

Mexico's Dionicio Ceron won his third straight London title on April 21 (2:10:00) over Belgium's Vincent Rousseau. Having an aversion to warm-weather races, Rousseau typically preferred not to start if the temperature exceeded 17°C (62.6°F). As the gun sounded, it was 18°C (64.4°F) and Rousseau decided to race anyway, achieving an excellent 2:10:26. Paul Evans led his home nation's contingent with a fine 2:10:40, good for third, but he was not selected to the British team! Those spots went to Richard Nerurkar (1993 IAAF World Marathon Cup winner and seventh at the 1995 IAAF World Athletics Championships at Göteborg), Peter Whitehead (fourth at Göteborg), and Steve Brace (second at the Houston Marathon in January with a time of 2:10:35).

The Mexicans were expected to be a top-level challenge in Atlanta. They were only one time zone and a short flight away, and they could use both altitude and tropical training to prepare. Ceron was selected, as were Benjamin Paredes and German Silva (only 11th at London, but known for his toughness ever since winning at New York in 1994).

One week later, Ethiopia's reigning world record-holder, Belayneh Dinsamo, won his fourth Rotterdam race (2:10:30). He accompanied Mekonnen and Turbo Tumo to Atlanta. Tumo (2:10:34) had beaten Steve Brace at Houston and, in keeping with his penchant for racing several marathons a year, had also finished 20th at Boston.

Gold for Thugwane in a Down-to-the-Wire Tussle

The men's marathon was originally scheduled to start at 1845 (6:45 p.m.), to conjoin with the Closing Ceremonies. Previous climatological data had suggested that the hot, sunny, humid conditions likely at that time of day in Atlanta could put athletes in medical danger for such a competition (Martin 1996; Roos 1996). Reasoned debate by the IAAF Council eventually agreed, and the men's race was changed to the women's format. And so, the following Sunday morning, August 4, the men assembled and experienced conditions similar to those on the day of the women's race. Start time was 0705 (7:05 a.m.), the stadium was nearly empty, and the weather was foggy and drizzly. The beginning temperature was a slightly warmer 23.0°C (73.4°F), but the humidity was a similar 92 percent. The cloud cover was more dense, however, and by the time the winner crossed the finish line it was 25.6°C (78.1°F), but still quite humid (80 percent).

Also in similar fashion to the women's race, it was the largest and most global marathon in Olympic history. Seventeen full teams of 3 started the race. Seventy-nine NOCs (7 more than at Barcelona) provided a field of 124 athletes (6 more than at Seoul). Europe did not dominate in numbers of athletes, full teams, or NOCs. Africa did that again, with 37 athletes from 24 NOCs and 5 full teams. Europe was next with 36 athletes, 21 NOCs, and also 5 teams. North and Central America sent 18 athletes representing 12 NOCs, with full teams from the United States, Canada, and Mexico. South America was represented by 13 athletes and 9 NOCs; Brazil had the only full team. Similarly, Asia sent 16 athletes from 11 NOCs. Oceania was the least represented, having a full Australian team and 1 athlete from New Zealand.

The dynamics of the race, however, were far different for the men than for the women. Instead of a runaway by a new superstar, it was a huge pack (figure 24.4) that required nearly the entire race distance to separate even the medalists. At 5 kilometers, 10 athletes were timed in 16:14 using the ChampionChip recording system. Most notable among these were Lee Bong-ju, Kim Yi-yong, Taniguchi, Peu, and Mekonnen. The third Korean, Kim Wan-ki never made it out of the stadium, testing an injured foot and deciding to withdraw early. At 10 kilometers, the lead pack numbered 16 in a time of 31:51, with Poland's Grzegorz Gadjus pushing the pace at 31:50. At 15 kilometers, 5 were timed at 47:37, but the next 15 were only 1 second behind. Replacing Gadjus in the lone pace-pushing front position was Zimbabwe's Tendai Chimusasa (47:36). At 20 kilometers, 8 were all timed in 1:04:06, with 13 more 1 second behind.

Figure 24.4 On the second of three laps, Ikaji Salum [TAN] (number 2267) leads the men's marathon, followed closely by Ahmed Salah [DJI] (number 1320). Others in the front rank include Laurence Peu [RSA] (number 2481), Diamantino dos Santos [BRA] (number 1161), Julius Sumaye [TAN] (number 2268), and behind him, Erick Wainaina [KEN] (number 1819). Farther back in the pack are Steve Moneghetti [AUS] (number 1055, wearing sunglasses), Mark Coogan [USA] (number 2343), and Richard Nerurkar [GBR] (number 1500). Courtesy David Martin.

The midpoint lead was officially given to world record-holder Belayneh Dinsamo (1:07:36), but alongside him were Lee, Steve Moneghetti, Thugwane, Peu, and Burundi's Tharcisse Gashaka. And then there were the accompanying hordes just behind. The 25 kilometers timing station was just before the posh Lenox shopping mall, not far from the start point of the well-known 10 kilometers Peachtree Road Race course, most of which was used for the marathon. Thirteen runners were abreast (1:19:54): Thys, Peu, and Thugwane of South Africa; Silva and Paredes of Mexico; Luiz Antonio dos Santos and Lima from Brazil; as well as Nerurkar, Moneghetti, Chimusasa, Pinto, Juzdado, and Zaire's Mwenze Kalombo. But 12 more were another second behind, including Korea's Lee Bong-ju, so the lead pack was still huge. The three South Africans moved out in front slightly at 26 kilometers, along with Lee, but this lead was short-lived, and by 30 kilometers, as runners dashed along the downgrade toward Peachtree Creek, seven were abreast at 1:35:24, with 12 more 1 second behind.

It was Thugwane who then made the move that changed the nature of the race. As runners proceeded up the long grade cresting at Piedmont Hospital (making the name "Cardiac Hill" quite apt), Thugwane increased his pace slightly, and Erick Wainaina was the only runner to stay with him. They passed 35 kilometers in 1:50:35, 3 seconds ahead of Lee, with Martin Fiz and German Silva another second behind. Richard Nerurkar was in sixth (1:51:00), 6 seconds behind Fiz and Paredes. The next 5 kilometers saw Thugwane, Wainaina, and Lee race essentially together, each trying unsuccessfully to break the others on this rolling section of roadway as they passed throngs of spectators edging the skyscraper-lined streets. At 40 kilometers, and within sight of the Olympic stadium complex, Thugwane (2:06:08) was 1 second in front of Lee, who was 1 second ahead of Wainaina.

As runners approached the stadium for the finish of the race, about 8,000 spectators had assembled within. This was the only event occurring in the stadium, and most locals were at home watching the event on live television. Thugwane led the final dash through the stadium tunnel onto the track, with Lee only 20 meters behind and Wainaina even closer to Lee (figure 24.5). After a gut-wrenching final lap, Thugwane finished only 3 seconds ahead of Lee—compared to a 13 seconds separation in 1920 between Kolehmainen and Lossman. Wainaina, in third place, was only 8 seconds behind the winner, which was closer than the 27 seconds separating Bordin from Salah in 1988. The three recovered remarkably quickly considering their grueling effort (figure 24.6). Reigning European and world champion Martin Fiz had to settle for fourth, only his second loss in five starts. Table 24.5 summarizes the order of top athletes as they proceeded through the race.

Thugwane's victory earned the first Olympic gold medal won by a black South African, coming four days after black countryman Hezekiel Sepang's silver in the 800 meters. Thugwane carried his nation's flag proudly around the stadium for a victory lap. For him, it was an emotional high: although South Africans competed in Barcelona, they did so under the Olympic emblem and not their own flag. Mexican athletes performed the best as a team, placing 6th (Silva), 8th (Paredes), and 15th (Ceron) for the unofficial team score. Thugwane's

Figure 24.5 Dashing into Olympic stadium, Josiah Thugwane is pursued closely by Lee Bong-ju, creating the closest Olympic marathon finish in history. Courtesy David Martin.

TABLE 24.5

Order of Top Placers Through Control Points

	Thugwane	*Lee*	*Wainaina*	*Fiz*	*Nerurkar*	*Silva*
5 km	=22-37	=1-10	=11-21	=54-60	=11-21	=22-37
10 km	=2-16	=2-16	=17-25	=26-41	=26-41	=26-41
15 km	=1-6	=1-6	=7-22	=7-22	=23-35	=23-35
20 km	=1-8	=9-22	=9-22	=47-52	=9-22	=9-22
25 km	=1-12	=13-25	=13-25	=13-25	=1-12	=1-12
30 km	=1-7	=1-7	=1-7	=8-19	=8-19	=8-19
35 km	=1, 2	3	=1, 2	=4, 5	6	=4, 5
40 km	1	2	3	4	5	6
Finish	1	2	3	4	5	6

Figure 24.6 In victory, the three marathon men medalists share smiles: from left are Lee Bong-ju, Erick Wainaina, and Josiah Thugwane. Courtesy David Martin.

teammates Peu (27th) and Thys (33rd) ran well enough for South Africa to place 2nd, ahead of the Australians. Table 24.6 presents race results.

Altogether, 111 of 124 finished, for a remarkably low attrition rate of only 11.5 percent considering the difficulty of the day. At 0935 (9:35 a.m.), the sun suddenly broke through the clouds, and the temperature rose dramatically during the period when those runners having the greatest difficulties were struggling home.

Fortunately, only 14 athletes were still out on the course, and all but 1 were back in the stadium by 1010 (10:10 a.m.). That one was Afghanistan's Abdel Baser Wasiqi. His left leg wrapped to ease a muscle strain, he was now exposed to the fierce subtropical sun that everyone had dreaded before these Olympic Games began—the fog had cleared. Inside the stadium (figure 24.7), spectators had long departed, but the officials and medical personnel cheered him enthusiastically as he crossed the finish line indicated by a makeshift piece of tape (Emmons 1997). As the slowest finisher (4:24:17) in this first Olympic marathon century—male or female—his spirit was a fitting tribute to all those who had finished ahead of him.

TABLE 24.6

1996 Atlanta Olympic Men's Marathon at a Glance

Date:	04 August	**Weather:**	23.0°C (73.4°F)
Start time:	0705	**Starters:**	124
Course:	Out-and-back loop	**Finishers:**	111
Course distance:	42.195 km	**GPEs:**	79

TOP RESULTS:

Place	*Athlete*	*GPE*	*Date of birth*	*Time*
1	Josiah Thugwane	RSA	15 Apr. 1971	2:12:36
2	Lee Bong-ju	KOR	11 Oct. 1968	2:12:39
3	Erick Wainaina	KEN	19 Dec. 1973	2:12:44
4	Martin Fiz	ESP	03 Mar. 1963	2:13:20
5	Richard Nerurkar	GBR	06 Jan. 1964	2:13:39
6	German Silva	MEX	09 Jan. 1968	2:14:29
7	Stephen Moneghetti	AUS	26 Sept. 1962	2:14:35
8	Benjamin Paredes	MEX	07 Aug. 1961	2:14:55
9	Danilo Goffi	ITA	03 Dec. 1972	2:15:08
10	Luiz Antonio dos Santos	BRA	06 Apr. 1964	2:15:55

New geopolitical entities represented: Ukraine [UKR], Venezuela [VEN], Kyrgyzstan [KGZ], Lithuania [LIT], Indonesia [INA], Trinidad and Tobago [TRI], Moldova [MOL], Andorra [AND], Cape Verde [CPV], St. Vincent and the Grenadines [STV], Yemen [YEM], Mauritius [MRI], Cambodia [CAM], Bosnia and Herzegovina [BIH], Afghanistan [AFG], Burundi [BUR]

Team score (unofficial):			
	1. MEX	29 points	(6-8-15)
	2. RSA	61 points	(1-27-33)
	3. AUS	64 points	(7-23-34)

Notes on the Men Medalists

Born in Bethal, South Africa, about 120 miles east of Johannesburg, **Josiah Thugwane's** rise to Olympic gold is as interesting as it is amazing. As a Ndebele tribesboy, he grew up in the abject poverty that characterized black South Africa. The choice for earning a living as an adult was either farming the veld or working the mines. He discovered that small amounts of prize money were offered at road races, but the competition even for such pittances was intense. He raced hard, and eventually his running skills landed him a mining job, which paid better than farming but had more dangers. The mines had intercompany competitions, and the company sought to benefit both from his racing excellence and his strong work ethic. Through an agent, he managed to secure an occasional international trip, but the arduous travel and strange environments

Figure 24.7 The final Olympic marathon finisher in the first Olympic century, Afghanistan's Abdel Baser Wasiqi smiles in delight as he completes his Olympic experience. Courtesy Perry H. Julien.

were challenging for even his tough constitution. He experienced four miserable race results: 13th at Honolulu at the end of 1993, 28th at Kyongju in the spring of 1994, a DNF at Chicago that fall, and another DNF in the bitter cold of New York in 1995. It was the fifth such experience that turned his fortune around. One month after the New York race, he found himself back in Honolulu. This was the year of its famous heat wave (90 percent humidity and 28.4°C or 83.1°F), and he won in 2:16:08.

He then set his sights on an Olympic team berth, but this meant that he had to win his national championship at Cape Town in February 1996. Because the team had already been determined, only the winner of this race could "bump" one of the team selectees from the roster. His 2:11:46 victory was a dream come true. His life was now coming together. His second daughter had just been born, and he was an Olympian. Unfortunately, tragedy struck when he picked up some local hitchhikers on the way home from work one day. Shots were fired in an unsuccessful attempt to rob him. One bullet's trajectory is still etched on his chin, where, luckily, it caused only a grazing scar (Montville 1996).

The South African marathon team traveled to Albuquerque, a city at altitude in the United States (1,507 meters, 4,945 feet), to reside and prepare. Four athletes were there, one as a reserve, with fitness in the final days determining who would watch the three compete. They were as diverse as South Africa itself: Lawrence Peu was a Pedi, Xolile Yawa was a Xhosa, Gert Thys was mixed ancestry ("colored"), and Thugwane was a Ndebele. One week before the Olympic Games race, Peu was substituted for Yawa, who had developed a stress fracture in his left leg. After experiencing the Opening Ceremonies, they went back to Albuquerque, returning to Atlanta three days before the race. Their race plan was to work together as long as possible to set up the best conditions for one of them to capture the gold medal. Thugwane took advantage of the opportunity.

From one perspective, Thugwane's life improved after the Games. He received a government bonus of $33,000, a Mercedes-Benz, sponsorship offers, and more. He now lives in a middle-class home on a paved street adjacent to the Koornfontein Mines property. But not all of life is rosy. His home must be protected. He travels with a bodyguard to help counter threats on his life and protect his wife and four children. During 1997, his training and racing went very successfully, and his third place at London and victory at Fukuoka were both personal bests. Since then, however, he has failed to finish three subsequent marathon attempts during 1998 and 1999. Table 24.7 presents a summary of Thugwane's marathon career.

Lee Bong-ju first entered the international marathon scene with a 7th-placed 2:19:18 effort at the December 1992 Honolulu Marathon. Winning at Kyongju the following March with a quick 2:10:58, his potential talent at distance running was obvious. Returning to Honolulu in December 1993, he won easily in 2:13:16, showing as well his ability to manage heat and humidity successfully. The Boston Marathon organizers were intrigued with his talent, too, and they invited him to their 1994 race. He scored another personal best of 2:09:57, which also was a national record, but the Boston field was so good that year that he placed only 11th! That experience toughened Lee as a competitor. He then focused on Korean competitions for the next 18 months, achieving a 2:09:54 victory at Chunchon in September 1994, a 2:10:58 victory at Kyongju in March 1995, and a 4th-placed 2:12:00 at Chunchon in October 1995. This consistency gave him confidence at his Olympic trial race at Kyongju in March 1996. His 2nd-placed 2:08:26 assured his place on the team.

Those who knew the Korean marathon scene thus knew that Lee would be strong in Atlanta. Since those Games, he has lowered his personal best (and the Korean record) to 2:07:44 at Rotterdam in 1998. Later that year, he was also the Asian Games champion in steamy Bangkok with an outstanding 2:12:32.

Born at altitude in Nyahururu, **Erick Wainaina** became the second Kenyan Olympic marathon medalist in this first century of the event. Judging from the enormous numbers of Kenyan distance runners who are making the marathon their specialty, he may be joined by more at Sydney and beyond. Following the pattern set by 1988 Olympic silver medalist Douglas Wakiihuri, he has lived and trained in Japan, which explains why his record contains only Japanese marathon performances except for major world championship competitions.

TABLE 24.7

Career Marathon Record of Josiah Thugwane

Date	Venue	Place	Time	Comments
21 Apr. 1990	Witbank	2nd	2:22:24	
02 Feb. 1991	Nelspruit	1st	2:18:00	
06 Apr. 1991	Ngodwana	1st	2:13:48	
20 July 1991	Durban	6th	2:14:00	
28 Mar. 1992	Cape Town	4th	2:13:36	
04 Apr. 1992	Ngodwana	1st	2:17:42	
05 Jan. 1993	Tiberias	3rd	2:18:42	
20 Mar. 1993	Cape Town	1st	2:14:25	
13 Nov. 1993	Pretoria	1st	2:15:57	
12 Dec. 1993	Honolulu	13th	2:29:16	
20 Mar. 1994	Kyongju	28th	2:24:52	
30 Oct. 1994	Chicago	DNF		
04 Dec. 1994	Soweto	5th	2:22:26	
01 Apr. 1995	Ngodwana	1st	2:18:47	
14 Oct. 1995	Bredasdorp	1st	2:26:39	
12 Nov. 1995	New York	DNF		
10 Dec. 1995	Honolulu	1st	2:16:08	
25 Feb. 1996	Cape Town	1st	2:11:46	
04 Aug. 1996	Atlanta	1st	2:12:36	Olympic Games
01 Dec. 1996	Fukuoka	DNF		
13 Apr. 1997	London	3rd	2:08:06	
07 Dec. 1997	Fukuoka	1st	2:07:28	
26 Apr. 1998	London	DNF		
01 Nov. 1998	New York	DNF		
18 Apr. 1999	London	DNF		
05 Dec. 1999	Fukuoka	26th	2:17:01	

Debuting at Sapporo in 1994 with a winning 2:15:03, he improved dramatically to 2:10:31 (still his personal best) with a victory at Tokyo in early 1995. This qualified him for the IAAF World Athletics Championships in 1995, where he placed only 18th (2:19:53). Following the same pattern, he was runner-up with another fine 2:10:37 at Otsu in February of 1996, which guaranteed his entry for Atlanta. His bronze medal effort is still his third-fastest performance, and he remains a top-level competitor. In 1997, he was again victorious in the summertime heat of Sapporo (2:15:03), and he remains a possible contender for a team berth to Sydney.

Looking Ahead: Brief Highlights 1996-1999

1996: Post-Olympic action saw Spanish debutante Abel Anton win at Berlin (September 29) in 2:09:15, with the 1995 winner Sammy Lelei only third. In Chicago (October 20), Britain's Paul Evans scored his first major victory (2:08:52), over a minute ahead of Jerry Lawson of the United States (2:10:04). Only Steve Jones and Charlie Spedding had run faster among British runners. Giacomo Leone was a surprise winner in the New York City Marathon on November 3 (2:09:54), beating, among others, Atlanta fourth placer Martin Fiz. Finally, despite snow and strong winds, the 50th Fukuoka Marathon saw an epic struggle on December 1. Lee Bong-ju outsprinted Alberto Juzdado to win by a couple of seconds (2:10:48). Thugwane didn't finish.

Among the women, South Africa's Colleen de Reuck won at Berlin (2:26:35), a personal best by more than four minutes. At New York, Romania's Anuta Catuna improved on her 1995 IAAF World Athletics Championships runner-up performance with a victory and national record (2:26:18). The prerace favorite, Tegla Loroupe, could not match her own 1995 and 1996 victories, and here she placed only seventh. Italy's Franca Fiacconi, having won her national championship two weeks earlier (2:28:22 at Carpi), was also impressive at New York with the runner-up time of 2:28:42.

1997: The European classics began with London (April 13), where the first six men all bettered 2:09:00. Antonio Pinto (a personal best 2:07:55) outlasted Stefano Baldini (a national record 2:07:57), with Atlanta Olympic champion Josiah Thugwane third in a personal best of 2:08:06. Seven days later, at Rotterdam, another Portuguese runner, Domingos Castro (2:07:51) won by 3 seconds over Alejandro Gomez, who further lowered the Spanish record.

The next day, April 21, the Boston Marathon was a showcase for Kenyans, as they placed one-two-five-six-seven. Lameck Aguta took the podium this time (2:10:34) as the seventh successive Kenyan to accept the winner's trophy. In Asia, Abel Anton overcame wind and rain to win the Korean Dong-A race on March 16 (2:12:37). Anton peaked again at the right moment and won the IAAF World Athletics Championships in Athens on August 10. His 2:13:16 was only 5 seconds faster than defending champion Fiz.

The Northern Hemisphere autumn saw a superfast result at Berlin on September 28 as Elijah Lagat (2:07:41) led a Kenyan sweep ahead of Eric Kimaiyo (2:07:43) and Sammy Lelei (2:08:00). Morocco's Khalid Khannouchi won at Chicago (October 19) in 2:07:10, for a national record and a debut record performance as well. Kenyan runners took the next four places. Later, at New York on November 2, two more Kenyans scored well as John Kagwe (2:08:12) and Joseph Chebet placed one-two. On the same day, another Kenyan, Sammy Lelei, having recovered from Berlin, won at Amsterdam with a course record 2:08:24. The year closed at Fukuoka on December 6, and this time Atlanta Olympic

(continued)

champion Josiah Thugwane was hungry to race. His 2:07:28 win was a national record. World champion Anton was a distant fourth, his first loss in four races.

Women marathon runners also performed very well. Katrin Dörre-Heinig scored her fourth win at Osaka (2:25:57) on January 26, her 21st career victory. In London, although Liz McColgan set a personal best of 2:26:52, she lost by a second to Joyce Chepchumba, who established a Kenyan national record. In third was Lidia Simon (2:27:11). One week later, in Rotterdam, Tegla Loroupe ran a Commonwealth record 2:22:07, making her the fourth-fastest all-time. Atlanta Olympic champion Fatuma Roba was a convincing winner in Boston (2:26:23) ahead of the South African duo of Elana Meyer (2:27:09) and Colleen de Reuck (2:28:03).

In the IAAF World Athletics Championships at Athens on August 9, Japan's Hiromi Suzuki, running her third marathon, challenged the reigning Maria Manuela Machado [POR] on a hot day over a hilly course, and won (2:29:48 to 2:31:12), with the consistent Simon in third (2:31:55). In the fall, Ireland's Catherina McKiernan became the sixth-fastest marathon debutante with her victory and national record 2:23:44 at Berlin. Not far behind were Madina Biktagirova (2:24:46) with a Belarus record, and Marleen Renders (2:26:18).

The United States fall classics at Chicago and New York had fewer marquee names than usual, but the top performances were excellent. Britain's Marian Sutton won at the former with a personal best (2:29:03), and Switzerland's Franziska Rochat-Moser won at the Big Apple (2:28:43) ahead of de Reuck (2:29:11). Victorious at Tokyo on November 30 was Makiko Ito (2:27:45), who had also placed third (2:26:03) at Rotterdam earlier in the year. Ito was 17 seconds ahead of London winner Chepchumba.

1998: Spanish runners dominated the Japanese men-only races early in the year. At Tokyo on February 8, Alberto Juzdado's 2:08:01 was a personal best and a course record. At Otsu on March 1, Martin Fiz's 2:09:33 was good for second behind Muneyuki Ojima, who ran 2:08:43 in only his fourth marathon. The Spaniards continued strongly in Europe later in the spring, as Fabian Roncero set a national record 2:07:26 with his Rotterdam victory on April 19. One week later, in London, Abel Anton also broke 2:08:00 (by 3 seconds) in staying ahead of Moroccan Abdelkader El Mouaziz (2:08:07) and Portugal's Anacleto Pinto (2:08:13). Anton missed Pinto's course record by just 2 seconds; Pinto had won in 1997. In Boston on April 20, three runners bettered 2:08:00 for the first time as 1996 winner Moses Tanui (2:07:34) outsprinted colleague Joseph Chebet by 3 seconds. Gert Thys was back in top form with his third-place 2:07:52, and Brazilian Andre Ramos set a South American continental record with 2:08:26, good for fourth.

The fall marathon season started out with drama on September 20 as Brazil's Ronaldo da Costa made history by shattering the 10-years-old world marathon record by 45 seconds at Berlin. He achieved his incredible 2:06:05 with even more amazing half marathon splits of 1:04:42 and 1:01:23! Da Costa's one previous marathon had been a fifth place at Berlin in 1997 (2:09:07). Three Kenyans trailed behind: Josephat Kiprono (2:07:27, his second marathon), Samson Kandie (2:09:11), and Reuben Chebutich.

Another Kenyan, Ondoro Osoro, set a men's world debut record with his 2:06:55 (third fastest in history) three weeks later, in Chicago on October 11. Four athletes bettered 2:08:00 in that race: 1997 winner Khalid Khannouchi was second (2:07:19), followed by the consistent Gert Thys (2:07:45), and Kenyan Joseph Kahugu (2:07:59, a personal best by more than three minutes). Kenyan runners continued their marathon domination with wins at both New York (John Kagwe in 2:08:44) and Amsterdam (Sammy Lelei, 2:08:13) on the same day (November 1). Both had won these races the previous year.

The women performed as spectacularly as the men in 1998. At Osaka on January 25, Simon scored her first major victory (2:28:31), holding off four-time winner Dörre-Heinig (2:28:38). Later, at Nagoya on March 8, Naoko Takahashi, running only her second marathon, amazed everyone with a national record 2:25:48.

On April 19, Tegla Loroupe clocked half marathon splits of 1:10:11 and 1:10:36 to cover the marathon distance in 2:20:47 at Rotterdam—the fastest in history. Unfortunately, she was paced by two Kenyan men, who effectively shielded her from the gusty winds and caused controversy over the appropriateness of such planned assistance in mixed races.

On the next day (April 20), in Boston, Olympic gold medalist Roba became the fifth-fastest all-time with another win and national record of 2:23:21, four minutes clear of her rivals. At London, McKiernan (2:26:26) scored her second victory in two marathon attempts, finishing ahead of a splendid field that saw five faster than 2:29:00.

Revealing the increasing strength of Kenyan women marathoners, 1997 London winner Chepchumba challenged a top-class Chicago field on October 11 and scored another personal best (2:23:57). South Africans de Reuck (2:27:04) and Meyer (2:27:20) had to settle for second and third. The Chicago Marathon was the first occasion where a Kenyan man and woman shared the winner's podium. Ireland's McKiernan ran even faster (2:22:23) to win a cold, windy Amsterdam Marathon on November 1, moving to fifth on the all-time list. On the same day, in New York, victory went to Italy's Franca Fiacconi (2:25:17), a new Italian national record.

Closing the year, at the Asian Games in Bangkok on December 6, Takahashi was again impressive on a steamy morning, running solo in a race that had only nine other competitors. Her 2:21:43 was the fastest point-to-point performance in a women-only race. The impressiveness of her performance was diluted because the course was slightly downhill and there was a favoring breeze.

1999: An attempt at breaking da Costa's new world best almost was successful at the Tokyo Marathon on February 14, with South Africa's Gert Thys (2:06:33) lowering his national record, well in front of Japan's Hiroshi Miki (2:08:05).

(continued)

The two-day period including April 18 and April 19 was unprecedented for fast marathon running. Major races occurred at Antwerp, Bordeaux, London, Nagano, Rotterdam, Santiago, and Boston. At Rotterdam, for the first time in history, five men were under 2:08:00, led by Kenyan Japhet Kosgei's 2:07:09 victory. Close behind, two Spanish athletes achieved personal bests: Fabian Roncero (2:07:23) and Julio Rey (2:07:37) (although Rey was later suspended from competition for a positive drug test for mesterolone). Kenyans Jackson Kabiga and Joseph Chebet won at Nagano (2:13:26) and Boston (2:09:52), respectively. In all, 23 Kenyan men broke 2:20:00 during these two days. Moroccan Abdelkader el Mouaziz dominated by 63 seconds at London (2:07:57) over 1997 London winner Antonio Pinto.

The major race of the year was the IAAF World Athletics Championships over a flat three-laps course through the streets of Seville. Scorching heat slowed performances, but Spain's Abel Anton delighted the home crowd with his 2:13:26, ahead of Italy's Vincenzo Modica by 27 seconds. It was his second world championship gold, making him a solid threat for a medal in Sydney.

For the women, the Osaka International Ladies Marathon on January 31 again was a thriller, as 1998 winner Lidia Simon challenged Tegla Loroupe, holder of the world's fastest time in a mixed race. They fought to the finish, with Simon the victor (2:23:24) by only 22 seconds. Simon eclipsed Lisa Martin's world best in a women-only out-and-back race, set at Osaka in 1988. Kenyans also dominated at the major April marathons. At London on April 18, Joyce Chepchumba was victorious over a superb field (2:23:22), while on the European continent on that same day, Loroupe scored the year's fastest time with 2:22:50 at Rotterdam. One day later, Atlanta Olympic champion Fatuma Roba captured her third Boston victory (2:23:25) with a decisive win over 1997 New York winner Franziska Rochat-Moser and Atlanta Olympic bronze medalist Yuko Arimori.

One week following that busy weekend, Katrin Dörre-Heinig amazed even herself with a personal best 2:24:35 in winning at Hamburg. She was already the most accomplished woman marathoner in history, and one could only be further astounded: this was her 40th career marathon completed, her 24th marathon victory over a span of 17 years, and her 20th sub-2:30:00 performance (compared with Grete Waitz's 13).

The IAAF World Athletics Championships in Seville in August featured an amazing upset as North Korea's entirely unheralded Jong Song-ok out-sprinted Japan's Ari Ichihashi on the track to win (2:26:59) by only 3 seconds. Lidia Simon took home the bronze (2:27:41), upsetting Atlanta Olympic champion Fatuma Roba in a race that saw an unprecedented 11 athletes under 2:30:00.

References

Anonymous. 1997. *The Official Report of the Centennial Olympic Games*. Vol. 3, *The competition results*. Atlanta: Peachtree Publishers.

Emmons, J. 1997. The last marathoner. *Marathon and Beyond* 1 (4): 57-64.

Jones, H. 1996. Improved Atlanta course profile. *Measurement News* 77: 3-4.

Lyberg, W.S. 1997a. Figures from Atlanta. *Journal of Olympic History* 5 (1): 28-29.
Lyberg, W.S. 1997b. I cannot say anything else but the truth! *Journal of Olympic History* 5 (2): 10-15.
Martin, D.E. 1996. Climatic heat stress studies at the Atlanta 1996 Olympic stadium venue, 1992-1995. *Sports Medicine, Training, and Rehabilitation* 6: 249-267.
Martin, D.E. 1999. Measurement of climatic heat stress at outdoor venues for endurance events at the Atlanta Olympic Games, 1996. *Sports Medicine, Training, and Rehabilitation* 8: 321-346.
Montville, L. 1996. Run for your life. *Sports Illustrated* 85 (17): 74-89.
Riegel, P. 1996. Distance and elevation data for the Olympic marathon. *Measurement News* 74: 7-8.
Roos, R. 1996. Heat stress in Atlanta. *Physician and Sportsmedicine* 24 (6): 89-99.
Saporta, M. 1996. *The Atlanta Journal-Constitution*, August 6.
Spangler, J. 1996. In their own words: The American women. *Runner's World* 31 (11): 86.

CHAPTER 25

2000—SYDNEY

Sydney's Sports Spectacle Ends the Second Millennium

The Games Go "Down Under" Once Again

While organizers of the Centennial Olympic Games of Atlanta were in the midst of preparations, on the evening of September 24, 1993, the IOC gathered at its 101st session to select the site for its Games of 2000. These festivities occurred in the Salle des Etoiles of the Sporting d'Eté in Monte Carlo, an elegant concert plaza and open air cinema. The choice was between Beijing, Berlin, Istanbul, Manchester, and Sydney—once again a broad spectrum of cultures and geography. Table 25.1 shows how the balloting proceeded, although for the first time, the voting delegates themselves did not see these numbers during the process, learning only which city was removed after each round (Anonymous 1997).

At 2030 (8:30 p.m.) in Monaco, IOC president Samaranch announced that Sydney had won over Beijing. Fireworks dazzled the predawn sky over Sydney (it was 4:30 in the morning), while back in Monte Carlo, signatures placed on

TABLE 25.1

Results of the 2000 Olympic Games Vote

City	*Round one*	*Round two*	*Round three*	*Round four*
Sydney	30	30	37	45
Beijing	32	37	40	43
Manchester	11	13	11	
Berlin	9	9		
Istanbul	7			

the official documents launched the Sydney Organizing Committee for the Olympic Games (SOCOG) into existence for a very busy seven years of preparations.

For all of Australia, this was an uplifting moment. A nation with only 17 million people prevailed over one that was home to more than a billion. Perhaps fittingly, Australia's support of the Olympic movement was in a real sense being honored; along with Greece, Great Britain, Switzerland, and France, it had never missed an Olympic Games. In recent years, its steadily improving sporting excellence had been noteworthy. Placing 15th in the Olympic medal count in 1988 with 14, Australia improved to 9th in 1992 with 27 medals, 5 ahead of Spain. In 1996 it finished 5th with 41 medals, behind the United States (101), Germany (65), Russia (63), and China (50). Recall how the Korean and Spanish athletes in 1988 and 1992 performed exceptionally well before their respective home crowds. The stage is now set for the Australians to follow suit.

With Sydney as far south of the equator (33.55°S) as Atlanta is north of it (33.45°N), the Olympic Games would return to the Southern Hemisphere for only the second time in their history. Back in 1956, the Games were in Melbourne (which won by only 1 vote over Buenos Aires, 21 to 20), then the primary financial center of influence in Australia. That center of focus eventually shifted to Sydney, which, with more than three million residents, is now also the nation's largest city.

These will be the final Olympic Games of the second millennium and the 20th century, and not the first Games of the third millennium and the 21st century. The explanation is simple (Baumel 1992): "the only way to unambiguously define the term 'millennium' is by the year numbers in the present Christian calendar. The key factor is that there never was a year zero (the year 1 A.D. was preceded by 1 B.C.). Thus, the first millennium extended from 1 A.D. through 1000 A.D. The second millennium from 1001 A.D. through 2000 A.D." If the first two millennia are indeed to each contain 1,000 years, the third millennium must begin on January 1, 2001, leaving 2000 a year of little note except for its rarity as a year with three zeroes. This proper reckoning of time seems to have been lost on the marketers of everything from tours to tee shirts welcoming January 1, 2000, incorrectly as the start of both the next millennium and century, with major celebratory marathons conducted in both Hamilton, New Zealand, and Rome.

Several aspects of Sydney's bid were attractive. One was the expectation of moderate weather. For marathon runners this is especially good news. Scheduled for September 15 through October 1, the Olympic Games occur during Australia's springtime. September is also Sydney's driest month, so the combination of moderate temperatures and low humidity create an ideal climate for excellent outdoor competition.

A second attractive feature involved the proposed centralization of facilities to optimize transportation logistics. Sydney's enormous Olympic Park was already rising from a vast reclaimed industrial and marshland area in suburban Homebush Bay, 14 kilometers west of the city center. For the first time, all athletes will be housed in just one Olympic Village, located in the park, which also has the main stadium for the ceremonies and track and field, along with stadia for aquatic events, gymnastics, baseball, tennis, and more. The media village is also planned for this region, along with the international broadcast center. A combination of ferries around the harbor, improved highways, and an expanded commuter rail system that will directly access the park should ensure manageable traffic flow for spectators.

A third desirable element of the Sydney bid was that it seemed "politically safe" (Findling and Pelle 1996). Virtually all local press and politicians wrote and spoke favorably about it. Sydney's infrastructure was superior to that of Beijing, often considered its stiffest competitor—particularly regarding air quality and availability of accommodations. And no governments had campaigned against Sydney, in contrast to criticism directed by the United States Congress against Beijing.

Some of the Sydney Games events will be shared among the other major cities of Australia. Large stadia in Adelaide, Brisbane, Canberra, and Melbourne will be used for the preliminary rounds of soccer. This means that the venerable Melbourne Cricket ground will once again become an Olympic venue. Previously, only the Los Angeles Coliseum has been a venue for more than one Olympic Games (the Panathenaikon stadium was also used for the Intercalated Games).

Even before the competition begins, some records have toppled, and several more may fall. One record already broken was by NBC television, which paid $715 million in cash for exclusive broadcast rights to the Sydney Games—dwarfing the $456 million that it doled out for the Atlanta Games. The network concluded the deal in private discussion with the IOC, with neither CBS nor ABC included. Totaling $1.26 billion, the package also includes the rights to broadcast the Salt Lake City Winter Games in 2002.

A second record already established includes the use of three Olympic mascots, not just one. Except for the Atlanta Games, whose computer morph, termed "Whatizit," failed to catch attention, mascots have successfully enhanced Games promotion, dating back to Munich's Waldi, the dachshund. Australia is showcasing the diversity of its native species, giving them names that reflect the global nature of the Olympic Games. There is Millie (for millennium), an echidna, or spiny anteater; Olly (for Olympic), a kookaburra bird; and Syd (for Sydney), a duckbilled platypus.

One record likely to be broken at Sydney is that for single-venue attendance. Whereas 101,022 attended the 1932 Los Angeles Olympic Opening Ceremonies (Anonymous 1933), Sydney's newly completed Stadium Australia seated 104,583 for its opening event, a rugby doubleheader on March 6, 1999. It was a world attendance record for any rugby match. Seating capacity for this mammoth venue has been announced as 110,000 for the Olympic Games, before subsequent planned reduction and reconfiguration to 80,000 for team sports.

Another record sure to fall is the unprecedented journey of 60,852 kilometers (37,820 miles) for the Olympic flame as it travels from Greece (Anonymous 1999a). It will be kindled in May and then will be taken on an unprecedented tour of all Pacific Ocean NOCs—American Samoa, the Cook Islands, Micronesia, Fiji, Guam, Nauru, New Zealand, Papua and New Guinea, the Solomon Islands, Tonga, Vanuatu, and Samoa—before reaching Australian soil on June 8. After arriving at the nation's symbolic center at Uluru near Ayre's Rock, it will make an equally complex trek through much of Australia and arrive in the Olympic stadium on September 15. Great care is being taken to ensure that the relay proceeds in a manner that prevents it from becoming a tool of political or commercial abuse, as has often occurred in the past (Cahill 1999).

Midway during SOCOG's preparations for the Olympic Games, a brief pause occurred for sharing in the excitement of the IOC's selection activities in choosing the 2004 Olympic Games site. This celebration occurred at the 106th IOC session at Lausanne on September 6, 1997. The meeting was historic, as IOC president Samaranch was reelected unanimously for another term of four years, and for the first time a woman was elected as an IOC vice president (Anita DeFrantz of the United States). When voting began for the 2004 host city, a tie occurred between Cape Town and Buenos Aires on round one of the voting. This required a special round two runoff that Cape Town won. Athens steadily gained support, although again those voting knew only which city was removed for each successive round. As table 25.2 shows, on the fifth ballot Athens gained a clear vote majority, and the Greeks delightedly started preparing to welcome the Games back to the site of their modern revival 108 years earlier.

TABLE 25.2

Results of the 2004 Olympic Games Vote

City	*Round one*	*Round two*	*Round three*	*Round four*	*Round five*
Athens	32		38	52	66
Rome	23		28	35	41
Cape Town	16	62	22	20	
Stockholm	20		19		
Buenos Aires	16	44			

Hills Replace Heat as a Challenge on the Marathon Course

The Sydney Olympic marathon route as outlined in the original bid proposal would have worried any elite runner advised of its details. Sydney is a hilly city surrounding a large harbor with multiple bays and inlets. The suggested route seemed like a tour of these hills with many sharp turns along the way. Fortunately, once the Olympic Games were awarded, the road events manager who was hired to supervise the marathons and race walks, Dave Cundy, had experience both as a marathon race director and as a top-level IAAF-certified course measurer. Sensible changes in course layout were incorporated successfully, and the final route is more favorably disposed to fast racing, with many fewer hills and turns.

The Opening Ceremonies are scheduled for Friday evening, September 15, with competition beginning the next day. As planned, the women's marathon occurs on the ninth day of competition (Sunday, September 24). It will start at 0900 (9:00 a.m.). No events are scheduled after this one on the morning program, so all athletes should finish in the main stadium. The men's race, which will close the competition for the Olympic Games, will begin at 1600 (4:00 p.m.) on Sunday, October 1, and is timed to coordinate with the Closing Ceremonies. Since 1984, the Closing Ceremonies have been timed to coincide with the completion of the men's marathon. Atlanta was an exception to this recent tradition in that the marathon was held early in the day to avoid the afternoon heat (Martin 1999). Any finishers slower than 3:10:00 will be directed to an alternate finish line, the adjacent Sydney International Athletics Field.

Figure 25.1 illustrates the plan for the course, current as of this writing, subject to changes following the official final course measurement. An opportunity for Olympic hopefuls as well as those "back in the pack" to experience the Olympic marathon course is being provided on April 30, 2000. Known as The Host City Marathon, this is the official SOCOG test event for the venue, incorporating the Australian marathon championship. It will also be Australia's final Olympic marathon team selection race, with its team being composed of those athletes delivering the best performances from either this event or from the IAAF World Athletics Championships in Seville during 1999. Preferred status will be given to 150 top runners from around the world who can be considered as Olympic team hopefuls. They will experience the same logistical support as will Olympic athletes at the Games in terms of transport to the start, special drinks along the way, and split timing of their performance. A people's race will be conducted simultaneously, open to those who believe they can meet the strictly enforced five hours time limit to complete the distance.

Organizers are eager for this test opportunity to discover in advance any remaining adjustments necessary to ensure a problem-free racing environment during the Olympic Games marathons. After these adjustments are made, the final official "group ride" will occur. A select small number of course measurement experts from around the world will use calibrated bicycles with Jones counters to precisely document the details of each kilometer.

The start is 13.6 kilometers from the finish, which is 32.2 percent of the race distance. IAAF guidelines suggest that greater than 30 percent start and finish separation shall categorize the course as "point-to-point." Also, because its net drop of 71 meters from start (80 meters) to finish (9 meters) is greater than 1 meter per kilometer (1.68 meters per kilometer), the course is considered as downhill, or potentially aided. However, this should not suggest that the course is easy, as will be clear in the description given below and as seen on the course map (figure 25.1).

The start is alongside the North Sydney Oval. This is a beautiful old cricket and football ground, with a grassy oval surrounded by grandstands maintained in the best of English tradition. These stands will be used for runner preparation, and the setting will provide a pleasant and private warm-up spot for athletes before starting the races. Competition, however, will start on adjacent Miller Street, where spectators will be able to watch the start of the race.

The majority of the course descent occurs in the first few kilometers. Proceeding southward, runners cross the spectacular Sydney Harbor Bridge and view its adjacent and equally renowned Opera House along the shoreline toward their left. They then skirt the city center, incorporate a 4 kilometers loop through Centennial Park, and continue to the turnaround point in suburban Kingsford.

Returning to the city center, the course then proceeds west toward Olympic Park. While there is little net change in elevation for the final 14 kilometers, the incessantly rolling terrain will demand ever-changing pace and/or work intensity. The portion between 25 and 37 kilometers is particularly challenging in this regard, but a noticeable uphill also occurs at 40 kilometers. The men will face the setting sun, as in Barcelona, while the sun will not pose a problem for the women. For both events, however, athletes will face a final 14 kilometers of prevailing west-to-east head winds. The races finish in the Olympic stadium at the standard track event finish line. Runners will enter the stadium from the northwest, arrive onto the track just behind the 100 meters sprint start line, continue to the finish line, and make one full lap before ending their journey. Thus, stadium spectators will see the final 500-plus meters of competition. A tentative listing of streets for the Sydney Olympic marathon course is provided in the course details box.

Scandal and the Specter of Drugs Cause Concern During Preparations

Perks for Votes

Unlike the approach to many previous Olympic Games, the end of the 1990s was relatively free of the kinds of external political strife that suggested Games disruption through boycott or global conflict. The IOC was stronger than ever

Course Details

The 2000 Sydney Olympic Marathon

Start on Miller Street, outside North Sydney Oval

Continue south (downhill) to Pacific Highway

Half left onto Pacific Highway to roadway entrance for Sydney Harbour Bridge

Enter lanes two, three, and four of roadway on the bridge, transitioning to lanes seven and eight

Cross Sydney Harbour (Routes 2, 40), proceed through the toll plaza

Angle left onto Cahill Expressway

Exit Cahill Expressway onto Bridge Street and then onto Macquarie Street

Left (south) onto Macquarie Street

Pass New South Wales Parliament House (~5 kilometers)

At Queens Square, where Macquarie Street ends, half left onto Prince Albert Road to College Street

Half right onto College Street, passing Hyde Park, to Whitlam Square

Half left onto Oxford Street to Taylor Square

Half right onto Flinders Street, which crosses South Darling Street and then becomes Anzac Parade

Continue south on Anzac Parade to Old Grand Drive

Left onto Old Grand Drive into Centennial Park, encircling the Park's central expanse for ~4.5 kilometers (~10 kilometers is near the Federation Pavilion) and returning to Anzac Parade

Left onto Anzac Parade, continuing past the University of New South Wales into suburban Kingsford

Continue south to turnaround point just north of Avoca Street intersection in suburban Kingsford

Return northward on Anzac Parade to Flinders Street (~23 kilometers)

Half left onto Flinders Street to Taylor Square

Half left onto Oxford Street to Liverpool Street

Left onto Liverpool Street, passing the south side of Hyde Park, to Elizabeth Street

Right onto Elizabeth Street alongside west side of Hyde Park to Bathurst Street

Left onto Bathurst Street (~25 kilometers) and proceed west to Anzac Bridge in suburban Pyrmont

After the bridge crossing, follow City West Link Road in suburban Lilyfield to Dobroyd Parade in suburban Haberfield

Continue on Dobroyd Parade to Ramsay Road

Right on Ramsay Road (~32 kilometers) to Fairlight Street in suburban Five Dock

Left onto Fairlight Street, crossing Great North Road and continuing as Queens Road past Williams Street (~35 kilometers)

Queens Road becomes Gipps Street in suburban Canada Bay

Continue on Gipps Street to Sydney Street in suburban Concord

Left onto Sydney Street to its end at Concord Road

Cross Concord Road onto the exit ramp off the M4 Motorway in suburban Strathfield

Continue along eastbound lanes of the M4, entering Sydney Olympic Park via bus tunnel ("mouse hole") in suburban Homebush Bay

Proceed on Olympic Boulevard around southeast and southwest sides of Olympic stadium to the marathon tunnel on the west side

Through the stadium tunnel onto the stadium track near the 100 meters sprint start

Continue to the finish line, then run one additional lap around to end at the standard finish line for running events

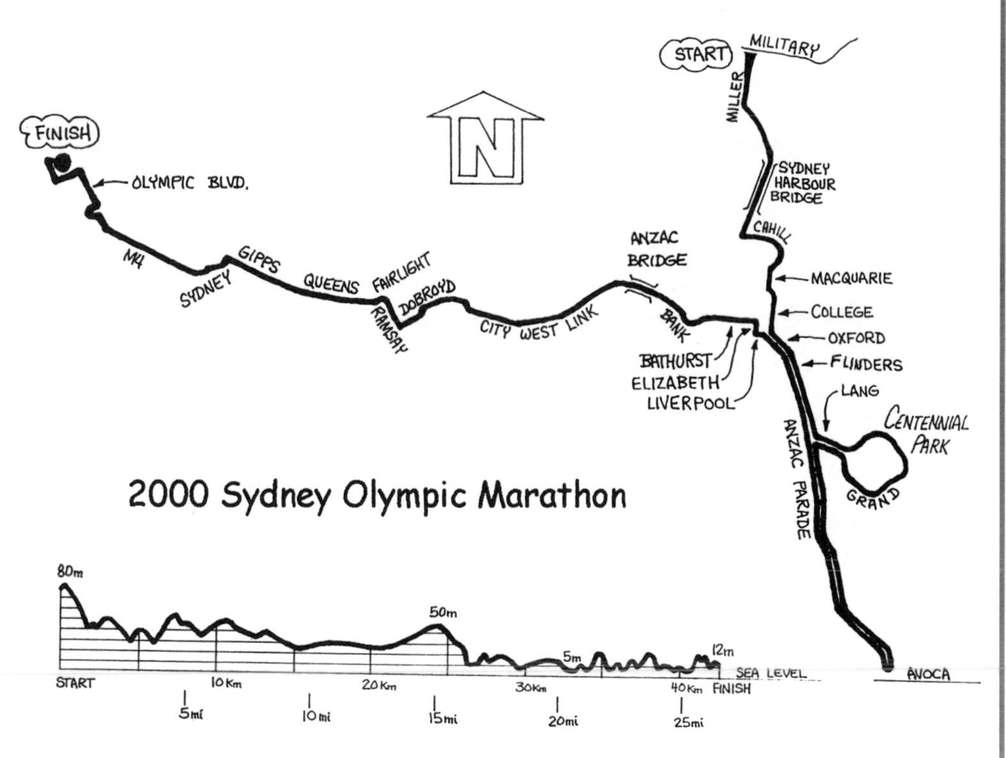

Figure 25.1 Sketch of the Sydney Olympic marathon course. Note that the various street descriptors (road, street, parade, etc.) have been omitted for simplicity. Prepared by Bob Letson.

financially, and the Olympic movement's stature as a positive social force for society had given the IOC continuing momentum and influence. However, in November 1998, revelations surfaced that the votes of some IOC members had been acquired through various perquisites, such as scholarships and gifts of excessive travel by Salt Lake City Winter Games bid organizers. This raised serious questions about the ethics of interactions between IOC members and potential host cities that were or are seeking support for their respective bids.

Further investigations revealed the unfortunate magnitude of the indiscretions—exceeding $1 million in the Salt Lake City scandal (Pound and Johnson 1999). Similar activities may have occurred in connection with bidding to secure the Atlanta, Nagano, and Sydney Games as well. To its credit, although it had little choice, the IOC launched an investigation into all aspects of its operational practices and demanded proper accounting of the actions of its committee members regarding Olympic Games site selection. President Samaranch convened an Extraordinary Session of the IOC at Lausanne on March 17 and 18, 1999, to discuss findings and create appropriate guidelines for future conduct of its members. At that session, three members resigned, six IOC members were expelled, and the IOC developed action plans. In particular, the organization created an IOC 2000 Commission and an Ethics Commission to address fundamental reform issues within the IOC, especially improving the system of selecting future sites, to ensure that inappropriate financial and/or unscrupulous activities would not reoccur (Anonymous 1999a).

Almost hidden among the news columns reporting this internal Olympic misbehavior came news during the spring of 1999 that Lord Killanin died, on April 25 at the age of 84. Having led the Olympic movement from 1972 until 1980 from the basement office of his Landsdowne Road home in Dublin (Anonymous 1999b), he "took over when the IOC was a struggling but more honest and more respected movement. The shenannigans of recent times must have saddened him."

Pharmacology and Athletic Performance

During this same period, the problem of performance-enhancing drug use in top-level sport became more pervasive, complex, and threatening. At least three aspects of the topic relate to marathon running. One concerns discovery of details of the former German Democratic Republic's (East Germany) state-supported systematic plan for improving athletic performance through clandestine pharmacology as a supplement to training. Through the investigative efforts of cellular biologist Werner Franke and his colleague Brigitte Berendonk, documents obtained from the Ministry of State Security (Stasi) files of the former German Democratic Republic have provided many details, which have been summarized in the scientific literature (Franke and Berendonk 1997). Athletes were assigned code numbers for secrecy and given specific drug regimens to improve their strength and/or endurance, depending upon event specialty. Some of these code numbers have now been matched to both athlete names and the drug regimens assigned. Several of the identified athletes are well known in the sports world, notably in the shorter distance races and field events. On the list of distance runners appear such marathoners as Waldemar Cierpinski and Jörg Peter. Cierpinski's code number was 62, but his assigned drug regimen has not been uncovered.

A second aspect relates to circumstantial but incriminating evidence obtained from world sport arenas that associates the presence of drugs with their possible use in competition or training. Two specific incidents can be mentioned. At the Tour de France cycling competition in July 1998, sizable quantities of erythropoietin (EPO) were seized from team support vehicles (Ferstle 1998a). Erythropoietin is a hormone produced by the kidneys that stimulates the bone marrow to produce more red blood cells, thereby increasing the oxygen-carrying capacity of blood. It could thus be an ideal clandestine drug of choice for endurance athletes hoping to succeed in intense competition, particularly because more than a decade of research has failed to develop an unequivocal test for its presence through exogenous (external) administration. The advent of EPO dates back to the Olympic Winter Games of 1988. Use of the drug must be controlled with extraordinary care, as minute doses can cause such a large increase in red blood cells that the blood becomes too thick for efficient pumping by the heart, with potentially tragic results.

The second incident occurred at the world swimming championships in Perth in January 1999, when an Australian customs officer found more than a dozen vials of human growth hormone (HGH) in the Chinese team's luggage. As with EPO, although HGH is on the IOC's list of banned substances, no testing procedure is in place for its detection.

A third aspect of the doping crisis relates to athletes failing established doping protocols, notably for steroids such as testosterone, followed by arguments presented by their legal counsel questioning the integrity of the tests themselves. Track runner Mary Slaney and marathoner Uta Pippig are just two of the more visible cases still under some form of legal involvement. A brief explanation indicates the difficulty in determining unequivocally that the use of exogenous banned substances has occurred.

Most of the scientific studies that quantify the extent of testosterone abuse date back to the period of the 1980 Moscow Olympic Games. At that time, Manfred Donicke, the IOC's chair of its Medical Commission's Doping Subcommission, analyzed the "B" sample urine specimens brought from Moscow to his laboratory in Cologne (Ferstle 1998a). Evidence of elevated testosterone levels in many of the samples suggested that either synthetic forms of the hormone or its precursors (such as androstenedione) were being administered exogenously. As a protein-synthesizing hormone, testosterone can increase skeletal muscle mass as well as increase hemoglobin and EPO production. Thus, both aerobic and anaerobic athletes could receive performance-enhancing benefits. Inasmuch as the body also produces an inactive accompanying mirror-image form of testosterone (T) in smaller quantities, called epitestosterone (E), Donicke suggested the use of the so-called T:E ratio to detect synthetic steroid use. Normally, this ratio does not exceed 6:1.

Staying one step ahead of those developing tests for doping, German Democratic Republic experts simply administered E to their athletes along with T, keeping the ratio within physiologically normal limits. In turn, to thwart these experts who specialize in clandestine chemistry for performance enhancement, a more recent and sophisticated advancement to the antidoping armamentarium involves the quantification of carbon isotopes by mass spectrometry. Synthetic testosterone and its precursors, such as androstenedione, have a different mix of two carbon isotopes, ^{12}C and ^{13}C, than do their naturally occurring counterparts. Thus, using the more expensive carbon isotope methodology, even if an athlete's T:E ratio is within normal limits, the presence of synthetic testosterone can be detected.

Pippig, who has won the Boston and Berlin Marathons three times each, tested positive for an elevated T:E ratio in a urine sample obtained during a random doping test conducted in April of 1998 in Colorado (Anonymous 1998). She claims the abnormality was due to her discontinuing birth control pill use, asserting that she had been tested many times before with acceptable results. The German track and field federation reported that carbon isotope analysis of her urine sample detected both natural and synthetic steroids (Eisfeld 1999). Her case is still in litigation as of this writing.

Mary Slaney tested positive for an elevated T:E ratio in a urine sample obtained at the United States Olympic track trials in Atlanta during June of 1996. Carbon isotope testing was not performed on her samples, but her attorneys suggest that a T:E ratio greater than 6:1 can occur in women as a result of the influence of oral contraceptive use, alcohol consumption, pregnancy, and interaction with certain medications. Thus, to apply the so-called rule of strict liability, which holds that exceeding this ratio *must* imply illegal steroid use, is inappropriate. It remains to be seen whether peer-reviewed scientific research supports the contentions of her attorneys or the IAAF regarding T:E ratios exceeding 6:1. Her case is also still in litigation.

Adjudication of such cases demands that the testing system be infallible. That is, the range of hormone values permitted must include all those that are physiologically explainable. But if this range includes high-end values that overlap the range of values also possible from administration of synthetic hormones, then the test becomes questionable because of its risk for producing false positives. Distinguishing between those exceptions that are legitimately biological and those that are created clandestinely is the real challenge.

Slaney and Pippig must be considered innocent until proven otherwise, but therein lies a crucial dilemma. Apart from the enormous legal expense and loss of potential earnings from not competing until the suspension is removed, the number of years required for movement of such cases through the legal system can be longer than the athlete's remaining competitive lifetime. A sense of urgency has thus fallen upon the IOC Medical Commission and the Sydney Games organizers to (1) improve urine testing procedures, (2) decide whether blood testing might be more informative, and (3) fund both the testing and the research into procedures that quickly and unequivocally identify those who opt to cheat in sport.

To help initiate progress, the IOC organized a World Conference on Doping in Sport, held February 2-4, 1999. The resulting Lausanne Declaration provided for the first time a written document outlining a broad-based joint effort between governments, sport federations, and the IOC—with significant IOC funding ($25 million) provided toward its successful implementation (Anonymous 1999a). By the time of the Sydney Olympic Games, the IOC hopes to have an independent International Antidoping Agency fully operational, the ultimate goal being to remove the likelihood of doping-influenced athletes reaching the medal platform in sport. As of this writing, however, it appears doubtful that testing procedures will be in place that will guarantee the detection of the use of EPO and HGH and end the controversy in quantifying steroid abuse.

Meanwhile, in July 1999, Spanish marathoner Julio Rey received a two-year IAAF suspension for two steroid-positive (mesterolone) urine tests, one at the Spanish national cross country championships in March, the second after his third place 2:07:37 at the Rotterdam Marathon in April.

What Does the Future Hold for Marathon Running?

The marathon footrace as a competitive sporting event is entering its 105th year. There have now been 21 men and 4 women who can call themselves Olympic marathon champions (22 men if we include Billy Sherring in 1906)—a truly elite group to whom this book is dedicated. The mystique and drama of the Olympic marathon have allowed it to flourish worldwide. More than a thousand varied venues now stage marathons on a more or less annual basis—from Antarctica to the Himalayas, from Anchorage to Zanzibar, from Boston to Berlin. The 100th Boston Marathon in 1996 saw 27,371 men and 8,497 women finish, still the record for participation in a single event.

A large percentage of the 210 IAAF member federations now stage an annual marathon championship, which often serves as a selection race for the various international championships, including the Olympic Games. The organizing committees of some races, such as those in New York, Boston, and London, have multimillion dollar budgets and eagerly court the world's fastest athletes to race for huge prize purses. Other races with very small budgets focus on participation by fitness runners who desire little more than drinks along the way, a tee shirt at the finish line, and the challenge of conquering the odd distance of 42.195 kilometers, or 26 miles, 385 yards. Thus, from the Olympic marathons to the smallest races, the marathon enjoys a global presence as a popular and exciting event in the sporting fabric of society.

Analyzing Past Performances

We can briefly summarize this first century of marathon racing and offer some thoughts for the future. Figure 25.2 shows that marathon race pace has quickened over time for the 23 men's Olympic marathons (24 if the 1906 Intercalated Games are included) but has remained relatively stable for the four women's Olympic races. The explanation for this difference is simple. Women were racing marathons at the highest level well *before* their first Olympic marathon was scheduled; that was a requirement for the event's inception. In contrast, the men's marathon began and grew in stature along with the Olympic Games, so the initial improvement of race pace at the Olympic marathons was a logical accompaniment to athletes developing their skills. Thus, the Olympic association with women's marathoning has done more to increase global participation than to enhance performance quality.

The overall improvement trend for the men displays three noticeable interruptions—for the years 1908, 1948, and 1968. Figure 25.2 illustrates these. In 1904, dusty roads, extreme heat in St. Louis, and the small global participation due to difficulty of reaching the central United States resulted in relatively poor performances. In 1948, the enormous loss of young athletic talent and training opportunities during World War II likewise yielded slower times. And in 1968, the challenge of the altitude of Mexico City slowed the race pace.

Much of the improvement in marathon performance occurred during the 28-years period between 1896 and 1924 for the men, and over the 9-years period between 1970 and 1979 for the women. Figure 25.3 shows the fastest marathon performance achieved each year by men since 1924 and by women since 1970. We selected 1924 as a starting point for the men's compilation because that was the first year that the now-standard distance of 42.195 kilometers (26 miles, 385 yards) was approved for the Olympic Games by the IAAF and the IOC. After 1924 and continuing until 1953, the rate of quickening for the annual men's fastest performance was much slower than for the 28 years preceding that era.

The pivotal period for records in distance running was between 1952 and 1956, when two British athletes—marathoner Jim Peters and miler Roger Banister—dramatically changed the thinking of top-level runners desirous of being the best. On June 14, 1952, Peters lowered the world marathon best by nearly five minutes at Chiswick, and improved on it three more times during this four-years period. He was the first under the 2:20:00 barrier. Then, on May 6, 1954, Banister broke the four minutes barrier for the mile at Oxford. Suddenly, it was as if athletes could now pursue their dreams of running ever faster, free of artificial constraints.

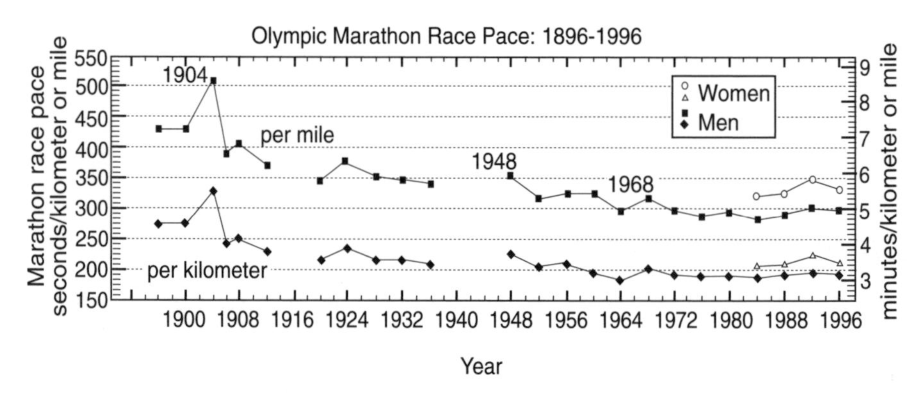

Figure 25.2 Plot of changes in Olympic marathon race pace during the history of the modern Olympic Games.

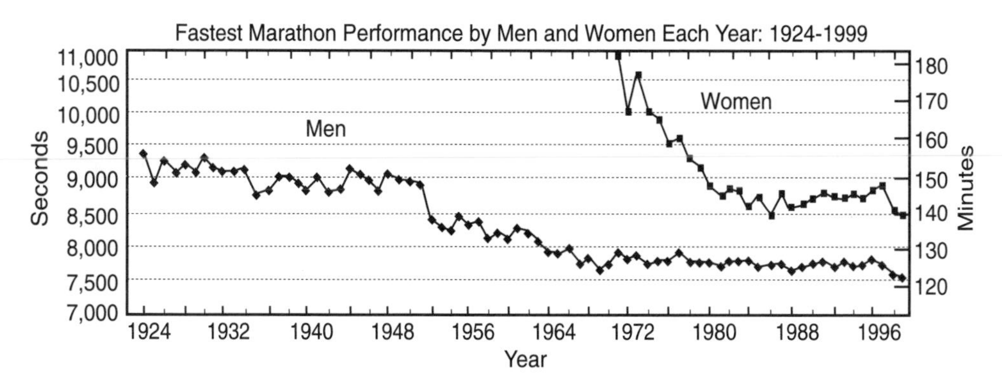

Figure 25.3 Plot showing the improvement in fastest annual marathon time by men and women from 1924 through 1999.

Sadly, Jim Peters joined the ranks of several Olympic sporting notables who passed on during the 26th Olympiad (from the start of the Atlanta Games to the start of the Sydney Games), losing a battle with cancer on January 9, 1999 at the age of 80. His great duel with Emil Zátopek at Helsinki in 1952, as well as his extraordinary athletic talent, give him a special place in the history of both the Olympic movement and the marathon.

Using data such as that summarized in figure 25.3, showing the progression of improving men's and women's marathon times, it is tempting to subject such data to mathematical modeling. Could we predict either the best performance for some year into the future, or suggest a theoretical performance limit? We have not done such modeling, but others have. Two renowned scientists attempted just this using data available in 1987 (Peronnet and Thibault 1989). They projected the best men's and women's world marathon performances for 2000 to be 2:05:23 and 2:18:43, respectively. These times have not been reached, and by viewing our data for annual best performance between 1924 and the present day, it can be seen that the rate of performance improvement still occurring during the 1980s has continued to slow. This recent trend was not factored into the model developed.

Since 1968 for the men and since 1983 for the women, the *rate* of quickening of the annual fastest marathon performance has slowed substantially. However, men and women are indeed still improving, as evidenced by the current world best times set relatively recently (in 1999) for both men (2:05:42, Khalid Khannouchi [MAR]) and women (2:20:43, Tegla Loroupe [KEN]). Interestingly, neither of these athletes has run an Olympic Games marathon. Only twice has a reigning marathon world record-holder achieved an Olympic marathon victory (Son in 1936 and Bikila in 1964). Perhaps the mild weather of Sydney will mesh with peak fitness to allow Loroupe the thrill of such an attempt.

Figure 25.4 plots the increasing *quantity* of top-level marathon performances each year from 1970 through 1998 using 2:20:00 (men) and 2:55:00 (women) as time limits. During the 1970s, breaking the 2:20:00 and 3:00:00 barriers for men and women, respectively, were achievements synonymous with world-class status in the marathon. Today, these standards have quickened to sub-2:10:00 and sub-2:30:00. As shown, an exponential rise in the numbers of top-class performances occurred between 1978 and 1982. From 1982 through 1998, the number of such performances has stabilized, with about 1,000 delivered each year by men under the 2:20:00 mark and about 1,150 by women faster than 2:55:00.

The Kenyan Marathon Phenomenon

If there is one nation poised to perform well at Sydney in the marathon, it is Kenya. Its athletes have recently become enamored with racing marathons to an extent almost never seen in other countries. In 1998, 128 Kenyan men delivered a total of 217 sub-2:20:00 performances (up from 163 the year previous)—a yearly total greater than that of any other nation in history except for the 268 performances (by 197 athletes) achieved by the far-larger United States during its peak of activity in 1983. Kenyan men won 34 major world marathons in 1998, compared with athletes from Morocco (11) and Ethiopia (9) (Martin 1999). Marathon racing by Kenyan women is smaller in numbers but very high in quality, largely stimulated by Tegla Loroupe, fastest woman marathoner on the planet as of this writing. Kenya, as with the other NOCs, will be permitted only three marathon entrants for each sex at the Sydney Olympic Games. At present, however, selection of the country's fastest three active men and women marathoners would make these the strongest entering teams.

Are Kenyan distance runners uniquely gifted for achieving performance excellence with such apparent dominance, or is it simply a fortuitous combination of their lifestyle, residence, and training? Understanding the physiological requirements of marathon running provides some clues. The marathon is an aerobic event, carried out using a high rate of complete fuel metabolism. Thus, the higher the rate of oxygen uptake and its use in metabolism, the faster one can run over long distances. This is measured in the laboratory as the maximum volume (V) of oxygen (O_2) consumed by the body in milliliters per kilogram of

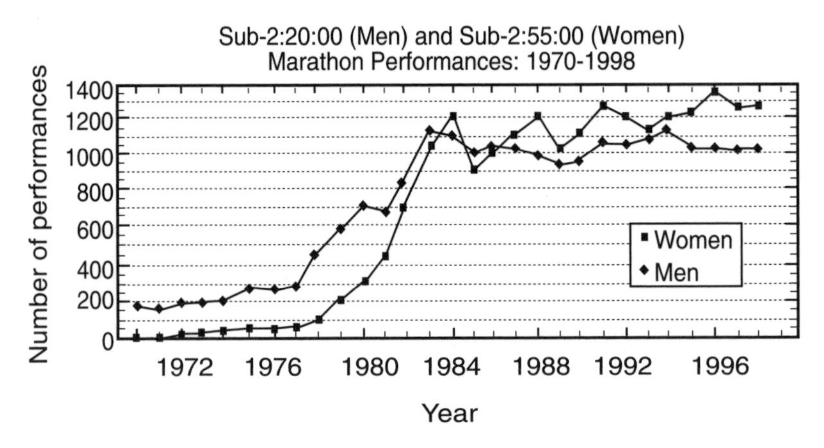

Figure 25.4 Plot showing the annual changes in numbers of top-level marathon performances among men and women from 1970 through 1998.

body weight per minute, symbolized as $\dot{V}O_2max$. However, as athletes quicken their pace, anaerobic metabolism—energy obtained by fuel breakdown without the use of oxygen—also starts to supplement the total energy output. An end product of anaerobic metabolism is lactic acid, which in turn inhibits aerobic metabolism if it starts to accumulate in the working tissues. Thus, optimum marathon race pace is only slightly below the workload at which lactic acid starts to accumulate. Typically, an athlete's so-called lactate threshold (LT) pace is at about 85 percent of the $\dot{V}O_2max$ pace.

With these basic facts, it can be seen that raising LT pace is the secret to success in marathon racing. This can be done in two ways. First, if LT pace normally remains at a similar percentage of $\dot{V}O_2max$ pace, training that raises $\dot{V}O_2max$ pace should also raise LT pace. The hypoxia (decreased tissue oxygen) occurring with residence at altitude (especially above 7,000 feet or 2,130 meters) and endurance-oriented (slower-paced) training at such altitude both increase EPO production, which increases red blood cell production. This increases available blood hemoglobin, which raises the blood's oxygen content and increases $\dot{V}O_2max$. Once this initial developmental training has been completed, the addition of faster-paced sessions, especially at lower altitudes, improves neuromuscular aspects of running efficiency, thereby raising LT pace further without necessarily raising $\dot{V}O_2max$. The resulting increased number and size of mitochondria in the working muscle cells provide additional enzymes used for complete fuel metabolism. These physiological adaptations occur in all runners to a variable extent, depending on genetic factors, response to training, and capability of enduring increasing training loads without injury.

Scientific studies conducted on elite-level Kenyan distance runners (Saltin et al. 1995) suggested that these athletes have a higher lactate threshold than top-level European distance runners, but not necessarily a higher $\dot{V}O_2max$. This difference is likely not due so much to genetics as it is to lifestyle and training effects. Running to and from school over hilly terrain at a young age improves running efficiency, and training at faster paces raises LT pace. Years of running over soft surfaces reduces risk of injury and develops resistance to injury. Later addition of very intense focused training to achieve supreme fitness for a short career of a few years of racing provides extraordinary performance output before injuries occurring from overuse begin to limit racing consistency.

In addition to the physiological attributes mentioned above that can be refined by all talented athletes for successful distance running, Kenyan athletes benefit from a unique synergism among several interacting factors (Ferstle 1998b). These include (1) effective management by foreign-based agents who secure their entry into races, (2) an effective family support system to permit athletes to leave home for long periods, (3) organized training camps based in Kenya to take advantage of climate, altitude, terrain, familiar food, and group motivation, (4) a sense of national pride in following in the footsteps of their earlier talented distance-running brethren, (5) an intense rivalry that has developed between runners of Kenya, Morocco, and Ethiopia, and (6) the desire to capture some of the nearly unimaginable local buying power of the cash prizes offered at the large city races (Ferstle 1998b).

Whether the rest of the sporting world can keep up with this juggernaut of well-managed talent, and whether the socioeconomic climate of Kenya remains sufficiently stable to permit this athletic development to continue will determine the influence of the Kenyan success story as the marathon enjoys its second century of popularity. Whatever the outcome, the excitement of this now-famous Olympic event promises to entertain and amaze!

References

Anonymous. 1933. *The Games of the Xth Olympiad, Los Angeles, 1932.* Los Angeles: Xth Olympiad Committee of the Games of Los Angeles.

Anonymous. 1997. Five finalist cities. *Olympic Review* XXVI-17: 21-24.

Anonymous. 1998. Uta Pippig suspended for failed drug test. *Runner's World OnLine*, October 7.

Anonymous. 1999a. Olympic news notes. *Journal of Olympic History* 7 (2): 28-37.

Anonymous. 1999b. Lord Killanin: A sporting gent who did Ireland proud. *Irish Independent OnLine*, April 26.

Baumel, B. 1992. Race to the millennium—solution to November puzzle. *Measurement News* 51: 9.

Cahill, J. 1999. Political influence and the Olympic flame. *Journal of Olympic History* 7 (1): 29-32.

Eisfeld, H. 1999. Zwei Jahre für Pippig. *Leichtathletik* 29, June 20.

Ferstle, J. 1998a. Drug scandals pervade sports: Could running be next? *Road Race Management* 193: 3.

Ferstle, J. 1998b. Exploring the Kenyan athlete. *Road Race Management* 188, 189, 191: 4-5.

Findling, J.E., and K.D. Pelle. 1996. *Historical dictionary of the modern Olympic movement.* Westport, CT: Greenwood Press.

Franke, W., and B. Berendonk. 1997. Hormonal doping and androgenization of athletes: A secret program of the German Democratic Republic government. *Clinical Chemistry* 43: 1262-1279.

Martin, D.E. 1999. World marathon review 1998. In *Athletics 1999.* Edited by P. Matthews. Surbiton, Great Britain: SportsBooks Ltd.

Peronnet, F., and G. Thibault. 1989. Mathematical analysis of running performance and world running records. *Journal of Applied Physiology* 67: 453-465.

Pound, E.T., and K. Johnson. 1999. Salt Lake gifts to IOC members top $1M. *USA Today*, February 1.

Saltin, B., C.K. Kim, N. Terrados, H. Larsen, J. Svedenhag, and C.J. Rolf. 1995. Morphology, enzyme activities and buffer capacity in leg muscles of Kenyan and Scandinavian runners. *Scandinavian Journal of Medicine and Science in Sports* 5: 222-230.

Appendixes

APPENDIX A: Abbreviations Used for Geopolitical Entities (GPEs)

AFG	Afghanistan - 1996
ALG	Algeria - 1980-88-92
AND	Andorra - 1996
ANG	Angola - 1988
ARG	Argentina - 1932-36-48-52-60-64-72-84-96 W-96**
ARU	Aruba - 1992 W-88-92
ASA	American Samoa - 1988
AUS	Australia - 1896-06-08-12-20-52-56-60-64-68-72-76-80-84-88-92-96* W-84-88-92-96
AUT	Austria - 1906-08-12-36-52-56-60-80-84-92
BEL	Belgium - 1906-08-20-24-28-36-48-52-56-60-64-68-72-76-80-84-96 W-84-88-96
BER	Bermuda - 1976
BHR	Bahrain - 1992
BIH	Bosnia and Herzegovina - 1996
BIR	Burma (later Myanmar) - 1956-60-64-68-72-80 W-88
BLR	Belarus - W-96
BIZ	Belize - 1988-96
BOH	Bohemia (later Czechoslovakia) - 1900-06-08-12
BOL	Bolivia - 1972-76-84-88-92-96 W-84
BOT	Botswana - 1984-88-92-96
BRA	Brazil - 1932-84-88-92-96 W-84-88-92-96
BUL	Bulgaria - 1936-68-96
BUR	Burundi - 1996
CAF	Central African Republic - 1984-88-92-96 W-96(unof)
CAM	Cambodia - 1996
CAN	Canada - 1900-06-08-12-20-24-28-32-36-48-52-60-68-76-84-88-92-96 W-84-88-92-96
CAY	Cayman Islands - W-88
CEY	Ceylon (later Sri Lanka) - 1960-68
CGO	Congo - 1980
CHI	Chile - 1920-24-28-36-48-52-56-60-64-68-84-88-92-96 W-84-96
CHN	People's Republic of China - 1936-48-88 W-88-96
CMR	Cameroon - 1992
COL	Colombia - 1932-68-72-76-80-84-88-92-96 W-96
CPV	Cape Verde - 1996
CRC	Costa Rica - 1968-84-88-92-96 W-92
CUB	Cuba - 1904-76-80-92
CYP	Cyprus - 1984
DEN	Denmark - 1906-08-12-20-24-28-32-36-48-52-60-68-72-76-80-84-88 W-84-96
DJI	Djibouti - 1984-88-92-96
ECU	Ecuador - 1924-68-92-96 W-96
EGY	Egypt - 1906-1952
ESA	El Salvador - W-88
ESP	Spain - 1924-28-60-68-72-76-80-84-88-92-96 W-96
EST	Estonia - 1920-24-28-32-96 W-96
ETH	Ethiopia - 1956-60-64-68-72-80-92-96 W-92-96
EUN	Equipe Unifiee (Unified Team) -1992 W-92
FIJ	Fiji - 1988-92
FIN	Finland - 1908-12-20-24-28-32-36-48-52-56-60-64-68-72-76-80-84-92-96 W-84-88-92-96
FRA	France - 96-00-04-06-12-20-24-28-32-36-48-52-56-60-68-72-76-80-84-88-92 W-88-92-96
FRG	Federal Republic of Germany - 1952-68-72-76-84-88 W-84-88
GBR	Great Britain & Northern Ireland - 00-06-08-12-20-24-28-32-36-48-52-56-60-64-68-72-76-80-84-88-92-96 W-84-88-92-96
GDR	German Democratic Republic - 1956-60-64-68-72-76-80-88 W-88
GER	Germany - 1906-08-28-32-36-92-96 W-92-96
GRE	Greece - 1896-04-06-08-12-20-24-36-48-76-80-84-96 W-96
GRN	Grenada - W-88
GUA	Guatemala - 1952-68-72-96 W-88
GUI	Guinea - 1988
GUM	Guam - 1988 W-88-92-96
GUY	Guyana - 1968
HAI	Haiti - 1972-76-84-88-92
HKG	Hong Kong - W-84
HON	Honduras - 1976-84-92 W-84
HUN	Hungary - 1896-12-24-28-48-52-60-64-68-72-80-92 W-88-92-96
INA	Indonesia - 1996
IND	India - 1920-24-36-48-52-60-64-76-80
IOP	Independent Olympic Participant - Yugoslav athletes in 1992
IRL	Ireland - 1906-48-52-60-64-68-72-76-80-84-88-92 W-84-88
IRN	Islamic Republic of Iran - 1956-88
ISR	Israel - 1984 W-84
ISV	British Virgin Islands - 1984-88-92-96 W-92
ITA	Italy - 1900-06-08-12-20-24-28-32-36-48-52-56-60-64-68-72-76-80-84-88-92-96 W-84-88-92-96
JAM	Jamaica - 1984-88-96
JOR	Jordan - 1984
JPN	Japan - 1912-20-24-28-32-36-52-56-60-64-68-72-76-84-88-92-96 W-84-88-92-96
KEN	Kenya - 1956-60-64-68-72-84-88-92-96 W-84-88-92-96

KGZ	Kyrgyzstan - 1996 W-96
KOR	Korea - 1948-52-56-60-64-68-84-88-92-96 W-88-92-96
KUW	Kuwait - 1968
LAO	Lao People's Democratic Republic - W-96
LAT	Latvia - 1928-36-96
LBN	Lebanon - 1980
LBR	Liberia - 1960-84
LBY	Libyan Arab Jamahiriya - 1980-92-96
LES	Lesotho - 1980-84-88-92-96
LIE	Liechtenstein - 1992
LIT	Lithuania - 1996 W-96
LUX	Luxembourg - 1964-84-88 W-88
MAD	Madagascar - 1980-84-92-96
MAR	Morocco - 1960-64-88-92-96
MAW	Malawi - 1972-84-88-92-96
MDV	Maldive Islands - 1988-92
MEX	Mexico - 1928-32-64-68-72-76-80-84-88-92-96 W-84-88-92-96
MGL	Mongolia - 1992 W-96
MLT	Malta - W-96
MOL	Republic of Moldova - 1996 W-96(unof)
MRI	Mauritius - 1996 W-88
MTN	Mauritania - 1992
MYA	Myanmar (formerly Burma) - 1992
NAM	Namibia - 1992-96 W-96
NCA	Nicaragua - 1972-92-96
NED	The Netherlands - 1908-20-24-28-52-60-68-76-80-84-88-92-96 W-84-88-96
NEP	Nepal - 1964-72-76-80-84-88-92-96 W-88-96
NGR	Nigeria - 1968-88 W-84
NIG	Niger - 1988-92-96
NOR	Norway - 1912-28-48-52-60-84-88 W-84-88-96
NRH	Northern Rhodesia (later Zambia) - 1964
NZL	New Zealand - 1956-60-64-68-72-76-84-88-92-96 W-84-88-92-96
OMA	Oman - 1984-88
PAK	Pakistan - 1952-56-64
PAR	Paraguay - 1976
PER	Peru - 1936-1996 W-84-92-96
PHI	Philippines - 1968-76-84-92-96
PNG	Papua New Guinea - 1976-84-88
POL	Poland - 1936-52-72-76-80-92-96 W-88-92-96
POR	Portugal - 1912-36-64-72-76-80-84-88-92-96 W-84-88-92-96
PRK	Democratic People's Republic of Korea - 1972-76-80-92-96 W-92-96
PUR	Puerto Rico - 1964-76-84-92-96 W-84
QAT	Qatar - 1984
ROM	Romania - 1928-36-52-64 W-92-96
RSA	Republic of South Africa (formerly South Africa) - 92-96 W-92-96
RUS	Russia - 1908-12
RUS	Russian Federation - 1996 W-96
RWA	Rwanda - 1988-92-96 W-88
SER	Serbia - 1912
SEY	Seychelles - 1980
SIN	Singapore - W-96
SLE	Sierra Leone - 1968-80-88
SLO	Slovenia - 1992 W-96
SMN	San Marino - 1992
SOA	South Africa (later Republic of South Africa) - 1904-08-12-20-24-28-36-48-52-56-60
SOL	Solomon Islands - 1988
SOM	Somalia - 1972-84-88-96
SRH	Southern Rhodesia (later Zimbabwe) - 1964
SRL	Sri Lanka (formerly Ceylon) - 1972-88-92
STV	St. Vincent and the Grenadines - 1996
SUD	Sudan - 1972-96
SUI	Switzerland - 1936-48-52-60-64-68-72-80-84-88-92 W-84-88-92-96
SWE	Sweden - 1900-06-08-12-20-24-28-36-48-52-56-60-76-80-84-96 W-84-88
SWZ	Swaziland - 1972-84-88-92-96
SYR	Syrian Arab Republic - 1992
TAN	United Republic of Tanzania - 1964-68-72-80-84-88-92-96
TCH	Czechoslovakia - 1924-28-32-36-52-56-60-64-80-88-92 W-88-92
THA	Thailand - 1964
TJK	Tajikistan - W-96
TPE	Chinese Taipei - 1984-96
TRI	Trinidad & Tobago - 1996
TUN	Tunisia - 1960-64-96
TUR	Turkey - 1948-52-68-72-76-84-88 W-96
UGA	Uganda - 1968-72-84-88-92
UKR	Ukraine - 1996 W-96
URS	Union of Soviet Socialist Republics - 1952-56-60-64-68-72-76-80-88 W-88
URU	Uruguay - 1968-92-96
USA	United States of America - 96-00-04-06-08-12-20-24-28-32-36-48-52-56-60-64-68-72-76-84-88-92-96 W-84-88-92-96
VEN	Venezuela - 1996
VIE	Vietnam - 1964-80-88-92 W-92
YEM	Yemen - 1996
YUG	Yugoslavia - 1928-36-52-56-60-68-88-96 W-96
ZAI	Zaire - 1984-88-92-96 W-92
ZAM	Zambia (formerly Northern Rhodesia) - 1968-80
ZIM	Zimbabwe (formerly Southern Rhodesia) - 1980-84-88-92-96 W-88

* Australia and New Zealand competed together as Australasia in 1908 and 1912.

** W signifies years of women participation.

APPENDIX B: Olympic Marathon Race Summary

Olympiad	Venue	Date	Distance	Shape of course	Weather	Start time	# GPEs**	Starters	Finishers
I	Athens	10-Apr-1896*	40,000m	Point-to-point	Cool, sunny	14:00	5	17	10***
II	Paris	19-Jul-1900	40,260m	Circular loop	35C–39C	14:36	8	16	7
III	St. Louis	30-Aug-1904	39,996m	Square loop	27.8C	15:03	5	32	15***
Intercalated	Athens	01-May-1906	41,860m	Point-to-point	Very warm	15:05	15	52	15
IV	London	24-Jul-1908	42,195m	Point-to-point	24.4C	14:30	16	55	28***
V	Stockholm	14-Jul-1912	40,200m	Out-and-back	30.0C	13:48	19	68	34
VI	Berlin	Not held							
VII	Antwerp	22-Aug-1920	42,750m	Out-and-back	Cool, damp	16:12	18	48	35
VIII	Paris	13-Jul-1924	42,195m	Out-and-back	Warm, breezy	17:23	20	58	30
IX	Amsterdam	05-Aug-1928	42,195m	Out-and-back	16.1C	15:15	23	69	57
X	Los Angeles	07-Aug-1932	42,195m	Square loop	22.2C	15:38	15	29	20
XI	Berlin	09-Aug-1936	42,195m	Out-and-back	24.0C	15:00	27	56	42
XII	Tokyo/Helsinki	Not held							
XIII	London	Not held							
XIV	London	07-Aug-1948	42,195m	Out-loop-back	22.8C	15:00	21	41	30
XV	Helsinki	27-Jul-1952	42,195m	Out-and-back	18.0C	15:28	32	66	53
XVI	Melbourne	01-Dec-1956	42,195m	Out-and-back	27.0C	15:15	23	46	33

XVII	Rome	10-Sep-1960	42,195m	Triangular	23.2C	17:30	35	69	62
XVIII	Tokyo	21-Oct-1964	42,195m	Out-and-back	20.0C	13:00	35	68	58
XIX	Mexico	20-Oct-1968	42,195m	Point-to-point	22.8C	15:00	41	75	57
XX	Munich	10-Sep-1972	42,195m	Out-back loop	21.0C	15:00	39	74	62
XXI	Montreal	31-Jul-1976	42,195m	Square loop	25.0C	15:30	36	67	60
XXII	Moscow	01-Aug-1980	42,195m	Out-and-back	26.0C	17:16	40	74	53
XXIII	Los Angeles Women	05-Aug-1984	42,195m	Point-to-point	20.0C	08:00	28	49	44
XXIII	Los Angeles Men	12-Aug-1984	42,195m	Point-to-point	23.2C	17:00	59	107	78
XXIV	Seoul Women	23-Sep-1988	42,195m	Out/back loop	19.5C	09:30	39	69	64
XXIV	Seoul Men	02 Oct-1988	42,195m	Out/back loop	24.5C	14:35	66	118	98
XXV	Barcelona Women	01-Aug-1992	42,195m	Point-to-point	27.2C	18:30	31	47	38***
XXV	Barcelona Men	09-Aug-1992	42,195m	Point-to-point	26.6C	18:30	73	112	87
XXVI	Atlanta Women	28-Jul-1996	42,195m	Out/back loop	21.3C	07:05	51	86	67***
XXVI	Atlanta Men	04-Aug-1996	42,195m	Out/back loop	23.0C	07:05	79	124	111
XXVII	Sydney Women	24-Sep-2000	42,195m	Point-to-point		09:00			
XXVII	Sydney Men	01-Oct-2000	42,195m	Point-to-point		16:00			
							Totals: 1,541/251 **men/women starters**		1,135/211 **men/women finishers**

* 29 March Julian = 10 April Gregorian calendars (see text)

** GPE = geopolitical entity

*** includes disqualifications

APPENDIX C: Summary of Top-Three Olympic Marathon Finishers*

Venue	*Date*	*First*	*Second*	*Third*
Athens	10-Apr-1896**	Spiridon Louis, GRE, 23	Kharilaos Vasilakos, GRE, 25/26	Gyula Kellner, HUN, 25
Paris	19-Jul-1900	Michel Theato, LUX, 22	Emile Champion, FRA, 21	Ernst Fast, SWE, 19
St. Louis	30-Aug-1904	Thomas Hicks, USA, 29	Albert Corey, FRA, 26/27	Arthur Newton, USA, 21
Athens	01-May-1906***	William Sherring, CAN, 25	Johan Svanberg, SWE, 23	William Frank, USA, 24
London	24-Jul-1908	John Hayes, USA, 24	Charles Hefferon, SOA, 32	Joseph Forshaw, USA, 29
Stockholm	14-Jul-1912	Kennedy McArthur, SOA, 30	Christian Gitsham, SOA, 23	Gaston Strobino, USA, 20
Berlin	Not held			
Antwerp	22-Aug-1920	Johannes Kolehmainen, FIN, 30	Juri Lossman, EST, 29	Valerio Arri, ITA, 28
Paris	13-Jul-1924	Albin Stenroos, FIN, 35	Romeo Bertini, ITA, 31	Clarence DeMar, USA, 36
Amsterdam	05-Aug-1928	Boughera El Ouafi, FRA, 29	Manuel Plaza, CHI, 26	Martti Marttelin, FIN, 31
Los Angeles	07-Aug-1932	Juan Zabala, ARG, 20	Samuel Ferris, GBR, 31	Armas Toivonen, FIN, 33
Berlin	09-Aug-1936	Kitei Son, JPN, 21	Ernest Harper, GBR, 34	Shoryu Nan, JPN, 23
Tokyo/Helsinki	Not held			
London	Not held			
London	07-Aug-1948	Delfo Cabrera, ARG, 28	Thomas Richards, GBR, 38	Etienne Gailly, BEL, 25
Helsinki	27-Jul-1952	Emil Zatopek, CZE, 29	Reinaldo Gorno, ARG, 34	Gustaf Jansson, SWE, 30
Melbourne	01-Dec-1956	Alain Mimoun, FRA, 35	Franjo Mihalic, YUG, 36	Veikko Karvonen, FIN, 30
Rome	10-Sep-1960	Abebe Bikila, ETH, 28	Rhadi ben Abdesselem, MAR, 31	Barrington Magee, NZL, 26
Tokyo	21-Oct-1964	Abebe Bikila, ETH, 32	Basil Heatley, GBR, 30	Kokichi Tsuburaya, JPN, 24
Mexico	20-Oct-1968	Mamo Wolde, ETH, 36	Kenji Kimihara, JPN, 27	Michael Ryan, NZL, 26
Munich	10-Sep-1972	Frank Shorter, USA, 24	Karel Lismont, BEL, 23	Mamo Wolde, ETH, 40
Montreal	31-Jul-1976	Waldemar Cierpinski, GDR, 25	Frank Shorter, USA, 28	Karel Lismont, BEL, 27
Moscow	01-Aug-1980	Waldemar Cierpinski, GDR, 29	Gerhardus Nijboer, NED, 24	Satymkul Dzhumanazarov, URS, 28
Los Angeles Women	05-Aug-1984	Joan Benoit, USA, 27	Grete Waitz, NOR, 30	Rosa Mota, POR, 26
Los Angeles Men	12-Aug-1984	Carlos Lopes, POR, 37	John Treacy, IRL, 27	Charles Spedding, GBR, 32
Seoul Women	23-Sep-1988	Rosa Mota, POR, 30	Lisa Martin, AUS, 28	Katrin Dorre, GDR, 26
Seoul Men	02-Oct-1988	Gelindo Bordin, ITA, 29	Douglas Wakiihuri, KEN, 25	Ahmed Salah Hussein, DJI, 31
Barcelona Women	01-Aug-1992	Valentina Yegorova, EUN, 28	Yuko Arimori, JPN, 25	Lorraine Moller, NZL, 37
Barcelona Men	09-Aug-1992	Hwang Young-cho, KOR, 22	Koichi Morishita, JPN, 24	Stephan Freigang, GER, 24
Atlanta Women	28-Jul-1996	Fatuma Roba, ETH, 22	Valentina Yegorova, RUS, 32	Yuko Arimori, JPN, 29
Atlanta Men	04-Aug-1996	Josiah Thugwane, RSA, 25	Lee Bong-ju, KOR, 27	Erick Wainaina, KEN, 22
Sydney Women	24-Sep-2000			
Sydney Men	01-Oct-2000			
	Average age	**27.8 men; 26.8 women**	**28.2 men; 28.9 women**	**27.3 men; 29.5 women**

* Excludes those who finished among the top three and later were disqualified: Belokas @ Athens '96; Lorz @ St. Louis '04; Pietri @ London '08

** 29 March Julian = 10 April Gregorian calendars (see text)

*** 18 April Julian = 01 May Gregorian calendars (see text)

APPENDIX D: Race Results for Men Listed Chronologically

First name	*Family name*	*GPE*	*Birth date*	*Time*	*Place*	*Venue*	*Race date*
Spiridon	Louis	GRE	12-Jan-1873	2:58:50	1	Athens	10-Apr-1896
Kharilaos	Vasilakos	GRE	1871	3:06:03	2	Athens	10-Apr-1896
Spiridon	Belokas	GRE		3:06:30	DQ	Athens	10-Apr-1896
Gyula	Kellner	HUN	11-Apr-1871	3:06:35	3	Athens	10-Apr-1896
Ioannis	Vrettos	GRE			4	Athens	10-Apr-1896
Eleitherios	Papasimeon	GRE			5	Athens	10-Apr-1896
Dimitrios	Deligiannis	GRE			6	Athens	10-Apr-1896
Evangelos	Gerakakis	GRE			7	Athens	10-Apr-1896
Stamatios	Masouris	GRE			8	Athens	10-Apr-1896
Sokratis	Lagoudakis	GRE			9	Athens	10-Apr-1896
Edwin	Flack	AUS	05-Nov-1873		DNF	Athens	10-Apr-1896
Arthur	Blake	USA	26-Jan-1872		DNF	Athens	10-Apr-1896
Albin	Lermusiaux	FRA	09-Apr-1874		DNF	Athens	10-Apr-1896
Ioannis	Lavrentis	GRE			DNF	Athens	10-Apr-1896
Ilias	Kafetzis	GRE			DNF	Athens	10-Apr-1896
Dimitrios	Khristopoulos	GRE			DNF	Athens	10-Apr-1896
Georgios	Grigoriou	GRE			DNF	Athens	10-Apr-1896
Michel	Theato	LUX	22-Mar-1878	2:59:45	1	Paris	19-Jul-1900
Emile	Champion	FRA	1879	3:04:17	2	Paris	19-Jul-1900
Ernest	Fast	SWE	21-Jan-1881	3:37:14	3	Paris	19-Jul-1900
Eugene	Besse	FRA		4:00:43	4	Paris	19-Jul-1900
Arthur	Newton	USA	31-Jan-1883	4:04:12	5	Paris	19-Jul-1900
Ronald	MacDonald	CAN	27-Sep-1874		6/7	Paris	19-Jul-1900
Richard	Grant	USA	03-Aug-1878		6/7	Paris	19-Jul-1900
Jacob	Walp	BOH			DNF	Paris	19-Jul-1900
Georges	Touquet-Daunis	FRA			DNF	Paris	19-Jul-1900
Auguste	Marchais	FRA	1872		DNF	Paris	19-Jul-1900
William	Saward	GBR	1858		DNF	Paris	19-Jul-1900
Ernest Ion	Pool	GBR	22-Nov-1857		DNF	Paris	19-Jul-1900
Derek Frank	Randall	GBR	05-Feb-1864		DNF	Paris	19-Jul-1900
Ettore	Zilia	ITA	1880		DNF	Paris	19-Jul-1900
Emilio	Banfi	ITA	1881		DNF	Paris	19-Jul-1900
Johan	Nystrom	SWE	16-Apr-1874		DNF	Paris	19-Jul-1900
Frederick	Lorz	USA	1880	3:13:00e	DQ	St. Louis	30-Aug-1904
Thomas	Hicks	USA	07-Jan-1875	3:28:53	1	St. Louis	30-Aug-1904
Albert	Corey	FRA	1878	3:34:52	2	St. Louis	30-Aug-1904
Arthur	Newton	USA	31-Jan-1883	3:47:33	3	St. Louis	30-Aug-1904
Felix	Carvajal	CUB	18-Mar-1875		4	St. Louis	30-Aug-1904
Dimitrios	Veloulis	GRE			5	St. Louis	30-Aug-1904
David	Kneeland	USA			6	St. Louis	30-Aug-1904
Henry	Brawley	USA	25-Aug-1880		7	St. Louis	30-Aug-1904
Sidney	Hatch	USA	06-Dec-1885		8	St. Louis	30-Aug-1904
Len	Tau	SOA			9	St. Louis	30-Aug-1904
Christos	Zekhouritis	GRE			10	St. Louis	30-Aug-1904
Frank	Devlin	USA			11	St. Louis	30-Aug-1904
Jan	Mashiani	SOA			12	St. Louis	30-Aug-1904
John	Furla	USA	13-Jan-1874		13	St. Louis	30-Aug-1904
Andreas	Ikonomou	GRE			14	St. Louis	30-Aug-1904
Frank	Pierce	USA			DNF	St. Louis	30-Aug-1904
Samuel	Mellor	USA	15-Feb-1878		DNF	St. Louis	30-Aug-1904
Edward	Carr	USA			DNF	St. Louis	30-Aug-1904
Michael	Spring	USA	14-Dec-1879		DNF	St. Louis	30-Aug-1904

First name	Family name	GPE	Birth date	Time	Place	Venue	Race date
John	Lorden	USA	1875		DNF	St. Louis	30-Aug-1904
William	Garcia	USA			DNF	St. Louis	30-Aug-1904
Robert	Fowler	USA	1882		DNF	St. Louis	30-Aug-1904
Thomas	Kennedy	USA			DNF	St. Louis	30-Aug-1904
Guy	Porter	USA	26-May-1875		DNF	St. Louis	30-Aug-1904
John	Foy	USA			DNF	St. Louis	30-Aug-1904
Robert	Harris	SOA			DNF	St. Louis	30-Aug-1904
Georgios	Vamkaitis	GRE			DNF	St. Louis	30-Aug-1904
Henrikos	Jenakas	GRE			DNF	St. Louis	30-Aug-1904
Georgios	Drosos	GRE			DNF	St. Louis	30-Aug-1904
Georgios	Louridas	GRE			DNF	St. Louis	30-Aug-1904
Ioannis	Lugitsas	GRE			DNF	St. Louis	30-Aug-1904
Petros	Pipiles	GRE			DNF	St. Louis	30-Aug-1904
William	Sherring	CAN	19-Sep-1878	2:51:23.6	1	Athens	01-May-1906
Johan	Svanberg	SWE	01-May-1881	2:58:20.8	2	Athens	01-May-1906
William	Frank	USA	12-Dec-1879	3:00:46.8	3	Athens	01-May-1906
Gustaf	Tornros	SWE	18-Mar-1887	3:01:00	4	Athens	01-May-1906
Ioannis	Alepous	GRE		3:09:25.4	5	Athens	01-May-1906
George	Blake	AUS		3:09:35	6	Athens	01-May-1906
Konstantinos	Karvelas	GRE		3:15:54	7	Athens	01-May-1906
Joseph	Roffi	FRA	1882	3:17.49.8	8	Athens	01-May-1906
Hermann	Muller	GER	18-Apr-1885	3:21:00	9	Athens	01-May-1906
Khristos	Davaris	GRE			10	Athens	01-May-1906
Georgios	Koundoumadis	GRE			11	Athens	01-May-1906
Joseph	Forshaw	USA	13-May-1881		12	Athens	01-May-1906
Vladimiros	Negrepontis	GRE			13	Athens	01-May-1906
Joseph	Cormack	GBR		3:35:00.0	14	Athens	01-May-1906
Arnost	Nejedly	BOH	1883	3:40:00.0	15	Athens	01-May-1906
Michael	Spring	USA	14-Dec-1879		DNF	Athens	01-May-1906
Robert	Fowler	USA	1882		DNF	Athens	01-May-1906
John	Daly	IRL	22-Feb-1880		DNF	Athens	01-May-1906
Dorando	Pietri	ITA	16-Oct-1885		DNF	Athens	01-May-1906
Valdemar	Lorentzen	DEN	16-Feb-1880		DNF	Athens	01-May-1906
Thure	Bergvall	SWE	23-Nov-1887		DNF	Athens	01-May-1906
Robert	Sennecke	GER			DNF	Athens	01-May-1906
Jules	Lesage	BEL	1880		DNF	Athens	01-May-1906
Emile	Bonheure	FRA	1885		DNF	Athens	01-May-1906
Felix	Kwieton	AUT	16-Nov-1877		DNF	Athens	01-May-1906
Arthur	Marson	EGY			DNF	Athens	01-May-1906
Andreas	Andreadis	GRE			DNF	Athens	01-May-1906
Spiridon	Belokas	GRE			DNF	Athens	01-May-1906
V	Boulakakis	GRE			DNF	Athens	01-May-1906
Nicolaos	Dialektos	GRE			DNF	Athens	01-May-1906
T	Dionisyotis	GRE			DNF	Athens	01-May-1906
Khristos	Ferarolakis	GRE			DNF	Athens	01-May-1906
G	Fotakis	GRE			DNF	Athens	01-May-1906
Mikhail	Giannarakis	GRE			DNF	Athens	01-May-1906
Konstantinos	Ioannou	GRE			DNF	Athens	01-May-1906
Diamantis	Kantzias	GRE			DNF	Athens	01-May-1906
V	Koskoris	GRE			DNF	Athens	01-May-1906
Ioannis	Kousoulidis	GRE			DNF	Athens	01-May-1906
Anastasios	Koutoulakis	GRE			DNF	Athens	01-May-1906
Nikolaos	Malintretos	GRE			DNF	Athens	01-May-1906
Khristos	Manarolakis	GRE			DNF	Athens	01-May-1906
M	Mantakis	GRE			DNF	Athens	01-May-1906
G	Marangoudakis	GRE			DNF	Athens	01-May-1906
Xenophon	Milonakis	GRE			DNF	Athens	01-May-1906
Panagiotis	Polimenos	GRE			DNF	Athens	01-May-1906
Mikhail	Rossidis	GRE			DNF	Athens	01-May-1906
G	Solidakis	GRE			DNF	Athens	01-May-1906
G	Stamoulis	GRE			DNF	Athens	01-May-1906

First name	*Family name*	*GPE*	*Birth date*	*Time*	*Place*	*Venue*	*Race date*
Tassos	Topsidellis	GRE			DNF	Athens	01-May-1906
Alkiviadis	Tzelopopoulos	GRE			DNF	Athens	01-May-1906
S	Velliotis	GRE			DNF	Athens	01-May-1906
Evangelos	Volonakis	GRE			DNF	Athens	01-May-1906
Dorando	Pietri	ITA	16-Oct-1885	2:54:46.4	DQ	London	24-Jul-1908
John	Hayes	USA	10-Apr-1886	2:55:18.4	1	London	24-Jul-1908
Charles	Hefferon	SOA	25-Jan-1878	2:56:06.0	2	London	24-Jul-1908
Joseph	Forshaw	USA	13-May-1881	2:57:10.4	3	London	24-Jul-1908
Alton	Welton	USA	1886	2:59:44.4	4	London	24-Jul-1908
William	Wood	CAN		3:01:44.0	5	London	24-Jul-1908
Frederick	Simpson	CAN	1876	3:04:28.2	6	London	24-Jul-1908
Harry	Lawson	CAN	1888	3:06:47.2	7	London	24-Jul-1908
Johan	Svanberg	SWE	01-May-1881	3:07:50.8	8	London	24-Jul-1908
Lewis	Tewanima	USA	1888	3:09:15.0	9	London	24-Jul-1908
Kaarlo	Nieminen	FIN	26-Apr-1878	3:09:50.8	10	London	24-Jul-1908
John	Caffery	CAN	21-May-1879	3:12:46.0	11	London	24-Jul-1908
William	Clarke	GBR	1873	3:16:08.6	12	London	24-Jul-1908
Ernest	Barnes	GBR		3:17:30.8	13	London	24-Jul-1908
Sidney	Hatch	USA	06-Dec-1885	3:17:52.4	14	London	24-Jul-1908
Frederick	Lord	GBR	11-Feb-1879	3:19:08.8	15	London	24-Jul-1908
William	Goldsboro	CAN		3:20:07.0	16	London	24-Jul-1908
James	Beale	GBR	07-Feb-1881	3:20:14.0	17	London	24-Jul-1908
Arnost	Nejedly	BOH	1883	3:26:26.2	18	London	24-Jul-1908
Georg	Lind	RUS		3:26:38.8	19	London	24-Jul-1908
Willem	Wakker	NED	08-Dec-1879	3:28:49.0	20	London	24-Jul-1908
Gustaf	Tornros	SWE	18-Mar-1887	3:30:20.8	21	London	24-Jul-1908
George	Goulding	CAN	16-Nov-1884	3:33:26.4	22	London	24-Jul-1908
Julius	Jorgensen	DEN	20-Jun-1880	3:47:44.0	23	London	24-Jul-1908
Arthur	Burn	CAN		3:50:17.0	24	London	24-Jul-1908
Emmerich	Rath	AUT	05-Nov-1883	3:50:30.4	25	London	24-Jul-1908
Carl	Hansen	DEN	13-Nov-1888	3:53:15.0	26	London	24-Jul-1908
George	Lister	CAN	06-Nov-1888	4:22:45.0	27	London	24-Jul-1908
William Victor	Aitken	AUS			DNF	London	24-Jul-1908
George	Blake	AUS			DNF	London	24-Jul-1908
Joseph	Lynch	AUS			DNF	London	24-Jul-1908
Francois	Celis	BEL			DNF	London	24-Jul-1908
Edward	Cotter	CAN	27-Dec-1887		DNF	London	24-Jul-1908
Thomas	Longboat	CAN	04-Jun-1887		DNF	London	24-Jul-1908
Frederick	Noseworthy	CAN			DNF	London	24-Jul-1908
John	Tait	CAN	25-Sep-1889		DNF	London	24-Jul-1908
Frederick	Appleby	GBR	30-Oct-1879		DNF	London	24-Jul-1908
Henry	Barrett	GBR	30-Dec-1879		DNF	London	24-Jul-1908
Alex	Duncan	GBR	24-Feb-1884		DNF	London	24-Jul-1908
Thomas	Jack	GBR	05-Feb-1881		DNF	London	24-Jul-1908
Jack	Price	GBR	1884		DNF	London	24-Jul-1908
Frederick	Thompson	GBR	04-Aug-1880		DNF	London	24-Jul-1908
Alfred	Wyatt	GBR			DNF	London	24-Jul-1908
Ferdinand	Resier	GER	1875		DNF	London	24-Jul-1908
Georgios	Koulkoumverdos	GRE			DNF	London	24-Jul-1908
Anastasios	Koutoulakis	GRE			DNF	London	24-Jul-1908
Umberto	Blasi	ITA	12-Oct-1886		DNF	London	24-Jul-1908
Wilhemus	Braams	NED	25-Aug-1886		DNF	London	24-Jul-1908
George	Buff	NED	23-Nov-1874		DNF	London	24-Jul-1908
Arie	Vosbergen	NED	10-Jun-1882		DNF	London	24-Jul-1908
James	Mitchell-Baker	SOA	14-Feb-1878		DNF	London	24-Jul-1908
Seth	Landqvist	SWE	08-Aug-1882		DNF	London	24-Jul-1908
Johan	Lindqvist	SWE	29-Aug-1882		DNF	London	24-Jul-1908
Thomas	Morrissey	USA	02-Sep-1888		DNF	London	24-Jul-1908
Michael	Ryan	USA	01-Jan-1889		DNF	London	24-Jul-1908
Kennedy	McArthur	SOA	10-Feb-1882	2:36:54.8	1	Stockholm	14-Jul-1912
Christian	Gitsham	SOA	15-Oct-1888	2:37:52.0	2	Stockholm	14-Jul-1912

First name	Family name	GPE	Birth date	Time	Place	Venue	Race date
Gaston	Strobino	USA	23-Aug-1891	2:38:42.4	3	Stockholm	14-Jul-1912
Andrew	Sockalexis	USA	11-Jan-1891	2:42:07.9	4	Stockholm	14-Jul-1912
James	Duffy	CAN	01-May-1890	2:42:18.8	5	Stockholm	14-Jul-1912
Sigfrid	Jacobsson	SWE	04-Jun-1883	2:43:24.9	6	Stockholm	14-Jul-1912
John	Gallagher	USA	13-Apr-1890	2:44:19.4	7	Stockholm	14-Jul-1912
Joseph	Erxleben	USA	15-Sep-1889	2:45:47.2	8	Stockholm	14-Jul-1912
Richard	Piggott	USA	06-Jul-1888	2:46:40.7	9	Stockholm	14-Jul-1912
Joseph	Forshaw	USA	13-May-1881	2:49:49.4	10	Stockholm	14-Jul-1912
Edouard	Fabre	CAN	21-Aug-1889	2:50:36.2	11	Stockholm	14-Jul-1912
Clarence	DeMar	USA	07-Jun-1888	2:50:46.6	12	Stockholm	14-Jul-1912
Jean	Boissiere	FRA	09-Apr-1883	2:51:06.6	13	Stockholm	14-Jul-1912
Henry	Green	GBR	15-Jul-1886	2:52:11.4	14	Stockholm	14-Jul-1912
William	Forsyth	CAN	20-Jan-1891	2:52:23.0	15	Stockholm	14-Jul-1912
Lewis	Tewanima	USA	1888	2:52:41.4	16	Stockholm	14-Jul-1912
Harry	Smith	USA	30-Jul-1888	2:52:53.8	17	Stockholm	14-Jul-1912
Thomas	Lilley	USA	19-Dec-1887	2:59:35.4	18	Stockholm	14-Jul-1912
Arthur	Townsend	GBR	07-Apr-1883	3:00:05.0	19	Stockholm	14-Jul-1912
Felix	Kwieton	AUT	16-Nov-1877	3:00:48.0	20	Stockholm	14-Jul-1912
Frederick	Lord	GBR	11-Feb-1879	3:01:39.2	21	Stockholm	14-Jul-1912
Jacob	Westberg	SWE	15-Dec-1885	3:02:05.2	22	Stockholm	14-Jul-1912
Axel	Simonsen	NOR	11-Mar-1887	3:04:59.4	23	Stockholm	14-Jul-1912
Carl	Andersson	SWE	03-Jan-1877	3:06:13.0	24	Stockholm	14-Jul-1912
Edgar	Lloyd	GBR	31-Jul-1885	3:09:25.0	25	Stockholm	14-Jul-1912
Herkules	Sakelloropoulos	GRE	01-Mar-1888	3:11:37.0	26	Stockholm	14-Jul-1912
Hjalmar	Dahlberg	SWE	04-Nov-1886	3:13:32.2	27	Stockholm	14-Jul-1912
Ivar	Lundberg	SWE	11-Nov-1878	3:16:35.2	28	Stockholm	14-Jul-1912
Johannes	Christensen	DEN	14-Feb-1889	3:21:57.4	29	Stockholm	14-Jul-1912
Olof	Lodal	DEN	06-Jul-1885	3:21:57.6	30	Stockholm	14-Jul-1912
Odon	Karpati	HUN	02-Jan-1892	3:25:21.6	31	Stockholm	14-Jul-1912
Carl	Nilsson	SWE	18-May-1888	3:26:56.4	32	Stockholm	14-Jul-1912
Emmerich	Rath	AUT	05-Nov-1883	3:27:03.8	33	Stockholm	14-Jul-1912
Otto	Osen	NOR	04-Jul-1882	3:36:35.2	34	Stockholm	14-Jul-1912
Stuart	Poulter	AUS	20-Jan-1889		DNF	Stockholm	14-Jul-1912
Karl	Hack	AUT	15-Jun-1892		DNF	Stockholm	14-Jul-1912
Bohumil	Honzatko	BOH	30-Dec-1875		DNF	Stockholm	14-Jul-1912
Vladimir	Penc	BOH	10-Sep-1893		DNF	Stockholm	14-Jul-1912
Frantisek	Slavik	BOH	25-Sep-1888		DNF	Stockholm	14-Jul-1912
James	Corkery	CAN	27-Jun-1889		DNF	Stockholm	14-Jul-1912
Aarne	Kallberg	FIN	27-Jul-1891		DNF	Stockholm	14-Jul-1912
Taavetti	Kolehmainen	FIN	21-Apr-1885		DNF	Stockholm	14-Jul-1912
Louis	Pautex	FRA	18-Apr-1883		DNF	Stockholm	14-Jul-1912
Henry	Barrett	GBR	30-Dec-1879		DNF	Stockholm	14-Jul-1912
James	Beale	GBR	07-Feb-1881		DNF	Stockholm	14-Jul-1912
Septimus	Francom	GBR	14-Feb-1882		DNF	Stockholm	14-Jul-1912
Henry	Kellaway	GBR	07-Oct-1891		DNF	Stockholm	14-Jul-1912
Henrik	Ripszam	HUN	01-Feb-1899		DNF	Stockholm	14-Jul-1912
Franco	Ruggero	ITA	22-Nov-1892		DNF	Stockholm	14-Jul-1912
Carlo	Speroni	ITA	13-Jul-1895		DNF	Stockholm	14-Jul-1912
Shizo	Kanaguri	JPN	20-Aug-1891		DNF	Stockholm	14-Jul-1912
Oscar	Fonbaek	NOR	06-Jul-1887		DNF	Stockholm	14-Jul-1912
Francisco	Lazaro	POR	08-Jan-1891		DNF	Stockholm	14-Jul-1912
Andrejs	Kapmals	RUS	05-Nov-1889		DNF	Stockholm	14-Jul-1912
Andrejs	Kruklins	RUS	10-Jan-1891		DNF	Stockholm	14-Jul-1912
Nikolai	Rasso	RUS	18-Oct-1890		DNF	Stockholm	14-Jul-1912
Elmar	Reimann	RUS	12-Dec-1892		DNF	Stockholm	14-Jul-1912
Alexandrs	Upmals	RUS	01-Sep-1892		DNF	Stockholm	14-Jul-1912
Dragutin	Tomashevic	SER	17-Jan-1891		DNF	Stockholm	14-Jul-1912
Arthur	St. Norman	SOA	20-Oct-1882		DNF	Stockholm	14-Jul-1912
Alexis	Ahlgren	SWE	14-Jul-1887		DNF	Stockholm	14-Jul-1912
Thure	Bergvall	SWE	23-Nov-1887		DNF	Stockholm	14-Jul-1912
Wilhelm	Gruner	SWE	06-May-1888		DNF	Stockholm	14-Jul-1912

First name	Family name	GPE	Birth date	Time	Place	Venue	Race date
David	Guttman	SWE	24-Jul-1883		DNF	Stockholm	14-Jul-1912
Ivan	Lonnberg	SWE	12-Nov-1891		DNF	Stockholm	14-Jul-1912
Gustaf	Tornros	SWE	18-Mar-1887		DNF	Stockholm	14-Jul-1912
John	Reynolds	USA	09-Aug-1889		DNF	Stockholm	14-Jul-1912
Michael	Ryan	USA	01-Jan-1889		DNF	Stockholm	14-Jul-1912
Johannes	Kolehmainen	FIN	09-Dec-1889	2:32:35.8	1	Antwerp	22-Aug-1920
Juri	Lossman	EST	04-Feb-1891	2:32:48.6	2	Antwerp	22-Aug-1920
Valerio	Arri	ITA	22-Jun-1892	2:36:32.8	3	Antwerp	22-Aug-1920
Auguste	Broos	BEL	09-Nov-1894	2:39:25.8	4	Antwerp	22-Aug-1920
Juho	Tuomikoski	FIN	14-Dec-1888	2:40:10.8	5	Antwerp	22-Aug-1920
Sofus	Rose	DEN	10-Apr-1894	2:41:18.0	6	Antwerp	22-Aug-1920
Joseph	Organ	USA	03-Aug-1892	2:41:30.0	7	Antwerp	22-Aug-1920
Rudolf	Hansen	DEN	30-Mar-1889	2:41:39.4	8	Antwerp	22-Aug-1920
Urho	Tallgren	FIN	10-Oct-1894	2:42:40.0	9	Antwerp	22-Aug-1920
Taavetti	Kolehmainen	FIN	21-Apr-1885	2:44:03.2	10	Antwerp	22-Aug-1920
Carl	Linder	USA	29-Dec-1890	2:44:21.2	11	Antwerp	22-Aug-1920
Charles	Mellor	USA	27-Dec-1893	2:45:30.0	12	Antwerp	22-Aug-1920
James	Dellow	CAN		2:46:47.0	13	Antwerp	22-Aug-1920
Arthur	Mills	GBR	16-Jan-1894	2:48:05.0	14	Antwerp	22-Aug-1920
Arthur	Scholes	CAN		2:48:30.0	15	Antwerp	22-Aug-1920
Shizo	Kanaguri	JPN	20-Aug-1891	2:48:45.4	16	Antwerp	22-Aug-1920
Gustav	Kinn	SWE	10-Jun-1895	2:49:10.4	17	Antwerp	22-Aug-1920
Albert	Moche	FRA	1884	2:50:00.2	18	Antwerp	22-Aug-1920
Phadeppa	Changule	IND		2:50:45.4	19	Antwerp	22-Aug-1920
Zensaku	Motegi	JPN	10-Feb-1893	2:51:09.4	20	Antwerp	22-Aug-1920
Kenzo	Yajima	JPN	06-Apr-1902	2:57:02.0	21	Antwerp	22-Aug-1920
George	Norman	CAN		2:58:01.0	22	Antwerp	22-Aug-1920
Rudolf	Wahlin	SWE	02-Nov-1887	2:59:23.0	23	Antwerp	22-Aug-1920
Yahei	Miura	JPN	02-Apr-1891	2:59:37.0	24	Antwerp	22-Aug-1920
Henri	Teyssedou	FRA	03-Apr-1889	3:00:04.0	25	Antwerp	22-Aug-1920
Hendrik	Wessel	NED	17-Dec-1887	3:00:17.0	26	Antwerp	22-Aug-1920
Charles	Melis	BEL		3:00:51.0	27	Antwerp	22-Aug-1920
Wilhelm	Gruner	SWE	06-May-1888	3:01:48.0	28	Antwerp	22-Aug-1920
George	Piper	GBR		3:02:10.0	29	Antwerp	22-Aug-1920
Thomas Sinton	Hewitt	AUS		3:03:27.0	30	Antwerp	22-Aug-1920
Leslie	Housden	GBR	30-Oct-1894	3:14:07.0	31	Antwerp	22-Aug-1920
Herkules	Sakelloropoulos	GRE	01-Mar-1888	3:14:25.0	32	Antwerp	22-Aug-1920
Juan	Bascunan	CHI		3:17:47.0	33	Antwerp	22-Aug-1920
Oscar	Blansaer	BEL	13-Nov-1890	3:20:00.0	34	Antwerp	22-Aug-1920
Eric	Robertson	NFD	12-Sep-1892	3:55:00.0	35	Antwerp	22-Aug-1920
Christian	Gitsham	SOA	15-Oct-1888		DNF	Antwerp	22-Aug-1920
Ettore	Blasi	ITA	18-Mar-1895		DNF	Antwerp	22-Aug-1920
Louis	Ichard	FRA	02-Jan-1901		DNF	Antwerp	22-Aug-1920
Amedee	Trichard	FRA			DNF	Antwerp	22-Aug-1920
Antonio	Persico	ITA			DNF	Antwerp	22-Aug-1920
Albert	Smoke	CAN			DNF	Antwerp	22-Aug-1920
Axel	Jensen	DEN	17-Sep-1899		DNF	Antwerp	22-Aug-1920
Arthur	Roth	USA	10-May-1892		DNF	Antwerp	22-Aug-1920
Hans	Schuster	SWE	07-Dec-1888		DNF	Antwerp	22-Aug-1920
Panayotis	Trivoulidas	GRE	1878		DNF	Antwerp	22-Aug-1920
Christian	Huygens	NED	25-Jan-1897		DNF	Antwerp	22-Aug-1920
Desire	van Remortel	BEL			DNF	Antwerp	22-Aug-1920
Sadashir	Datar	IND			DNF	Antwerp	22-Aug-1920
Albin	Stenroos	FIN	24-Feb-1889	2:41:22.6	1	Paris	13-Jul-1924
Romeo	Bertini	ITA	21-Apr-1893	2:47:19.6	2	Paris	13-Jul-1924
Clarence	DeMar	USA	07-Jun-1888	2:48:14.0	3	Paris	13-Jul-1924
Lauri	Halonen	FIN	24-Mar-1894	2:49:47.4	4	Paris	13-Jul-1924
Samuel	Ferris	GBR	29-Aug-1900	2:52:26.0	5	Paris	13-Jul-1924
Manuel	Plaza	CHI	19-Mar-1902	2:52:54.0	6	Paris	13-Jul-1924
Boughera	El Ouafi	FRA	18-Oct-1898	2:54:19.6	7	Paris	13-Jul-1924
Gustav	Kinn	SWE	10-Jun-1895	2:54:33.4	8	Paris	13-Jul-1924

First name	Family name	GPE	Birth date	Time	Place	Venue	Race date
Dionisio	Carreras	ESP	09-Oct-1890	2:57:18.4	9	Paris	13-Jul-1924
Juri	Lossman	EST	04-Feb-1891	2:57:54.6	10	Paris	13-Jul-1924
Axel	Jensen	DEN	17-Sep-1899	2:58:44.8	11	Paris	13-Jul-1924
Jean	Manhes	FRA	04-Feb-1897	3:00:34.0	12	Paris	13-Jul-1924
John	Cuthbert	CAN	1894	3:00:44.6	13	Paris	13-Jul-1924
M. Victor	MacAulay	CAN	1889	3:02:05.4	14	Paris	13-Jul-1924
Marcel	Alavoine	BEL	03-Apr-1898	3:03:20.0	15	Paris	13-Jul-1924
Frank	Wendling	USA	25-Aug-1897	3:05:09.8	16	Paris	13-Jul-1924
Anthony	Farrimond	GBR	1894	3:05:15.0	17	Paris	13-Jul-1924
Frank	Zuna	USA	02-Jan-1893	3:05:52.2	18	Paris	13-Jul-1924
Harry	Phillips	SOA	20-Jun-1883	3:07:13.0	19	Paris	13-Jul-1924
Auguste	Broos	BEL	09-Nov-1894	3:14:03.0	20	Paris	13-Jul-1924
Waldemar	Carlsson	SWE	20-May-1897	3:14:21.4	21	Paris	13-Jul-1924
Tullio	Biscuola	ITA	12-Jul-1894	3:19:05.0	22	Paris	13-Jul-1924
William	Churchill	USA	07-Oct-1886	3:19:18.0	23	Paris	13-Jul-1924
Mohammed	Ghermati Kader	FRA	1898	3:20:27.0	24	Paris	13-Jul-1924
Charles	Mellor	USA	27-Dec-1893	3:24:07.0	25	Paris	13-Jul-1924
Pierre	Leclercq	BEL		3:27:54.0	26	Paris	13-Jul-1924
Jack	McKenna	GBR	14-Apr-1889	3:30:40.0	27	Paris	13-Jul-1924
Antal	Lovas	HUN	20-Dec-1884	3:35:34.0	28	Paris	13-Jul-1924
Mahadeo	Hingh	IND	1888	3:37:36.0	29	Paris	13-Jul-1924
Elmar	Reimann	EST	12-Dec-1892	3:40:52.0	30	Paris	13-Jul-1924
Gerardus	Steurs	BEL	13-Jun-1901		DNF	Paris	13-Jul-1924
Felicien	Vandeputte	BEL	1898		DNF	Paris	13-Jul-1924
Belisario	Villacis	ECU	1899		DNF	Paris	13-Jul-1924
Vilho	Hietakari	FIN	06-Apr-1894		DNF	Paris	13-Jul-1924
Johannes	Kolehmainen	FIN	09-Dec-1889		DNF	Paris	13-Jul-1924
Ville	Kyronen	FIN	14-Jan-1891		DNF	Paris	13-Jul-1924
Gabriel	Ruotsalainen	FIN	13-Mar-1893		DNF	Paris	13-Jul-1924
Gabriel	Verger	FRA	1896		DNF	Paris	13-Jul-1924
Ernest	Leatherland	GBR	23-Jun-1894		DNF	Paris	13-Jul-1924
Arthur	Mills	GBR	16-Jan-1894		DNF	Paris	13-Jul-1924
Duncan McLeod	Wright	GBR	22-Sep-1896		DNF	Paris	13-Jul-1924
Vassilos	Athanassiadis	GRE	1900		DNF	Paris	13-Jul-1924
Alexandros	Kranis	GRE	1897		DNF	Paris	13-Jul-1924
Herkules	Sakelloropoulos	GRE	01-Mar-1888		DNF	Paris	13-Jul-1924
Pal	Kiraly	HUN	07-Nov-1897		DNF	Paris	13-Jul-1924
Emilio	Alciati	ITA	03-Dec-1901		DNF	Paris	13-Jul-1924
Ettore	Blasi	ITA	18-Mar-1895		DNF	Paris	13-Jul-1924
Alberto	Cavallero	ITA	14-Sep-1900		DNF	Paris	13-Jul-1924
Angelo	Malvicini	ITA	01-May-1895		DNF	Paris	13-Jul-1924
Shizo	Kanaguri	JPN	20-Aug-1891		DNF	Paris	13-Jul-1924
Yahei	Miura	JPN	02-Apr-1891		DNF	Paris	13-Jul-1924
Kikunosuke	Tashiro	JPN	10-Jun-1898		DNF	Paris	13-Jul-1924
Cornelius	Brouwer	NED	17-Dec-1900		DNF	Paris	13-Jul-1924
Teunis	Sprong	NED	16-Feb-1889		DNF	Paris	13-Jul-1924
Josef	Eberle	TCH	1901		DNF	Paris	13-Jul-1924
Bohumil	Honzatko	TCH	30-Dec-1875		DNF	Paris	13-Jul-1924
Jan	Kalous	TCH	1902		DNF	Paris	13-Jul-1924
Ralph	Williams	USA	24-Aug-1900		DNF	Paris	13-Jul-1924
Boughera	El Ouafi	FRA	18-Oct-1898	2:32:57.0	1	Amsterdam	05-Aug-1928
Manuel	Plaza	CHI	19-Mar-1902	2:33:23.0	2	Amsterdam	05-Aug-1928
Martti	Marttelin	FIN	18-Jun-1897	2:35:02.0	3	Amsterdam	05-Aug-1928
Kanematsu	Yamada	JPN	16-Sep-1903	2:35:29.0	4	Amsterdam	05-Aug-1928
Joie	Ray	USA	13-Apr-1894	2:36:04.0	5	Amsterdam	05-Aug-1928
Seiichiro	Tsuda	JPN	26-Jul-1906	2:36:20.0	6	Amsterdam	05-Aug-1928
Yrjo	Korholin-Koski	FIN	03-May-1900	2:36:40.0	7	Amsterdam	05-Aug-1928
Samuel	Ferris	GBR	29-Aug-1900	2:37:41.0	8	Amsterdam	05-Aug-1928
Albert	Michelsen	USA	16-Dec-1893	2:38:56.0	9	Amsterdam	05-Aug-1928
Clifford	Bricker	CAN	23-Apr-1904	2:39:24.0	10	Amsterdam	05-Aug-1928
Harold	Wood	GBR	28-Nov-1902	2:41:15.0	11	Amsterdam	05-Aug-1928

First name	Family name	GPE	Birth date	Time	Place	Venue	Race date
Verner	Laaksonen	FIN	07-Nov-1895	2:41:35.0	12	Amsterdam	05-Aug-1928
Harry	Payne	GBR	05-Sep-1892	2:42:29.0	13	Amsterdam	05-Aug-1928
Eino	Rastas	FIN	17-Jul-1894	2:43:08.0	14	Amsterdam	05-Aug-1928
Vaino	Sipila	FIN	24-Dec-1897	2:43:08.0	15	Amsterdam	05-Aug-1928
Alois	Krof	TCH	08-Jul-1903	2:43:18.0	16	Amsterdam	05-Aug-1928
John	Miles	CAN	30-Oct-1905	2:43:32.0	17	Amsterdam	05-Aug-1928
Leon	Broers	BEL		2:44:37.0	18	Amsterdam	05-Aug-1928
Hans-Ludwig	Stelges	GER	06-Jun-1901	2:45:27.0	19	Amsterdam	05-Aug-1928
Duncan McLeod	Wright	GBR	22-Sep-1896	2:45:30.0	20	Amsterdam	05-Aug-1928
Herbert	Bignall	GBR	28-Jan-1906	2:45:44.0	21	Amsterdam	05-Aug-1928
Ernest	Harper	GBR	02-Aug-1902	2:45:44.0	22	Amsterdam	05-Aug-1928
Jean	Gerault	FRA	08-May-1904	2:46:08.0	23	Amsterdam	05-Aug-1928
Ilmari	Kuokka	FIN	23-Jul-1901	2:46:34.0	24	Amsterdam	05-Aug-1928
Gustav	Kinn	SWE	10-Jun-1895	2:47:35.0	25	Amsterdam	05-Aug-1928
Silas	McLennan	CAN		2:49:33.0	26	Amsterdam	05-Aug-1928
Clarence	DeMar	USA	07-Jun-1888	2:50:42.0	27	Amsterdam	05-Aug-1928
Marcel	Denis	FRA	31-Jan-1896	2:51:15.0	28	Amsterdam	05-Aug-1928
Guillaume	Tell	FRA	08-Jul-1902	2:51:18.0	29	Amsterdam	05-Aug-1928
Henri	Landheer	NED	27-Apr-1899	2:51:59.0	30	Amsterdam	05-Aug-1928
Paul	Hempel	GER	30-Jun-1890	2:52:01.0	31	Amsterdam	05-Aug-1928
Aurelio	Terrazas	MEX		2:52:22.0	32	Amsterdam	05-Aug-1928
Frantisek	Zyka	TCH	03-Mar-1902	2:52:42.0	33	Amsterdam	05-Aug-1928
Giuseppe	Ferrera	ITA		2:53:10.0	34	Amsterdam	05-Aug-1928
Juan	Torres	MEX		2:54:00.0	35	Amsterdam	05-Aug-1928
Johan	Stoa	NOR	13-Jun-1900	2:54:15.0	36	Amsterdam	05-Aug-1928
Gerardus	Steurs	BEL	13-Jun-1901	2:54:48.0	37	Amsterdam	05-Aug-1928
Arturs	Motmillers	LAT	01-Oct-1900	2:56:45.0	38	Amsterdam	05-Aug-1928
James	Henigan	USA	25-Apr-1892	2:56:50.0	39	Amsterdam	05-Aug-1928
Marthinus	Steytler	SOA	1890	2:57:21.0	40	Amsterdam	05-Aug-1928
Harvey	Frick	USA	13-Oct-1893	2:57:24.0	41	Amsterdam	05-Aug-1928
Jean	Linsen	BEL	1904	2:58:08.0	42	Amsterdam	05-Aug-1928
Frank	Hughes	CAN		2:58:12.0	43	Amsterdam	05-Aug-1928
William	Agee	USA	25-Dec-1905	2:58:50.0	44	Amsterdam	05-Aug-1928
Percival	Wyer	CAN	23-Jan-1888	2:58:52.0	45	Amsterdam	05-Aug-1928
Georg	Hoerger	GER	08-Sep-1897	2:59:01.0	46	Amsterdam	05-Aug-1928
Hans	Schneider	GER	03-Feb-1900	2:59:36.0	47	Amsterdam	05-Aug-1928
Juichi	Nagatani	JPN	27-Jan-1903	3:03:34.0	48	Amsterdam	05-Aug-1928
Jozsef	Galambos	HUN	15-Oct-1900	3:05:58.0	49	Amsterdam	05-Aug-1928
Paul	Gerhardt	GER	06-Dec-1901	3:09:30.0	50	Amsterdam	05-Aug-1928
Gottlieb	Bach	DEN	04-Feb-1900	3:10:30.0	51	Amsterdam	05-Aug-1928
Emilio	Ferrer	ESP		3:11:05.0	52	Amsterdam	05-Aug-1928
Dimitrije	Stevanovic	YUG	21-Jan-1896	3:11:35.0	53	Amsterdam	05-Aug-1928
Johannes	Vermeulen	NED	21-Oct-1907	3:13:47.0	54	Amsterdam	05-Aug-1928
Pleun	van Leenen	NED	02-Jan-1901	3:14:37.0	55	Amsterdam	05-Aug-1928
Joseph	Marien	BEL	25-Jan-1900	3:16:13.0	56	Amsterdam	05-Aug-1928
Wilhemus	van der Steen	NED	09-Nov-1905	3:19:53.0	57	Amsterdam	05-Aug-1928
Aksel	Madsen	DEN	29-Jul-1899		DNF	Amsterdam	05-Aug-1928
Hans Orla	Olsen	DEN	31-Aug-1899		DNF	Amsterdam	05-Aug-1928
Karl	Laas	EST	17-Apr-1908		DNF	Amsterdam	05-Aug-1928
Romeo	Bertini	ITA	21-Apr-1893		DNF	Amsterdam	05-Aug-1928
Attilio	Conton	ITA	02-Sep-1902		DNF	Amsterdam	05-Aug-1928
Stefano	Natale	ITA	16-Apr-1903		DNF	Amsterdam	05-Aug-1928
Abraham	Groeneweg	NED	13-Mar-1905		DNF	Amsterdam	05-Aug-1928
Teunis	Sprong	NED	16-Feb-1889		DNF	Amsterdam	05-Aug-1928
Vintila	Cristescu	ROM			DNF	Amsterdam	05-Aug-1928
Axel	Elofs	SWE	20-Nov-1903		DNF	Amsterdam	05-Aug-1928
Vilis	Cimmermanis	LAT	31-Dec-1896		DNF	Amsterdam	05-Aug-1928
Franz	Wanderer	GER	20-Feb-1901		DNF	Amsterdam	05-Aug-1928
Juan	Zabala	ARG	21-Sep-1911	2:31:36.0	1	Los Angeles	07-Aug-1932
Samuel	Ferris	GBR	29-Aug-1900	2:31:55.0	2	Los Angeles	07-Aug-1932
Armas	Toivonen	FIN	20-Jan-1899	2:32:12.0	3	Los Angeles	07-Aug-1932

First name	Family name	GPE	Birth date	Time	Place	Venue	Race date
Duncan McLeod	Wright	GBR	22-Sep-1896	2:32:41.0	4	Los Angeles	07-Aug-1932
Seiichiro	Tsuda	JPN	26-Jul-1906	2:35:42.0	5	Los Angeles	07-Aug-1932
Onbai	Kin	JPN	21-Aug-1913	2:37:28.0	6	Los Angeles	07-Aug-1932
Albert	Michelsen	USA	16-Dec-1893	2:39:38.0	7	Los Angeles	07-Aug-1932
Oskar	Heks	TCH	10-Apr-1908	2:41:35.0	8	Los Angeles	07-Aug-1932
Taika	Gon	JPN	02-Jun-1906	2:42:52.0	9	Los Angeles	07-Aug-1932
Anders	Andersen	DEN	01-Feb-1907	2:44:38.0	10	Los Angeles	07-Aug-1932
Hans	Oldag	USA	02-Mar-1901	2:47:26.0	11	Los Angeles	07-Aug-1932
Clifford	Bricker	CAN	23-Apr-1904	2:47:58.0	12	Los Angeles	07-Aug-1932
Michele	Fanelli	ITA	14-Sep-1907	2:49:09.0	13	Los Angeles	07-Aug-1932
John	Miles	CAN	30-Oct-1905	2:50:32.0	14	Los Angeles	07-Aug-1932
Paul	de Bruyn	GER	07-Oct-1907	2:52:39.0	15	Los Angeles	07-Aug-1932
Francois	Begeot	FRA	11-Apr-1908	2:53:34.0	16	Los Angeles	07-Aug-1932
Fernando	Ciccarelli	ARG	18-Jul-1905	2:55:49.0	17	Los Angeles	07-Aug-1932
Edward	Cudworth	CAN	1911	2:58:35.0	18	Los Angeles	07-Aug-1932
Joao Clemente	da Silva	BRA		3:02:06.0	19	Los Angeles	07-Aug-1932
Margarito	Pomposo	MEX		3:10:51.0	20	Los Angeles	07-Aug-1932
Jose	Ribas	ARG	01-Oct-1899		DNF	Los Angeles	07-Aug-1932
Matheus	Marcondes	BRA	1897		DNF	Los Angeles	07-Aug-1932
Jorge	Perry	COL			DNF	Los Angeles	07-Aug-1932
Alfred	Maasik	EST	26-Jan-1897		DNF	Los Angeles	07-Aug-1932
Ville	Kyronen	FIN	14-Jan-1891		DNF	Los Angeles	07-Aug-1932
Lauri	Virtanen	FIN	03-Aug-1904		DNF	Los Angeles	07-Aug-1932
Francesco	Roccati	ITA	09-Jun-1908		DNF	Los Angeles	07-Aug-1932
Santiago	Hernandez	MEX			DNF	Los Angeles	07-Aug-1932
James	Henigan	USA	25-Apr-1892		DNF	Los Angeles	07-Aug-1932
Kitei	Son	JPN	29-Aug-1914	2:29:19.2	1	Berlin	09-Aug-1936
Ernest	Harper	GBR	02-Aug-1902	2:31:23.2	2	Berlin	09-Aug-1936
Shoryu	Nan	JPN	23-Nov-1912	2:31:42.0	3	Berlin	09-Aug-1936
Erkki	Tamila	FIN	05-May-1911	2:32:45.0	4	Berlin	09-Aug-1936
Vaino	Muinonen	FIN	30-Dec-1898	2:33:46.0	5	Berlin	09-Aug-1936
Johannes	Coleman	SOA	05-Jun-1910	2:36:17.0	6	Berlin	09-Aug-1936
Donald McNab	Robertson	GBR	07-Oct-1905	2:37:06.2	7	Berlin	09-Aug-1936
Henry	Gibson	SOA	31-Mar-1914	2:38:04.0	8	Berlin	09-Aug-1936
Mauno	Tarkiainen	FIN	18-Aug-1904	2:39:33.0	9	Berlin	09-Aug-1936
Thore	Enochsson	SWE	17-Nov-1908	2:43:12.0	10	Berlin	09-Aug-1936
Stylianos	Kyriakidis	GRE	04-May-1910	2:43:20.9	11	Berlin	09-Aug-1936
Nouba	Khaled	FRA	11-Dec-1905	2:45:34.0	12	Berlin	09-Aug-1936
Henry	Palme	SWE	04-Sep-1907	2:46:08.4	13	Berlin	09-Aug-1936
Franz	Tuschek	AUT	27-Mar-1899	2:46:29.0	14	Berlin	09-Aug-1936
James	Bartlett	CAN	29-Dec-1907	2:48:21.4	15	Berlin	09-Aug-1936
Emile	Duval	FRA	05-Jul-1907	2:48:39.8	16	Berlin	09-Aug-1936
Manuel	Dias	POR	13-Apr-1905	2:49:00.0	17	Berlin	09-Aug-1936
John A.	Kelley	USA	06-Sep-1907	2:49:32.4	18	Berlin	09-Aug-1936
Miroslav	Lunak	TCH	02-Feb-1902	2:50:26.0	19	Berlin	09-Aug-1936
Felix	Meskens	BEL	14-Feb-1906	2:51:19.0	20	Berlin	09-Aug-1936
Jan	Takac	TCH	02-Feb-1909	2:51:20.0	21	Berlin	09-Aug-1936
Rudolf	Wober	AUT	10-Oct-1911	2:51:28.0	22	Berlin	09-Aug-1936
Ludovic	Gall	ROM	10-Jan-1900	2:55:02.0	23	Berlin	09-Aug-1936
Robert	Nevens	BEL	02-May-1914	2:55:51.0	24	Berlin	09-Aug-1936
Anders	Andersen	DEN	01-Feb-1907	2:56:31.0	25	Berlin	09-Aug-1936
Gabrielo	Mendoza	PER	22-Jun-1906	2:57:17.8	26	Berlin	09-Aug-1936
Thomas	Lalande	SOA	31-Dec-1904	2:57:20.0	27	Berlin	09-Aug-1936
Arturs	Motmillers	LAT	01-Oct-1900	2:58:02.0	28	Berlin	09-Aug-1936
Eduard	Braesicke	GER	30-Nov-1905	2:59:33.4	29	Berlin	09-Aug-1936
Percival	Wyer	CAN	23-Jan-1888	3:00:11.0	30	Berlin	09-Aug-1936
Fernand	Leheurteur	FRA	27-Sep-1905	3:01:32.0	31	Berlin	09-Aug-1936
Wilhelm	Rothmayer	AUT	18-Dec-1910	3:02:32.0	32	Berlin	09-Aug-1936
Bronislaw	Gancarz	POL	31-Oct-1906	3:03:11.0	33	Berlin	09-Aug-1936
Max	Beer	SUI	15-Sep-1912	3:06:26.0	34	Berlin	09-Aug-1936
Guillermo	Suarez	PER	08-Sep-1912	3:08:18.0	35	Berlin	09-Aug-1936

First name	Family name	GPE	Birth date	Time	Place	Venue	Race date
Boris	Haralambiev	BUL	08-Feb-1908	3:08:53.8	36	Berlin	09-Aug-1936
Arul	Swami	IND	18-Dec-1913	3:10:44.0	37	Berlin	09-Aug-1936
Josef	Sulc	TCH	12-Sep-1907	3:11:47.4	38	Berlin	09-Aug-1936
Franz	Eha	SUI	07-Feb-1907	3:18:17.0	39	Berlin	09-Aug-1936
Tsungling	Wang	CHN	21-Oct-1912	3:25:36.4	40	Berlin	09-Aug-1936
Stane	Sporn	YUG	01-Apr-1904	3:30:47.0	41	Berlin	09-Aug-1936
Jose	Farias	PER	20-Oct-1909	3:33:24.0	42	Berlin	09-Aug-1936
Luis	Oliva	ARG	21-Jun-1908		DNF	Berlin	09-Aug-1936
Juan	Zabala	ARG	21-Sep-1911		DNF	Berlin	09-Aug-1936
Harold	Webster	CAN	18-Jan-1895		DNF	Berlin	09-Aug-1936
Juan	Acosta	CHI	16-Apr-1907		DNF	Berlin	09-Aug-1936
Albert	Norris	GBR	05-Nov-1898		DNF	Berlin	09-Aug-1936
Franz	Barsicke	GER	15-May-1905		DNF	Berlin	09-Aug-1936
Paul	de Bruyn	GER	07-Oct-1907		DNF	Berlin	09-Aug-1936
Giannino	Bulzone	ITA	09-May-1911		DNF	Berlin	09-Aug-1936
Aurelio	Genghini	ITA	01-Oct-1907		DNF	Berlin	09-Aug-1936
Tamao	Shiaku	JPN	12-May-1906		DNF	Berlin	09-Aug-1936
Kazimierz	Fialka	POL	02-Jul-1907		DNF	Berlin	09-Aug-1936
Jaime	Mendes	POR	28-Aug-1913		DNF	Berlin	09-Aug-1936
Ellison	Brown	USA	22-Sep-1914		DNF	Berlin	09-Aug-1936
William	McMahon	USA	03-Mar-1910		DNF	Berlin	09-Aug-1936
Delfo	Cabrera	ARG	12-Nov-1919	2:34:51.6	1	London	07-Aug-1948
Thomas	Richards	GBR	15-Mar-1910	2:35:07.6	2	London	07-Aug-1948
Etienne	Gailly	BEL	26-Nov-1922	2:35:33.6	3	London	07-Aug-1948
Johannes	Coleman	SOA	05-Jun-1910	2:36:06.0	4	London	07-Aug-1948
Eusebio	Guinez	ARG	16-Dec-1906	2:36:36.0	5	London	07-Aug-1948
Thomas Sydney	Luyt	SOA	11-Dec-1925	2:38:11.0	6	London	07-Aug-1948
Gustav	Ostling	SWE	17-Dec-1914	2:38:40.6	7	London	07-Aug-1948
John	Systad	NOR	20-Mar-1917	2:38:41.0	8	London	07-Aug-1948
Armando	Sensini	ARG	21-Sep-1909	2:39:30.0	9	London	07-Aug-1948
Henning	Larsen	DEN	12-Dec-1910	2:41:22.0	10	London	07-Aug-1948
Viljo	Heino	FIN	01-Mar-1914	2:41:32.0	11	London	07-Aug-1948
Anders	Melin	SWE	31-Jul-1921	2:42:20.0	12	London	07-Aug-1948
Jussi	Kurikkala	FIN	12-Aug-1912	2:42:46.0	13	London	07-Aug-1948
Theodore	Vogel	USA	17-Jul-1925	2:45:27.0	14	London	07-Aug-1948
Enrique	Inostroza Arancibia	CHI		2:47:48.0	15	London	07-Aug-1948
Lloyd	Evans	CAN	31-Jul-1915	2:48:07.0	16	London	07-Aug-1948
Gerard	Cote	CAN	28-Jul-1913	2:48:31.0	17	London	07-Aug-1948
Stylianos	Kyriakidis	GRE	04-May-1910	2:49:00.0	18	London	07-Aug-1948
Jozsef	Kiss	HUN	29-Apr-1909	2:50:20.0	19	London	07-Aug-1948
Sevki	Koru	TUR	01-Apr-1913	2:51:07.0	20	London	07-Aug-1948
John A.	Kelley	USA	06-Sep-1907	2:51:56.0	21	London	07-Aug-1948
Kaspar	Schiesser	SUI	28-Jan-1916	2:52:09.0	22	London	07-Aug-1948
Walter	Fedorik	CAN	30-Jan-1918	2:52:12.0	23	London	07-Aug-1948
Aulis Olavi	Manninen	USA	09-Jan-1917	2:56:49.0	24	London	07-Aug-1948
Chong-Oh	Hong	KOR	07-Jul-1925	2:56:52.0	25	London	07-Aug-1948
Frank Paddy	Mulvihill	IRL	08-Dec-1915	2:57:35.0	26	London	07-Aug-1948
Yun-Bok	Suh	KOR	09-Jan-1923	2:59:36.0	27	London	07-Aug-1948
Sven	Hakansson	SWE	14-Nov-1909	3:00:09.0	28	London	07-Aug-1948
Jakob	Jutz	SUI		3:03:55.0	29	London	07-Aug-1948
Stanley	Jones	GBR	26-Dec-1914	3:09:16.0	30	London	07-Aug-1948
Weng-au	Lou	CHN			DNF	London	07-Aug-1948
Mikko	Hietanen	FIN	22-Sep-1911		DNF	London	07-Aug-1948
Pierre	Cousin	FRA	14-Jun-1913		DNF	London	07-Aug-1948
Rene	Josset	FRA	28-Jul-1910		DNF	London	07-Aug-1948
Arsene	Piesset	FRA	31-Jul-1919		DNF	London	07-Aug-1948
Jack	Holden	GBR	13-Mar-1907		DNF	London	07-Aug-1948
Athanasios	Ragazos	GRE	23-Aug-1913		DNF	London	07-Aug-1948
Chhota	Singh	IND			DNF	London	07-Aug-1948
Salvatore	Costantino	ITA	11-Jan-1919		DNF	London	07-Aug-1948
Yoon-Chil	Choi	KOR	19-Jul-1928		DNF	London	07-Aug-1948

First name	Family name	GPE	Birth date	Time	Place	Venue	Race date
Hans	Frischknecht	SUI	31-Dec-1922		DNF	London	07-Aug-1948
Emil	Zatopek	TCH	19-Sep-1922	2:23:03.2	1	Helsinki	27-Jul-1952
Reinaldo	Gorno	ARG	18-Jun-1918	2:25:35.0	2	Helsinki	27-Jul-1952
Gustaf	Jansson	SWE	05-Jan-1922	2:26:07.0	3	Helsinki	27-Jul-1952
Yoon-Chil	Choi	KOR	19-Jul-1928	2:26:36.0	4	Helsinki	27-Jul-1952
Veikko	Karvonen	FIN	05-Jan-1926	2:26:41.8	5	Helsinki	27-Jul-1952
Delfo	Cabrera	ARG	12-Nov-1919	2:26:42.4	6	Helsinki	27-Jul-1952
Jozsef	Dobronyi	HUN	17-Jun-1917	2:28:04.8	7	Helsinki	27-Jul-1952
Erkki	Puolakka	FIN	17-May-1925	2:29:35.0	8	Helsinki	27-Jul-1952
Geoffrey	Iden	GBR	08-Oct-1914	2:30:42.0	9	Helsinki	27-Jul-1952
Wallace	Hayward	SOA	10-Jul-1908	2:31:50.2	10	Helsinki	27-Jul-1952
Thomas Sydney	Luyt	SOA	11-Dec-1925	2:32:41.0	11	Helsinki	27-Jul-1952
Gustav	Ostling	SWE	17-Dec-1914	2:32:48.4	12	Helsinki	27-Jul-1952
Victor	Dyrgall	USA	08-Oct-1917	2:32:52.4	13	Helsinki	27-Jul-1952
Luis	Celedon	CHI	16-Dec-1926	2:33:45.8	14	Helsinki	27-Jul-1952
Adrianus	van der Zande	NED	16-Sep-1924	2:33:50.0	15	Helsinki	27-Jul-1952
Victor	Olsen	NOR	05-Feb-1924	2:33:58.4	16	Helsinki	27-Jul-1952
Mikko	Hietanen	FIN	22-Sep-1911	2:34:01.0	17	Helsinki	27-Jul-1952
Charles	DeWachtere	BEL	22-Dec-1927	2:34:32.0	18	Helsinki	27-Jul-1952
William	Keith	SOA	26-Nov-1925	2:34:38.0	19	Helsinki	27-Jul-1952
Yakov	Moskachenkov	URS	07-Aug-1916	2:34:43.8	20	Helsinki	27-Jul-1952
Mihaly	Esztergomi	HUN	13-Jun-1912	2:35:10.0	21	Helsinki	27-Jul-1952
Doroteo	Flores	GUA	11-Feb-1922	2:35:40.0	22	Helsinki	27-Jul-1952
Jean	Simonet	BEL	05-May-1927	2:35:43.0	23	Helsinki	27-Jul-1952
Jakob	Kjersem	NOR	02-Aug-1925	2:36:14.0	24	Helsinki	27-Jul-1952
Katsuo	Nishida	JPN	24-Jan-1929	2:36:19.0	25	Helsinki	27-Jul-1952
Keizo	Yamada	JPN	30-Nov-1927	2:38:11.2	26	Helsinki	27-Jul-1952
Feodosiy	Vanin	URS	25-Feb-1914	2:38:22.0	27	Helsinki	27-Jul-1952
Grigoriy	Suchkov	URS	1917	2:38:28.8	28	Helsinki	27-Jul-1952
Henry	Norrstrom	SWE	28-Jan-1918	2:38:57.4	29	Helsinki	27-Jul-1952
Dieter	Engelhardt	FRG	24-Feb-1926	2:39:37.2	30	Helsinki	27-Jul-1952
Cristea	Dinu	ROM	10-Aug-1911	2:39:42.2	31	Helsinki	27-Jul-1952
Jean	Leblond	BEL	02-Jun-1920	2:40:37.0	32	Helsinki	27-Jul-1952
Choong-Sik	Choi	KOR	19-Sep-1931	2:41:23.0	33	Helsinki	27-Jul-1952
John	Systad	NOR	20-Mar-1917	2:41:29.8	34	Helsinki	27-Jul-1952
Jaroslav	Sourek	TCH	07-Sep-1927	2:41:40.4	35	Helsinki	27-Jul-1952
Thomas	Jones	USA	18-Nov-1916	2:42:50.0	36	Helsinki	27-Jul-1952
Robert	Prentice	AUS	04-Nov-1923	2:43:13.4	37	Helsinki	27-Jul-1952
Muhammad Havildar	Aslam	PAK	10-Oct-1921	2:43:38.2	38	Helsinki	27-Jul-1952
Adolf	Gruber	AUT	15-May-1920	2:45:02.0	39	Helsinki	27-Jul-1952
Paul	Collins	CAN	22-Jul-1926	2:45:58.0	40	Helsinki	27-Jul-1952
Vasile	Teodosiu	ROM	21-Dec-1916	2:46:00.8	41	Helsinki	27-Jul-1952
Erik	Simonsen	DEN	05-Aug-1915	2:46:41.4	42	Helsinki	27-Jul-1952
Ludwig	Warnemunde	FRG	10-Oct-1916	2:50:00.0	43	Helsinki	27-Jul-1952
Theodore	Corbitt	USA	31-Jan-1920	2:51:09.0	44	Helsinki	27-Jul-1952
Claude	Smeal	AUS	22-Sep-1918	2:52:23.0	45	Helsinki	27-Jul-1952
Asfo	Bussotti	ITA	02-Dec-1925	2:52:55.0	46	Helsinki	27-Jul-1952
Winandiusz	Osinski	POL	22-Aug-1913	2:54:38.2	47	Helsinki	27-Jul-1952
Olaf	Sorensen	DEN	30-Nov-1917	2:55:21.0	48	Helsinki	27-Jul-1952
Joseph	West	IRL	04-Dec-1924	2:56:22.8	49	Helsinki	27-Jul-1952
Rudolf	Morgenthaler	SUI	22-Mar-1926	2:56:33.0	50	Helsinki	27-Jul-1952
Hassan Abdel Gani	Abdelfattah	EGY	23-Oct-1920	2:56:56.0	51	Helsinki	27-Jul-1952
Surat	Singh Matur	IND	22-Aug-1930	2:58:09.2	52	Helsinki	27-Jul-1952
Artidoro	Berti	ITA	29-Jul-1920	2:58:36.2	53	Helsinki	27-Jul-1952
Stanley	Cox	GBR	15-Jul-1918		DNF	Helsinki	27-Jul-1952
James	Peters	GBR	24-Oct-1918		DNF	Helsinki	27-Jul-1952
Corsino	Fernandez	ARG	12-Nov-1920		DNF	Helsinki	27-Jul-1952
Raul	Inostroza Donoso	CHI	10-Feb-1921		DNF	Helsinki	27-Jul-1952
Luis	Velasquez	GUA	30-Dec-1919		DNF	Helsinki	27-Jul-1952
Egilberto	Martufi	ITA	05-May-1926		DNF	Helsinki	27-Jul-1952
Yoshitaka	Uchikawa	JPN	04-Apr-1931		DNF	Helsinki	27-Jul-1952

First name	Family name	GPE	Birth date	Time	Place	Venue	Race date
Chong-Oh	Hong	KOR	07-Jul-1925		DNF	Helsinki	27-Jul-1952
Muhammad	Banaras	PAK	13-Sep-1930		DNF	Helsinki	27-Jul-1952
Constantin	Radu	ROM	13-Feb-1912		DNF	Helsinki	27-Jul-1952
Ahmet	Aytar	TUR	1922		DNF	Helsinki	27-Jul-1952
Lionel	Billas	FRA	03-Feb-1929		DNF	Helsinki	27-Jul-1952
Franjo	Krajcar	YUG	07-Sep-1914		DNF	Helsinki	27-Jul-1952
Alain	Mimoun	FRA	01-Jan-1921	2:25:00.0	1	Melbourne	01-Dec-1956
Franjo	Mihalic	YUG	09-Mar-1920	2:26:32.0	2	Melbourne	01-Dec-1956
Veikko	Karvonen	FIN	05-Jan-1926	2:27:47.0	3	Melbourne	01-Dec-1956
Chang-Hoon	Lee	KOR	21-Mar-1935	2:28:45.0	4	Melbourne	01-Dec-1956
Yoshiaki	Kawashima	JPN	10-May-1934	2:29:19.0	5	Melbourne	01-Dec-1956
Emil	Zatopek	TCH	19-Sep-1922	2:29:34.0	6	Melbourne	01-Dec-1956
Ivan	Filin	URS	10-Mar-1926	2:30:37.0	7	Melbourne	01-Dec-1956
Evert	Nyberg	SWE	28-Feb-1925	2:31:12.0	8	Melbourne	01-Dec-1956
Thomas	Nilsson	SWE	09-Apr-1926	2:33:33.0	9	Melbourne	01-Dec-1956
Eino	Oksanen	FIN	07-May-1931	2:36:10.0	10	Melbourne	01-Dec-1956
Arnold	Vaide	SWE	17-Apr-1926	2:36:21.0	11	Melbourne	01-Dec-1956
Choong-Sik	Choi	KOR	19-Sep-1931	2:36:53.0	12	Melbourne	01-Dec-1956
Paavo	Kotila	FIN	26-Aug-1927	2:38:59.0	13	Melbourne	01-Dec-1956
Mercer	Davies	SOA	10-Dec-1924	2:39:48.0	14	Melbourne	01-Dec-1956
Harry	Hicks	GBR	06-Aug-1925	2:39:55.0	15	Melbourne	01-Dec-1956
Hideo	Hamamura	JPN	17-Jul-1928	2:40:53.0	16	Melbourne	01-Dec-1956
Albert	Richards	NZL	1924	2:41:34.0	17	Melbourne	01-Dec-1956
John	Russell	AUS	1932	2:41:45.0	18	Melbourne	01-Dec-1956
Lothar	Beckert	GDR	26-Jul-1931	2:42:10.0	19	Melbourne	01-Dec-1956
Nicholas	Costes	USA	03-Aug-1926	2:42:20.0	20	Melbourne	01-Dec-1956
John J.	Kelley	USA	24-Dec-1930	2:43:40.0	21	Melbourne	01-Dec-1956
Muhammad Havildar	Aslam	PAK	10-Oct-1921	2:44:33.0	22	Melbourne	01-Dec-1956
Adolf	Gruber	AUT	15-May-1920	2:46:20.0	23	Melbourne	01-Dec-1956
Aurele	Vandendriessche	BEL	04-Jul-1932	2:47:18.0	24	Melbourne	01-Dec-1956
Keith	Ollerenshaw	AUS	28-Sep-1928	2:48:12.0	25	Melbourne	01-Dec-1956
Naw	Myitung	BIR	28-Dec-1933	2:49:32.0	26	Melbourne	01-Dec-1956
Pavel	Kantorek	TCH	08-Feb-1930	2:52:05.0	27	Melbourne	01-Dec-1956
Kurt	Hartung	GDR	17-Apr-1925	2:52:15.0	28	Melbourne	01-Dec-1956
Feleke	Bashay	ETH	1920	2:53:37.0	29	Melbourne	01-Dec-1956
Abdul	Rashid	PAK	25-Apr-1928	2:57:47.0	30	Melbourne	01-Dec-1956
Arap-Sum	Kanuti	KEN	1934	2:58:42.0	31	Melbourne	01-Dec-1956
Gebre	Birkay	ETH	1926	2:58:49.0	32	Melbourne	01-Dec-1956
Kurao	Hiroshima	JPN	05-Dec-1928	3:04:18.0	33	Melbourne	01-Dec-1956
Giuseppe	Lavelli	ITA	12-Nov-1928		DNF	Melbourne	01-Dec-1956
Johannes	Barnard	SOA	21-Oct-1929		DNF	Melbourne	01-Dec-1956
Ronald	Clark	GBR	09-Mar-1930		DNF	Melbourne	01-Dec-1956
Eduardo	Fontecilla	CHI	09-Nov-1929		DNF	Melbourne	01-Dec-1956
Ali	Baghanbashi	IRN	06-Sep-1924		DNF	Melbourne	01-Dec-1956
Boris	Grishayev	URS	21-Jun-1928		DNF	Melbourne	01-Dec-1956
Leslie	Perry	AUS	29-Jan-1923		DNF	Melbourne	01-Dec-1956
Juan	Jorquera	CHI	24-Jun-1930		DNF	Melbourne	01-Dec-1956
Albert	Ivanov	URS	01-Sep-1931		DNF	Melbourne	01-Dec-1956
Klaus	Porbadnik	GDR	24-Mar-1930		DNF	Melbourne	01-Dec-1956
Frederick	Norris	GBR	04-Sep-1921		DNF	Melbourne	01-Dec-1956
Hwa-Dong	Lim	KOR	1938		DNF	Melbourne	01-Dec-1956
Dean	Thackwray	USA	07-Mar-1933		DNF	Melbourne	01-Dec-1956
Abebe	Bikila	ETH	07-Aug-1932	2:15:16.2	1	Rome	10-Sep-1960
Rhadi	ben Abdesselem	MAR	28-Feb-1929	2:15:41.6	2	Rome	10-Sep-1960
Barrington	Magee	NZL	06-Feb-1934	2:17:18.2	3	Rome	10-Sep-1960
Konstantin	Vorobiev	URS	30-Oct-1930	2:19:09.6	4	Rome	10-Sep-1960
Sergey	Popov	URS	21-Sep-1930	2:19:18.8	5	Rome	10-Sep-1960
Thyge	Togersen	DEN	04-Nov-1926	2:21:03.4	6	Rome	10-Sep-1960
Abebe	Wakgira	ETH	21-Oct-1921	2:21:09.4	7	Rome	10-Sep-1960
Benaissa	Bakir	MAR	07-Apr-1931	2:21:21.4	8	Rome	10-Sep-1960
Osvaldo	Suarez	ARG	17-Mar-1934	2:21:26.6	9	Rome	10-Sep-1960

First name	Family name	GPE	Birth date	Time	Place	Venue	Race date
Franjo	Skrinjar	YUG	17-May-1920	2:21:40.2	10	Rome	10-Sep-1960
Nikolay	Rumyantsev	URS	31-May-1930	2:21:49.4	11	Rome	10-Sep-1960
Franjo	Mihalic	YUG	09-Mar-1920	2:21:52.6	12	Rome	10-Sep-1960
Keith	James	SOA	05-Nov-1934	2:22:58.6	13	Rome	10-Sep-1960
Pavel	Kantorek	TCH	08-Feb-1930	2:22:59.8	14	Rome	10-Sep-1960
Gumersindo	Gomez	ARG	13-Jan-1929	2:23:00.0	15	Rome	10-Sep-1960
Dennis	O'Gorman	GBR	22-May-1928	2:24:16.2	16	Rome	10-Sep-1960
Miguel	Navarro	ESP	21-Nov-1929	2:24:17.4	17	Rome	10-Sep-1960
Jeffrey	Julian	NZL	09-Oct-1935	2:24:50.6	18	Rome	10-Sep-1960
John J.	Kelley	USA	24-Dec-1930	2:24:58.0	19	Rome	10-Sep-1960
Chang-Hoon	Lee	KOR	21-Mar-1935	2:25:02.2	20	Rome	10-Sep-1960
Arnold	Vaide	SWE	17-Apr-1926	2:25:40.2	21	Rome	10-Sep-1960
Gerald	McIntyre	IRL	22-May-1929	2:26:03.0	22	Rome	10-Sep-1960
Olavi	Manninen	FIN	20-Jul-1928	2:26:33.0	23	Rome	10-Sep-1960
Eino	Oksanen	FIN	07-May-1931	2:26:38.0	24	Rome	10-Sep-1960
Arthur	Keily	GBR	18-Mar-1921	2:27:00.0	25	Rome	10-Sep-1960
Tor	Torgersen	NOR	20-Mar-1928	2:27:30.0	26	Rome	10-Sep-1960
Naw	Myitung	BIR	28-Dec-1933	2:28:17.0	27	Rome	10-Sep-1960
Bruno	Bartholome	GDR	23-Aug-1926	2:28:39.0	28	Rome	10-Sep-1960
Brian	Kilby	GBR	26-Feb-1938	2:28:55.0	29	Rome	10-Sep-1960
Alexander	Breckenridge	USA	17-Apr-1932	2:29:38.0	30	Rome	10-Sep-1960
Kurao	Hiroshima	JPN	05-Dec-1928	2:29:40.0	31	Rome	10-Sep-1960
Kazumi	Watanabe	JPN	25-Dec-1935	2:29:45.0	32	Rome	10-Sep-1960
Juan	Jorquera	CHI	24-Jun-1930	2:31:18.0	33	Rome	10-Sep-1960
Alain	Mimoun	FRA	01-Jan-1921	2:31:20.0	34	Rome	10-Sep-1960
Paul	Geneve	FRA	30-Jul-1925	2:31:20.0	35	Rome	10-Sep-1960
Franciscus	Kunen	NED	17-Apr-1930	2:31:25.0	36	Rome	10-Sep-1960
Francesco	Perrone	ITA	03-Dec-1930	2:31:32.0	37	Rome	10-Sep-1960
Silvio	de Florentiis	ITA	01-Jan-1935	2:31:54.0	38	Rome	10-Sep-1960
Linus	Diaz	CEY	23-Sep-1933	2:32:12.0	39	Rome	10-Sep-1960
Chand	Nil Lal	IND	19-Jul-1928	2:32:13.0	40	Rome	10-Sep-1960
Johannes	Lauridsen	DEN	25-Dec-1930	2:32:32.2	41	Rome	10-Sep-1960
William	Dunne	IRL	12-Sep-1933	2:33:08.0	42	Rome	10-Sep-1960
Ian	Sinfield	AUS	03-Oct-1934	2:34:16.0	43	Rome	10-Sep-1960
Arthur	Wittwer	SUI	15-Nov-1927	2:34:42.0	44	Rome	10-Sep-1960
Jagmal	Singh Ragho	IND	20-Mar-1923	2:35:01.0	45	Rome	10-Sep-1960
Nobuyoshi	Sadanaga	JPN	07-Feb-1929	2:35:11.0	46	Rome	10-Sep-1960
Sang-Chul	Lee	KOR	01-Nov-1934	2:35:14.0	47	Rome	10-Sep-1960
Gordon	McKenzie	USA	26-Jun-1927	2:35:16.0	48	Rome	10-Sep-1960
Ahmed ben Dali	Labidi	TUN	04-May-1922	2:35:43.0	49	Rome	10-Sep-1960
Walter	Lemos	ARG	13-Mar-1930	2:36:55.0	50	Rome	10-Sep-1960
Raymond	Puckett	NZL	17-Dec-1935	2:37:36.0	51	Rome	10-Sep-1960
Adolf	Gruber	AUT	15-May-1920	2:37:40.0	52	Rome	10-Sep-1960
Antti	Viskari	FIN	01-May-1928	2:38:06.0	53	Rome	10-Sep-1960
Allan	Lawrence	AUS	09-Jul-1930	2:38:46.0	54	Rome	10-Sep-1960
Gordon	Dickson	CAN	11-Sep-1939	2:38:46.0	55	Rome	10-Sep-1960
Lothar	Beckert	GDR	26-Jul-1931	2:40:10.0	56	Rome	10-Sep-1960
Gunther	Havenstein	GDR	14-Dec-1928	2:41:14.0	57	Rome	10-Sep-1960
Evert	Nyberg	SWE	28-Feb-1925	2:42:59.0	58	Rome	10-Sep-1960
Arap-Sum	Kanuti	KEN	1934	2:46:55.0	59	Rome	10-Sep-1960
Ranjit	Bhatia	IND	27-May-1936	2:57:06.0	60	Rome	10-Sep-1960
Allal	Saoudi	MAR	1932	2:59:41.0	61	Rome	10-Sep-1960
Alifu Albert	Massaquoi	LBR	06-Apr-1937	3:43:18.0	62	Rome	10-Sep-1960
Vito	Di Terlizzi	ITA	07-Aug-1930		DNF	Rome	10-Sep-1960
Albert	Messitt	IRL	28-Jul-1928		DNF	Rome	10-Sep-1960
Yun-Bum	Kim	KOR	10-Dec-1934		DNF	Rome	10-Sep-1960
Aurele	Vandendriessche	BEL	04-Jul-1932		DNF	Rome	10-Sep-1960
Gerhard	Hecker	HUN	11-Sep-1933		DNF	Rome	10-Sep-1960
Mouldi	Essalhi	TUN	28-Dec-1932		DNF	Rome	10-Sep-1960
Hamadi	Dhaoui	TUN	10-Jan-1940		DNF	Rome	10-Sep-1960
Abebe	Bikila	ETH	07-Aug-1932	2:12:11.2	1	Tokyo	21-Oct-1964

First name	*Family name*	*GPE*	*Birth date*	*Time*	*Place*	*Venue*	*Race date*
Basil	Heatley	GBR	25-Dec-1933	2:16:19.2	2	Tokyo	21-Oct-1964
Kokichi	Tsuburaya	JPN	13-May-1940	2:16:22.8	3	Tokyo	21-Oct-1964
Brian	Kilby	GBR	26-Feb-1938	2:17:02.4	4	Tokyo	21-Oct-1964
Jozsef	Suto	HUN	09-Sep-1937	2:17:55.8	5	Tokyo	21-Oct-1964
Leonard	Edelen	USA	22-Sep-1937	2:18:12.4	6	Tokyo	21-Oct-1964
Aurele	Vandendriessche	BEL	04-Jul-1932	2:18:42.6	7	Tokyo	21-Oct-1964
Kenji	Kimihara	JPN	20-Mar-1941	2:19:49.0	8	Tokyo	21-Oct-1964
Ronald	Clarke	AUS	21-Feb-1937	2:20:26.8	9	Tokyo	21-Oct-1964
Demissie	Wolde	ETH	08-Mar-1937	2:21:25.2	10	Tokyo	21-Oct-1964
Sang-Hoon	Lee	KOR	30-Sep-1938	2:22:02.8	11	Tokyo	21-Oct-1964
Benaissa	Bakir	MAR	07-Apr-1931	2:22:27.0	12	Tokyo	21-Oct-1964
Eino	Oksanen	FIN	07-May-1931	2:22:36.0	13	Tokyo	21-Oct-1964
William	Mills	USA	30-Jun-1938	2:22:55.4	14	Tokyo	21-Oct-1964
Toru	Terasawa	JPN	04-Jan-1935	2:23:09.0	15	Tokyo	21-Oct-1964
Yun-Bum	Kim	KOR	10-Dec-1934	2:24:40.6	16	Tokyo	21-Oct-1964
Giorgio	Jegher	ITA	28-Aug-1937	2:24:45.2	17	Tokyo	21-Oct-1964
Vaclav	Chudomel	TCH	27-Sep-1932	2:24:46.8	18	Tokyo	21-Oct-1964
Ronald	Hill	GBR	25-Sep-1938	2:25:34.4	19	Tokyo	21-Oct-1964
Paavo	Pystynen	FIN	03-Feb-1932	2:26:00.6	20	Tokyo	21-Oct-1964
Fidel	Negrete	MEX	23-Feb-1932	2:26:07.0	21	Tokyo	21-Oct-1964
Nikolay	Tikhomirov	URS	21-Dec-1930	2:26:07.4	22	Tokyo	21-Oct-1964
Peter	McArdle	USA	22-Mar-1930	2:26:24.4	23	Tokyo	21-Oct-1964
Heinrich	Hagen	GDR	17-Dec-1935	2:26:39.8	24	Tokyo	21-Oct-1964
Pavel	Kantorek	TCH	08-Feb-1930	2:26.47.2	25	Tokyo	21-Oct-1964
Nikolay	Abramov	URS	10-Dec-1933	2:27:09.4	26	Tokyo	21-Oct-1964
Raymond	Puckett	NZL	17-Dec-1935	2:27:34.0	27	Tokyo	21-Oct-1964
Eino	Valle	FIN	18-Feb-1932	2:27:34.8	28	Tokyo	21-Oct-1964
Jeffrey	Julian	NZL	09-Oct-1935	2:27:57.6	29	Tokyo	21-Oct-1964
Ricardo	Vidal	CHI	10-Sep-1930	2:28:01.6	30	Tokyo	21-Oct-1964
Robert	Vagg	AUS	02-Feb-1940	2:28:41.0	31	Tokyo	21-Oct-1964
Guido	Vogele	SUI	17-Nov-1937	2:29:17.8	32	Tokyo	21-Oct-1964
Akotkar	Balakrishan	IND	01-Jul-1937	2:29:27.4	33	Tokyo	21-Oct-1964
Jean	Aniset	LUX	15-Sep-1934	2:29:52.6	34	Tokyo	21-Oct-1964
Wegam	Sumb	BIR	12-Mar-1930	2:30:35.8	35	Tokyo	21-Oct-1964
Constantin	Grecescu	ROM	07-Jan-1929	2:30:42.6	36	Tokyo	21-Oct-1964
Janos	Pinter	HUN	28-Feb-1936	2:30:50.2	37	Tokyo	21-Oct-1964
Gerhard	Honicke	GDR	25-Mar-1930	2:33:23.0	38	Tokyo	21-Oct-1964
Manfred	Naumann	GDR	21-Jun-1933	2:33:42.0	39	Tokyo	21-Oct-1964
Antonio	Ambu	ITA	10-May-1936	2:34:37.6	40	Tokyo	21-Oct-1964
Oskar	Leupi	SUI	17-Nov-1932	2:35:05.4	41	Tokyo	21-Oct-1964
Ivan	Keats	NZL	16-Apr-1937	2:36:16.8	42	Tokyo	21-Oct-1964
Harbans	Lal	IND	11-Apr-1938	2:37:05.8	43	Tokyo	21-Oct-1964
Armando	Aldegalega	POR	23-Nov-1937	2:38:02.2	44	Tokyo	21-Oct-1964
Christantus	Nyakwayo	KEN	1944	2:38:38.6	45	Tokyo	21-Oct-1964
Constantino	Kapambwe	NRH	21-Jul-1940	2:39:28.4	46	Tokyo	21-Oct-1964
Omari	Abdallah	TAN	05-May-1943	2:40:06.0	47	Tokyo	21-Oct-1964
Muhammad	Yousaf	PAK	10-Jan-1938	2:40:46.0	48	Tokyo	21-Oct-1964
Naftali	Temu	KEN	20-Apr-1945	2:40:46.6	49	Tokyo	21-Oct-1964
Hyung-Kil	Joo	KOR	20-Aug-1939	2:41:08.2	50	Tokyo	21-Oct-1964
Mathias	Kanda	SRH	02-Jun-1942	2:41:09.0	51	Tokyo	21-Oct-1964
Anthony	Cook	AUS	18-Sep-1936	2:42:03.6	52	Tokyo	21-Oct-1964
Victor	Peralta	MEX	16-Sep-1942	2:44:23.6	53	Tokyo	21-Oct-1964
Trevor	Haynes	NRH	17-Nov-1929	2:45:08.6	54	Tokyo	21-Oct-1964
Abraham	Fornes	PUR		2:46:22.6	55	Tokyo	21-Oct-1964
Robson	Mrombe	SRH	22-Jul-1941	2:49:30.8	56	Tokyo	21-Oct-1964
Laurent	Chifita	NRH	03-Aug-1943	2:51:53.2	57	Tokyo	21-Oct-1964
Chanom	Srirangsri	THA	12-Mar-1935	2:59:25.6	58	Tokyo	21-Oct-1964
James	Hogan	IRL	28-May-1933		DNF	Tokyo	21-Oct-1964
Bahadur	Ganga	NEP	1935		DNF	Tokyo	21-Oct-1964
Bahadur	Bhupendra	NEP			DNF	Tokyo	21-Oct-1964
Viktor	Baikov	URS	09-Feb-1935		DNF	Tokyo	21-Oct-1964

First name	Family name	GPE	Birth date	Time	Place	Venue	Race date
Haddeb Mohamed	Hannachi	TUN	1938		DNF	Tokyo	21-Oct-1964
Andrew	Soi	KEN	1938		DNF	Tokyo	21-Oct-1964
Osvaldo	Suarez	ARG	17-Mar-1934		DNF	Tokyo	21-Oct-1964
Mamo	Wolde	ETH	12-Jun-1932		DNF	Tokyo	21-Oct-1964
Hedhili	Ben Boubaker	TUN	1938		DNF	Tokyo	21-Oct-1964
Nguyen Van	Li	VIE	30-May-1942		DNF	Tokyo	21-Oct-1964
Mamo	Wolde	ETH	12-Jun-1932	2:20:26.4	1	Mexico City	20-Oct-1968
Kenji	Kimihara	JPN	20-Mar-1941	2:23:31.0	2	Mexico City	20-Oct-1968
Michael	Ryan	NZL	26-Dec-1941	2:23:45.0	3	Mexico City	20-Oct-1968
Ismail	Akcay	TUR	09-Jul-1942	2:25:18.8	4	Mexico City	20-Oct-1968
William	Adcocks	GBR	11-Nov-1941	2:25:33.0	5	Mexico City	20-Oct-1968
Merawi	Gebru	ETH	12-Dec-1932	2:27:16.8	6	Mexico City	20-Oct-1968
Derek	Clayton	AUS	17-Nov-1942	2:27:23.8	7	Mexico City	20-Oct-1968
Timothy	Johnston	GBR	11-Mar-1941	2:28:04.4	8	Mexico City	20-Oct-1968
Akio	Usami	JPN	31-May-1943	2:28:06.2	9	Mexico City	20-Oct-1968
Andrew	Boychuk	CAN	17-May-1941	2:28:40.2	10	Mexico City	20-Oct-1968
Gaston	Roelants	BEL	05-Feb-1937	2:29:04.8	11	Mexico City	20-Oct-1968
Patrick	McMahon	IRL	01-Feb-1942	2:29:21.0	12	Mexico City	20-Oct-1968
Alfredo	Penaloza	MEX	31-May-1947	2:29:48.8	13	Mexico City	20-Oct-1968
Kenneth	Moore	USA	01-Dec-1943	2:29:49.4	14	Mexico City	20-Oct-1968
Jurgen	Busch	GDR	24-Dec-1942	2:30:42.6	15	Mexico City	20-Oct-1968
George	Young	USA	24-Jul-1937	2:31:15.0	16	Mexico City	20-Oct-1968
Manfred	Steffny	FRG	14-Aug-1941	2:31:23.8	17	Mexico City	20-Oct-1968
Wegam	Sumb	BIR	12-Mar-1930	2:32:22.0	18	Mexico City	20-Oct-1968
Naftali	Temu	KEN	20-Apr-1945	2:32:36.0	19	Mexico City	20-Oct-1968
Maurice	Peiren	BEL	28-Dec-1937	2:32:49.0	20	Mexico City	20-Oct-1968
Antonio	Ambu	ITA	10-May-1936	2:33:19.6	21	Mexico City	20-Oct-1968
Ronald	Daws	USA	21-Jun-1937	2:33:53.0	22	Mexico City	20-Oct-1968
Karl-Heinz	Sievers	FRG	02-Oct-1942	2:34:11.8	23	Mexico City	20-Oct-1968
Gyula	Toth	HUN	12-Apr-1937	2:34:49.0	24	Mexico City	20-Oct-1968
Huseyin	Aktas	TUR	25-Mar-1941	2:35:09.5	25	Mexico City	20-Oct-1968
Pablo	Garrido	MEX	22-Jun-1938	2:35:47.8	26	Mexico City	20-Oct-1968
Adrianus	Steylen	NED	01-Aug-1935	2:37:42.0	27	Mexico City	20-Oct-1968
Anatoliy	Sukharkov	URS	10-Feb-1938	2:38:07.4	28	Mexico City	20-Oct-1968
Myung-Jung	Lee	KOR	15-Apr-1945	2:38:52.2	29	Mexico City	20-Oct-1968
Ivailo	Charankov	BUL	18-Nov-1933	2:39:49.6	30	Mexico City	20-Oct-1968
Gioacchino	de Palma	ITA	21-May-1940	2:39:58.2	31	Mexico City	20-Oct-1968
Josef	Gwerder	SUI	12-Jan-1939	2:40:16.0	32	Mexico City	20-Oct-1968
Hubert	Riesner	FRG	13-Aug-1940	2:41:29.0	33	Mexico City	20-Oct-1968
George	Olsen	DEN	05-May-1937	2:42:24.6	34	Mexico City	20-Oct-1968
Douglas	Sinkala	ZAM	15-Jul-1944	2:42:51.0	35	Mexico City	20-Oct-1968
Ezequiel	Baeza	CHI	08-May-1944	2:43:15.6	36	Mexico City	20-Oct-1968
David	McKenzie	NZL	16-Mar-1943	2:43:36.6	37	Mexico City	20-Oct-1968
Bong-Lee	Kim	KOR	15-Jul-1942	2:43:56.0	38	Mexico City	20-Oct-1968
Carlos	Cuque	GUA	24-Nov-1945	2:45:20.4	39	Mexico City	20-Oct-1968
Godwin	Kalimbwe	ZAM	27-Feb-1946	2:45:26.8	40	Mexico City	20-Oct-1968
Michael	Molloy	IRL	13-Mar-1938	2:48:13.6	41	Mexico City	20-Oct-1968
Nikola	Simeonov	BUL	19-Nov-1939	2:48:30.4	42	Mexico City	20-Oct-1968
John	Farrington	AUS	02-Jul-1942	2:50:16.8	43	Mexico City	20-Oct-1968
Helmut	Kunisch	SUI	26-Nov-1936	2:50:58.2	44	Mexico City	20-Oct-1968
Alifu Albert	Massaquoi	SLE	06-Apr-1937	2:52:28.0	45	Mexico City	20-Oct-1968
Sang-Hoon	Lee	KOR	30-Sep-1938	2:52:46.2	46	Mexico City	20-Oct-1968
Thein	Hla	BIR	25-Apr-1944	2:54:03.6	47	Mexico City	20-Oct-1968
Paul	Mose	KEN	14-Jul-1949	2:55:17.0	48	Mexico City	20-Oct-1968
Benjamin	Silva Netto	PHI	27-Apr-1939	2:56:19.4	49	Mexico City	20-Oct-1968
Harry	Prowell	GUY	10-Jul-1936	2:57:01.4	50	Mexico City	20-Oct-1968
Wimalasena	Perera	CEY	30-May-1945	2:59:05.8	51	Mexico City	20-Oct-1968
Fulgencio	Hernandez	GUA	01-Jan-1941	3:00:40.2	52	Mexico City	20-Oct-1968
Gustavo	Gutierrez	ECU	26-Sep-1939	3:03:07.0	53	Mexico City	20-Oct-1968
Martin	Ande	NGR	12-Apr-1948	3:03:47.6	54	Mexico City	20-Oct-1968
Musa	Mustapha	UGA	25-Jul-1947	3:04:53.8	55	Mexico City	20-Oct-1968

First name	Family name	GPE	Birth date	Time	Place	Venue	Race date
Enock	Mweemba	ZAM	18-Jun-1947	3:06:16.0	56	Mexico City	20-Oct-1968
John	Stephen	TAN	1942	3:25:17.0	57	Mexico City	20-Oct-1968
Edgar	Friedli	SUI	28-Oct-1933		DNF	Mexico City	20-Oct-1968
Mraljeb	A'yed-Mansoor	KUW	1939		DNF	Mexico City	20-Oct-1968
Mukhamed	Shakirov	URS	19-Mar-1933		DNF	Mexico City	20-Oct-1968
Saoud	Obaid Daifallah	KUW	1944		DNF	Mexico City	20-Oct-1968
Carlos	Perez	ESP	01-Jun-1935		DNF	Mexico City	20-Oct-1968
James	Alder	GBR	10-Jun-1940		DNF	Mexico City	20-Oct-1968
Seiichiro	Sasaki	JPN	02-Sep-1945		DNF	Mexico City	20-Oct-1968
Peter	Buniak (Drayton)	CAN	10-Jan-1945		DNF	Mexico City	20-Oct-1968
Guy	Texereau	FRA	14-May-1935		DNF	Mexico City	20-Oct-1968
Nedjalko	Farcic	YUG	12-Oct-1941		DNF	Mexico City	20-Oct-1968
Rene	Combes	FRA	24-Jun-1937		DNF	Mexico City	20-Oct-1968
Armando	Gonzalez	URU	20-Apr-1940		DNF	Mexico City	20-Oct-1968
Abebe	Bikila	ETH	07-Aug-1932		DNF	Mexico City	20-Oct-1968
Juan Rafael	Perez	CRC	03-Jul-1946		DNF	Mexico City	20-Oct-1968
Lajos	Mecser	HUN	23-Sep-1942		DNF	Mexico City	20-Oct-1968
Jozsef	Suto	HUN	09-Sep-1937		DNF	Mexico City	20-Oct-1968
Jose	Gaspar	MEX	20-Mar-1946		DNF	Mexico City	20-Oct-1968
Pentti	Rummakko	FIN	12-Oct-1943		DNF	Mexico City	20-Oct-1968
Frank	Shorter	USA	31-Oct-1947	2:12:19.8	1	Munich	10-Sep-1972
Karel	Lismont	BEL	08-Mar-1949	2:14:31.8	2	Munich	10-Sep-1972
Mamo	Wolde	ETH	12-Jun-1932	2:15:08.4	3	Munich	10-Sep-1972
Kenneth	Moore	USA	01-Dec-1943	2:15:39.8	4	Munich	10-Sep-1972
Kenji	Kimihara	JPN	20-Mar-1941	2:16:27.0	5	Munich	10-Sep-1972
Ronald	Hill	GBR	25-Sep-1938	2:16:30.6	6	Munich	10-Sep-1972
Donald	Macgregor	GBR	23-Jul-1939	2:16:34.4	7	Munich	10-Sep-1972
John	Foster	NZL	23-May-1932	2:16:56.2	8	Munich	10-Sep-1972
Jack	Bacheler	USA	30-Dec-1943	2:17:38.2	9	Munich	10-Sep-1972
Bedane	Lengisse	ETH	08-May-1945	2:18:36.8	10	Munich	10-Sep-1972
Seppo	Nikkari	FIN	06-Feb-1948	2:18:49.4	11	Munich	10-Sep-1972
Akio	Usami	JPN	31-May-1943	2:18:58.0	12	Munich	10-Sep-1972
Derek	Clayton	AUS	17-Nov-1942	2:19:49.6	13	Munich	10-Sep-1972
Yuriy	Velikorodnikh	URS	18-Feb-1942	2:20:02.2	14	Munich	10-Sep-1972
Anatoliy	Baranov	URS	02-Feb-1940	2:20:10.4	15	Munich	10-Sep-1972
Paul	Angenvoorth	FRG	10-Aug-1945	2:20:19.0	16	Munich	10-Sep-1972
Richard	Mabuza	SWZ	03-Mar-1946	2:20:39.6	17	Munich	10-Sep-1972
Demissie	Wolde	ETH	08-Mar-1937	2:20:44.0	18	Munich	10-Sep-1972
Reino	Paukkinen	FIN	20-Sep-1945	2:21:06.4	19	Munich	10-Sep-1972
Colin	Kirkham	GBR	30-Oct-1944	2:21:54.8	20	Munich	10-Sep-1972
Antonio	Brutti	ITA	02-May-1945	2:22:12.0	21	Munich	10-Sep-1972
David	McKenzie	NZL	16-Mar-1943	2:22:19.2	22	Munich	10-Sep-1972
Daniel	McDaid	IRL	04-Aug-1941	2:22:25.2	23	Munich	10-Sep-1972
Renato	Martini	ITA	12-Nov-1949	2:22:41.4	24	Munich	10-Sep-1972
Eckhard	Lesse	GDR	01-Dec-1948	2:22:49.6	25	Munich	10-Sep-1972
Jacinto	Sabinal	MEX	12-Aug-1942	2:22:56.6	26	Munich	10-Sep-1972
Gyula	Toth	HUN	12-Apr-1937	2:22:59.8	27	Munich	10-Sep-1972
Fernand	Kolbeck	FRA	11-Oct-1944	2:23:01.2	28	Munich	10-Sep-1972
Hernan	Barreneche	COL	25-Jul-1939	2:23:40.0	29	Munich	10-Sep-1972
Jorgen	Jensen	DEN	10-Apr-1944	2:24:00.2	30	Munich	10-Sep-1972
Manfred	Steffny	FRG	14-Aug-1941	2:24:25.4	31	Munich	10-Sep-1972
Lutz	Philipp	FRG	14-Oct-1940	2:24:25.4	32	Munich	10-Sep-1972
Ferenc	Szekeres	HUN	21-Mar-1947	2:25:17.6	33	Munich	10-Sep-1972
Terry	Manners	NZL	19-Oct-1939	2:25:29.2	34	Munich	10-Sep-1972
Igor	Shcherbak	URS	09-Jun-1943	2:25:37.4	35	Munich	10-Sep-1972
Yoshiaki	Unetani	JPN	06-Oct-1944	2:25:59.0	36	Munich	10-Sep-1972
Chang-Son	Kim	PRK	11-Apr-1952	2:26:45.6	37	Munich	10-Sep-1972
Francesco	de Menego	ITA	08-Sep-1944	2:26:52.2	38	Munich	10-Sep-1972
Agustin	Fernandez	ESP	11-May-1938	2:27:24.2	39	Munich	10-Sep-1972
Edward	Stawiarz	POL	16-Jun-1940	2:28:12.4	40	Munich	10-Sep-1972
Armando	Aldegalega	POR	23-Nov-1937	2:28:24.6	41	Munich	10-Sep-1972

First name	Family name	GPE	Birth date	Time	Place	Venue	Race date
Desmond	McGann	IRL	21-Jul-1945	2:28:31.6	42	Munich	10-Sep-1972
Carlos	Cuque	GUA	24-Nov-1945	2:28:37.0	43	Munich	10-Sep-1972
Alfons	Sidler	SUI	01-Nov-1934	2:29:09.2	44	Munich	10-Sep-1972
Alfredo	Penaloza	MEX	31-May-1947	2:29:51.0	45	Munich	10-Sep-1972
Walter	van Renterghem	BEL	09-Feb-1949	2:29:58.4	46	Munich	10-Sep-1972
Donal	Walsh	IRL	28-May-1949	2:31:12.0	47	Munich	10-Sep-1972
Alvaro	Mejia	COL	15-May-1940	2:31:56.4	48	Munich	10-Sep-1972
Man-Hyong	Ryu	PRK	08-Jan-1942	2:32:29.4	49	Munich	10-Sep-1972
Carlos	Perez	ESP	01-Jun-1935	2:33:22.6	50	Munich	10-Sep-1972
Rafael	Tadeo	MEX	28-Sep-1949	2:35:48.4	51	Munich	10-Sep-1972
Victor	Mora	COL	24-Nov-1944	2:37:34.6	52	Munich	10-Sep-1972
Fernando	Molina	ARG	09-Apr-1938	2:38:18.6	53	Munich	10-Sep-1972
Julio	Quevedo	GUA	17-Oct-1939	2:40:38.6	54	Munich	10-Sep-1972
Ramon	Cabrera	ARG	30-May-1938	2:42:37.2	55	Munich	10-Sep-1972
Matthews	Kambale	MAW	27-Dec-1953	2:45:50.0	56	Munich	10-Sep-1972
Thein	Hla	BIR	25-Apr-1944	2:48:53.2	57	Munich	10-Sep-1972
Ricardo	Condori	BOL	07-Feb-1950	2:56:11.4	58	Munich	10-Sep-1972
Fulgence	Rwabu	UGA	23-Nov-1947	2:57:04.4	59	Munich	10-Sep-1972
Bahadur	Jit	NEP	1947	2:57:58.8	60	Munich	10-Sep-1972
Crispin	Quispe	BOL	13-May-1946	3:07:22.8	61	Munich	10-Sep-1972
Maurice	Charlotin	HAI	06-Dec-1944	3:29:21.0	62	Munich	10-Sep-1972
Nazario	Araujo	ARG	25-May-1945		DNF	Munich	10-Sep-1972
Pekka	Tiihonen	FIN	29-Jun-1947		DNF	Munich	10-Sep-1972
Rudolfo	Gomez	NCA	09-Aug-1946		DNF	Munich	10-Sep-1972
Shagi Musa	Medani	SUD	17-Oct-1948		DNF	Munich	10-Sep-1972
Juvenal	Rocha	BOL	03-May-1948		DNF	Munich	10-Sep-1972
Jama	Awil	SOM	02-Sep-1948		DNF	Munich	10-Sep-1972
Ismail	Akcay	TUR	09-Jul-1942		DNF	Munich	10-Sep-1972
Bahadur	Bhakta	NEP	1950		DNF	Munich	10-Sep-1972
Lucien	Rosa	SRL	11-Feb-1944		DNF	Munich	10-Sep-1972
Julius	Wakachu	TAN	01-Jan-1948		DNF	Munich	10-Sep-1972
Gaston	Roelants	BEL	05-Feb-1937		DNF	Munich	10-Sep-1972
Richard	Juma	KEN	19-Jul-1945		DNF	Munich	10-Sep-1972
Waldemar	Cierpinski	GDR	03-Aug-1950	2:09:55.0	1	Montreal	31-Jul-1976
Frank	Shorter	USA	31-Oct-1947	2:10:45.8	2	Montreal	31-Jul-1976
Karel	Lismont	BEL	08-Mar-1949	2:11:12.6	3	Montreal	31-Jul-1976
Donald	Kardong	USA	22-Dec-1948	2:11:15.8	4	Montreal	31-Jul-1976
Lasse	Viren	FIN	22-Jul-1949	2:13:10.8	5	Montreal	31-Jul-1976
Jerome	Drayton (Buniak)	CAN	10-Jan-1945	2:13:30.0	6	Montreal	31-Jul-1976
Leonid	Moiseyev	URS	21-Oct-1952	2:13:33.4	7	Montreal	31-Jul-1976
Franco	Fava	ITA	03-Sep-1952	2:14:24.6	8	Montreal	31-Jul-1976
Aleksandr	Gozki	URS	25-Oct-1947	2:15:34.0	9	Montreal	31-Jul-1976
Hendrik	Schoofs	BEL	06-Oct-1950	2:15:52.4	10	Montreal	31-Jul-1976
Shivnath	Singh	IND	11-Jul-1946	2:16:22.0	11	Montreal	31-Jul-1976
Chang-Sop	Choi	PRK	18-Jul-1955	2:16:33.2	12	Montreal	31-Jul-1976
Massimo	Magnani	ITA	04-Oct-1951	2:16:56.4	13	Montreal	31-Jul-1976
Goran	Bengtsson	SWE	25-Nov-1949	2:17:39.6	14	Montreal	31-Jul-1976
Kazimierz	Orzel	POL	26-Aug-1943	2:17:43.4	15	Montreal	31-Jul-1976
Hakan	Spik	FIN	18-Aug-1951	2:17:50.6	16	Montreal	31-Jul-1976
John	Foster	NZL	23-May-1932	2:17:53.4	17	Montreal	31-Jul-1976
Mario	Cuevas	MEX	22-Jul-1949	2:18:08.8	18	Montreal	31-Jul-1976
Rodolfo	Gomez	MEX	30-Oct-1950	2:18:21.2	19	Montreal	31-Jul-1976
Shigeru	Soh	JPN	09-Jan-1953	2:18:26.0	20	Montreal	31-Jul-1976
Noriyasu	Mizukami	JPN	06-Oct-1947	2:18:44.0	21	Montreal	31-Jul-1976
Anacleto	Pinto	POR	25-Feb-1948	2:18:53.4	22	Montreal	31-Jul-1976
Jose	de Jesus	PUR	18-Sep-1954	2:19:34.8	23	Montreal	31-Jul-1976
Yuriy	Velikorodnikh	URS	18-Feb-1942	2:19:45.6	24	Montreal	31-Jul-1976
Josephus	Hermans	NED	08-Jan-1950	2:19:48.2	25	Montreal	31-Jul-1976
George Jeffrey	Norman	GBR	06-Feb-1945	2:20:04.8	26	Montreal	31-Jul-1976
Jukka	Toivola	FIN	07-Sep-1949	2:20:26.6	27	Montreal	31-Jul-1976
Jorgen	Jensen	DEN	10-Apr-1944	2:20:44.6	28	Montreal	31-Jul-1976

First name	Family name	GPE	Birth date	Time	Place	Venue	Race date
Michael	Koussis	GRE	10-Oct-1953	2:21:42.0	29	Montreal	31-Jul-1976
Thomas	Howard	CAN	20-Sep-1948	2:22:08.8	30	Montreal	31-Jul-1976
Keith	Angus	GBR	05-Apr-1943	2:22:18.6	31	Montreal	31-Jul-1976
Akio	Usami	JPN	31-May-1943	2:22:29.6	32	Montreal	31-Jul-1976
Rigoberto	Mendoza	CUB	04-Jan-1946	2:22:43.2	33	Montreal	31-Jul-1976
Fernand	Kolbeck	FRA	11-Oct-1944	2:22:56.8	34	Montreal	31-Jul-1976
Christopher	Wardlaw	AUS	03-Mar-1950	2:23:56.8	35	Montreal	31-Jul-1976
Wayne	Yetman	CAN	08-Oct-1946	2:24:17.4	36	Montreal	31-Jul-1976
Huseyin	Aktas	TUR	25-Mar-1941	2:24:30.0	37	Montreal	31-Jul-1976
Veli	Balli	TUR	10-Dec-1949	2:24:47.0	38	Montreal	31-Jul-1976
James	McNamara	IRL	17-Apr-1938	2:24:57.2	39	Montreal	31-Jul-1976
William	Rodgers	USA	23-Dec-1947	2:25:14.8	40	Montreal	31-Jul-1976
Hipolito	Lopez	HON	07-Feb-1952	2:26:00.0	41	Montreal	31-Jul-1976
Daniel	McDaid	IRL	04-Aug-1941	2:27:07.2	42	Montreal	31-Jul-1976
Eusebio	Cardozo	PAR	15-Aug-1950	2:27:22.8	43	Montreal	31-Jul-1976
Chang-Son	Kim	PRK	11-Apr-1952	2:27:38.8	44	Montreal	31-Jul-1976
Barrington	Watson	GBR	13-Feb-1944	2:28:32.2	45	Montreal	31-Jul-1976
Agustin	Fernandez	ESP	11-May-1938	2:28:37.8	46	Montreal	31-Jul-1976
Jerzy	Gross	POL	21-Feb-1945	2:28:45.8	47	Montreal	31-Jul-1976
Jairo	Cubillos	COL	20-Aug-1954	2:29:04.4	48	Montreal	31-Jul-1976
Luis Antonio	Raudales	HON	21-May-1956	2:29:25.0	49	Montreal	31-Jul-1976
Baikuntha	Manandhar	NEP	24-Dec-1952	2:30:07.0	50	Montreal	31-Jul-1976
Antonino	Banos	ESP	07-Dec-1945	2:31:01.6	51	Montreal	31-Jul-1976
Chun-Son	Goe	PRK	02-Jun-1952	2:31:54.8	52	Montreal	31-Jul-1976
Victor	Serrano	PUR	20-Sep-1949	2:34:59.6	53	Montreal	31-Jul-1976
Gunter	Mielke	FRG	30-Nov-1942	2:35:44.8	54	Montreal	31-Jul-1976
Neil	Cusack	IRL	30-Dec-1951	2:35:47.2	55	Montreal	31-Jul-1976
John Tau	Tokwepota	PNG	25-Jun-1956	2:38:04.6	56	Montreal	31-Jul-1976
Victor	Idava	PHI	28-May-1956	2:38:23.2	57	Montreal	31-Jul-1976
Raymond	Swan	BER	07-Dec-1938	2:39:18.4	58	Montreal	31-Jul-1976
John	Kokinai	PNG	17-May-1951	2:41:49.0	59	Montreal	31-Jul-1976
Lucio	Guachalla	BOL	19-Oct-1949	2:45:31.8	60	Montreal	31-Jul-1976
David	Chettle	AUS	14-Sep-1951		DNF	Montreal	31-Jul-1976
Ross	Haywood	AUS	18-Feb-1947		DNF	Montreal	31-Jul-1976
Rafael	Mora	COL	04-Jun-1952		DNF	Montreal	31-Jul-1976
Santiago	Manguan	ESP	25-Jul-1956		DNF	Montreal	31-Jul-1976
Thancule	Dezart	HAI	15-Apr-1947		DNF	Montreal	31-Jul-1976
Giuseppe	Cindolo	ITA	05-Aug-1945		DNF	Montreal	31-Jul-1976
Kevin	Ryan	NZL	22-Jul-1949		DNF	Montreal	31-Jul-1976
Waldemar	Cierpinski	GDR	03-Aug-1950	2:11:03.0	1	Moscow	01-Aug-1980
Gerhardus	Nijboer	NED	18-Aug-1955	2:11:20.0	2	Moscow	01-Aug-1980
Setymkul	Dzhumanazarov	URS	17-Sep-1951	2:11:35.0	3	Moscow	01-Aug-1980
Vladimir	Kotov	URS	21-Feb-1958	2:12:05.0	4	Moscow	01-Aug-1980
Leonid	Moiseyev	URS	21-Oct-1952	2:12:14.0	5	Moscow	01-Aug-1980
Rodolfo	Gomez	MEX	30-Oct-1950	2:12:39.0	6	Moscow	01-Aug-1980
Dereje	Nedi	ETH	10-Oct-1955	2:12:44.0	7	Moscow	01-Aug-1980
Massimo	Magnani	ITA	04-Oct-1951	2:13:12.0	8	Moscow	01-Aug-1980
Karel	Lismont	BEL	08-Mar-1949	2:13:27.0	9	Moscow	01-Aug-1980
Francois Robert	de Castella	AUS	27-Feb-1957	2:14:31.0	10	Moscow	01-Aug-1980
Hans-Joachim	Truppel	GDR	24-Mar-1951	2:14:55.0	11	Moscow	01-Aug-1980
Ferenc	Szekeres	HUN	21-Mar-1947	2:15:18.0	12	Moscow	01-Aug-1980
Marc	Smet	BEL	05-Feb-1951	2:16:00.0	13	Moscow	01-Aug-1980
Emmanuel	Ndiemandoi	TAN	1957	2:16:47.0	14	Moscow	01-Aug-1980
Gidamis	Shahanga	TAN	04-Sep-1957	2:16:47.0	15	Moscow	01-Aug-1980
Anacleto	Pinto	POR	25-Feb-1948	2:17:04.0	16	Moscow	01-Aug-1980
Domingo	Tibaduiza	COL	22-Nov-1949	2:17:06.0	17	Moscow	01-Aug-1980
Hendrik	Schoofs	BEL	06-Oct-1950	2:17:28.0	18	Moscow	01-Aug-1980
Kjell-Erik	Stahl	SWE	17-Feb-1946	2:17:44.0	19	Moscow	01-Aug-1980
Michael	Koussis	GRE	10-Oct-1953	2:18:02.0	20	Moscow	01-Aug-1980
Jurgen	Eberding	GDR	03-Dec-1955	2:18:04.0	21	Moscow	01-Aug-1980
Eleuterio	Anton	ESP	30-Mar-1950	2:18:16.0	22	Moscow	01-Aug-1980

First name	Family name	GPE	Birth date	Time	Place	Venue	Race date
Leodigard	Martin	TAN	08-Jan-1960	2:18:21.0	23	Moscow	01-Aug-1980
Moges	Alemayehu	ETH	06-Dec-1948	2:18:40.0	24	Moscow	01-Aug-1980
Jules	Randrianarivelo	MAD	28-Nov-1951	2:19:23.0	25	Moscow	01-Aug-1980
Zbigniew	Pierzynka	POL	21-Oct-1951	2:20:03.0	26	Moscow	01-Aug-1980
Chun-Son	Goe	PRK	02-Jun-1952	2:20:08.0	27	Moscow	01-Aug-1980
Christopher	Wardlaw	AUS	03-Mar-1950	2:20:42.0	28	Moscow	01-Aug-1980
Jong-Hyong	Li	PRK	03-Mar-1956	2:21:10.0	29	Moscow	01-Aug-1980
Tommy	Persson	SWE	23-Dec-1954	2:21:11.0	30	Moscow	01-Aug-1980
Hari	Chand	IND	01-Apr-1953	2:22:08.0	31	Moscow	01-Aug-1980
Hakan	Spik	FIN	18-Aug-1951	2:22:24.0	32	Moscow	01-Aug-1980
Chang-Sop	Choi	PRK	18-Jul-1955	2:22:42.0	33	Moscow	01-Aug-1980
Luis	Barbosa	COL	21-Jan-1953	2:22:58.0	34	Moscow	01-Aug-1980
Marco	Marchei	ITA	02-Aug-1954	2:23:21.0	35	Moscow	01-Aug-1980
Gabashane	Rakabaele	LES	03-Sep-1948	2:23:29.0	36	Moscow	01-Aug-1980
Baikuntha	Manandhar	NEP	24-Dec-1952	2:23:51.0	37	Moscow	01-Aug-1980
Richard	Hooper	IRL	26-Aug-1956	2:23:53.0	38	Moscow	01-Aug-1980
Josef	Steiner	AUT	24-Sep-1950	2:24:24.0	39	Moscow	01-Aug-1980
Joseph	Peter	SUI	23-Dec-1949	2:24:53.0	40	Moscow	01-Aug-1980
Cornelis	Vriend	NED	08-Nov-1949	2:26:41.0	41	Moscow	01-Aug-1980
Patrick	Hooper	IRL	12-May-1952	2:30:28.0	42	Moscow	01-Aug-1980
Gabriel Halwand	Buumba	ZAM	23-Sep-1947	2:36:51.0	43	Moscow	01-Aug-1980
Issa Ali	Chetoui	LBY	1953	2:38:01.0	44	Moscow	01-Aug-1980
Mukunda Hari	Shrestha	NEP	14-Dec-1955	2:38:52.0	45	Moscow	01-Aug-1980
Baba Ibrahim	Suma-Keita	SLE	20-Apr-1947	2:41:20.0	46	Moscow	01-Aug-1980
Soe	Khin	BIR	01-Nov-1950	2:41:41.0	47	Moscow	01-Aug-1980
Damiano Musonda	Ngwila	ZAM	15-Aug-1945	2:42:11.0	48	Moscow	01-Aug-1980
Enemri	Al Marghani	LBY	1953	2:42:27.0	49	Moscow	01-Aug-1980
Nguyen	Quyen	VIE	21-Oct-1952	2:44:37.0	50	Moscow	01-Aug-1980
Tapfumaeyi	Jonga	ZIM	13-Nov-1959	2:47:17.0	51	Moscow	01-Aug-1980
Emmanuel	Mpioh	CGO	24-May-1952	2:48:17.0	52	Moscow	01-Aug-1980
Abel	Nkhoma	ZIM	1951	2:53:35.0	53	Moscow	01-Aug-1980
Shivnath	Singh	IND	11-Jul-1946		DNF	Moscow	01-Aug-1980
Ryszard	Marczak	POL	25-Nov-1945		DNF	Moscow	01-Aug-1980
Andrzej	Sajkowski	POL	21-May-1952		DNF	Moscow	01-Aug-1980
Vlastimil	Zwiefelhofer	TCH	20-Nov-1952		DNF	Moscow	01-Aug-1980
Radames	Gonzalez	CUB	04-Feb-1956		DNF	Moscow	01-Aug-1980
David	Black	GBR	02-Oct-1952		DNF	Moscow	01-Aug-1980
Bernard	Ford	GBR	03-Aug-1952		DNF	Moscow	01-Aug-1980
Lasse	Viren	FIN	22-Jul-1949		DNF	Moscow	01-Aug-1980
Jean-Michel	Charbonnel	FRA	25-Apr-1952		DNF	Moscow	01-Aug-1980
Albert	Marie	SEY	03-Mar-1957		DNF	Moscow	01-Aug-1980
Abdelmadjid	Mada	ALG	06-Apr-1953		DNF	Moscow	01-Aug-1980
Gerard	Barrett	AUS	31-Dec-1956		DNF	Moscow	01-Aug-1980
Goran	Hogberg	SWE	20-Dec-1948		DNF	Moscow	01-Aug-1980
Josef	Jansky	TCH	24-Nov-1940		DNF	Moscow	01-Aug-1980
Nabil	Choueri	LBN	1955		DNF	Moscow	01-Aug-1980
Ian	Thompson	GBR	16-Oct-1949		DNF	Moscow	01-Aug-1980
Jouni	Kortelainen	FIN	09-Jun-1957		DNF	Moscow	01-Aug-1980
Patrick	Chiwala	ZAM	10-Jan-1953		DNF	Moscow	01-Aug-1980
Kebede	Balcha	ETH	07-Sep-1951		DNF	Moscow	01-Aug-1980
Jorn	Lauenborg	DEN	14-Sep-1944		DNF	Moscow	01-Aug-1980
Kenneth	Hlasa	LES	02-Mar-1955		DNF	Moscow	01-Aug-1980
Carlos	Lopes	POR	18-Feb-1947	2:09:21	1	Los Angeles	12-Aug-1984
John	Treacy	IRL	04-Jun-1957	2:09:56	2	Los Angeles	12-Aug-1984
Charles	Spedding	GBR	19-May-1952	2:09:58	3	Los Angeles	12-Aug-1984
Takeshi	Soh	JPN	09-Jan-1953	2:10:55	4	Los Angeles	12-Aug-1984
Francois Robert	de Castella	AUS	27-Feb-1957	2:11:09	5	Los Angeles	12-Aug-1984
Juma	Ikangaa	TAN	19-Jul-1960	2:11:10	6	Los Angeles	12-Aug-1984
Joseph	Nzau	KEN	14-Apr-1952	2:11:28	7	Los Angeles	12-Aug-1984
Djama	Robleh	DJI	31-Dec-1958	2:11:39	8	Los Angeles	12-Aug-1984
Jeremiah	Kiernan	IRL	31-May-1953	2:12:20	9	Los Angeles	12-Aug-1984

First name	Family name	GPE	Birth date	Time	Place	Venue	Race date
Rodney	Dixon	NZL	13-Jul-1950	2:12:57	10	Los Angeles	12-Aug-1984
Peter	Pfitzinger	USA	29-Aug-1957	2:13:53	11	Los Angeles	12-Aug-1984
Hugh	Jones	GBR	01-Nov-1955	2:13:57	12	Los Angeles	12-Aug-1984
Jorge	Gonzalez	PUR	20-Dec-1952	2:14:00	13	Los Angeles	12-Aug-1984
Toshihiko	Seko	JPN	15-Jul-1956	2:14:13	14	Los Angeles	12-Aug-1984
Alberto	Salazar	USA	07-Aug-1958	2:14:19	15	Los Angeles	12-Aug-1984
Mehmet	Terzi	TUR	05-May-1955	2:14:20	16	Los Angeles	12-Aug-1984
Shigeru	Soh	JPN	09-Jan-1953	2:14:38	17	Los Angeles	12-Aug-1984
Ralf	Salzmann	FRG	06-Feb-1955	2:15:29	18	Los Angeles	12-Aug-1984
Henrik	Jorgensen	DEN	10-Oct-1961	2:15:55	19	Los Angeles	12-Aug-1984
Ahmed Salah	Hussein	DJI	31-Dec-1956	2:15:59	20	Los Angeles	12-Aug-1984
Agapius	Masong	TAN	12-Apr-1960	2:16:25	21	Los Angeles	12-Aug-1984
Gidamis	Shahanga	TAN	04-Sep-1957	2:16:27	22	Los Angeles	12-Aug-1984
Eloi	Schleder	BRA	26-Jul-1951	2:16:35	23	Los Angeles	12-Aug-1984
Karel	Lismont	BEL	08-Mar-1949	2:17:07	24	Los Angeles	12-Aug-1984
Allan	Zachariassen	DEN	04-Nov-1955	2:17:10	25	Los Angeles	12-Aug-1984
Michael	Koussis	GRE	10-Oct-1953	2:17:38	26	Los Angeles	12-Aug-1984
Pertti	Tiainen	FIN	15-Nov-1954	2:17:43	27	Los Angeles	12-Aug-1984
Alain	Lazare	FRA	23-Mar-1952	2:17:52	28	Los Angeles	12-Aug-1984
Vincent	Ruguga	UGA	12-Dec-1959	2:17:54	29	Los Angeles	12-Aug-1984
Armand	Parmentier	BEL	15-Feb-1954	2:18:10	30	Los Angeles	12-Aug-1984
Cesar	Mercado	PUR	25-Oct-1959	2:19:09	31	Los Angeles	12-Aug-1984
Charmarke Cochine	Omar Abdillahi	DJI	1954	2:19:11	32	Los Angeles	12-Aug-1984
Oyvind	Dahl	NOR	12-May-1951	2:19:28	33	Los Angeles	12-Aug-1984
Derek	Froude	NZL	20-Apr-1959	2:19:44	34	Los Angeles	12-Aug-1984
Giovanni	D'Aleo	ITA	01-Jul-1959	2:20:12	35	Los Angeles	12-Aug-1984
Jesus	Herrera	MEX	22-Mar-1962	2:20:33	36	Los Angeles	12-Aug-1984
Hong-Yul	Lee	KOR	15-Mar-1961	2:20:56	37	Los Angeles	12-Aug-1984
Juan	Camacho	BOL	04-Jun-1959	2:21:04	38	Los Angeles	12-Aug-1984
Cornelis	Vriend	NED	08-Nov-1949	2:21:08	39	Los Angeles	12-Aug-1984
Frans	Ntoale	LES	08-Aug-1950	2:21:09	40	Los Angeles	12-Aug-1984
Johan	Geirnaert	BEL	09-Jan-1951	2:21:35	41	Los Angeles	12-Aug-1984
Jacques	Boxberger	FRA	16-Apr-1949	2:22:00	42	Los Angeles	12-Aug-1984
Marco	Marchei	ITA	02-Aug-1954	2:22:38	43	Los Angeles	12-Aug-1984
Arthur	Boileau	CAN	09-Oct-1957	2:22:43	44	Los Angeles	12-Aug-1984
Samuel	Hlawe	SWZ	21-Jul-1952	2:22:45	45	Los Angeles	12-Aug-1984
Baikuntha	Manandhar	NEP	24-Dec-1952	2:22:52	46	Los Angeles	12-Aug-1984
Ahmed Mohamed	Esmail	SOM	06-Jun-1964	2:23:27	47	Los Angeles	12-Aug-1984
Hong-Nak	Chae	KOR	29-May-1961	2:23:33	48	Los Angeles	12-Aug-1984
Joseph	Otieno	KEN	19-May-1958	2:24:13	49	Los Angeles	12-Aug-1984
Bruno	Lafranchi	SUI	19-Jul-1955	2:24:38	50	Los Angeles	12-Aug-1984
Richard	Hooper	IRL	26-Aug-1956	2:24:41	51	Los Angeles	12-Aug-1984
Derrick	Adamson	JAM	24-Mar-1958	2:25:02	52	Los Angeles	12-Aug-1984
Claudio	Caban	PUR	25-Mar-1963	2:27:16	53	Los Angeles	12-Aug-1984
Marco	Agosta	LUX	07-May-1948	2:27:41	54	Los Angeles	12-Aug-1984
Wilson	Theleso	BOT	25-Jun-1960	2:29:20	55	Los Angeles	12-Aug-1984
Changming	Chen	TPE	02-Dec-1955	2:29:53	56	Los Angeles	12-Aug-1984
Alejandro	Silva	CHI	28-Jul-1958	2:29:53	57	Los Angeles	12-Aug-1984
Won-Sik	Kim	KOR	21-Jan-1963	2:30:57	58	Los Angeles	12-Aug-1984
Ruben	Aguiar	ARG	21-Jul-1956	2:31:18	59	Los Angeles	12-Aug-1984
Shemtov	Sabag	ISR	13-Apr-1959	2:31:34	60	Los Angeles	12-Aug-1984
Gabashane	Rakabaele	LES	03-Sep-1948	2:32:15	61	Los Angeles	12-Aug-1984
Marios	Kassianides	CYP	16-Sep-1954	2:32:51	62	Los Angeles	12-Aug-1984
Arjun	Pandit	NEP	21-Jun-1959	2:32:53	63	Los Angeles	12-Aug-1984
Ismaiel	Mahmoud	JOR	01-Jan-1961	2:33:30	64	Los Angeles	12-Aug-1984
Alain	Bordeleau	CAN	07-Oct-1956	2:34:27	65	Los Angeles	12-Aug-1984
John Tau	Tokwepota	PNG	25-Jun-1956	2:36:36	66	Los Angeles	12-Aug-1984
Patrick	Nyambariro-Nhauro	ZIM	01-Aug-1957	2:37:18	67	Los Angeles	12-Aug-1984
Kirmurgor	Ngeny	KEN	10-Jul-1951	2:37:19	68	Los Angeles	12-Aug-1984
Amira Prasad	Yadav	NEP	13-Jul-1959	2:38:10	69	Los Angeles	12-Aug-1984
Adolphe	Ambowode	CAF	13-Feb-1958	2:41:26	70	Los Angeles	12-Aug-1984

First name	Family name	GPE	Birth date	Time	Place	Venue	Race date
Carlos	Avila	HON	15-Sep-1951	2:42:03	71	Los Angeles	12-Aug-1984
Jules	Randrianarivelo	MAD	28-Nov-1951	2:43:05	72	Los Angeles	12-Aug-1984
Ahmed	Abdullahij	SOM		2:44:39	73	Los Angeles	12-Aug-1984
George	Mambosasa	MAW	31-Jan-1964	2:46:14	74	Los Angeles	12-Aug-1984
Marlon	Williams	ISV	09-Sep-1956	2:46:50	75	Los Angeles	12-Aug-1984
Johnson	Mbangiwa	BOT	28-Feb-1956	2:48:12	76	Los Angeles	12-Aug-1984
Leonardo	Illut	PHI	21-Sep-1956	2:49:39	77	Los Angeles	12-Aug-1984
Dieudonne	Lamothe	HAI	29-Jul-1954	2:52:19	78	Los Angeles	12-Aug-1984
Matthews	Kambale	MAW	27-Dec-1953		DNF	Los Angeles	12-Aug-1984
Alawi	Altahir	QAT			DNF	Los Angeles	12-Aug-1984
Domingo	Tibaduiza	COL	22-Nov-1949		DNF	Los Angeles	12-Aug-1984
Mehmet	Yurdadon	TUR	02-Jun-1954		DNF	Los Angeles	12-Aug-1984
Tommy	Persson	SWE	23-Dec-1954		DNF	Los Angeles	12-Aug-1984
Bigboy	Matlapeng	BOT	04-Feb-1958		DNF	Los Angeles	12-Aug-1984
Awadh	Al-Sameer	OMA	06-May-1961		DNF	Los Angeles	12-Aug-1984
David	Edge	CAN	11-Nov-1954		DNF	Los Angeles	12-Aug-1984
Cidalio	Caetano	POR	22-Jan-1952		DNF	Los Angeles	12-Aug-1984
John	Tuttle	USA	16-Oct-1958		DNF	Los Angeles	12-Aug-1984
Wilson	Achia	UGA	18-Jun-1959		DNF	Los Angeles	12-Aug-1984
Gerhard	Hartmann	AUT	12-Jan-1955		DNF	Los Angeles	12-Aug-1984
Cornelis	Lambregts	NED	04-Aug-1958		DNF	Los Angeles	12-Aug-1984
Tommy	Lazarus	ZIM	15-Oct-1962		DNF	Los Angeles	12-Aug-1984
Ronaldo	Lanzoni	CRC	21-Feb-1959		DNF	Los Angeles	12-Aug-1984
Rodolfo	Gomez	MEX	30-Oct-1950		DNF	Los Angeles	12-Aug-1984
Gerhardus	Nijboer	NED	18-Aug-1955		DNF	Los Angeles	12-Aug-1984
Santiago	de la Parte	ESP	18-Aug-1948		DNF	Los Angeles	12-Aug-1984
Ahmet	Altun	TUR	25-Jan-1958		DNF	Los Angeles	12-Aug-1984
Juan	Traspaderne	ESP	02-Sep-1956		DNF	Los Angeles	12-Aug-1984
Kjell-Erik	Stahl	SWE	17-Feb-1946		DNF	Los Angeles	12-Aug-1984
Geoffrey	Smith	GBR	24-Oct-1953		DNF	Los Angeles	12-Aug-1984
Stig Roar	Husby	NOR	12-Sep-1954		DNF	Los Angeles	12-Aug-1984
Delfim	Moreira	POR	11-Dec-1955		DNF	Los Angeles	12-Aug-1984
Miguel	Cruz	MEX	29-Sep-1955		DNF	Los Angeles	12-Aug-1984
Omar	Aguilar	CHI	01-Dec-1959		DNF	Los Angeles	12-Aug-1984
Nimley	Twegbe	LBR	09-Sep-1963		DNF	Los Angeles	12-Aug-1984
Filippos	Filippou	CYP	29-Sep-1956		DNF	Los Angeles	12-Aug-1984
Kumbanza	Situ	ZAI	21-Oct-1955		DNF	Los Angeles	12-Aug-1984
Gelindo	Bordin	ITA	02-Apr-1959	2:10:32	1	Seoul	02-Oct-1988
Douglas	Wakiihuri	KEN	26-Sep-1963	2:10:47	2	Seoul	02-Oct-1988
Ahmed Salah	Hussein	DJI	31-Dec-1956	2:10:59	3	Seoul	02-Oct-1988
Takeyuki	Nakayama	JPN	20-Dec-1959	2:11:05	4	Seoul	02-Oct-1988
Stephen	Moneghetti	AUS	26-Sep-1962	2:11:49	5	Seoul	02-Oct-1988
Charles	Spedding	GBR	19-May-1952	2:12:19	6	Seoul	02-Oct-1988
Juma	Ikangaa	TAN	19-Jul-1960	2:13:06	7	Seoul	02-Oct-1988
Francois Robert	de Castella	AUS	27-Feb-1957	2:13:07	8	Seoul	02-Oct-1988
Toshihiko	Seko	JPN	15-Jul-1956	2:13:41	9	Seoul	02-Oct-1988
Ravil	Kashapov	URS	15-Nov-1956	2:13:49	10	Seoul	02-Oct-1988
Jesus	Herrera	MEX	22-Mar-1962	2:13:58	11	Seoul	02-Oct-1988
John	Campbell	NZL	06-Feb-1949	2:14:08	12	Seoul	02-Oct-1988
Gerhardus	Nijboer	NED	18-Aug-1955	2:14:40	13	Seoul	02-Oct-1988
Peter	Pfitzinger	USA	29-Aug-1957	2:14:44	14	Seoul	02-Oct-1988
Martin	ten Kate	NED	16-Dec-1958	2:14:53	15	Seoul	02-Oct-1988
Orlando	Pizzolato	ITA	30-Jul-1958	2:15:20	16	Seoul	02-Oct-1988
Masanari	Shintaku	JPN	20-Dec-1957	2:15:42	17	Seoul	02-Oct-1988
Won-Tak	Kim	KOR	21-Jul-1964	2:15:44	18	Seoul	02-Oct-1988
Piergiovanni	Poli	ITA	05-Nov-1957	2:16:07	19	Seoul	02-Oct-1988
Dieudonne	Lamothe	HAI	29-Jul-1954	2:16:15	20	Seoul	02-Oct-1988
David	Long	GBR	21-Nov-1960	2:16:18	21	Seoul	02-Oct-1988
Henrik	Jorgensen	DEN	10-Oct-1961	2:16:40	22	Seoul	02-Oct-1988
Ralf	Salzmann	FRG	06-Feb-1955	2:16:54	23	Seoul	02-Oct-1988
Richard	Hooper	IRL	26-Aug-1956	2:17:16	24	Seoul	02-Oct-1988

First name	Family name	GPE	Birth date	Time	Place	Venue	Race date
Miroslav	Vindis	YUG	08-Nov-1963	2:17:47	25	Seoul	02-Oct-1988
Shangyan	Cai	CHN	19-Jul-1962	2:17:54	26	Seoul	02-Oct-1988
Joaquim	Silva	POR	13-Jan-1961	2:18:05	27	Seoul	02-Oct-1988
Arthur	Boileau	CAN	09-Oct-1957	2:18:20	28	Seoul	02-Oct-1988
Edward	Eyestone	USA	15-Jun-1961	2:19:09	29	Seoul	02-Oct-1988
Noureddine	Sobhi	MAR	27-Jun-1962	2:19:56	30	Seoul	02-Oct-1988
Jae-Sung	Yoo	KOR	20-Feb-1960	2:20:11	31	Seoul	02-Oct-1988
Mehmet	Terzi	TUR	05-May-1955	2:20:12	32	Seoul	02-Oct-1988
Kevin	Forster	GBR	27-Sep-1958	2:20:45	33	Seoul	02-Oct-1988
Bigboy	Matlapeng	BOT	04-Feb-1958	2:20:51	34	Seoul	02-Oct-1988
Allaoua	Khellil	ALG	24-Jul-1954	2:21:12	35	Seoul	02-Oct-1988
Justin	Gloden	LUX	22-Mar-1953	2:22:14	36	Seoul	02-Oct-1988
Alexandre	Gonzalez	FRA	16-Mar-1951	2:22:24	37	Seoul	02-Oct-1988
Guowei	Zhang	CHN	04-Jan-1959	2:22:49	38	Seoul	02-Oct-1988
Pedro	Ortiz	COL	26-Feb-1956	2:23:34	39	Seoul	02-Oct-1988
Ronaldo	Lanzoni	CRC	21-Feb-1959	2:23:45	40	Seoul	02-Oct-1988
Bradley	Camp	AUS	25-Dec-1964	2:23:49	41	Seoul	02-Oct-1988
Adolphe	Ambowode	CAF	13-Feb-1958	2:23:52	42	Seoul	02-Oct-1988
John	Burra	TAN	20-Nov-1965	2:24:17	43	Seoul	02-Oct-1988
Samuel	Hlawe	SWZ	21-Jul-1952	2:24:42	44	Seoul	02-Oct-1988
Juan	Amores	CRC	25-Oct-1963	2:24:49	45	Seoul	02-Oct-1988
Peter	Maher	CAN	30-Mar-1960	2:24:49	46	Seoul	02-Oct-1988
Abdou	Monzo	NIG	01-Jan-1959	2:25:05	47	Seoul	02-Oct-1988
Diamantino	dos Santos	BRA	03-Feb-1961	2:25:13	48	Seoul	02-Oct-1988
Moussa	Omar	DJI	08-Feb-1961	2:25:25	49	Seoul	02-Oct-1988
Carlos	Retiz	MEX	13-Aug-1961	2:25:34	50	Seoul	02-Oct-1988
Gary	Fanelli	ASA	24-Oct-1950	2:25:35	51	Seoul	02-Oct-1988
John	Woods	IRL	08-Dec-1955	2:25:38	52	Seoul	02-Oct-1988
Gideon	Mthembu	SWZ	25-Sep-1963	2:25:56	53	Seoul	02-Oct-1988
Baikuntha	Manandhar	NEP	24-Dec-1952	2:25:57	54	Seoul	02-Oct-1988
Karel	David	TCH	08-Feb-1964	2:26:12	55	Seoul	02-Oct-1988
Ivo	Rodrigues	BRA	15-Oct-1960	2:26:27	56	Seoul	02-Oct-1988
Martin	Mondragon	MEX	11-Nov-1953	2:27:10	57	Seoul	02-Oct-1988
Thomas	Dlamini	SWZ	28-Aug-1958	2:28:06	58	Seoul	02-Oct-1988
Inni	Aboubacar	NIG	1948	2:28:15	59	Seoul	02-Oct-1988
Yohanna	Waziri	NGR	01-Jan-1964	2:29:14	60	Seoul	02-Oct-1988
Nqheku	Nteso	LES	01-Aug-1962	2:29:44	61	Seoul	02-Oct-1988
Benjamin	Longiross	UGA	03-Mar-1963	2:30:29	62	Seoul	02-Oct-1988
Vincent	Ruguga	UGA	12-Dec-1959	2:31:04	63	Seoul	02-Oct-1988
Alfonso	Abellan	ESP	21-Jul-1951	2:31:10	64	Seoul	02-Oct-1988
Vithanakande	Samarasinghe	SRL	16-Jan-1962	2:31:29	65	Seoul	02-Oct-1988
Tika	Bogate	NEP	26-Sep-1962	2:31:49	66	Seoul	02-Oct-1988
David	Edge	CAN	11-Nov-1954	2:32:19	67	Seoul	02-Oct-1988
Luis	Lopez	CRC	14-Jul-1949	2:32:43	68	Seoul	02-Oct-1988
Juan	Camacho	BOL	04-Jun-1959	2:34:41	69	Seoul	02-Oct-1988
Abbas	Mohammed	NGR	27-Oct-1963	2:35:26	70	Seoul	02-Oct-1988
Ahmet	Altun	TUR	25-Jan-1958	2:37:44	71	Seoul	02-Oct-1988
James	Gombedza	ZIM	11-Apr-1962	2:38:13	72	Seoul	02-Oct-1988
Kamana	Koji	ZAI	13-Mar-1967	2:38:34	73	Seoul	02-Oct-1988
Joao	Carvalho	ANG	04-Nov-1950	2:40:45	74	Seoul	02-Oct-1988
Aaron	Dupnai	PNG	27-Aug-1968	2:41:47	75	Seoul	02-Oct-1988
Bineshwar	Prasad	FIJ	18-Jul-1963	2:41:50	76	Seoul	02-Oct-1988
Calvin	Dallas	ISV	02-Apr-1952	2:42:19	77	Seoul	02-Oct-1988
Telesphore	Dusabe	RWA	15-May-1965	2:42:52	78	Seoul	02-Oct-1988
Eugene	Muslar	BIZ	28-Mar-1959	2:43:29	79	Seoul	02-Oct-1988
Hassane	Karinou	NIG	1959	2:43:51	80	Seoul	02-Oct-1988
Wallace	Williams	ISV	23-Oct-1946	2:44:40	81	Seoul	02-Oct-1988
Mohala	Mohloli	LES	12-Nov-1961	2:44:44	82	Seoul	02-Oct-1988
Awadh	Al-Sameer	OMA	06-May-1961	2:46:59	83	Seoul	02-Oct-1988
Derrick	Adamson	JAM	24-Mar-1958	2:47:57	84	Seoul	02-Oct-1988
Krishna Bahadur	Basnet	NEP	17-Feb-1959	2:47:57	85	Seoul	02-Oct-1988

First name	Family name	GPE	Birth date	Time	Place	Venue	Race date
Fred	Schumann	GUM	09-Aug-1959	2:49:52	86	Seoul	02-Oct-1988
John	Mwathiwa	MAW	01-Mar-1967	2:51:43	87	Seoul	02-Oct-1988
Marlon	Williams	ISV	09-Sep-1956	2:52:06	88	Seoul	02-Oct-1988
Kaleka	Mutoke	ZAI	07-Jul-1966	2:55:21	89	Seoul	02-Oct-1988
James	Walker	GUM	18-Aug-1954	2:56:32	90	Seoul	02-Oct-1988
Muhiddin Mohamed	Kulmiye	SOM	1958	2:58:10	91	Seoul	02-Oct-1988
Jackson	Ogwang	UGA	16-Jun-1959	2:59:35	92	Seoul	02-Oct-1988
Naser	Bahadur	IRN	06-Nov-1957	3:00:20	93	Seoul	02-Oct-1988
Ricardo Joseph	Taitano	GUM		3:03:19	94	Seoul	02-Oct-1988
Suma	Keita	SLE	20-Apr-1958	3:04:00	95	Seoul	02-Oct-1988
Alassan	Bah	GUI	1960	3:06:27	96	Seoul	02-Oct-1988
Nguyen Van	Thuyet	VIE	10-Jan-1956	3:10:57	97	Seoul	02-Oct-1988
Apolinario	Belisle	BIZ	02-Jul-1966	3:14:02	98	Seoul	02-Oct-1988
Omar	Aguilar	CHI	01-Dec-1959		DNF	Seoul	02-Oct-1988
Alain	Lazare	FRA	23-Mar-1952		DNF	Seoul	02-Oct-1988
Joseph	Kipsang	KEN	25-Sep-1962		DNF	Seoul	02-Oct-1988
Jorg	Peter	GDR	23-Oct-1955		DNF	Seoul	02-Oct-1988
Hussain	Haleem	MDV	05-Mar-1969		DNF	Seoul	02-Oct-1988
Mark	Conover	USA	28-May-1960		DNF	Seoul	02-Oct-1988
El Mostafa	Nechchadi	MAR	15-Feb-1962		DNF	Seoul	02-Oct-1988
Paulo	Catarino	POR	30-Sep-1963		DNF	Seoul	02-Oct-1988
Martin	Vrabel	TCH	21-Sep-1955		DNF	Seoul	02-Oct-1988
Geir	Kvernmo	NOR	29-Oct-1955		DNF	Seoul	02-Oct-1988
Abdullatheef	Abdul Hadi	MDV	10-Oct-1970		DNF	Seoul	02-Oct-1988
Ibrahim	Hussein	KEN	03-Jun-1958		DNF	Seoul	02-Oct-1988
John	Treacy	IRL	04-Jun-1957		DNF	Seoul	02-Oct-1988
George	Mambosasa	MAW	31-Jan-1964		DNF	Seoul	02-Oct-1988
Bruno	Lafranchi	SUI	19-Jul-1955		DNF	Seoul	02-Oct-1988
John	Maeke	SOL	06-Jun-1962		DNF	Seoul	02-Oct-1988
Honorato	Hernandez	ESP	29-Jun-1956		DNF	Seoul	02-Oct-1988
Dirk	Vanderherten	BEL	09-Mar-1957		DNF	Seoul	02-Oct-1988
Ahmed Mohamed	Esmail	SOM	06-Jun-1964		DNF	Seoul	02-Oct-1988
Seon-Lak	Kwon	KOR	19-Dec-1964		DNF	Seoul	02-Oct-1988
Young-Cho	Hwang	KOR	22-Mar-1970	2:13:23	1	Barcelona	09-Aug-1992
Koichi	Morishita	JPN	05-Sep-1967	2:13:45	2	Barcelona	09-Aug-1992
Stephan	Freigang	GER	27-Sep-1967	2:14:00	3	Barcelona	09-Aug-1992
Takeyuki	Nakayama	JPN	20-Dec-1959	2:14:02	4	Barcelona	09-Aug-1992
Salvatore	Bettiol	ITA	28-Nov-1961	2:14:15	5	Barcelona	09-Aug-1992
Salah	Qoqaiche	MAR	10-Jul-1967	2:14:25	6	Barcelona	09-Aug-1992
Jan	Huruk	POL	27-Jan-1960	2:14:32	7	Barcelona	09-Aug-1992
Hiromi	Taniguchi	JPN	05-Apr-1960	2:14:42	8	Barcelona	09-Aug-1992
Diego	Garcia	ESP	12-Oct-1961	2:14:56	9	Barcelona	09-Aug-1992
Jae-Ryong	Kim	KOR	25-Apr-1966	2:15:01	10	Barcelona	09-Aug-1992
Harri	Hanninen	FIN	18-Oct-1963	2:15:19	11	Barcelona	09-Aug-1992
Steven	Spence	USA	09-May-1962	2:15:21	12	Barcelona	09-Aug-1992
Edward	Eyestone	USA	15-Jun-1961	2:15:23	13	Barcelona	09-Aug-1992
Boniface	Merande	KEN	13-Feb-1962	2:15:46	14	Barcelona	09-Aug-1992
Albert	van Vlaanderen	NED	25-Nov-1964	2:15:47	15	Barcelona	09-Aug-1992
Rex	Wilson	NZL	10-Apr-1960	2:15:51	16	Barcelona	09-Aug-1992
Robert	Kempainen	USA	18-Jun-1966	2:15:53	17	Barcelona	09-Aug-1992
Rodrigo	Gavela	ESP	05-Jan-1966	2:16:23	18	Barcelona	09-Aug-1992
Karel	David	TCH	08-Feb-1964	2:16:34	19	Barcelona	09-Aug-1992
Leszek	Beblo	POL	08-Jul-1966	2:16:38	20	Barcelona	09-Aug-1992
Wieslaw	Perszke	POL	18-Feb-1960	2:16:38	21	Barcelona	09-Aug-1992
Yakov	Tolstikov	EUN	20-May-1959	2:17:04	22	Barcelona	09-Aug-1992
Tena	Negere	ETH	05-Oct-1972	2:17:07	23	Barcelona	09-Aug-1992
Osmiro	de Souza Silva	BRA	09-Oct-1961	2:17:16	24	Barcelona	09-Aug-1992
Abel	Mokibe	RSA	03-Jul-1962	2:17:24	25	Barcelona	09-Aug-1992
Francois Robert	de Castella	AUS	27-Feb-1957	2:17:44	26	Barcelona	09-Aug-1992
Stephen	Brace	GBR	07-Jul-1961	2:17:49	27	Barcelona	09-Aug-1992
Wan-Ki	Kim	KOR	08-Jul-1968	2:18:32	28	Barcelona	09-Aug-1992

First name	Family name	GPE	Birth date	Time	Place	Venue	Race date
Jose Isidro	Ricorangel	MEX	15-May-1961	2:18:52	29	Barcelona	09-Aug-1992
Ahmed Salah	Hussein	DJI	31-Dec-1956	2:19:04	30	Barcelona	09-Aug-1992
Dominique	Chauvelier	FRA	03-Aug-1956	2:19:09	31	Barcelona	09-Aug-1992
Jose Esteban	Montiel	ESP	20-Sep-1962	2:19:15	32	Barcelona	09-Aug-1992
Thabiso	Moqhali	LES	07-Dec-1967	2:19:28	33	Barcelona	09-Aug-1992
Juma	Ikangaa	TAN	19-Jul-1960	2:19:34	34	Barcelona	09-Aug-1992
Derek	Froude	NZL	20-Apr-1959	2:19:37	35	Barcelona	09-Aug-1992
Douglas	Wakiihuri	KEN	26-Sep-1963	2:19:38	36	Barcelona	09-Aug-1992
Ibrahim	Hussein	KEN	03-Jun-1958	2:19:49	37	Barcelona	09-Aug-1992
Gyula	Borka	HUN	03-Jun-1959	2:20:46	38	Barcelona	09-Aug-1992
David	Long	GBR	21-Nov-1960	2:20:51	39	Barcelona	09-Aug-1992
Miroslav	Vindis	SLO	08-Nov-1963	2:21:03	40	Barcelona	09-Aug-1992
Paul	Davies-Hale	GBR	21-Jun-1962	2:21:15	41	Barcelona	09-Aug-1992
Elphas	Gimindaza	SWZ	23-Aug-1967	2:21:15	42	Barcelona	09-Aug-1992
Rolando	Vera	ECU	27-Apr-1965	2:21:30	43	Barcelona	09-Aug-1992
Alessio	Faustini	ITA	10-Jun-1960	2:21:37	44	Barcelona	09-Aug-1992
Luis	Soares	FRA	24-Mar-1964	2:21:57	45	Barcelona	09-Aug-1992
Paul	Kuete	CMR	20-Dec-1967	2:22:43	46	Barcelona	09-Aug-1992
Helmut	Schmuck	AUT	07-Apr-1963	2:23:38	47	Barcelona	09-Aug-1992
Stephen	Moneghetti	AUS	26-Sep-1962	2:23:42	48	Barcelona	09-Aug-1992
Konrad	Dobler	GER	27-Apr-1957	2:23:44	49	Barcelona	09-Aug-1992
Mwenze	Kalombo	ZAI	07-Jun-1967	2:23:47	50	Barcelona	09-Aug-1992
John	Treacy	IRL	04-Jun-1957	2:24:11	51	Barcelona	09-Aug-1992
Herman	Suizo	PHI	19-Jan-1959	2:25:18	52	Barcelona	09-Aug-1992
Kimball	Reynierse	ARU	10-Jan-1961	2:25:31	53	Barcelona	09-Aug-1992
Nelson	Zamora	URU	05-Apr-1959	2:25:32	54	Barcelona	09-Aug-1992
Daniel	Boltz	SUI	17-Jul-1962	2:25:50	55	Barcelona	09-Aug-1992
Joseildo	da Silva	BRA	20-Feb-1965	2:26:00	56	Barcelona	09-Aug-1992
Juan	Camacho	BOL	04-Jun-1959	2:26:01	57	Barcelona	09-Aug-1992
Cephas	Matafi	ZIM	24-May-1971	2:26:17	58	Barcelona	09-Aug-1992
Mohamed	Salmi	ALG	11-Nov-1963	2:26:56	59	Barcelona	09-Aug-1992
Ildephonso	Sehirwa	RWA		2:27:44	60	Barcelona	09-Aug-1992
Zerehune	Gitaw	ETH	21-Mar-1965	2:28:25	61	Barcelona	09-Aug-1992
Jaime	Ojeda	CHI	03-Aug-1963	2:28:39	62	Barcelona	09-Aug-1992
Smartex	Tambala	MAW	30-Jul-1965	2:29:02	63	Barcelona	09-Aug-1992
Pascal	Zilliox	FRA	19-Jun-1962	2:30:02	64	Barcelona	09-Aug-1992
Luis	Lopez	CRC	14-Jul-1949	2:30:26	65	Barcelona	09-Aug-1992
Gian Luigi	Macina	SMN	17-Dec-1963	2:30:45	66	Barcelona	09-Aug-1992
Abdou	Monzo	NIG	01-Jan-1959	2:31:15	67	Barcelona	09-Aug-1992
Roland	Wille	LIE	01-Aug-1961	2:31:32	68	Barcelona	09-Aug-1992
Tuihaleni	Kayele	NAM	12-Feb-1964	2:31:41	69	Barcelona	09-Aug-1992
Hari Bahadur	Rokaya	NEP	02-Sep-1965	2:32:26	70	Barcelona	09-Aug-1992
Kuruppu	Karunaratne	SRL	29-Apr-1960	2:32:26	71	Barcelona	09-Aug-1992
Thomas	Hughes	IRL	08-Jan-1960	2:32:55	72	Barcelona	09-Aug-1992
William	Aguirre	NCA	27-Oct-1962	2:34:18	73	Barcelona	09-Aug-1992
Ferdinand	Amadi	CAF	18-Sep-1970	2:35:39	74	Barcelona	09-Aug-1992
Mohamed Khamis	Taher	LBY	30-Dec-1959	2:35:46	75	Barcelona	09-Aug-1992
Dieudonne	Lamothe	HAI	29-Jul-1954	2:36:11	76	Barcelona	09-Aug-1992
Myint	Kan	MYA	13-Sep-1965	2:37:39	77	Barcelona	09-Aug-1992
Calvin	Dallas	ISV	02-Apr-1952	2:38:11	78	Barcelona	09-Aug-1992
Saad	Mubarak Ali	BHR	18-Sep-1960	2:39:19	79	Barcelona	09-Aug-1992
Ok-Hyon	Ryu	PRK	18-Apr-1965	2:40:51	80	Barcelona	09-Aug-1992
Alain Claerk	Razahasoa	MAD	30-Mar-1966	2:41:41	81	Barcelona	09-Aug-1992
Michael	Lopeyok	UGA	16-Feb-1962	2:42:54	82	Barcelona	09-Aug-1992
Benjamin	Keleketu	BOT	06-Feb-1965	2:45:57	83	Barcelona	09-Aug-1992
Moussa	Al Hariri	SYR	01-Oct-1966	2:47:06	84	Barcelona	09-Aug-1992
Vang Hung	Luu	VIE	03-Oct-1966	2:56:42	85	Barcelona	09-Aug-1992
Hussain	Haleem	MDV	05-Mar-1969	3:04:16	86	Barcelona	09-Aug-1992
Pyambuu	Tuul	MGL	17-Feb-1959	4:00:44	87	Barcelona	09-Aug-1992
Andrew	Ronan	IRL	19-Jul-1963		DNF	Barcelona	09-Aug-1992
Luketz	Swartbooi	NAM	07-Feb-1966		DNF	Barcelona	09-Aug-1992

First name	Family name	GPE	Birth date	Time	Place	Venue	Race date
Jan	Tau	RSA	18-Nov-1960		DNF	Barcelona	09-Aug-1992
Peter	Maher	CAN	30-Mar-1960		DNF	Barcelona	09-Aug-1992
Ignacio Alberto	Cuba	CUB	31-Jul-1962		DNF	Barcelona	09-Aug-1992
Dionisio	Castro	POR	22-Nov-1963		DNF	Barcelona	09-Aug-1992
Antonius	Dirks	NED	12-Feb-1961		DNF	Barcelona	09-Aug-1992
Zithulele	Singe	RSA	09-Jun-1963		DNF	Barcelona	09-Aug-1992
Bineshwar	Prasad	FIJ	18-Jul-1963		DNF	Barcelona	09-Aug-1992
Antonio	Pinto	POR	22-Mar-1966		DNF	Barcelona	09-Aug-1992
Dionicio	Ceron	MEX	09-Oct-1965		DNF	Barcelona	09-Aug-1992
Joaquim	Pinheiro	POR	20-Dec-1960		DNF	Barcelona	09-Aug-1992
John	Burra	TAN	20-Nov-1965		DNF	Barcelona	09-Aug-1992
Gelindo	Bordin	ITA	02-Apr-1959		DNF	Barcelona	09-Aug-1992
Jorge	Gonzalez	PUR	20-Dec-1952		DNF	Barcelona	09-Aug-1992
Apolinario	Belisle	HON	02-Jul-1966		DNF	Barcelona	09-Aug-1992
Csaba	Szucs	HUN	29-Jan-1965		DNF	Barcelona	09-Aug-1992
Khalifa	Mohamed	MTN	04-Nov-1966		DNF	Barcelona	09-Aug-1992
Abebe	Mekonnen	ETH	09-Jan-1964		DNF	Barcelona	09-Aug-1992
Simon Robert	Naali	TAN	09-Mar-1966		DNF	Barcelona	09-Aug-1992
Diamantino	dos Santos	BRA	03-Feb-1961		DNF	Barcelona	09-Aug-1992
Talal	Omar Abdillahi	DJI	12-May-1967		DNF	Barcelona	09-Aug-1992
Carlos	Grisales	COL	24-Aug-1966		DNF	Barcelona	09-Aug-1992
Salvador	Garcia	MEX	01-Nov-1962		DNF	Barcelona	09-Aug-1992
Vladimir	Bukhanov	EUN	01-Oct-1961		DNF	Barcelona	09-Aug-1992
Josiah	Thugwane	RSA	15-Apr-1971	2:12:36	1	Atlanta	04-Aug-1996
Bong-Ju	Lee	KOR	11-Oct-1968	2:12:39	2	Atlanta	04-Aug-1996
Erick	Wainaina	KEN	19-Dec-1973	2:12:44	3	Atlanta	04-Aug-1996
Martin	Fiz	ESP	03-Mar-1963	2:13:20	4	Atlanta	04-Aug-1996
Richard	Nerurkar	GBR	06-Jan-1964	2:13:39	5	Atlanta	04-Aug-1996
German	Silva	MEX	09-Jan-1968	2:14:29	6	Atlanta	04-Aug-1996
Stephen	Moneghetti	AUS	26-Sep-1962	2:14:35	7	Atlanta	04-Aug-1996
Benjamin	Paredes	MEX	07-Aug-1961	2:14:55	8	Atlanta	04-Aug-1996
Danilo	Goffi	ITA	03-Dec-1972	2:15:08	9	Atlanta	04-Aug-1996
Luiz Antonio	dos Santos	BRA	06-Apr-1964	2:15:55	10	Atlanta	04-Aug-1996
Carlos	Grisales	COL	24-Oct-1966	2:15:56	11	Atlanta	04-Aug-1996
Yi-Yong	Kim	KOR	20-Sep-1973	2:16:17	12	Atlanta	04-Aug-1996
Tendai	Chimusasa	ZIM	28-Jan-1971	2:16:31	13	Atlanta	04-Aug-1996
Antonio	Pinto	POR	22-Mar-1966	2:16:41	14	Atlanta	04-Aug-1996
Dionicio	Ceron	MEX	09-Oct-1965	2:16:48	15	Atlanta	04-Aug-1996
Mwenze	Kalombo	ZAI	07-Jun-1967	2:17:01	16	Atlanta	04-Aug-1996
Leszek	Beblo	POL	08-Jul-1966	2:17:04	17	Atlanta	04-Aug-1996
Alberto	Juzdado	ESP	20-Aug-1966	2:17:24	18	Atlanta	04-Aug-1996
Hiromi	Taniguchi	JPN	05-Apr-1960	2:17:26	19	Atlanta	04-Aug-1996
Salvatore	Bettiol	ITA	28-Nov-1961	2:17:27	20	Atlanta	04-Aug-1996
Peter	Fonseca	CAN	05-Oct-1966	2:17:28	21	Atlanta	04-Aug-1996
Rolando	Vera	ECU	27-Apr-1965	2:17:40	22	Atlanta	04-Aug-1996
Roderic	de Highden	AUS	15-Jan-1969	2:17:42	23	Atlanta	04-Aug-1996
Jose Luis	Molina	CRC	08-Mar-1965	2:17:49	24	Atlanta	04-Aug-1996
Domingos	Castro	POR	22-Nov-1963	2:18:03	25	Atlanta	04-Aug-1996
Tahar	Mansouri	TUN	09-Jan-1965	2:18:06	26	Atlanta	04-Aug-1996
Lawrence	Peu	RSA	13-Feb-1966	2:18:09	27	Atlanta	04-Aug-1996
Keith	Brantly	USA	23-May-1962	2:18:17	28	Atlanta	04-Aug-1996
Thabiso	Ralekhetla	LES	03-Mar-1960	2:18:26	29	Atlanta	04-Aug-1996
Khristo	Stefanov	BUL	21-Dec-1970	2:18:29	30	Atlanta	04-Aug-1996
Robert	Kempainen	USA	18-Jun-1966	2:18:38	31	Atlanta	04-Aug-1996
Harri	Hanninen	FIN	18-Oct-1963	2:18:41	32	Atlanta	04-Aug-1996
Gert	Thys	RSA	12-Nov-1971	2:18:55	33	Atlanta	04-Aug-1996
Sean	Quilty	AUS	16-May-1966	2:19:35	34	Atlanta	04-Aug-1996
Carey	Nelson	CAN	04-Jun-1963	2:19:39	35	Atlanta	04-Aug-1996
Spiridon	Andriopoulos	GRE	01-Aug-1962	2:19:41	36	Atlanta	04-Aug-1996
Oleg	Strizhakov	RUS	18-Jul-1963	2:19:51	37	Atlanta	04-Aug-1996
Jung-Won	Kim	PRK	20-Jan-1973	2:19:54	38	Atlanta	04-Aug-1996

First name	Family name	GPE	Birth date	Time	Place	Venue	Race date
Bruce	Deacon	CAN	05-Dec-1966	2:19:56	39	Atlanta	04-Aug-1996
Jong-Su	Kim	PRK	09-Apr-1970	2:20:19	40	Atlanta	04-Aug-1996
Mark	Coogan	USA	01-May-1966	2:20:27	41	Atlanta	04-Aug-1996
Ahmed Salah	Hussein	DJI	31-Dec-1956	2:20:33	42	Atlanta	04-Aug-1996
Petr	Sarafenyuk	UKR	28-Sep-1965	2:20:37	43	Atlanta	04-Aug-1996
Abdelkader	El Mouaziz	MAR	01-Jan-1969	2:20:39	44	Atlanta	04-Aug-1996
Albert	van Vlaanderen	NED	25-Nov-1964	2:20:48	45	Atlanta	04-Aug-1996
Manuel	Matias	POR	30-Mar-1962	2:20:58	46	Atlanta	04-Aug-1996
Vanderlei	de Lima	BRA	11-Aug-1969	2:21:01	47	Atlanta	04-Aug-1996
Konrad	Dobler	GER	27-Apr-1957	2:21:12	48	Atlanta	04-Aug-1996
Borislav	Devic	YUG	09-Jan-1963	2:21:22	49	Atlanta	04-Aug-1996
Davide	Milesi	ITA	27-Dec-1964	2:21:45	50	Atlanta	04-Aug-1996
Aleksandr	Prokopchuk	LAT	02-May-1967	2:21:50	51	Atlanta	04-Aug-1996
Lameck	Aguta	KEN	10-Oct-1971	2:22:04	52	Atlanta	04-Aug-1996
Diego	Garcia	ESP	12-Oct-1961	2:22:11	53	Atlanta	04-Aug-1996
Masaki	Oya	JPN	11-Jul-1966	2:22:13	54	Atlanta	04-Aug-1996
Peter	Whitehead	GBR	03-Dec-1964	2:22:37	55	Atlanta	04-Aug-1996
Ezequiel	Bitok	KEN	15-Feb-1966	2:23:03	56	Atlanta	04-Aug-1996
Gisheng	Hsu	TPE	02-Jan-1964	2:23:04	57	Atlanta	04-Aug-1996
Pavel	Loskutov	EST	02-Dec-1969	2:23:14	58	Atlanta	04-Aug-1996
Ruben	Maza	VEN	09-Jun-1967	2:23:24	59	Atlanta	04-Aug-1996
Stephen	Brace	GBR	07-Jul-1961	2:23:28	60	Atlanta	04-Aug-1996
Grzegorz	Gajdus	POL	16-Jan-1967	2:23:41	61	Atlanta	04-Aug-1996
Isaac	Simelane	SWZ	20-Apr-1962	2:23:43	62	Atlanta	04-Aug-1996
Nazirdin	Akylbekov	KGZ	14-Mar-1966	2:23:59	63	Atlanta	04-Aug-1996
Anders	Szalkai	SWE	17-Apr-1970	2:24:27	64	Atlanta	04-Aug-1996
John	Mwathiwa	MAW	01-Mar-1967	2:24:45	65	Atlanta	04-Aug-1996
Leonid	Shvetsov	RUS	28-Mar-1969	2:24:49	66	Atlanta	04-Aug-1996
Eddy	Hellebuyck	BEL	22-Jan-1961	2:25:04	67	Atlanta	04-Aug-1996
Ahmed Adam	Salah	SUD	10-Jan-1966	2:25:12	68	Atlanta	04-Aug-1996
Ikaji	Salum	TAN	15-Feb-1967	2:25:29	69	Atlanta	04-Aug-1996
Pavelas	Fedorenka	LIT	05-Oct-1964	2:25:41	70	Atlanta	04-Aug-1996
Miguel	Mallqui	PER	10-Dec-1971	2:25:56	71	Atlanta	04-Aug-1996
Ethel	Hudson	INA	02-Feb-1970	2:26:02	72	Atlanta	04-Aug-1996
Diamantino	dos Santos	BRA	03-Feb-1961	2:26:53	73	Atlanta	04-Aug-1996
Tika	Bogate	NEP	26-Sep-1962	2:27:04	74	Atlanta	04-Aug-1996
Ronnie	Holassie	TRI	29-Jul-1971	2:27:20	75	Atlanta	04-Aug-1996
Joseph	Tjitunga	NAM	21-Jul-1970	2:27:52	76	Atlanta	04-Aug-1996
Valeri	Vlas	MOL	06-Aug-1971	2:28:36	77	Atlanta	04-Aug-1996
Daniel	Sibandze	SWZ	28-Jan-1964	2:28:49	78	Atlanta	04-Aug-1996
Waldemar	Cotelo	URU	12-Mar-1964	2:28:50	79	Atlanta	04-Aug-1996
Petko	Stefanov	BUL	19-Jan-1972	2:29:06	80	Atlanta	04-Aug-1996
Abebe	Mekonnen	ETH	09-Jan-1964	2:29:45	81	Atlanta	04-Aug-1996
Luis	Martinez	GUA	19-Nov-1966	2:29:55	82	Atlanta	04-Aug-1996
Sean	Wade	NZL	03-Feb-1966	2:30:35	83	Atlanta	04-Aug-1996
Abderrahim	Benredouane	MAR	02-Mar-1966	2:30:49	84	Atlanta	04-Aug-1996
Abdou	Monzo	NIG	01-Jan-1959	2:30:57	85	Atlanta	04-Aug-1996
Marcelo	Barrientos	CHI	09-May-1970	2:31:05	86	Atlanta	04-Aug-1996
Toni	Bernado	AND	09-Dec-1966	2:31:28	87	Atlanta	04-Aug-1996
Adel	Adili	LBY	06-Sep-1974	2:32:12	88	Atlanta	04-Aug-1996
Carlos	Tarazona	VEN	14-Aug-1965	2:32:35	89	Atlanta	04-Aug-1996
Tharcisse	Gashaka	BUR	18-Dec-1962	2:32:55	90	Atlanta	04-Aug-1996
Policarpio	Calizaya	BOL	10-Sep-1962	2:33:08	91	Atlanta	04-Aug-1996
Simon	Qamunga	TAN	20-Nov-1967	2:33:11	92	Atlanta	04-Aug-1996
Kenjiro	Jitsui	JPN	16-Dec-1968	2:33:27	93	Atlanta	04-Aug-1996
Antonio Carlos	Zeferino	CPV	17-Jan-1966	2:34:13	94	Atlanta	04-Aug-1996
Pamenos	Ballentyne	STV	09-Dec-1973	2:34:16	95	Atlanta	04-Aug-1996
Kaleka	Mutoke	ZAI	07-Jul-1966	2:34:40	96	Atlanta	04-Aug-1996
Ernest	Ndissipou	CAF	24-Sep-1972	2:35:55	97	Atlanta	04-Aug-1996
Ali	Ettounsi	MAR	01-Jan-1966	2:36:01	98	Atlanta	04-Aug-1996
William	Aguirre	NCA	27-Oct-1962	2:37:02	99	Atlanta	04-Aug-1996

First name	***Family name***	***GPE***	***Birth date***	***Time***	***Place***	***Venue***	***Race date***
Roy	Vence	PHI	22-Feb-1966	2:37:10	100	Atlanta	04-Aug-1996
Mohamed	Al Saadi	YEM	01-Jan-1968	2:40:41	101	Atlanta	04-Aug-1996
Julio	Hernandez	COL	20-Aug-1958	2:41:56	102	Atlanta	04-Aug-1996
Ajay	Chuttoo	MRI	14-Nov-1969	2:42:07	103	Atlanta	04-Aug-1996
Nils	Antonio	JAM	31-Mar-1963	2:44:10	104	Atlanta	04-Aug-1996
Rithya	To	CAM	10-Oct-1967	2:47:01	105	Atlanta	04-Aug-1996
Maximo	Oliveras	PUR	02-Feb-1962	2:47:15	106	Atlanta	04-Aug-1996
Islam	Djugum	BIH	01-Jun-1960	2:47:38	107	Atlanta	04-Aug-1996
Marlon	Williams	ISV	09-Sep-1956	2:48:26	108	Atlanta	04-Aug-1996
Eugene	Muslar	BIZ	28-Mar-1959	2:51:41	109	Atlanta	04-Aug-1996
Abdi	Isak	SOM	01-Jan-1966	2:59:55	110	Atlanta	04-Aug-1996
Abdel Baser	Wasiqi	AFG	12-Jul-1975	4:24:17	111	Atlanta	04-Aug-1996
Tumo	Turbo	ETH	23-Feb-1970		DNF	Atlanta	04-Aug-1996
Patrick	Ishyaka	RWA	28-Jul-1972		DNF	Atlanta	04-Aug-1996
Belayneh	Dinsamo	ETH	28-Jun-1965		DNF	Atlanta	04-Aug-1996
Antonio	Silio	ARG	09-May-1966		DNF	Atlanta	04-Aug-1996
Victor	Razafindrakoto	MAD	28-Feb-1972		DNF	Atlanta	04-Aug-1996
Ceslovas	Kundrotas	LIT	03-Jan-1961		DNF	Atlanta	04-Aug-1996
Stephan	Freigang	GER	27-Sep-1967		DNF	Atlanta	04-Aug-1996
Julius	Sumaye	TAN	12-Sep-1965		DNF	Atlanta	04-Aug-1996
Benjamin	Keleketu	BOT	06-Feb-1965		DNF	Atlanta	04-Aug-1996
Dainius	Virbickas	LIT	12-Nov-1971		DNF	Atlanta	04-Aug-1996
Risto	Ulmala	FIN	07-May-1963		DNF	Atlanta	04-Aug-1996
Moussa	Omar	DJI	08-Feb-1961		DNF	Atlanta	04-Aug-1996
Wan-Ki	Kim	KOR	08-Jul-1968		DNF	Atlanta	04-Aug-1996

APPENDIX E: Race Results for Women Listed Chronologically

First name	Family name	GPE	Birth date	Time	Place	Venue	Race date
Joan	Benoit	USA	16-May-1957	2:24:52	1	Los Angeles	05-Aug-1984
Grete	Waitz	NOR	01-Oct-1953	2:26:18	2	Los Angeles	05-Aug-1984
Rosa	Mota	POR	29-Jun-1958	2:26:57	3	Los Angeles	05-Aug-1984
Ingrid	Kristiansen	NOR	21-Mar-1956	2:27:34	4	Los Angeles	05-Aug-1984
Lorraine	Moller	NZL	01-Jun-1955	2:28:34	5	Los Angeles	05-Aug-1984
Priscilla	Welch	GBR	22-Nov-1944	2:28:54	6	Los Angeles	05-Aug-1984
Lisa	Martin	AUS	12-May-1960	2:29:03	7	Los Angeles	05-Aug-1984
Sylvie	Ruegger	CAN	23-Feb-1961	2:29:09	8	Los Angeles	05-Aug-1984
Laura	Fogli	ITA	05-Oct-1959	2:29:28	9	Los Angeles	05-Aug-1984
Tuija	Toivonen	FIN	22-Sep-1958	2:32:07	10	Los Angeles	05-Aug-1984
Joyce	Smith	GBR	26-Oct-1937	2:32:48	11	Los Angeles	05-Aug-1984
Alba	Milana	ITA	17-Mar-1959	2:33:01	12	Los Angeles	05-Aug-1984
Dorthe	Rasmussen	DEN	27-Jan-1960	2:33:40	13	Los Angeles	05-Aug-1984
Sarah	Rowell	GBR	19-Nov-1962	2:34:08	14	Los Angeles	05-Aug-1984
Sinikka	Keskitalo	FIN	29-Jan-1951	2:35:15	15	Los Angeles	05-Aug-1984
Charlotte	Teske	FRG	23-Nov-1949	2:35:56	16	Los Angeles	05-Aug-1984
Anne Marie	Malone	CAN	28-Jul-1960	2:36:33	17	Los Angeles	05-Aug-1984
Marie-Louise	Hamrin	SWE	19-Apr-1957	2:36:41	18	Los Angeles	05-Aug-1984
Nanae	Sasaki	JPN	08-Feb-1956	2:37:04	19	Los Angeles	05-Aug-1984
Paola	Moro	ITA	14-Aug-1952	2:37:06	20	Los Angeles	05-Aug-1984
Maria	van Landeghem	BEL	19-Jul-1957	2:37:11	21	Los Angeles	05-Aug-1984
Carolina	Beurskens	NED	15-Feb-1952	2:37:51	22	Los Angeles	05-Aug-1984
Regina	Joyce	IRL	07-Feb-1957	2:37:57	23	Los Angeles	05-Aug-1984
Marie-Christine	Deurbroeck	BEL	01-Feb-1957	2:38:01	24	Los Angeles	05-Aug-1984
Maria	Trujillo	MEX	19-Oct-1959	2:38:50	25	Los Angeles	05-Aug-1984
Bente	Moe	NOR	02-Dec-1960	2:40:52	26	Los Angeles	05-Aug-1984
Mary	O'Connor	NZL	19-Jun-1955	2:41:22	27	Los Angeles	05-Aug-1984
Carey	May	IRL	19-Jul-1959	2:41:27	28	Los Angeles	05-Aug-1984
Francine	Peeters	BEL	23-Feb-1957	2:42:22	29	Los Angeles	05-Aug-1984
Zehava	Shmueli	ISR	19-May-1955	2:42:27	30	Los Angeles	05-Aug-1984
Winnie	Lai-Chu Ng	HKG	07-Aug-1952	2:42:38	31	Los Angeles	05-Aug-1984
Monica	Regonessi	CHI	27-Apr-1961	2:44:44	32	Los Angeles	05-Aug-1984
Naydi	Nazario	PUR	10-Sep-1956	2:45:49	33	Los Angeles	05-Aug-1984
Yuko	Gordon	HKG	23-Feb-1951	2:46:12	34	Los Angeles	05-Aug-1984
Ena	Guevara	PER	07-Feb-1959	2:46:50	35	Los Angeles	05-Aug-1984
Julie	Brown	USA	04-Feb-1955	2:47:33	36	Los Angeles	05-Aug-1984
Gabrielle	Andersen	SUI	20-May-1945	2:48:42	37	Los Angeles	05-Aug-1984
Rita	Borralho	POR	21-Mar-1954	2:50:58	38	Los Angeles	05-Aug-1984
Maria Conceicao	Ferreira	POR	13-Mar-1962	2:50:58	39	Los Angeles	05-Aug-1984
Maria del Carmen	Cardenas	MEX	13-Feb-1959	2:51:03	40	Los Angeles	05-Aug-1984
Maria Luisa	Ronquillo	MEX	12-Dec-1956	2:51:04	41	Los Angeles	05-Aug-1984
Nelly	Wright	BOL	17-Dec-1945	2:51:35	42	Los Angeles	05-Aug-1984
Mary	Wagaki	KEN	20-Jun-1954	2:52:00	43	Los Angeles	05-Aug-1984
Eleonora	Mendonca	BRA	13-Nov-1948	2:52:19	44	Los Angeles	05-Aug-1984
Ifeoma	Mbanugo	NGR	03-Mar-1952		DNF	Los Angeles	05-Aug-1984
Anne	Audain	NZL	01-Nov-1955		DNF	Los Angeles	05-Aug-1984
Jacqueline	Gareau	CAN	10-Jan-1953		DNF	Los Angeles	05-Aug-1984
Leda	Diaz de Cano	HON	28-Oct-1946		DNF	Los Angeles	05-Aug-1984
Julie	Isphording	USA	05-Dec-1961		DNF	Los Angeles	05-Aug-1984
Akemi	Masuda	JPN	01-Jan-1964		DNF	Los Angeles	05-Aug-1984
Rosa	Mota	POR	29-Jun-1958	2:25:40	1	Seoul	23-Sep-1988
Lisa	Martin	AUS	12-May-1960	2:25:53	2	Seoul	23-Sep-1988

First name	Family name	GPE	Birth date	Time	Place	Venue	Race date
Katrin	Dorre	GDR	06-Oct-1961	2:26:21	3	Seoul	23-Sep-1988
Tatyana	Polovinskaya	URS	14-Mar-1965	2:27:05	4	Seoul	23-Sep-1988
Youfeng	Zhao	CHN	05-May-1965	2:27:06	5	Seoul	23-Sep-1988
Laura	Fogli	ITA	05-Oct-1959	2:27:49	6	Seoul	23-Sep-1988
Daniele	Kaber	LUX	20-Apr-1960	2:29:23	7	Seoul	23-Sep-1988
Maria	Curatolo	ITA	12-Oct-1963	2:30:14	8	Seoul	23-Sep-1988
Zoya	Ivanova	URS	14-Mar-1952	2:30:25	9	Seoul	23-Sep-1988
Angela	Pain	GBR	08-Feb-1962	2:30:51	10	Seoul	23-Sep-1988
Odette	Lapierre	CAN	28-Jan-1955	2:30:56	11	Seoul	23-Sep-1988
Susan	Tooby	GBR	24-Oct-1960	2:31:33	12	Seoul	23-Sep-1988
Karolina	Szabo	HUN	17-Nov-1961	2:32:26	13	Seoul	23-Sep-1988
Francoise	Bonnet	FRA	08-Apr-1957	2:32:36	14	Seoul	23-Sep-1988
Mi-Ok	Lee	KOR	10-Mar-1968	2:32:51	15	Seoul	23-Sep-1988
Raisa	Smekhnova	URS	16-Sep-1950	2:33:19	16	Seoul	23-Sep-1988
Nancy	Ditz	USA	25-Jun-1954	2:33:42	17	Seoul	23-Sep-1988
Maria	Lelut	FRA	29-Jan-1956	2:33:47	18	Seoul	23-Sep-1988
Jocelyne	Villeton	FRA	17-Sep-1954	2:34:02	19	Seoul	23-Sep-1988
Maria Conceicao	Ferreira	POR	13-Mar-1962	2:34:23	20	Seoul	23-Sep-1988
Kerstin	Pressler	FRG	02-Feb-1962	2:34:26	21	Seoul	23-Sep-1988
Marianna Wanda	Panfil	POL	26-Jan-1959	2:34:35	22	Seoul	23-Sep-1988
Antonella	Bizioli	ITA	29-Mar-1957	2:34:38	23	Seoul	23-Sep-1988
Eriko	Asai	JPN	20-Oct-1959	2:34:41	24	Seoul	23-Sep-1988
Evy	Palm	SWE	31-Jan-1942	2:34:41	25	Seoul	23-Sep-1988
Lizanne	Bussieres	CAN	20-Aug-1961	2:35:03	26	Seoul	23-Sep-1988
Gabriela	Wolf	FRG	28-Oct-1960	2:35:11	27	Seoul	23-Sep-1988
Kumi	Araki	JPN	11-Oct-1965	2:35:15	28	Seoul	23-Sep-1988
Misako	Miyahara	JPN	29-May-1962	2:35:26	29	Seoul	23-Sep-1988
Huandi	Zhong	CHN	23-Oct-1967	2:36:02	30	Seoul	23-Sep-1988
Helene	Rochefort	CAN	22-Nov-1954	2:36:44	31	Seoul	23-Sep-1988
Susan	Crehan	GBR	12-Sep-1956	2:36:57	32	Seoul	23-Sep-1988
Carolina	Beurskens	NED	15-Feb-1952	2:37:52	33	Seoul	23-Sep-1988
Lorraine	Moller	NZL	01-Jun-1955	2:37:52	34	Seoul	23-Sep-1988
Magda	Ilands	BEL	16-Jan-1950	2:38:02	35	Seoul	23-Sep-1988
Sissel	Grottenberg	NOR	17-Aug-1956	2:38:17	36	Seoul	23-Sep-1988
Eun-Joo	Lim	KOR	05-Mar-1961	2:38:21	37	Seoul	23-Sep-1988
Marcianne	Mukamurenzi	RWA	11-Nov-1959	2:40:12	38	Seoul	23-Sep-1988
Margaret	Groos	USA	21-Sep-1959	2:40:59	39	Seoul	23-Sep-1988
Cathy	O'Brien	USA	19-Jul-1967	2:41:04	40	Seoul	23-Sep-1988
Tuija	Jousimaa	FIN	22-Sep-1958	2:43:00	41	Seoul	23-Sep-1988
Sinikka	Keskitalo	FIN	29-Jan-1951	2:43:00	42	Seoul	23-Sep-1988
Blanca	Jaime	MEX	03-Nov-1965	2:43:00	43	Seoul	23-Sep-1988
Angelica	de Almeida	BRA	25-Mar-1965	2:43:40	44	Seoul	23-Sep-1988
Ludmila	Melicherova	TCH	06-Jun-1964	2:43:56	45	Seoul	23-Sep-1988
Ailish	Smyth	IRL	18-Sep-1958	2:44:17	46	Seoul	23-Sep-1988
Genoveva	Eichenmann	SUI	12-Sep-1957	2:44:37	47	Seoul	23-Sep-1988
Rosmarie	Muller	SUI	27-Mar-1958	2:47:31	48	Seoul	23-Sep-1988
Pascaline	Wangui	KEN	30-Nov-1960	2:47:42	49	Seoul	23-Sep-1988
Apollinaire	Nyinawabera	RWA	1962	2:49:18	50	Seoul	23-Sep-1988
Maryse	Justin	MRI	25-Aug-1958	2:50:00	51	Seoul	23-Sep-1988
Michele	Bush	CAY	03-Oct-1961	2:51:30	52	Seoul	23-Sep-1988
Maria	Menendez de Cox	GUA	12-Oct-1954	2:51:33	53	Seoul	23-Sep-1988
Juan	Li	CHN	05-Oct-1966	2:53:08	54	Seoul	23-Sep-1988
Linda	Hunter	ZIM	10-Dec-1963	2:53:17	55	Seoul	23-Sep-1988
Cornelia	Melis	ARU	23-Feb-1960	2:53:24	56	Seoul	23-Sep-1988
Marie-Louise	Rollins	IRL	23-Mar-1959	2:54:37	57	Seoul	23-Sep-1988
Kriscia	Garcia	ESA	20-Sep-1963	3:04:21	58	Seoul	23-Sep-1988
Julie	Ogbourn	GUM	01-Aug-1958	3:06:05	59	Seoul	23-Sep-1988
Rajkumari	Pandey	NEP	13-Dec-1969	3:10:31	60	Seoul	23-Sep-1988
Menuka	Rawat	NEP	1972	3:11:17	61	Seoul	23-Sep-1988
Arlene	Vincent Mark	GRN	06-Oct-1954	3:23:56	62	Seoul	23-Sep-1988
Lourdes	Klitzkie	GUM	02-Feb-1940	3:25:32	63	Seoul	23-Sep-1988

First name	Family name	GPE	Birth date	Time	Place	Venue	Race date
Mariana	Ysrael	GUM		3:42:23	64	Seoul	23-Sep-1988
Grete	Waitz	NOR	01-Oct-1953		DNF	Seoul	23-Sep-1988
Agnes	Pardaens	BEL	09-Oct-1956		DNF	Seoul	23-Sep-1988
Mi-Kyong	Kim	KOR	19-Feb-1967		DNF	Seoul	23-Sep-1988
Bente	Moe	NOR	02-Dec-1960		DNF	Seoul	23-Sep-1988
Mar Mar	Min	MYA	18-Jul-1958		DNF	Seoul	23-Sep-1988
Valentina	Yegorova	EUN	16-Feb-1964	2:32:41	1	Barcelona	01-Aug-1992
Yuko	Arimori	JPN	17-Dec-1966	2:32:49	2	Barcelona	01-Aug-1992
Lorraine	Moller	NZL	01-Jun-1955	2:33:59	3	Barcelona	01-Aug-1992
Madina	Biktagirova	EUN	20-Sep-1964	2:35:39	DQ	Barcelona	01-Aug-1992
Sachiko	Yamashita	JPN	20-Aug-1964	2:36:26	4	Barcelona	01-Aug-1992
Katrin	Dorre	GER	06-Oct-1961	2:36:48	5	Barcelona	01-Aug-1992
Gyong-Ae	Mun	PRK	08-Apr-1969	2:37:03	6	Barcelona	01-Aug-1992
Maria Manuela	Machado	POR	09-Aug-1963	2:38:22	7	Barcelona	01-Aug-1992
Ramilya	Burangulova	EUN	11-Jul-1961	2:38:46	8	Barcelona	01-Aug-1992
Colleen	de Reuck	RSA	13-Apr-1964	2:39:03	9	Barcelona	01-Aug-1992
Cathy	O'Brien	USA	19-Jul-1967	2:39:42	10	Barcelona	01-Aug-1992
Karolina	Szabo	HUN	17-Nov-1961	2:40:10	11	Barcelona	01-Aug-1992
Francie	Larrieu-Smith	USA	23-Nov-1952	2:41:09	12	Barcelona	01-Aug-1992
Sally	Eastall	GBR	05-Jan-1963	2:41:20	13	Barcelona	01-Aug-1992
Ritva	Lemettinen	FIN	09-Sep-1960	2:41:48	14	Barcelona	01-Aug-1992
Birgit	Jerschabek	GER	17-May-1969	2:42:45	15	Barcelona	01-Aug-1992
Veronique	Marot	GBR	16-Sep-1955	2:42:55	16	Barcelona	01-Aug-1992
Marcia	Narloch	BRA	28-Mar-1969	2:44:32	17	Barcelona	01-Aug-1992
Emma	Scaunich	ITA	01-Mar-1954	2:46:14	18	Barcelona	01-Aug-1992
Odette	Lapierre	CAN	28-Jan-1955	2:46:18	19	Barcelona	01-Aug-1992
Anna	Villani	ITA	21-Jun-1966	2:46:44	20	Barcelona	01-Aug-1992
Janis	Klecker	USA	18-Jul-1960	2:47:17	21	Barcelona	01-Aug-1992
Marianna Wanda	Panfil	POL	26-Jan-1959	2:47:27	22	Barcelona	01-Aug-1992
Bettina	Sabatini	ITA	21-Mar-1966	2:50:09	23	Barcelona	01-Aug-1992
Alena	Peterkova	TCH	13-Nov-1960	2:53:30	24	Barcelona	01-Aug-1992
Mi-Ok	Lee	KOR	10-Mar-1968	2:54:21	25	Barcelona	01-Aug-1992
Malgorzata	Birbach	POL	17-Feb-1960	2:54:33	26	Barcelona	01-Aug-1992
Sally	Ellis	GBR	17-May-1958	2:54:41	27	Barcelona	01-Aug-1992
Pascaline	Wangui	KEN	30-Nov-1960	2:56:46	28	Barcelona	01-Aug-1992
Yumi	Kokamo	JPN	26-Dec-1971	2:58:18	29	Barcelona	01-Aug-1992
Addis	Gezahegn	ETH	01-Jan-1969	2:58:57	30	Barcelona	01-Aug-1992
Janete	Mayal	BRA	19-Jul-1963	3:00:23	31	Barcelona	01-Aug-1992
Elena	Murgoci	ROM	20-May-1960	3:01:46	32	Barcelona	01-Aug-1992
Vilma	Sanchez Pena	CRC	26-Mar-1960	3:03:34	33	Barcelona	01-Aug-1992
Ena	Guevara	PER	07-Feb-1959	3:05:50	34	Barcelona	01-Aug-1992
Ana	Gutierrez	ISV	18-Sep-1961	3:14:02	35	Barcelona	01-Aug-1992
Jen	Allred	GUM	17-Dec-1961	3:14:45	36	Barcelona	01-Aug-1992
Bakombo	Kungu	ZAI	07-Aug-1962	3:29:10	37	Barcelona	01-Aug-1992
Maria	Rebelo	FRA	29-Jan-1956		DNF	Barcelona	01-Aug-1992
Lisa	Ondieki	AUS	12-May-1960		DNF	Barcelona	01-Aug-1992
Thi Teo	Dang	VIE	19-Jul-1968		DNF	Barcelona	01-Aug-1992
Olga	Avalos	MEX	02-Aug-1963		DNF	Barcelona	01-Aug-1992
Aurora	Cunha	POR	31-May-1959		DNF	Barcelona	01-Aug-1992
Marguerite	Buist	NZL	19-Dec-1962		DNF	Barcelona	01-Aug-1992
Cornelia	Melis	ARU	23-Feb-1960		DNF	Barcelona	01-Aug-1992
Lizanne	Bussieres	CAN	20-Aug-1961		DNF	Barcelona	01-Aug-1992
Franziska	Moser	SUI	17-Aug-1966		DNF	Barcelona	01-Aug-1992
Fatuma	Roba	ETH	18-Dec-1973	2:26:05	1	Atlanta	28-Jul-1996
Valentina	Yegorova	RUS	16-Feb-1964	2:28:05	2	Atlanta	28-Jul-1996
Yuko	Arimori	JPN	17-Dec-1966	2:28:39	3	Atlanta	28-Jul-1996
Katrin	Dorre	GER	06-Oct-1961	2:28:45	4	Atlanta	28-Jul-1996
Rocio	Rios	ESP	13-Mar-1969	2:30:50	5	Atlanta	28-Jul-1996
Lidia	Simon	ROM	04-Sep-1973	2:31:04	6	Atlanta	28-Jul-1996
Maria Manuela	Machado	POR	09-Aug-1963	2:31:11	7	Atlanta	28-Jul-1996
Sonja	Krolik	GER	24-Feb-1973	2:31:16	8	Atlanta	28-Jul-1996

First name	Family name	GPE	Birth date	Time	Place	Venue	Race date
Xiujuan	Ren	CHN	14-Sep-1974	2:31:21	9	Atlanta	28-Jul-1996
Anne Marie	Lauck	USA	07-Mar-1969	2:31:30	10	Atlanta	28-Jul-1996
Malgorzata	Sobanska	POL	25-Apr-1969	2:31:52	11	Atlanta	28-Jul-1996
Izumi	Maki	JPN	10-Dec-1968	2:32:35	12	Atlanta	28-Jul-1996
Ornella	Ferrara	ITA	17-Apr-1968	2:33:09	13	Atlanta	28-Jul-1996
Monica	Pont	ESP	03-Jun-1969	2:33:27	14	Atlanta	28-Jul-1996
Angelina	Kanana	KEN	16-Dec-1965	2:34:19	15	Atlanta	28-Jul-1996
Elizabeth	McColgan	GBR	24-May-1964	2:34:30	16	Atlanta	28-Jul-1996
Junko	Asari	JPN	22-Sep-1969	2:34:31	17	Atlanta	28-Jul-1996
Franziska	Rochat-Moser	SUI	17-Aug-1966	2:34:48	18	Atlanta	28-Jul-1996
Griselda	Gonzalez	ARG	04-Dec-1965	2:35:12	19	Atlanta	28-Jul-1996
Song-Ok	Jong	PRK	18-Aug-1974	2:35:31	20	Atlanta	28-Jul-1996
Irina	Bogachova	KGZ	30-Apr-1961	2:35:44	21	Atlanta	28-Jul-1996
Inglandini	Gonzalez	COL	02-May-1966	2:35:45	22	Atlanta	28-Jul-1996
Serap	Aktas	TUR	25-Sep-1971	2:36:14	23	Atlanta	28-Jul-1996
Yelena	Mazovka	BLR	30-Jun-1967	2:36:22	24	Atlanta	28-Jul-1996
Marleen	Renders	BEL	24-Dec-1968	2:36:27	25	Atlanta	28-Jul-1996
Chang-Ok	Kim	PRK	27-May-1975	2:36:31	26	Atlanta	28-Jul-1996
Albertina	Dias	POR	26-Apr-1965	2:36:39	27	Atlanta	28-Jul-1996
Kerryn	McCann	AUS	02-May-1967	2:36:41	28	Atlanta	28-Jul-1996
Aniela	Nikiel	POL	01-Nov-1965	2:36:44	29	Atlanta	28-Jul-1996
Mi-Ja	Oh	KOR	03-Jul-1970	2:36:54	30	Atlanta	28-Jul-1996
Linda	Somers	USA	07-May-1961	2:36:58	31	Atlanta	28-Jul-1996
Danuta	Bartoszek	CAN	19-Aug-1961	2:37:06	32	Atlanta	28-Jul-1996
Maria del Carmen	Diaz	MEX	15-Jul-1970	2:37:14	33	Atlanta	28-Jul-1996
Nelly	Glauser	SUI	27-Jan-1966	2:37:19	34	Atlanta	28-Jul-1996
Ramilya	Burangulova	RUS	11-Jul-1961	2:38:04	35	Atlanta	28-Jul-1996
Judit	Nagy	HUN	09-Sep-1965	2:38:43	36	Atlanta	28-Jul-1996
Erika	Olivera	CHI	04-Jan-1976	2:39:06	37	Atlanta	28-Jul-1996
Yvonne	Danson	SIN	22-May-1959	2:39:18	38	Atlanta	28-Jul-1996
Marcia	Narloch	BRA	28-Mar-1969	2:39:33	39	Atlanta	28-Jul-1996
Stefanija	Statkuviene	LIT	06-Mar-1963	2:39:51	40	Atlanta	28-Jul-1996
Antje	van Schuppen	NED	11-Oct-1960	2:40:46	41	Atlanta	28-Jul-1996
Valentina	Yenaki	MOL	15-Feb-1966	2:41:30	Unof.	Atlanta	28-Jul-1996
Maria	Polizou	GRE	10-Nov-1968	2:41:33	42	Atlanta	28-Jul-1996
Guadaloupe	Loma	MEX	12-Dec-1967	2:41:56	43	Atlanta	28-Jul-1996
Anuta	Catuna	ROM	01-Oct-1968	2:42:01	44	Atlanta	28-Jul-1996
Karen	Macleod	GBR	24-Apr-1958	2:42:08	45	Atlanta	28-Jul-1996
Lorraine	Moller	NZL	01-Jun-1955	2:42:21	46	Atlanta	28-Jul-1996
Maria Albertina	Machado	POR	25-Dec-1961	2:43:44	47	Atlanta	28-Jul-1996
Anita	Haakenstad	NOR	19-Feb-1968	2:43:58	48	Atlanta	28-Jul-1996
Ana Isabel	Alonso	ESP	16-Aug-1963	2:44:12	49	Atlanta	28-Jul-1996
Natalya	Galushko	BLR	18-Sep-1971	2:44:21	50	Atlanta	28-Jul-1996
Adriana	Fernandez	MEX	04-Apr-1971	2:44:23	51	Atlanta	28-Jul-1996
May	Allison	CAN	29-Oct-1964	2:44:38	52	Atlanta	28-Jul-199
Helena	Javornik	SLO	26-Mar-1966	2:46:58	53	Atlanta	28-Jul-1996
Marilu	Salazar	PER	27-Oct-1965	2:48:58	54	Atlanta	28-Jul-1996
Suzana	Ciric	YUG	12-Jul-1969	2:49:30	55	Atlanta	28-Jul-1996
Nadia	Prasad	FRA	06-Oct-1967	2:50:05	56	Atlanta	28-Jul-1996
Suzanne	Malaxos	AUS	30-Dec-1961	2:50:46	57	Atlanta	28-Jul-1996
Suzanne	Rigg	GBR	29-Nov-1963	2:52:09	58	Atlanta	28-Jul-1996
Elizabeth	Mongudhi	NAM	15-Jun-1966	2:56:19	59	Atlanta	28-Jul-1996
Solange	de Souza	BRA	05-Feb-1969	2:56:23	60	Atlanta	28-Jul-1996
Guylsara	Dadabayeva	TJK	04-Jul-1976	3:09:08	61	Atlanta	28-Jul-1996
Bimala	Rana Magar	NEP	02-Jul-1971	3:16:19	62	Atlanta	28-Jul-1996
Erhemsaihan	Davaajargal	MGL	19-May-1969	3:19:06	63	Atlanta	28-Jul-1996
Sirivanh	Ketavong	LAO	01-Sep-1970	3:25:16	64	Atlanta	28-Jul-1996
Marie	Benito	GUM	09-Aug-1965	3:27:28	65	Atlanta	28-Jul-1996
Virginie	Gloum	CAF	23-Aug-1972	3:32+	Unof.	Atlanta	28-Jul-1996
Gitte	Karlshoj	DEN	14-May-1959		DNF	Atlanta	28-Jul-1996
Uta	Pippig	GER	07-Sep-1965		DNF	Atlanta	28-Jul-1996

First name	Family name	GPE	Birth date	Time	Place	Venue	Race date
Cristina	Pomacu	ROM	15-Sep-1973		DNF	Atlanta	28-Jul-1996
Soon-Duk	Kang	KOR	29-Oct-1974		DNF	Atlanta	28-Jul-1996
Kamila	Gradus	POL	19-Mar-1967		DNF	Atlanta	28-Jul-1996
Lyubov	Klochko	UKR	26-Sep-1959		DNF	Atlanta	28-Jul-1996
Kirsi	Rauta	FIN	17-Mar-1962		DNF	Atlanta	28-Jul-1996
Maura	Viceconte	ITA	03-Oct-1967		DNF	Atlanta	28-Jul-1996
Carmen	de Oliveira	BRA	17-Aug-1965		DNF	Atlanta	28-Jul-1996
Martha	Tenorio	ECU	17-Feb-1966		DNF	Atlanta	28-Jul-1996
Alla	Zhilyayeva	RUS	05-Feb-1969		DNF	Atlanta	28-Jul-1996
Elana	Meyer	RSA	10-Oct-1966		DNF	Atlanta	28-Jul-1996
Jane	Salumae	EST	17-Jan-1968		DNF	Atlanta	28-Jul-1996
Mi-Kyung	Lee	KOR	26-May-1975		DNF	Atlanta	28-Jul-1996
Lisa	Ondieki	AUS	12-May-1960		DNF	Atlanta	28-Jul-1996
Madina	Biktagirova	BLR	20-Sep-1964		DNF	Atlanta	28-Jul-1996
Carol	Galea	MLT	24-Oct-1962		DNF	Atlanta	28-Jul-1996
Maria	Curatolo	ITA	12-Oct-1963		DNF	Atlanta	28-Jul-1996
Joyce	Chepchumba	KEN	06-Nov-1970		DNF	Atlanta	28-Jul-1996
Salina	Chirchir	KEN	08-Aug-1968		DNF	Atlanta	28-Jul-1996
Jennifer	Spangler	USA	20-Jul-1963		DNF	Atlanta	28-Jul-1996

Marital Name Changes
Lelut=Rebelo
Martin=Ondieki
Toivonen=Jousimaa

APPENDIX F: Fastest 200 Olympic Men's Marathon Performances

First name	*Family name*	*GPE*	*Birth date*	*Time*	*Place*	*Venue*	*Race date*
Carlos	Lopes	POR	18-Feb-1947	2:09:21	1	Los Angeles	12-Aug-1984
Waldemar	Cierpinski	GDR	03-Aug-1950	2:09:55.0	1	Montreal	31-Jul-1976
John	Treacy	IRL	04-Jun-1957	2:09:56	2	Los Angeles	12-Aug-1984
Charles	Spedding	GBR	19-May-1952	2:09:58	3	Los Angeles	12-Aug-1984
Gelindo	Bordin	ITA	02-Apr-1959	2:10:32	1	Seoul	02-Oct-1988
Frank	Shorter	USA	31-Oct-1947	2:10:45.8	2	Montreal	31-Jul-1976
Douglas	Wakiihuri	KEN	26-Sep-1963	2:10:47	2	Seoul	02-Oct-1988
Takeshi	Soh	JPN	09-Jan-1953	2:10:55	4	Los Angeles	12-Aug-1984
Ahmed Salah	Hussein	DJI	31-Dec-1956	2:10:59	3	Seoul	02-Oct-1988
Waldemar	Cierpinski	GDR	03-Aug-1950	2:11:03.0	1	Moscow	01-Aug-1980
10							
Takeyuki	Nakayama	JPN	20-Dec-1959	2:11:05	4	Seoul	02-Oct-1988
Francois Robert	de Castella	AUS	27-Feb-1957	2:11:09	5	Los Angeles	12-Aug-1984
Juma	Ikangaa	TAN	19-Jul-1960	2:11:10	6	Los Angeles	12-Aug-1984
Karel	Lismont	BEL	08-Mar-1949	2:11:12.6	3	Montreal	31-Jul-1976
Donald	Kardong	USA	22-Dec-1948	2:11:15.8	4	Montreal	31-Jul-1976
Gerhardus	Nijboer	NED	18-Aug-1955	2:11:20.0	2	Moscow	01-Aug-1980
Joseph	Nzau	KEN	14-Apr-1952	2:11:28	7	Los Angeles	12-Aug-1984
Setymkul	Dzhumanazarov	URS	17-Sep-1951	2:11:35.0	3	Moscow	01-Aug-1980
Djama	Robleh	DJI	31-Dec-1958	2:11:39	8	Los Angeles	12-Aug-1984
Stephen	Moneghetti	AUS	26-Sep-1962	2:11:49	5	Seoul	02-Oct-1988
20							
Vladimir	Kotov	URS	21-Feb-1958	2:12:05.0	4	Moscow	01-Aug-1980
Abebe	Bikila	ETH	07-Aug-1932	2:12:11.2	1	Tokyo	21-Oct-1964
Leonid	Moiseyev	URS	21-Oct-1952	2:12:14.0	5	Moscow	01-Aug-1980
Charles	Spedding	GBR	19-May-1952	2:12:19	6	Seoul	02-Oct-1988
Frank	Shorter	USA	31-Oct-1947	2:12:19.8	1	Munich	10-Sep-1972
Jeremiah	Kiernan	IRL	31-May-1953	2:12:20	9	Los Angeles	12-Aug-1984
Josiah	Thugwane	RSA	15-Apr-1971	2:12:36	1	Atlanta	04-Aug-1996
Rodolfo	Gomez	MEX	30-Oct-1950	2:12:39.0	6	Moscow	01-Aug-1980
Bong-Ju	Lee	KOR	11-Oct-1968	2:12:39	2	Atlanta	04-Aug-1996
Dereje	Nedi	ETH	10-Oct-1955	2:12:44.0	7	Moscow	01-Aug-1980
30							
Erick	Wainaina	KEN	19-Dec-1973	2:12:44	3	Atlanta	04-Aug-1996
Rodney	Dixon	NZL	13-Jul-1950	2:12:57	10	Los Angeles	12-Aug-1984
Juma	Ikangaa	TAN	19-Jul-1960	2:13:06	7	Seoul	02-Oct-1988
Francois Robert	de Castella	AUS	27-Feb-1957	2:13:07	8	Seoul	02-Oct-1988
Lasse	Viren	FIN	22-Jul-1949	2:13:10.8	5	Montreal	31-Jul-1976
Massimo	Magnani	ITA	04-Oct-1951	2:13:12.0	8	Moscow	01-Aug-1980
Martin	Fiz	ESP	03-Mar-1963	2:13:20	4	Atlanta	04-Aug-1996
Young-Cho	Hwang	KOR	22-Mar-1970	2:13:23	1	Barcelona	09-Aug-1992
Karel	Lismont	BEL	08-Mar-1949	2:13:27.0	9	Moscow	01-Aug-1980
Jerome	Drayton (Buniak)	CAN	10-Jan-1945	2:13:30.0	6	Montreal	31-Jul-1976
40							
Leonid	Moiseyev	URS	21-Oct-1952	2:13:33.4	7	Montreal	31-Jul-1976
Richard	Nerurkar	GBR	06-Jan-1964	2:13:39	5	Atlanta	04-Aug-1996
Toshihiko	Seko	JPN	15-Jul-1956	2:13:41	9	Seoul	02-Oct-1988
Koichi	Morishita	JPN	05-Sep-1967	2:13:45	2	Barcelona	09-Aug-1992
Ravil	Kashapov	URS	15-Nov-1956	2:13:49	10	Seoul	02-Oct-1988
Peter	Pfitzinger	USA	29-Aug-1957	2:13:53	11	Los Angeles	12-Aug-1984
Hugh	Jones	GBR	01-Nov-1955	2:13:57	12	Los Angeles	12-Aug-1984
Jesus	Herrera	MEX	22-Mar-1962	2:13:58	11	Seoul	02-Oct-1988
Jorge	Gonzalez	PUR	20-Dec-1952	2:14:00	13	Los Angeles	12-Aug-1984

First name	*Family name*	*GPE*	*Birth date*	*Time*	*Place*	*Venue*	*Race date*
Stephan	Freigang	GER	27-Sep-1967	2:14:00	3	Barcelona	09-Aug-1992
50							
Takeyuki	Nakayama	JPN	20-Dec-1959	2:14:02	4	Barcelona	09-Aug-1992
John	Campbell	NZL	06-Feb-1949	2:14:08	12	Seoul	02-Oct-1988
Toshihiko	Seko	JPN	15-Jul-1956	2:14:13	14	Los Angeles	12-Aug-1984
Salvatore	Bettiol	ITA	28-Nov-1961	2:14:15	5	Barcelona	09-Aug-1992
Alberto	Salazar	USA	07-Aug-1958	2:14:19	15	Los Angeles	12-Aug-1984
Mehmet	Terzi	TUR	05-May-1955	2:14:20	16	Los Angeles	12-Aug-1984
Franco	Fava	ITA	03-Sep-1952	2:14:24.6	8	Montreal	31-Jul-1976
Salah	Qoqaiche	MAR	10-Jul-1967	2:14:25	6	Barcelona	09-Aug-1992
German	Silva	MEX	09-Jan-1968	2:14:29	6	Atlanta	04-Aug-1996
Francois Robert	de Castella	AUS	27-Feb-1957	2:14:31.0	10	Moscow	01-Aug-1980
60							
Karel	Lismont	BEL	08-Mar-1949	2:14:31.8	2	Munich	10-Sep-1972
Jan	Huruk	POL	27-Jan-1960	2:14:32	7	Barcelona	09-Aug-1992
Stephen	Moneghetti	AUS	26-Sep-1962	2:14:35	7	Atlanta	04-Aug-1996
Shigeru	Soh	JPN	09-Jan-1953	2:14:38	17	Los Angeles	12-Aug-1984
Gerhardus	Nijboer	NED	18-Aug-1955	2:14:40	13	Seoul	02-Oct-1988
Hiromi	Taniguchi	JPN	05-Apr-1960	2:14:42	8	Barcelona	09-Aug-1992
Peter	Pfitzinger	USA	29-Aug-1957	2:14:44	14	Seoul	02-Oct-1988
Martin	ten Kate	NED	16-Dec-1958	2:14:53	15	Seoul	02-Oct-1988
Hans-Joachim	Truppel	GDR	24-Mar-1951	2:14:55.0	11	Moscow	01-Aug-1980
Benjamin	Paredes	MEX	07-Aug-1961	2:14:55	8	Atlanta	04-Aug-1996
70							
Diego	Garcia	ESP	12-Oct-1961	2:14:56	9	Barcelona	09-Aug-1992
Jae-Ryong	Kim	KOR	25-Apr-1966	2:15:01	10	Barcelona	09-Aug-1992
Danilo	Goffi	ITA	03-Dec-1972	2:15:08	9	Atlanta	04-Aug-1996
Mamo	Wolde	ETH	12-Jun-1932	2:15:08.4	3	Munich	10-Sep-1972
Abebe	Bikila	ETH	07-Aug-1932	2:15:16.2	1	Rome	10-Sep-1960
Ferenc	Szekeres	HUN	21-Mar-1947	2:15:18.0	12	Moscow	01-Aug-1980
Harri	Hanninen	FIN	18-Oct-1963	2:15:19	11	Barcelona	09-Aug-1992
Orlando	Pizzolato	ITA	30-Jul-1958	2:15:20	16	Seoul	02-Oct-1988
Steven	Spence	USA	09-May-1962	2:15:21	12	Barcelona	09-Aug-1992
Edward	Eyestone	USA	15-Jun-1961	2:15:23	13	Barcelona	09-Aug-1992
80							
Ralf	Salzmann	FRG	06-Feb-1955	2:15:29	18	Los Angeles	12-Aug-1984
Aleksandr	Gozki	URS	25-Oct-1947	2:15:34.0	9	Montreal	31-Jul-1976
Kenneth	Moore	USA	01-Dec-1943	2:15:39.8	4	Munich	10-Sep-1972
Rhadi	ben Abdesselem	MAR	28-Feb-1929	2:15:41.6	2	Rome	10-Sep-1960
Masanari	Shintaku	JPN	20-Dec-1957	2:15:42	17	Seoul	02-Oct-1988
Won-Tak	Kim	KOR	21-Jul-1964	2:15:44	18	Seoul	02-Oct-1988
Boniface	Merande	KEN	13-Feb-1962	2:15:46	14	Barcelona	09-Aug-1992
Albert	van Vlaanderen	NED	25-Nov-1964	2:15:47	15	Barcelona	09-Aug-1992
Rex	Wilson	NZL	10-Apr-1960	2:15:51	16	Barcelona	09-Aug-1992
Hendrik	Schoofs	BEL	06-Oct-1950	2:15:52.4	10	Montreal	31-Jul-1976
90							
Robert	Kempainen	USA	18-Jun-1966	2:15:53	17	Barcelona	09-Aug-1992
Henrik	Jorgensen	DEN	10-Oct-1961	2:15:55	19	Los Angeles	12-Aug-1984
Luiz Antonio	dos Santos	BRA	06-Apr-1964	2:15:55	10	Atlanta	04-Aug-1996
Carlos	Grisales	COL	24-Aug-1966	2:15:56	11	Atlanta	04-Aug-1996
Ahmed Salah	Hussein	DJI	31-Dec-1956	2:15:59	20	Los Angeles	12-Aug-1984
Marc	Smet	BEL	05-Feb-1951	2:16:00.0	13	Moscow	01-Aug-1980
Piergiovanni	Poli	ITA	05-Nov-1957	2:16:07	19	Seoul	02-Oct-1988
Dieudonne	Lamothe	HAI	29-Jul-1954	2:16:15	20	Seoul	02-Oct-1988
Yi-Yong	Kim	KOR	20-Sep-1973	2:16:17	12	Atlanta	04-Aug-1996
David	Long	GBR	21-Nov-1960	2:16:18	21	Seoul	02-Oct-1988
100							
Basil	Heatley	GBR	25-Dec-1933	2:16:19.2	2	Tokyo	21-Oct-1964
Shivnath	Singh	IND	11-Jul-1946	2:16:22.0	11	Montreal	31-Jul-1976
Kokichi	Tsuburaya	JPN	13-May-1940	2:16:22.8	3	Tokyo	21-Oct-1964
Rodrigo	Gavela	ESP	05-Jan-1966	2:16:23	18	Barcelona	09-Aug-1992

First name	Family name	GPE	Birth date	Time	Place	Venue	Race date
Agapius	Masong	TAN	12-Apr-1960	2:16:25	21	Los Angeles	12-Aug-1984
Kenji	Kimihara	JPN	20-Mar-1941	2:16:27.0	5	Munich	10-Sep-1972
Gidamis	Shahanga	TAN	04-Sep-1957	2:16:27	22	Los Angeles	12-Aug-1984
Ronald	Hill	GBR	25-Sep-1938	2:16:30.6	6	Munich	10-Sep-1972
Tendai	Chimusasa	ZIM	28-Jan-1971	2:16:31	13	Atlanta	04-Aug-1996
Chang-Sop	Choi	PRK	18-Jul-1955	2:16:33.2	12	Montreal	31-Jul-1976
110							
Karel	David	TCH	08-Feb-1964	2:16:34	19	Barcelona	09-Aug-1992
Donald	Macgregor	GBR	23-Jul-1939	2:16:34.4	7	Munich	10-Sep-1972
Eloi	Schleder	BRA	26-Jul-1951	2:16:35	23	Los Angeles	12-Aug-1984
Leszek	Beblo	POL	08-Jul-1966	2:16:38	20	Barcelona	09-Aug-1992
Wieslaw	Perszke	POL	18-Feb-1960	2:16:38	21	Barcelona	09-Aug-1992
Henrik	Jorgensen	DEN	10-Oct-1961	2:16:40	22	Seoul	02-Oct-1988
Antonio	Pinto	POR	22-Mar-1966	2:16:41	14	Atlanta	04-Aug-1996
Emmanuel	Ndiemandoi	TAN	1957	2:16:47.0	14	Moscow	01-Aug-1980
Gidamis	Shahanga	TAN	04-Sep-1957	2:16:47.0	15	Moscow	01-Aug-1980
Dionicio	Ceron	MEX	09-Oct-1965	2:16:48	15	Atlanta	04-Aug-1996
120							
Ralf	Salzmann	FRG	06-Feb-1955	2:16:54	23	Seoul	02-Oct-1988
John	Foster	NZL	23-May-1932	2:16:56.2	8	Munich	10-Sep-1972
Massimo	Magnani	ITA	04-Oct-1951	2:16:56.4	13	Montreal	31-Jul-1976
Mwenze	Kalombo	ZAI	07-Jun-1967	2:17:01	16	Atlanta	04-Aug-1996
Brian	Kilby	GBR	26-Feb-1938	2:17:02.4	4	Tokyo	21-Oct-1964
Anacleto	Pinto	POR	25-Feb-1948	2:17:04.0	16	Moscow	01-Aug-1980
Yakov	Tolstikov	EUN	20-May-1959	2:17:04	22	Barcelona	09-Aug-1992
Leszek	Beblo	POL	08-Jul-1966	2:17:04	17	Atlanta	04-Aug-1996
Domingo	Tibaduiza	COL	22-Nov-1949	2:17:06.0	17	Moscow	01-Aug-1980
Karel	Lismont	BEL	08-Mar-1949	2:17:07	24	Los Angeles	12-Aug-1984
130							
Tena	Negere	ETH	05-Oct-1972	2:17:07	23	Barcelona	09-Aug-1992
Allan	Zachariassen	DEN	04-Nov-1955	2:17:10	25	Los Angeles	12-Aug-1984
Richard	Hooper	IRL	26-Aug-1956	2:17:16	24	Seoul	02-Oct-1988
Osmiro	de Souza Silva	BRA	09-Oct-1961	2:17:16	24	Barcelona	09-Aug-1992
Barrington	Magee	NZL	06-Feb-1934	2:17:18.2	3	Rome	10-Sep-1960
Abel	Mokibe	RSA	03-Jul-1962	2:17:24	25	Barcelona	09-Aug-1992
Alberto	Juzdado	ESP	20-Aug-1966	2:17:24	18	Atlanta	04-Aug-1996
Hiromi	Taniguchi	JPN	05-Apr-1960	2:17:26	19	Atlanta	04-Aug-1996
Salvatore	Bettiol	ITA	28-Nov-1961	2:17:27	20	Atlanta	04-Aug-1996
Hendrik	Schoofs	BEL	06-Oct-1950	2:17:28.0	18	Moscow	01-Aug-1980
140							
Peter	Fonseca	CAN	05-Oct-1966	2:17:28	21	Atlanta	04-Aug-1996
Michael	Koussis	GRE	10-Oct-1953	2:17:38	26	Los Angeles	12-Aug-1984
Jack	Bacheler	USA	30-Dec-1943	2:17:38.2	9	Munich	10-Sep-1972
Goran	Bengtsson	SWE	25-Nov-1949	2:17:39.6	14	Montreal	31-Jul-1976
Rolando	Vera	ECU	27-Apr-1965	2:17:40	22	Atlanta	04-Aug-1996
Roderic	de Highden	AUS	15-Jan-1969	2:17:42	23	Atlanta	04-Aug-1996
Pertti	Tiainen	FIN	15-Nov-1954	2:17:43	27	Los Angeles	12-Aug-1984
Kazimierz	Orzel	POL	26-Aug-1943	2:17:43.4	15	Montreal	31-Jul-1976
Kjell-Erik	Stahl	SWE	17-Feb-1946	2:17:44.0	19	Moscow	01-Aug-1980
Francois Robert	de Castella	AUS	27-Feb-1957	2:17:44	26	Barcelona	09-Aug-1992
150							
Miroslav	Vindis	YUG	08-Nov-1963	2:17:47	25	Seoul	02-Oct-1988
Stephen	Brace	GBR	07-Jul-1961	2:17:49	27	Barcelona	09-Aug-1992
Jose Luis	Molina	CRC	08-Mar-1965	2:17:49	24	Atlanta	04-Aug-1996
Hakan	Spik	FIN	18-Aug-1951	2:17:50.6	16	Montreal	31-Jul-1976
Alain	Lazare	FRA	23-Mar-1952	2:17:52	28	Los Angeles	12-Aug-1984
John	Foster	NZL	23-May-1932	2:17:53.4	17	Montreal	31-Jul-1976
Vincent	Ruguga	UGA	12-Dec-1959	2:17:54	29	Los Angeles	12-Aug-1984
Shangyan	Cai	CHN	19-Jul-1962	2:17:54	26	Seoul	02-Oct-1988
Jozsef	Suto	HUN	09-Sep-1937	2:17:55.8	5	Tokyo	21-Oct-1964
Michael	Koussis	GRE	10-Oct-1953	2:18:02.0	20	Moscow	01-Aug-1980

First name	Family name	GPE	Birth date	Time	Place	Venue	Race date
160							
Domingos	Castro	POR	22-Nov-1963	2:18:03	25	Atlanta	04-Aug-1996
Jurgen	Eberding	GDR	03-Dec-1955	2:18:04.0	21	Moscow	01-Aug-1980
Joaquim	Silva	POR	13-Jan-1961	2:18:05	27	Seoul	02-Oct-1988
Tahar	Mansouri	TUN	09-Jan-1965	2:18:06	26	Atlanta	04-Aug-1996
Mario	Cuevas	MEX	22-Jul-1949	2:18:08.8	18	Montreal	31-Jul-1976
Lawrence	Peu	RSA	13-Feb-1966	2:18:09	27	Atlanta	04-Aug-1996
Armand	Parmentier	BEL	15-Feb-1954	2:18:10	30	Los Angeles	12-Aug-1984
Leonard	Edelen	USA	22-Sep-1937	2:18:12.4	6	Tokyo	21-Oct-1964
Eleuterio	Anton	ESP	30-Mar-1950	2:18:16.0	22	Moscow	01-Aug-1980
Keith	Brantly	USA	23-May-1962	2:18:17	28	Atlanta	04-Aug-1996
170							
Arthur	Boileau	CAN	09-Oct-1957	2:18:20	28	Seoul	02-Oct-1988
Leodigard	Martin	TAN	08-Jan-1960	2:18:21.0	23	Moscow	01-Aug-1980
Rodolfo	Gomez	MEX	30-Oct-1950	2:18:21.2	19	Montreal	31-Jul-1976
Shigeru	Soh	JPN	09-Jan-1953	2:18:26.0	20	Montreal	31-Jul-1976
Thabiso	Ralekhetla	LES	03-Mar-1960	2:18:26	29	Atlanta	04-Aug-1996
Khristo	Stefanov	BUL	21-Dec-1970	2:18:29	30	Atlanta	04-Aug-1996
Wan-Ki	Kim	KOR	08-Jul-1968	2:18:32	28	Barcelona	09-Aug-1992
Bedane	Lengisse	ETH	08-May-1945	2:18:36.8	10	Munich	10-Sep-1972
Robert	Kempainen	USA	18-Jun-1966	2:18:38	31	Atlanta	04-Aug-1996
Moges	Alemayehu	ETH	06-Dec-1948	2:18:40.0	24	Moscow	01-Aug-1980
180							
Harri	Hanninen	FIN	18-Oct-1963	2:18:41	32	Atlanta	04-Aug-1996
Aurele	Vandendriessche	BEL	04-Jul-1932	2:18:42.6	7	Tokyo	21-Oct-1964
Noriyasu	Mizukami	JPN	06-Oct-1947	2:18:44.0	21	Montreal	31-Jul-1976
Seppo	Nikkari	FIN	06-Feb-1948	2:18:49.4	11	Munich	10-Sep-1972
Jose Isidro	Ricorangel	MEX	15-May-1961	2:18:52	29	Barcelona	09-Aug-1992
Anacleto	Pinto	POR	25-Feb-1948	2:18:53.4	22	Montreal	31-Jul-1976
Gert	Thys	RSA	12-Nov-1971	2:18:55	33	Atlanta	04-Aug-1996
Akio	Usami	JPN	31-May-1943	2:18:58.0	12	Munich	10-Sep-1972
Ahmed Salah	Hussein	DJI	31-Dec-1956	2:19:04	30	Barcelona	09-Aug-1992
Cesar	Mercado	PUR	25-Oct-1959	2:19:09	31	Los Angeles	12-Aug-1984
190							
Edward	Eyestone	USA	15-Jun-1961	2:19:09	29	Seoul	02-Oct-1988
Dominique	Chauvelier	FRA	03-Aug-1956	2:19:09	31	Barcelona	09-Aug-1992
Konstantin	Vorobiev	URS	30-Oct-1930	2:19:09.6	4	Rome	10-Sep-1960
Charmarke Cochine	Omar Abdillahi	DJI	1954	2:19:11	32	Los Angeles	12-Aug-1984
Jose Esteban	Montiel	ESP	20-Sep-1962	2:19:15	32	Barcelona	09-Aug-1992
Sergey	Popov	URS	21-Sep-1930	2:19:18.8	5	Rome	10-Sep-1960
Jules	Randrianarivelo	MAD	28-Nov-1951	2:19:23.0	25	Moscow	01-Aug-1980
Oyvind	Dahl	NOR	12-May-1951	2:19:28	33	Los Angeles	12-Aug-1984
Thabiso	Moqhali	LES	07-Dec-1967	2:19:28	33	Barcelona	09-Aug-1992
Juma	Ikangaa	TAN	19-Jul-1960	2:19:34	34	Barcelona	09-Aug-1992
200							

APPENDIX G: Fastest 100 Olympic Women's Marathon Performances

First name	Family name	GPE	Birth date	Time	Place	Venue	Race date
Joan	Benoit	USA	16-May-1957	2:24:52	1	Los Angeles	05-Aug-1984
Rosa	Mota	POR	29-Jun-1958	2:25:40	1	Seoul	23-Sep-1988
Lisa	Martin	AUS	12-May-1960	2:25:53	2	Seoul	23-Sep-1988
Fatuma	Roba	ETH	18-Dec-1973	2:26:05	1	Atlanta	28-Jul-1996
Grete	Waitz	NOR	01-Oct-1953	2:26:18	2	Los Angeles	05-Aug-1984
Katrin	Dorre	GDR	06-Oct-1961	2:26:21	3	Seoul	23-Sep-1988
Rosa	Mota	POR	29-Jun-1958	2:26:57	3	Los Angeles	05-Aug-1984
Tatyana	Polovinskaya	URS	14-Mar-1965	2:27:05	4	Seoul	23-Sep-1988
Youfeng	Zhao	CHN	05-May-1965	2:27:06	5	Seoul	23-Sep-1988
Ingrid	Kristiansen	NOR	21-Mar-1956	2:27:34	4	Los Angeles	05-Aug-1984
10							
Laura	Fogli	ITA	05-Oct-1959	2:27:49	6	Seoul	23-Sep-1988
Valentina	Yegorova	RUS	16-Feb-1964	2:28:05	2	Atlanta	28-Jul-1996
Lorraine	Moller	NZL	01-Jun-1955	2:28:34	5	Los Angeles	05-Aug-1984
Yuko	Arimori	JPN	17-Dec-1966	2:28:39	3	Atlanta	28-Jul-1996
Katrin	Dorre	GER	06-Oct-1961	2:28:45	4	Atlanta	28-Jul-1996
Priscilla	Welch	GBR	22-Nov-1944	2:28:54	6	Los Angeles	05-Aug-1984
Lisa	Martin	AUS	12-May-1960	2:29:03	7	Los Angeles	05-Aug-1984
Sylvie	Ruegger	CAN	23-Feb-1961	2:29:09	8	Los Angeles	05-Aug-1984
Daniele	Kaber	LUX	20-Apr-1960	2:29:23	7	Seoul	23-Sep-1988
Laura	Fogli	ITA	05-Oct-1959	2:29:28	9	Los Angeles	05-Aug-1984
20							
Maria	Curatolo	ITA	12-Oct-1963	2:30:14	8	Seoul	23-Sep-1988
Zoya	Ivanova	URS	14-Mar-1952	2:30:25	9	Seoul	23-Sep-1988
Rocio	Rios	ESP	13-Mar-1969	2:30:50	5	Atlanta	28-Jul-1996
Angela	Pain	GBR	08-Feb-1962	2:30:51	10	Seoul	23-Sep-1988
Odette	Lapierre	CAN	28-Jan-1955	2:30:56	11	Seoul	23-Sep-1988
Lidia	Simon	ROM	04-Sep-1973	2:31:04	6	Atlanta	28-Jul-1996
Maria Manuela	Machado	POR	09-Aug-1963	2:31:11	7	Atlanta	28-Jul-1996
Sonja	Krolik	GER	24-Feb-1973	2:31:16	8	Atlanta	28-Jul-1996
Xiujuan	Ren	CHN	14-Sep-1974	2:31:21	9	Atlanta	28-Jul-1996
Anne Marie	Lauck	USA	07-Mar-1969	2:31:30	10	Atlanta	28-Jul-1996
30							
Susan	Tooby	GBR	24-Oct-1960	2:31:33	12	Seoul	23-Sep-1988
Malgorzata	Sobanska	POL	25-Apr-1969	2:31:52	11	Atlanta	28-Jul-1996
Tuija	Toivonen	FIN	22-Sep-1958	2:32:07	10	Los Angeles	05-Aug-1984
Karolina	Szabo	HUN	17-Nov-1961	2:32:26	13	Seoul	23-Sep-1988
Izumi	Maki	JPN	10-Dec-1968	2:32:35	12	Atlanta	28-Jul-1996
Francoise	Bonnet	FRA	08-Apr-1957	2:32:36	14	Seoul	23-Sep-1988
Valentina	Yegorova	EUN	16-Feb-1964	2:32:41	1	Barcelona	01-Aug-1992
Joyce	Smith	GBR	26-Oct-1937	2:32:48	11	Los Angeles	05-Aug-1984
Yuko	Arimori	JPN	17-Dec-1966	2:32:49	2	Barcelona	01-Aug-1992
Mi-Ok	Lee	KOR	10-Mar-1968	2:32:51	15	Seoul	23-Sep-1988
40							
Alba	Milana	ITA	17-Mar-1959	2:33:01	12	Los Angeles	05-Aug-1984
Ornella	Ferrara	ITA	17-Apr-1968	2:33:09	13	Atlanta	28-Jul-1996
Raisa	Smekhnova	URS	16-Sep-1950	2:33:19	16	Seoul	23-Sep-1988
Monica	Pont	ESP	03-Jun-1969	2:33:27	14	Atlanta	28-Jul-1996

First name	Family name	GPE	Birth date	Time	Place	Venue	Race date
Dorthe	Rasmussen	DEN	27-Jan-1960	2:33:40	13	Los Angeles	05-Aug-1984
Nancy	Ditz	USA	25-Jun-1954	2:33:42	17	Seoul	23-Sep-1988
Maria	Lelut	FRA	29-Jan-1956	2:33:47	18	Seoul	23-Sep-1988
Lorraine	Moller	NZL	01-Jun-1955	2:33:59	3	Barcelona	01-Aug-1992
Jocelyne	Villeton	FRA	17-Sep-1954	2:34:02	19	Seoul	23-Sep-1988
Sarah	Rowell	GBR	19-Nov-1962	2:34:08	14	Los Angeles	05-Aug-1984
50							
Angelina	Kanana	KEN	16-Dec-1965	2:34:19	15	Atlanta	28-Jul-1996
Maria Conceicao	Ferreira	POR	13-Mar-1962	2:34:23	20	Seoul	23-Sep-1988
Kerstin	Pressler	FRG	02-Feb-1962	2:34:26	21	Seoul	23-Sep-1988
Elizabeth	McColgan	GBR	24-May-1964	2:34:30	16	Atlanta	28-Jul-1996
Junko	Asari	JPN	22-Sep-1969	2:34:31	17	Atlanta	28-Jul-1996
Marianna Wanda	Panfil	POL	26-Jan-1959	2:34:35	22	Seoul	23-Sep-1988
Antonella	Bizioli	ITA	29-Mar-1957	2:34:38	23	Seoul	23-Sep-1988
Eriko	Asai	JPN	20-Oct-1959	2:34:41	24	Seoul	23-Sep-1988
Evy	Palm	SWE	31-Jan-1942	2:34:41	25	Seoul	23-Sep-1988
Franziska	Rochat-Moser	SUI	17-Aug-1966	2:34:48	18	Atlanta	28-Jul-1996
60							
Lizanne	Bussieres	CAN	20-Aug-1961	2:35:03	26	Seoul	23-Sep-1988
Gabriela	Wolf	FRG	28-Oct-1960	2:35:11	27	Seoul	23-Sep-1988
Griselda	Gonzalez	ARG	04-Dec-1965	2:35:12	19	Atlanta	28-Jul-1996
Sinikka	Keskitalo	FIN	29-Jan-1951	2:35:15	15	Los Angeles	05-Aug-1984
Kumi	Araki	JPN	11-Oct-1965	2:35:15	28	Seoul	23-Sep-1988
Misako	Miyahara	JPN	29-May-1962	2:35:26	29	Seoul	23-Sep-1988
Song-Ok	Jong	PRK	18-Aug-1974	2:35:31	20	Atlanta	28-Jul-1996
Madina	Biktagirova	EUN	20-Sep-1964	2:35:39	DQ	Barcelona	01-Aug-1992
Irina	Bogachova	KGZ	30-Apr-1961	2:35:44	21	Atlanta	28-Jul-1996
Inglandini	Gonzalez	COL	02-May-1966	2:35:45	22	Atlanta	28-Jul-1996
70							
Charlotte	Teske	FRG	23-Nov-1949	2:35:56	16	Los Angeles	05-Aug-1984
Huandi	Zhong	CHN	23-Oct-1967	2:36:02	30	Seoul	23-Sep-1988
Serap	Aktas	TUR	25-Sep-1971	2:36:14	23	Atlanta	28-Jul-1996
Yelena	Mazovka	BLR	30-Jun-1967	2:36:22	24	Atlanta	28-Jul-1996
Sachiko	Yamashita	JPN	20-Aug-1964	2:36:26	4	Barcelona	01-Aug-1992
Marleen	Renders	BEL	24-Dec-1968	2:36:27	25	Atlanta	28-Jul-1996
Chang-Ok	Kim	PRK	27-May-1975	2:36:31	26	Atlanta	28-Jul-1996
Anne Marie	Malone	CAN	28-Jul-1960	2:36:33	17	Los Angeles	05-Aug-1984
Albertina	Dias	POR	26-Apr-1965	2:36:39	27	Atlanta	28-Jul-1996
Marie-Louise	Hamrin	SWE	19-Apr-1957	2:36:41	18	Los Angeles	05-Aug-1984
80							
Kerryn	McCann	AUS	02-May-1967	2:36:41	28	Atlanta	28-Jul-1996
Helene	Rochefort	CAN	22-Nov-1954	2:36:44	31	Seoul	23-Sep-1988
Aniela	Nikiel	POL	01-Nov-1965	2:36:44	29	Atlanta	28-Jul-1996
Katrin	Dorre	GER	06-Oct-1961	2:36:48	5	Barcelona	01-Aug-1992
Mi-Ja	Oh	KOR	03-Jul-1970	2:36:54	30	Atlanta	28-Jul-1996
Susan	Crehan	GBR	12-Sep-1956	2:36:57	32	Seoul	23-Sep-1988
Linda	Somers	USA	07-May-1961	2:36:58	31	Atlanta	28-Jul-1996
Gyong-Ae	Mun	PRK	08-Apr-1969	2:37:03	6	Barcelona	01-Aug-1992
Nanae	Sasaki	JPN	08-Feb-1956	2:37:04	19	Los Angeles	05-Aug-1984
Paola	Moro	ITA	14-Aug-1952	2:37:06	20	Los Angeles	05-Aug-1984
90							
Danuta	Bartoszek	CAN	19-Aug-1961	2:37:06	32	Atlanta	28-Jul-1996
Maria	van Landeghem	BEL	19-Jul-1957	2:37:11	21	Los Angeles	05-Aug-1984
Maria del Carmen	Diaz	MEX	15-Jul-1970	2:37:14	33	Atlanta	28-Jul-1996
Nelly	Glauser	SUI	27-Jan-1966	2:37:19	34	Atlanta	28-Jul-1996

First name	Family name	GPE	Birth date	Time	Place	Venue	Race date
Carolina	Beurskens	NED	15-Feb-1952	2:37:51	22	Los Angeles	05-Aug-1984
Carolina	Beurskens	NED	15-Feb-1952	2:37:52	33	Seoul	23-Sep-1988
Lorraine	Moller	NZL	01-Jun-1955	2:37:52	34	Seoul	23-Sep-1988
Regina	Joyce	IRL	07-Feb-1957	2:37:57	23	Los Angeles	05-Aug-1984
Marie-Christine	Deurbroeck	BEL	01-Feb-1957	2:38:01	24	Los Angeles	05-Aug-1984
Magda	Ilands	BEL	16-Jan-1950	2:38:02	35	Seoul	23-Sep-1988
100							

Index

Page references followed by *t* or *f* indicate tables or figures, respectively.

About the Authors

David E. Martin, PhD, is a Fellow in the American College of Sports Medicine (ACSM), as well as a contributing member of the Association of Track and Field Statisticians (ATFS), the International Marathon Medical Directors Association (IMMDA), the Association of International Marathons (AIMS), and the International Society of Olympic Historians (ISOH). This multidisciplinary approach to the study of top-level marathon performance—from a scientific as well as an historical viewpoint—gives him a unique perspective. In 1978, Martin was selected by the U.S. Olympic Academy to be one of three representatives to the International Olympic Academy. Even before then, he had begun to compile a database of top-level men's and women's performances. His work has continued, and the list now tops 44,000 performances. This provides an unparalleled resource for his research on the use of mathematical modeling techniques to assess performance trends in distance running.

Martin is coauthor of *The Marathon Footrace* (1979, with Gynn), *Training Distance Runners* (1991), and *Better Training for Distance Runners* (1997). Since 1979, he has served prominently as chair of various committees within USA Track and Field, applying his sport science and coaching skills to the guidance of many of America's top distance runners. In addition, since 1989, he has been the marathon statistician for the ATFS, taking over the role pioneered by coauthor Roger Gynn. Martin lives in Decatur, Georgia.

Roger W.H. Gynn began documenting marathons in the late 1950s and is today one the world's foremost experts on marathon statistics. He was the marathon statistician for the Association of Track and Field Statisticians (ATFS) from 1968 to 1988. In this role, he was responsible for producing documentation on the marathon for the *ATFS Annual,* the definitive source for track and field performance statistics. Gynn also spent 20 years preparing annual marathon rankings for *Track and Field News.*

Over the years, Gynn has served as the marathon statistician for the *British Union of Track and Field Statisticians, Running* magazine, and *Athletics Weekly.* He has also been the main compiler of marathon lists for *Track and Field Performance Through the Years,* volumes 1-4. Gynn is coauthor of *The Marathon Footrace* (with Martin) and compiler of both *The Guinness Book of the Marathon* and *International Marathon Statistics.* He is a member of the Association of Track and Field Statisticians and the National Union of Track and Field Statisticians. Gynn resides in Watford, Hertfordshire.